CUNARD

Library

Out of respect for your fellow guests, please return all books as soon as possible. We would also request that books are not taken off the ship as they can easily be damaged by the sun, sea and sand.

Please ensure that books are returned the day before you disembark, failure to do so will incur a charge to your on board account, the same will happen to any damaged books.

www.oceanbooks.com

THE TEN TYPES OF HUMAN

THE
TEN TYPES OF
HUMAN

A New Understanding of Who We Are
and Who We Can Be

Dexter Dias

WILLIAM HEINEMANN: LONDON

1 3 5 7 9 10 8 6 4 2

William Heinemann
20 Vauxhall Bridge Road
London SW1V 2SA

William Heinemann is part of the Penguin Random House group of companies
whose addresses can be found at global.penguinrandomhouse.com.

Penguin
Random House
UK

First published by William Heinemann in 2017

www.penguin.co.uk

A CIP catalogue record for this book is available from the British Library.

ISBN 9781785150166 (Hardcover)
ISBN 9781785150173 (Trade paperback)

Typeset in India by Integra Software Services Pvt. Ltd, Pondicherry

Printed and bound by Clays Ltd, St Ives PLC

Penguin Random House is committed to a sustainable future for
our business, our readers and our planet. This book is made
from Forest Stewardship Council® certified paper.

MIX
Paper from
responsible sources
FSC® C018179
FSC
www.fsc.org

For Katie,
Fabi and Hermione

CONTENTS

CONTENTS

FROM THE AUTHOR

The book you are about to read is part of a project to forge a new understanding of who we are and who we can be. It is based on research that began ten years ago and that has been conducted on four continents. It is also grounded in my work as a human rights lawyer. But the project would not have been possible without the participation, collaboration and generous contribution of a great number of people, many of who appear in the course of the text. Later in the book I pay proper tribute to them and explain the distinctive nature of their indispensable contribution. There I also acknowledge my deep gratitude to the friends and colleagues who have been instrumental in facilitating this endeavour. However, at the outset I must acknowledge the advice and support of close colleagues at the University of Cambridge, especially Professor Loraine Gelsthorpe, Director of Research at the Centre for Community, Gender and Social Justice, which I am proud to be affiliated to, my academic collaborator Dr Caroline Lanskey at the Institute of Criminology, and Dr Nicola Padfield at the Faculty of Law. Equally, at Harvard I am particularly indebted to Professor James Sidanius, the William James Professor of Psychology and Director of the Intergroup Relations Lab, who offered me a residency as Visiting Researcher, Dr Mariska Kappmeier (my next door neighbour on the 14th floor), and Professor Joshua Greene, who kindly invited me to present elements of my research at his groundbreaking Moral Cognition Lab. I am also indebted to numerous colleagues in sub-Saharan Africa, Haiti and Central Asia, in London and New York, at UNICEF (especially the astounding Judith Léveillée and Sabrina Avakian) and at the Bar Human Rights Committee (particularly its Chair, Kirsty Brimelow QC, and my colleague on fighting FGM Zimran Samuel). However, it would be a serious omission not to point out that of the numerous people I've interviewed, followed, consulted, contested, travelled with and tormented, during the research for this book, only a small proportion actually appear in the text. Nevertheless my other correspondents, confrères, intellectual comrades and combatants have informed my thinking and approach and thus are present as well. A comprehensive list of those I can name appears at the end of the book. However, given the particular nature of this research inquiry, and while many people appear bearing their real names, others have necessarily had their names altered. In respect of several, identifying characteristics and certain circumstances have had to be changed. The reason has been to protect the participants – both in terms of protecting their privacy and in certain instances their personal security, or that of people closely connected to them. Some have been or remain at considerable risk. Others have had their lives threatened. Several have been hurt or injured. A few have taken great risks in telling what they have. They have done so in the hope that it will help others, an aspiration I share and one of the chief animating ideas of the book.

Some are embarking on perilous ventures – among the great secret journeys of our age – across treacherous terrain frequented by treacherous people. Others are returning to dangerous countries or regions acknowledged by international agencies to be hazardous and unsafe. Therefore I make it plain that where necessary, as in the unforgettable *Love's Executioner* by Irvin Yalom, I have endeavoured to create an impenetrable 'disguise' (to use Yalom's apt phrase). In some cases, as in his book, the best course to safeguard the identity of the participant has been to make what Yalom calls 'symbolic substitutions' or to 'graft', as he puts it, one person's background or identity onto another's, an approach also used by Barack Obama in respect of certain characters in *Dreams from My Father*. In making such elisions, I have sought to preserve what the great Oliver Sacks in *The Man Who Mistook His Wife for a Hat* calls 'the essential "feeling" of their lives'. Where this has been done it is because it has been the only way to ensure that their privacy and personal safety are maximally protected. Thus this book contains the full spectrum of material, from accounts that appear with names and essential details listed as they occurred, to those where there has had to be some or a substantial degree of disguise, to those where accounts have been blended or collaged. In the latter case, my solution has been to create connecting material and endeavour to develop a different kind of writing, melding fictive with non-fiction elements. Throughout, dialogue has had to be redacted for reasons of confidentiality or sensitivity; some dialogue has been modified, reconstructed from memory, condensed or paraphrased for length, or deduced for continuity or coherence from accounts of events provided. I have tried to convey the sense of accents and modes of speech and where – as frequently occurred – discussion took place in more than one language, I have usually (but not always) simplified it into one. Where participants have communicated dialogue or scenes with third parties, I have endeavoured to reconstruct them as authentically as possible and in the spirit of the overall narrative. Where there are gaps in the account or for reasons of confidentiality and/or security I have had to find a substitute, my approach has been informed by that of John Berendt in the seminal *Midnight in the Garden of Good and Evil*, which is to combine the 'strict non-fiction' (his term) with elements constructed with the intention of remaining, as Berendt puts it, 'faithful to the characters and to the essential drift of events', but those are acts, it is essential to emphasise, that necessarily draw on both the inquisitional and imaginative faculties, concisely described by John le Carré (in a different context) as an exercise in 'blending experience with imagination'. Thus some parts are necessarily a fictive reimagining of certain events grounded in the best available evidence. When done, this has been with the clear objective of protecting the personal safety of a contributor or preserving their privacy. The non-scientific narratives are based on what people have said about their lives. This is not an exercise in investigative journalism, nor an official inquiry. That would be a different book. Interesting, but different. Instead it contains accounts of how people have thought and talked about their lives and an attempt to convey what those lives are like. What is elevated to centre stage in this inquiry is what Oliver Sacks in *Awakenings* calls the 'landscapes of being in which these [people] reside' necessitating 'an active exploration of images and views . . . and imaginative *movement*' (his emphasis). Thus I have explored developing a somewhat different type of book, blending science with narrative, non-fiction with fictive elements. This is not the place for an epistemological (or any other) disquisition, but I should observe that my approach has also been heavily influenced by two of the foremost critical thinkers of the last 30 years, Pierre Bourdieu and Loïc Wacquant (including invaluable correspondence with the latter, particularly in relation to my Cambridge research), and their advocacy of an active and immersive engagement with the subject. You will find references and suggestions for further reading in the Methodology section of the Note on Sources at the end of the book. Due to the text's length, the full referencing can be found at the book's dedicated page at the penguin.co.uk website. I should also state that I am an adherent of a critical school of thought that considers social forces and the social construction of both the individual and society as extraordinarily important. But I am also persuaded that there is something more in addition to and combining intricately with those already intricate processes. This book seeks to explore (but does not claim to resolve) that entanglement. Put simply: both nature and nurture are important. Our behaviour is not biology *or* environment, genetic inheritance *or* social learning, but both – and our social learning mechanisms are in any event probably shaped by evolution. The approach and moral stance of this book are a world away from 'social Darwinism' – in fact, they strenuously oppose it. Evolution is a fact, not a value. Therefore the book aims to lend itself to the project luminously articulated by philosopher Peter Singer: the reclamation of the penetrating explanatory power of Darwin's thought for progressives. Very occasionally (rarely) there are biographical sketches that rely entirely on secondary sources. In such cases, all the originating source documents are cited in the reference section. Several thought experiments or hypotheticals appear in the book. They are entirely fictional except where the text refers to a particular case or event that has informed them. This book is based on research that began nine years ago and that has extended to four continents; it is also grounded in my practice as a human rights lawyer for over 25 years. Where protective measures have been adopted, they have been the ones wished for by the contributor. I am indebted to them all, not least for their companionship in the mound of months I was away, in the dust of every astounding, eye-opening day. They have been and remain the very heart and life pulse of the book.

DDQC
London/Cambridge
May 2017

THE TEN TYPES OF HUMAN

How does one fashion a book of resistance,
a book of truth in an empire of falsehood?
Is it possible for freedom and independence
to arise in new ways under new conditions?

Philip K. Dick

PROLOGUE

Some books begin with an idea, others with an event. This book is of the latter kind. The event that triggered the book took place in a quiet corner of rural England, with a name that conjures shaded streams, gently running with water: Rainsbrook. That place was a prison. The event was the death of a child.

A small boy – he is 4 foot 10, weighs 6½ stone – pads along a corridor in silence. My view is from a high CCTV camera on a metal stanchion on a smoothed brick wall, black-and-white footage (it may not be, but that's how I remember it), no sound, and the boy walks slowly with his back to me towards a room, which is his cell. He turns left, enters. I never see his face. Can you be haunted by a face you never see? He disappears, shuts the door. Minutes later, two prison officers walk, faster, along the same corridor. They walk in silence, but their sheer size compared to the boy seems to fill the frame with noise, with chaos. They also turn left, enter the room, shut the door. A third prison officer comes along, enters, shuts the door. Within minutes, the boy is dead. His name was Gareth Myatt.

What happened in that room?

It was my professional duty – it became my quest – to find out. On a day of pale blue March skies high above the crenulated towers of the Palace of Westminster, when I was appointed Queen's Counsel, my thoughts kept turning to Gareth and his mother Pam. At the inquest into his death, during which I represented their family, Pam asked me a question: 'Why did they do it – why did they do that to my son?'

I didn't have an answer, or a good enough one for her. Truth in a courtroom is only part of human truth. She didn't mean to affect me like that. She is a quietly courageous person who bears so much, wants to burden no one. What she really wanted was her son back. I couldn't make that happen, but I could try to find a better answer. I took a sabbatical, went back to university. People did not understand. I'm not sure I did. But I was determined to find out what happened in that room.

You do the case. Finish it. Move on. But the case isn't always finished with you. My ensuing investigation, for investigation it was – and mystery, and secret story – was in pursuit of an elusive fugitive: a culprit and quarry which was at the same time the hero of the piece – us. Or more precisely the hidden parts of us. It took me first to the Institute of Criminology at Cambridge University. I was lured on by those few frames: a corridor, a boy disappearing, a door shutting, a question: what happened in that room?

When I continued my research at another place an ocean away, the labs of the Department of Psychology at Harvard, people asked 'What are you doing?' It was difficult to answer succinctly. I was tempted to say I want to know – we *need* to know – what happened in that room. I never said what I actually felt: I owed it to someone to find out.

In my mind, over time, Pam's question slowly began to change. Not why did they do that, but why do *we*? A larger truth loomed behind what she asked. Why do we hurt the most fragile things? What are we? Who are we?

The quest in part was to save a boy it was impossible to save. I see that now. I was chided by an ominously named legal principle: the law of impossible attempts. This is an account of an attempt that was impossible. The data, the clues – the evidence – took me, over the next ten years, on a series of 'journeyings' (as Wittgenstein calls them) to four of the six humanly habitable continents and ranged from ancient Greece and imperial Rome, to modern southern Siberia and the ice mountains of Pluto. Again and again it was necessary to try to penetrate the inner recesses, the secret sanctuaries, of our brain. It resulted in my meeting people undaunted in the face of unimaginable conditions, people who have stolen, people who have killed, people who have spoken out at enormous personal risk, people who have performed feats of unimaginable heroism. And many, many others: people who, I am willing to wager, number among the most extraordinary we have. Remember this bet and hold me to it.

The more I researched the science and the far-flung frontiers of the human experience – the unguessable edges of what we know and what we are, of life and human longing – the more I realised that I was not just researching what happened in that room, that corridor, but in many. There are many such rooms and corridors in our mind. What is more, they are populated by a number of regularly recurring kinds of people. Types. In this book you will also meet them.

In a way, you already know them. Only you don't – not really. You carry them around inside you. But you probably don't know it. In a sense, they are you. Only they're not – not entirely. They inform and shape the most important decisions in your life. But you're almost certainly unaware of their intervention. They are the essence and instinct of the people you meet. They are the Ten Types of Human.

Who are they? What are they for? How did they get into our head?

For years our brain was thought to function like a general-purpose computer, a little like an old-fashioned telephone system in those black-and-white movies, with everything going through a central switchboard. This view is being challenged. New findings in neuro-science and evolutionary biology indicate that the brain may be more intriguingly fragmented than that. Instead of a computer, the brain instead may be better understood as a series of highly special-ised 'modules' – assemblages of banks of neurons and neurotrans-mitters and the connective pathways between them – each developed in response to specific adaptive problems or evolutionary goals. In other words, to help cope with certain key, recurring problems in human life. This is the concept of 'modularity'.

Indeed the brain may not be just modular – it may be *massively* modular. It may possess many such mechanisms. In what follows, we're going to restrict our focus. We're going to focus on a select number of critical life problems and the processes we are equipped with to respond to them. We're going to focus on ten.

Our brain is not immune to evolution. How it works today tells us as much about our ancestral past as the collections of bones of early humans scattered around the museums of the world. As biophysicist Max Delbrück said, 'Any living cell carries with it the experience of a billion years of experimentation by its ances-tors.' The modules that were relied upon for survival in millennia past still shape our lives in important ways. So:

Ten critical life problems
Ten modules in our mind
Ten characteristic types of human behaviour
Ten 'Types' of human

The book examines ten problems that have haunted humanity, and ten types of characteristic human behaviours that can occur in response. Some of this behaviour will be instantly recognisable; some will be shocking. We shall see.

We are, it turns out, not entirely alone. We carry within us a number of evolved modules. We are, in important respects, an aggregation of the decisions these modules have informed. The concept of the 'Type' of human is an idea, a way of trying to understand a complex process. It is not a precise description of the world, but a way to think about it. As we're going to see in the coming analysis, neuroscience and genetics are vitally important, but they do not provide a complete picture. Culture is also critical. We are unashamedly social beings. Our behaviour is influenced by where we are, what we are taught, what we learn, what we experience. Nurture matters. But so does biology.

But what do these Types do? Why do we still need them? And what do they tell us about human nature today?

I have been a human rights lawyer for over 25 years. My practice has been about carnage. The hidden parts of us that are the stuff of the book have significantly affected the triumph and tragedy of the human race. As Harvard professor E. O. Wilson states, 'The worst in our nature coexists with the best' – the 'monster in the fever swamp'. This is not a new thought. In fact, it is almost our oldest. Sophocles saw it. In his imperishable *Antigone* he tells us, 'Many things are both wonderful and terrible, but none more so than humans.' We want to believe humankind is good, but we see so much wrongdoing – carnage – around us. Where does the truth lie? Each time the chaos comes it is new and very old.

All this led to the three core questions the book asks. They are these:

Who are we?
What are we?
Who is inside us?

Ultimately the book brings to bear the latest cutting-edge research science to offer a different way to think about these and a series of linked questions that flow from them: *Why are we like this? Why do we do the things we do? What choice do we have? Who (or what) in the end does the choosing?*

Let us begin to find out. For that, I will have to take you to another corridor – one in a school. But it is a very particular type of school. And I must introduce you to a person – a very particular type of person. The Kinsman.

The Kinsman

It is every parent's nightmare.

You come out of the coffee shop blinking in the late morning sunshine and you realise your mobile's been on silent. You instinctively glance at its screen as you do one hundred times a day – *must* clean it properly. A text message arrives, then another, a flurry of them. You notice a series of missed calls. Something's happened – but what? You begin to read the texts – they're all telling you the same thing, the message horribly the same. The one you never dreamed you'd hear.

You hardly notice your coffee splashing over your shoes. A man is prowling around your child's school. The man is armed with a gun.

You're just a couple of streets away, you rush down there, but find that all is unnervingly quiet. Summer sunshine casts soft shadows of the schoolyard trees, a lone bird skims across the pale blue sky, but there on the periphery of your vision you see the door to the classrooms – kicked open. Two police officers sprawl on the concrete by the entrance, dead. The bird disappears into the treeline as you enter the corridor – the one with your daughter's classroom. Then you hear them: shots in the next hallway.

You advance, more urgently now, until you glimpse through the glass in the classroom door the many traumatised pupils, wide-eyed, huddled together, hiding under tables. You try in vain to see your daughter. You can't. You gesture to the children, but they're frozen with fear. You are literally going to have to pull and drag them out. But where is your daughter? Then you hear heavy breathing, heavier footsteps – approaching. Heavy boots, a click, more: click, click, *click* . . . a gun being loaded. Time is running out. Suddenly you hear a voice from a broom cupboard by the exit, all the way back down the corridor: it cries your name. Your daughter. What do you do?

Do you abandon the class with the 24 children? Do you stay and try to defend them? At the far end of the corridor, your eyes fall on another body, a teacher who tried and failed to stop the gunman. Then another shape, sprawling, motionless – another teacher who met the same fate.

This could be about being heroic. All of us have the capacity for extreme courage. But if you confront the gunman, assume it's certain that like the police officers and the two teachers before you, you will be killed. So confronting him will be futile: he will shoot you as he has shot them. He will shoot you then shoot all the children, including your daughter, but you will have tried to be heroic – and we all want to think of ourselves as heroic. But what other choices do you have? If you go to the class you can lead them out of the window to safety. If you go to your daughter, you will be able to get her out before the gunman arrives. *There is just not time to do both.*

So what do you do? It's not easy. Something like this never is. But people in these situations have to make a choice. What's yours?

Save the 24 innocent children of other decent parents or save a single child of your own. That is your dilemma. The worst of your life. Perhaps of anyone's. But there it is.

You can hear the gunman's footsteps approaching, the clicks of the weapon being primed, you can see the eyes of the children, you can hear the voice of your daughter calling you, beseeching you – what are you going to do?

You are probably experiencing a whirl of emotions. So to make things clearer, let me reduce your choice to three equations:

1. Confront the gunman, everyone dies = 26 deaths (24 + 1 + 1)
2. Abandon the class, the other children die = 24 deaths
3. Abandon your daughter, only she dies = 1 death

What do you do?

You Were Not Alone

I know what you would do. I know what you'd do because I would do the same. Because virtually everyone we know would do the same.

But can I try to change your mind?

Imagine the choice is between your child and 50 children. Does that alter things? It must surely alter things: 50 lives for one. Below are 50 dots. Imagine each has a child's name. I plucked some from a random name generator on the Internet.

Todd, Sarah, Suresh.

Ellen, David, Jacinth.

Aston, Tiresias (the blind prophet of Thebes – it *was* random). Imagine each is the face of a different child.

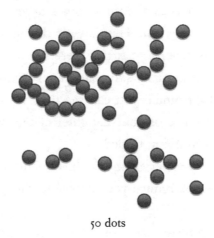

50 dots

Will you save these 50 dots, these 50 children? Or just your own?

What about 100 children? No change? What about 1,000 children? Twenty boxes full of dots, full of children? Still no.

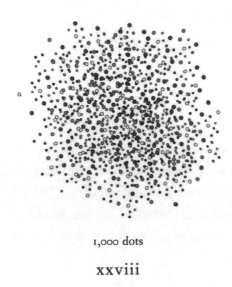

1,000 dots

What about one million — one thousand *thousand* other children — surely that changes your decision? Let us write it out in numbers so you can see the sheer magnitude of the lives at stake: 1,000,000 — all those noughts, that's how many lives you can save, if only you give up one.

Still not enough? What if it were a choice between your child and a young brilliant scientist, and she's stumbled on the vital breakthrough to curing cancer. But here's the problem: she hasn't yet had time to tell anyone about her world-altering discovery. Think of all the generations of unspeakable suffering and grief you will save. Or do you save your child? Can you live with the condemnation of the generations if you choose your child? Can you live with yourself if you don't?

If it's possible, step back. Think about what you're seriously considering. You're contemplating consigning generation after future generation to suffering the continuing blight of cancer, just to save one child. What would you do?

I know what you would do. I know what we'd both do. But why?

This is what the book is about. This and questions like it. The truth is that as you rushed down that corridor towards the broom cupboard, there is one fact you may not have realised:

You were not alone.

The argument of this book is that with you at every step, in fact helping *inform* every step — to advance, retreat, waver — was the first of the Ten Types of Human that are the central subject-matter of what follows. You've just met the first one. Let's give it a name — the Kinsman.

How did this character get into your head? What is it there for? What is it like? This book proposes that it is a psychological mechanism that has evolved over great stretches of our evolutionary past to respond to certain repeating life problems. Its functioning interacts with our learned behaviour, our socialisation. Thus nature and nurture connect and complicate. While you were in the school corridor you may have caught yourself saying that you *ought* to be doing one thing, but something deep inside you *wants* to do something else: to head to the classroom, to head back to the broom cupboard. You will find out much more about the Kinsman soon, but you already know something tremendously important: it will sacrifice dozens or even hundreds of other children — even a thousand — for just one of its own. We all want to protect our children. Everyone knows that. But do we really appreciate the frightening strength of that drive? How aware are we of the ruthless extent that it chooses our child over others? Why is it like this?

Did you 'break'? This is the term we've pretty quickly settled on when I've spoken to groups about this problem. Did you reach a point at which you left your child? Some people — very few — break at 24. Far more when it gets to 50 other children. Many more find their breaking point is closer to 100. I have a friend who did not break even if the toll would be every single other child on the planet. Until she realised that she wanted a child for her daughter to play with — so everyone else minus one, that was her number. That friend (she's still a friend) is a lawyer.

We all have a number. What's yours? What do these numbers say about us? By our numbers shall we be known? These are the kind of questions this book is about. Questions and characters. Characters like the Kinsman. This has been just a brief introduction to one – the Kinsman will come again. But there are others of the Ten Types we must meet first. Like the subject of the next section: the Perceiver of Pain. Here they are in the order you will meet them:

The Perceiver of Pain
The Ostraciser
The Tamer of Terror
The Beholder
The Aggressor
The Tribalist
The Nurturer
The Romancer
The Rescuer
And finally, again, the Kinsman

But in order to understand the Ten Types, we must have examples. Thus in the following ten parts of the book — one for each Type – I triangulate my approach.

Firstly, we explore the mental modules involved, invoking the latest research in psychology and neuroscience.

Secondly, personal narratives, human stories from a number of exceptional people I've worked with and met, will show how the Types affect people in their everyday lives – and how these remarkable individuals have found ways to face and face down their more damaging effects.

Thirdly, a number of hypotheticals will offer you the opportunity to experience some of these mechanisms for yourself.

In this way I hope you will not only hear about the Types, but see them, *feel* them, and thus arrive at a richer answer to those core questions: *Who are we? What are we? Who is inside us?*

Therefore I hope that the coming pages will reveal why we are not what we think – and how this is a good thing. How it opens up intriguing possibilities for knowing ourselves in a new way and seeing the world differently. We will see a number of things that are not right with the world. The book will offer ways to challenge them. These solutions are grounded in the approach of Spanish philosopher Manuel Castells, who said that in order to challenge harmful power and its abuse, we must unveil its presence in the workings of our minds. This is the most essential mission of this book.

It offers a new examination of the nature of human nature. It is a quest. To look in a new way at how human beings hurt other human beings – and in doing so, to find ways to change this. Ultimately that is what *The Ten Types of Human* is about: finding fresh ways to be free.

Throughout my work on this book, I constantly kept close at hand an increasingly tattered news report about the boy I never met and could not save. Sometimes those few frames from the high CCTV camera would flicker in my mind; sometimes the screen would go blank, then slowly the picture would reassemble: a corridor, a boy disappearing from it, a door shutting, a question: what happened in that room?

My other constant companion was the simple question of his mother Pam – why?

PART I

THE PERCEIVER OF PAIN

It is true that I suffered captivity in the fortress of Yakub the Afflicted.

Richard Francis Burton, *The Lake Regions of Central Africa* (1860)

ONE

The Argument

The tension you felt when agonising between protecting the 24 children in the classroom and saving your own child, was in part generated by an aspect of your mental make-up – a 'Type'. The Kinsman. What are these Types? What do they consist of neurologically, functionally, practically in everyday life? What sort of a thing are they?

To understand, take a boy like Anthony.

'Why do you want to talk to me?' he asked. 'I'm nobody.'

At the beginning, it's true, my mastery of our language of mutual communication was too rusty to explain why I believed he had something crucial we needed to hear. My fault: I should have brushed up better. But I persevered. More accurately, he did. And here it is: the story of the boy who thought he was nobody. We met in an old shack, just close enough to the shore to feel the sea breeze, but which offered scant shade from the unsparing African sun. So Africa: the other side from those ancestral savannahs, but Africa nonetheless.

'When it happened,' he said, 'I was doing nothing.'

A chicken wandered past our feet on vital business of its own. So: nobody doing nothing. How very promising. At the time he was talking about, a few years before, Anthony was 11 years old, and like many 11-year-olds he would do a great deal to get this one thing, the object of his desire. Although the world – and I mean the *entire* world – knows it as an iconic American product (it was conceived by Atlanta pharmacist John S. Pemberton in 1886), few realise that one of its constituents, the kola nut, is actually native to Africa. But at that precise point in his life, Anthony couldn't care less: he would just give almost anything to get it. And that's how it started: with Coca-Cola.

That first time we met, in a shack surrounded by boxing gyms and signs for Ovaltine and the Almighty's undying love, near the Gulf of Guinea, near an old slaver fort (those things are connected), I was perplexed. Anthony reminds you of a ball. Not because he is round – he most certainly is not – but because like a rubber ball there is something elastic and durable about him. Something that bounces back; that's had to. His greatest love is indeed boxing, and he finds it hard to stay still, forever bobbing and swaying as if constantly in some imaginary bout in the ring. He has limbs that look like linguine, but in fact are steel wire. He has big almond eyes. At times, later, when he was telling me what actually happened, his eyes would well up and he'd fight it, fight himself and everything he knows – too much for a teen-aged boy to know: the strange underwater forests, the snakes (*'Les serpents, les serpents'*), the day of rain and lightning, the body in the boat. But it started off joyously. With the chance of Coca-Cola.

4

Fictional depictions of human trafficking portray it as starting with predatory snatch squads, kidnapping, abduction. Sometimes it does. But other times it's much more mundane. With Anthony it started by going to the local store. The shop was in his small town in Ghana. 'My father sent me to the store,' he said. Anthony and I communicate mainly in French – his mother is from the French-speaking country of Benin further along the coast; he had come to Ghana to be with his father.

After that first meeting, I wrote in my notebook:

Does he like me? Does he _need_ to like me?
The British barrister, the boy from Benin.
He needs to trust me.
What's trust?

At the shack near the seafront, Anthony told me, 'You know, my father, he gave me money. He said I could buy a Coca-Cola.'

That day that changed his life was in the long, dry season and everyone was thirsty. It was as though the rain had forgotten how to come. Anthony went to the store to get a Coke. He never returned.

The story of Anthony you are about to read – why he never returned, what happened on the other side of that door – tells us something vital about one part of who we are. But right from the start, let me be clear about what the book is seeking to do: it will present an account of human nature. Not *the* account. An account.

We all have pet theories about human nature. As do all religions and political parties. Think of some of the truth claims produced by less gender-sensitive times:

All men are sinners. (Pet theory)
Man is born free, yet everywhere he is in chains. (Theory)
We hold these truths to be self-evident, that all men are created equal. (Theory)
All animals are equal; some are more equal than others. (Counter-theory)

The Uber driver who conveyed me across Florida in an unnervingly militaristic Jeep (we'll come to Florida in Part II), well, he had a very distinctive theory of human nature. It involved Donald J. Trump and people from the other side of the wall Trump says he wants to build. Thus this book is not offered to you as 'the one and only Truth'. It is grounded in two things: scientific fact and scientific theory. A scientific theory is a wider kind of theory than the simple truth claims above. It is a series of propositions from which you can make predictions that are testable. The book's prime theory is based on a mass of research science and converging lines of evidence in evolutionary biology, neuroscience and several branches of experimental psychology – what has been called a second Darwinian revolution. Our prime theory is as follows:

Theory #1

THE HUMAN MIND IS MODULAR

By this we mean that the architecture of the mind includes certain specialised, information processing, computational programmes. Same old brain; new way to understand it. A better way, a growing number of scientists now argue. Here is how the argument leads to and then flows on from that prime theory:

6

1. Our physical bodies have been shaped by evolution.
2. They consist of a series of highly specialised (adapted) components or organs.
3. The mind has also been shaped by evolution.
4. It also consists of a series of highly specialised components.
5. These components – or modules – have evolved when confronting certain repeating, real, highly relevant survival and reproductive challenges.

Propositions 1 and 2 are obvious to most people. So forgive me for not labouring them. If you are interested in them . . . actually, why *shouldn't* you be? How many more interesting things are there than why life *is* – just is. Why there is life rather than non-life and *this* kind of life. To get at this, we're blessed with Richard Dawkins' *The Selfish Gene*, Daniel Dennett's *Darwin's Dangerous Idea*, Stephen Jay Gould's *Wonderful Life*, a magisterial account of the stunning burgeoning of new life forms in the Precambrian. More recently, a concise but compelling addition to the evolution literature is Jerry Coyne's *Why Evolution Is True*.

These works are backdrop, run-up to the wicket, advance battalions. In the pages that follow, the concept of evolution is so pervasively important that here is Coyne's brief refresher:

> Life on Earth evolved gradually beginning with one primitive species – perhaps a self-replicating molecule – that lived more than 3.5 billion years ago; it then branched out over time, throwing off many new and diverse species; and the mechanism for most (but not all) of evolutionary change is natural selection.

This book does not seek to *prove* evolution. It examines its implications for the human mind. It does not provide an anatomical or physiological disquisition of the human body and its functional subunits or organs. Instead it considers how an equivalent functional specialisation may apply to our brain and thus our mind (approximately: what the brain does). So it uses Propositions 1 and 2 as building blocks. From them we infer what our mind might be like. It is an argument from analogy. We infer some qualities of the mind from how our physical bodies have been built and developed over time by genes. Some gene mutations were better, some worse for survival and reproduction. Microscopic advantages, when elongated over aeons, mattered greatly. Thus some arrangements survived, were reproduced, flourished and spread through populations in the grand and gruesome cosmic sorting process, the unsparing battle for existence in a world of scarcity and limit. And here we are. With our module-packed physical bodies. But what about our mind?

I first began to understand this because of Anthony. Shortly, I will return to him so you can see for yourself. But there is something else you need to know before we go to those underwater forests infested by water snakes and simultaneously grapple with the question posed in the single most famous case in English law: who is my neighbour – what duty do we owe to one another? First we must follow the overarching argument through and understand two things: the evolved mind and modularity. Then we will go to the lake that is not a lake and meet children who, in almost every way, are not children. One of them is Anthony.

Thus we come to **Proposition 3**: the evolved mind.

The argument from analogy is supported by a growing mass of evidence that the mind has also been shaped by this same process of cosmic sorting – evolution by natural selection. Indeed, the evidence and research you will read in this book supports this plank of the argument. But nonetheless I invite you to read the material with an open mind and reach your own conclusion. Darwin foresaw these developments about the human mind. As he drew his world-changing *Origin of Species* to a conclusion, he wrote that

> In the distant future I see open fields for **far more important researches. Psychology** will be based on a new foundation, that of the necessary **acquirement** of each mental power and capacity **by gradation**. (my emphasis)

Yes: mental powers acquired by *gradation* – by gradual, incremental change. Evolution by natural selection. A simple question puts the point. If almost everything about our physical being has evolved, why not our brain? The brain has billions of neurons: nerve cells that carry and transmit information. It may have something like 100 billion of them. Via networks of neurons, the brain processes information received externally from the environment, internally from ourselves. Like the rest of our body, the brain is built by genes. The process is, after all, *genetic* evolution. Some genes are 'selected' because they confer durable survival and reproductive benefits; others are not because they do not. Natural selection is simply the process regulating what gets through to the next generation, who gets through – ultimately, what works in a particular environmental setting. If our bodies have evolved, and our brains have evolved, why should what our brains *do* not evolve? Simply: some of the variants in what the brain has done may not have worked so well. They may well have not 'got through'. Seen in this light, why should our mind be immune to evolution? Put the other way around:

has virtually everything of serious importance about our body evolved except our brain and what it does?

The best statement by far of this approach is by Australian philosopher Peter Singer, whose work we'll come to shortly. Singer states that it is time 'to take seriously the fact that we are evolved animals, and that we bear the evidence of our inheritance, not only in our anatomy and DNA, but in our behaviour too.'

On **Proposition 4**, modularity, just look around.

Modularity is everywhere. When we deliberately set about building complex systems to perform complex tasks, we build them modularly. That is, with a lot of smaller component parts. Cars, phones and fridges, planes and political systems. In doing so, we are imitating nature. The principle of division and subdivision of tasks yielding outcome benefits can be found everywhere. In engineering, computer science and coding — on the back of a banknote. Consider the rear of the £20 note.

Here is the Bank of England celebrating functional modularity. Adam Smith wrote in his *Wealth of Nations* about the division of labour in a pin factory and the great increase in the quantity of work that results (you may just be able to read that on the note). The meta-task of making a pin was broken down into smaller specialist units or modules. It's appropriate to mention Smith for while at Cambridge, Darwin read *The Wealth of Nations*. Then when Darwin wrote *On the Origin of Species*, Smith's 'invisible hand' of the market became the silent and insensible workings of the 'hand of time' and natural selection. It is this unobservable process that produced mental modules over what Darwin calls 'the long lapses of ages'. A module is simply a functional subunit. Its job is to perform a specific task – like part of the process of making a pin. You'll find modules everywhere in nature. So what about the human mind? Can natural selection have created specialised programmes like the Kinsman?

For us, all this leaves two important takeaways. First, modules in nature are ubiquitous. Second, it is very likely that one of the most sophisticated and complex mechanisms in the known universe – the human mind – is modular. And, as we'll see, that's what the evidence indicates.

Meticulous neurophysiological experimentation has shown that the brain has different areas implicated in different functions. But note two things. Each area of the brain is not restricted to performing only one function. Equally, each area works in a network with others. The occipital lobe at the lower rear of the brain, for example, makes sense out of the visual information that pours in through the eyes to the retina, and which is then transmitted via the thalamus to the back of the brain (and from there to the parietal and temporal lobes). A series of structures, together called the limbic system, is associated with what is sometimes called the Four Fs: Feeding, Fighting, Fleeing and – getting lucky. And the limbic system is a perfect example of what we were considering: it is a network of structures, including the amygdala, the hippocampus and the hypothalamus, working in concert. So in the brain, unquestionably, function is to some extent localised.

There is therefore a growing weight of scientific evidence indicating that the human mind has organisational units or modules. But what are they like?

Proposition 5: these modules evolved in response to certain important regularly recurring life problems. What these modules are like and how they affect our behaviour is the substance of the book.

These mental modules, embedded in the human nervous system, process information, particularly emanating from stimuli and challenges in the environment. The argument is that these modules developed over evolutionary time, as many things develop, due to selection pressures, in the ongoing struggle to fulfil the two fundamental evolutionary drives: to survive and reproduce. Thus the modules are the work of natural selection. They have encountered, engaged with, and helped us solve life problems – existential threats to our survival and flourishing. They are functionally specialised, directed at key adaptive problems. They have enhanced 'fitness': the relative frequency of the genes of their host in subsequent generations of the relevant population, the gene pool. They do not determine behaviour robotically, but they do influence our feelings, thoughts and actions. This is particularly so when we are confronted with the branching sub-problems of survival and reproduction, such as mate selection, raising offspring, living in groups, avoiding predators, punishing transgressors. We will look at ten such problems in the ten parts of this book.

So those are the five planks of the argument. Leda Cosmides and John Tooby, two founders (legends) of evolutionary psychology, nail it, as they often do:

. . . our abilities to see, to speak, to find someone beautiful, to reciprocate a favor, to fear disease, to fall in love, to initiate an attack, to experience moral outrage, to navigate a landscape, and myriad others – are possible only because there is a vast and heterogenous array of complex computational machinery supporting and regulating these activities.

Of the five propositions – I make no bones about it – 1 and 2 are *assumed*. They are taken as a base to proceed from. Others, the more interesting and controversial 'stuff', the ten parts of the book will examine. Propositions 1 to 5 together constitute building blocks for formulating a theory about human nature. It is a theory in the sense that it can help explain the evidence and generate some predictions about how humans are (probabilistically) likely to behave. The Ten Types build on this theory.

Here is our prime theory, fleshed out – supersized:

Theory #1A

The human mind is an array of highly specialised mental modules that perform different functions, and which evolved through natural selection to solve life challenges that recurrently confronted our ancestors over long stretches of evolutionary time.

Building on that theory, the Ten Types is a tool to understand something unique and extraordinary about our evolved nature. As Daniel Dennett reminds us, in the history of thought, thinkers have always used vignettes, models, stories – for example, Plato's Cave, or Descartes' Demon. They help us think about the problem.

Modularity is a theory that helps to explain some of the mysteries of human behaviour. Particularly of what human beings do to other human beings. Both good and bad. The Ten Types help us to explore and understand some features of the modular mind. What its working out might mean on a human level.

There have been many analyses and postulations about the complicated and fragmented nature of the self. Neuroscientist V. S. Ramachandran puts it starkly: the idea of 'a single unified self "inhabiting" the brain may indeed be an illusion'. Robert Kurzban and Athena Aktipis state that 'the self that talks and controls muscles is but one subsystem in the modular architecture'. Psychologists Douglas Kenrick and Vladas Griskevicius have identified from the mass of our complex behaviour a number of 'subselves' – versions of ourself subconsciously selected by our nervous system to take the 'driver's seat' at any given time.

In this book, I conceive of these complex systems, and the other 'selves' associated with them, as 'Types' because they exemplify and embody particular types of human behaviour. The book's deepest purpose is to understand how and why these Types are implicated in harmful human behaviours and then suggest ways to change those patterns of harm.

Our first example is Anthony.

To understand what happened to him, why this child in sub-Saharan Africa who thought he was nobody, and was doing nothing, matters, why he casts light on one of our evolved mental modules – the Perceiver of Pain – you must understand the place. And to understand the place you must understand its geography. It is like none other on earth.

TWO

The 21,000

If you unfold an old-fashioned map of the world – the Imperial Federation map of 1886 for example, an imperial relic with the British Empire inked in salmon pink– and slowly trace your finger 3,000 miles due south from the UK, you will pass over Morocco and Mauretania and Mali until you reach sub-Saharan Africa's vast Volta basin.

This basin of the Volta river is a complex meshing of hundreds of tributaries and waterways that spread across six West African countries: Mali, Ivory Coast, Burkina Faso, Togo, Benin and Ghana. And in Ghana lies an immense body of brooding water: Lake Volta. Through its deceptively placid surface – the area suffers from severe sudden thunderstorms that make the lake lethal – denuded tree branches stick out, thin fossilised fingers, frozen in time, pointing to the sky. But the lake is not real. At least, it did not exist, not even as an idea, until 1915 when British geologist A. E. Kitson, KBE, CMG thought, with the kind of colonial swagger characteristic of the best and worst of Empire, 'Let's stop that river in its tracks.'

Albert Ernest Kitson — 'Kittie' to his friends — led a remarkable life. He was born in Audenshaw, a Cheshire cotton town now swallowed up by the sprawl of Greater Manchester. His parents, a Mancunian and his Scottish bride, emigrated first to Nagpur in India, then to rural Australia, where Kitson learned to handle snakes, a feat that the Ghanaians he would later meet thought imbued Kittie with mystical powers. He was an outstanding geologist and was knighted in 1927. His aptitude and vast imagination led to a simple, staggering suggestion: dam the Volta, dam the whole damn thing. Like many things in the British Empire, Kitson's idea was about transformation. The wild power of the river water would be transformed into electricity, which would transform the bauxite from the Kwahu Mountain area into alumina and then into aluminium ingots, with the result that the soil and substance of Ghana would be transformed into money.

In 1937 Kitson died of pneumonia and influenza at Beaconsfield, Buckinghamshire. A eucalyptus tree and a fossil eucalypt were named after him — as was a reptile (*Panaspis kitsoni*), a kind of little slithery eel-like lizardy thing with legs. But in 1965, a full 50 years after his initial idea, there was a much more significant legacy. Ghana's first post-independence president, Kwame Nkrumah, authorised work on Kitson's dam. An enormous pile of stone and rock was dropped in the way of the water at Akosombo. The result was devastating: the creation of the largest man-made lake by surface area on the planet. Lake Volta is over 200 miles long. That fact is easy to state. But imagine a lake stretching from London to Liverpool or from the Brooklyn Bridge to Boston. That's how long.

The White Volta and Black Volta rivers were restrained by the immense Akosombo Dam with its six gushing spillways, generating hydroelectric power not only for Ghana but for eastern neighbour Togo as well, and even for the next country to the east again: Benin. (We will return to Benin.) The scheme was to play a crucial part in Ghana's socio-economic development, the plan being to produce 200,000 tons of aluminium per year. There is indeed now a smelter at the port of Tema on the coast. But the result was devastating in another way.

The river upstream of the dam flows with a very flat gradient, about one foot per mile. This meant that the backed-up water created a deluge that flooded 740 villages. In total 78,000 people were made refugees in their own land. But human beings are resilient. Soon a series of small fishing communities sprang up around the fringes of the newly formed lake. There are now over 1,200. Some were populated by local people who previously had been pastoralists and farmers. But there was an influx of migrants from other parts of Ghana, tough coastal people with fishing expertise, intent on harvesting the lake's 120 species of fish, including many types of tilapia. The new migrants now outnumber the historic locals and came notwithstanding the dangers. The area is notorious for onchocerciasis – river blindness, caused by repeated bites from blackflies.

The fishing that takes place at the lake is of a very particular kind: long, arrow-like wooden boats, small catches, and fish that are ever smaller as the waters are over-exploited. It is desperately subsistence stuff. Therefore there's the need to cut costs to the very minimum. Small fingers are needed to pick the small fish from the nets. Children are needed.

But the margins are so small that for some fishermen not only is child labour needed, but the cheapest form of it: child slave labour. And that's what you've got. Estimates vary, but there are thought to be 21,000 children engaged in hazardous work at the lake – labour that is potentially life-threatening. Of that number, it is not known how many have been sold into slavery.

What has this to do with any of us? I knew only a few of these details before I met Anthony. Still, again the question: what has this to do with us? Slave children fishing in arrow-like wooden boats on a lake in a land hardly any of us really know. I began to understand it because of him. Although he did not know, it was his gift to me.

You don't even have to force yourself to get up early.

It's the thrill of getting away, of leaving the city; the simple, silent intoxication of cleaner air. And so you're walking in the early sunshine, relaxed – didn't even recharge your mobile. The lake is a local beauty spot, remarkably close to the metropolitan area, but on the other side of a heavily wooded hill from the clogged arteries feeding cars and commuters into the city. But here it is: a haven, an oasis, something like a minor miracle. It all seems perfect. Only it's not. Something is wrong.

You've been told that local kids go night fishing at the lake in the holidays, and a number of rare species of bird rest there before heading south – some flying 3,000 miles to sub-Saharan Africa and the Equator. You pass through the outer fringe of trees: chestnuts, beech, mature oaks. You glance down towards the water, the sun dazzling as it bounces off the sheet mirror stillness of the surface. When two things force their way into your thoughts. Yes. Something is definitely wrong.

First, you notice a small bike, carelessly propped against a tree. It's slid down, handlebars turned invitingly askew. The sheer brilliance of the water-reflected light blinds you, a low spotlight beam shining into your face. You shield your eyes with your cupped hand. And then you notice the second thing.

Something in the water. Bobbing above the water, then just as suddenly gone. Perhaps you're imagining things.

In the distance the low growl of the commuter traffic slowly increases as the morning rush hour begins its laborious winding up. There is a foldaway chair, patio furniture, at the edge of the lake. Lurid yellow and white stripes, but somehow festive. The stillness of the lake is broken by something. You squint. Something moving in the water. You squeeze your eyes, move your head left, right, for a better view. There *is* something in the water.

Someone.

A child. Drowning.

Your head snaps around, scans the trees. No one anywhere. It's just past dawn. From the apron of trees, slippery embankments run treacherously down to the water, which is black and dangerous. The child – a boy. His head appears above the water, then disappears below. There are reeds and bulrushes. He splutters something, his mouth, nose, full of water. His head vanishes below the surface. He can't call for help. You do. You call out. No one anywhere. His hand appears above the water. Fingers outstretched. Just the top of his head, not even his eyes. He's fighting but something's dragging him down, dragging him under – the reeds? The mud? He's about 30 feet out from the bank. It's down to you. No one else can save him. He is going to drown. It's down to you. You'll have to go in.

You rush down to the edge of the water. The bank's so steep, hazardous with morning dew. You lose your footing, your soles fly into the air. You skid down the bank, hurtling towards the water yourself. You see another skid mark. This is what happened to him? You see a sign. A red warning triangle. Two hands disappearing beneath sinister black waves with the words below: *Danger of Drowning – No Swimming.*

The boy is not swimming. He is drowning.

For a fleeting, fateful second, your eyes, his eyes, meet. No words are exchanged. But you know what he's saying: *Are you going to save me?*

Are you?

You can save him. No one else can. Your peripheral vision is drawn magnetically back to that sign: *Danger of Drowning – No Swimming.*

Another red warning sign further along the bankside: *It only takes seconds to drown.* Do you risk yourself? Do you go in? Your feet are wet. Your jeans now drenched up to the knees, but that's all. You don't have to be where he is. You don't have to be in the water. That's his life, not yours. You don't have to imperil yourself. You didn't ask for this. You went on a walk. You didn't even have to force yourself to get up early. But you want to do something. Your mobile. You snatch it out of your pocket. It's dead. There is no other help. You shout out again. Your words lost in the trees. No one else is going to intercede. Your eyes lock again – you and the boy. You see his bike with its skewed handlebars. You see his face. He's looking at you. You *feel* his gaze. You feel his fear, his terror that he's about to die. If not for you. There are only two people. One in the water, one out. One drowning. The other can try to stop it.

You think of those you love. Wouldn't they want you to help him?

Think of those who depend on you: would they want you to risk your life? *It only takes seconds to drown.* But so many people do depend on you. *Danger of Drowning – No Swimming.*

Do you go in?

THREE

Here Be Dragons

This was almost exactly the dilemma that faced the friends of Dylan Aaron in 2010. Dylan was 17 years old and he ended up in John Pit pond, a local beauty spot near the metropolitan area of Wigan. The water is black and dangerous. Beneath the surface reeds and plants await. Along with the sucking mud they tangle the legs and trap the feet of anyone swimming in it. People have died there. Locally it is known as Deep Pit.

Dylan's family had been involved in an ongoing feud with another local family, the McGrails. After a series of skirmishes, the events culminated in a fateful confrontation in May 2010. At 3am after a night out with his friends Dylan returned home. He saw that their family car had a stone slab smashed through the windscreen. He knew who was responsible. And he was right.

Drew McGrail was night fishing at Deep Pit. As Dylan approached, a fight broke out. The two tumbled down the steep bank towards the water. It was then that McGrail, ten years older, threw Dylan into the lake. He said, 'Drown, you little bastard.' Struggling to keep his head above water, Dylan cried out, 'Help me, I can't kick my legs.' McGrail said, 'Let him die. If he gets out, I'm going to kill him anyway.'

Friends of Dylan, desperate, tried to get in the water. At first McGrail stopped them, but one managed to jump in. It was too late. Dylan's head, his outstretched arm, disappeared beneath the waters of Deep Pit, where he died.

I mention this for two reasons. Firstly, to indicate how deceptively lethal the lake is – it is so easy to drown in a place like that, beautiful or not. But secondly, because despite the obvious danger, one of Dylan's friends tried to save him. What is all the more stirring is that he tried to save Dylan despite the fact that there had been another incident at John Pit pond just three years before. Another death. One that received national attention.

On the day Anthony's life changed, he simply did something he'd done several dozen times before: he walked to the local store in Ghana. As he did so, he could smell someone cooking fowl: the enticing odour wafted into his nose and jumped straight into his brain. He was hungry, so hungry – but despite the heat, his feet were lured on by one thought . . . Co-ca Co-la. He *was* 11. And his father had said he could get a Coke. What if he could get a Coke *and* some of the bird to eat? Life was good. It had been hard in Benin; they had struggled. His mother had tried her best. But now life was good. Sometimes his father beat him, but it was to make him tough. Anthony wanted to be tough.

Sometimes when you're speaking to him, he'll narrow those almond eyes, squint at you. A gunslinger look. He would later tell me what he really felt at our first meeting. 'I was thinking, "Who is this person? He speaks worse than me."'

All true: my French *was* rusty.

'Why did you come here?' he asked me, genuinely.

Frankly, I didn't know where to start. I said that a boy had died in a prison in England and I was trying to understand what had happened. It meant speaking to lots of different people about lots of different things. This surprised him, not my diffuse and imprecise search, but the location in which the death occurred. What he knew of the UK was Premiership football.

'They *kill* children in England?' he said incredulously.

'*C'est compliqué,*' I said and immediately regretted it. In truth, having to admit this so far from home, I was ashamed. But in truth, yes, we had. I should have said it.

'But why are you doing this?' he asked.

I tried to explain that I was the family's lawyer, but am not sure I was able to help him understand what a lawyer does. The more I talked, the stranger it sounded to me, there under the hot West African sun, what a lawyer actually is. In that moment, we both seemed a long way from home. 'I'm trying to find out why he died,' I said.

'For who?' Anthony asked.

It was a question worthy of any lawyer. The answer, it was – *compliqué*. Life, like the law, is not an exact science. 'I want to know,' I finally said.

Later, almost at the end of our time together, he told me, 'That first time we met, I was going to leave. Then I thought, "Okay, I give him *one* chance."'

Which is interesting. No one had ever given Anthony much of one. In my notes I wrote: *Chances. When do we give each other chances?*

*

On 3 May 2007, Jordon Lyon was out with his step-sister Bethany, aged eight, collecting tadpoles from the edge of Deep Pit. But the banks are treacherously steep. Bethany slipped into the cloying water and mud. Without thinking, Jordon dived in to save her. Two anglers were able to pull the girl free, but Jordon was sucked further in. He disappeared.

As the alarm was raised, two PCSOs (Police Community Support Officers) turned up on bicycles. They arrived minutes after Jordon vanished beneath the water. What they did next caused what the major newspapers called a 'national outcry'. What they did was heavily criticised by Conservative party leader David Cameron. Cameron said it was an 'extraordinary farce'. The PCSOs did not go in after ten-year-old Jordon.

As the controversy intensified, a Home Office spokesperson came to the defence of the much-maligned officers. She said, 'Guidance advises PCSOs not to enter into life-threatening situations for which they are not trained.' That was the official line. They are not trained, so they had no obligation to help.

But this official stance begs a question of the most fundamental importance: trained in what? They may have not been police-trained to intervene, but were they not trained by life? Are we? What would you have done? As Jordon's stepfather Anthony Ganderton said, 'You don't have to be trained to jump in after a drowning child.' Indeed Paul Kelly, the chair of the Police Federation in the area, accepted, 'People throw themselves into rivers and ponds to save people every day because it's the right thing to do.'

The drowning of Jordon Lyon raises the question of what our obligations to one another consist of. What do we owe to those around us and how do our evolved mental structures affect it? It was the central question in the most famous case in English law, *Donoghue v Stevenson*, the case that many people who know nothing of the law nevertheless have heard of, the modern launch pad of the law of negligence: the case of the snail in a bottle of ginger beer in the Wellmeadow Café in Paisley. When it was appealed all the way up to the highest court, the House of Lords, Lord Atkin – as he often did – crisply posed the critical question in its simplest form: 'Who is my neighbour?'

The Atkin formulation resonates with a much more ancient question, much cited, but rarely understood, which even more people have heard of. It is this: am I my brother's keeper?

To understand whether, and in what way, you are your brother's keeper, we are going to meet another of your evolved selves, another Type: the Perceiver of Pain.

Anthony entered the store in Ghana.

It was slightly more than a shack, had brick walls, a tin roof. The shopkeeper told him that in the backroom he had a couple of fake football shirts. Not the real thing, but to an 11-year-old boy in a country obsessed with Barclays Premiership football irresistible. Anthony's history is complex. The family are Ewe, a tribal group that spans the eastern reaches of Ghana, the south of Togo and the neighbouring country to the east – Benin. Anthony's father is Ghanaian, and Anthony was born there. But his mother's family is part Beninese, and when his father abandoned the family, she returned with Anthony and his three younger sisters to Benin. In Benin people generally speak their local language, and French. Benin has had a tangled relationship with France ever since the French built a slaving fort there in late 1600s. The area officially became a French protectorate during the 19th century.

Benin itself is a long thin strip of land in central West Africa. It extends for 400 miles like a bulbous finger pointing north up towards the Sahara from the Bight of Benin, from which the former French colony of Dahomey took its new name on independence in 1960. It's situated near that continental elbow where West Africa bulges out in a right angle into the Atlantic spray. And though its shoreline is narrow – a modest 75 miles – the sea has played a critical part in Benin's history. Its seaboard was part of the infamous Slave Coast, a centre of the Atlantic slave trade. As the old sea shanty warned:

> Beware, beware the Bight of Benin;
> Few come out though many go in.

It was a variation of the admonition of old map-makers: Here Be Dragons. As a tribute to all the slaves torn from their homes and shipped to the Americas, there is a memorial arch above the beach of the coastal city of Ouidah (pronounced 'why-da'). Above the slowly breaking Atlantic waves is the 'Door of No Return'. It commemorates the many millions who died in the Atlantic slave trade.

Economically, Benin is severely underdeveloped and is ranked by the IMF among the world's poorest countries, comparable in GDP with South Sudan and Rwanda. Extreme poverty affects much of life in Benin. It is one of the critical factors that contributes to many social ills, including malnutrition and death from a number of preventable diseases, like malaria and diarrhoea. It also contributes to a modern form of slavery.

Still, Anthony's father said he'd have the boy back in Ghana. He'd pay for his schooling. He'd give him a future – set him up in life. 'I would miss my mother and sisters,' Anthony told me. 'But I was happy also because I wanted to learn. I wanted to go to school.' So Anthony was sent back to Ghana to be with his father. And now his father had sent him to the shop with the tin roof.

Anthony went through the door, never to return.

FOUR

A More Total Darkness

To recap: the argument of the book is that we've evolved a number of mental modules. They are associated with characteristic types of human behaviour. Through Anthony we are exploring one of them: the Perceiver of Pain. But what do these modules look like? Can we *see* them? If so, where?

Though they operate like discretely functioning subunits, remember that they are systems. Thus they're not plug-ins like the SIM card in a phone or the spark plugs of your car. They are likely to be smeared across several connected areas of the brain: it is networks of structures that are important. They could look, as Steven Pinker memorably put it, like roadkill.

They are unlikely to depend on one gene. They are likely to be associated with many. They are unlikely to be neatly isolatable. They're likely to be messily integrated with other systems, overlapping, connecting, co-opting. So we're unlikely to be able to prod and probe them with tweezers. But they work. And thus we do. Therefore, just as our bodies have evolved to house numerous

27

specialised organs tailored for specific tasks (the eyes for seeing; the heart for pumping precious oxygen-carrying blood), so it is likely that the mind has also evolved with specialised units fit for purpose – tailored for the task.

I cannot emphasise too strongly how controversial views like this once were – and indeed have recently been. In 1616 Galileo was informed by the Roman Inquisition that the suggestion that the Earth revolved around a stationary sun was 'foolish and absurd in philosophy; and formally heretical since it explicitly contradicts in many places the sense of Holy Scripture.'

Galileo was ordered to abstain from teaching or defending his blasphemous heresy. By publicly recanting, he saved himself from the purifying fires of blind faith. I have often hoped that it's true that after his forced renunciation, Galileo whispered, '*E pur si muove*' – 'And still it moves'. Darwin finally published *On the Origin of Species* in 1859, but if at the time of Galileo, some precocious visionary had had the temerity to say, 'Oh, and by the way, in addition to the Earth moving around the Sun, our bodies and minds have developed glacially slowly over countless millennia through a biological process that seems to govern all nature,' they would have been burnt at the stake.

In the 20th century, another kind of orthodoxy gained a great deal of prominence, this time within academic circles. It was the view that we, *Homo sapiens*, have no inherent nature. It was put by Spanish philosopher Ortega y Gasset thus, 'Man has no nature; what he has is history.' Medieval philosopher (and Catholic saint) Thomas Aquinas said there is 'nothing in the intellect which was not previously in the senses'. This is the 'blank slate' thesis. It builds upon the idea of Oxford philosopher John Locke, who while never quite using the precise term, helped develop the idea. We are all only social learning and experience. We come into the world with no inheritance – with a blank slate. Therefore our behaviour is learning, not legacy. In the 1970s, when some scholars began to suggest there may just be a genetic component in what we do, there was outrage. There were metaphorical lynchings and intellectual burnings at the stake.

Be under no misapprehension: the ideas I want to share with you have been considered subversive. But that can be a good thing. Subversion is justified – it is *necessary* – when it is countering superstition, bigotry, prejudice or just simple but damaging error.

Nowadays, while these ideas may not be universally accepted, they are less controversial, grounded in research examining an extraordinary variety of areas of human life. A study published in 2014 by Yale psychologists Annie Wertz and Karen Wynn indicated that six-month-old babies are born with an evolved learning mechanism for identifying which plants can be eaten. This ability was present 'prior to any formalized instruction, and mirrors the ancestrally recurrent problem humans faced with respect to identifying edible plant resources.'

In similar vein, just this morning on Radio 4 there was a piece about how the 'food fussiness' and 'neophobia' (rejection of unfamiliar food) of some children may be hereditary. Anyone who has tried to introduce some virtuous new foodstuff to a child will have been scarred on this particular battlefield. As one child I tried to persuade to eat alfalfa sprouts put it, 'What is the difference between this and grass?' Radio 4's *Today* programme showcased an extensive study of 1,921 families with twins, aged 16 months at the time of the research. The study examined to what extent food fussiness and neophobia were contributed to by genetic or environmental influences – nature or nurture.

Comparisons between twins are particularly useful in unpacking the contribution of genes and environment. Identical twins share the same genes. If reared apart in different environments, do they nevertheless share some common behavioural patterns? Do they independently have a serious loathing of cauliflower? The findings demonstrated how the reluctance to be thrilled about eating certain foods may show 'considerable heritability'. Yet hope was offered to dispirited parents: it is possible with a supportive, nurturing environment to 'overcome' these inbuilt disinclinations. Nurture can help smooth some of the rougher edges of nature. The authors gamely suggest 'repeated exposure to the problem food'. Good luck with that.

So: genetic inheritance *and* social learning contribute to our behaviour. There. Was that so terrible?

As the late Stephen Jay Gould said, 'There is inheritance, of course there is . . . but heritable doesn't mean you can't change it. I have an inheritable defect of vision so I go to the drugstore and I get this . . .' He puts on some glasses. So inheritance isn't always or necessarily the final word.

But let's not get ahead of ourselves. For I am going to take the argument one step further. Using Theory #1A (supersized version), I'll further suggest that the genetic component of human behaviour is informed and influenced by various evolved specialised computational modules of the mind.

Let us note in passing (we'll return to it) that there remains an important – and unresolved – debate about which of these modules are prime evolutionary adaptations and which are second-order side effects. There is the acrimonious debate between evolutionary psychologists and those like Gould who warn against 'adaptationism' – the fallacy of believing everything is an adaptation. So what is an adaptation? Simply put, it is an evolved trait prevalent within a population that may offer improved function or survival benefit. The key is differential success: the tendency to leave more genes in the next generation.

One example. Is the human belief in God, a spiritual world, or the practice of religion itself (in whatever form) an evolved adaptation? For Karl Marx, religion was the opium of the masses, a form of social control. The full quotation bears repeating: 'Religion is the sigh of the oppressed creature, the heart of a heartless world, and the soul of soulless conditions. It is the opium of the masses.' Is it? Of course, it could be *both* a form of social control and provide survival advantages. Or is it simply a 'spandrel', as Gould claimed – a secondary by-product of some other adaptation? For Richard Dawkins, religious sentiment may be a 'misfiring' of other psychological systems. Others suggest it could be a distorted offshoot of in-group preferences and/or coalitional behaviour.

We don't need to resolve religion here. You may be relieved about that. But it deftly illustrates the scholarly debate. We should understand that these are all heavily contested claims. Within the academy, entire books are written on such confined but compelling intricacies. But not this one. Indeed in this chapter we are investigating something a vast number of scholars *would* consider an evolutionarily advantageous adaptation: our ability to perceive pain – and particularly, since we are social animals, the ability to perceive the pain of others.

Let's get to work. To begin to access these ideas, let's revisit the problem of the boy drowning in the lake in a different way.

Imagine you have £1,000 to give to charity. You can give it to a reputable NGO that will make a great difference to the lives of two orphaned children in Romania. Here's the chance for you to materially improve the lives of two vulnerable young people. It all seems entirely reasonable. But let me suggest a simple alternative.

Instead: how about giving the money to an equally reputable charity that will make a great difference to the life of just one orphaned child? The difference is that the child is in your home town.

What do you do? Benefit two children abroad or one at home?

The research evidence suggests you'll find it difficult to donate the money to the Romanian charity. And even if you do, you will have had to struggle against a number of serious objections around giving the money to the distant children, even if you are going to be helping twice as many as locally. Why does this happen?

Think again about the problem of the lake. If it's a member of your family in the water, you're going in. If it's a friend, someone you know, you're going in. But if it's a stranger – then what?

As the social distance between 'us' and 'them' increases, the likelihood of intervention goes down. This problem was posed by Australian philosopher Peter Singer when trying to analyse why there was such poor response to the catastrophic famine in East Bengal (now Bangladesh) in the early seventies. Although estimates vary, it is likely that more than 1 million people died. Singer's point is that although distant people are *morally equivalent* to those we know and love, we don't act as though they are. In other words, our instincts steer us towards giving money to the local charity rather than the Romanian one.

Singer poses this dilemma via his thought experiment of a young girl drowning in a lake. You can rescue her. It will ruin your shoes, your suit. It will cost you a few hundred dollars. But you will have saved a child – a child in front of your eyes. Practically everyone would do it. For the same money (in fact almost certainly less) you could save a child in the Global South, one of the many millions dying each year from preventable diseases like malaria, measles and diarrhoea. But we don't. Or don't very much. Why? And what has this to do with the Perceiver of Pain and the make-up of our brain?

In the rest of Part I, we will examine a number of ideas that offer us insight into our dilemma on the edge of the lake. They are the three principles of pain.

The first is the Principle of Emotional Blindsight – how we can see even when we don't. It is a strange phenomenon, one against all our intuitions, a mechanism constructed by evolution that enables us to see other people's pain, even when we can see nothing else.

Next is the Rule of Effective Invisibility – how we can make the visible invisible. We will examine how after severe damage to the brain, some stroke patients develop an extraordinary indifference to one half of the world even though their eyes see it. We explore how this may offer a clue to how we respond to the pain and suffering of other people, acting as if for all intents and purposes they don't exist.

Finally we'll examine the Cognitive Cost of Compassion, scrutinising a much-misunderstood concept. We'll examine the risks and rewards of opening ourselves up to other people, of being compassionate.

Together these precepts will equip us with ways to dissect our dilemma about the drowning boy with the bike: both what might be going on in our mind and our reaction to another scenario I want to introduce you to. For I will take you to a place I recently visited, which has one of the biggest lakes in the world – Lake Volta. And I will introduce you to children I met, who each day face the real risk of drowning. Two boys, Anthony and Michael, will provide us with a way into understanding this mental module, this Type, that inhabits our mind: the Perceiver of Pain.

The volunteer – let us call him Patient A – was alert and focused as the experiment began. He was a doctor, somewhere near the peak of his powers, and right-handed. But being alert is not the same as being able to see. Less than six months before the experiment, then aged 52, he had suffered a stroke. Within 36 days, another seizure silently tore through his brain. The effect was disastrous.

The first stroke destroyed the principal visual areas on the left of the brain; the second did the same on the right, devastating the right occipital lobe and wiping out his remaining visual field. Consequently, regrettably, inevitably, he was blind.

The stroke damage to his visual cortex was so severe that he was unable to detect colours, or movement, or a low spotlight beam shone directly into his eyes. If you showed him pictures of shapes – triangles or a bunch of circles, even 200 of them – no matter how big or small, he had no way of distinguishing between them. For all intents and purposes, as Milton wrote about his own blindness, his 'light was spent'. Regrettably, inevitably, given the severity of the strokes. But his complete cortical blindness was not the end of the story. There was something else, something that puzzled his doctor Alan Pegna.

Pegna is a gloriously affable man with the soft, comforting contours of his face matching his soothing voice. He has bound-less enthusiasm – precisely the kind of person you'd want as your clinician. When he speaks his ideas and interests pour out, drawing you in, uplifting the listener. And that is what is so unusual about what happened with Patient A, because on the day it happened Pegna was being uncharacteristically quiet. Pegna thinks deeply about the brain and has cutting-edge ideas about what it is – about what we are.

'As a teenager, I dreamed of asking questions that no one at the time was much asking. I became interested in the intersection of biology and philosophy, how the brain can determine how we see the world and what it means to us. It remains astonishing to me.'

And it still astonishes Pegna that one day, out of the blue, the physical evidence pointing to one of the most profound discoveries in his research career was there, right in front of his eyes.

'That day I walked into the consulting room to see this patient as normal. Nothing unusual, but I was thinking – about something – and instead of saying hello I smiled and nodded. And that was what was amazing. My patient nodded and smiled back. He nodded as I'd nodded, he returned my smile a fraction of a second after my smile, and yet he was blind. I said to him, "Why did you do that? How *could* you do that?" He said he didn't know what I was talking about. I said that he returned my smile and he must be improving, because he must have seen me. He said that he had no idea what I was talking about. He said, "I'm in total darkness." And yet, I was thinking, how could he do that? How could he return my smile? How could he "see"?'

There is a long and remarkable history of scientific serendipity – the happy occurrence of events. In 1928 Alexander Fleming was cultivating the bacterium *Staphylococcus aureus* as part of his study of influenza. He left for his holiday in August, but when he returned to St Mary's Hospital, Paddington in September, he noticed the growth of an unwanted mould in his Petri dishes. 'That's *funny*,' he immortally said. For bizarrely enough, the bacteria around the mould had died. The uninvited fungal intruder had killed them. He had discovered penicillin.

In 1964 Robert Wilson and Arno Penzias were using a type of radio telescope to scan the skies from Holmdel, New Jersey, when there was an annoying background buzzing, an incessant interference they just couldn't get rid of whatever they did. But the buzzing wasn't a system fault – it was the system itself. The buzzing was the cosmic microwave background, thermal radiation blown across time and space by the birth of the universe. The buzzing was the remnants of the Big Bang.

Just after the millennium, Dr Alan Pegna was checking on one of his clinical patients who was cortically – thus for all intents and purposes *totally* – blind, when something serendipitous happened, when he had his own 'That's *funny*' moment. Pegna slowly realised that his patient could somehow 'see' the smile on his face.

Being a researcher as well as a clinician, Pegna immediately resolved to test the curious phenomenon. For the circles of serendipity worked in another way also: a complex chain of coincidental events that led to Patient A being in the examining room in Geneva of a doctor who was also a neurological research frontiersman.

When Pegna began his research into the links between anatomy and emotion, he was told by supervisors that emotions can't be measured, are too subjective – it wasn't really science. But Pegna didn't give up. Time (and technology) has proved his hunch right.

Patient A hails from the Republic of Burundi, in the Great Lakes region of Central Africa. He was a physician working for the World Health Organisation in Chad. It was in Chad that he suffered a severe stroke. Because he happened to be working for the UN's coordinating health authority at that moment, he was flown to Geneva for treatment.

But the nature of the remarkable condition Patient A possesses would not have come to light if he had not suffered a second stroke. Coincidentally, it was in virtually the same brain region as the first, but on exactly the opposite side. I say coincidentally advisedly, since this degree of symmetry in damage is really rather rare. Nevertheless the bilateral damage resulted in total cortical blindness. But at the same time there was – *serendipitously* – a vital part of his brain that remained intact and fully functioning. And that was to change everything.

And finally, when he unconsciously mirrored the smile of his clinician in Geneva's University Hospital, the man standing before him was Dr Alan Pegna, who was not only a doctor but a researcher intensely concerned with exploring the secret pathways of the human brain. This catalogue of contingencies is how science sometimes works.

'I *am* in total darkness,' Patient A told Pegna. 'I can't see you. But for some reason, I was under the impression you were smiling.'

How could a blind person form such an impression? For 'some' reason? What reason?

FIVE

Once I Was Blind

Alan Pegna made Patient A as comfortable as it was possible to make him. The necessary formalities were completed and the physician from Burundi gave his informed consent as his wife, also a doctor, read out the ethical release form. Then the testing began.

In front of him, two ruler lengths away, was a laptop. On it 'stimuli' were flashed: 200 black squares or circles on a white background. The patient was asked to guess the shape before his eyes. Obviously, by pure luck he could be right 50 per cent of the time. As it turned out, he did a little worse than that (45 per cent), but his overall task performance was not statistically different from pure chance. Then the stimuli were changed. Now instead of geometric shapes, he was presented with human faces.

The faces were chosen from the renowned IAPS database, developed by the University of Florida's Center for the Study of Emotion and Attention based in Gainesville. IAPS (pronounced 'eye-apps'), the International Affective Picture System, consists of a large database of colour photographs developed to provide a standardised set of emotionally evocative images to test for a variety of emotional states. The database includes sets of human faces. Starting off with a neutral face, they move up through the emotional gears from happy, surprised, sad, to disgusted, angry and fearful.

Pegna initially presented his patient with faces in two conditions: angry and happy. Each face was presented for 2,000 milliseconds with a rest interval of 2,000 milliseconds before the next image. Although the patient was blind, he was asked to keep his eyes open. Although he could not see, he was asked to stare directly ahead. Once more he was asked to guess. Was the face angry or happy? He was not timed, but he was instructed to give his answer as swiftly as possible. It was then that something remarkable happened.

His score leapt. For identifying happy versus fearful faces, he scored 58 per cent. For happy versus angry faces, he scored 59 per cent. And for happy versus sad, he scored 61.5 per cent. Suddenly this was statistically significant. Something was happening.

Alan Pegna and his colleagues Asaid Khateb, François Lazeyras and Mohamed Seghier needed to perform a control experiment to cross-check these startling results. They showed the physician another series of faces, either male or female, but neutral, displaying no emotion, and asked him to state the gender. His score plummeted back down to 44.5 per cent, back to where he was for the circles and squares. So was he, for all his visual impairment, somehow able to respond to images depicting emotion? They needed to control for that.

To do so, Pegna chose animal faces from the IAPS database. 'We looked for all the threatening animals we could find there,' he tells me. 'There was a dog snarling and baring its teeth, a mean-looking German shepherd, possibly a bear. We also chose some less menacing animals. I think there were four bunny rabbits.' These were shown to the patient. The bear and the bunny rabbits. How did he now do?

No more than mere chance level. He could not distinguish between different animal emotions. So what had been happening? Although he was blind, the physician was able to detect not any kind of emotion, but *human* emotion on *human* faces.

The next step was to identify the neural mechanism that had permitted what appears to be a conjuring trick to happen. But the computer analysis would take time. Hoping but unsure whether the analysis would turn up something, anything, Pegna was transferred from Switzerland to his next academic post. It was in Wales. And there in Wales he waited.

To identify which brain structures were activated, Pegna had used fMRI (functional magnetic resonance imaging). The brain scan comes up as a kind of X-ray and is then minutely examined for any telltale blips. The scan is scoured in search of voxels.

A voxel is a cross between a pixel and volume. It is a computer representation of a three-dimensional structure. With the fMRI results, it would appear as coloured flashes denoting the brain structures activated in response to the various stimuli. As Pegna recalls, 'I'd moved to Bangor University, so it was my research assistant who first looked at the results. I was eagerly waiting and he eventually got in touch and told me that there was nothing much there. I thought, oh, well. It was worth a try, but to tell the truth I was a little disappointed. Then later I had time to look at the scans myself. Then I was really . . . jubilant. So *jubilant*. There was really something happening there.'

What actually appeared on the axial scan, that is, a horizontal slice image of the patient's brain, was a small but unmistakable cluster of orangey-yellow illumination. Pegna was right: something *was* happening – Patient A, despite being blind, was using another neural pathway to 'see' emotion.

'Initially I was worried it was a false finding,' Pegna says. 'But the more I examined it, the more it became clear that it was a solid scientific finding. It was my number one hope.'

Anthony was ambushed. In a crushing moment, all his hopes were dashed.

Anthony found himself in a cluttered back storeroom. There were no football shirts. He'd get no fowl, no Coke. Instead two men stared hard at him. One with a stick – sun-bleached, the colour of bone – the other with a chain. Not a chain that could be used to bind people. A bicycle chain, not oiled, wrapped around the man's fist, with a long end dangling down like a menacing tail. They each grabbed one of the boy's arms. Anthony was suspended, a few inches off the floor, his feet scrabbling in the air.

'The first one, Stick, he says, "Your father, he's sending you for education." Then the second says, "You must work to pay for education." I didn't understand. Why had my father not told me this? They said, "Your father says you fight with other boys." [This, Anthony told me, was true. He loved boxing.] They said, "You fight with us and we will hurt you." I said to them, "Why did my father not tell me?" And Stick, he says, "Your father orders this." And Chain, he says, "This is his wish. We must take you away for education." And I said my mother would never agree. And Chain says, "Who?"'

And as children everywhere in the world do, and always have done, Anthony cried out for his mother as they dragged him out of the store. But she was in distant Benin. He gave this detail at our second meeting. He was too embarrassed to mention crying out for his mother when we first met. 'I kicked him and then he hits me with the chain. *Schhhukkkk*. It cuts my leg and it opens . . .' He points to his trousers. Like a zip.

They threw him into the back of a van parked behind the store. They shut the doors. He couldn't believe his father would have done this. He struggled with the back door to get out. Inside the small box-like rear, like the back of a dog van, the air was rancid with stale cigarette smoke. 'There were old cigarettes and birdcages and I thought: Do they catch birds as well as children?' Then Anthony's heart sank.

As the engine coughed to life and tyres rolled over the rutted road, he saw him. Out on the roadside leading away from the shop. He stood with his hands in his pockets beneath the fronds of a palm – his father. Anthony stopped struggling with the door handle. He knew it was true. Chain was right. This is what his father wanted.

They drove and drove and drove. He kept thinking of his mother and Benin, whether he would see it again – see her. He'd once heard of the high hills in the north of the country where, his mother said, spirits of ancestors roamed. He'd always wanted to go there: he was scared, but curious, more curious than scared. How could it be true? His father said no: there was no magic, only men.

In the van, the heat was incessant. The strangers said nothing to him. Where they were taking him, he didn't know. Why, they wouldn't tell him, except that he would work for his education. Sometimes there were huge trees with climbers spiralling up them towards the sky; sometimes none. Through the back windows he saw the world disappearing in the clouds of dust the vehicle threw up, as if he were being carried away on a storm.

'Then we stopped,' he said. 'There were lots of trucks. They handed me to two other men. The two men spoke in a language

I didn't know. They kept saying this word to me. Again and again.'
The word was a threat and a curse. It was slave.

The neural signal that Alan Pegna found beamed out from a
particular part of Patient A's brain – the amygdala.

The amygdala – the name deriving from the Greek for almond–
is a brain structure located deep in the temporal lobe. However,
the characteristic almond shape that captivated 19th-century anatomists actually only accounts for one part of its complex structure.
Subsequently our understanding of its extent – and importance
– has expanded. To locate it in your head, imagine drawing a line
through the ear and another going through your eye. At the junction – there. The amygdala, or more precisely amygdalae, for you
have one on each side, are slightly bigger in males than females,
certainly for adult humans – and adult rats.

They are known to be associated with memory and emotion.
By the middle of the last century, it was observed that damage to
the amygdala is associated with alterations in emotional behaviour,
particularly fear reactivity, phobias and panic.

For the 52-year-old physician, the brain damage from the stroke
had taken place within five months of the experiment, and so there
was very little time for the brain's networks to reorganise themselves. What Alan Pegna and his colleagues had observed was
the result of the neural network constructed by evolution that
allows humans to 'see' the joy and pain of other human beings –
even when they can see nothing else. It may not be the principal
pathway that conveys and processes sensory information, but as
Pegna says, 'It may have less information, but very relevant
information. It might be a bit faster. It might give us a slight
evolutionary edge when faced with danger.' Patient A had what
is known as 'blindsight'.

What follows is the remarkable prospect that if he were close enough, he could have detected the terror on the face of the boy drowning in the lake, *even if he could not see him* – nor the bike with the turned handlebars, nor the fringe of trees, nor the bulrushes, nor even the lake; though cortically blind, Patient A could have told you with a reliability statistically higher than mere chance by pure blindsight that the boy was in fear. Why does this happen – and what does it say about us? This is the problem that preoccupied Alan Pegna.

SIX

The Rule of Effective Invisibility

In the deep heartland of Ghana is located one of the densest concentrations of child trafficking and forced labour in sub-Saharan Africa. In proportional terms, sub-Saharan Africa has by a significant margin the highest incidence of children in child labour in the world.

The International Labour Organization (ILO) estimated in 2012 that worldwide there were 168 million child labourers. It also estimated that of all the people in modern slavery around the world (a figure in excess of 20 million), around 25 per cent were children. Thus the ILO estimates that around 5.5 million children at this moment live their lives as slaves.

It is hard to comprehend what this means. As psychologist Paul Slovic states, when we hear these terms, the sheer enormity of the problem results in a kind of 'psychic numbing'. Our Perceiver of Pain, the mechanism by which we monitor the plight of other people, cannot absorb the information. It results in our developing a kind of cognitive paralysis. As Slovic writes, we suffer an 'utter collapse of compassion'.

Anthony did not know how much money his father received for selling him into slavery. Judging the matter as best I can – I met several children sold into slavery from the region and people who work rescuing and rehabilitating them – it is likely to have been around 80 Ghanaian cedis, that is, around USD 20 or £16.

It is likely that the men his father contacted were so-called 'labour agents'. His father would have taken the money and then what happened to his son would be up to them. Anthony's father may not even have known what was going to happen to his son: where precisely he was going; what exactly his future enslavement would involve. Or perhaps he knew all too well and didn't care.

I listen to Anthony and what happens slowly comes to life, unfolding in front of me like those reels of film of test dummies in cars being slowly smashed against a wall. I want to stop what is going to happen, but at the same time realise that it has already taken place. And that is, I think, the structure of tragedy.

On an early winter afternoon, with a weak low sun being slowly snuffed out by drizzle, I went to a drop-in travel clinic in west London. Christmas decorations were just appearing along the length of High Street Kensington. The windows were all misted up like something out of a Dickens novel. When I told the practice nurse I wished to visit up-country Ghana and wanted to know which vaccinations were needed, she smiled and simply said, 'Everything.' It was only just an exaggeration.

I'd quickly checked the requirements on Google while travelling to High Street Ken on the Tube. It said I'd have to have typhoid and it could be uncomfortable.

'Can I have it in my right arm?' I said. 'I'm left-handed.'

'Roll up both your sleeves,' she replied.

As well as typhoid, I was inoculated against diphtheria, polio, yellow fever (you need a valid medical certificate just to enter Ghana), tetanus, hepatitis A, as well as having to take malaria tablets and use weapons-grade insect repellent. I was also warned about dengue fever and tsetse flies carrying sleeping sickness which infests the central nervous system causing neurological damage and a confused wakefulness throughout the night.

The route Anthony took was one where drivers are exposed to crushing heat. It is worse for their cargo, the trafficked children. For them no injections, medication, tablets or sprays. In many ways Ghana is a transit route for child trafficking, with routes running through it to and from Benin and Togo, Niger, Mali, and Burkina Faso. But there are a couple of exceptions. There is one notable destination point for child trafficking within Ghana. That destination is Lake Volta.

To Western sensibilities, these appear as remote, almost mythical lands. Few of us know much about Mali, Niger, Burkina, Benin. About the countries – about the mass of humanity teeming in them. In 1759 Scottish political economist Adam Smith postulated in his *Theory of Moral Sentiments* the case of a catastrophic earthquake in China. Smith argued that for all the myriads of sentient human beings suddenly swallowed up, a humane and thoroughly decent person in Europe 'would pursue his business or his pleasure, take his repose or his diversion, with the same ease and tranquillity, as if no such accident had happened.'

So Burkina, Benin, Lake Volta. What do we care? Why should we? Perhaps we don't – can't – never really will. Perhaps.

'It drives me crackers,' Peggy says.

Peggy Palmer is an elderly English woman, with impeccably cut snowy white hair. It's styled into a neat bob with a perfect parting on the left. Reading glasses dangle from her neck on a long chain. She is someone who could comfortably walk onto the set of an Agatha Christie Miss Marple mystery deep in the middle of Middle England. What drives Peggy to distraction, however, is best illustrated when she tries to describe the world around her. When she draws daisies.

Pretty much anyone can draw daisies. When children first draw flowers, they're basically daisies. There is something winning and perennially appealing about the simplicity of the common, lawn or English daisy (*Bellis perennis*: Latin for everlasting prettiness). The symmetrical fan of white petals, the yellowy sun-like blob in the middle. The name itself is a corruption of 'day's eye', reflecting the fact that the petals fold into a tight ball at night and then open to eye the world in the morning. Except that after she suffered a serious stroke, Peggy's daisies are forever different to those you and I know. Only half of the petals will open – those on the right-hand side.

To understand her condition, imagine a clock face with a second hand sweeping smoothly from 12 to 2 to 4 then on to 5 and 6 – and then, not even stopping, but *vanishing*, disconcertingly disappearing, the left half of the clock face a blank. Peggy, and stroke patients like her, suffer from something like the opposite of blindsight, those who see without seeing. Sufferers of her condition, hemispatial (or visual) neglect, don't see – even though they do. Half the world is effectively invisible to them.

Alan Burgess, for example, was a draughtsman, and then a driver, when at the age of 59 he suffered a stroke that damaged the right parietal lobe of his brain. The majority of people suffering from visual neglect suffer this right-sided brain damage. The resulting effect is usually 'contralesional': the damage affects the opposite side. And thus, like Peggy and many others, when Alan Burgess is asked what lies on the other side of the midpoint from his nose to his navel, the answer is short and shocking: 'Nothing,' he says. The left-hand side of the world has vanished.

It is not a problem with his eyes. His retinas are fit and functioning, receiving visual information, passing it on. That's not the problem. It's what then happens to it. For a critical part of his brain ignores what the eyes are telling it. This damage to the parietal lobe, the part of the brain that helps us construct space around us, results in a complete indifference to one part of the world. As if it no longer counted. As if it were no longer there.

Patients suffering from visual neglect might eat only the right half of their pizza, but always the same half – as if the other identical slices topped with melting cheese simply do not exist. They might shave only one side of their chin; apply lipstick to only one half of their mouth – always the same half. Their lives narrow into a long half-moon corridor with exit doors only on the right. Consequently for them, and for all intents and purposes, one huge part of the world, which they see and yet fail to see, has simply ceased to be.

Theirs is a physical processing problem. But when we ignore the suffering of others that we intellectually *know* must be going on, when we act as though it does not exist, is it also somehow being processed out? If so, how and why? What are the mechanisms in our mind that do this?

Anthony had no idea how long the journey would last, or when it would end – if it would end. Then suddenly it did. The two new men flung open the truck doors, and gestured that he should get out. One of them, he's never forgotten this, 'He bows to me, like he is my servant.' They delivered Anthony outside someone's compound, a simple collection of huts and shacks. It was over – the journey was over. The worst experience of his life. He glanced around, squinting in the sudden sunlight. Finally he was able to stretch out his legs, start to get over his travel sickness, breathe fresh air. Before long he would have given anything to be back in the truck.

In this new place there was water. He did not know what it was. 'I wondered if it was the sea,' Anthony said. 'There was so much water. I never knew there could be so much dirty water.' In fact it was a lake. And the lake was waiting.

On the water he saw long thin wooden boats, canoes, with sharply pointed bows like arrows, darting across the heavily silted water of the biggest man-made lake on the planet. Within hours, he was on one; he was working and he was terrified.

'I was scared getting on the boat, scared getting off. I was scared of being on the boat. I couldn't swim well. I was afraid of falling asleep. Scared of waking up. Scared to eat anything. Scared of dying of hunger. I was always hungry.'

There was in this place by the lake nowhere and nothing that was safe. But what scared him the most, terrified him totally, was the people. There were new strangers now: a man, a woman, their two daughters, their son. They owned him.

The man was a fisherman and he would be called Master. The woman, his wife, was Mistress. The two girls, younger than Anthony, barely registered his existence, as if he were a phantom. There was also a son called Korku. When Anthony arrived, the son was the eldest of the three boys that formed the extended household: Anthony was 11 and Korku 13, and there was another boy, this one aged 12 – another slave. His name was Michael. Anthony became confused about Korku. 'I didn't know what he really wanted. Later, Michael explained it all to me.'

The renowned Austrian psychiatrist Viktor Frankl often asked his patients who believed they were on the verge of ending it all, 'Well, if life is so grim, why don't you commit suicide?' Frankl had earned the right to speak with such directness. He was a survivor of four concentration camps during the Holocaust. He understood something about carrying on. What he found was that when people are presented with that unadorned question, when they are pressed for an answer, invariably they find – something. A talent, a cherished memory, another person they cannot bear to leave, for all the pain they have to endure. They find a reason to go on. And if you asked Anthony the same question, how he was able to continue as a slave at Lake Volta, he would answer instantly. Michael.

SEVEN

The Cognitive Cost of Compassion

The female partner in each of the volunteer couples was eased into the huge doughnut-shaped contraption like a roast into the oven. Once that was done, the experiment could begin.

The assumption made by the researchers in the Department of Imaging Neuroscience at London's University College was not an outlandish one. As a hypothesis upon which to base an experiment, it was entirely reasonable. It was that each individual in the pairs of experimental volunteers was likely to feel sympathy for the person sitting next to them. Not unreasonable as they were all suffering from a painfully common, much discussed, little comprehended, human condition. What Ambrose Bierce in his *Devil's Dictionary* calls that temporary loss of sanity curable by marriage – love.

The research team had found 16 pairs of volunteers. The female partner was carefully inserted into an MRI scanner – an enormous, bulky, jaw-droppingly expensive machine (they can cost over £1 million). The scanner oozes out a magnetic field and then projects pulse after pulse of radio waves into the inner recesses of your body. In this case, into each woman's brain.

For within the brain are anatomical structures, and within them atoms, and within them, lying at their heart, protons. While the MRI's magnetic field lines up the protons in the head like a row of compass needles (MRI stands for magnetic resonance imaging), the radio waves knock them out of position. Then the radio wave is suddenly cut off. Free of the disturbance, the protons shoot back, emitting a telltale signal. And it's this that appears on the scanner and can be read. And through all this, sitting next to her, quietly, adoringly, no doubt a little anxiously, is the woman's partner. And the anxiety for both is deepened since on the back of each of their right hands are strategically placed electrodes. These slivers of metal are there to administer another kind of signal: a pulse of pain.

Sometimes there would be none. Otherwise the pain would be 'high'. Sometimes to him; sometimes to her. This would be communicated on a large screen. When the woman is shocked, the pain matrix in her brain is activated. It flashes on the scanner. The brain regions activated include the anterior insula and the anterior medial cingulate cortex. That is what the UCL researchers expected – textbook stuff. But when the woman's partner is shocked, something remarkable happens.

Before the experiment, the lead investigator, Tania Singer (now Professor in the Department of Social Neuroscience at the prestigious Max Planck Institute for Human Cognition and Brain Sciences in Leipzig) said that some doubters suspected that her team's efforts would be wasted – that they'd find 'an empty brain'. When the data on the computer scanner was actually analysed, however, there was a small but unmistakable signal – a telltale message from the protons. What were the protons saying?

*

For child labourers at Lake Volta, the working day often begins at 3 or 4am. It can run through until 6 or 7pm. It all depends on the fish. But sometimes the fishermen will be out on the water until the next morning, trying to grab sleep on the undulating, leaking boat. Like fishermen through the ages, their lives are determined by the fish. Everyone follows the fish. For Anthony and Michael, the work was seven days a week. There was no rest day. The master pursued the fish with an unrelenting fury, as though it were his personal mission to empty the lake of every one of them. As Anthony said, 'The Master says, "When the fish don't swim, you don't swim." So we work every day.'

Children work on the lake for different reasons. Some work with their families who are local fishing folk. Others have been sent to join distant relatives. Most of these children get at least some education. Then there are those sent by parents via agents for money. They are the lowest of the low. That was Anthony. For them there is little or no education, just work.

But what was expected of a child labourer fishing on the lake? The boats are flat-bottomed and many have no engines. They need paddling. One sees small boys with grotesquely developed muscles from propelling the boat through the silty water day after day. Children are involved in casting the nets, hauling them in, even when they are laden with fish. And then once out of the water, the catch needs to be unpicked from the nets. And during all this, they are outdoors without protection, exposed to sun and wind with little food or water. But the worst thing of all, the thing they dread, is the diving. I'll come to the diving.

'Michael helped me with everything,' Anthony said. 'He was from [a town in Ghana]. His mother sold him for five years. He didn't know how much for. He'd been there four years when I came. He was a good swimmer. He taught me to swim better. But I never liked it. I was frightened of the water.'

'How were you able to work on the lake when you were frightened of it?' I asked.

'I always think of Benin,' Anthony said. 'And Michael looked after me. He explained to me about the fishing. He explained to me about Korku. We were standing next to the lake, in the shadow of a tree. He said be careful about Korku.'

Sometimes the son of the slave owner was friendly to them. But it never lasted. Then he would pick a fight, usually over nothing.

'I hate him,' Anthony said.

'Think how hard it is for him,' Michael replied. 'Now there are two more boys in his family.'

'We are not family.'

'We live with them,' Michael insisted. 'But if you fight him, the Master will beat you. You must never fight him. If you do, the Master will beat you. Do you understand?'

'I said I understood but wasn't scared,' Anthony told me. 'I love to box. Michael grabbed my arm. He pushed me against the tree. He turned and showed me the marks on his back. Where he had been beaten. "Do you *understand*?" he said. I said I did.'

Since Lake Volta was created by the flooding of an area of trees and villages, there are many hazards just below the surface. There are forests beneath the water, waiting. Forests of tropical hardwood: ebony, mahogany. They snag the nets. When this happens, it is the job of one of the children to dive under the boat and free the fishing tackle, disappearing into the depths to untangle the knots, lungs bursting, trying to hang onto life-saving breath. But the forests do not just snag the netting. Sometimes they catch children.

All the boys working the boats know it. But in the way that one child will torment another, it was Korku who told Anthony.

A couple of months after Anthony arrived, Korku crept into the flimsy compound shack that Anthony shared with Michael.

'One night, Michael is asleep and I am lying thinking, thinking of my sisters, and Korku comes. He whispers in my ear. He says "When you dive under the boat, you see them." He made his hand dive under and his eyes all big. I said nothing, because he wanted me to be scared, so I just say nothing. So he says, "You see them, the dead boys." I said nothing but I was scared. I began to have dreams about dead boys swimming in the trees.

'When we wake early the next morning, I ask Michael if he's scared of the dead boys. "Why?" he says. I said because they're dead. He said, "We are lucky. We are alive. They are dead. I'm sad for them. Not scared."'

Michael was always prepared to dive off, dive under, swim through the dark water, working in the silty darkness. But it was extremely dangerous work, with the constant risk of getting trapped in the nets and drowning. So I asked – I was bound to ask: 'Why did Michael always do it, the diving?' Anthony shrugged. I continued, 'It's the most dangerous thing, isn't it? But he kept doing it. Do you know why?' Anthony shook his head. His bobbing and moving stopped, and he was uncharacteristically still.

When he shook his head, I had my own kind of 'That's *funny*' moment. But not a positive one. It was the only thing Anthony did that didn't convince me.

What Tania Singer's team had found was that the same areas in the woman's brain flashed whether she was shocked or her partner was. They flashed when she received the shock; they flashed when she knew that her partner was shocked. What does this mean? What does it tell us about the Perceiver of Pain?

When we say 'I feel your pain', very often it is empty hyperbolic platitude. But sometimes it is true. Your pain registers in my brain. The implications of this, Singer and her team appreciated, are far-reaching. In fact they are immense.

It seems that our ability to 'feel' what other people are feeling – to empathise – has evolved from the same brain structures that we use to monitor ourselves. They provide a bridge from our inner state of well-being or distress projecting out – reaching out – to the well-being or distress of others. We are not alone; we do not live alone; we do not *feel* alone. This all sounds good. It presents the possibility of an unseen cognitive connection with humans beyond the boundaries of our being, past the perimeters of our skin. But there's a problem.

Helping others can cost. Research science has shown that the cost is more than the expensive shoes or new suit ruined by jumping in the lake to save the drowning child that Peter Singer postulated in his hypothetical. Opening ourselves up to helping others can carry pain. Neuroscientific data show that. Empathy is invariably, and most reasonable people would say quite rightly, regarded as a laudable emotion. But empathic resonance, placing oneself in a position where one observes, absorbs, and thus 'feels' the suffering of others, can lead to burnout. It has the potential to be a highly aversive experience: in other words, it's one we would habitually want to avoid. We withdraw to protect our core self from feeling negative and distressing emotions. We all know this; we understand it: the switching of channels during a particularly harrowing charity appeal or documentary, the glancing away from that young man, broken and begging, under the arch by the Tube station as we walk by with our mobiles and takeaway lattes. One part of us wants to do something. But do what? And there are so many people in need.

This is one reason why we are unable to connect to the suffering of many others: we have a defence mechanism to protect ourselves from overload. It is likely that, for all the flowery pronouncements of greetings cards and greatly followed spiritual and moral leaders, our ability to show genuine compassion is limited. It's limited because we do not have the cognitive equipment to process it.

The human brain is three pounds of flesh. If you spread your fingers and keep still, you would be able to hold it in the palm of your hand. Its outer surface is crinkled and canyoned, like the place that haunted the dreams of Arnold Schwarzenegger's character in *Total Recall*, the Mountains of Mars – like the strange peaks NASA's New Horizons space probe would photograph in 2015 on the dwarf planet Pluto. Cut through this and you enter the white realm. Here gelatinous matter sprawls. At its core, the human brain is dark.

Yet this thing you can hold in your hand can contemplate the immensity of deep space, the infinitesimal shenanigans of atoms, the causes of the fall of the Roman Empire, and (occasionally, imperfectly) why the love of one's life is annoyed with you. Three pounds of flesh that thinks. And yet thinking does not come free. It costs. It costs in calories. Although our brain accounts, typically, for 2 to 3 per cent of our body mass, it uses up about 20 per cent of our calorific intake. It is very high maintenance matter.

The Volta region is full of ghosts and spirits – so it is said. It is an area where folk tales and belief in the supernatural abound, and so Korku's ominous tales of dead boys resonate with deeply engrained tradition. Around Volta, for example, the practice of *trokosi* is found. In the Ewe language, the word means 'slave to the gods'. In this traditional practice young girls are sent to live at shrines to appease the gods for wrongs other members of their family have committed. Such beliefs form part of the fabric of rural life in this area. It is a situation ripe for exploitation by slave masters. They imbue their young charges with the belief that should they try to escape their servitude, the spirits will catch them in the bush around the lake and drag them under the water.

Captured escapees are severely punished. 'When he was 11,' Anthony said, 'Michael tried to escape. They caught him in a village down the lake. He was so hungry, he tried to steal some food. They tied him up and the Master came. They held his hand on a wooden stump. The Master cut his finger with a knife. Not all of it. A mark so he remembers.'

Then the slave master cut Michael again in a different way. He told him, 'Your mother doesn't want you.'

The Master used an additional form of deterrence on Anthony, another kind of psychology. 'He said, "If you try to escape, I will beat Michael with a paddle. I will beat him till he dies."'

I asked if Michael knew what the Master said. Anthony said Michael did. I asked if the boys ever spoke about it.

'When we were in the hut, Michael once showed me his finger. He said, "If you escape, promise me you'll do it better than this. Promise me you'll get free."'

'But then they'll beat you,' Anthony said.

Michael shrugged. 'Then you'll be free,' he replied.

Dr Kate Danvers qualified in clinical psychology at Oxford, before spending the first years of her career in the NHS. I met her in Winneba, along Ghana's coastline. Danvers was on a two-year placement with the NGO Challenging Heights. It rescues and rehabilitates children enslaved at the lake.

'We have found children punished in all kinds of ways,' she says. 'Hit on head with paddle so hard that they pass out. Hands held in the fire till they burn. Pepper put in open wounds.'

'Children?' I say.

'There is a level of severe sadism inflicted which is designed to control them, keep them enslaved, deter them from even trying to escape.' She pauses. 'It's harsh.'

'Diving wasn't only to free the nets,' Anthony told me. I didn't understand. What else could it be for? 'Sometimes we dive to find the fish.' I was silent, confused. 'You understand?' he continued. It was such an unexpected notion that all I could respond with was the utterly inadequate, 'Really?' (*Vraiment?*)

'But Michael used to do this,' he said.

'You didn't?'

'Sometimes. But almost every time Michael did.'

'There were trees under the water?'

'And snakes.'

'It was dangerous, but Michael dived?'

'Yes,' he said.

The dangers reminded me of a conversation I had with one of the members of the rescue teams that liberate children from the lake. When asked why fishermen use children, he said that adults expect payment, children don't; adults want a share of the catch, children don't; adults refuse to dive, children won't. So why do slave masters use children? Because they can. From that time, I've kept thinking of Michael, this boy diving into the murky water, looking at the fish, as the fish looked at him.

So life on the lake continued into Anthony's second year. I asked why Michael had not been released then as his five years' bonded labour was up. 'The slave master took him for another five years,' Anthony said. 'He paid his mother more money. He said that he'd get a boat for Michael at the end. But Michael didn't believe it.'

Michael told Anthony he knew the truth: his mother didn't want him; no one did. He would live at the lake. He would die at the lake and there was nothing else.

It is not uncommon for parents who have sold their children to resell them. At home, the economic pressures are unlikely to have improved – in fact, there's every chance they've got worse. There may be new mouths to feed, so the prospect of another lump sum of cash for the child they had not seen for half a decade can be too much to resist. The best I can gauge it, this is what happened to Michael. And so he stayed at the lake. And life continued for the two boys for another year: Anthony now 13, Michael 14. They endured a relentless cycle of work without weekend break or holiday, little food, beatings, lightning storms on the lake, risk of disease and serious injury, attack from water snakes, and the greatest risk of all, what their thoughts on the boats kept coming back to – diving.

Despite appearances, despite what some believe about the mass of empty-headed people around them, we all do an awful lot of thinking. The thing about human thinking is that it is thinking of a very particular kind. It uses up a disproportionate amount of energy. It is, to use the phrase of Oxford's Robin Dunbar and his colleagues, 'very expensive in computational terms'. Dunbar's team won the British Academy's research competition to explore 'what it means to be human'. They investigated what we are doing that is differently cognitively from other primates. They plotted and charted the brain sizes and social groups of our near neighbours and more distant evolutionary relations. And they zeroed in on one of the factors that distinguishes us from virtually every other living being creation has known: our unfeasibly high 'neocortex ratio'.

The neocortex is the 'newer' part of the brain. (From 'neo': new; 'cortex': shell or husk, from the Latin for tree bark.) It consists of the frontal and temporal regions, areas vital for something humans constantly do: mind reading. Getting into someone else's head. It is this deft trick, to begin to divine the thoughts and motivations of others, that is strongly correlated with the size of the social groups we live in. More neocortical power, more complex social groups – and there are none more complex than those of *Homo sapiens*. To simplify, the higher the neocortical ratio – the greater the preponderance of newer, more sophisticated brain regions over old – the more intelligent the animal. But Dunbar's team found that all this comes at a cost, a high one computationally.

The reason is that while living in a social group of the same size (say, an extended family of six), the neurons in the human brains will be working harder than those of a similarly sized group of macaque monkeys. The neurons in the neocortex of humans will be in overdrive gauging all the permutations and problems of family life – or imagining them. And that is effortful. It uses energy. It is tiring and trying. Welcome to the human family. Now imagine extending that to others around us. To those we are not related to. To those we are not even closely connected to socially. As the ripple of concentric circles radiates out, as more and more people come within what Dunbar calls our 'circles of intimacy', we are using more and more of our cognitive resources. We are not, as the Prince of Denmark speculated, infinite in faculty. Rather more circumspectly, Dunbar claims that we reach a limit – we run into buffers of the brain.

We just cannot meaningfully extend the process beyond a certain point. Because for all our thousands of Facebook friends or Twitter followers, the effective limit of our social circle is 150 – what has come to be known as Dunbar's Number (he is unaware of the precise origins of the term, but is quite content to adopt it). What can we deduce from all this? Thinking of others comes at a price. It has a cognitive cost. And that affects how we view and treat other people.

Once we start worrying, caring, or just plain thinking of other people outside our family and familiar circles, we begin to load up our system. As Dunbar's team conclude, this cognitive load 'acts as a brake on our social ambitions'. It's good to know this. It does not have to be viewed as a mordantly negative thing. It just is. It's not that we don't care. It's just that in an important but critical sense we just cannot keep caring indefinitely. As Samantha Power poignantly puts it in her account of the historic failure to engage with genocide, we just can't 'wrap our minds around it'.

We should stop beating ourselves up about this. Because there is a risk: our inability to care for the many, to act on a massive scale, can preclude us from engaging on a more modest but essentially achievable level – a human level. When we reach out to other human beings, we expose ourselves to pain. This is the classic sense of the Latin root of the word compassion: *compati* – to suffer with another. But that might not be the end of the story.

The latest research science may hold the secret key to another, subtler, more startling insight into our ability to show compassion towards others. And it may also explain what happened between Anthony and Michael at the lake.

EIGHT

The Promise

Anthony often felt it would have been better if he had been there – on the boat – when it happened.

They lived in a state of constant hunger. It wasn't unusual. As Kate Danvers told me, often the children are fed koko, a sludgy porridge, or dried ground cassava mixed with lake water. The lake contains numerous diseases, including bilharzia, caused by parasites in the water itself and which affects the liver. Sometimes Anthony and Michael would risk a beating to scavenge food from neighbouring compounds. What they had found the previous day must have been off as it resulted in Anthony constantly being sick. His temperature soared and he was so weak that he collapsed on the way to the boat.

'What? You *want* the fish to escape?' the Master shouted at the boy. He did not want to spare a single one of his personal finned enemies, not one of them. But Anthony could not stand. So swearing it was a ruse of some kind to rob him of his rightful income, the Master relented. Anthony had a day off. For the first time he could remember, he didn't work. He didn't understand how the bad food hadn't affected Michael also, but Michael had been at the lake four more years, so was more accustomed to it.

'I lay in the hut,' Anthony said, 'and Michael left for the lake and he says to me, "I'll catch fish for you also."'

As he was lying there, Anthony couldn't help thinking about the fish. Sometimes they'd pass like smoke through the water. Then Michael would suddenly surface, water streaming out of his nose and mouth. 'I've found them. I've found them,' he would beam. These were the good times.

It was a very strange day with winds and rain and terrible lightning. The first he knew that something had happened came from the Mistress. She ran to their neighbours; she shouted, panicked.

Anthony rushed outside. He grabbed people, asked what had happened. Everyone ran down to the water. He still felt queasy, but did the same. On the shore, the men used ropes to pull up the Master's boat. The villagers clustered around it.

'The Master's clothes were all wet,' Anthony said. 'Then I knew something was wrong. The Master didn't like going in the water.'

Once on the strand, the boat tipped over on one side like a great beast slowly toppling. And there in the bowels of the skiff, splayed out and motionless, was Michael. No one said anything to Anthony. No one needed to.

The children of the lake are vulnerable to a long list of serious injuries. Some have physical deformities, their backs misshapen due to the excessive crouching and paddling from a young age (sometimes as young as four) while the skeleton is still being formed. Others cannot spread open their hands fully because their fingers are habituated to clutching the paddle. So their hands are constantly in a claw-like shape. Rehabilitation staff use 'pomade' to try and manipulate the tendons slowly back.

Children brought back from the lake are often found with the three big diseases: typhoid, malaria and of course bilharzia. And then there is the invisible damage. The behavioural disorders from the deeply scarring trauma. Not only from their own maltreatment, but from having witnessed the serious injury and death of others. Of their friends.

A few days after Michael died – Anthony cannot say how many – Korku came back to the hut.

'Korku is so happy. He cannot keep still. He says, "Let's see. Let's see if you see your friend down there now."'

Anthony hurled himself at the bigger boy. This was what Korku had been waiting for. Michael had warned him that Korku wanted to fight the boys so his father would beat them. 'Michael said to me, "Promise me you'll never fight him." I promised.'

But now Anthony fell willingly into his trap. 'I didn't care. I didn't care what happened.'

Anthony set about Korku. He landed two blows – 'Hard, very hard' – on his face. The second made Korku's nose bleed. At first Korku was shocked: the jolt of pain; the dripping of blood. Then he must have realised that the blood running down his face was the best evidence. Korku had prepared well. He had concealed a paddle behind the nets. Now armed with this weapon he mounted a severe counter-attack, smashing the thick slab of wood over the head of the smaller boy. With the fourth or fifth blow, Anthony's knees gave way. As he crumpled to the ground, he became aware of others arriving in the hut. 'I could hear the Mistress scream. I could not see her. The Master took the paddle. He took it.' The slave master set about ending what his son had started. As Anthony began slipping out of consciousness, as his eyes 'filled with water' as he put it, he saw feet, fishing nets, then nothing.

When the heat of the sun finally roused him – he didn't know how long after – he found himself lying in the compound outside the hut, motionless. From time to time Korku's friends would come by. At first they were excited and stared at him. But they didn't know what they were supposed to make of the devastation inflicted on Anthony and moved on. Blood from the gashes in his head was now caked hard by the remorseless sun. He didn't have the strength to move. But the pain that paralysed his body taught him the decisive lesson of his life: if he stayed in that place he would die. They would kill him. Perhaps slowly, perhaps quickly and painfully; perhaps at their hands, perhaps by the lake, but he would die. There in the yard, prostrate, he learned the law of the lake: that enslaved children were nothing. There would be no education that many of their parents had been promised. There would be no end to the slavery, except just possibly one distant day to become a slave master and buy children to paddle *his* boat and dive to untangle *his* nets. He would never do it.

'So I made a promise. I promised I will escape. I didn't know how. If you try to get a ride in a boat, the boat owner will know your master. He takes you back. You're beaten or they cut your finger. So I didn't know how to do it, but I promised Michael that one day I will escape.'

A significant body of recent research has been exploring the connection between our ability to focus, to keep paying attention and different forms of motivation. To what extent does the enticing possibility of reward concentrate the minds of healthy humans? Unsurprisingly enough, it does rather significantly. Research scientists have taken this cue to examine whether a similar motivational mechanism may operate in cases where attention has been impaired because of physical factors, as in visual neglect.

Charlotte Russell, now at King's College London, systematically explored this intellectually intriguing lead with colleagues at Brunel. They tested ten patients suffering from hemispatial neglect, all having suffered right hemisphere strokes. Like Peggy Palmer and Alan Burgess, for these people the left-hand side of space had disappeared. Russell sat them down in front of a sheet on which 106 circles were printed. Around one half were golden circles. They acted as 'distractors'. The remaining were the real targets, images of £1 coins. The patients were asked to ring all the coins they could see. Of course, since they suffered from left neglect, they largely ignored those on the left-hand side of the sheet. After the task, the patients received a £15 voucher. Critically, they were told that this was based on their performance in circling the £1 coins. On a subsequent day, the same patients performed the same task again. They were reminded that they would be rewarded in accordance with the number of coins they ringed. This time they found significantly more coins. But they also almost doubled the number of coins they could find on the 'invisible' left-hand side (from 6 to 11). Russell concluded that with the right motivation, the world that was treated as invisible could be reclaimed and recognised. However, there was a problem.

Out of the ten patients, for two the enticement of reward made no difference whatsoever. You couldn't incentivise them. They could not be 'bribed'. Like the others they suffered from left neglect. Like the others this was due to right hemisphere stroke. But there was a difference in their cases. These two also had damage to another brain structure – the striatum (a brain structure we will return to). And this clue connects their story to the children of the lake.

When I met Anthony, he wasn't sure what his age actually was. He said he thought he was 18. He said 'thought' because he'd lost track of his precise age. Kate Danvers told me this was not unusual. Many of the children have not had their births registered by parents and have little numeracy. Numbers mean little to them. They just have not been exposed to them. One boy she met, who they estimated at 17 or 18 said that he was 8.

For a few years – again he finds it hard to be exact – Anthony had eked out a living, eventually ending up in Ghana's capital, Accra. We met in the historic heart of the city, Old Accra, down on the seafront. The forts of the European traders – Dutch, Danish, Portuguese, British – were built along that stretch of coast, a prized location as it connected the growing European maritime presence with the trading routes that ran deep into the heart of sub-Saharan Africa and the Sahel.

Our first meeting was in Jamestown, named after the forbidding Fort James, built in 1673 by the British. At first the encampment was used to trade ivory and gold. But by the beginning of the 1700s, Fort James began trading in the lucrative new international commerce: slaves.

When we spoke at our various meetings our conversation ranged over what you have just read, but not in the order here recorded. I asked him how he escaped Lake Volta. Attuned to escape stories and movies, I expected some tense, heart-stopping drama. It was in fact as banal as walking to the store to buy Coca-Cola.

'I just got up one night and left,' he said. 'I saved bits of food. I stole a couple of things, a torch, a knife. I sold them for more food. I knew if I got a boat, the owner would take me back. So I walked, mostly at night.'

He lived rough. He nearly starved. But he knew that life at the lake would kill him. So he took his chance. Physically, Anthony actually walked out of the hut the boys had once shared several months after the drowning, but in truth he began escaping the day Michael died.

He left the lake when he was about 14 and was now living in Old Accra's shanty town, a place called Bukom, an area of both brick buildings dating from colonial times and also shacks with corrugated iron roofs all alongside the venues that have made Bukom famous – boxing gyms. This maze of streets has produced an extraordinary number of African boxing champions and five world champions, including the legendary triple world title winner Azumah 'The Professor' Nelson. They are tough people, hardened by straitened circumstances and sea fishing, and here Anthony, strong beyond his years from the forced labour at the lake, found a place. Sometimes he'd beg at traffic lights. Occasionally he'd go down to the old port where women sell the day's catch propped against the sea walls covered in Biblical edicts ('I can do all things through him who strengthens me', Philippians 4:13; 'Give, and you shall receive', Luke 6:38; 'I have overcome the world', John 16:33). Anthony didn't go back on the water.

While we spoke in Bukom, the nearby lighthouse and the old British fort with its imposing peeling stucco walls loomed over everything. Forts used as holding pens for slaves awaiting shipment were known as 'factories', facilities for the systematic processing of human beings. After such use, Fort James became a prison. It was used by the Ghanaian government to incarcerate 700 prisoners until its decommission in 2008. Another type of human processing.

'So we meet here, when I return to Accra, after Winneba?' I said.

We were drinking Coca-Cola in bottles with straws in a shack in Bukom. We chinked them in agreement. We were just hanging out and it was fun. Another chicken, two, strutted by. There was a sign for Ovaltine and another for Coca-Cola, another heralding a big boxing match – a massive event in the lifeblood of Bukom. I'd discovered that the Coca-Cola's creator John S. Pemberton was seriously injured during the very last battle of the American Civil War at Columbus, Georgia, and devised Coke as a form of pain relief.

'Meet here? This place?' Anthony said, gesturing at the shack. He gave the premises his gunslinger look – he didn't like them. I never found out why.

'Or by the walls,' I said. 'Whatever you prefer.' I was conscious of the warping of time: we were where slaves and slave-drivers had once been; me and a boy who recently had been enslaved.

Pemberton, a Confederate colonel, became addicted to the opium he used to relieve his pain. He realised how dangerous a drug it was, so experimented with opium-free concoctions to find another way to ease his suffering. He came up with a mysterious, dark, caramel syrup. It contained cocaine and kola extract. Ten billion gallons of Coke later (the amount of water crashing over the Niagara Falls in 3½ hours), we finished the latest bottles of Pemberton's potion.

A woman walked by with a baby held against her back by gravity-defying folds in her wrap dress. The child was enjoying the ride and looked squarely at Anthony and smiled. He smiled back briefly, unconsciously, I think. Just as quickly, his smile faded. Perhaps he thought of his sisters, away in Benin. That strange loss of those who are living.

'Not here,' Anthony replied.

So it was agreed: we'd meet in a few days near the walls of the prison. We clinked our bottles of Coke again.

John Stith Pemberton died in 1888, two years after he created Coca-Cola, still addicted to opium.

As we have seen, research evidence has demonstrated that engaging with the suffering of others can cost; it can cause us pain. But that is not all that the research evidence shows. Tania Singer and her colleagues found another mechanism. To understand it, they needed a monk. A Buddhist one.

Matthieu Richard, philosopher, photographer – and Buddhist monk – was asked to contemplate distressing images of a Romanian orphanage from a BBC documentary. The children kept there were neglected, in an emaciated state, spending hours rocking backwards and forwards listlessly. Some of them died. The hour Richard spent visualising the suffering of these children exhausted him. He felt 'burnt out'. But now the real experiment began.

He was asked to switch mindset to think now towards the children 'compassionately' – projecting positive, benevolent 'warmth', wanting to approach and not be deterred by the children. Two things happened.

Firstly, although his mental images of the beleaguered children were just as vivid as before, he felt energised and restored. Secondly, the fMRI registered a different mental mechanism at work. Adopting a compassionate approach does not deny the suffering of others, but it activates a different neural network: the medial orbitofrontal cortex, the pregenual anterior cingulate cortex – and the ventral striatum. (Remember the striatum?)

So activated here, among others, was the striatum structure that had been damaged in Charlotte Russell's patients who didn't respond to the reward of the £1 coins. The group of structures activated in

Matthieu Richard together form a network related to positive emotions, affiliation, reward – even love. It presents the empirical prospect that when we feel compassionately towards someone suffering, when we adopt a mindset of wanting to approach or help them, we trigger the reward mechanisms of the mind.

The positive surge of feelings we project towards another person in distress may result in the flow back of positive feeling from the reward centres in our own brain. Tania Singer and colleagues are devising programmes to promote compassion. She believes it has the potential to be a 'trainable strategy'. The evidence suggests it might help insulate us from the pain of exposing ourselves to other people. It may promote behaviour that helps.

Give and you shall receive – literally, neurologically. And with that final piece of research in place, we must turn back for the last time to the lake.

I left Accra, heading west along the old slave coast. I visited a human rights project that provided support and education for children who were once enslaved at the lake. The coastal town of Winneba is one of the 'source' communities for child slavery at Volta, even though it's situated over 100 miles from the Akosombo Dam, and 300 miles from the main lake town of Yeji. I asked Anthony whether I could mention his case to the NGO, to see if they could help him – it was the kind of thing they did. He didn't want me to. He remained fiercely independent and didn't want other people's assistance. 'I do all this myself,' he said.

At Winneba, I listened intently to team leaders as they explained how they organise the missions to free children in forced labour at Lake Volta, planning the intervention like a military operation. Indeed it is so dangerous that sometimes their operations are accompanied by armed police or the Navy.

I heard many stories that were similar to Anthony's: extreme poverty, parents desperate or duped, grinding remorseless labour, injury, disfigurement, death. The accounts were alarming and distressing. But my thoughts kept returning to Anthony. I thought of the quote from John 16:33, painted in blue on a sign propped against that old sea wall — somehow, almost inconceivably, Anthony had overcome the world. By himself.

When I returned to the capital a few days later, I went back down into Old Accra to find him. Boys were playing football on the beach, using pieces of driftwood stuck vertically into the sand as makeshift goalposts. The place smelled of the morning's catch, fresh out of the sea and displayed in gleaming metal bowls on low tables, or already being salted and drying in the sun in the hulls of beached boats. Red snapper, barracuda, live crabs still clawing the air in slow motion. But I couldn't find Anthony. He had gone. I did everything I could to find him in Bukom. But nothing. Nothing anywhere except the morning's catch.

NINE

The Blank Face of Oblivion

I n Rudyard Kipling's *Jungle Book*, when Mowgli is finally leaving his adopted friends and the forest, he suddenly feels a pain he's not previously felt.

> Then something began to hurt Mowgli inside him as he'd never been hurt in his life before, and he caught his breath and sobbed, and the tears ran down his face. 'What is it? What is it?' he said. '. . . Am I dying, Bagheera?'

No, the great black panther told him. 'That is only tears such as men use.'

The persistent problem of other people's pain is one that evolution has not resolved. It is evolutionarily adaptive, in other words valuable to our general survival and propagation, to understand what those around us are feeling. On the other hand, projecting ourselves too much – feeling too much – can be debilitating and dangerous.

There are all kinds of paralysis. Just as there are all kinds of denial of it. As we've seen through Charlotte Russell's work, with some patients suffering from visual neglect it's possible to 'reintroduce' them to that part of the world that is invisible to them. It is also possible for us.

Perhaps what we need is a recalibration – a rethinking – of our understanding of empathy. One that is more scientifically accurate and emotionally honest. We should face the fact that empathising – opening ourselves to 'empathic resonance' in Tania Singer's phrase – is painful. It should be if we engage in it genuinely rather than in a superficial voyeuristic way. It is also likely to be tiring, in the sense that carrying the additional cognitive load wears us out, as Dunbar and colleagues found. But here is the good news.

That pain and additional computational work is not the end of the story. With compassion comes the analgesic of reward. We get the glow. What we believed were metaphors and folklorish nostrums turn out to have a demonstrable empirical basis. That's good to know. It's good to know that when we give, after all, and in the end, and via mechanisms we might never have imagined, we receive.

I rushed around in my hotel in the central embassy sector of Accra, and threw clothes into suitcases for the flight back to London. It was an overbearingly hot day. Yet in the courtyard outside a mass choir was patiently practising Christmas carols. That haunting quote by the old harbour wall had seeped under my skin and I momentarily paused the packing to check the reference online. 'I have overcome the world.' What did it mean? I found out that in fact the full quote from John is:

> In the world you shall have tribulations.
> But take heart: I have overcome the world.

76

I checked my passport, travel documents. Inside the leather wallet I'd got from the travel agents, alongside the insurance policy, a folded slip of paper. I knew what it was instantly. It was a bit tattered now, but I opened it, smoothed it out on the desk with a fan that did not work. And there, staring at me was Gareth Myatt. When Michael drowned in Lake Volta, he would have been similar in age to Gareth when he died at Rainsbrook Secure Training Centre 3,200 miles away. A couple of hours before my flight was due to leave Ghana, I received a call. It was Anthony.

The carol practice was coming to an end – they were fantastic singers, framed by the African sky – people, immaculately dressed in tuxedos and formal dresses with orchids and other unknown flowers, milled about near the pool. They chatted quietly, exchanged greetings. I had the chance to speak to Anthony. I could smell the orchids and flowers, even over my insect repellent. The singers were drinking. It was the long, dry season and people were thirsty.

Our conversation, as always, was in Anthony's Beninese French and my broken schoolboy one – coincidentally, I'd been in a French boarding school near Paris for a short time when I was roughly Anthony's age. I tried to keep it light. I told him that next time my French would be better. He laughed. He told me it needed to be. Next time, I told myself, I'd be ready. Next time I'd be fluent. What is below is as much as I can remember of the rest. I made no notes at the time, nor later that day. I'm not sure why – whether it was out of respect or shock or sadness. I now wish I had made a record so I could tell you more, but everything of importance is here – except for one or two details I've excluded that would reveal details Anthony wanted to keep private.

DD: So . . . Mr Big Boxing Man. (Anthony laughs.) Are you all right?

A: Yes, yes.

DD: I've been trying to find you everywhere. (*Je cherche partout.*)

A: Did you find me?

DD: Very funny. Are you sure you're all right?

A: *Ça va, ça va.*

DD: So what's been going on?

A: Oh, nothing, nothing. You know, talking to you, it makes me think a lot about what happened.

DD: Yes, I'm sorry. I said it might.

A: No, not sorry. Is good and bad. I think hard what to do now.

DD: I'm just about to leave for the airport. I'm flying back to London tonight. But we can meet when I come back to Africa?

A: No problem.

DD: Okay. You just tell me where. In Bukom?

A: Not Bukom. Benin.

DD: Benin?

A: I'm going home. (He paused, and I said nothing.) I think my mother still wants me.

There was another silence. Perhaps like me, he was thinking about Michael and what he was told about his own mother.

A: I think she does want me.

DD: That would be great. And you'll see your sisters.

A: They will not recognise me. I'm training in the gym. Big boxing man.

I thought of him walking through that grand memorial arch on the waterfront at Ouidah. The boy from Benin returning through the Door of No Return. He wouldn't, of course. He needn't. And anyway, triumphs can be much more understated.

A: I must go. Is not my credit.

DD: I can call you back.

A: I've got to go.

DD: Okay.

A: We see each other again.

Yes, I said. But I was not convinced.

A: You know, I was feeling very bad to tell you before. When you ask why Michael dives. Michael says, 'I dive so you do not have to.' That's why. I'm sorry I didn't tell you.

There was a pause.

DD: Why sorry? There's nothing to be sorry for.

A: So you buy me Coca-Cola in Benin?

DD: I will buy you Coca-Cola in Benin. Are you going to keep boxing back home?

The call cut out. I tried ringing back but it didn't connect. I rushed down to the swimming pool for better reception. A waiter carefully skimmed slimy leaves, twigs and insects out of the water with a net. I thought about the lake, fishing, kept trying to connect to Anthony. A bug crawled past my foot, seeking the water. A hawk circled high above. Soon I'd be up there, higher. Time was short. For the rest of that day until I boarded the BA flight back to London late that night, the same thing happened. I had lost the connection. The connection had been lost.

Back in my room, I carefully folded the report of Gareth's death. I smoothed the wrinkles from the paper and thought again about what happened in that room in that corridor in that prison.

A dispute developed between Gareth and the prison officers when they tried to remove a piece of paper with his mother's number on it. They were removing the personal items from his room as a punishment: he refused to clean the toaster after making a toastie and then was sent to his room and wouldn't calm down – they said. The three prison officers 'restrained' him. They used a technique called the Seated Double Embrace. It had been approved by the government, but not properly safety checked. It was, the experts at the inquest agreed, potentially lethal. Two officers held Gareth's torso, one 'controlled' his head. They bent him forward. He complained he couldn't breathe, then he shouted he couldn't breathe. During the inquest, we discovered that many other children had complained of the same when restrained. No one had done anything. The prison continued to use this method, this 'embrace': two on the torso, one on the head. Witnesses outside stated that they could hear Gareth screaming, like he was in pain. Gareth Myatt asphyxiated.

The Seated Double Embrace has now been banned.

So here is one part of the answer to the why of Pam's question. It happened because we didn't listen. We didn't listen to the voice of the child. One of the officers said after the incident, 'I shouldn't have PCC'd [restrained] him, he was half my size.' Then he bemoaned the operation of chance. 'It was rather like having run over a cat and then thinking . . . if I hadn't gone down that street, it wouldn't have happened.'

Rather like running over a cat.

Our lives are full of concentric circles. Circles of serendipity; circles of disaster. They clash and stretch and tear and vanish like fading ripples at the distant edge of a distant lake. So a barrister from Britain and a boy from Benin. Two circles that touched and overlapped for a very short period of time. And it was short, when both of us were a long way from home, in Bukom, in Accra, in Ghana. What happened?

I met several children of the lake; I visited an extraordinary rehabilitation centre where remarkably resilient children who have experienced the unimaginable begin the slow struggle to recover. But there was something about Anthony.

What had we in common? What was the nature of the connective tissue? The starting point is the lake. The lake that is not a lake, the consequence of the vision of the snake-handling colonial geologist from the old cotton town of Audenshaw. The starting point is that lake full of underwater forests – what it is, what it stands for. Children die at the lake. Die in the lake. Child slaves and labourers, getting seriously injured, drowning in the lake as they are forced to work, or do work no child should do. *In the 21st century*, I have to keep telling myself. I am astonished. I am appalled that I have to write words for you like 'slave master' and 'child slave', and that they are accurate descriptors of our world today, not lawyer's licence, the writer's hyperbole. But such emotions – predictable human reactions – little count unless accompanied by action. Otherwise they are an indulgence.

This section has not been about a great and famous figure, about someone who was enslaved and whose plight came to represent the obscenity of child labour. It's been the story of a boy. Two boys. The story of two boys whose intense struggle you have just read because I met one of them in one of a myriad of chaotic streets full of boxing gyms and chickens, in the shadow of a slaver fort, in a cacophonous capital in sub-Saharan Africa. His journey began, this boy who thought he was nobody, because he went to a store with a tin roof to buy Coca-Cola, a drink that was created an ocean away to relieve pain, by an officer in an army that fought to keep their African slaves.

I am conscious of the cautionary words of Paul Slovic: once we start to scale up and generalise, once we try to open ourselves up to the enormity of a human problem like child slavery – even at that moment – something else within us shuts down. A kind of cognitive paralysis spreads through our bodies like cracks through a sheet of ice, and the human in the human tragedy is lost. The boy is lost. Anthony is; Michael is.

How do we find them? How do we listen to the voice of these children? Let's face the truth: the enslaved children of sub-Saharan Africa, they are not our children. But they are still children of the world. They are nevertheless enslaved. How can we know them? By knowing of their lives, their stories, which is what I was falteringly, imperfectly trying to do. Through that process, I kept vividly recalling the words of the outstanding coroner who presided over Gareth's inquest, His Honour Judge Richard Pollard, a humane man in semi-retirement, brought in to preside over the traumatic case because of his vast legal experience. He wrote urgently to the Secretary of State for Justice after the verdict; he said that it would be 'wholly unforgivable and a double tragedy' if we did not listen to the lessons to be learned from Gareth's death – if we failed to listen to the voice of the child. Can the same be said for Lake Volta?

For thousands of children around its shores, the lake is waiting. It's what it does. Marcel Proust wrote that the real voyage of discovery lies 'not in seeking new landscapes but in having new eyes'. Ultimately I think that's what it is. These boys opened my eyes. By their fierce struggle, I could begin to see – to understand – what was happening to children in forced labour in a new way. Through them my Perceiver of Pain was able to see the human in the human rights violation. And that may be one explanation for what I felt about Gareth's case, why it did not let go of me. At times during the inquest proceedings, certain members of the jury were in tears. They were hearing about strangers – prisoners, yes – but children whom we collectively put there and who then in certain instances, like Gareth's, have been treated unimaginably. We are capable of perceiving that pain.

For all that, it seems that the human brain – that monumental accomplishment of evolution – is plagued by paradox. We have evolved an inconceivable range of emotions, but aren't very well equipped to do emotion at long range. That is no one's fault. It is a consequence of our evolutionary history. Evolution as a cause and a curse? Peter Singer forcefully makes the argument that from a moral standpoint at-risk children in distant lands – those suffering from 'preventable evils' – are no different from those in our backyard. From a moral obligation perspective, they are the same as those we come across floundering in our parish ponds, in the Deep Pits in front of our eyes. But it doesn't feel like that. This social distancing would make evolutionary sense in our deep past when our affiliations and interactions were with much smaller groups of people living immediately around us. But the world is changing. It's shrinking. With globalisation and IT, we're connected to people around the globe like never before; we're much more aware of their problems and their lives. We may not live in a global village. But few in the Global North do any longer live in a village.

In this section of the book, I have focused on just one injustice in a world in which there is no shortage. There are, it appears, all kinds of serpents. How do we adjudicate between the claims of this practice, forced fishing on Lake Volta – albeit recognised by international bodies as among the worst forms of child labour – and others such as children forced into labour and exposed to mercury poisoning while mixing toxic chemicals during gold mining (also in Ghana), or enslaved on plantations in the industrial picking of cocoa – the bitter truth of our chocolate. How?

We learned from Alan Pegna's serendipitous discovery that evolution has equipped us with a distinct neural network for recognising the pain of others, even when we may be blind to almost everything else. That is remarkable. It is perhaps in part due to this that Patient A, a doctor, continues to do what he can to practise medicine. In his country in the equatorial lake region, he still 'sees' patients when he can. A nurse acts as his 'eyes'. As the internecine bloodshed spreads around him, he strives to help those who suffer.

However, evolution has not equipped us with a limitless capacity for empathy. That is because feeling other people's pain comes at a cognitive cost. We have limited bandwidth. There is only so much cognitive load we can carry, only so much processing of other people's pain our mental module can do. All the same, we can partially insulate ourselves from the emotional burn by seeking the analgesic of reward on offer when we adopt a compassionate stance towards other people in pain. We can, after all, get something back.

The notion that compassion costs, but that the cost can be budgeted for, managed, absorbed – *paid* – is not the most intuitive one. In fact it runs counter to many prevalent media messages about compassion fatigue and the futility of attempting to engage with 'big' social problems. (What's the point? What difference could I make, anyway?) But nevertheless the idea is a profoundly empowering one. We *can* care about Michael or Anthony without being Michael or Anthony – or even socially or genetically connected to them, or even in the same country or continent as them. The Perceiver can do this work.

It means we can politely acknowledge the defeatism that surrounds vast social justice issues like human trafficking and child slavery, and put it to one side. Alexander Pope famously wrote that to err is human. Perhaps. But the research in this section suggests that to *care* also is, in the sense of feeling the pain of other human beings. It's just that it costs. We should not pretend that it does not. Nor should we confuse hesitations and misgivings with signs of weakness, moral or otherwise. It's just our mind doing the maths. Perhaps we cannot entirely overcome the world. But we can engage with it in a meaningful way so that it does not overcome us. I wrote in my notebook: *Protect the Perceiver.* Why? So it can be used boldly, imaginatively, decisively.

But beware of the written word. The difference between what you write and what you do. Protect the Perceiver. You'll see in Part VI, I didn't. I didn't really get it. Not until it got me.

Philip K. Dick asks whether in 'the empire of falsehood' in which we live it remains possible for freedom and independence to arise in new ways. Anthony found a way: he found the strength, mental and physical, to walk to freedom through some of the most inhospitable and punishing terrain in the world. His freedom was born in pain: the death of his friend. But things can be so born: all human life is, even Coca-Cola was, born in pain. It was a minor miracle Anthony survived. He was 14 years old.

But we cannot evade the more difficult question – Michael. He chose to risk himself for someone else. For his friend. Is that a kind of freedom? If so, what kind? The bonded labourer, the child slave, chooses to swim through underwater forests so his friend does not have to, and in that choice he is less unfree. Chances. Was it also about chances? He gave Anthony a chance.

Anthony did not know what happened to Michael's body. No one ever told him. He saw his friend motionless in the hull of the boat, and then never again. But while Michael was here he was able to make a scratch, a mark. A mark on what William Faulkner, like Pemberton another haunted Southerner, calls 'the blank face of oblivion to which we are all doomed'. What was Michael's mark? It was, I think, Anthony. The fact that he survived and lived to leave the lake, to be able to see that he was worth more than to live and die there.

So finally, then, what of that executive system attuned to the fates and foundering of others, the Perceiver of Pain? What of the hypothetical I posed earlier, the boy with the bike, the child drowning in the lake? I've thought long and hard about whether Michael would have dived in. I never met Michael – I must emphasise that. But I believe he would. Certainly Anthony was his friend, but Michael risked his life by diving under the boat almost every day. When he did so, he dived into waters that were as dangerous as those of Wigan's Deep Pit. Unlike the Police Community Support Officers, he did not stand by.

One of the earliest documented human questions is found in the first book of the Bible. There in the Book of Genesis, Cain – for whatever part of the human psyche he represents – asks, 'Am I my brother's keeper?' In other words, is what happens to my brother my responsibility?

To this eternal human dilemma, Michael, a boy sold into slavery in sub-Saharan Africa, simply answered yes.

PART II

THE OSTRACISER

But the well is poisoned. Are you insane?

Henrik Ibsen, *An Enemy of the People* (1882)

ONE

Take Elpinice and Go

S ometimes it is hard to see at all.

If you turn around – you really don't *want* to because of the magnetic pull of the slowly breaking waves – but if you do, the sun is just beginning to drop out of the sky somewhere to the west of Cape Canaveral and into the Banana River Lagoon. Along the beach to the south, in the direction of Miami, you can actually just discern a rocket, almost a cartoon caricature of a skyrocket, something out of *Flash Gordon*, squatting there ready to do battle with Ming the Merciless.

Cocoa Beach, Florida. The kind of glorious day that makes Florida, Florida – not just the Sunshine State (everyone knows that), but where, as its anthem goes, 'the sawgrass meets the sky'. And there was a lot of sky. Above me, hanging imperiously in it, a flight of pelicans, seven of them in precise, geometric formation, strafed the shoreline on their way towards the Kennedy Space Center. But it was on the simple incline of sand folding down to the sea, where at this time of year sea turtles clamber up to nest

('Sea Turtle Season has begun! The first leatherback nest has been laid in Jupiter, FL'), it was there that it happened.

I cup my hand over my eyes to cut out the glare, to track the pelicans. Along the water, a low sloop with sharp triangular sails glides past, rising and falling on the waves. In the haze the boat resolves itself into something else, sharp in another way: an arrow boat, and suddenly the Atlantic is unnaturally still, brooding – a lake – Lake Volta. Two boys work busily pulling nets into the boat. I fear one of them will dive off.

'Of the children we have rescued and interviewed,' Kate Danvers told me in Ghana, '80 per cent found themselves in situations where at some point they believed they were actually going to die at the lake. It is an entirely legitimate fear. Forty per cent of girls and 62 per cent of boys have actually witnessed someone drown at the lake.'

Often the drowned child is left in the water; no attempt is made to bring him or her back to the shore. They dive off, swim under, are never seen again. The lake has them.

A Frisbee rolls along the beach like a lost cartwheel and I'm back on Cocoa. Three men in Bermuda shorts, two with tattooed torsos as ornate as the Bermudas, are tossing the Frisbee between themselves. The Atlantic breeze gets under the shimmering disc and propels it dramatically right towards my face. And then, just as suddenly, someone switches the wind off. The Frisbee falls to earth.

I pick it up and prepare to launch. But I'm thinking about those nets. What is a net? How do we escape them?

The Frisbee heading in my direction was one of those bizarre coincidences of life. I write it, but still barely believe it. I was due to fly back to the UK the next day and then skype the person most qualified on the entire planet (and this is no exaggeration) to explain what happens with people throwing Frisbees to strangers. The thing is, it had happened to him. And when it did, it changed the course of Kip Williams's academic and professional life forever.

Another sea.

About 50 miles east off the Queensland coastline, near the Tropic of Capricorn. Here 42 acres of land barely peek above the surrounding Coral Sea. It is called Heron Island for the numerous reef herons that adorned it when in January 1843 it was discovered by the British exploratory vessel HMS *Fly*. The highest point of the little platform of land is barely more than a ceiling height above the encompassing turquoise waters.

Beneath that shining surface on all sides sprawls the southern section of the Great Barrier Reef. This staggering complex of coral, built by – and out of – living creatures, stretches in excess of 1,250 miles, and shadows the north-eastern coastline of Australia. It has taken hundreds of thousands of years in the building, and consists of the skeletal and calcareous remains of an inconceivably vast array of once-living marine organisms. European exploration of the reef began when Captain James Cook ran aground on it in 1770. Today, for all the depredations of pollution and climate change (large swatches are being 'bleached'), a small, rather ugly-looking fish flourishes. And that fish has a connection to Frisbees.

The coral-dwelling goby, of the genus *Paragobiodon*, a small reef fish that may well have been picked off by the herons HMS *Fly* spotted, inhabits the coral complexes off Heron Island and behaves in a very distinctive way. Its behaviour casts light on some of the perennial, intractable problems not only of fish life, but of those other creatures that once were also sea-dwelling but that took to dry land, lost their gills (though their embryos still go through a stage where they have slits in their neck – a kind of proto-gill), started propelling themselves on two legs and became addicted to mobile phones.

The coral-reef gobies are usually around an inch long. Some a little more, some less. They live in small groups or colonies and tenaciously defend a minute patch of the reef. In general there is one male with a number of females within the group. Their life is full of challenge since the teeming reef waters present a significant risk: they constantly run a predation gauntlet. Should the dominant male perish, something remarkable happens.

The largest female changes. The prime breeding female becomes the breeding male and the next largest non-breeding female in the hierarchy thereafter becomes the breeding female. Thus the principal *she* changes into dominant *he*. She becomes a male.

For the fish are protogynous hermaphroditic. They have the capacity to develop male sexual organs having started out female. This sexual 'fluidity' is relatively rare among vertebrates. Among invertebrates it is far more commonly found.

But it is not this extraordinary behaviour of these gender-bending fish that is of interest to us, remarkable though it is. It is something else that they do, which illuminates one of the most pervasive and persistent problems of human social behaviour. And thus these tiny tropical fish provide a way in to understanding another of our mental modules, another of the adaptations we have evolved. An acute sensitivity to one of social life's most persistent problems: being excluded from it. Ostracism.

So we have met the Kinsman and the Perceiver of Pain. Next there is the Ostraciser.

Sree Dasari came to the UK from India. Academically he came to study for a master's degree in international business at the University of Hertfordshire. But burning inside him was a deeper need: to court public acclamation. In his host college, he put himself forward for student union president. Undoubtedly an extrovert, with a mass of unkempt ink-black hair, Dasari – bizarrely – appeared to be smaller than he actually was. Nevertheless by sheer force of personality he won. But the arriviste from the Indian subcontinent had bigger ideas. Literally far 'bigger' plans.

He would tell people that he'd like to be a film star, or at least a celebrity, not for the sake of it, of course, but so he could raise money for deserving charitable causes. So what quicker way to accomplish all that in the post-millennial world than reality TV? He applied for *Big Brother 10* in 2009. He said he intended to remain a virgin until he married. His ideal woman was Beyoncé. Once more, by dint of personality, an irrepressible energy as if he were being drip-fed Red Bull, he won out. He entered the Big Brother House.

But things did not go well for him on *BB10*.

Perhaps conscious of his otherness (it was his first time out of India), he entered the House on launch night wearing a Union Jack shirt. But he remained an outsider. His heavy Indian accent was ridiculed by sideburn-infested fellow contestant and Wolverine wannabe Marcus Akin. Dasari, 25, sporting a number of elaborate hairstyles, frequently misread social cues and misinterpreted the fragile personal politics of the House. He earned the collective opprobrium of housemates by drinking the alcohol allowance of Russian resident, Angel. The Russian boxer was a teetotaller anyway, but it made no difference: the group considered that Dasari had violated the norm. He was perceived as a disruptive and destabilising presence in the House.

But the vilification of the Asian business student reached a more savage pitch when he very publicly fell for another resident of the

House: Irish athlete Noirin Kelly. In the merciless glare of the constant surveillance cameras, his romantic advances were just as publicly rejected.

Dasari spiked his hair; he slicked his hair; he changed his look; he claimed he was only ever looking for friendship. Increasingly isolated, he tried to find ways to be accepted within the bosom of the group. He tried to be liked. He was not.

The structure of the show, infamously, is to stage a weekly eviction. The two least popular housemates go head to head. Dasari was pitted against a resident from Market Drayton called Halfwit. Dasari lost. He received an enormous 85 per cent of the public's eviction vote.

Perhaps he could draw some comfort from the fact that he was not the first resident to be ejected. But he was out. He then had to run a gauntlet of a different kind. He emerged down the gangway leading out of the Big Brother House and onto a platform surrounded by a baying crowd, many of whom had voted for his life within the programme to be terminated. He stepped out hiding behind oversized aviator shades. He was met with a deafening barrage of boos.

Dasari put on a brave smile. Or at least a smile. The booing and abuse did not abate. He gamely endured the rituals of rejection: being interviewed on the eviction show, where the programme psychologist told him that she 'would like to take your ego and pickle it for science'. He smiled again gamely. Sort of. Played the game, went home.

Now cast out, he returned to his student hall of residence in Hatfield. From the sanctuary of his room he settled down to watch subsequent evictions from the Big Brother House. He said in his eviction show that he didn't care about being evicted as it 'wasn't about winning or losing. It was about the experience.' A few weeks later, Sree Dasari slashed his wrists.

The *BB10* contestant was rushed to the the Queen Elizabeth II Hospital in Welwyn Garden City, one of the nation's first new towns. Statements of concern were issued by the programme producers. Questions were asked by the Mental Health Foundation and the British Psychological Society about the levels of public vilification and humiliation inherent within the format. But the programme went on. The evictions went on.

A year later, the UK Border Agency investigated Dasari's visa status. He had to leave the country. Perhaps thinking of the day he stepped down the gangway from the Big Brother House into the cauldron of boos behind his aviator shade glasses, he suffered eviction once more.

Of all facets of shows like *Big Brother* and *Survivor*, and even *The X Factor* and *Strictly Come Dancing* – our new coliseums – it is the moment of eviction, the slow build to an artificially staged weekly crescendo, where the thumb will go up or down, that represents the pinnacle of the gladiatorial drama. It constantly fascinates people. Why? What is it about that ritual of rejection that compels? To understand, we need to travel to its historically documented origins.

Some inscriptions gave both the name and accompanying piti-less advice: 'Cimon son of Miltiades, take Elpinice and go.' Others simply stated Cimon's name, his given name and that of his family. Elpinice was his sister, and the inscriptions amounted to a public accusation of transgression and taboo violation – of incest.

One can imagine his neighbours, his enemies, those who were both, squatting down near to the Agora and etching away with a slow deliberation into the ceramic and stone, inscribing the angular marks, the early script, the alphabet.

Allegations of immoral conduct against political enemies are hardly unfamiliar to us today. But this was 461 BCE, Athens. And Cimon was a statesman and general. He was unquestionably a prominent public figure, hailing from a distinguished aristocratic family. They had contributed greatly to the city, to the very survival of Athens. His father Miltiades had famously defeated the enormous Persian invading army in a battle three decades before, in 490 BCE, at a place called Marathon. It was already the stuff of legend. But it didn't save his son.

For his part, Cimon also displayed conspicuous courage when the Persians came again and were defeated once more in one of history's greatest sea battles, at Salamis in 480. According to Plutarch, he donated funds to beautify the city, planting trees for shade in the marketplace, turning the Academy into a well-watered grove. But it didn't insulate him from gossip and envy. In 461 his name was inscribed on piles of broken pottery at the Agora. The cutting words were cut – literally – into a fragment of ceramic, what was called an *ostrakon*. And now we get our word for it, from this small shard of broken pottery: ostracism.

The Athenian democracy was in its infancy. But a threat hung over the young city and haunted its populace: the restoration of tyranny.

Burnt into the Athenians' memory was their struggle to free themselves from a string of tyrants. A widespread suspicion of the powerful remained. Could they be trusted? Were they honest? As the ascetic philosopher Diogenes was famed to have done in the next century, it was necessary to wander the streets of Athens in broad daylight with a blazing lantern to find a single honest man.

The two millennia following the time of Cimon and Diogenes have obligingly taught us that democracy is a fragile thing, painstakingly constructed, ever needing nourishment, easily lost. Many mechanisms have been developed to protect the health of the social group. For its part, fifth-century Athens devised a system whereby every year a motion would be put to the assembly of eligible voting citizens. Should there be an ostracism?

If there were sufficient support for the motion, citizens proceeded to the designated gathering place, the Agora, to write a name on a shard of pottery. Once all the *ostraka* were counted, the person whose name was most mentioned was given ten days to leave Athens. He would be banished – ostracised – for ten years. He would be evicted. Premature return resulted in death.

It was not so much a popularity contest as an unpopularity one. If the accusers had only cared to glance up, their spirits could have been elevated by the transporting beauty of the Parthenon, standing high above them on the Acropolis. But malice was on their mind. Because instead they looked down to the shard of broken pottery and cut a name into it. Why? What function did this serve? To understand we need to return from Athens to Australia.

Off the Queensland shores there are a number of subtly differing types of goby. One of them, *Paragobiodon xanthosomus*, is typically a yellowy-emerald colour (*xanthos* is Greek for yellow), but is not celebrated for its beauty or grace. It is in truth a rather unlovely fish.

'I don't mean to be harsh,' I say, 'but they're not nature's finest.'

'Oh, *noooo*,' says Marian Wong, laughing. 'I just *love* them.' She spends a significant proportion of her professional life studying goby and other small fish. 'But I know what you mean, a lot of people say that. They say, "Marian, couldn't you find a prettier fish to follow?" People say, "Marian, why are you studying the ugliest fish on the reef? Why can't you study a cute one like Nemo?" But I love goby. I'm happy to stare at them the entire time. I'm beyond redemption.'

We break off temporarily as the Skype connection falters. Wong is at the opposite end of the earth to me. She has followed the fish. Wong, now in her thirties, has straight, immaculate shoulder-length dark hair and an accent that is hard to pin down. 'It's a bastardisation of everywhere I've been,' she says. Hailing from a family of Malaysian origins, she was born in the UK and did her undergraduate degree in zoology at Girton College, Cambridge. Then she followed the fish. First to Queensland, then to Canada, and now back to Australia, at Wollongong University, where she is a Senior Lecturer at the School of Biological Sciences. She laughs a lot. At fish, at us, our pretensions.

'But why, Marian?' I ask.

'Why what?'

I had to ask. 'Why you and fish?'

'I blame my father. He was a dedicated aquarist who annoyed my mum by keeping fish tanks in their tiny one-bed flat in London back in the day. Didn't see many fish in the River Cam, of course, so after Cambridge I was very pleased to go to Australia.'

And why not fish? Fish have found ways to survive for 450 million years – they have earned the right to be studied. Wong did her doctorate work at James Cook University in Queensland, a college instituted on 20 April 1970, the inauguration chosen to be exactly 200 years to the day that the restless Yorkshire lad from Marton, Captain James Cook, first sighted Australia. Wong's research site was Lizard Island, another speck in the surrounding sea, but 750 miles to the north of Heron Island, basking in the northern reach of the Barrier Reef. (Cook actually ran HMS

Endeavour aground on the reef.) Around Lizard Island the ugly little goby swims along the best it can and tries to find a life in the wild and dangerous sea within a complex social group of similarly vulnerable and unlovely fish. It pretty much keeps to the coral. It's safe if it keeps to its little patch of coral. But while there it does something unusual, even remarkable.

'You see them,' Wong says, 'all lining up. They are careful not to touch each other, but they are there lined up and it couldn't be by chance. It was performative – a real event, a performance. And then we knew: this is important. It's not random, it's not by chance they're redoing this. We had to investigate it academically. It means something.'

But what? The point of scholarship, of the Academy, begun in 387 BCE when Plato opened his school on that patch of land that Cimon had beautified, is to understand. (Plato's most famous pupil, Aristotle, in large part was a biologist.) So what was this goby behaviour about?

'We watched and watched. We began to realise what they were doing,' Wong says. 'It's all to do with the 9–3. We knew something was going on around the 9–3.'

Each group consists of a principal pair of dominant fish, male and female, the breeding pair, and then a number of non-breeding females, up to around 15 such subordinates.

'They were *displaying*. We began to get what was going on down there. Think of it this way: the coral is safety. The group is. But there's no such thing for fish as a free lunch. They have to pay to stay.'

'Pay? And the cost?' I ask.

She laughs. 'Okay, this is the thing,' Wong says. 'Fasting. The fish fast.'

*

Female goby exhibit a careful gradation in size, diminishing in stature progressively. In fish such as goby, social rank – where in the queue one is – is determined primarily by size. Relative body size matters greatly and group members are acutely attuned to minute variations.

'So when they're lining up,' Wong says, 'they're actually evaluating one another. Literally, they're sizing each other up.'

These assessments constitute critical clues about where you are in the hierarchy, and consequently what you are entitled to – and what is expected of you. But the dilemma of social groups is that without some kind of restraint, subordinates would have a strong motivation to usurp their immediate 'superiors' and claw their way up the ladder. Such ambition, if replicated by all or even significant numbers of subordinates, who themselves would have sub-subordinates immediately below them, would be a nightmare. It would degenerate into the fearful dreamscape that haunted Oxford philosopher Thomas Hobbes: incessant mass conflict – *bellum omnium contra omnes*. Ethnological evidence, however, indicates that it doesn't happen like that. There are certainly contests for supremacy. But social animals tend to form themselves into relatively stable societies of functioning communal groups over time. How does that happen?

One contributory mechanism is the threat of eviction – of ostracism. As Wong puts it, 'Once they're outside the coral, they're basically eaten. Stay in the coral, you're safe. Out? Eaten. So it's pretty serious. It's a credible threat.'

Thus the threat of ostracism acts as an effective mechanism to control the behaviour of subordinates and promote the relative peace and durable stability of the group. For animals like goby where size matters greatly, the unrestrained growth of subordinates would threaten dominant fish. This problem is accentuated by the fact that fish grow asymptotically (smaller fish grow more rapidly than larger ones). Therefore the closer that subordinates grow to superior fish, the more of a threat they become: the more likely it is that in a contest they would be able to successfully evict their immediate dominant. Thus mechanisms have evolved whereby – to an extraordinarily precise degree – the growth of subordinates is regulated.

In coral-dwelling goby the figure is 0.93.

'We knew something was going on around the 9–3 threshold,' Wong says. 'That was the magic number.' It is different in other fish, but for goby it's 0.93. In other words, if subordinate fish are below this precise proportion smaller than their immediate neighbour in the social queue, they do not constitute a threat. They would not have the physical prowess to defeat them.

'We wanted to get a better understanding of what was happening. It was fascinating watching them go about their lives. You get to know the characters in the group. The bigger dominant ones, the smaller upstarts, trying to push the boundaries. It's addictive.'

'Like a soap opera?'

'It's like *Big Brother*. Yeah, you can't wait to get on the flippers and see what's going on today out on the reef.'

'You go diving?' I say.

'Yeah, it's such fun,' she replies.

It was good to hear: diving not just about fear. Diving for fun. I resolve to tell her about Anthony, Michael, the lake.

Wong and her team conducted their research from the Centre of Excellence for Coral Reef Studies in Queensland. She had a research grant for Lizard Island. In a carefully regulated procedure, they gathered samples of fish and then measured them, anaesthetising them in a clove oil solution to ensure they would not be harmed. Calipers were used to measure their size precisely;

sex was determined using a microscope. They were then released back into the colony and observed over the course of two weeks (every other day) using scuba equipment. In all 420 fish from 54 groups were examined. The purpose: to test how the risk of being evicted varied with the size ratio between the dominant and subordinate fishes.

But because the consequences of eviction are so extreme, it rarely happens. It rarely has to. 'I've only seen it two or three times in the wild,' Wong says. 'So we had to find another way to research it experimentally.' Wong's team staged a series of 'contest experiments', placing unrelated fish in an experimental coral environment. The live coral was the more desirable destination – the West End. But there was also a patch of less salubrious dead coral rubble at another location – the slum.

Conflict in these types of goby has been observed to involve chasing, the butting of heads, and biting of fins. 'They'll engage each other in a fight, then the smaller one usually backs down but gets chased, and is hounded until it's pushed out.' Following these trials of strength, the 'losing' fish was condemned to the other place, the slum, a proxy for being effectively evicted from the group. Wong's team found that once the subordinate's size was over 0.95 of the dominant's, the probability of eviction was doubled.

So the fish regulate their growth. By remaining relatively small and unthreatening, they are able to enjoy the collective benefits of group social life. Wong's research indicates that as subordinate fish approach the critical coefficient, they begin to carefully curtail their eating.

'They suddenly cease feeding,' Wong says. They fast. 'What is extraordinary is that even if we provide them with excess food, if they're at the 9–3, they just wouldn't eat it. The goby were doing it to themselves. The threat of being ejected was likely doing that. It's not a fake threat. It works.'

This was the 'pay-to-stay' rule. The cost of social inclusion was watching your waistline. Or equivalent. Research indicates that other fish, such as Nemo's clownfish (*Amphiprion percula*), have their own 'regulation coefficient' – their own magic number. Thus the threat of ostracism restrains, here literally, dangerously disruptive behaviour: getting greedy, unrestrained growth, threatening the status quo. It acts to stabilise the group, reducing the amount of costly conflict and dominance contests. Taken cumulatively, the threat of such eviction acts to enhance the viability and cohesiveness of the group. Ostracism, therefore, functions as a form of threat management on two levels. Firstly, it protects the dominant. Secondly, and at the same time, it promotes and prolongs the viability of the group. It is a deft combination of punishment and cooperation.

'What do your experiments tell us about ostracism?' I ask.

'Well, this kind of conflict resolution promotes the stability of social groups. The threat of social ejection probably acts as a powerful form of social control. We believe we're likely to find these kinds of mechanisms in a wide range of animal societies. Other colleagues have been looking at meerkats, mongooses. And mole rats – have you looked yet at mole rats?'

'I'd love to look at mole rats,' I say.

She laughs. 'You *must* look at mole rats.'

'What about humans?'

'Humans,' Marian Wong says, 'are animals. I think we all live under the threat of being punished. On all sorts of levels, in all sorts of ways. It does govern our behaviour. Being ejected hurts. When I see people around the university or the city, and they're doing some stuff, I think, "Oh, that's *so* damselfish. Come on, are you serious – that's such *goby* acting out." Of course, humans are a lot more complicated, but the basic social behaviours are the same.'

By sheer coincidence, as we speak an article comes up on my Twitter feed. It's entitled, 'How loneliness can affect your health'. A study reveals that social isolation can increase your risk of having a stroke or coronary artery disease by 30 per cent. 'I feel like I am completely unloveable,' says interviewee Miley, aged 32, who constantly suffers from depression.

'These are very real social problems,' Wong says. 'The shame and shunning across social animal species, same thing – to maintain the norms. We humans are such a social species that ostracism is bound to have a very powerful effect on us.'

'In what way? To do what?'

'To make us do what we wouldn't otherwise do. Our research shows just how amenable social animals are to being manipulated. That's the thing: the group norm *influences* us, whether the norm is a good one . . .' she pauses, 'or not. Yes, that's the thing – whether what the group's doing is good or not.'

That moment, when there was absolutely no turning back – when she agonised over whether to actually press Send – Kathy Bolkovac didn't know her life would change so utterly. More precisely: that her old life as she knew it would be over. She paused.

She knew what she was contemplating was massive – no doubt about that. But *that* momentous? Yet she also knew herself: there was only one way she could go.

Send.

At that point, in 2000, Bolkovac was just a very, very small cog in the vast machinery of international post-conflict transitional justice. She was a mother of three, twice divorced, and working away from home for the first time.

Home was Lincoln, the state capital of Nebraska, nestling deep in the Great Plains and prairie lands of the US between the Mississippi and the Rocky Mountains. Bolkovac has thick waves of blonde hair and eyes that look right at you. Direct, no-nonsense, straightforward – Plains people. 'Where we lived,' she says, 'it's farm country, ranch country. What people think of as the Big Country. That was our home.'

Her family name is actually Croatian in origin and her grandfather came to the United States from the Balkans in the 1920s. His granddaughter, who by the turn of the century had for ten years been a cop in Nebraska, would return. It all happened because of a simple flyer.

Bolkovac, then in her late thirties, saw it one day pinned up on the noticeboard in the police department, an opportunity to join the UN's International Police Task Force. Shining out enticingly there in the Nebraskan plains: a chance to join an *international* task force. Then there was an ominous dash, separating the role from the region – Bosnia, it added.

Bolkovac discussed the opening in detail with her children. It was a big step. Bosnia was a long way from the rolling farmlands of Nebraska. But the work would be similar to that she had been doing, for she had specialised in sex crime work, had flourished in it. The UN job was in Sarajevo, investigating sex violations. Bolkovac was confident in her professional abilities. She had a conviction rate of almost 100 per cent. 'The secret,' she says, 'is to extract confessions.'

At that point in her life, she was financing her kids' education – the elder two were in college – and thus the salary of $85,000, twice what she was earning at Lincoln PD, was tempting. But there was one curious feature to the advert, one she did not pay much heed to at the time, sort of noticed it, kind of registered it, before her eyes went back to the 85K. For at the top of the printed sheet was the logo of the corporate contractor the US State Department had outsourced the recruitment to: DynCorp.

She'd never heard of DynCorp Aerospace. But they were working with the United Nations and the State Department, so at that time she didn't think anything more of it. The project was an enormous international initiative and she was just a cop from Nebraska looking to do her duty and make money for her kids' tuition. She would do her bit to the utmost of her abilities, as she always did; she'd throw herself into it. But she'd been round the block enough times not to be a dewy-eyed romantic about it all. 'I was going to be the Big 4–o soon,' she says. 'It was a job. So, no, not Kathy saves the world stuff, but knuckle down, do the work, cash the cheques, secure the kids' future.'

Having said that, the sheer exotic allure of that single word 'Bosnia' there on the noticeboard in the middle of Nebraska was intriguing. She couldn't deny it. She appreciated that if she were lucky enough to be accepted, it would be an incredible experience. But then the contract would end and she'd go home. Thank you, DynCorp – whoever you are. DynCorp had been appointed by the State Department. They were working closely with the United Nations, and that had to be reassuring.

TWO

The Wounded City

To be evicted from a group, any group, involves a kind of social death. The ensuing pain was put best by psychologist William James:

> If no one turned round when we entered, answered when we spoke, or minded what we did, but if every person we met 'cut us dead,' and acted as if we were nonexisting things, a kind of rage and impotent despair would ere long well up in us, from which the cruellest bodily tortures would be a relief.

But on the other hand, as Richard Alexander, a zoologist at the University of Michigan, put it in 1974, 'There is no automatic or universal benefit from group living.' And therein lies the dilemma of social life.

For many species, humans included, it's hard to live within a group but almost impossible to live without it. Wherever group living has been found, various modes of ostracism have often been found to follow.

The ostracising of certain other group members has been found in numerous non-human animal species. It exists in virtually every human society. But one must be careful before concluding definitively that because non-human animals socially exclude conspecifics (members of same species), they do so for the same reasons that humans do. However, it suggests a similar process; it at the very least raises an inference. Very often the target of the social opprobrium has violated, or is perceived to have violated, some group norm. And in this light ostracism can be understood as a distancing from potentially problematic social partners – from the fish that grow too threateningly big.

In Tanzania in the mid-1990s, a juvenile chimpanzee that refused to conform to the rule of showing deference to dominant males was seriously assaulted in a group attack involving eight males. It was forcibly evicted from the group. Leading primatologist Jane Goodall observed comparable behaviour a decade earlier in Tanzania's Gombe National Park. Two chimpanzees were acting strangely. They were in fact suffering from polio. But their unconventional behaviour led to their being shunned and marginalised. They were physically isolated; they were attacked.

Analysis of the historical, anthropological and cross-cultural record attests to the ubiquitous presence of human ostracisation across time and space. In humans it can occur in a highly formalised fashion, as at Athens, and in practices steeped in ritual such as shunning among close-knit communities like the Amish. It will be found in virtually every children's playground and in other kinds of playgrounds: the Internet and social media. The human inclination towards living in groups of other humans derived from a stark evolutionary fact: lone individuals were likely to die; left alone, the solitary human being was, on average, more likely to be doomed to disaster and death.

Human beings lacked the obvious defence mechanisms of other animals: speed, strength, formidability. But what they could do, what they were unsurpassingly good at in a way nature had never quite seen, was to band together in cooperating groups. Hunting together; dividing labour; sharing out scarce essentials like food or safer habitats. Further, the vulnerability and slow development of the human child also created a need for group living. But sociality has limits.

Living with other human beings, as well as being the solution, is also a significant survival problem: the perennial problem of other people.

As I was speaking to Marian Wong on Skype, the penny suddenly dropped.

'Marian,' I said. 'How much do you know about Frisbees?'

'Sorry,' she said, 'didn't get that. Did you say Frisbees?'

'Yes, Frisbees.'

'Frisbees?'

'You see,' I said, 'I was on this beach in Florida.'

'A beach in Florida – with Frisbees?'

'Marian,' I said. 'I think there is something you need to know.'

The group Kathy Bolkovac joined in Bosnia was of international personnel from around the world seeking to help a country rebuild itself after the bitterest of wars. Things happened here that didn't have names. The Bosnian war bequeathed them: the conflict introduced a new term to the lexicon – ethnic cleansing.

Maybe someone, somewhere, had used it before, but because of Bosnia, everyone now knew it. Even in rural Nebraska, people had heard. It was a long way off, across an ocean, but when the United States and NATO started bombing, people would talk occasionally at the mall about the terrible tragedy that had been unfolding in the heart of Europe. In Europe – it was hard to believe.

Kathy's friends and family were understandably concerned. But this was part of the international community's next step in helping the communities deal with the trauma and return to some semblance of peaceful life. Transitional justice, capacity building, asserting the principles of the rule of law – investigating sex crime violations. It was worthy work.

But she knew there would be risks. It was a judgement call – a gamble – but those college tuition fees kept on coming. Besides, she didn't spook easily, a 5 foot 10, as she puts it, 'big-boned' cop. She'd been in dangerous situations. She'd been in danger. She'd been hurt, concussed, bloodied, bandaged up. 'I don't scare easy,' Bolkovac says.

Her kids were encouraging. She could reassure them that the role, an investigative one, wouldn't put her in the direct line of fire.

'But what did you think you were getting yourself into?' I ask.

Bolkovac pauses. Where did she start? How to? There is a pause. Outside my window is a tree. Leaves fall from it and spin rapidly like tops as they float down. 'Well,' Kathy says, 'wow . . .'

When she arrived she looked aghast at the wasted and wounded city. Sarajevo itself was a victim. Shattered windows, shrapnel-spattered walls, shell craters – the signs of siege, of carnage. What was this place? she wondered. What had happened here? 'But I kept telling myself, people, they still live here, they lived, somehow, through that thing. You know, we were working to make things better.'

She was a cop. She'd stick to her knitting: do cop things. She'd investigate.

What?

Bosnia had a potentially incendiary mix of Muslim Bosniaks, Orthodox Serbs and Catholic Croats. Between 1992 and 1995 war raged pitilessly. But it did not simply take the form of conventional conflict between armed belligerents. The distinctive and defining nature of the conflict was the terrorising of civilian populations of the opposing ethnic groups. They were forcibly removed, detained in concentration camps, starved, tortured, sexually violated, raped, murdered individually, massacred communally. In the heart of Europe, in the last decade of the 20th century. It was hard to believe.

In the aftermath of this mayhem, Kathy's job was to run a project on violence against women. The job of the IPTF was to assist local police in the effective investigation of human rights abuses. Their mandate derived from the UN Security Council itself.

There was a time of a lot of rain. Then a time of snow. The snow covered things, concealed them. It lay like a beautiful blanket over the damaged city. Under snow, Sarajevo was again a beautiful place, like it had once been, a city of medieval bridges over a quiet river. Despite it all, people still lived here. She'd help them.

After a few months, she was transferred to the city of Zenica, an hour's drive north-west of Sarajevo. She was put in charge of another UN project, again to combat violence against women. Soon she succeeded in prosecuting the first conviction in Bosnia for an offence of domestic violence.

Then one day in the Bosna river, which rises high in the Igman mountain plateau and then flows down through Zenica, a body was found. It was of a young Ukrainian girl. The back of her head had been caved in. She had been killed before her body was disposed of in the river.

Shortly after this another young woman, a Moldovan girl, lost and bewildered, was found in a daze stumbling along the riverbank. She was picked up by the local police. They didn't know what to do with her. They took her to Kathy's office.

Bolkovac tried to interview her, but the girl was deeply traumatised. She wore a swatch of cloth so short it could barely be called a skirt. Her top glittered brilliantly with sequins; above it, her neck was patterned with bruises, her chest and arms too. She was barely more than a child. She asked for a cigarette.

As the two women faced each other, the younger one kept repeating again and again, mantra-like, a single word: Florida . . . Florida . . . *Flor-i-da.*

At first bemused, Bolkovac recalled – just something she'd registered with her peripheral vision – that there was a ramshackle bar or club called the Florida – she thought that was what it was called. She drove out to take a look.

When she finally arrived in a UN truck, the shabby building on the edge of town was empty. Maybe the girl (her name of Viktorija) was wrong, or had got the wrong place. There was nothing here. It was deserted. But then again, the intensity, the sheer compelling repetition of the word Florida, had convinced Bolkovac that there had to be something to it. She'd interviewed so many people in her time as a cop. She knew when people were telling the truth. It's what she did.

The door was open. Strange. Tables and chairs were tipped over, half-consumed beers littered the bar. Behind the bar was a metal box. In it were wads of US dollars – so much money in a country where foreign currency was gold dust – but it was what she found below the cash that chilled her. A stack of passports. They were all the same: young women from a variety of East European countries. Romania, Ukraine, Moldova – Viktorija's passport. A happier, healthier Viktorija. Smiling, hopeful, unbruised. Viktorija was right. It was happening here.

Bolkovac went outside. Barely clinging to the outer wall was a dilapidated fire exit. With some trepidation, she climbed the steps, metal grilles rattling under her feet, rattling the building itself. At the top was a wooden door. It was locked, but weathered, in disrepair. Everything was in disrepair; Bosnia was. Bolkovac kicked it open.

Behind it, terrified and cowering, in a room with two soiled mattresses on the floor, were seven young women.

THREE

Do Not Read This

Kipling D. Williams – known to most people as Kip – is today in his early sixties, with very short salt-and-pepper hair echoed by a matching tightly trimmed beard and moustache. He is now Professor of Psychology at Purdue University, Indiana, but started lab research work when an undergraduate at Washington University. It involved a lot of rats. After a couple of years, he realised he'd had enough of rats. Really he'd like to work with humans. And particularly in his area of chief interest: social influence. He got his wish. By the mid-1980s, Williams was a young Assistant Professor at Drake University, Des Moines, Iowa. The day that changed his life was like any other. He was simply taking his dog for a walk in a park.

'She was a mutt,' Williams says. 'Her name was Michelob. I know, I know, like the beer. I was a student when I got her. She was a mix of German shepherd, collie, some other stuff. Such an affectionate dog.'

Man and dog were taking a rest on the grass by a lake, sitting on a blanket, pretty much minding their own business, when something rolled along the ground and into his back. Williams turned to see it was a Frisbee.

'I turned and saw two guys waiting for it. So I picked it up and threw it back to them and thought nothing more of it. Who wouldn't do that? But to my surprise, the guy who caught it threw it back towards me. Actually threw it back to *me*. We didn't speak, but we started playing Frisbee.'

In the complex lexicon of park politics, where we come up close to unsorted strangers, it was, Williams says, 'an invitation'. The game proceeded with the usual forehand flicks, backhands and hammer throws. Then after about two minutes, and just as suddenly, the men stopped tossing the Frisbee in Williams's direction.

'At first, I found it kind of funny. Like they were playing around with me. Then I realised that Frisbee is not heading in my direction again.'

Williams was out.

'The thing made me feel foolish. Bad, tremendously bad. It was awkward, a kind of humiliation. I felt *hurt*.'

He tried to rationalise it. Just a few minutes before he didn't even know of the existence of these people. In all likelihood would never see them again. 'So why am I feeling this bad for something this trivial? Why should I actually care?'

Why should we? Why, recognisably, *do* we? It feeds into our fear of something inside us – the Ostraciser.

Kathy Bolkvac was wrong: the nameless things had not ended. They were still happening now. How were they happening? She was a cop. She'd investigate.

The young women Kathy Bolkovac found behind the upstairs door of the Florida nightclub were emaciated, exhausted, terrified. Too terrified to talk. They were victims in another kind of war. But who were the combatants? What were the spoils?

The young women, she discovered, were trapped in a form of debt bondage: passports confiscated, forced to repay their 'transport and board expenses'. As the Human Rights Watch report into Bosnia and Herzegovina details, the only employment offered to them was sex work. In reality the real debt incurred was the price their traffickers paid to buy their bodies. Young women were sometimes sold on multiple times. There was a market where they were traded. In Sarajevo, the actual physical marketplace in which they were ushered, stripped, prodded, inspected, was called the Arizona.

Girls that tried to escape this grim prospect were recaptured, beaten, or would end up floating in the river. More and more young women came to Bolkovac. They originated from countries as far afield as Russia; they told similar stories: how they were duped, deceived, degraded, bought and sold and then sexually exploited. In all there were over 200 such nightclubs scattered across towns and cities in Bosnia trading in trafficked young women.

Bolkovac discovered something more: many members of the international police force were not only having sex with these vulnerable young women, but were also in the traffickers' pay, rewarded for tip-offs about raids or where rescued girls could be recaptured to be 'recycled' for further sexual exploitation.

Kathy determined to do something about it. Whatever it took, she was going to expose the abuse. First, everyone who mattered needed to know.

She drafted an email setting out everything she'd discovered about the abuse. She sent it out to dozens of the most senior staff – both DynCorp and UN – all the way to the head of the UN mission in

Bosnia. Her hope was it would burst the bubble. With it people would be brought to their senses. They'd wake up. How could they not? In the subject line of the email window she typed:

DO NOT READ THIS
IF YOU HAVE A WEAK STOMACH
OR A GUILTY CONSCIENCE

She pressed Send.

Kathy was summoned to high-level meetings immediately. She was thanked for exposing so egregious a practice. A board of inquiry was urgently established with emergency resources to support her work and the abused and exploited young women. Kathy Bolkovac's courageous step was regarded as a vindication of the UN mission. It was why they were there.

That's what should have happened. This is what did.

The sun still rose and shone down. The abuse of hundreds of young women went on. The more Kathy spoke about sexual enslavement, the more she was frozen out by colleagues. She was isolated in the cafeteria. She was avoided as if she carried a contagion.

Around her, it was as if stones were being carved; her name, like Cimon's, was being inscribed. The ancient practice, the silent ritual, began. There was a deep mystery about it, as if time were circling, and the canteen became the Agora – the Balkans, Athens.

People started interfering with her files.

Papers went missing.

Superiors removed her from cases.

Her investigations were sabotaged.

Her position became intolerable. She was redeployed, away from the Trafficking Office, away from human rights work. She was reassigned to check radios and answer the phone. Then she was suspended.

A series of allegations were levelled against her. Then she was dismissed. The death threats began.

As Kathy Bolkovac says, 'You better be prepared to lose your job, lose your career, lose your financial savings, to lose your retirement, because you will be discredited, and they will do everything they can to harm you.'

As a core survival strategy, humans (along with other animals) have to be acutely attuned to signs of disease. It might be as simple as recoiling from someone who sneezes. But there is a complex overlap between disease and difference. Different behaviour, such as that exhibited by Goodall's polio-riddled chimpanzees, may be an indicator of risk. Such systems, however, may also alert us to signs of risk from different social behaviour such as doing something different from the norm. That was what Kathy Bolkovac did in Bosnia.

We have many modern forms of ostracism, ranging from unfriending and unfollowing someone on Facebook and Twitter, to the latest policy suggestion by the UK government that naturalised citizens convicted of terrorism-related offences should have their citizenship stripped. Prisons are a form of ostracism.

In the research I conducted with colleagues from Cambridge following the death of Gareth Myatt in a Secure Training Centre, we found ostracism operating on a number of levels. What was striking was not just the social isolation and the containment of these young people. It was how they were viewed. As a kind of contagion. They were seen as offences rather than children. The staff regarded these children as fundamentally different – a different 'type'. The language staff used to describe them involved animal imagery: having to move them around the institution 'like cattle'; having to 'feed and water' them; having to be careful about their 'dog eat dog' ways.

At the inquest into Gareth's death, we discovered that some prison officers who were tasked to look after some of our community's most highly vulnerable children, gave themselves names like Clubber, Crusher, Mauler and Breaker (this is not to suggest that the three restraining officers did so). We discovered that, it being a youth institution, the staff ran a competition with a star chart for 'Star of the Week'. The star was the child who was forcibly restrained the most by adult officers. This led to a dangerous spiral of denigration, demonisation and finally dehumanisation. It created the conditions for the dangerous use of physical force by prison officers on detained young people, a practice that was happening across the country. It led to injury. Some children lost consciousness; others suffered broken bones. One young person had both wrists broken. The spiral led to death.

When answering questions at the beginning of the inquest into Gareth's death, his mother Pam said, 'When the authorities took him away from me I thought he was going to be safe and that he would be coming home to me.' She said that she received no apology or offer of support after his death. 'It has virtually stopped my life,' she said.

So this is another part of Pam's question, another clue to what happened in that room. Gareth, like many detained children, was socially ostracised. Other detained children were demeaned, ignored, ill-treated. Far too frequently, physical force was used upon them when it shouldn't have been. After the jury returned its verdict, Pam told the awaiting press pack that it was hard enough dealing with what happened to her son, but hearing that the injuries had happened again and again over years to others, that children were complaining and no one listened and nothing was done, that made it harder. Deborah Coles, co-director of the organisation INQUEST, which acts in contentious death cases, said Gareth's death, 'was entirely preventable and a disaster waiting to happen'.

The fact is, these young people were incarcerated, imprisoned, cast out. We care less about those things we cast out.

Asked in court what would help her move on, Pam said, 'To get the truth.'

Kathy Bolkovac had been trying to expose the truth. But now she was out. She was ostracised. She sued DynCorp for unlawful dismissal. Her claim was that she was demonised and ostracised because she had made what in law is called a 'protected disclosure'. She blew the whistle. It led to a bitterly contested court case. During the proceedings, DynCorp admitted that three of its staff had been sacked for using prostitutes. One of them, the company accepted, had 'bought' a 'sex slave' and kept her in his apartment. He'd paid $700.

Bolkovac won. The court found that DynCorp had sacked her because of her efforts to raise awareness of human trafficking cases and exposing corruption. As the court ruled, the company 'had a knife in the applicant and was determined that she be removed from her role as gender monitor'. The tribunal chair said, 'It is hard to imagine a case in which a firm has acted in a more callous, spiteful and vindictive manner.'

But she has found it impossible to resume her career in international law enforcement. As the court found, because of what she had done, Kathy had become a 'marked woman'. She next lived with her husband near Amsterdam and went 'back to school', as she puts it. As she says, 'I'm still trying to figure out what my cause is.'

None of the officers implicated in the sex trafficking and prostitution in Bosnia has ever been prosecuted. DynCorp subsequently won a series of lucrative military contracts in Iraq, Afghanistan and Haiti, among other places – in Part VI, we'll come to Haiti. DynCorp announced being awarded a US State Department contract to provide policing services in Iraq three days after dropping its appeal against Kathy's unfair dismissal verdict.

'When you blow the whistle,' Bolkovac says, 'history and experience over the years show that the odds will be stacked against you. That's what I've learned from the whistleblowers I've met since.'

Why did that happen when she was doing the right thing, exposing a pernicious pattern of human exploitation? When she revealed how young women were burned, beaten, desensitised and degraded for systematic sexual exploitation? How did it happen that the organisations she was working with not only ignored her but froze her out – ostracised her?

Science may have the answer.

FOUR

The Circle and the Suffering

K ip Williams knew it was important; he knew it spoke to
something important in us. It *hurt* him. 'By cutting me out
of the game, they made me feel invisible,' he says. 'As though
I had never existed.' The Frisbee game had only lasted two minutes.
How and why did that rejection actually hurt? he wondered. What
kind of pain was it? He knew he had to bring it under experimental
control.

Social ostracism is something he had wanted to research for
eight years and hadn't worked out a way to do it. Now a Frisbee
rolling into his back when he was on the blanket with Michelob
gave him the clue. He would play Frisbee. Cyber versions of it.
'It was a really clean way to manipulate it in a lab.'

In the laboratory at Purdue, Williams and his colleagues began
using a number of strategies to manipulate human encounters.
They load the dice in carefully constructed cyber games; direct
the pain; exclude some volunteers; have others ignored or rebuffed.
Some people are ejected from chat rooms. For others, it's simply

the sting of an averted glance. Whatever the device, it's directed at delivering social pain.

'We wanted to see how minimal we could make this event and still get feelings of ostracism,' Williams says. He succeeded. There is now a substantial body of experimental research documenting how the brain registers this pain. The research shows that we recruit the same or similar neural systems as when we experience trauma that is physical. Thus brain structures are activated such as the anterior insula, which assesses pain severity, and the dorsal anterior cingulate cortex, which is linked to the emotion of physical pain.

Naomi Eisenberger of the Psychology Department at UCLA states in her article 'Broken Hearts and Broken Bones' that although we are able to distinguish between the two types of pain, it appears that they share neurobiological and neural substrates. She makes the point that when people speak of social rejection, they use phrases like 'he hurt my feelings' or 'she broke my heart'. This applies across cultures, with social pain described in terms of physical pain in almost every language. In fact, over the course of evolutionary history, she believes, the social bonding/attachment system may have 'piggy-backed' onto the physical pain one. Thus the mental module may not have developed independently. It may not be entirely freestanding. But the social pain people describe is more than just a metaphor. It actually hurts.

One of the remarkable findings of this line of research is that for all our bluster and posturing, as Williams says, social pain 'hurts us all about the same in its initial effect and personality doesn't appear to make much difference at first. The variance is in how we cope, that's where the individual differences kick in, but we are all hurting about as much.'

Pain is a method of social control. It is used across the animal kingdom by all kinds of social animals. Groups that ostracise deviant or onerous members become more cohesive. Concomitantly, however, the prospects for ostracised animals are not good. As Marian Wong said, 'When you're out, you're eaten.' Such extreme outcomes are not restricted to non-human animals.

In 2013 Joshua Unsworth was in Year 11 at St Cecilia's Roman Catholic High School in Longridge, Lancashire. He lived with his mother and father in a converted farmhouse in the nearby ancient village of Goosnargh. But Joshua was also on ask.fm. The site is a social media hub created by two Russian entrepreneurs, Ilya and Mark Terebin, the sons of a Red Army soldier. It is based in Riga, Latvia, beyond real regulation. Controversially, the site allows users to post comments or questions to other users anonymously. This feature has been called by child protection charities a 'stalker's paradise'.

While he was on ask.fm, Joshua was repeatedly told over a period of time that no one liked him. One of the messages read, 'honestly no one cares for you even your parents don't want you, there gunna put you in care'.

On 4 April 2013, at 6.50am, Joshua Unsworth was found on land behind the family's farmhouse. He had hanged himself. Paramedics were called but he was pronounced dead at the scene.

Just months before these events, Josh had posted a YouTube video in which he said he'd seen how much despair there was on social media among young people. He said he had come up with an idea to help. He would try to support anyone who felt isolated and alone by posting his mobile phone number; he offered anyone who needed it 'a friendly chat'. Joshua Unsworth was 15 years old when he died.

*

In 2000, Williams and colleagues published a study he had conducted with colleagues at Purdue. Using a computerised version of the Frisbee throwing in the park that he called Cyberball, they had 1,486 people play a ball-toss game. The cover story they told participants was that the study was interested in 'mental visualisation' of who was playing, what the temperature was like, and it was irrelevant who got the ball. In fact, it was all about who got the ball. After a few early inclusions, the research volunteer would be excluded as the other players on the computer screen carried on without them – as if the volunteer was no longer there. Invisible. Those who suffered this social rebuff – albeit a virtual one – when subsequently interviewed reported significantly reduced levels of self-esteem, control, belonging and meaning in their life. It wasn't 'real': it was a virtual game with anonymous others they did not and would never meet. Nevertheless they experienced it as real pain.

'This was in contrast to those who were included, so it is a statistically reliable reduction. Something real happened,' Williams says. Even when some selected subjects were told the 'absolute truth', that the on-screen players were in fact computer-generated and not other humans down the cyberconnection, they still were adversely affected. This led Williams and his colleagues to conclude this was a pretty 'primitive' reaction, something deep down.

'We could see it,' Williams says. 'They were in an MRI magnetic chamber, and their brain activates when they don't get the ball. We could see a significant activation of the dorsal anterior cingulate cortex which is the same region of the brain that is activated when people experience physical pain.'

There are now over 175 published papers of studies or analyses of Cyberball alone. People have been studied playing it from the ages of 7 to 85. In one parallel study in the Netherlands, participants kept feeling the pain of rejection, even when being passed the ball would cost them financially. People continued to want to play with others even if the game involved tossing an imaginary explosive that could at any moment obliterate everything.

'Think of it this way,' Williams explains, 'it's the conceptual equivalent of feeling bad when you're not invited to play Russian roulette. That's how strong the urge is.'

Ostracism threatens our need to feel we belong, that we are worthy of attention – are not invisible. It is a pain, Williams says, 'that keeps on giving'. The reaction to such social rejection can be both fundamental and fierce.

On Wednesday 24 November 2004, it was the first period of the last school day before the Thanksgiving holiday at Valparaiso High School, Indiana – a 90-mile drive due north up Interstate 65 from the Purdue Cyberball lab. In Spanish, Valparaiso means Paradise Valley, and coincidentally it was a Spanish class when a video was going to be played that it happened. It was just before 8 o'clock.

James Lewerke, a 15-year-old class member, offered to close the classroom door and turn off the lights for the video. He stood. His teacher, Ashley Dobis, daughter of the State Representative Chet Dobis, thought he was just being polite. Students tended to behave well with her. They *liked* her (her stellar review on rate-myteacher.com: 'she ROCKS she is the best Spanish teacher or any teacher in the entire world I LOVE HER – 5stars'). So when Miss Dobis gave permission, Lewerke got up. He was a generally quiet boy with pretty good grades. But when he turned to face the class, Dobis says, 'He just had that look in his eyes.' James Lewerke pulled out a machete and a serrated tree saw.

He slashed seven of his classmates with the weapons.

As he rushed out of the room, several courageous teachers tackled him. One of them kicked a weapon along the school corridor. Later Lewerke told the police that he targeted his fellow pupils indiscriminately because 'they all were the same to him'. In the aftermath of his rampage, it was reported by the *Indianapolis Star* that 'He was so invisible at High School this fall that students who sat next to him didn't even know his name.'

'To repair the pain of invisibility,' Kip Williams says, 'we may provoke other people into paying attention to us, to force others to recognise our existence. Ostracism is a thread that weaves through case after case after case of school violence.'

In 2003, Mark Leary and colleagues published a meta-analysis of school shootings in the US since 1995. They called it, 'Teasing, Rejection, and Violence'. They found that 87 per cent of incidents had as a major contributory factor acute or chronic social rejection. In that period, 40 children had been shot dead in their school corridors and classrooms.

'They are past wanting to be liked or readmitted into society,' Williams says. 'They may even want to be immortalised for their actions, even their death. By doing what they're doing, they're going to get noticed. They'll be invisible no more.'

'When animals experience extreme physical pain,' Naomi Eisenberger, speaking in *Reject,* a film on social ostracism, says, 'one of their first responses is to attack whatever's nearby. This sheds some light on why people may be aggressive after they feel rejected. The extent to which there's some overlap between the system that regulates physical pain and the system regulating pain of rejection, means people may become aggressive in response to social rejection.'

*

'I am not insane,' Luke Woodham, 16, said to psychiatrists, 'I'm angry.' Woodham had been arrested in October 1997 for opening fire with a hunting rifle in the cafeteria at the Pearl High School, Mississippi. He killed two, wounded seven. 'All throughout my life,' he said, 'I was ridiculed, beaten, hated.'

It was, said Adam Scott, one of the students shot by Woodham, 'like a horror movie'.

We scan our social horizons for clues about our acceptance or threats to it. Further, research suggests that humans have developed behavioural immune systems to regulate and restrict contact with threats to fitness such as pathogens and parasites. Such a system may however be extremely sensitive to signs of other kinds of 'difference', such as actions by an individual that violate established group norms or patterns of behaviour.

Indeed we have seen how with different forms of 'pain', similar neural structures are recruited, whether the pain is physical (which is where in evolutionary terms the system is likely to have first evolved) or social, which is likely to have developed more recently – in evolutionary time, that is, which would encompass the previous several million years in which hominids have lived in social groups. Indeed there is evidence of how people who are viewed as having violated a group norm are deemed to be diseased. My research around detained children and young people also found evidence of the same phenomenon. More: some children believed themselves to be contaminated. Some like Anthony in Ghana believed they were nothing. Or worse.

What are we doing?

On this analysis, cognitive systems are likely to have developed to solve recurring vital survival problems, including the problems of group living. Deviance from the norm may trigger similar systems to those directed at distancing from contagion. Group members who loyally hold onto the pervasive group norm avoid individuals who depart from or transgress it in a similar way to that in which they avoid disease-bearers. As such, ostracism amounts to a social isolation which can be viewed as a kind of quarantine, with the ultimate sanction being total group exclusion.

Kathy Bolkovac was in the end excluded from the group. She has not subsequently returned. She *did* carry a contagion. It was the truth. In the opaque twilight world of illicit brothels and backstreet bars in which young women were incarcerated and outside which international agency vehicles would pull up for business, she had indeed violated a norm. She had dared challenge the squalid status quo. She had disrupted the quiet complicity of the strange micro-world that was raw and ravaged post-conflict Bosnia.

If ostracism is indeed used by group members as a form of threat management and social control, in the dysfunctional world that operated almost autonomously in post-conflict Bosnia, Kathy Bolkovac was considered a threat. Not only was *she* a threat, but the truth was.

It was too dangerous to the status quo; disastrous to the perpetuation of the harmful and profitable practices that had flourished following the international intervention. It would threaten jobs, careers and wallets, greed, lust, power; it would call into sharp question the legitimacy of the international mission.

How could a risk of that magnitude be managed? By ostracising the messenger.

Her ostracism performed the two threat management functions that were observed in the regulation of goby colonies in the Great Barrier Reef: it protected and promoted. It protected those benefiting from the exploitation of young trafficked women – the dominant; it promoted and prolonged the (dysfunctional) status quo of the group, the norm.

In behavioural ecology terms, the 'pay-to-stay' model prevalent within social animal groups suggests that for Kathy Bolkovac to stay within the malfunctioning microcosm of post-conflict Bosnia, she would have to pay. The price was her silence. It was a price she was not prepared to meet.

As it floated and shimmered through the air towards him, the Frisbee that changed Kip Williams's intellectual life carried with it a message about human communication and connection. Of course, tossing a ball or a Frisbee by oneself can provide the same aerobic and energetic workout, more so if we wish. It's just not phenomenologically rewarding for humans. It's not much fun. Broadly, we want to be around other humans – at least some of the time. But simultaneously, we have a residual, often unvoiced, fear of the fun stopping, of it being taken away, of our being unfriended, unfollowed.

What is all this for?

Beyond a few, relatively rare exceptions, most of us *need* the impromptu Frisbee games of life with strangers. The opportunity for fruitful future interaction means that they represent an acceptable risk. But risk of what? Rejection. Degrees of ostracisation, social death.

Naomi Eisenberger believes that the sting of social rejection may be an avoidance adaptation to encourage steering clear of behaviours that may lead to exclusion, a method for promoting social bonds. In broad agreement, Williams says, 'I think it has an evolutionary basis. We have evolved as social animals, and it's important for the survival of a social animal to maintain a connection with others. So we are wired to detect hints that we could lose it.'

But that group connection is not free. It comes at a cost.

Groups have norms – rules. They act as regulators, producers and reproducers of social order. Ostracism or its threat operates as a form of social control, the enforcement of norm conformity – even if that order is not fair or equitable, even if it is pathological and harmful. The power of ostracism derives from its targeting of our vulnerabilities and insecurities: the fear of not belonging – ultimately, of being alone.

'So we have seen,' Williams says, 'interesting patterns of behavioural responses to ostracism. For many people, they will conform more to a unanimous group, even if that group is clearly wrong in their perceptual judgements. They will just go along with it. They will be more likely to comply, to obey a command.' In other words, they become more susceptible to social influence, to avoid, as Williams puts it, the 'kiss of social death'.

There is another reaction. A more violent one. As we saw at Valparaiso High School – and one hundred others.

Fear of social rejection, of being seen not to conform, of *not belonging*, may have contributed to the institutional indifference to the human rights abuses that Kathy Bolkovac uncovered. Other people suffer; we stay within the safe circle. And so it continues: the circle and the suffering.

It feeds on our need to fit in. It preys on the pain that keeps on giving. It takes the courage of a Kathy Bolkovac to defy it.

Eventually Bolkovac's tireless advocacy of the rights of young exploited women led to officials suspected of being implicated in the trafficking having to resign. More needs to be done, much more.

THE TEN TYPES OF HUMAN

None of them was prosecuted. 'Charges were never brought because no one allowed any of the investigations to be completed,' she says.

When in 2010 a film about what she had done was screened at the UN, Kathy was invited to speak. At another event, the Secretary General Ban Ki-moon led a panel discussion about sexual abuse, human trafficking and forced prostitution in post-conflict situations. Kathy harboured misgivings then about whether the lessons had really been learned. She still does. She has every right to remain dubious. As I write several years later, there are allegations of serious sexual exploitation of women in the Central African Republic (CAR) by international peace-keepers, both UN and non-UN personnel. We'll come to CAR later.

In Henrik Ibsen's play *An Enemy of the People*, Thomas Stockmann, doctor at an affluent Norwegian spa town, becomes the object of collective fury when he points out that the town's well is poisoned. He tells his neighbours they have to stop profiting from a lie. The windows of the Stockmann home are smashed; the family members are evicted by their landlord; his daughter is sacked from her teaching job at the school; the town passes a resolution that no one should ever employ the doctor again. Thomas Stockmann is forced out of the town because he refuses to be silent about the truth.

I asked Kathy Bolkovac if she knew the play.

'I had my own,' she says, her eyes staring right at you.

'But you didn't want it.'

'Didn't want it, didn't need it, but what are you going to do?' That Plains stoicism. 'You know, over the years people keep asking me where I got my strength from. How I did it and didn't back down, even though I was shut out, targeted, attacked. Well, it's a pretty simple thing.'

Outside my window there is that tree. Leaves keep coming off it, being shed, discarded, falling as she speaks.

'Right is right and wrong is wrong,' she says. 'I think it pretty much comes down to that.'

'So, yes,' I said to Marian Wong. 'I said Frisbees.'

And so I told her what I knew. I sent Wong the Williams research, and sent him her research on fish. We're planning a small (but perfectly formed) research group. Something new. Because their startling work – the fish and the Frisbees – kept grating on me. It wouldn't let me rest. There was another connection it took me a while to pin down. And then I got it.

I profoundly believe that the goby fish and the Frisbee players are surreptitiously connected to another form of creaturely behaviour we will reach later in the book, something I've been trying to fight: FGM – female genital mutilation.

The pelicans fly overhead again – I assume it is the same group – their long beaks scything through the Florida sky on another strafing run. I throw the Frisbee back towards the Bermuda-shorted men. But the wind suddenly gets up. The disc almost reaches them, hovers elusively, an inch beyond their fingertips, before suddenly boomeranging back towards me.

'Looks like it wants to come back to you,' the nearest of them says.

'It likes me,' I reply, picking it up again. 'Looks like you're having fun.'

'It's the best,' he says. 'You all visiting?'

'From London.'

'Man, I have got to go there. I have family there.'

'In London?'

'Yessir, in Slough.'

Which to us is not quite the same thing. But that's a British thing. John Betjeman famously had a rather severe assessment, 'Come friendly bombs and fall on Slough / It isn't fit for humans now.'

'You know Slough?' the Frisbee-er asks.

Things change. Post-Betjeman Slough has different problems: one of the highest incidences of FGM in the UK. It also has people fighting against it. 'I know Slough,' I say.

'Man, I have to go.'

'Yes, do. Definitely do.'

Unlike Kip Williams, I don't manage to enter into a game with strangers. But I talk. Which is another kind of game.

We ostracise; we are ostracised. We are the Ostraciser; we are its victim. Ostracism lances surgically straight into our mind. Neural systems fire; avoidance systems are engaged; social pain feels like real pain. It *is* real. Whether the mental module has developed independently or recruited pre-existing systems for physical pain, we are constantly alive to its signals. Acceptance, rejection, they matter. Rejection can lead to serrated tree saws in the classroom; bloodied knives being kicked along school corridors; the slashing of wrists after a reality TV eviction; a well-meaning boy like Joshua Unsworth walking quietly out of his parents' farmhouse and into the trees.

The men on Cocoa Beach continue their Frisbee game without me. I turn towards the water again, but do not see the arrow boat now, nor the two boys, Anthony and Michael. The Atlantic remains reassuringly the Atlantic. Silhouettes dart above in geometric pattern; I cup my hand over my eyes and watch as the pelicans disappear over Cape Canaveral and the sun slides into the Banana River Lagoon.

PART III
THE TAMER OF TERROR

A single glance at the landscape was sufficient
to show me how widely different it was from
anything I had ever beheld.

Charles Darwin, diary entry on sighting Tierra del Fuego,
17 December 1832

ONE

The Time Has Come

In the distance, beyond the windows, there is a faint yelping. You enter your daughter's bedroom in the darkness and see a letter she's composed on her iPad. It's addressed to you.

Outside, more yelping, horrid screeching in the night. The iPad rests on her stomach as your daughter rests on her bed. You notice the charge left on the tablet: 49%. Something is strange.

Normally (you've seen it a thousand times before) there would be the screensaver – an old photo of her sprinting across the sand with her favourite dog, a beagle she used to have called Cindy. But that was a long time ago, and so much has happened. For such a long time you've had to look after her. But now the fact that you can read these two thick paragraphs of text can only mean one thing: she's deactivated the screensaver. She *wants* you to find what she's written.

It is a starry night. The yelping, fox cubs in the distance – there has been a new litter – gets worse. The night air carries an unmistakable chill. As you read, as your eyes pass with mounting horror over the words, a chill of a different kind seeps through you.

Dear Mum and Dad,

I know you love me, perhaps more than I deserve — we all know I can be a right misery guts. But I hope you also know that this is not — not really *— me. It hasn't been for a long time. I'm the girl ripping wrapping paper off presents under the Christmas tree too fast, with both of you laughing and saying hold your horses. I'm the girl inside the slightly naff costumes you made, Mum, for school concerts and Joseph's Technicolour Dreamcoat (but I loved them anyway). That's me. This is the illness. We all know it's ruined my life and yours. You know the pain I'm constantly in, in every little part of my body. My fingernails hurt, my scalp hurts, my heart is broken up and hurts. I can't have children. I can't give life. I don't* have *a life, not one to speak of. I still don't understand why someone, anyone, has to suffer like this for so many years. I want to get free of this pain, and think I've done it. But pls help me if I messed it up like last time. I need this time for it to work. So I have injected all the morphine. If it doesn't work, I* need *you to give me some more M. I've used everything in the syringe so it's my responsibility. But if it's not enough, if it comes to it, pls, pls help me. I hope it won't and when you read this I will be free.*

I'm sorry for not saying goodbye, but it was too hard. Don't you ever stop thinking of me, okay? I know that's selfish but I want you to keep thinking of me because I will be thinking of you. But now you can stop worrying and have your lives back. I'm really sorry to have taken up so much of them so unfairly. I can't live with the illness anymore, and I don't want you to have to. I love you both and know we will all see one another again, only not in a place with so much pain. And then when

we meet, you will see that I was <u>right all along</u> and I will be with Cindy.
Because this is not me. I'm the girl paddling on the beach in Cornwall
and finding that seahorse. Pls never forget <u>that</u> me.

Love you always, B xx

The syringe which held the morphine is entirely empty. The plunger has been pushed right in. Your daughter went through with it. She injected it all. But.

But she is still alive. Her breathing is shallow, horribly strained. She is still alive and not yet free of the pain. You can help her. You have it in your power to help her. To help her in what she has discussed many, many times and now is on the brink of succeeding in doing: getting free of the pain. Your beautiful daughter. The girl on the beach in Cornwall, who found that rarest of seahorses. Only a dozen have been found in Cornwall over the past 30 years. The mesmerising name: *Hippocampus hippocampus*. That minute snub-nosed creature, delicate and proud.

In the medicine cabinet, safely stored away, out of direct heat and light just as the doctors directed, is the morphine. Enough to end your daughter's life. It is impossible to contemplate. And yet this is what she wants. She has tried before, and did not succeed, and her life was so much worse afterwards. You have no doubt – none whatsoever – that this is what she wants: an end to the years of suffering, to be with her beloved Cindy again, not just to be with her adored pet, but to be restored to a time, a life, unclouded by pain. And yet it *is* your daughter.

People speak about mercy killing. What is merciful about any of this – either way? This would be the taking of a life you helped create. And yet you are consumed with terror. Terror that she is suffering even more now. Terror that you will let her down. Terror that you will not help her bring that suffering to an end.

Slowly, some part of you grasps the smooth metal handle of the medicine cabinet. The door glides open silently. Your mind spins dizzyingly with competing thoughts: your daughter running unrestrained and unharmed on the beach . . . your daughter lying on her bed with a devastating quantity of morphine coursing through her veins. You see the tide coming in on the beach. You see the dangerous drug seeping through her body. You secretly always knew this day would come. That you'd be put to this test. And you have prepared your answer. Only now, there appears to be no answer. Or rather, there are two.

The fox cubs scrap and yelp in the night chill.

Your hand reaches for the morphine bottle. Drops.

Reaches for the morphine bottle. Drops.

Reaches . . .

First, there was Tony.

On the Internet you will find grainy video footage of him floating. He hangs in the air from the tenuous tendrils of a parachute. It has a corrugated yellowish canopy and a little pilot chute, neon pink and cupcake-shaped, above it. Tony wears a lime green jumpsuit. The sky above him, all around him, is unblemished cobalt blue. He waves to the camera.

'It was somewhere over the Emirates,' his wife Jane says. She has collar-length chestnut hair in a no-nonsense get-on-with-it style. She used to be a nurse, too busy to waste time on irrelevancies. A faint warm burr is just detectable in her accent, revealing her Dorset roots. Now in her mid-fifties, she's back working in the NHS, but not as a nurse. She's done enough nursing. Enough, she tells me, for a lifetime.

'Yes, that was taken when we were in the Middle East,' she says. 'If you're going to skydive, that's the place to do it. Perfect blue skies, see for miles. It was a birthday present. Tony got it for himself. He liked experiencing all sorts of things.'

She paints a picture of perfection in her Dorset burr. But something slightly unbalances me. I realise and ask, 'He liked skydiving?'

She laughs. 'Oh, loved, *loved* it. Diving for him was freedom.'

A third type of diving: Anthony's fear, Marian Wong's fun, Tony's freedom. 'Would you do it?' I ask her for the first time. I knew I'd have to ask her the same question – *would you do it?* – in an entirely different context again later. I didn't want to ask it – the crucial question, the only real question – now. It didn't seem right for either of us. Jane is direct and tough, but there are limits.

'Would I dive out of a plane with a parachute?' she says. 'No chance. You wouldn't get me up there in a million years. What's the point?' More irrelevancies; she was unimpressed. 'But Tony, he loved doing mad things like that. He was fun and loud and a real show-off. It was a wonderful, mad world with Tony.'

On the footage, Tony falls through the Emirates sky, waving to the camera, doing just that – joyously showing off.

Jane and Tony met, of all places, on a blind date in Dubai. That was in 1984. It was at, of all things, a Dionne Warwick concert. 'I know it sounds a bit cheesy, but it was love at first sight. He was this tall, dark, handsome guy. Very funny. The life and soul.'

He was indeed tall: 6 foot 4½, a keen rugby player (in fact obsessed with rugby), a dabbler in extreme sports. You may have heard of him. His name was Tony Nicklinson.

What happened in June 2005 changed all their lives. Tony was on a business trip to Athens. He was a civil engineer, working for a

Greek company, and although settled with his family in the Emirates, he had to regularly travel back to Greece, no time for the tourist stuff, the Parthenon, the Agora, but for work – graft. He played hard, but he grafted.

In his hotel a headache came on. Crushingly so; it wouldn't shift. He lost consciousness and was rushed to hospital. Tony had suffered a massive stroke. It left him paralysed. At that point he was 51 years old, married to Jane and father of two daughters, Lauren and Beth. The way Jane describes it, her husband's body suddenly disappeared from his control, like the sudden vanishing of the safety of a plane to man in terrifying freefall. Tony Nicklinson was cast adrift. Only one small – minuscule – islet of control remained: blinking. And the torment was deepened because his mind had been left unharmed, completely unimpaired. He had locked-in syndrome.

His sphere of control had shrunk and so had his world. Whereas once he travelled the globe – South Africa, New Zealand, the Emirates, Thailand – now his life had shrivelled to a room in a bungalow in a village in Wiltshire. And a blinking of an eye within that room.

In his own words, Tony put it like this: 'My life now is nothing like my life before the stroke. Then my family and I were living outside Dubai. I was chairman of the local sports club and president of the Middle East rugby association. I had a nice home, an excellent job as a senior manager in a construction company, and I earned enough for all of us to have a comfortable life. We weren't rich but we didn't want for anything. Now my wife and I live on benefits and I'm totally dependent on others for everything.'

Every day after Athens, he had to contend with the terror. This vibrant, vital man was trapped in a body unresponsive and unknowable to him. But torment is not choosy. It's quite prepared to spread itself about.

'Athens changed everything,' Jane says. 'Of all the places.'

'How do you think of it now?'

'As the end. Of so much. It affected us all, our little family. Our lives as we knew it were over. For a good year afterwards, every morning I'd wake up and for a split second it would be like it was not real, a bad dream, and we were going to go back to normal. And then slowly you'd gather your thoughts and know it was the real thing. This was our life.'

What was that life? When he was finally able to communicate with Jane using a Perspex alphabet board, staring at particular letters to select them, blinking confirmations, he had a simple but unmistakable message for her.

'When we were first able to communicate,' Jane says, 'one of the very first things he told me was that he wanted to die.'

What was life inside that unknowable body like? 'I go out once a year to the dentist,' Tony said. 'I don't see people who call to see us. That's because I get upset sitting there unable to contribute to the conversation. I prefer not seeing anyone – it's the lesser of two evils. I am resigned to a miserable existence. I can't move. I can't talk. I live in constant mental anguish. I can't live like this.'

Once, for a BBC documentary, the former Lord Chancellor Charlie Falconer visited him. Falconer was chairing an independent commission on assisted dying. His committee opposed the right to die for those like Tony who were not terminally ill but who remained incapable of initiating the process of suicide themselves – who needed assistance to die.

'So what do *you* suggest I do?' Tony asked Falconer. There was no satisfactory response. How could there be?

'I view the next 20 years with trepidation,' Tony said. 'There is no light at the end of the tunnel. Knowing that today is the same as tomorrow and the day after is soul-destroying. I am fed like a baby with baby food, cannot do anything for myself. I have this for the rest of my life.'

Fluid was inserted directly into his stomach through the abdominal wall using percutaneous endoscopic gastrostomy, a PEG tube. In his affidavit to the High Court, Tony said that the loss of control of his bodily functions was 'by far the hardest thing'.

As Jane explains, 'It all caused him a lot of distress. The daily indignities. You have no privacy, no control. Everything has to be done for you. It's humiliating and really upset him. He was handsome, athletic, funny and popular. All the things he loves about his life, he can't now do. He used to love going out to the pub with his mates to watch the rugby.'

Tony's life – its remnants – settled into an unvarying routine: every morning he had to be unceremoniously lifted vertically out of his bed with a mechanical hoist. He was then set down in a wheelchair. He also had an armchair. Every evening he was hoisted back into bed. That was his world: two chairs and a bed. Tony wrote to the High Court that his life could best be summed up as 'miserable, demeaning, undignified and intolerable'.

But one thing added greatly to his ordeal. He could not control how he would meet his death. Suicide was not an option for him.

'I am so severely disabled that I can't commit suicide. I need someone else to kill me,' he said.

But who?

That was when I had to ask the question.

'Until Tony's stroke,' Jane told me, 'to be honest, I didn't have any opinion on it, assisted dying. I can kind of remember reading about it in the paper, but it always happens to someone else, doesn't it? Not to people like us. We're just an ordinary working family. Not to people like us. And then it did.'

'When did Tony reach his final decision that he wanted to die?'

'When he first started communicating with the board, he said it, and I kind of expected it, knowing his character, how much he loved his old life. It was entirely predictable that would be his first reaction. So I kind of expected it. But then there was the other side to him, the determined side, so we just waited a bit.'

They waited for those crosswinds to pass, talking it through, not being rash. Trying to assess where they were now.

'We went through all the discussions trying to change his mind and that and it worked. He said he'd give life a go for a couple of years to see if he could adjust. He did try. It was so difficult, every single day for him, but he did try. Then in December 2007 [2½ years after the stroke], he was just worn down. He couldn't take much more and decided that he wanted to start . . . making plans. He took himself off all his life-prolonging drugs. He made one of those directives. It said if he had another stroke he was not to be resuscitated. He said he wasn't to be treated, that we should let him go.'

Tony Nicklinson had made what is known as an advance directive, a living will, a formalised set of instructions about his future medical care. It specified that in case of further collapse he was not to receive any life-sustaining treatment.

'I saw the way Tony suffered,' Jane said, 'and I don't believe that anyone should suffer like that. He lived through eight years of hell.'

'So,' I said, 'would you do it?'

Jane paused. In truth, there's been a pause in her life since Tony checked into the Athens hotel in June 2005 and was carried out with a stroke. Her life's been on pause since then.

'Would I do it?' she said. 'Someone's got to. If we couldn't have found a doctor, I would have done it. I would have done it for Tony. I think I probably could have done it.'

'But that's you, his wife, killing the husband you love,' I said. 'Could you really have done that?'

'How could you possibly do that, people often ask. But it's *because* I love him that I could have. Because it was the one thing he wanted.'

'Did you discuss it, how he actually wanted to – do it?'

'In an ideal world, he wanted me to give him a sedative and be with him as he slipped away. Then a doctor would come in later and give him the lethal dose so I wouldn't actually be the one who killed him. In an ideal world, that's what he wanted.'

In an ideal world. Out of respect for Tony, she continues to fight for the principle of the right to choose to die with dignity, taking the test case to the European Court of Human Rights. Out of respect, out of love. It is hard to conceive the extent of the devastation inflicted upon the lives of two ordinary decent people so that the carefully considered process of injecting lethal toxins to deliberately kill someone with a perfectly intact and active mind becomes 'an ideal world'.

In the summer of 2012, Tony Nicklinson lost his case in the High Court. The specially convened three-judge tribunal – a reflection of the tremendous importance of the issue – rejected his claim that he had a right to die. Although as is convention, the family was privately informed of the court's ruling a couple of days before, the public pronouncement of the judgment was on Thursday 16 August 2012.

'It was after the High Court decision that he broke down,' Jane says. 'It was the enormity of it. Tony was devastated and very, very frightened.'

The terror that Tony had so courageously contended with returned. The chance for any light at the end of the tunnel was snuffed out. His lawyer Saimo Chahal QC, a senior partner in the famous human rights firm Bindmans, says, 'Tony was the best kind of client. I often tell young lawyers what you need is a client who is difficult and challenging, because they become bloody-minded and refuse to compromise where there is an obvious injustice. That was the situation with Tony. He'd spend hours contacting me, devising ingenious arguments he'd thought out in his living room. He was irrepressible. And then when the court handed down its judgment, he was just broken. He cried and cried, this extremely tough man. I've never seen anything like it. It was such a moving thing. But he just couldn't understand: it was such a terrible injustice. How could someone in a fair and compassionate society be condemned to years of suffering and anguish? He sent me an email on the Sunday night, asking how long he'd have to hang on for an appeal.'

Things were moving very quickly, but in a dark direction. 'The decision was announced in court on the Thursday,' Jane told me. 'Then on Saturday he became poorly. By Monday he was very ill. The doctor said if he didn't get any treatment he would die.'

One of Tony's lungs had collapsed. He refused antibiotics.

'He was gone by the Wednesday,' Jane says. 'The doctors say he died of pneumonia. But he died of a broken heart. I lost the love of my life, but at least he's not suffering any more.'

One of the last things Tony did was to compose a tweet. He had over 50,000 followers on Twitter. In doing so, and a little like the footage of his skydive, there he is, preserved, looking at us and waving. The tweet said, 'Goodbye world, the time has come, I had some fun.'

Tony Nicklinson died in his bungalow in Melksham, Wiltshire on Wednesday 22 August 2012. He was 58 years old. He left his wife Jane and his daughters Lauren and Beth.

TWO

The Broken Circuit

G iven the sheer implausibility of our own existence, how glorious is it to be alive? Better: how transcendentally glorious to be alive and know it. As we evolved and developed greater cognitive capacities, one of them was the astounding ability to reflect upon the fact that we are actually here and existing and – from time to time – *loving* it.

The difficulty with this burgeoning self-awareness is that we would undoubtedly have pretty rapidly developed an understanding that the party would not last. Life giveth and life taketh away. It is perhaps telling then that from extremely early in the record of human cultural activity there is evidence of a belief in the supernatural – an indication that there may be something greater than life on earth. Neanderthals were burying their dead up to 100,000 years ago. It could have just been to prevent stench, disease or scavengers. Something happened subsequently with humans. In the Upper Palaeolithic period, perhaps 40,000 years ago, *Homo sapiens* started leaving trinkets and food with their dead. It began to look like they believed death was not the end: there may be a further journey. Why did such beliefs evolve? The recognition that death is annihilation is an unsettling, annoying, astonishing thought. Everything around us will continue. Without us. How do we cope with that thought? It presents a persistent and profound risk of severe anxiety. In a paper he wrote with colleagues in 2007, psychologist Sheldon Solomon stated that 'death obliterates control, social connections, meaning, pleasure and everything else that people seek in life . . . and there is a massive literature that death-related thought is indeed uniquely potent'. Such potentially debilitating anxiety and threat to daily functioning sounds like a life problem we need to manage. And if we have devised mechanisms to do so, what have they to do with evolution?

When he was a boy, growing up in a working-class Jewish family in the Bronx, Sheldon Solomon's parents would sometimes deliberately take a detour and drive him through Harlem. They would point to the street people, destitute and down at heel, and say, 'Sheldon, some of them are there because it's their fault. But others are not. Your first duty, never forget this, is to look after yourself. But after you've done that, then you should reach out and help those who need help.' It was a lesson Solomon never forgot.

His family, like many similar families in the area, had endured much. Not only the Depression, but the Holocaust. The consolations that they could find to deal with such unimaginable horror did not come from any supernatural or spiritual quarter. It was a proudly secular family. But the question about what it all meant – or perhaps more precisely, how to make meaning out of it all – preoccupied young Sheldon.

Solomon is now a gravelly-voiced, intensely animated man in his early sixties, but still sporting impressively shoulder-length surfer-dude hair. There is a touch of Jim Morrison and the Doors about him, and that makes sense in another way also: he has spent his adult life trying to peer through our doors of perception to see what is on the other side. His sartorial preferences range from being interviewed in Bob Marley T-shirts to making prestigious scholarly presentations in tie-dyed shirts with shorts. He has eclectic interests, extending to the culinary. With one of his former students he opened Esperanto, a restaurant on Caroline Street in Saratoga Springs. There they sell the famous 'doughboy', a concoction Solomon himself devised of sautéed chicken, spices, cheese and cream all baked in a pizza dough wrap. 'I am hard pressed to understand why people like them,' Solomon says. But love them people do. Esperanto sells a thousand a night in the summer.

Having completed a first degree in psychology at Franklin and Marshall College in Pennsylvania, he proceeded to the PhD programme in experimental social psychology at Kansas University. Solomon loved Kansas. Even if he at first found it unnerving. It was not that the natives were unfriendly. It was the opposite. They were too friendly.

'You've got to understand that I'd grown up in the Bronx,' he says. 'With some time in New Jersey also. But in Kansas people in the street, folks I'd never met, would say hi, and how are you, and my reaction was – Stop! Why are you doing this? Stop *persecuting* me.'

It was at Kansas that he met two fellow psychologists who would become lifelong collaborators: Jeff Greenberg and Tom Pyszczynski. 'We were almost Pythonesque in our inclination to annoy,' he tells me. 'We had two big questions we were obsessed with, which we thought were unconnected. On Monday and Wednesday we looked at self-esteem. On Tuesday and Thursday we looked at prejudice and destructive behaviour. On Friday we went bowling. But at that point we didn't know how they were connected or what lay behind both.' As Solomon was to realise, in fact something decidedly dark did lie behind both.

In 1980 Solomon took an academic post at Skidmore, an affluent private liberal arts college in upstate New York. 'I remember when I arrived and my mother said, "Sheldon, look at all the BMWs and Porsches in the car park," and I said, "Mom, that's the students' parking lot."'

The cars for the staff were rather less salubrious.

'Still, I found Skidmore a great place,' he says. 'I had to teach a course in personality theory (which I knew nothing about – I neglected to tell them that in the interview), and was going up and down the library stacks looking for Freud, which seemed a good place to start, when something caught my eye. It was a book called *The Birth and Death of Meaning*. It was the title that grabbed my attention, and the green spots on the cover – literally. It was by some cultural anthropologist, this guy called Becker.'

Finding that book changed everything. It was, as Solomon says, 'like finding the Rosetta Stone'. Suddenly the hidden hieroglyphics of life made sense. What was it in Becker that had such a tremendous effect?

When we think of the unthinkable dilemma facing Tony and Jane Nicklinson, we recognise the dread of suffering and loss of control – the obvious terror it engenders. I think we understand that. But Becker examines something even more pervasive. Tony Nicklinson belongs to a certain class of people who are demonstrably, excruciatingly, forced to live each day face to face with death. For Becker there is a lesson in this – one that affects the rest of us.

We can begin to understand by asking a single question. What is the single most famous piece of writing in history? This could be endlessly debated, so I'm going to make a claim about a likely contender. It is Hamlet's 'To be or not to be' speech. Here the young prince contemplates how

> . . . the dread of something after death,
> The undiscover'd country from whose bourn
> No traveller returns, puzzles the will,
> And makes us rather bear those ills we have
> Than fly to others that we know not of?

We see in *Hamlet* something we profoundly and painfully recognise. We see the paralysing effect of thinking about our mortality. And it is this that the work of Ernest Becker not only examines, but exhumes.

It is not only, as in Tony Nicklinson's case, how life runs into death, it is the opposite: how death looms over life – every life. Because for Becker one of the 'great rediscoveries of modern thought' is how the terror of death – invariably without our realising – lies at the heart of so much human activity. The question is how serious a challenge to functioning it is. We all know that some people are crippled by death anxieties. But what about the rest of us? Is it present, even holographically, in our lives? If so, its presence may plausibly assume the dimensions of a recurrent life problem affecting our efficacy, survival, even reproductive ability, that may need to be met – that may require a specific adaptation. If death is inevitable, the anxiety about our inescapable extinction must be managed. But how? Sheldon Solomon believes that evolution does – *must* – play a part.

Becker himself knew something about death. He was born in Springfield, Massachusetts in 1924 into a Jewish family, and then served in a US infantry battalion that liberated one of the Nazi concentration camps at the end of World War II. More than that, when Becker came to his own end, it was merciless and tragic.

For many years, his ideas were far from fashionable. The grim subject matter and sobering message of Becker's work found little traction. Worse still, the supposed impossibility of subjecting the ideas to empirical verification meant that they were deemed 'unscientific'. Becker paid a heavy personal and professional price. He wandered from academic post to post, finally ending up in Canada. He was deprecated, marginalised, ignored professionally. Undeterred, however, he continued to develop his ideas since it was increasingly, glaringly, obvious to him that how human beings deal with the terror of our inevitable demise lies at the very heart of much human striving. His work culminated in the last book published during his lifetime, *The Denial of Death*.

Finally his work would be recognised. The book was widely acclaimed. It won the 1974 Pulitzer Prize. That was two months after Becker had died from colon cancer. He was 49 years old.

'In 1980 when I found out about Becker's ideas,' Solomon says, 'I wanted to tell *everybody* about them.' With Greenberg and Pyszczynski, he spent the next few years both worked up by the ideas and working them up for scholarly consumption. The opportunity came in 1984, at a meeting of the Society of Experimental Social Psychology.

'It was a big academic conference,' Solomon says, 'and there were over 300 psychologists there. But when I started talking they began elbowing each other to get out of there, like some mortified mob at a soccer match when the stadium was on fire. Jeff and Tom said, "Look at all those people go, I don't think they like it." And I said, "Nah, they love it. They're just trying to find the paper we haven't written yet."'

So they did write a paper. A formal academic article. 'We sent it to this place called *American Psychologist*, which is a big journal in our field. And we were so psyched, but we got this review back. And it is just one sentence. It says, "I have absolutely no doubt that these ideas are of no interest to any psychologist living or dead." And Tom and Jeff are again like, "I don't think they like it." But I thought they were being coy – they wanted us.'

In fact, they didn't want Solomon and his colleagues. Nor did they much want the theory they had developed, grounded as it was in Becker's work. The next years were full of academic frustration and rejection. But slowly, painstakingly, they did what Becker never got round to doing: they built up a significant body of empirical data verifying their ideas. They became convinced that what they were researching was intimately connected to evolution. Undoubtedly the extraordinary development of the cognitive abilities of our species tens of thousands of years ago, a progression that was and remains evolutionarily unprecedented, would have been put to immediate and practical use in solving survival, resource and reproductive problems. *Homo sapiens* began to reflect on their lot. Every living thing around them died. Their parents did; their greatest hunters or chiefs did; sometimes their children did. No one was immune. Everyone would die. At the beginning of the play, Hamlet's father is dead; by the end, Hamlet is dead, as is Ophelia, her father Polonius, her brother Laertes, Hamlet's mother, her new husband and even the hapless Rosencrantz and Guildenstern. Death, it would have been rapidly understood, was inevitable. Solomon and his colleagues suspected that it would be become necessary to find ways to cope with the implications of this stark reality, with the fallout such ruminations produced – the terror.

Solomon, Greenberg and Pyszczynski worked and argued and pulled these thoughts together. They called the result terror management theory.

And then there was Kay.

Jane Nicklinson faced up to the unimaginable: deliberately ending the life of someone we love. In her mind, she'd made a decision. She was prepared to help her husband die. But it never came to it. Jane Nicklinson never had to stand next to her loved one with a syringe of morphine and wonder if she could go through with pressing the plunger. But Kay Gilderdale did.

The family lived in the glorious East Sussex village of Burwash, sitting within the High Weald Area of Outstanding Natural Beauty. It was an area, in wilder times, once frequented by high-waymen and smugglers. Rudyard Kipling lived half his life here. For her part, Kay Gilderdale practised as an auxiliary nurse and her husband Richard was the local policeman. They were the perfect couple: liked, respected. In 1977 they had a daughter. They named her Lynn. She was an exceptional child, not only beautiful and popular, but very talented: a bright, bubbly girl, the school netball captain, a prizewinning ballet dancer, who also loved sailing and swimming.

They led an idyllic, quiet rural life. Then in November-1991, following a BCG injection at school when she was 14, the standard inoculation against tuberculosis, Lynn inexplicably weakened. Her mother was telephoned by the school and asked to take Lynn home. One illness soon followed another in the life of this previously entirely healthy girl, one affliction after another: flu, bronchitis, tonsillitis, glandular fever.

Very gamely, Lynn intermittently tried to return to school, but it always proved too much. Around six months after the injection she was in a wheelchair. She became paralysed from the waist down. She couldn't swallow and had to be fed every meal through a nasogastric tube. From the summer of 1992 she was bedridden, and the much-loved daughter of the auxiliary nurse and policeman would never recover. There followed 16 years of abject misery and constant pain as myalgic encephalomyelitis – the neurological disease ME, an inflammation of the brain and spinal chord – slowly destroyed Lynn's life.

Kay said, 'I made a conscious decision. I said to her, however long it takes, I'll be there to look after you.' And she was. With her child constantly. The only other constant companion Lynn had was the pain. Always the pain. Lynn went to hospital 50 times in the next 16 years. It was one thing after another. Daylight hurt her eyes, so she lived in a room with the curtains constantly drawn, shrouding her from the world. She developed anaemia, renal failure, liver dysfunction, hypothalamic dysfunction, premature ovarian failure and osteoporosis with 50 per cent bone loss. Just moving her could fracture her bones. Always, always the pain.

At the end of those 16 years, Lynn was 31 years old and had, as she put it, 'never kissed a boy properly, let alone done anything else.' But what hurt her most was that her ovaries had shrunk. She could never have children. Another kind of pain.

'Still, she wasn't difficult to look after,' Kay has said. 'She might lie there and cry with pain, but she didn't complain. She was very determined. She was very strong, a real fighter. But she felt the only escape was to die.'

It can be hard to understand this. But Lynn's own words provide a route to forming an understanding. Some of this was read out in the court case that was to subsequently take place.

> I can't keep hanging on to this miserable excuse of a life. I'm tired and my spirit is broken. My body and mind is broken. I'm desperate to end the never-ending carousel of pain and suffering. I've just had enough of being in such pain and feeling so sick every second of every day. I have nothing left and I am spent.

At 1.45am on 3 December 2008, Lynn injected herself with a massive dose of morphine. When her mother arrived, she told her, 'I want the pain to go.' We read this without fully absorbing what it actually means. Your child looks you in the eyes and lets you know unmistakably that she is trying to kill herself.

Kay tried to dissuade her daughter, but she saw the determination on Lynn's face. She asked her mother to get more morphine. Kay did. But Lynn wouldn't let her mother go near the syringes. She knew she had to inject the chemical, the toxic substance, into her bloodstream herself. With remarkable presence of mind, Lynn was at the same time trying to kill herself and save her mother from blame. Purely coincidentally at that early hour, the lights went out in the house. A circuit broke. Lynn pushed the plunger in. She became unconscious immediately.

In the end it took 30 hours for Lynn to die. Eventually at 7.10am on the morning after, it was over.

It had been an agonising ordeal. The morphine had not been enough. Lynn was languishing between life and death. It had gone, as the court would later be told, 'horribly wrong'. Kay gave Lynn yet more morphine. Then, as the family GP Dr Jane Woodgate would relate, Kay told her that she had three times injected syringes of air into Lynn's Hickman line. She told the doctor that she was terrified her daughter would be left brain-damaged. Injecting air into someone's bloodstream – creating an air embolism – can block the flow of blood from the heart to the lungs. It can kill you.

'I know I did the right thing for Lynn,' Kay has said. 'She was free and in peace. I had no right to make her stay and suffer more.'

Bridget Kathleen Gilderdale, aged 55, known as Kay, was charged with the attempted murder of her daughter.

The terror management theory (TMT) that Solomon and his colleagues developed borrows, as does Ernest Becker, from a line of thinkers including Kierkegaard, Freud, William James, Otto Rank and Charles Darwin. The essence is captured by Becker's statement that 'to live fully is to live with an awareness of the rumble of terror that underlies everything'.

We begin (as in so much else) with Darwin. Organisms have an incessant, irrepressible drive for self-preservation. It isn't the only drive. It may be subservient to the deeper drive to propagate their own genes. Later we will come to this, the gene-eyed view, the argument that the gene and not the individual human husk is the fundamental unit. Indeed, there is a highly technical – and occasionally fractious – academic debate about this. But whether the urge to survive is more or less free-standing or ultimately a device to afford the opportunity for the replication of genes in the next generation, we can state two things.

We recognise, do we not, a deep urge for our own survival. We share that with most of the rest of the animal kingdom. Perhaps that impulse is not unqualified, perhaps we do not wish to live at all costs, and in all circumstances, but it exists. We understand it. Let us put it another way: in most situations, we would prefer to be alive tomorrow rather than dead. As Spinoza tells us, 'Everything endeavours to persist in its own being.' But for human beings, here's the difference – the paradoxical problem – the second thing we recognise.

Unlike other living things, we have the capacity for abstract thought. As psychoanalyst Otto Rank said, human beings have the capacity 'to make the unreal real'. And with this exceptional power, we can project ourselves into the future. For looming ahead is the one certainty, the one thing we glumly know: life, for whatever else it is or has in store for us, will end.

And that creates the most fundamental of tensions: our will to live; our knowledge of the inescapability of death. As Becker himself put it, 'The idea of death, the fear of it, haunts the human animal like nothing else.' We do not know when it will happen. But we know that happen it will. It torments and terrorises. And yet . . . most of us, despite all this, get along pretty fine. How?

This is where terror management theory provides a challenging and thought-provoking answer. One that has now been scientifically tested in dozens of research labs around the world. One that has generated an impressive stock of hypotheses that have been empirically tested and confirmed. But it remains contentious.

How could it not? It deals with some of the deepest, most disturbing features of our mental life. It tries to explain them. How we build defences against the incapacitating intrusion of death anxiety in our lives. For as Philip Roth wrote in *The Dying Animal*, 'In every calm and reasonable person there is hidden a second person scared witless about death.'

The trial that came to be called the Queen against Gilderdale came on in January 2010 at the Crown Court in Lewes, the historic county town of East Sussex, perched up in the South Downs. It was here that infamously between 1555 and 1557 a total of 17 Protestant Martyrs were burned to death in front of what was then the Star Inn. It is now the Town Hall, a stone's throw along the High Street from the white pillared front of the Crown Court.

On the day the trial started, Tuesday 12 January, it was snowing. The Crown's case was prosecuted by senior barrister Sally Howes QC. She fully acknowledged that the defendant had indeed been a 'caring and loving' mother. She further accepted that Lynn suffered from a 'profound illness with a quality of life that was unimaginably wretched'. But that, for all the sympathies any of us may have, was not the point. So what was?

It was simply whether or not the actions of Kay Gilderdale 'fell outside the law'. The law that is there, as Howes put it, 'to protect us all – sometimes from ourselves'. In deciding the case, she said, the jury should never lose sight of the fact that what Kay Gilderdale did was not designed to make her sick daughter better. Instead it was done with a different intention: 'to make sure she died'.

The prosecution witnesses were called. Lynn's father Richard was summonsed as a witness during the *prosecution* case. As such, he had to attend court as a material witness. Dr Jane Woodgate, the family's GP, was also summonsed. The trial was to last two fraught and distressing weeks.

On Monday 25 January, a jury of six men and six women slowly returned to the dark wooden confines of Court Number One at Lewes. A man, the foreperson, stood up and was asked the following question by the clerk of the court.

'Members of the jury, on Count 1, have you reached a verdict on the defendant upon which you are all agreed?'

'We have,' he replied.

'Members of the jury, do you find the defendant Bridget Kathleen Gilderdale guilty or not guilty of attempted murder?'

Kay Gilderdale was later to say that in that moment she thought, whatever the outcome, whatever the verdict, she would have done nothing different.

It was a very widely reported news story. Headline stuff. After they returned their verdict, the trial judge Mr Justice David Bean said to the assembled court:

> I do not normally comment on the verdicts of juries but in this case their decision shows common sense, decency and humanity which makes jury trials so important in a case of this kind.

Outside on the steps of the court, backed by the austere pillars, it was Kay's son Stephen, blinking in the media spotlights and camera flashes, who provided the family's response. Kay Gilderdale was later to observe in an interview that her legal ordeal was akin to having her heart ripped out. Another circuit was broken.

The jury verdict was unanimous. Key Gilderdale was found not guilty of attempting to murder her daughter Lynn.

In October 2010, two years after Kay helped her daughter die, Lynn's ashes were scattered at a beach near Eastbourne. It was where this close-knit family had holidayed when Lynn was a child.

Of course, attempted murder is one of the most serious of charges. But the case of Kay Gilderdale and her daughter reminded me of a case of my own, one at the very opposite end of the scale of seriousness, but which involved a mother and a daughter and terror and death.

THREE

The Case of Schwarzenegger's Farm

Researchers at Bar-Ilan University in Israel fitted volunteers with a head-fixed video system. It consisted of an infrared source and camera. The objective was to beam light into the eye while the camera recorded the eye's movements. What does it look at? Where does it go? What the researchers wanted to know was whether and how images of physical injury interfere with our management of terror.

So they exposed participants to images of different forms of human injury. The pictures had been graded with a representative population group for their 'valence' – how much they affected or upset the viewer. But then here was the magic: in the control condition the Hebrew word *kova* was secretly flashed on the screen. It was flashed for one-thirtieth of a second, too fast for the human eye to consciously register it. It was a subliminal prime. But a neutral one. *Kova* means hat. No one, quite correctly, thought flashing the word 'hat' would much affect how people responded to pictures of personal injury. However, that was the control condition, the comparator. What researchers really wanted to know was what would happen if volunteers were primed about death.

Thus for those volunteers in the experimental group – the real guinea pigs – another word was flashed. Again for one-thirtieth of a second. It was *mavet*. In Hebrew it means death.

The participants were then presented with a group of four images, an array, including both neutral images and those of physical injury to humans. Using the infrared camera system, it was possible to measure with great precision how long volunteers looked at the images of injury. Of course, most average well-adjusted people are not in their ordinary lives much inclined to look at injury. That much is obvious. The real question is whether unconsciously priming the volunteer with death thoughts will affect their responses to injury. So what did the Bar-Ilan team find?

For neutral pictures (not of injury), it didn't matter what secret prime was used – whether *kova* or *mavet*. There was no significant difference in the time spent gazing at the images. However, once researchers examined the results for physical injury, there was a distinct difference. It was statistically significant. Once primed with death, people did not look at images of physical injury for so long. In fact, they looked at them significantly less. They avoided them. Remember: the volunteers had no idea that they had been unconsciously fed the word *mavet* – death. It remained a mystery to them, yet it mattered. And this finding, along with many other converging lines of evidence that support it, is significant.

It shows that even the slightest reminders of death, even when they are below the radar of consciousness, result in our desire to avoid images of injury. The microscopic, faintest eye movements for fractions of a second reveal a world within the individual, in which he or she is unconsciously managing the terror of death, dealing with Roth's hidden, scared witless person.

It is an ongoing and surreptitious act of containment, finding practical ways to make the best and the most out of a journey with only one destination. At the time, when I conducted the case I'm about to tell you about, I did not realise the significance of these matters. If I had known, the case would have made more sense, for it was unquestionably one of the most baffling I ever had.

It was only a small legal brief. But that made the mystery correspondingly greater, more bewildering, because it should have been so straightforward. Later, I came to think of it as the case of Arnold Schwarzenegger's farm.

Miss L was a young woman of exceptional intelligence and considerable beauty. She was an accomplished cellist and a postgraduate at one of our top universities, launching herself into a career of research in astrophysics, looking at the death of stars. Her family were of Huguenot extraction, Protestants who came to England in the late 1600s seeking refuge from France after the intensification of persecutions by the Sun King, Louis XIV. Once here, they had flourished, as had Miss L. Then, amazingly, she was before the court for shoplifting.

For some reason that no one who knew her could understand, she was on the brink of throwing away her glittering future.

'Most of the stuff, I didn't even want,' she told me outside court.

For example, one of the items she had stolen was a video of Arnold Schwarzenegger's 1977 film about winning the Mr Universe bodybuilding competition *Pumping Iron*. I'd watched the film back then when I was still at school, and loved the mind games Schwarzenegger played with Lou (Incredible Hulk) Ferrigno. Be lenient: I was a teenage boy. But why Miss L would have had the remotest interest in any of that was to me completely unfathomable.

The case had been adjourned for a pre-sentence report (it was called something different back then). There was a rather glib probation officer, a young woman of similar age, who concluded that my client was 'self-sabotaging' (as she put it) because she couldn't live up to the perfect image that everyone had constructed of her. It was a valiant attempt to explain the unexplainable. But something about that theory didn't feel right.

'Who does she think she is?' Miss L said to me, when I read her this analysis from the report's concluding paragraph. 'Sigmund fucking Freud?'

More self-sabotage, lashing out at those who were trying to help her? There was something snarling within her, snarling at herself. The probation officer's report was in fact very sympathetic. Miss L was also cuttingly abrupt towards me at various points, but barristers grow thick skin. We take perverse pride in it.

'She's jealous of me,' Miss L said.

'The probation officer?' I replied. 'I rather doubt it.'

'Really. I guarantee.'

'What has she got to be jealous of?'

'My university. When I told her which college I was in, she was all interested and asked dozens of questions.'

'She's a probation officer.'

'No, turns out she applied, but not to my college, didn't get a place. When she told me all this, she announced it in this witheringly judgemental way, like you got to go to one of the greats and *now* look at you. She was sitting in judgement of me. She really rather relished it.'

'Okay, okay, it's not important. Let's focus. Is anyone coming today?'

'Coming?'

'You know, to support you.'

'One of my supervisors was going to, but he's written a reference. And then someone from the Music Soc.'

'Yes, you're a cellist, aren't you?'

'Was,' she said. 'All this has kind of . . .'

'Got in the way.'

'Fucked the whole thing up. I feel bad. I've let down my friends. We were going to perform Beethoven's *Geistertrio*. No doubt they'll find someone who won't butcher the Largo like me.'

I didn't tell her that I'd been to see a performance of Beethoven's haunting 'Ghost Trio' in London a couple of months previously. I didn't think it would help.

'But no one's coming from the University,' she said. 'In case whatever I've got is catching. You're probably immune to it by now.'

I chose not to rise to her bait. 'Actually,' I said. 'I really meant the family. Who's coming from your family?'

She was silent.

'There's absolutely *no one* here for you?' I said.

Nothing in the case made sense to me. At that exact moment, I felt I understood more about the death of stars than I did about Miss L and her case.

What was going on? A young, brilliant woman in front of the criminal court for stealing things she did not want and there was no one at court to support her. Then I remembered the marginal notes I'd made in the report: there were no details of her family life in the text. What *was* going on? Maybe it was her mentioning of the Beethoven, but at that precise instant it was as if standing in front of me was a ghost. A ghost who'd taken to shoplifting things that positively repulsed her.

'What about your mum?' I said.

At that, she started to weep.

Miss L had been straining to hold things together. She couldn't any longer. Infuriatingly on cue, the court usher appeared and called on our case. I went up and spoke quietly to her, asking permission to talk to my client outside the court precinct. It was obviously all getting too much. I said I would make the application to the magistrates if necessary, but the usher said she would have a word with the court clerk and get the case put back further down the list. I thanked her. She looked at Miss L and whispered to me, 'Poor luv.'

We stood by the court steps in the sunshine. It was a late spring day, the kind where the season has turned just enough so you don't mind being outside, for a while, anyway.

'So tell me about our sun,' I said, trying to take her mind off the case just for a moment.

She didn't look up, her eyes fixed on the concrete steps. She lit a cigarette. A Gauloise, I noticed. She offered me one. I told her I didn't. 'Good,' she said, 'I'm almost out. Our sun? Just a bog-standard star.'

'So what will happen to it?'

'It will run out of fuel at its core.'

'That doesn't sound good.'

She ignored me. 'When it does, it will massively expand in size and become so bloated it will swallow up all the inner planets, Earth included.'

'Sounds pretty grim.'

'No. It will be spectacular, but everything on Earth will have long been incinerated. We're about halfway through its rather mundane life cycle. Thus far, painfully unremarkable.'

'I quite like that,' I said.

'Cue clichéd lawyerly speech about the extraordinary coming from the ordinary.'

I smiled. I actually was going to say something frighteningly similar. 'But it *is* remarkable,' I said. 'Life.'

'In what sense?'

'In the sheer improbability of it.'

'Life somewhere in the wretched universe – or universes – is almost inevitable, probabilistically. Life on Earth, well, yes, the odds are remote, I'll grant you that.'

'Thank you for the granting.'

This time she smiled, but only briefly. She tapped the ash off the end of her cigarette. 'Mum, she was diagnosed with breast cancer. She had a mastectomy. But they were going to have to cut away more and she couldn't bear it. She was incredibly beautiful when she was young.'

I could believe it.

'You know, one of the last of the debs kind of thing. She used to say that her family once owned a country estate, but I found out she grew up on a farm. I think she was happy there. But the C, as she called it, it just terrified her. She had constant nightmares about the painful death she thought lay ahead. So she asked me.'

'Asked you?'

'If I'd . . . help her . . .'

I thought I understood, but needed her to spell it out in her own way. 'Help her?'

'End it,' she replied.

In a second study, the Bar-Ilan research team investigated whether the effect that they found – that subliminal priming about death decreased the amount of time we gaze at physical injury – was simply a reaction to a 'negative' word like death. What they wanted – needed – to know was whether there is something unique in how being reminded of death affects us.

So they compared the flashing of the word for death with the word *koev*. It is Hebrew for pain. However, the pain prompt did not reduce the time that lab volunteers gazed at the images of physical injury. What does this mean?

We are arguably engaged in an ongoing process of dealing with death – 'managing' it, as TMT theorists like Sheldon Solomon say. As in Ingmar Bergman's film *The Seventh Seal*, constantly playing chess with it. Death and its prospect affect our behaviour like nothing else.

I said to Miss L, 'You don't have to tell me about this.'

She shook her head, but said nothing. I was a young lawyer – a baby barrister, we call it, only recently 'on my feet' in court – and many of my clients were my age or older. Somehow I had been tasked to represent them and their lives. I hadn't learned how to speak to them, or to myself.

'I *mean* it,' I said. It was more authoritative than I felt. 'We can just deal with this case, get the minimum possible sentence for all those stupid vids, and get out of here so you can get on with your life.'

She snorted. I'm not sure she was even aware of doing so. 'What life?' she said.

'You've got an amazing future.'

'That's what my mother said.'

'Well, she was right.'

'No, she must have thought when she was my age that *she* had an amazing future. And what does it come to? Asking your daughter to help you OD.'

I was silent briefly, then said, 'That's not all it comes to. And there's all the stuff along the way.'

'She didn't think she'd have the guts to do it on her own. She was terrified of cancer. But petrified of death itself.'

'So what did you do?'

'You've got to understand that she'd been a bitch to me all my life. *Hated* me. "You ruined my figure. You ruined my social life." When Dad left and she had to bring me up on her own: "You ruined my chance of happiness". So she thought I owed her. That I was actually obliged to pay her back.'

'By killing her?'

'It wouldn't be me killing her, would it – just giving her the pills.'

'It would,' I said.

'Oh.'

'Look, let me repeat: you don't have to tell me any of this. You're only up for shoplifting.'

She wasn't listening. She took another drag on the Gauloise and exhaled. A long pale purple plume rose above us. There was no wind. The sun kept shining evenly. 'The cancer came back. Worse. Angrier. Fucking cancer. Our family came to this country to escape persecution. That's why Britain is great. To me. To us. It gave us shelter. But you can't escape it, can you, cancer. Fucking cancer, and she was terrified. She begged me to help her. But I didn't. I couldn't.'

'Because it was wrong?'

She nodded. 'And because, if I'm being truthful, and I wasn't truthful for one second to Little Miss Snotty Probation Officer, but also because a part of me wanted her to suffer. For all she'd done to me.'

'Is that what you really think?'

'Possibly,' she said unconvincingly.

171

'And possibly,' I said, 'all these videos [there were so many that the case had been adjourned for the compilation of a report] are your way of punishing yourself because you couldn't bring yourself to put an end to all her fear.'

'She kept saying she was so alone. And I could understand that. But if she . . . went, that's what I'd be – alone.'

And now she was alone at court. It was plain to me that my client's life was suffused with death, encircled by it. In her research about the end of stars, in her family. In psychological terms, death was 'salient': she was being constantly primed about it. One of the ways we tame terror is together, but it's difficult when there's serious illness in the family. Being reminded of death, as the Bar-Ilan researchers found, makes us look away from injury and images of suffering, the reminders of our own mortality. But what do we do when the thing reminding us about death and the image of suffering – the thing we have an impulse to look away from – is one and the same thing, and someone we love? I wish I had understood this better all those years ago.

'She did end it,' Miss L said. 'Without me.' She started to cry.

We were both quiet for a while. The court usher silently appeared from behind us. She nodded towards me and pointed to her clipboard with the court list on it. The bench was waiting.

'What do you want me to tell the court?' I asked Miss L.

She stubbed out the cigarette and roughly wiped her face with the heel of both palms. 'That I'm sorry,' she said.

And I did. It was the shortest plea in mitigation I have ever made. It was possibly the most effective.

Before we knew it, it was over. We were once more outside on the court steps in the sunshine and saying goodbye. She had received a conditional discharge for the Arnold Schwarzenegger video and the others, just about the lowest sentence it was possible to receive. Why had she taken those videos she didn't want? Not to tame the terror made vivid by her mother's impending death, but because she *couldn't* — and life's shining, illusory meaning and coherence was crumbling around her? It's hard to say. But back then, even though a young and inexperienced barrister, I was convinced as I watched her slowly disappear into the market-day crowds that the sentence Miss L imposed upon herself daily far exceeded the severest sanction of any court of law I knew.

I didn't hear anything about Miss L for a long time. I held my breath; I feared a great calamity. But there was no news. The only other thing she told me was such a small one, but I thought about it a lot. It was a school trip. They went to Paris, like so many English schools, visited Versailles. It was the palace of Louis XIV, the man who decreed the resumption of the persecution of her family at the end of the 17th century. 'It felt like a betrayal,' Miss L told me. 'But it was beautiful, everyone said it, and fair enough. But I saw it all mixed up, the beauty and the horror. Funny that I came to research stars and suns.'

'Why?' I said.

'That was his symbol, all over Versailles, the Sun King.'

A few years later, through a mutual contact, I found out that my former client had given up her research and had relocated to the West Country. She had gone back to her music, I was delighted to hear. Miss L was happily married and lived on a farm. She had three children. She named one after her mother.

I took that as an act of leniency towards her mother, towards her herself and maybe even (I'd like to think) towards life. I was told that when Miss L's mother came to end it all, she left her daughter a note. It simply said, 'My darling, I'm sorry.'

FOUR

The Ice Age

How being sensitised to death can impinge on life can be seen in a series of unexpected consequences beyond what happened to Miss L. These range from those as innocuous as being disinclined to have a foot massage (yes, really: being unconsciously primed about death makes us less enthusiastic about pampering and pedicure as we become averse to our physicality), to being less tolerant to breastfeeding in public and (for men at least) being less eager to have sex. But there are other more serious manifestations at the darker end of the spectrum.

Take the experiment with the Arizona judges. They're now pretty legendary, those Arizona judges, in TMT research circles. Why?

In 1987 Sheldon Solomon and his colleagues endeavoured to see just what would happen when those in authority were reminded of death. Their working hypothesis was that we can try to inure ourselves from the debilitating effects of death anxiety in our lives by bolstering our self-esteem and maintaining an absolute conviction and faith in our view of the world. These acts provide meaning; they help counteract the meaninglessness of extinction; they help manage the terror. If this is right, then should someone be primed about death, that may affect their world view in a measurable way.

To test this prediction, they recruited 22 judges in Tucson, Arizona. They were judges of the municipal court, so the kind of judicial officer that dealt with high-volume, lower end legal problems. The kind of judge you were most likely to come across. Fifteen of them were male and seven female.

Solomon's team chose prostitution as the subject matter of a hypothetical case to emphasise the moral nature of the crime. With prostitution there is no obvious 'victim', save for the woman herself and perhaps society's sense of what is proper. Therefore for the purposes of Solomon's experiment, prostitution was perfect.

They used a 'cover story', a widely accepted distraction device in psychological research. It was that investigators were developing a new kind of personality and life attitude testing. There was indeed a standard personality questionnaire, but embedded in it were the two vital questions – the 'death manipulation'.

These consisted of two open-ended questions the judges were invited to answer with their 'first, natural response', for researchers stated that they were interested in 'gut-level' reactions. One question asked the judges to describe the emotions the thought of their own deaths aroused in them. Next they were asked to detail as clearly as they could what they imagined would happen to them when they were dying and when they were actually physically dead.

And that was all it took. Short. To the point. Deadly.

When judges were given a hypothetical brief about whether, and with what bond, they should release a young sex worker arrested the previous evening on Tuscon's Miracle Mile, the judges came down hard on such an archetypal moral transgressor once they were reminded of their own death. In the Arizona municipal courts, *nine* times as hard.

The judges who were given the standard questionnaire set a bail bond of around $50 – a typical figure at the time. However, those judges who had been primed with the death manipulation set bail on average at $455.

But that was an experiment. A manipulation by ingenious experimental social psychologists. It couldn't be true in real-life situations, could it?

Sheldon Solomon observes, 'We think of judges as supremely rational creatures, unswayed by emotion or sentiment. But that's not what our data were telling us.'

And that is exactly the point – the 'creaturely' quality of judges, of us all. I know.

It was the last bank holiday of the year. I was standing at a bus stop, off to see *Ice Age 3* (or *303*). Let me put it this way: it was not my number-one choice. It was a soothingly warm late August day and about 15 other people were waiting for the bus with me. I was standing there, blithely checking my iPhone for Chelsea's latest covert ops in the transfer window, when it happened.

From the other side of the road I suddenly heard screaming. Repeated screaming.

I glanced up. There at the junction – she was halfway across the road – was a young blonde woman. I would later find out that she was Australian. And looming over her, legs astride a bike frame, was a very large man in a hoodie. He was repeatedly hitting her, punching her hard on the arm, the back, the side of the head. He was mugging her for her iPhone. It is a cliché that everything happens very slowly at such moments, but it does.

She was trying to pull away, he was viciously punching her with one arm and trying to pull the mobile phone from her with the other. She would not give up. But she was wilting under the ferocious assault. What I did next was ill-advised. I ran across the busy road barely looking either way, my total attention focused on a blow he landed on her ear, her screaming out in response. I shouted as loudly as I could, 'Leave her alone. Leave her *alone*.' He glanced quickly at me, hit her hard on the back of the head, a sickening blow. She released the phone. He pushed the bike off. By now I was almost with them. I tried to grab the rear wheel, to knock him off, but missed. He was too quick. He cycled off, disappearing into the maze of residential streets, his escape route probably well planned and travelled. She slumped onto the tarmac, shaking. I have never seen anyone trembling so much.

I took her home (it was 200 yards away), made her some sugary tea (what else do the British do?), and waited for the police.

In due course, I made a short statement describing the assailant. I thought I would hear nothing more of it. This is London. There was an article around the same time in the *Independent* that said that there were 56,680 mobile phone thefts in London in the preceding six-month period alone. I had just witnessed another.

I want to emphasise that I tell you all this not because of what I did, but because of what I did *afterwards*. Something that would have made sense to Sheldon Solomon.

At precisely the same time, I was undergoing my judicial training. To sit as a part-time judge not only do you have to be selected after a competitive public examination, but you then have the joys of an intense week at Judicial College. And it is intense. I was about to go.

By way of preparation, you are asked to work up what seem like dozens of sentencing judgments (it's probably about ten) for hypothetical cases. Just that morning, before the mugging, I had been agonising over one that had particularly troubled me.

It was the robbery of an inebriated businessman at an underpass late at night by three young people. The youngest defendant was female, a girl of 15 or 16 with a history of neglect and maltreatment. The pre-sentence report explained in some detail how she had been dealt a rotten lot by life. But she was the most serious of the offenders: she had held a knife to the victim's throat. It hadn't really injured him but it would unquestionably have been terrifying. I totally accepted that. But could I find a way to keep her out of prison? The pre-sentence report said that a period of intense supervision might provide her with a chance to get out of crime and lead a positive life. But I kept returning to the knife at the throat. No real injury, but still: a naked blade at a naked throat.

My research at Cambridge had demonstrated just how self-defeating much youth custody can be, and many experts agree. After a period of deeply troubling custodial inflation, we had finally begun to recognise that we are sending too many young people to prison in the UK. Although our rates of youth incarceration are still high, and we must go further, we had systematically reduced them by half over the previous few years. Was I going to add this girl to those mournful statistics? In the end, I decided to go with the report recommendation and give her a final chance. I thought nothing more of it. I went to see *Ice Age*. Later that day I went to Warwick University where the Judicial College training course is based. I became immersed in mock trials and the structure of the summing-up and tried to keep at bay the creeping exhaustion all new judicial appointees feel during the boot camp. And then a couple of days later that week I got the call.

It was from the police. They needed to take a statement from me. I said, 'But I already gave a statement about the mugging.'

'We need to take another one, I'm afraid,' the female detective said.

It had been a male detective before. 'I don't understand,' I said. 'Why? Was something left out?'

'No, no, it's not that. We just need to go over the whole thing again and see if you can provide us with any more detail. It's just that – and I don't want you to be unduly concerned, sir – but yesterday there was another very similar incident up the road from where you stepped in.'

'Well, I tried to, but missed,' I said.

'It's probably as well you did.'

Again I didn't understand.

The officer continued, 'Someone tried to intervene like you did. The mugger stabbed him through the heart. He's just died.'

I didn't sleep that night. But here's the strange thing. It wasn't that I was thinking 'It could have been me', although various people at Warwick made exactly that point. I stayed up for hours drafting and redrafting my sentencing judgment on the hypothetical girl with the knife in the underpass. I sent her to prison.

What was going on? Once we are primed about death, made – however briefly – to think about it, we tend to resort to endorsing and validating shared, dominant social norms. This sensitisation, 'mortality salience' as Solomon and his colleagues call it, appears to affect our judgement of the behaviour of others – which side of the line it falls on.

Solomon noted the same after 9/11. 'Every time Bush spoke about the terror threat,' Solomon says, 'and his crusade to rid the world of evildoers, his approval ratings shot up.' Margaret Thatcher, famously, benefited from the Falklands Factor. Ronald Reagan chose to invoke the Evil Empire.

According to TMT, all this is because our culture – the rules and values we construct to give life meaning – is a defence against potentially paralysing terror, against Hamlet's dread. It is our buffer against the catastrophe of non-existence. When we are reminded of our mortality, we rally round. We more vehemently denounce aliens, we forcefully deprecate opponents. Like Arizona judges, we punish prostitutes more harshly.

The central claims of terror management theory have now received evidential support in over 500 research studies conducted in over 20 countries on five continents. There is something in it.

What is interesting is that the effects that Sheldon Solomon and researchers like him have observed – the punitiveness and preju- dice – are not produced by reminders of other undesirable events, such as failure in exams. There is something unique about what death does to us. It skews our thoughts and our judgement like nothing else.

I now know this to be the case. For finally – and most tellingly – there was Dawn.

FIVE

Facing into the Sun

To begin with, my contacts with Dawn were exclusively by email. I wasn't able to speak to her on the phone. I felt it was too intrusive to visit, even to suggest a visit. So we emailed. Dawn is a stupendous emailer – as will become clear. But it all started off conventionally enough. In response to my short query message sent through an intermediary, I received this:

> Dear Dexter
> I would be happy for you to email me using this email address.
> Best wishes
> Dawn

I got the email when I turned on my iPhone when emerging from Westminster after a long and intense meeting where I'd been advising parliamentarians about the new law on female genital mutilation. I had been trying to persuade MPs and peers about the urgent need to strengthen the UK's protective mechanism not only to comply with our obligations under international law, but to better protect young women and girls from genital mutilation. Had the politicians really understood the extreme risk young women and girls faced at this very moment? I was unsure I'd properly persuaded them. Dawn's email – as I would find with others she sent me – seemed to arrive at precisely the perfect moment. I quickly dashed off a reply:

> Dear Dawn
> I've finally got clear of Parliament and wanted to touch base with you again. Firstly, thanks for responding to my email – I really appreciate it. Where to begin? Let me just introduce myself properly, perhaps . . .

I then proceeded to (undoubtedly) bore her with details of who I am, the kind of human rights work I do, and why I wanted us to speak.

> I guess this is all a rather long-winded way of wondering if you'd like to correspond a bit further. It would be great if you would. I look forward to hearing from you.
>
> > Best rgds
> > Dexter

Would I hear from her again? I wasn't sure – not now that I'd explained what I wanted. Would it be too personal – too painful? I waited anxiously. I heard nothing for the rest of that day, nor the next morning. The next afternoon, the answer came.

Dear Dexter,

Glad to hear that you eventually escaped from the round-heads!
I will gladly answer any questions that you have and help in any
way I can, if I am a bit slow in replying its because I am mid-way
through an essay for my Master's Degree.

Best wishes,

Dawn

Delight. And relief. I needed to understand Dawn, what had
happened to her, and what she had done as a result. What I knew
of her story preoccupied me in a way Sheldon Solomon would
have much to say about. I replied:

You're a star. Actually, being bugged by round-heads right now.
Can I send you a couple of Qs tomorrow — and absolutely no
rush in getting back to me. Btw, what's the essay?

I had so many questions, but there was one question I did want
to ask straight away. Probably the least important thing, but just
something I wanted to know. I'd read somewhere about her liking
for heavy metal band Black Sabbath. Many years previously, I'd
been to one of their concerts and it was something — despite
everything else that divided us — that we seemed to have in
common. I also gathered that she lived in Staffordshire and Sabbath
were from Birmingham.

One last thing for now: your love of Black Sabbath — is it a
Midlands thing?

Best rgds

Dexter

I fully appreciate that it was slightly idiotic, gloriously pointless, as is so much human curiosity and correspondence.

> Dear Dexter
> Liking Black Sabbath is a Midlands thing as much as liking Abba is a Swedish thing.
>
> > Best wishes
> > Dawn

I received this message when I was on the District Line, coming back from a case conference in Legal London. In response, I wrote:

> Okay, okay, I asked for that! Got your email as I was sitting on Tube and burst out laughing – other passengers think I'm a bit crazy, I think.
>
> To kick off, how would you feel if I sent a list of simple Yes/No questions to cover a lot of ground as quickly as possible with just Y/Ns from you? Of course, you can Take the 5th (as my US colleagues say) on any Q or deem them boring, trivial or just plain dumb. Witnesses in court not infrequently attach all of the aforementioned labels to my questions. Oh, and must tell you at some point about when I went to a B. Sabbath concert . . .
>
> > Best rgds
> > Dexter

The next day I received this response:

Dear Dexter

I have developed a five point answering system: Y, N, D, B, ?.
This stands for Yes, No, Dumb, Boring and What are you on?

Best wishes

Dawn

The legal conference I was coming back from took place just behind the same High Court that two years earlier had rejected Tony Nicklinson's claim for the right to die. Dawn – Dawn Faizey Webster – aged 42, mother of an 11-year-old son Alexander, former grammar school IT teacher from Rugeley, Staffordshire, composed all of what you've just read by blinking at a computer screen with her one remaining working eye, the left.

What happened illustrates how, as Edgar Allan Poe once put it, the 'character of calamity' can sometimes be banal – how, as happened to Dawn, it can sidle up to you on a sofa.

It was supposed to be the happiest event of her life. In 2003, life could not have been much better for Dawn. Married, a degree in psychology and computing, working as a successful and much-loved teacher at Stafford Grammar. 'I was a sort of get down with the kids kind of teacher. That said, they knew not to cross me. Fortunately, I didn't turn green like the Incredible Hulk – it doesn't suit me.' Her colour, as I would find out, is red.

Dawn was pregnant with her first child. Everything she wanted in life was coming true.

And then in June 2003, she developed a pain in her neck that just wouldn't shift. At the same time her blood pressure started to climb, higher and higher, and showed little sign of coming down. Her ankles were swelling. But she was pregnant – only 26 weeks pregnant, admittedly, but pregnant, and maybe that explained it all. In truth,

185

it had been an uneventful pregnancy, but then her baby's appearance into the world came in a bewildering rush. Dawn had to have an emergency Caesarean. So on 15 June 2003, weighing in at a mighty 1 pound 8 ounces, Alexander was born. He had to remain in the neonatal unit at the City General Hospital, Stoke-on-Trent when Dawn was discharged home. To be fair, she had been told this was a possibility, had braced herself for it, went home without her child. But as the next few days wore on, Dawn was subtly deteriorating.

From time to time dizzy spells would wash over her. Sometimes they were so crippling that she couldn't drive to the hospital to see Alexander. Still, her parents were able to take her, so (as they do) the family found a way. Slowly Dawn's world was becoming blurry, its sharp edges smudged. It was as though the tide was going out on Dawn. All her molecules were drifting away on a dark stream she didn't understand. Like Tony Nicklinson jumping out of that plane in the cobalt blue Emirates sky, she was being stranded.

As she was sitting on the sofa at home, her vision became curiously disjointed, the world degenerating into a sinister series of fairground distortions, a horrid House of Mirrors. Finally it fractured: the images through her right eye loomed dizzyingly over the left. Dawn collapsed. This was Friday. On Saturday she sank into a deep coma.

For the next week at Stafford Hospital she slipped in and out of consciousness. In this dreamlike drifting, she was aware of people ghosting around her. She was screaming at them, but no one could hear her. She couldn't move any part of her body except her eyes – left, right; right, left – she was shouting as loud as she could at the doctors, her family, and no one in Ward 24 heard a thing. Would anyone ever know that she was still inside her body? She'd had a catastrophic stroke at the base of her brainstem. Her brain had been assaulted, ambushed. Her mind functioned acutely – frantically, fearfully. Her body was totally paralysed. She was locked in.

I remember reading about Richard Marsh from California, a retired police officer and lecturer in forensic science. He had a massive stroke and became locked in. As he lay in his hospital bed, he was conscious of doctors telling his wife Lili that he only had a minute chance of surviving – only 2 per cent – and even if he did, he would 'be a vegetable'. And all the while Marsh was there in a Ward 24 of his own, screaming silently at them, unbeknown to anyone in the room. For they were discussing turning off his life support machine.

'I knew that my cognitive abilities were 100 per cent,' he said in interview. 'I could think, I could hear, I could listen to people, but I couldn't speak. I couldn't move.'

The doctors stood at the bottom of his bed and discussed what they were going to do. How they would withdraw his life support and he would die. They spoke as if he wasn't in the room, because they assumed he wasn't. And yet Richard Marsh was watching, hidden in plain sight, staring out through the portals of his eye, unable to move. He was buried within his own body. What he says about it is intriguing. He says that it was his brain that protected him. His brain that had betrayed him when he had the stroke itself, then set about protecting him, enabling him to cope. It kept him calm. It let him cope with the terror.

It is this predicament that has again and again preoccupied writers, all the way from the character of Noirtier de Villefort in *The Count of Monte Cristo* to *Alfred Hitchcock Presents*. In his episode 'Breakdown', Hitchcock, still sporting the East End accent of a boy born in Leytonstone, looks warningly at the camera and tells his audience that tonight's tale is 'proper terrifying'. And indeed the fate of Hitchcock's protagonist, still alive but treated as if he were not, echoes the fate of a number of reported medical cases. In some instances it has taken four to six years. The patient, all the time aware and sensitive, is trapped inside their immobile body and not recognised as being conscious. In fact, in their review of the treatment of locked-in patients 'Blink and you live', Marie-Aurélie Bruno of the Coma Science Group of the University of Liège and colleagues found that in more than half of cases physicians fail to recognise early signs that the patient is still there.

Many years ago, walking aimlessly through central London, I suddenly came across the poster for the first of the *Alien* films. It was on a huge billboard in Leicester Square. The poster was a vast deep-space backdrop, with a sinister ashen egg, cratered like the surface of the moon. Monstrous, literally. I can remember shuddering when I read the strapline: 'In space no one can hear you scream.'

I shudder now at the thought and want to know what it is like – how do humans cope with this kind of damage? Anatomically, the brainstem is a small area of the brain. Within it lie a multiplicity of still smaller structures with wondrous names: aqueducts, canals, pyramids. The brainstem controls and regulates the heart rate, breathing, sleeping, eating, maintaining consciousness, swallowing – almost everything. In June 2003 the stroke struck here. Dawn's damage is here. It is this devastation – among the aqueducts, canals and pyramids in her head – that she lives with.

Dawn, how did you do it? How do you?

SIX

A H N T

When and how we can safely attribute consciousness to another human being is one of the most vexing questions in science and morality. It is not just morbidly intriguing, a factually formidable challenge. But it can have far-reaching practical consequences: it can determine whether we turn off the machines.

Therefore the dividing lines between the various disorders of consciousness have proved contentious. This problem has been one of the least understood and most ethically problematic challenges in modern medicine. Even the names have been controversial. For example, the term persistent vegetative state (PVS), first used in the *Lancet* in 1972, has been discarded by the Royal College of Physicians after a series of difficult cases and misdiagnoses. Indeed, the European Task Force on Disorders of Consciousness jettisons the term 'vegetative' itself and uses unresponsive wakefulness syndrome (UWS). This approach focuses on the fact that for this group of patients who have suffered severe 'brain insult' (whether by traumatic injury or hypoxia – the brain being starved of oxygen), critical functions like the ability to breathe unaided remain intact. But unlike coma patients, they maintain more or less normal sleep-wake cycles (hence 'wakeful-ness' syndrome). When they are 'awake', their eyes open. The eyes rove around the room. However, there is complete unaware-ness of the environment and the self – they are unresponsive. Thus it was thought that such patients were insensible to their surroundings and themselves, in a state of wakeful unconscious-ness, a state of limbo. That was the orthodoxy, what many experts believed. Then in 2006 a team of neuroscientists led by Adrian Owen, then at Cambridge University, challenged that view.

Using brain scanning technology, they showed that some UWS or vegetative patients were in fact aware of their surroundings – and of themselves. There were 'islands' of undetected awareness obscured by the mental mists. Owen believed that some of these patients knew what was going on around them.

He and his team set about finding a way through to them. They did this by an extraordinary expedient: asking the patient to imagine playing tennis. Here were people who were believed to be, although technically alive, for all intents and purposes effectively dead to the world. They weren't.

Deep inside their bodies, they were still consciously there. They just had no means of communicating. Some had been in this condi-tion for many months. It was as if they were tightly wrapped in cling film, layers of it wound tightly over their mouth and face, so much so that they were cocooned, waiting within while no one knew.

Owen's key patient was a 23-year-old woman. In 2005 she suffered severe brain injury in a road accident. She was diagnosed by a multidisciplinary team in accordance with prevailing inter-national standards as being in a vegetative state. Moreover, she had been in this state for five months. But when she was asked to imagine playing tennis, brain signals were suddenly activated in certain regions of her brain, for a full 30 seconds – until she was told to 'rest'. These were in an area called the supplementary motor area (SMA). This brain structure is known to be associated with purposefully imagining coordinated movements – hitting a tennis ball. The woman's responses were compared with those of a control group of 12 healthy volunteers. When they imagined playing tennis, their brains also lit up. In the same area, the SMA. In fact, in a way that was statistically indistinguishable from the patient. Of course, it could have been a freak result. So Owen's team pressed on.

The patient was next asked to imagine walking through all the rooms of her home, one by one. This time three very different brain regions were activated: the parahippocampal gyrus, the posterior parietal lobe and the lateral premotor cortex. Together they form the parahippocampal place area – the PPA. The PPA is known to be frequently activated when someone either performs or imagines acts of spatial navigation – like walking through a house. Then it was the turn of the healthy volunteers. You know what Owen found.

The unavoidable conclusion was that his patient, despite the diagnosis of being in vegetative state, imagined what the volunteers imagined; she planned what they planned. She was responding to Adrian Owen's instructions. She was still there.

What her awareness must have felt like is almost impossible to determine. It should never be forgotten that she had suffered severe brain injury. But for all that, she was responding; for all that, she was not, as the definition had her, 'unresponsive'. What she imagined, what she thought was going on, might be something akin to dreaming or delirium – but it was *something*. And whatever that dreamlike drifting something actually was, she was able to latch onto what the researchers said to her. On their cue, she was able to imagine herself – where? – on the Centre Court at Wimbledon, perhaps, sending a fizzing backhand down the line. She was able to imagine herself home.

Owen and his colleagues continued. Out of a group of 54 patients with severe brain injuries who were examined, five were able to respond. Five patients – five *people* – previously believed to be unresponsive, were able (in scientific terms) to 'wilfully modulate' their brain activity. That's what neuroscientists call it. You and I call it communicating.

Additional tests were performed on one patient in particular. Before using the brain scanner, it was once more established that he was in a vegetative state. Indeed he had suffered a serious road traffic accident and was diagnosed as being in a permanent vegetative state 17 months after it. This diagnosis was confirmed after 3½ years. And now, 5 years later, he was to be retested. He was inserted into the MRI. Owen's group devised a communication protocol:

> For yes, imagine playing tennis.
> For no, imagine walking through streets of a town you know well or your home.

The patient was asked to imagine swinging an arm to hit the tennis ball back and forth over the net or to envisage walking from room to room in his home – visualise what you see there. Tennis for yes; home for no. He was then asked a number of questions.

They were questions such as 'Do you have any brothers?' The first five questions he was able to answer with 100 per cent accuracy. This man, who for five years was believed to have no awareness of his surroundings, was there. He remembered. He answered. He knew.

As Poe has written, 'The boundaries which divide Life from Death are at best shadowy and vague.' I wondered where Owen's patient had gone in his mind for those five – *five* – years. What had he thought? What was it like? Poe is surely right when he says that to be buried alive, to be trapped in a confined space with no one knowing you're trapped, is just about the most terrifying prospect that can befall 'the lot of mere mortality'.

Do you have any brothers?

It was Dawn's brother Mark who realised she was still in there. Immediately after the stroke, Dawn experienced her own dreamlike drifting something. She recalls a number of strange dreams. In one she imagined she had to be cryogenically frozen, just as the crew of the *Nostromo* spaceship in *Alien* had to be to travel to the far reaches of deep space. In another dream Dawn became an Iraqi soldier (all this had happened about the time of the invasion of Iraq). Jean-Dominique Bauby, the editor-in-chief of French fashion magazine *Elle*, wrote after he became locked in that his imagination took flight even as his body stagnated, carrying him to Tierra del Fuego or the court of King Midas. What about Adrian Owen's vegetative patient: over the years, what realms had he visited, what distant lands had he seen?

Finally, Dawn and I arranged to meet. I travelled to her home town in pursuit of an answer to my question (what is it like – how do humans cope?). I took the train, I prepared my notes, I met Dawn. I was crushed.

The sheer unfathomable injustice of it all, the unfairness of a universe that doesn't seem to care. How could this have happened to such a decent person – to anybody? The French have a term for locked-in syndrome: *maladie de l'emmuré vivant* – being walled in alive. And this, for all the hyperbole, is the most factually accurate description of the condition.

It is a commonplace and a cliché to say that 'nothing prepared me for what I then found'. To guard against this, I had endeavoured to make every possible preparation for meeting Dawn. I read as much as I could about locked-in syndrome – and there is a sprawling literature. I watched and rewatched the film about Bauby, *The Diving-Bell and the Butterfly*. I played and replayed the frustratingly brief news clips about Dawn on YouTube. I think I can state hand on heart that I did my Dawn due diligence.

Not even close.

When confronted by the devastation inflicted on Dawn's life by the brainstem stroke, I was stunned. In part what had disarmed me was the easy affability of our email correspondence. It was in many ways like correspondence with many others of my legal and academic colleagues – only funnier. But that correspondence did not now *correspond*, not with what I found in front of my eyes, not with the sheer savagery of the damage.

Dawn is confined to a wheelchair. She cannot move any part of her body, save for her left eye (her right has had to be closed) and a slight movement of her head. Her arms sit folded neatly in her lap, but she cannot control them. Occasionally as we speak her body goes into full spasm. She cannot speak; she cannot swallow. She is fed with liquid through a tube. But her left eye works. It works overtime. It is magnificent. Her father Alec, now 80, was telling me about his hardships and privations growing up as a boy in the war, but breaks off. 'Dawn wants to say something,' he

says. He patiently goes through their meticulous routine, the reci-
tation of letters, with Dawn acknowledging the correct one with
a blink of an eye.

'V-I-O-L . . . yes, very funny Dawn,' he says.

I don't understand.

Alec shakes his head solemnly. 'Violins,' he tells me. 'She's
bored of my war stories. Violins.' To emphasise the point, Dawn
lets her head sink dramatically into her chest as if she's been shot
by a sniper.

She wears her hair long, down past the shoulders, as she did
when she was a student. Much later, to prompt my memory, I ask
her to remind me what colour it is: 'Same as my piano,' she emails
back. There in the family's immaculate living room, I point out
that we are both wearing red jumpers, it's just the smallest of
small talk – I'm trying to buy time, to get my bearings with the
complex physical reality of Dawn right in front of my eyes. Dawn
begins spelling out.

Her father duly obliges. 'I . . . W-E-A . . . I wear . . . oh, Dawn,'
he breaks off.

I look at him. She is looking unrelentingly at my red jumper.

'She says she wears it better,' Alec says.

Dawn lives with her parents in the quiet Staffordshire market
town of Rugeley, on the banks of the River Trent. It is 20 miles
down the A51 from Stoke-on-Trent, where Pam lived with Gareth
before he was committed to custody. I sit there and quietly tell
her about my legal work, my cases, Pam, Gareth.

Occasionally, Dawn raises her left eye skywards which means
both yes and I'm still listening. On her father's side, the family
are Faizeys, solid Midland folk, with a Norman name traceable
back to William the Conqueror and the time that wolves still
roamed through England. Alec did the genealogical detective

work. It's official: they have a framed certificate in the hall. The Faizeys long outlasted the wolves, whose end came soon after Edward I ordered their extermination in 1281. Dawn's grandfather fought with the Royal Engineers in many of the main European battles of World War II, in North Africa, Italy and Germany. He was at Dunkirk, being evacuated in one of the legendary Little Ships. 'He didn't really talk about it,' Alec says, 'he didn't like to make a fuss.'

And the family then survived the dire storm that passed over the British Isles as enemy warplanes rained down fire and steel. And that's the thing: the family does not make a fuss. Not about what's happened to Dawn, to them all.

Alec worked for years as a joiner and now, instead of relaxing in comfortable retirement, is in his ninth decade a full-time carer for his immobilised daughter. As is his wife Shirley. They met 60 years ago at a wedding when Shirley's friend married Alec's brother. Shirley left her earrings in Alec's pocket during the festivities and he tracked her down after that. She was 17; he was 22. They've been together ever since.

As I'm talking to Dawn, Shirley brings me in the most spectacular plate of chocolate biscuits I've ever encountered. When I leave, she makes me a cheese sandwich for the train. ('Just in case you get peckish.') I ask for the best number for a taxi for the station. 'It's called Dad,' Dawn spells out. That's the kind of people they are.

When I looked Rugeley up, searching for points of interest, Google presented Rugeley reindeer park on the Uttoxeter Road, 'home to the largest working reindeer herd in England'. Working reindeer – what work do they do? I emailed Dawn in advance to ask if this much-vaunted local attraction was worth a visit.

I once took my son Alexander to see the reindeer. He was not impressed. Rugeley is better known for its murders. More than one. Dr Palmer – the Rugeley Poisoner. And the murder at the Bloody Steps. Luckily Morse solved it!

Best wishes
Dawn

You see, that's the problem. You read her email in one smooth survey, and imagine Dawn speaking to you, voicing the words she cannot now speak. And she was of course right: William Palmer was a physician who in 1856 was hanged at Stafford Prison for murder. Although convicted after trial at the Old Bailey of one murder by poisoning (that of his friend John Cook), he was strongly suspected of killing many more victims, including adult members of his own family and four of his infant children. Dickens called him 'the greatest villain who ever stood in the Old Bailey'. I thought of Palmer (and Dawn) when shortly after that I sat as a judge at the Bailey.

Being there with Dawn, I remember all her quips – Black Sabbath and ABBA; her objection to Oliver Cromwell ('thirteen years without Christmas and dressed for a funeral'); the wretched Rugeley reindeer – her mild rebukes, her incisive comments. They ring in my head as I sit next to her and her one working eye gives signs and cues to her adoring parents who painstakingly recite the alphabet. *A, H, N, T.* We spend time discussing Rugeley's murder at the 'Bloody Steps' leading up from the Trent and Mersey Canal, where in 1839 a young woman called Christina Collins was killed by drunken bargemen. It is said that the steps still ooze with the victim's blood. Collins's grave is in the small parish church of St Augustine's, just up the road. The case featured in the Inspector

Morse mystery *The Wench is Dead.* I resolve to visit Christina's grave on the day I visit Dawn's house.

We proceed, glacially, one letter at a time. *A, H, N, T.* Alec or Shirley recites the specially adapted alphabet, a system devised by her sister-in-law, the head of science in a school in Uttoxeter. It divides the 26 letters into quadrants in a 7–6–6–7 arrangement for speedier navigation. Dawn blinks to indicate the letter. Blinking out one letter at a time, she has embarked on a rigorous programme of serious academic study. Dawn has earned a degree in ancient history like this; Dawn is doing a master's in history of art, along the way phenomenologically critiquing Hans Holbein's famous painting *The Ambassadors* invoking Heidegger and Merleau-Ponty, like this. Dawn lives like this. I marvel. It's not just her obvious courage and calm composure. It's that when her soaring mind's connection to the outside world is viciously shrivelled to the flicker of an eye, I must admit to feeling embarrassed by the sheer abundance of the opportunities open to me. In the taxi leaving Dawn's house, driving through Rugeley, its windows now glowing warm gold in the winter night, I try not to think about the sheer profligacy of my life.

I can only remember snatches of our conversation. I was in a daze.

On the windswept platform of Rugeley Trent Valley station, the clouds scud in overhead, rapid, low, lowering. The train races the clouds back to London. The engine bites its way through the Midlands countryside, but unnervingly quietly as if the snow has subdued everything. Except Dawn. Irrepressible Dawn. Fiercely alive Dawn. She is not silent. Her vocal chords can still generate a deeply resonant sound. I hadn't known about it until we met. It surprised me. I imagine it can disconcert the unprepared, but in fact it is a triumph. ('So much glorious sound,'

I later text her. 'I'm part Wookie,' she responds with frightening rapidity. 'Wait till I try my farmyard animals on you.')

Nearer London it starts raining, water sluicing through trees along the railway tracks, their branches all winter-bare, barren like the protuberances in Lake Volta. I find myself thinking of Anthony. I'd love Anthony to meet Dawn. Two worlds within our world, two humans, two types. And Dawn is what? A Tamer. She tames the terror. But to understand the sheer extent of her courage, I need to tell you how it all started.

SEVEN

Locked Out

It was her mother who first noticed.

'Dawn, your ankles are swollen,' Shirley told her daughter.

Pregnant with swollen ankles – in the immortal phrase, it was time to call the midwife. Dawn's ankles were indeed swollen, and not only did the midwife find protein in her urine, but her blood pressure was high – and climbing. In a flurry of flashing lights and sirens, the ambulance rushed Dawn to Stafford Hospital. The emergency doctor was concerned. What to do? To protect Dawn, it would be best to operate immediately. To protect her child, it would be best to wait. The gynaecologist told her, 'Every day you can hang on to your baby, you give him a better chance of living.'

Dawn held on. For six heroic days.

All the time her blood pressure was climbing. Every day she put herself at greater and greater risk. But she refused to harm her unborn baby. She protected him. In doing so, Dawn gave Alexander every chance of life, and although a mere 11 inches when born prematurely, he grabbed it tenaciously. Today he is not 11 inches but 12 years old. I see a picture of him and realise that he is now around the age that Anthony was when his father sold him into slavery. Alexander is quite small. But then so was Gareth Myatt. Across time and space, I see these boys in a curiously linked chain.

The fact is that by her sacrifice, Dawn may well have wrought upon herself a life of almost complete paralysis. Emboldened by the utter honesty of all her correspondence and the connection I'd hoped we'd made, I decided to ask her.

> DD: Knowing what you now know would happen to you, would
> you do it again, hang on for Alexander?

She replied simply, and in the code she devised for us: Y.

How to make sense of the senseless? How to make it mean something – anything? Dawn tames the terror of a mind trapped within an almost entirely paralysed body with a straightforward understanding of the connection between the devastation of her life and the delivery of her son. She refused to do something that would harm her child. She exposed herself to the most grievous risk and would do it again. She does not want our violins.

What happened to Dawn Faizey Webster was not meaningless. In a broader sense, it has been life-augmenting – when one computes the dread calculus, when you do all the sums: adding her life (albeit altered) plus her son's. This is certainly her view. We must, however, be clear: Dawn's is not a triumph over adversity; it is a triumph *with* adversity, at every laborious blink of the eye. She meets the terror head on. She drags it with her on an extraordinary journey.

In his dark and disturbing composition of 1611, 'Ignatius His Conclave', John Donne wrote an account of a restless soul that had 'liberty to wander through all places, and to survey and reckon all the rooms, and all the volumes of the heavens, and comprehend the situation, the nature, the people, and the policy.'

The tethering of life and limbs that severe stroke damage inflicts has the deeply paradoxical effect, related by survivor after survivor, of untethering the mind. It affords the mind an unwelcome, savage but rare, opportunity to view the world afresh, to wander through all places and comprehend the people and the policy. To, as Ernest Becker puts it, 'expand into dimensions of worlds and time without moving a physical limb'.

By the determined device of blinking an eye, Dawn travelled intellectually – and imaginatively – all the way to Ancient Greece and Rome for her degree. 'Who is your favourite figure from the classical world,' I once asked. 'Alexander,' she instantly replied.

We speak about how Alexander the Great famously tamed his horse. It is a story that comes down to us from Plutarch's *Life of Alexander* (and also from Arrian of Nicomedia). Philonicus the Thessalian had brought a massive horse, a magnificent specimen with a jet-black coat, for which he demanded 13 talents, only the beast was so wild and unruly that no one could control it. The 13-year-old Alexander, despite the failure of many others, believed he could accomplish this seemingly impossible task. No one believed him. But he did. By one deft adjustment. To the astonishment of all, he was able to approach the great rearing animal and nimbly mount him. How did he do it? He realised that Bucephalus was unnerved by his own shadow: he turned the horse to face directly into the sun.

Why did she so admire the Macedonian? 'Because he achieved so much,' Dawn says. 'When Alexander the Great died in 323 BC, he was only 32 years old. Imagine what he could have accomplished if he had lived longer.'

And that is the key – or one of the critical ones – to Dawn Faizey Webster. Despite the bleakness and almost total physical devastation of the stroke, Dawn remains determined not only to live, but to make it mean something, to make it count – not only to tame the terror, but batter it into some meaning. Like the unruly horse of Alexander, she appreciates that the seemingly impossible is within grasp – if you approach it from the right side. If you turn to face the sun.

'After the stroke, I just experience life differently. But it's just as precious. Your dreams may have to change. But they're still yours. I wanted to show people I'm still Dawn. That I'm still here. What can I do about the past, the stroke? Nothing. But you can change your future. I'm going to.'

Like the great Macedonian, she has a detailed list of things to do and worlds to conquer. After six years of painstaking work, when she was finally awarded her degree in ancient history, her father said to her, 'Are we going to have a bit of a rest now, Dawn?'

She said to Alec, 'You can. I'm doing a master's.'

'What did you say to her?' I asked.

He shook his head slowly. 'I said, "Oh, Dawn."'

It will take her two more years of unrelenting slog to blink her way to a history of art master's degree at 50 words per hour. Just *this* slender paragraph, for example, will take her an hour to compose. She is then determined to embark on a PhD. I have not the slightest doubt she will achieve it.

Dawn Faizey Webster's case intriguingly resonates with a further research study by Marie-Aurélie Bruno and colleagues. They surveyed 44 patients with locked-in syndrome, seeking to understand to what extent their 'massively changed bodies' extinguished their sense of self – who they were after the stroke. The researchers examined whether they felt like the same person, recognised their new bodies as 'theirs', and found their life still meaningful, notwithstanding almost total paralysis.

What is significant about this study is that the answers of locked-in patients were compared with a control group. They were 20 medical practitioners from Avicenne Hospital, in rue de Stalingrad, Paris. These health professionals were asked to respond to the same questions *as if* they had suffered total paralysis. But according to Bruno and her colleagues, they 'failed in predicting patients' experience'. And this must make us pause for thought. For the most robust responses from real locked-in patients were that although their body had become 'a jail', it was still them inside; despite the disability, they still felt active in their lives; despite the paralysis, they still contributed to their families; despite all this they could still express who they really were. In other words, they still found a way to find meaning in their lives. Thus despite the haunting terror of *maladie de l'emmuré vivant* – being walled in alive – when it comes to it, human beings *can* find a way to tame the terror.

It is likely that we have been doing it a long time. Sheldon Solomon is probably correct: for almost as long as we have been conscious that (1) we are alive; and (2) that it will not last. The taming of the terror is an ongoing act of maintenance and repair, a constant painting of the Forth Bridge of fear with this caveat: as we age, death becomes more salient – it looms larger. Such a ubiquitous human need with such far-reaching and potentially crippling consequences makes a strong case for there being an executive system, a mental module, that engages with it. Or maybe it co-opts others. Indeed in a position piece in the journal *Evolutionary Psychology*, Solomon and his colleagues concluded that they believed further research will result in a 'further integration' of terror management theory and evolutionary perspectives. We shall see.

Viktor Frankl cautions us against seeking some external, overarching, definitive meaning to life – something that is going to settle the question, tame the terror, once and for all. Instead of asking 'What is the meaning of life?', he argues, we should 'instead think of ourselves as those who were being questioned by life – daily and hourly.'

It is the notion of life putting us to the test. It is appealing but contains dangers.

Because what if we don't pass? What if like Tony Nicklinson or Lynn Gilderdale we don't want to go on? Therefore can we rather think of life as extending a complex kind of invitation? As in Edvard Munch's psychologically haunting masterpiece *Dance of Life*, painted in 1899, life asks whether we want to dance. Let us recognise that taking up life's invitation is hard. And let us not forget that death extends its invitation also.

In the end, we may simply cling on to the former because of Hamlet's dread of something after death, as did Miss L's mother for a time – wanting to die, scared of dying. In all this, Dawn Faizey Webster's struggle can be viewed not as a search for meaning, but as a making of it. By what Dawn does, she daily makes meaning for herself. Thus we are not just seekers of meaning but makers of it. And that is a complex kind of freedom: living free of the anguish and overwhelming mental suffering that consumed Tony Nicklinson.

On one occasion Dawn said to me, 'Once I was a successful teacher.'

'Really – *you*?' I said. We tend to tease each other.

'The most successful by *far*.'

'You?' I repeat.

'At wheelie races on the swivel chairs in the computer lab. Once I was a very good teacher.'

Here's a truth: Dawn still teaches, should we have the wit to listen. After Dawn, I begin to appreciate what Charles Darwin must have seen on that day in December 1832 when the *Beagle* cut through the south Atlantic waves and he rubbed the salted spray from his eyes, seeing rise before him Tierra del Fuego: a landscape that reveals the world in an unimagined way. All this, after Dawn.

There are, of course, two ways to look at it. The ever-present prospect of the greatest mystery of all, death, can appear to consign our lives to the trivial. Viewed through the wrong end of the cosmic telescope, we evaporate and vanish. But I think there is something more. Something better. Turn that device around, look at our lives through the microscope – communicate it all, like Dawn Faizey Webster, through the blinking of an eye – and everything is imbued with passion and intensity, the chance to just move where you want and speak the words that you want is infused with the deepest, simplest pleasure. All at once, the opportunities ahead of us, around us at this precise moment, shimmer with almost irresistible allure. After Dawn the world is vast; it pulses with dizzying possibility. I find myself stretching out my fingers and curling my toes and try to track the perfectly unbroken neural signal from the brain down through the limbs ('Mine just aren't on speaking terms with my brain,' she writes to me. 'The Do Not Disturb sign is up.')

There are all kinds of terror we have to tame. I try to imagine scenes from Dawn's life – imagine because these are things I feel I have no right to ask her. When her baby boy is brought into her hospital room for the first time after the stroke, and she cannot touch him; when she, a new mother, hears her child cry, and cannot feed him; when she cannot move a single finger towards him. These things.

What is this state? In Harold Pinter's play *A Kind of Alaska*, about Deborah, a woman who has awoken after being in the deep 'sleep' of encephalitis lethargica for 29 years, she asks what she had been doing all that time and where she has been. And the thing is, as the doctor at her side tells her candidly, we don't really know.

Why does Dawn Faizey Webster matter? She has been forced to a far fringe, a frontier, of the human experience and gained some bitterly purchased knowledge. In a world beset by terror and the loss of life itself, she reminds us that life's little daily losses also matter. She reminds us that we can do something about them. We can reclaim dreams we have cast adrift. But more: she shows how these little things are daily defences against oblivion. They are not only all we can do, they are all we need to.

Here's one way to think about Dawn: she's just like us.

Here's another: she is extraordinary and exceptional.

And here is what I think: she has accessed the extraordinary and exceptional within us, not because she wanted to, but because she had to, for herself and Alexander. Yes, she had almost total paralysis from that brainstem stroke; yes, she was locked in (Dawn, forgive me for using the term); but she was also a young mother. Only being able to blink her left eye, she's been ever-present in her son's life. She's brought him up. When they come to my home to see a recording of the final of *The Apprentice* (Dawn and I both missed the original broadcast), Alex spends a lot of time on the computer playing games like Uncharted 4. It is kind of reassuring. I show him my old globe, where I'd recently been, where Lake Volta is. I tell him about the children fishing. He says he isn't particularly pleased with all this and we have to find a way to stop it happening. He is right.

My index finger traces across the minute bumps and burrows of the worn globe in my back room followed by Dawn's son's finger, before he returns to his computer gaming and chocolate roll. I begin to understand what she fought for.

There are all kinds of terror. Terror is what happened in the stem of Dawn's brain, what it did to her. Taming also takes many forms. It includes telling your son to get off the PlayStation. That too. That gloriously too.

Where did time go? Where does it? I acknowledge the terror of the death anxiety Becker writes about. But there is another type of anxiety as well: one about life. Dawn hates the term 'locked-in'. I understand that now. But I wonder whether we're locked *out*, shut out by the press of life from so much of the wonder of the world. It's not a criticism, just a fact. The lesson Dawn Faizey Webster teaches is that it doesn't have to be so. I have never met anyone whose every waking day, whose every blink of the eye, is so injected with urgency and ardour. The 19th-century French neurologist Jean-Martin Charcot wrote of the merciless Parkinson's disease afflicting his patients that it offered them no truce. Nor does Dawn. She is unrelenting, irrepressible. Through her we can understand the rebellious work the Tamer of Terror must do. It is hard. It can be heroic.

In the distance, beyond the windows, there is a faint yelping. You enter your daughter's bedroom in the darkness and see a letter she's composed on her iPad. It is addressed to you.

Dear Mum and Dad,
I know you love me, perhaps more than I deserve ...

We are back in that bedroom. But where are *you* now – what are you going to do? Are you where Jane Nicklinson was, prepared to help your loved one die? Jane, a nurse; Jane, a loving wife. *It was because I loved him that I could have done it.* Tony died so swiftly. Of pneumonia, the doctors say; of a broken heart, says Jane. So it never came to it. But for Kay Gilderdale it did.

... if it comes to it, pls, pls help me.

And that's the choice in front of you now. Are you actually able to do what it takes – whatever it takes – to ensure your own flesh and blood will be free of all the pain? You cannot help but think of Dawn. Gloriously, rebelliously defiant Dawn. There is one more thing I should tell you before you decide.

When she was finally able to communicate by blinking, when her family and the doctors finally realised she was still in there, Dawn made a simple request of her former husband, Alexander's father. It was this: 'Please help me die.'

But Dawn changed her mind. She was able to tame the terror to this extent at least: even if she could not totally defeat it, she would not let it defeat her. And then there was Miss L. I think often of my client and her children on that West Country farm, which in my mind's eye – I know this is sentimental – is always bathed in sunshine. I never found out her mother's name. Gradually I began to realise that it didn't actually matter because it could be any name – it *is* any name.

Like Dawn, Miss L was able to step back from the brink, she fought herself free of meaninglessness. Like Alexander the Great, she turned directly into the sun. So those are the people with you in the room: Jane and Kay; Dawn and Miss L.

The fox cubs scrap and yelp.

Your hand reaches for the morphine bottle. Drops.

Reaches for the morphine bottle. Drops.

Reaches . . .

PART IV

THE BEHOLDER

Time is short and the water is rising.

Raymond Carver

ONE

All They Saw Was My Face

'When I was growing up,' Rana says, 'you know, a teenager, there was this girl in school no one liked.'

She liked playing chess a lot that other girl, which made her seem very clever, but also slightly threatening. Yet it was something else that caused her to be treated with suspicion by the rest of the class in their school in a city in a state in the vast Indian subcontinent.

'She had this mark, a birthmark, on her face,' Rana says. 'Like a map. You know how bitchy young girls can be. Not just young girls, but especially young girls.'

Rana's words spill out, rapid, intense, almost agitated, as if there is not enough time left. Then again, she has lost so much time. Rana found herself constantly staring at the girl's face. She became obsessed: what was it a map of? The girl had no friends – people were put off, couldn't see past the chess or the mark or both.

'I tried speaking to her, but my friends, they were like, "Rana, what are you speaking to *her* for? What is now wrong with you?"'

Rana didn't want to lose her friends. She didn't want to stand out. The girl left the school.

'Do you keep in touch with the other girls?' I ask.

She pauses. 'Since what happened,' by which she meant the reason we were speaking, 'most of them have dropped me. Sometimes one of them, I think because they are feeling real guilty, messages me to see how I'm doing. They say, "Oh, Rana, you are so brave." And I say, "What would you do?" They ask me how I spend my days. I'm too embarrassed to say.'

What Rana does – it was the last thing she expected – is to read. And in particular about one place, which she would argue, *does* argue, has the greatest story of all.

Two castaway children, the offspring of a vestal virgin, float down a river in a basket, which snags on some reeds or rushes. The vulnerable babes are approached by a wolf. But the wolf is a she-wolf and instead of devouring them, she lets them suckle. The children, two boys, survive and grow up to found a hilltop town on the site of their salvation.

That town became a city, and that city became Rome. For seven centuries Rome enjoyed unmatched conquest and triumph. Then it paused for breath. The Republic became the Empire and Augustus Caesar relinquished the grand plan to subdue the whole earth and prosecute distant wars. The City of the Seven Hills would consolidate. But there was one piece of unfinished business. What Tacitus, one of Rome's chief chroniclers, describes as a mysterious isle 'obscured by continual rain and cloud' – Britannia.

'I love the pages in Gibbon about your land,' Rana says. 'How you got conquered.'

I thanked her for the interest. Later, I looked it up. Gibbon tells us that it took 40 years of blood-soaked war to subdue Britain, a project, 'undertaken by the most stupid [Claudius], maintained by the most dissolute [Nero], and terminated by the most timid [Domitian]'. These stories, I slowly realised, had not just stimulated Rana, but in a way it's hard to conceive, they had saved her.

'And what I found in Gibbon is what he says about hope,' Rana says. 'Do you know it?' I didn't. 'It's the best comfort,' she says.

Gibbon's quote in full states that: 'Hope, the best comfort of our imperfect condition.' I looked that up too. I knew what Rana hoped for. But it took a long time for us to talk about it. It was too painful. So I was happy in the meantime to read about the Romans in Britain.

It all began almost a century before Claudius, even before the birth of Christ, on a beach on Kent's chalky coast, where the first Caesar, Gaius Julius, having found fortune with a favourable wind and tide for his warships and spy sloops, landed 10,000 legionaries and centurions on a level shore of shingle and shale. That was near Deal. And that was where, two millennia later, they found her.

The Middle Street Fish Bar is a quaint olde worlde eatery in Deal. It is a seven-minute drive along the A258 from where Caesar's squadrons landed. Working there was Florence – Florence Colgate – and for a while this 18-year-old became the object of international attention for one thing.

'I had to send in a picture,' Colgate says, 'like wearing no make-up, and from that I got called to say that I'd got through to the last five out of 8,000 people.'

Of the five finalists, Colgate won, and in doing so provoked a stream of researchers to pore over the ratios and precise proportions of her physiognomy.

'I think I just look at my face and I see me,' she says. 'I don't really see the science.'

Colgate won the television competition on ITV's *Lorraine* to find Britain's most 'natural' beauty – no make-up, no plastic surgery, just 'you'. Following her triumph, Colgate appeared on posters and promotional materials in Superdrug stores all over the nation. At least her face did.

Florence Colgate

In China in 2015 the high-profile actor and supermodel Angelababy (real name Yeung Wing) underwent the most nerve-racking audition of her life.

At the Chinese Academy of Medical Sciences, 'Baby', hailed as the Kim Kardashian of China, whose $31 million wedding was possibly the most expensive in Chinese history (and live-streamed online), exposed herself to a battery of intrusive tests – in public. Yeung Wing was forced to go to court to sue for defamation when the Beijing cosmetic clinic Ruili claimed she'd had plastic surgery: 'Angelababy's plastic surgery fails, netizens say her chin is extremely unnatural.'

Baby needed to protect the authenticity of her image, the naturalness of her beauty – of her face.

Across the Pacific Ocean, on the west coast of the United States, Stanford MBA and Silicon Valley wealth manager Michelle Miller was causing controversy of her own. She developed a theory of beauty – the 'theory of seven'.

Miller, the author of weblog *The Underwriting*, who famously claimed to easily step into the head of her male characters by (1) shutting off 80 per cent of her brain, then (2) committing half of what was left to thinking about sex, revealed the secret of her success. It is, Miller claims, by being 'a seven'. You don't want to be too pretty. That is too intimidating and off-putting. But nor do you want to have an unattractive face.

You need to be attractive enough to be noticed, but not so unnervingly beautiful to be written off. Seven out of ten, that's the 'sweet spot', Miller claims, between beauty and bland oblivion for a woman's face.

Across another ocean, on the other side of the Atlantic, Laura Fernee claims to have missed that sweet spot – but on the high side. The former medical research scientist who has a first-class degree from the University of London says that her life is being ruined – by her face.

'The truth is,' the 33-year-old says, 'my good looks have caused massive problems for me . . . It's not my fault . . . I can't help the way I look.' She adds that stricken male colleagues leave 'romantic gifts' on her desk. Even when she is in the lab in scrubs, they cannot help themselves, even 'with no make-up they still come on to me because of my natural attractiveness. There was nothing I could do to stop it.'

Following her doctorate, Fernee worked for a series of medical research companies in the development of drug treatments. Her interest in the field was sparked by the fact that her mother suffers from an autoimmune disease and so her research was intensely personal. But due to the intolerable attention visited upon her, Fernee left research science to set about writing a book: on what it's like to have too pretty a face for work. 'They were only interested in me for how I looked,' Fernee complains. 'All they saw was my face.'

Inevitably, Fernee suffered a backlash because of daring to state such a thing. It was ferocious. She became overnight, according to that barometer of public vitriol and vituperation the *Daily Mail*, 'the most hated woman in Britain'.

Along with the predictable deluge of social media comments – 'get over yourself', 'you're not all that, luv', 'you're wearing too much slap', 'you look like my mum' – came the advice that there was nothing in her problems that could not be 'sorted out' by having something administered to her face. Acid.

TWO

Penalising Plainness

They found the bust at the bottom of the Rhone in southern France. Luc Long, its discoverer, said that the features on the face were so lifelike that it was almost as if they were 'carved in human flesh.' The bust now sits on a white plinth in the Museum of Antiquity in Arles, surrounded by other artefacts dragged from the river waters. The French minister of culture Christine Albanel hailed it as 'the oldest representation of the emperor'. But others were less convinced.

Mary Beard, Professor of Classics at Cambridge, for example, wrote in her *A Don's Life* blog for *The Times*, 'There is, I suppose, a remote possibility that it does represent Julius Caesar, but no particular reason at all to think that it does.' Another blogger ('rogueclassicist') observed, 'It looks more like George Bush to me.'

But from the start, Caesar's face has been important. It has been the crucial clue to his exceptional achievements and character. Controversial Victorian scholar James Anthony Froude, Regius

Professor of Modern History at Oxford between 1892 and 1894, famously wrote of Caesar:

> His features were more refined than was usual in Roman faces; the forehead was wide and high, the nose large and thin, the lips full, the eyes dark gray like an eagle's, the neck extremely thick and sinewy. His complexion was pale. His beard and mustache were kept carefully shaved.

We infer character from face, infer the entire human being. It is a heuristic, a tool. It's also a trap.

Rana knows about this trap; she is now in one of her own. For since it – the reason for our communication – happened, which was in fact around the same time that in a river in southern France, 4,000 miles from where Rana ended up in hospital, a bust of a man that may or may not have been Gaius Julius Caesar was fished out of the water, Rana has become obsessed with people's faces. She has every right to.

Affiliate behaviour in animals – both human and non-human – is highly dependent on the physical cues others present. How they look. It regulates how we associate and bond, reject and recoil from others. The human animal extracts an inordinate amount of valuable information from the faces of other people.

Attractive people are more likely to be hired than less attractive people. They are more likely to be promoted and be better remunerated. There is a 'beauty premium' or, regarded the other way, a 'plainness penalty'. Attractive defendants are more likely to be both bailed and acquitted than less attractive people in the dock. Thus attractiveness can affect not only financial well-being but also freedom. And when the face absolutely does not fit, the consequences can be disastrous. As Jennifer Eberhardt's devastating study showed, defendants convicted of homicide 'with stereotypically "black-looking" features are more than twice as likely to get the death sentence than lighter-skinned African American defendants found guilty of killing a white person.' Therefore, for better or for worse, what you look like matters greatly. What the module in the mind that processes all this information – the Beholder – beholds can be metaphorically, and sometimes literally, a matter of life or death.

'He kept looking at me,' Rana said. 'You know how guys sometimes do. A little look, and then when you catch them, they look away. So when I caught him, I would try to smile back at this boy to say, "It's okay, you're allowed, yah." I *liked* him looking at me for sure.'

Rana is now in her late twenties. All this happened several years ago on the Indian subcontinent. Rana was having a year out before she went to university and was volunteering for an NGO that helped children from poorer backgrounds with literacy. But it wasn't all about doing good. 'I was crazy about fashion then, really, really crazy. Nonsense, huh, but it was my life.'

'Why?' I ask.

She laughs. It is a laugh with an edge. 'I don't have a good answer for this. I just liked beautiful things. That was my life. I enjoyed helping out at the learning centre, but what I really loved was having a good time, looking good, fashion. I was a little selfish, you know.' She pauses. 'I mean, I was young.'

'And the boy?'

'It was *nice*,' she tells me, 'to be noticed. The best feeling ever. I was never the pretty, pretty one.'

She shows me photographs from just before that time. I have to differ. They depict a young woman with an open, unblemished, gentle face. She is in a garden full of trees.

'In our home,' she tells me, 'we have fruit trees. They flower and fruit every year as I grow up. It is like magic, only magic.'

Due to reasons of confidentiality, which are tremendously important to Rana (as you will soon appreciate), I will not describe her or the location in greater detail. The truth is that Rana doesn't like to look at those photos. She holds them up for me to see, the image turned away from her, but does not look. They are a torment to her.

In fact, she cannot bear it.

Michelle Miller states that in her financial career she found a lot of women whose accomplishments and brains were undermined by the surface effects – because, as Miller puts it, 'They were too hot.' They fell outside the narrow band of beneficial professional attractiveness. This preference for professional 'sevens' is, Miller suggests, 'an unconscious bias – these heuristics we use to see the world really happen.'

Unquestionably her theory of seven has garnered her precious column inches and airtime. But has it any objective basis? What about the proportions of Florence Colgate's much pored-over face: the 44 per cent ratio between the space between her pupils and the width of her face; the 32.8 per cent ratio between the distance from eyes to mouth and hairline to chin. When we see facial 'perfection' like this, what are we seeing?

As importantly, who – or what – 'sees' it?

Is the old saying about beauty being in the eye of the beholder descriptively adequate? Beauty comes through the eyes, but then it seeps into our brain. Here's where the puzzle deepens, darkens. What things does it do there? To what – to *whom*?

*

'But then,' Rana said, 'as I got to know him a bit more, started to spend time with him, I realised there was something wrong. I mean, he was a very good-looking guy and my friends, they kept saying I was lucky he was interested, but they didn't actually know what it was like, how he was like when we were together. That's the thing, one face in public, when there are people there, and then this . . . *other*, when we were alone. He kept asking me which other boys I spoke to. How many, when, what about. We were not even in a proper full-on relationship, but it began to make me feel funny. I felt something was wrong.'

She was right. As the time went on, something became very wrong. Her admirer – I'm going to call him Yuvraj – began following her.

'I would be out with my friends, my girlfriends, and there across the street he would be. Just watching. Sometimes taking photos on his phone. It wasn't me who first noticed but my best friend. She said, "Why is that boy taking photos of us on his phone?" And I looked up and, you know, it was Yuvraj. There he was.'

Once more he quickly looked away. But now Rana didn't smile. She didn't want him to look at her. Not like that. It was not looking; it was guarding. It was devouring.

'For a few days I didn't hear anything from him,' she said. 'Then suddenly he came to my house. And he was pretending like it never happened. I asked him why he was following me. And he said he was not, that I must be mistaking him for someone else.'

She wasn't. It happened again. Then again.

'I sent him a text,' Rana said. 'I said, very, very polite, that, please, Yuvraj, please, I don't think it would work out between us and so, you know, we should not meet any more. So please, don't visit my house or message me.'

There was a sudden radio silence.

'The silence was even kind of worse,' Rana said. 'I kept thinking, what is going on in his head for him to act like this? But at least I'd told him, not to bother me any more now. That's what I was trying to say to him, but politely. What I wanted. Why couldn't I tell him what I wanted?'

It was not what he wanted. Hell broke loose. All of it.

It begins with babies.

Unquestionably, during our formative years there is a deluge of messaging flooding us with images and ideations of perfect or even just preferred standards of beauty. There is undoubtedly a colossal feat of social construction around this. But there may be something else at work also. Research evidence indicates that the systems in our mind that evaluate and respond positively or negatively to attractiveness operate from a very young age. Human infants prefer to look at physically attractive human faces compared to faces judged by adults to be less attractive. In early studies by Judith Langlois and her team at the University of Texas, attractive face preference in babies was detected from as young as six months old. It extended across different types of faces, to 'stimulus' (observed) faces of different races, ages and gender. Thus the finding was robustly found when there were matched faces of entirely different fundamental structures, two young white female faces or two elderly black male faces. There is a persistent preference for beauty.

In more recent studies by Alan Slater at Exeter University, this clear aesthetic preference was also detected in newborns, two days old (that was the average of his sample group). The phenomenon was even found in babies just a few hours old. When presented with a choice of two perfectly matched faces with the only distinguishing feature being the level of attractiveness, newborn human babies spend on average 80 per cent of the time gazing at the attractive face. Slater's conclusion is that humans are 'born with a very detailed representation of the human face'. This leads to the startling conclusion that our ability to sort and filter the world in aesthetic terms is not simply a social construct, something we learn from others. It may have a more innate component. As Slater states, 'Attractiveness is not simply in the eye of the beholder, it is in the brain of the newborn infant right from the moment of birth and possibly prior to birth.'

Indeed, Slater's team in a follow-up experiment detected infant preference for attractive faces in non-human animals that the three-month-old infant had no experience of (here, matched pairs of attractive and unattractive tigers). The results suggest an innate mechanism we come into the world with. But why? Is it an adaptation for future mate choice or a by-product of more general information processing (perceptual-cognitive) mechanisms?

While the academic and scientific debate about this continues, what is clear is that the visual pattern that human infants respond to and recognise first (and fastest) is the human face. Indeed, the preference for gazing at faces is activated within the first 24 hours of human life: it is one of the very first things we do. It has obvious adaptive implications. As stated by Russell Revlin in his analysis of human cognition, this rapid ability to recognise faces 'emerges from basic human brain structure and is a biologically based universal'.

Evolutionarily, the early onset of accurate and reliable facial recognition is an indispensable survival tool: identifying kin and caregivers, being alert to strangers and thus being aware of possible threat. But why should this facial detection and distinguishing mechanism exhibit a preference for attractiveness? Features that are found to be on average more appealing may be cues not just of fitness (reproductive potential, even if some time away) but health and immuno-robustness, indications that the possessor lacks disease or deformity – and even that the person may be resistant to parasites. Signs of self-care may suggest that the individual is equipped and competent to provide care to others.

If this deep pull of the pleasing is something – at least in some measure – wired within us, what happens to us when we look on beauty? And what of the opposite: what happens when we are deprived of it?

On the day it happened, there were pure blue skies – just as on the day Tony Nicklinson skydived over the Emirates.

Rana had been to a clothes store with her girlfriends and they had swooned over this beautiful print dress with luxurious tapered sleeves. She fell in love with it, with the sheer romance of it. ('It was like something out of a fairy tale, out of a dream.') The fabric was deep burnt orange, and that is what she most recalls – perhaps the memory intensified by what was to take place – the deep burnt orange of the dress, the cornflower blue of the skies above filling her eyes, the simple joy of the vivid combination.

'But it was *soooo* expensive,' she says. 'So hardcore. Could I really afford it? But it was super dreamy and my friends, they were saying, "Can you really afford not to get it? It's you, Rana, it's you." We were like that in those days. Serious things in life like debt were not a matter of concern for us. Nothing really bothered us then, yah?'

She speaks about eight years ago as if it were a different era, a different life. Perhaps it was.

They went to a restaurant where they had milkshakes. Then they went their separate ways. 'I had to buy my mother a present. It was her birthday the next day and she is like the best mother in the world. I wanted to get her something special.'

As she wandered through the streets, Rana became aware of someone following her. Just that sixth sense, the disturbance on the back of the neck, the chill. But when she looked round there was no one. Once she glimpsed a figure slip quickly into an alley behind her. She turned to go and investigate, then thought twice about it. So on she went in search of her mother's present. She had two thoughts in her mind: a white porcelain horse or a scarf. But the horse, it was not right, not appropriate (there were too many memories). So a scarf, she thought, a gloriously coloured scarf. Every now and then she glanced behind.

There was no one. She must have been mistaken. She had been on edge for a while. It was getting like every shadow was a stalker, every fleeting reflection a threat. That was no way to live, and she wouldn't. She thought of something better. She thought of fabrics: the scarf for her mother, the dress. The hell with the price, life was too short. What was money for, anyway?

She turned down a little alley, a shortcut. One minute there was a thin ribbon of blue sky high above, then there was a blur suddenly directly in front of her, then there was nothing, except the purring sound, which one part of her brain understood to be a motorbike idling – that's why the shape had suddenly appeared, it was the screeching to a halt of a motorbike at the mouth of the alley – so there was nothing except that sound of the motorbike, like it was growling at something, at her, and the other thing, the only other thing, was the intense pain – blinding pain, slicing pain, cutting into her. The world disappeared, as – slowly – did her face. Almost all of it.

As Rana was walking through an alley in the garment district, someone rode in front of her on a motorbike and threw a beaker of acid in her face.

THREE

The Pool of Fire

I tzhak Aharon and colleagues at the Motivation and Emotion Neuroscience Center at Massachusetts General Hospital used functional MRI imaging to study the human brain response pattern to provocative visual stimuli. Put more simply, they were trying to crack an age-old mystery. What is it that happens in a man's head when he views an attractive woman?

Where does it happen?

There are certain distinct structures of the brain – the reward circuitry – that are activated when we anticipate gratification. These systems have been documented as being engaged when the observer is faced with stimulants offering gratification such as drugs (whether nicotine or cocaine or amphetamine) or money or something to remedy a deficit state (being cold, or thirsty, or hungry, part of the body's regulation of equilibrium activity, its 'homeostatic' tendency). But what effect does the presentation of a human face have? Were these same reward systems triggered? In other words, the object of Aharon's study was to analyse whether human faces are not just objects about which we can make an aesthetic judgement ('That's a beautiful face'), but also the objects of anticipated reward.

Functional MRI equipment was used to focus on six brain regions known through previous research to be associated with reward in human and non-human animals. These included the amygdala, the hypothalamus, the orbitofrontal cortex and the nucleus accumbens (NAc). To examine this, they assembled a cohort of heterosexual males to view a selection of faces. Eighty faces, male and female. Some were attractive, others significantly less so.

By the design of the computer viewing system, the screen would present each image for 8 seconds. However, the viewers could determine how long the face would stay on the screen. They could press a key to reduce the exposure time and another to prolong the time they could look at the face: keep it or delete it. The total observation time for the set of 80 images was 40 minutes, and the participant could view the set as many times as they wished, dependent on their keystroke interventions. On average they viewed the set three or four times.

Out of the four categories (male/female, attractive/not), it was only when the participants were exposed to attractive female faces that they expended effort to prolong the viewing time. Perhaps that was to be expected. But what might not have been anticipated was the finding that, on average, men gazed for longer at attractive male faces than less attractive female faces. Why was this?

Was it an inclination to gauge potential rivals, or a manifestation of a deeply sublimated homoerotic sentiment, or do people, generally, prefer to look at beautiful things? Aharon's team sought to understand this process better by monitoring which brain systems were engaged during the observation time.

The results indicated that male heterosexual volunteers found the attractive male faces aesthetically pleasing, but not 'rewarding'. By contrast, observation of aesthetically pleasing female faces activated the brain's neural reward circuitry. One of the key findings is that the viewing of attractive women engaged the nucleus accumbens. The NAc has complex reward functions, and in particular is associated with expectation of reward. Thus when the male observers viewed the attractive female faces not only did they register them as aesthetically pleasing (as they did with the attractive male faces), but the neural systems that are activated in anticipation of reward were triggered.

The implications of this study are that (in young heterosexual males at least) two different brain processes are engaged. One is concerned with aesthetic judgements – whether a face is attractive. The other – the reward circuitry – is also engaged when viewing attractive female faces. Young men are prepared to expend effort to view attractive females – even when there is no other direct reward forthcoming for that effort other than the act of viewing. The viewing in itself is pleasurable. This second neural network is concerned with the expectation – hope – of reward, of future gratification. In this way, young males live in hope. But what happens in their head when those hopes are dashed?

In an edition of *New Vision*, one of her country's leading national daily newspapers, there is a picture of Hanifa Nakiryowa, then 30, sitting with her two children. She is wearing a stylish grey jacket with an ornate button and large lapels and a delicate rust-coloured headscarf. She is described by the report, with some accuracy, as a 'beautiful woman'. But that phrase doesn't capture her real essence. There is a calmness about her, which radiates powerfully from the picture. It is a quality she would later need. Desperately.

'I grew up in western Uganda, near the Rwanda border. It was such an amazing place – so pretty. My father was stationed there as part of a religious mission, but we were struggling with money. I was one of six children. It was there that I saw many things I did not like. The way women and girls were treated. From a very young age, at ten years, I could see those disparities, so I developed a passion for education because I saw how educated women had a voice, a platform. They were more respected. So I was determined to advance myself somehow – somehow. I knew the only way I could get to university was to work hard and limit the time I went out to play and hang out with my friends. I had to have that discipline, that strength, to stay longer, harder over my books. It became more difficult for us all because my parents separated and we were left all alone. It was complicated. Really, it was chaos. I cannot tell you how I made it. I now keep asking myself how I made it. I was the firstborn, I was in charge of my younger siblings as well.'

The calmness kicked in through the chaos and she forced herself to work hard in the middle of it. Her relentless toil led to Nakiryowa winning a coveted government scholarship to university in the capital, Kampala. She runs ahead in her story, 'Later, after university when the problems began, I got a job I loved so much,' she says. 'It made me so proud that I was able to stand on my own and support my children with it.' She was employed on a UNICEF project in the capital to protect women and children from violence and abuse. 'We were trying to counter religious teachings that ended up in harming vulnerable people. We tried to offer other ways of thinking, showing people that there was another way with respect and human rights. It was a very effective model. We were trying to show them how education can empower them. It was a community-based approach, also having dialogue with men and community elders, spiritual leaders, challenging the role of religion in limiting the role and life chances of women and young girls.'

Hanifa Nakiryowa is now in her late thirties and has relocated to the United States, studying for a master's degree in international development at the University of Pittsburgh, Pennsylvannia. When we speak, it is at 4am US time. She gets up every day at 3am.

'That's pretty impressive,' I say to her.

'No, it's necessary. It's while the babies are asleep, so I can do my study and research. I love UPitt. I know it's a long way from home and people tell me it's going to get so cold, but it's okay for now.'

When we first spoke it was early October. I warned her about the beguiling charm of the fall. I told her how the New England fall took me in when I was at Harvard – then within no time the polar vortex fell upon us. It was hitting −25°C.

'Minus?' she asked.

'I'm afraid so,' I replied.

She paused. One of those pauses in a conversation when you can almost hear the other person thinking. 'Hmm. I'll be ready,' she said. 'After what happened back home, I'm now always ready.'

Following Aharon and colleagues' study, the Canadian team of Margo Wilson and Martin Daly investigated another aspect of how males respond to attractive females. They looked at the concept of discounting.

Generally organisms prefer present goods over the promise or prospect of future ones. The bread today–jam tomorrow principle (often attributed to Lewis Carroll's White Queen in *Through the Looking Glass*). It is a *carpe diem* form of behaviour, and can be adaptive. It can make sense. Discounting across the life course can enhance both survival and reproductive prospects. It is the calculus of life, the 'scheduling of reproductive effort' – it is, as Wilson and Daly state, 'a gamble'.

The rate of discounting varies. For example, worker bees are prepared to undertake more dangerous foraging missions if there is a higher prevalent mortality rate. If you're more likely to die, you take greater risks. We see it in the obvious dangers that refugees expose themselves to by clambering onto flimsy boats to cross the Mediterranean. Studies show that heroin addicts discount the future more. They are more focused on present reward and gratification. The future, any kind of meaningful future, blurs and fades.

Typically human discounting – 'time preference' effects – has been investigated in research settings under controlled conditions by offering either real or notional choices with differing financial rewards over differing timescales. Would you prefer less now or more later?

Wilson and Daly hypothesised that if men were primed with images of attractive women, they would be more likely to discount the future: they would prefer to have money now rather than later. This flows from the research base on the human pursuit of reward. The pursuit of natural rewards such as food or drink affect human behaviour and engage reward systems. But the question is whether a human face could act as a similar stimulus, engaging the same reward system in the pursuit (not necessarily consciously) of mating opportunity – of sex.

The study used 96 male and 113 female undergraduates. They were first assessed for their discounting proclivities (they vary slightly from human to human), then they were presented with 12 opposite-sex faces, then reassessed for their discounting. The discounting was assessed by offering participants a smaller sum ($15 to $35) tomorrow or a larger sum ($50 to $75) much later (a week to several months later).

What Wilson and Daly found was that the sight of attractive female faces led to men discounting the future more. By the simple act of viewing these women's faces, male participants were more prepared to take the money immediately. They would opt for less money now. Those male volunteers who were exposed to less attractive female faces did not increase their discounting.

This was a significant result since, as the authors stated, 'We believe that this is the first demonstration of an experimentally induced change in human discounting.' Why did it happen?

Wilson and Daly suggest (as Aharon and his colleagues found) the stimulus of attractive faces has an arousing effect which activates neural pathways 'associated with cues of sexual opportunity'. In other words, when viewing attractive faces, men become more present-oriented.

Once primed in a 'mating opportunity' mindset, they were more likely to prefer the money now, resources that could in theory be used, as Wilson and Daly term it, in 'mating effort'. It is unlikely, of course, that any of this was conscious. But here was a change of behaviour generated by the expedient of viewing the picture of a beautiful woman.

As an undergraduate studying for a degree in economics, Hanifa Nakiryowa was very interested in just these kinds of human decision choices and behaviours. While studying at the college in Kampala, she met a professor who lectured on one of the modules.

He was very struck by the stellar student, the class rep – committed, ambitious, obviously attractive – but at first she rejected his interest and overtures. However, since she was the official class representative, they were in frequent contact. He persisted, term after term, and in time he convinced her of his seriousness by proposing marriage. It was in her final year and she accepted.

At first the marriage went well – at least as far as her husband was concerned. 'There was a honeymoon period,' she says. 'But I think it was him who was happy, because looking back, I don't think I was. He was starting to tell me everything to do, but I took it as this is what marriage is like, what a woman of character does, and at first you don't have a problem doing these small things, giving in, just to have peace in the home.'

But after five months, Hanifa could not bear it any more.

'I tried to run away. I told my cousin I was not comfortable with what was happening in my marriage, so I ran away. I was so unhappy and worried. But my family took me back to my husband.'

'Your family?'

'They told me that I would shame myself and also my family. What would the community think of me? It is the woman's responsibility to make the marriage work, that's your job. If you're failing in your marriage, you're not being the right woman you should be in the home. If he is being abusive, then you are doing something wrong. You are the problem. You must change, find a way to make it work. "Hanifa," they said, "why are you disappointing your husband? What are you doing wrong? You must change, you must please your husband."'

But he became progressively more possessive, more obsessively controlling.

'He told people he could not control a woman who earned twice his salary. The UNICEF project paid well compared to his university stipend. He said he was my husband and he had the right to choose who I see, who I meet, even how I dress up. He would check my phone, my computer, check who I was speaking to. He became paranoid and sometimes would beat me. Even in front of the children. The last time was because I bought a USB without telling him.'

'Your husband,' I said, 'the lecturer?'

'I feel embarrassed telling you this. Violence against women can be this. It has no class. He would lecture in the university and beat me at home, the same day, almost the same hour. He came home that time and found I had bought a USB. I think so many women stay silent about this. They are shocked at first. Then they are ashamed. Deep, deep shame. It is not our fault, our failure, but it feels like it somehow.'

'Did you leave after the abuse?'

'I did what too many women do.'

I had seen it so many times in court.

'I stayed,' Hanifa continued. 'I think we stay in these conditions because we hope.'

'Hope?' I recalled what Rana said about Gibbon. Hope – the best comfort in our imperfect condition. It didn't sit right.

'Hope it is going to get better and change if we do what they say,' Hanifa said, 'what we are told. But eventually you are disarmed. There is nothing left of you. So I knew I had to go or I would be completely lost.'

In a study at Arizona University, participants were divided into two groups. One was shown pictures of an ordinary street. They were asked to write for three minutes about what would be the ideal weather to be there. This was the neutral (control) condition.

In the experimental group, volunteers were shown three pictures of attractive members of the opposite sex and invited to select the most alluring one. They were also given three minutes. But now they had to describe their ideal date with such a person. All participants from both groups were then asked to imagine they had $5,000 in their bank account. How much would they be prepared to spend on luxuries (five were listed, including watches, a new mobile phone, a holiday abroad).

For women participants, there was no statistical difference in the amount of money they would spend, irrespective of whether they had been primed with the street or an attractive man. For men, the situation was significantly different.

As the research team had hypothesised, exposure to the images of attractive women (even for simply a matter of minutes) resulted in men engaging in displays of conspicuous consumption. This costly 'signalling' by purchasing lavish luxuries was animated by mate attraction strategies. It was part of a complex process that would contribute to that male being able to signal that he was resource-rich. It was a highly strategic self-presentation. It was the making of a statement. And it was triggered by an attractive face. An attractive female face can make men do things they wouldn't otherwise do. As Hanifa was to find out.

Hanifa left with her children. Her desire was to wrest back control of her life.

'I wanted to do everything for myself. Show I could. At the same time in my work I was helping other women and their children. That was in August 2011. In October I started receiving threatening text messages. They said I would be killed. When he spoke to me, my husband was pleading for me to come back, pleading with my family, but I was not reliant on anyone, burdening anyone, I was supporting myself and my children so I could make decisions for myself. I let him see our children regularly because none of this was their fault. On December 11 he asked me to pick up the children after they'd been with him for two days. I went to his apartment at the university campus as he asked. When I arrived at the building, I could hear footsteps. I thought it may be my husband, but it was a young man waiting for me. I thought he was a security guard. I paused. I didn't understand. Why did he want to speak to me? It was just a second. What did he want? What was the point, this young man who had walked up to me?'

The unknown male at Hanifa's husband's house had a red plastic bottle, a brake fluid bottle, that had been cut in half and wrapped in a black 'kaveera', a polythene bag. He threw acid in Hanifa's face. Then poured the rest on the floor. She recalls that: on the floor.

'Suddenly your life changes. Your old life is gone. It was like you've been thrown into a pool of fire.'

FOUR

The Water is Rising

The fire was everywhere on her. She felt she was burning to death and drowning at the same time.

'He threw the liquid in my face,' Hanifa says, 'then he poured the rest on the floor. At first the liquid was cold, and then – *fire*. My clothes were dripping with acid and falling apart. My face was. You burn in invisible flames. I cannot even describe what this world is like. Neighbours took me to hospital.'

Once at the Mulago Hospital in Kampala, Hanifa began a long and tortuous process of medical intervention. She was hospitalised for many months and has subsequently had to endure 20 operations. So far all of the surgery is reconstructive as the primary task has been to rebuild and reconstitute her face. Cartilage from her ribs has been used to help rebuild her nose.

'People are shocked when they see my face,' she says. 'My dad fainted when he first came to see me. I was so sorry, so hurt that I did that to my father – that my face did that. I would be shocked too. Before this I had not heard about acid violence. But while I was in hospital I met other women. They'd come in on a weekly basis, more and more women victims, their faces attacked. The attackers try to take away who you are, your self-esteem.' The calmness kicked in again. 'I thought, "Hmm, Hanifa, are you going to let them do that?" You see in people's facial expressions when they see you, by how they judge you. But why should people judge my capability, who I am, what I am worth, what I am capable of doing, because of my facial features? This was a choice for me. What my life would be. I was determined to show them.'

Hanifa Nakiryowa is an intensely intelligent and articulate person. She is intent on using what has happened to her to (as she puts it) 'mobilise' others who have suffered, to give them courage to step forward as she has stepped forward, to – literally – face the world.

Many survivors simply cannot cope with the devastating trauma. They give up, self-harm, take their own life. Others are shunned by their communities and even their families and take to the streets in destitution.

'People always say to me that after we talk to you, Hanifa, we cease to see your scars. But that's the problem.'

In fact there are two. How to stop these attacks happening. And then, if they do, how to get people to just speak to you, to listen, when your face has been disfigured. It should be a simple human transaction: listening. But, it appears, we also listen with our eyes.

Jaf Shah, the Executive Director of ASTI (the Acid Survivors Trust International, based in London), speaks of a woman they have tried to support in Cambodia. After her attack, she wears a veil, even though she has lost sight in both eyes. She understands what her face now looks like, even though she cannot see it herself. The shame of how other people will react distresses her too much and so she covers herself. Constantly.

And this reflects the fate of survivors more generally in countries with a high incidence of attacks such as India and Bangladesh as well as Cambodia. Here survivors not only have to endure the physical pain and mental anguish of the attack and its aftermath, but something more.

A research team at Cornell University's International Human Rights Clinic conducted research on behalf of the UN's Office of the High Commissioner for Human Rights. It found that survivors face marginalisation and stigmatisation. This social isolation may in part be explained by the fact that the victims, as Cornell states, have in a 'significant majority' of cases transgressed subordinate gender roles; they have dared – as Hanifa Nakiryowa did, as Rana did – to stand up for themselves, sought to challenge those who would constrain, coerce or control them.

But there is another aspect. The fact of their disfigurement transgresses in another way: it is at variance with people's understanding of what humans should look like. The Beholder in us, the wiring for beauty and fine form, struggles. Tragedy is heaped upon tragedy. Because the victims are so visible, society acts to neutralise the deviation from the norm, the disfigurement. It invisibilises them, makes the deviation disappear. So victims of such violence become outcasts. Literally, they are cast out.

As Cornell's report into acid attacks states, perpetrators 'aim for a woman's face in an attempt to destroy what many members of society consider to be one of her most important assets – her beauty.'

It is a joy forever, Keats wrote about a thing of beauty, in his poem *Endymion*. That line is so well known that much of its motive force has been stripped away by deadening repetition and overfamiliarity. But Keats added that beauty will not pass into nothingness. And that is what survivors of violence directed against their faces like Hanifa Nakiryowa are resisting. They refuse to be defined by what has happened to their face; by the theft of their features; by the social rejection they experience because of their disfigurement. They refuse to be beaten by the dehumanising effects of the attack, to pass into nothing.

Rana has not yet bought the dress. 'But I will,' she said. 'I will buy a special, special one.'

'Do you know when?'

'Oh, god, yeah, I know in the smallest detail when: when my last operation is done, then I'm going. That's my when.'

'Okay.'

'You are thinking it's silly, for me to think so much about buying a dress?'

I paused, then said, 'Yes. Definitely. It's an outrage, Rana,' and she laughed. 'Send me a picture,' I said.

'Oh, my god, *totally*,' Rana said. She adjusted the headscarf that covers most of her face.

She wants to become a teacher, carry on what she began at the literacy centre. My thoughts circled back to Dawn: driven in exactly the opposite direction, from teaching to study.

'Since all this happened,' Rana said, 'I have so much time. I read and read and read.'

What would you read if suddenly you had a year, two years, at home, away from the world?

'I read about you,' Rana said, laughing. 'Your country. The history of Britain. How Julius Caesar went there. Britain ruled my country, but it was ruled too, by the Romans. That's what I read. About the Romans. What is it like to be ruled? What is it to come up from being ruled? I love Gibbon's *Decline and Fall of the Roman Empire*. It's all online. It's like *Game of Thrones*. Almost better.' She laughed again. It was good to hear it. 'You think I'm joking. The Romans brought elephants to your cold country. Did you know that?'

Time to be insufferable. I agonised for the briefest moment whether to say it; couldn't resist. 'Britain had elephants before the Romans,' I said as casually as I could. 'But not for thousands of years.'

'Your cold country?'

So I told her. A couple of years earlier I'd read about the Ebbsfleet elephant, a straight-trunked mammal about twice the size of the modern African elephant. It was killed by early humans, possibly four of them, 420,000 years ago. At that time Britain may still have been connected to mainland Europe. The British Isles were not yet islands. The elephant was discovered during digging for a high-speed rail link to the coast. The place the elephant rested for almost half a million years is now buried beneath the B259 Southfleet Road.

'I *love* all this,' Rana said. '*Twice* the size? So that's what I'm going to do: teach – teach history. I am definitely, *definitely* going to teach history one day. Maybe even history of fashion. And like your Mr Edward Gibbon, one day I want to stand there in the Forum. Imagine that, yah? Me in the Forum of Rome. Me in the streets where Julius Caesar's chariot drove.'

She paused and so did I. She went off to get a drink. I checked some emails. Dawn Faizey Webster had texted me.

'What do you know about Foucault?' she asked.

'Step into my office,' I texted back. I was about to be exceedingly boring. One of the things Foucault investigated was the way people don't just find freedom but manufacture it, construct it, even in the most unpromising situations, the dance between the controller and the controlled. It would be tempting to say that this is the project Dawn had been engaged in, but that's too simplistic. Anyway, she was researching an essay. When Rana returned, we continued to talk about history, but of a different kind – her own.

'When my father died, I went a little bit, you know, wild,' she told me. 'My head was very strong. Wilful, my mother said. "Rana," she said, "you are becoming a wilful child." Only I wasn't a child, or didn't think of myself like that.'

'It's understandable, isn't it?' I said. 'After something like that, to have a reaction?' We never quite know what form it will take. After my father died, for several years I couldn't play the piano. I don't know why. The first thing I tried to play after I'd been told the news of his death was some Beethoven I'd been practising. I couldn't.

'I've thought a lot about what went wrong with me,' Rana said, 'what was happening. I used to come home drunk, fall over. For a long, long time I did not understand, but then after . . . Yuvraj, I began reading history on the Internet, to see the lives of famous people. You can read about them all. It's all there on the Internet, in the *Parallel Lives*.'

It was a reference to first-century Greek author Plutarch, who wrote famous biographies of the lives, deeds and follies of notable Greeks and Romans. Plutarch spanned the Greek and Roman worlds, having studied philosophy and mathematics in Athens, but he visited Rome several times. He may even have met Emperor Trajan.

'And I begin to read those lives,' Rana said, 'and I think, oh, these are just big stories. You read one, have one browser open, then you have to read another, then just one more, you know, because so many are connected.'

That night, I used the link she provided. I became, I must confess, addicted. I read the life of Sulla, then Solon, about Sertorius and Coriolanus.

'And when you read,' Rana said, 'you see, really see.'

'What?'

'That they are most definitely people. You realise that the greatest of the great people, they are real people. And they do so many damn fool things. Like I did.'

At first, I didn't grasp what she was saying. But slowly, painstakingly, like the sunken bust being raised inch by inch out of the river waters, the picture emerged. There wasn't just one boy. There were two.

The loss of a face can inflict a pain that is so debilitating and devastating that the sufferer cannot continue. Hanifa Nakiryowa saw that happen to women around her in the hospital in Uganda. She was adamant she'd find a way not to succumb. 'Despite all that was done to me,' she says, 'I was determined to tell myself and tell the world that my life is not finished. I have a future. That I will face it.'

So she has fought back.

The year after the attack, Nakiryowa sought to do something to help other women who were suffering as she had been. She co-founded CERESAV, the Center for Rehabilitation of Survivors of Acid and Burns Violence. Through intense campaigning and an online petition through change.org signed by 300,000 people, they were able to lobby the Ugandan government to take acid violence seriously. In January 2016, the Attorney General announced that the Toxic Chemicals Prohibition and Control Bill would be passed into law. It is a first step to controlling the availability of corrosive substances, but more needs to be done to create criminal sanctions reflective of the gravity of acid violence. Nevertheless, what she has accomplished is a victory for Hanifa and her fellow survivors. It is a fight they did not choose. But one they will not turn away from.

At one of the city's chicest bars, with trees growing within the white walls and a dance floor, Rana's gaze fell on the face of a young man. She fell in love.

'This other boy,' Rana said, 'he was *beautiful*. You know, some guys, they are very hot. But this one, he was beautiful. And what was better, he didn't really know it. Or it wasn't just this big, big thing with him. He would look at you, you know, with these sad, sad eyes, and oh . . .

'But my mother, she did not approve. The family, they had found someone for me to marry. This future husband, he was doing very, very well. He had a business here, also in Dubai, making a lot of money. We'd gone out a couple of times and he was a very smart guy, sharp, but I just didn't like him enough. My mother and I, we had a big row. And I said, "Please, please, Maa, I don't love him. I can never love him. I love this other boy." And my mother said no, never. You cannot. You must not. His people are not our people.'

By which she meant they were of a different caste. The other match was also one her father had approved. Rana loved her father deeply. She did not want to disrespect his memory.

'So I did it,' Rana said. 'I smashed her favourite thing.'

It was a little white horse with blue eyes. It was made of porcelain. Once in a bazaar in their city her mother had bought this little white thing.

'I don't know why she got it. But I threw it on the floor and saw it smash. Then I thought: what have I done? Then I thought: what else could I have done?'

For many weeks Rana and her mother did not speak. They shared the same house but avoided each other, one in, the other out – another kind of parallel lives. Sometimes Rana would come home drunk, twice she collapsed, her mother would clean her up, say nothing, disappear. Then one day, Rana's mother burst into her room.

'I was so surprised to see her,' Rana said, 'I stood up. She holds my face tight in her hands. She looks straight in my eyes. She looks hard, hard. Is the answer there? But what is her question? She says, "You love this boy." She doesn't say, "Do you love him?" She looks in my face and says you *do* love him. She can see it. She sees how unhappy I am. And she says, "Okay, okay, Rana, I will find a way to do it."'

And that was why Rana went out that day with her girlfriends, to celebrate her mother's change of heart. And that is why she was particularly intent on buying her a birthday present, not just to celebrate the day, but to say thank you and sorry. She thought for a moment that she would buy another horse, if she could find one. But then she thought that no, that is broken and gone and the new horse would remind her mother of the old. So she would buy her mother something else. A scarf, perhaps.

While she was going back and forth in her mind about all this, someone else had been watching. Whether it was Yuvraj or someone else, she didn't know. The attack was a blur: a motorbike appeared, it growled at her, the world disappeared – she's still not sure exactly what happened. And she had no proof about who it was. No witnesses came forward.

After the attack, the boy with the sad eyes could not cope, would not wait for the operations and what Rana one distant day might look like. And so she was alone. With her mother who diagnosed her lovesickness by looking at her face, and who has stood by her ever since.

Hanifa has found her own way, a fresh way, to be free. 'You know, I never used to take selfies. For so long I couldn't bring myself to do it. But now I do. When I look at my photos, I see a freer person. I have a different face. When I blink, you wouldn't know because the scarring has restricted my eyelids. So I sleep with my eyes open. So today, yes, I'm a different person. But I am also more vocal, more . . . strong. I want to share what happened to me because I think many women in different ways go through what I go through. It isn't just acid, it is how they are hurt and controlled and have taken away from them who they are. And that is happening to women in so many different walks of life, and part of the reason people get away with it is because we lose our confidence and who we are. We become ashamed.

'So what we're trying to tell girls now is that even if from the outside your relationship looks silver and gold, but on the inside you're trapped and suffering, do something. Don't just take it. It is difficult because in Africa there is a culture of silence, you don't talk about what happens behind the walls.'

I told her that I was not sure it was restricted to Africa. Whether our inclination to prefer things of beauty is a by-product of other cognitive processing or a distinct module, there is a disconcertingly prevalent outcome: destruction of the attractive thing we cannot have. A mania of possessiveness; a need to defile. The reward systems in our brain are powerful. The frustration of them can also provoke a powerful reaction.

'This is the work I'm doing,' Hanifa says, 'to break the cycle. Because young girls are otherwise modelling what they are seeing, that their mothers or older sisters are controlled or abused or beaten and they are obliged to take it, to deal with it, to accept it. But it is not something anyone should accept and I want to change that. So I want people to know that I didn't sit down and mourn my loss. I am more than the face I lost. I look at the photos of me from before. I *read* them.'

'Read?' I say, unsure whether I heard correctly down the Skype connection.

'Yes. Read. And when I read these pictures of the me from before, I see a sad young woman from back then who may be smiling at the camera but is still sad and unfree. Life is so brief. We can't waste it being unfree.'

Time is short, Raymond Carver wrote. Time is short and the water is rising.

'So much has happened to me,' Hanifa Nakiryowa says. 'So much has changed, but I am freer now. That young woman I see in those photos, she smiles, she smiles out at me, but she is unfree.'

'How do you know?' I ask.

'I see it,' Hanifa says. 'I see it in her face.'

I imagine Rana standing in the splendour of Rome's ancient Forum – decreed by Emperor Trajan, designed by Apollodorus of Damascus – as a light breeze, the same that cooled the faces of the Caesars, ruffles her headscarf. For that moment, I would like there to be no one else around, so for a minute she has

Rome's ruins to herself, and she can remove the fabric that shields her face from the world and the world from her, and look.

'Some people, I know this, sometimes they find it . . . difficult to see me and I'm sorry. I always apologise.' *She* apologises. 'Once I saw my reflection. I thought it's like there's been a car crash, but there was no car. I'm trying to move forward now. There's so much poverty here. You know it, but you never really *see* it. We spend billions on cricket and cars and phones and pretend, yah, we don't see all this human flesh. We are, I think, like Roman emperors. It's not, you know, this . . . thing has made me a better person. I'm still me. The Rana that loves fashion. Everything that happens teaches us something,' she said. 'Everything.'

There was a lull in our conversation. Finally, she said, 'You're a judge, yes? You punish people.'

'I have to sentence them,' I replied. 'When they break the law.'

She waited, absorbed my answer, said, 'What if all this is so I am punished?'

'You? Punished for what?'

'Because I didn't try to help her.'

'Her?'

'That girl in our school. She was deep, deep lonely. All she wanted was a friend.' Rana paused, said, 'Do you believe in fate?'

'How do you mean?'

'Like the Romans did.'

I was tempted to say, 'I'm not Roman.' But it was too glib, too easy. I want to believe we are the authors of our lives. Heavily circumscribed by society and circumstance, influenced by genes, but still with power to change things, do things, be things. It's hard to say that convincingly to someone who has experienced what Rana has. I invoked a Greek, not a Roman. I used a method handed down to us by the man famed to be the wisest who ever lived because he knew that he knew nothing – Socrates. I was troubled by Rana's belief that the implacable hand of fate had inflicted all this on her. So I did what Socrates encouraged us to do: I asked a question.

'The other girls in your class,' I said, 'what has happened to them?'

'Some are still at uni, some married, some have children.'

'Do you think they are being punished?' She was silent. 'At least you tried to speak to her,' I said.

'Someone said she hangs out on Facebook,' Rana said. 'Do you think I should search her up?'

'What do you think?'

'I think I should search her up.'

'I think that sounds like a plan,' I said.

At the time of writing this, I don't know whether Rana has found that other girl. She'll tell me when she's ready, I'm pretty confident of that. At the other end of the connection, I heard a voice, a few words from another room. It was Rana's mother. I couldn't hear what she said. I didn't need to. I never saw her mother or the fruit trees. It is enough to know they are there.

Later, on Rana's suggestion, I looked up the passage that fired her imagination. Edward Gibbon, born in Putney in 1737, writes of the birth of his magnum opus, 'It was among the ruins of the Capitol that I first conceived the idea of a work that has amused and exercised near twenty years of my life.'

Rana's own long work continues. It is now some years since the attack and her mother hasn't stopped crying about what happened to her daughter the day she went shopping for her birthday present. She never will. Life marks us. But the trees in their garden still flower and fruit and the seasons slowly turn them away from that time of torment and pain.

Trajan's Forum, Rome

Once, in a courtroom that rattled with the final approach of airliners to one of the world's busiest airports, I sentenced a man to prison. After I'd done so, he stood there in the dock and bowed and thanked me. Something quietly passed between us that I didn't understand at the time. He had let down his family terribly, thrown away his freedom and his reputation, and I had sent him to prison. He bowed after I passed sentence, before he was led away to the cells. I thought of him after speaking to Rana. The Beholder in us also beholds itself. We look at ourselves and judge. We reserve our severest sentences for ourselves. As is required when passing sentences of imprisonment, I told him how long he would have to serve before he would be eligible for parole, for release. Perhaps it was that: the act of being told that at some point in the future there could be some release.

I kept thinking of Rana's words – everything that happens can teach – and wondered what was I learning. Around me, the news was full of images of a world in tumult. Whole populations were in motion. In an insignificant way, so was I. People in flimsy boats were crossing the Mediterranean. The water was rising. Where were they coming from? Why were they coming? Who were they?

There was a lot of extraordinary coverage, but there remained another story, I felt, that had not been told. I sent Dawn some of my favourite passages of Foucault, on 'technologies of the self' – how we can make our lives and our selves – then went searching for my travel documents: the leather wallet, the insurance policy, passport – the folded picture of Gareth. I gathered them, gathered myself, and resolved to go back. I got out my old globe and, slowly turning its surface, found the place.

PART V

THE AGGRESSOR

Werner,

I was dreaming for the second time that crabs were invading the earth. Large orange crabs coming out of the sea. Nobody cared about them at first. But, in the end, there were so many that I became scared. They covered the whole world.

A letter from Michael Goldsmith to Werner Herzog

ONE

Ordinance 72.058

When I told colleagues – human rights lawyers, international aid workers, journalists – that I wanted to go, people thought I was mad. They actually used that word – mad. The UN had said, ominously, that the country had experienced a total breakdown in law and order; it was a threat to the stability of the entire region; it risked spiralling into genocide.

When I told friends, the reaction was different. Few people even knew it existed. It is one of the greatest humanitarian crises on the planet, happening to, as Rana put it, all that human flesh, yet few of the people I spoke to even know the country exists. Those that do, don't really understand what it is – a region, an area? And those who do know, the few that do, are filled with sadness and despair. It is what the UN has described as 'the world's most silent crisis'.

As Judith Léveillée, UNICEF's Deputy Representative in the country told me, 'I've never seen such destruction before. I've been stationed in Cambodia, Albania during the Kosovo crisis,

Yemen, but nothing, *nothing*, like this. I've never seen such devastation.'

'You could see the storm coming,' Léveillée, a Canadian national, says. 'It was a narrow escape. The Sangaris [French troops] came to the country in December. If they hadn't, the blood and death would have been incredible. Everything has been pillaged, more than once. Everything destroyed, devastated. We had such a problem just to ensure the rats wouldn't eat the high protein biscuits we brought in for the hungry children. We had to weld the door to our warehouse shut every night and cut it open with blowtorches every morning, just to stop looters, militias. The worst thing, I think, was the fact that this could be a prosperous country, but there was a grab of resources by the powerful. The elites used atrocious means to keep them. Diamonds, gold, natural resources. It's a water-rich, forest-rich country – was. So much illegal logging. Large trucks with tree trunks sliced down, lying there flat out on trailers, horizontal, coming through Cameroon. Have you seen them?' I had. 'They're the forests of this beautiful country. Senior humanitarian coordinators were offered diamonds. Just like that. Right out in the open. No one was worried because there was no rule, no law. It was the Wild West, only in the middle of Africa. This forgotten country in the middle of Africa.'

The site of one of the world's worst humanitarian crises is the Central African Republic. For reasons that will become clear, I needed to go.

During my planning time, I would dream about the capital Bangui. The old French colonial city (pronounced 'bahn-ghee'), established on the *rive droite* of a massive, brooding river, the city a former playground of the country's European masters, known as Bangui la Coquette, a place of patisseries and boulangeries in the middle of Africa, but also a base for the notoriously cruel Compagnie forestière, which would ruthlessly exploit 'native employees' in rubber gathering in the dense tropical forests, where colonial administrators and private agents colluded to kidnap the workers' wives and children to concentrate the minds of the men. Many of the hostages died in unspeakable conditions.

I needed to go to the capital that takes its name from the river that runs through this troubled place, the Oubangui, a river that you've probably not heard of either, but which is one of the major tributaries of something you will certainly know. And perhaps that explains my preoccupation with it. For the Oubangui is one of the principal sources of the river Congo.

The Central African Republic, also known as CAR, is a landlocked sprawl right at the heart of Africa. When European colonial maps were drawn up in the great 'scramble for Africa', at the solemn conferences convened by rapacious European powers in Berlin between 1884–85 and Brussels in 1890, the area that is now the Central African Republic was little more than a blank.

But that is a European thing. People have lived in this area for many thousands of years. They have raised their children, and loved and eked out a life on the undulating plains – the vast 'prairies' as André Gide once famously called them – or in the tropical rainforests of the south-west, inhabited by pygmy hunter-gatherers, the great Aka people, whose oral histories are proclaimed by UNESCO as one of the masterpieces of humanity.

These rainforests are one of the world's few remaining great natural sanctuaries, described by the Pulitzer Center as 'one of the last truly wild places'. *National Geographic* put it more starkly, it is 'the last place on earth'. But now large areas of the country have been devastated and I needed to go. I was about to pay the airfare to Bangui – the flights are infrequent and inconvenient – when I got the call. As it happens, I was in France, visiting friends who live on a wonderfully wooded bank of the Seine, downstream from Paris.

My legal colleague back in the UK said down the phone, 'Dex, I can hardly hear you. What's that music?'

I put my hand over my ear. 'Dancing fountains. They just spring up and this deafening music plays.'

We were doing the obligatory while in the area – visiting Versailles. Miss L was right: it was stunning, obviously. But I thought also about the horror, the persecutions the Sun King ordained along with the fountains.

'Yes, very interesting,' he said. He wasn't the slightest bit interested. 'Just wondering, have you seen the Foreign Office warning?'

'What warning?'

'On that place you're going.'

'What does it say?'

'It's dressed up in the usual lily-livered officialese.'

'But what does it say?'

There was a pause. 'Well. . . Don't go.'

There is not a single mile of railway track in the Central African Republic. There are fewer paved roads than anywhere else on the entire African continent. So travel might be tough; travel some-times is. I looked at the Foreign and Commonwealth Office (FCO) travel advice site. The map of any particular country can be coloured three ways, coded for three advisory levels. Green means it is broadly safe to travel, but check advice on, for example, health risks before travel. A yellow warning means that the FCO advises against all but essential travel. Don't go unless you absolutely have to. And then there is red.

In official terminology it indicates that the FCO 'advises against all travel'. Do not go. Some countries, say Nigeria, where the majority of the country is green, including the capital Abuja and the coastal city of Lagos, have trouble hotspots. There are patches of yellow or red – in Nigeria's north-east, for example, where Boko Haram operates.

I checked the map of the Central African Republic – perhaps I could avoid the hotspots. At that point, such was my plan. I looked again at the map: the entire country was red. Every inch of it lurid red. I looked down through the FCO's country summary:

> British nationals should leave now if practical means are available, if it is safe to do so, and if a safe destination is available. Those who remain should take all precautions and maintain sufficient stocks of food and water. Those who remain or visit against our advice should be aware that the FCO is not able to provide consular services nor organise or assist your evacuation from the country.

It didn't sound promising. The site was being constantly updated. I checked it for the latest advice. It was just as bleak:

> There have been a number of kidnappings of government ministers and humanitarian and UN workers.

But this was an official site. Don't governments err on the side of caution to safeguard their citizens? I spoke to someone who knows someone I know. He works for the Foreign Office, on one of the Africa desks. What's the inside story on the Central African Republic?

'Take the advice seriously,' he said. 'It's based on the government's best intelligence.'

'Well, there's nothing like the government's best intelligence,' I said.

'Human rights lawyer to the end, eh? Okay, what's your security plan and exit strategy?'

'*Security* plan?

'Yes, security plan.'

'I'm visiting. I'm not planning a coup.'

'You need contingency planning.'

'I *am* taking out travel insurance,' I said.

He laughed. 'Please tell me you're going to do a proper security risk assessment. Who's assessing the mission risk?'

'Come on.'

'You need to walk through all the steps. I know it's not glamorous and save-the-worldsy. It might just save your life. What vehicles will you be met with? Who will be your guards – government or private contractor? If so, who? How many? How many armed? What weapons? Have you formulated the evacuation plan? The FCO is not going to Black Hawk Down you. We're not coming in to get you. You're just not that important an asset. You're on your own in there.'

I thanked him – as it happens, genuinely. He'd opened my eyes. It mattered not a jot to him – we'd never met before.

'I'm still getting insurance,' I said. 'What if they lose my luggage?'

He laughed. 'Just don't fucking go.'

As pitches go, it was persuasive. I'll give him that. But then – as your mind does when you really, really want to do something – I began to construct all the counterarguments: doesn't he, at the end of the day, work for the government? Wasn't this the repetition of the official party line? Aren't civil servants, however well intentioned, paid to play it safe – I'd seen that in dozens of legal cases: institutional caution. I needed a second opinion.

I contacted good friends, South Africans, with connections in conservation and commerce throughout sub-Saharan Africa. They would know – or would know people who did. I sent a text, as casual as I could make it. Greetings from Paris. How are things? Is Steffan back in London? Oh, I'm thinking of heading on over to CAR – any views?

Very rapidly, a text came back 'Do NOT go.'

Then more details: 'My friend's conservation team had three deaths, one ear cut off, and four kidnappings in six months.'

Curiously, what resonated with me was that single detail: an ear cut off. It tallied with my research into the human rights history of the Republic. For on 29 July 1972 President-for-Life, dictator – later self-appointed 'Emperor' – Jean-Bédel Bokassa, like a mad medieval monarch, or the more savage of the Caesars, introduced Ordinance 72.058:

1. One ear amputated for first offence of theft.
2. Other ear amputated for second offence of theft.
3. Right hand amputated for third offence of theft.

These 'operations' were to be performed with scissors and knives within 24 hours of the sentence being passed. In its *World Population Prospects* published in 2011, the UN's Department of Economic and Social Affairs listed the 194 countries of the world in order of life expectancy. The Central African Republic came 194th. And this was *before* the sectarian violence really degenerated into mass violence in the next 18 months.

Médecins Sans Frontières witnessed the execution of one health-care worker and violent attacks on humanitarian staff. Camille Lepage, 26, a freelance French journalist whose work has appeared in *Le Monde* and the *New York Times*, travelled independently to CAR. In May 2014, she was found in the back of a militia jeep. Lepage had been murdered in the west of the country, near the Cameroon border. It was where I was hoping to go. As I was planning the trip, a 67-year-old French woman, an aid worker for the charity Caritas, was kidnapped in Bangui at gunpoint. As Judith Léveillée said, there were 'unprecedented levels of attacks on humanitarian workers'.

Thus the grim picture was more or less complete. And yet there was the persistent pull of the centre of Africa, the continent which is, as Graham Greene puts it, 'the shape of the human heart'. And that was ultimately the thing I wanted to explore, not all of that pulsing organ, but a tiny corner – and something that may or may not be part of it: aggression. I had to find another way.

But it wasn't as pure as intellectual curiosity. There's a perverseness and pigheadedness in us. Something that bristles when we're told no, no you don't, don't you dare. I wanted to try and know this unknowable place. What is such preoccupation for? It became my mission: to find another way to access this land of dereliction and cruelty, of lynchings and amputations, where people have been burnt alive and impaled; where churches and mosques have been incinerated, but which is also a place of unimaginable natural beauty, home of lowland gorillas, forest-dwelling elephants and almost extinct antelopes. That then was my mission: to reach the last place on earth.

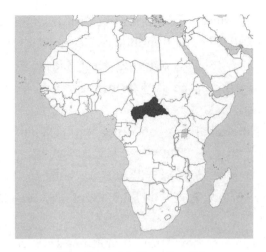

The Central African Republic

This is an account of that other way.

Almost at the end, when Patrice and I met for the last time, the rubble-strewn truck stop had disintegrated into a muddy mess. During the night it had rained, angry tropical rain. I couldn't complain: it was the rainy season, even if the 'low' one. Puddles formed in the cratered surface. They began emitting faint wisps of vapour in the heat. Sullen birds squatted in roadside trees. They seemed dark blue in the early light, crosses between crows and jays with strange elongated heads, but in truth I didn't know what the birds in this continent actually were. We were a little distance outside Yaoundé, the capital of Cameroon, 265 miles north of the equator.

On my first arrival, my guide and contact François, a huge jovial man, told me as we were driving up yet another of Yaoundé's many inclines, 'Is known as the Rome of Central Africa. The City of Seven Hills. We're very proud, proud of our city.'

It's hard to see far in Yaoundé precisely because of those hills, some covered with the hint of the many mysteries of the tropical rainforests that cover vast tracts of the country.

'That way,' François said, pointing over his shoulder with his massive bejewelled hand, 'Republic of Congo, Gabon, Equatorial Guinea. There,' he said, pointing west, 'so much water, Gulf of Guinea. Up there,' he said, pointing north-west and north, 'Nigeria, Chad. Lake Chad too.'

But it was the east I was concerned with. 'What's over there?' I asked.

François paused. Perhaps without his realising, his foot eased off the accelerator. 'There?' he said. 'Nothing.' He paused again. 'Everything.'

I would later learn how both his answers were true. But freshly arrived from fair London, I could not begin to understand. For to the east, Cameroon shares a long and poorly policed border with – for want of a better word – chaos.

If you drive from Yaoundé in an easterly direction, after a few hours you will reach the Central African Republic. François, who lived in Yaoundé, had links with the CAR community which I didn't at first fully understand. He loved playing old Motown music as we were driving. It was through him that I met Patrice.

At the truck stop at the other end of my trip, at our final meeting, Patrice and I approached each other from opposite directions, like envoys from two worlds. The sullen birds watched, were silent.

'Amazing morning,' I said to him.

He half-agreed by shrugging as if to say, 'What do you expect?'

'Okay, okay, you want amazing?' For some reason I didn't entirely understand, over time a competitive edge had developed between us. I took my iPhone out of my jeans pocket. 'Look at this,' I said, pointing the device up to the sky. 'I'll show you amazing.'

He pressed his face up to it. I clicked on the app and suddenly on the screen an extraordinary array of stars appeared.

'You can't see them in the sky now, but they are there,' I said. 'The app tells you what is the name of every major star in the sky.'

'And for you, this is amazing?'

The names of stars, presently invisible in the morning light, started to appear on the star field on the screen – Sirius, Andromeda, Perseus. My interest in space was sharpened by reports that the New Horizons space probe was approaching Pluto after nine years of lonely travel. 'In the UK,' I said, 'for years – all my life I can remember – there is this big star I see at night. I thought it was what we call the Pole Star, this big thing in the sky we see all the time, often near the moon, but I was wrong.'

Every now and then the air around us quivered with the tremendous disturbance of a truck cab hauling the wheeled carcass behind it out of the yard, sniffing out the way to a *route nationale*. Some were laden with huge tree trunks, terrible piles of them, horizontal, bleeding sap. Some trucks trek south, through Gabon, Equatorial Guinea, Angola, even to South Africa. Others go in the opposite direction, up towards Chad, or through Nigeria, towards the Sahara, Niger, Libya and onwards all the way to the Med.

'That light,' I said, 'it wasn't a star.'

'*Pas une étoile?*' he said. Not a star?

'No, a planet. The planet Jupiter.'

He looked at me and was silent. On the road, the vehicles ground their wheels left or right, east or west, to another part of the vast and waiting continent.

In the wet earth beneath our feet, I drew a circle with my finger. 'That's the Sun, okay?' It was surfacing at that very moment from the horizon to the east, rising out of the very heart of Africa, a pale, serene semicircular disc. I drew another blob in the mud and a tight orbit around the Sun. 'The planet Mercury,'

I said, and drew more. 'Venus, us – Earth, Mars, and then this one, the biggest one: Jupiter. It's the biggest thing in our solar system, bigger than all the other planets put together. It is in our sky every night. I had been looking at this light in the sky for many years and didn't know what it was. But the app has told me it is Jupiter. For me, that is amazing.'

I didn't even get the chance to tell him what else I knew: how Jupiter was observed through a telescope for the first time by Galileo Galilei in 1610, that he realised it had its own moons, and that this was a definitive moment in the history of an utter revolution in thought that challenged received wisdom, that challenged power, dogma, superstition, uncritical thinking – that seeing this light in the sky, the same thing I'd been looking at, was a flaring moment of freedom. I wanted to tell him about Pluto – man's mechanical envoy, the New Horizons probe, about to reach there, an incredible feat. I didn't have a chance to tell him any of this. Because he spoke.

'In Africa,' Patrice said, 'we don't need phones to see stars.'

I was quiet for a while with the rebuke.

'You're lucky,' I said.

Patrice, this son of Central Africa, a self-styled 'man of business', who would reveal to me one of the handful of most perilous human journeys in the underground history of our times, paused. He had told me how he had killed a man in the Central African Republic. He looked around. In that moment, no one was near us. Unnervingly, nothing moved and no one was watching, except those birds in the trees, whose names I did not know. They stared disapprovingly. But otherwise on the fringes of a city teeming with 2 million souls, we were momentarily alone.

'I will show you amazing,' he said.

And he did.

TWO

The Golden Box

The Kinsman. The Perceiver of Pain. The Ostraciser. The Tamer of Terror. The Beholder. What else? What more? Is there a system in the human brain that foments and feeds aggression? If so, why is it there? What is it like? What, in the end, can we know about it? When I sit in the criminal court as a part-time judge, I see violence in a hundred different forms. Where does it come from?

On 9 February 1864 the evening edition of the *Adams Sentinel and General Advertiser* in Pennsylvania ran a story on page four about the birth of Queen Victoria's fifth grandchild, a boy. The *Advertiser* stated that such was the bountiful fecundity of Victoria and her children that the royal succession seemed assured. On the same page, a story from closer to home appeared. It was about a discovery made in the local Pennsylvanian meadows.

The report stated that '28,000 muskets have been gathered upon the fields'. That is a lot of muskets. The firearms were gathered up after a plainly very substantial armed confrontation. The newspaper continued:

> Of these 24,000 were found to be loaded, 12,000 containing two loads, and 6,000 from three to ten loads. In many instances half a dozen balls were driven in on a single charge of powder.

The fields in question were situated to the south of the county seat of Adams borough, a town called Gettysburg.

So here's the thing: in this defining battle of the American Civil War it appears that thousands upon thousands of muskets were loaded but not fired. Many thousands were loaded again and again and not fired. What was going on?

Could the soldiers with these muskets not fire them? Did they not have the chance to fire? Or was it something else? Was it that in the fields to the south of the town of Gettysburg, thousands of soldiers could not *bring* themselves to fire? And if not, why not?

For almost as long as she could remember, Saira wanted a golden box. It was not real gold, but to her youthful eyes looked like it, and more than anything in the world that is what she wanted after her baby brother died.

They lived in a town in the east-central region of the Central African Republic, an area dominated by the great Kotto River with its thunderous falls and racing rapids. When her father took her to see the waterfalls, the sunlight bounced and darted off the tumbling water. She stood hand in hand with him laughing as a pleasing, fine spray coated them.

Her father was short-sighted and had to take off the thick glasses he habitually wore. 'He says to me, "Never forget, Saira, we are people of the first land. Africa is the first land."'

The way her father spoke about it, it was a land of light and water – the very opposite of the 'dark continent' that *les Européens* called it. There were constantly brilliant expanses of sky above them; light everywhere, even caught in the tiniest things, even trapped in the rock beneath them – in diamonds. For Saira lived in one of the country's two principal diamond-mining areas. Her father was part of the diamond supply and purchasing chain in which the country's Muslim minority population flourished.

Her father dreamed of one day seeing the wide boulevards of Paris – a rep from a diamond-buying office, possibly a Lebanese, had once lived there. In Paris, the man said, was a metal bar that was exactly one metre long. The Lebanese knew because his 'friend' studied science in Paris. Saira's father thought they were men who liked other men, but he couldn't be sure, and it didn't matter anyway. He was progressive in his views. As for Saira, she thought many metal bars would be one metre long – so what? No, her father said, this was the *first* metre ever. It was an extra-ordinary thought: the first metre ever.

The buying office, the Bureau d'Achat de Diamant en Centrafrique, is more simply known as Badica. In the Central African Republic, this was the principal diamond supply chain: miner – collector – Badica – commercial market (eventually, usually, Antwerp) – the world. Thus the diamonds you see on the fingers of young women in Europe and North America could have come from the Central African Republic, from Saira's home region.

'The miners find the diamonds hiding in our soil,' Saira said. 'My father, he says, "See, Saira, we come from the same soil. We are like diamonds."'

The friend of the possibly gay Lebanese man was almost right about the metre bar in Paris. But why is a metre a metre at all? In 1791 the

French Academy of Sciences, in a post-Revolutionary fervour to start everything afresh, decided the new measurement of length – the metre – would be one ten-millionth of the distance of the earth's circumference from the North Pole to the equator running through Paris – thus reaching the equator just to the west of the Central African Republic. Although there were earlier metre bars placed in the National Archives in Paris (the Parisian student was right about that), in 1889 a new improved one made of 90 per cent platinum and 10 per cent iridium was devised. It was not in Paris but Sèvres. Nowadays, however, the length of a metre is defined by wavelength and the speed of light in a vacuum.

One hundred and fifty kilometres – 150,000 metres – below the earth's crusted surface, in its mantle, is a region of intense pressure where diamonds are formed. Here carbon is crushed in temperatures of 1,500°C. Something new is created: a lattice structure – a diamond. The hardest naturally occurring substance on the planet.

It is from this nether region of banished light that diamonds begin their journey to the ring on the finger of a newly engaged young woman on Fifth Avenue or Bond Street. But before coming to rest on a black velvet cushion in a deftly lighted showcase, the stone is propelled out of its subterranean combustion chamber in vents – 'pipes' – of kimberlite, a molten volcanic rock. It appears in unprepossessing and unexpected spots – for the unstoppable molten rock does not care. And one of the principal places where these crushed carbon crystals meet the light is the Central African Republic.

Some mysterious blessing – perhaps it is a curse – has ordained that significant proportions of the diamonds found in CAR are amongst the most brilliant and clear in the world. They are superior to industrial diamonds. They are destined for gemstones, for jewellery in the luxurious adverts of glossy magazines. Overall,

Central African diamonds are particularly *precious* precious stones. And that has been part of the problem.

Saira went to school and was good at her studies. Her father insisted that she was attentive to her work. To supplement the lessons, he used to read to her at night. He told her that books were more precious than diamonds. And she did agree, but that didn't stop her wanting the golden box.

'One year I was playing in the street and I trip and fall. There in the ground is a broken bottle. It is bit in, bit out. I fall on it and it cuts my hand. I scream and scream. My father, he is so calm. He says so quietly, "It is all right, Saira. It is all right." He uses the things [she indicates tweezers] and he takes out the broken glass from my hand. Then he washes the hand and wraps it up. It hurts, but my father kisses me on the top of the head and I stop crying.'

She had to go to the clinic in the big town, where she had stitches. Today she still has the scar.

'The next day he comes back after work. He has his hands behind his back and says, "Saira, I have something for you, but you must find it." I run around behind his back and there he is holding the box. I take it and look at it. It is so beautiful and I am pleased. But he says, "You haven't found it." I say, "I have," pointing to the box. "No, *look*, Saira," he says.'

And she did. She slowly unclasped the lid. Inside the box was empty except for a note, on see-through, thin blue-lined paper, folded over and over again. Slowly, carefully, Saira unfolded it. In her father's elegant, meticulous hand it simply said: *Tout est possible* – Anything is possible.

She finds it hard to speak about it because there was no escaping the fact: diamonds gave her family its living; they could afford the box because of them. But it was diamonds – the insatiable lust for the glinting light trapped in these chips of rock – that was contributing to the carnage and bloodshed around her.

Villages were being destroyed. People were being destroyed. Even ideas were. For example, she thought she understood the idea of being a child. But some children around her were changing. They were joining armed groups. They were becoming soldiers, fighters, killers. Was everyone, she wondered, deep inside a killer? Was everyone, somewhere inside, filled with aggression?

They discovered the remains when they were building a dam.

It was the Aswan High Dam, soaring 364 feet above the Nile waters and stretching from bank to bank in an imperious curtain of stone, the ambition of which the great pharaohs themselves would have understood.

The building of the dam submerged the original site of the Egyptian temple complex at Abu Simbel built by the mighty Ramses II, and the ruins had to be relocated. But there were other sites threatened with inundation. In particular, three of them, two on one side of the river, another on the opposite bank. During the preservation project at Jebel Sahaba in what is now northern Sudan, the conservation team found the remains of 24 women, 19 men and 13 children. There were also a further three people who could not be satisfactorily identified – too many of their bones were missing.

The skeletons were carbon-dated as approximately 13,000 years old. Getting on for half of the people who have been lying there for these millennia had died a violent death. A team of research anthropologists from a number of universities, from Liverpool to Alaska, have pored over these remains from the shifting sands, as perhaps others will one day pore over us. They found wounds to the back and skull, coming through the jaw and neck. One body had 39 pieces of flint lodged within it from arrows and spears. It was a brutal death.

Jebel Sahaba is on the fringes of the Sahara Desert. Experts on Early Egypt from the British Museum state that this Nubian cemetery, Site 117, is the earliest evidence we have of mass human violence, of coalitional killing – of war. And now, 13 millennia later, you can go and see the slaughter. The remains of people slain at Jebel Sahaba are displayed in Room 64 of the British Museum.

Why were parents killed with their children at this site; why this aggression; why these acts of war? Why any? Inside us is there a system, an adaptation, an Aggressor?

THREE

Like a Torch

In May 1986 a group of 20 of the world's most prominent social and natural scientists met at the 6th International Colloquium on the Brain and Aggression to examine questions such as those posed by Site 117. The conference was held in what was once an ancient Phoenician settlement in the Andalusian region of southern Spain. The city has a harbour 50 miles from the sea, and it was from here, in Seville in 1519, that Ferdinand Magellan set off for the first circumnavigation of the globe. The Colloquium statement – it came to be known as the Seville Statement on Violence – was jointly drafted by ethologists, behavioural geneticists, neurophysiologists and political and social psychologists. It read:

> It is scientifically incorrect to say that we have inherited a tendency to make war from our animal ancestors . . . that war or any other violent behaviour is genetically programmed into our human nature . . . [and] that humans have a 'violent brain'.

The Statement was promulgated during the UN's International Year of Peace. In 1989 it was adopted by UNESCO at its 25th General Conference Session. The pronouncement has become a touchstone, a totem, a creed – almost a prayer from a beleaguered planet to the better part of ourselves.

Five years later, between 800,000 and 1 million human beings were massacred in 100 days in Rwanda, and the world, including the same UN institutions, looked on and did – effectively – nothing. The next year, 1995, saw what the International Criminal Tribunal deemed the genocidal killing of Bosnians by Serb para-military 'Scorpion' units. A huge white stone stands in silent memorial of the Srebrenica massacre. It has the number 8372 carved into it, the number of people killed in the worst act of ethnic cleansing Europe has witnessed since the Holocaust.

In the following 20 years we have seen a pestilential number of conflicts, not necessarily between first-rank power blocs, but smaller wars, often internecine, that have been marked by extraordinary and escalating brutality. What has been remarkable is not necessarily the number of casualties, but the nature and extent of atrocity. No doubt most reasonable people would prefer the Seville Statement to be right. We don't want a world, or to belong to a species, programmed for war. Indeed the Seville Statement itself was animated by a genuine professional responsibility felt by its authors to address 'the most dangerous and destructive activities of our species, violence and war'. However, despite those laudable intentions, it has subsequently received heavy criticism. Harvard psychologist Steven Pinker believes it suffers from 'moralistic fallacy'. Elsewhere it has been said to be the product of 'ideology and fear'.

But if we put the arguments from each camp to one side for the moment, we are bound to observe that something has been happening on the planet around us. The world has been witnessing chronic outbursts of human aggression that is localised, severe and atrocious. These bouts of concentrated violence provide a vivid if alarming insight into the functioning of human aggression. And in this dismal catalogue of atrocity, one of the most atrocious is the Central African Republic.

Saira had been the proud owner of her golden box for two years when there was terrible conflict in her town. Rebels and armed groups began sweeping in from the north and east. People also spoke darkly about even more terrifying dangers from the south-east: the LRA – the Lord's Resistance Army of Joseph Kony from Hanifa Nakiryowa's homeland, Uganda. They made repeated raids into CAR. They terrorised the local population. They were brutal and merciless.

'My father comes into my bedroom with my mother one day and says, "We may have to leave, Saira." But I love my town. My friends are here, I tell him. "It has become too dangerous to stay," he says. I ask why these people make so much trouble for our town.'

Saira said that her father was unable to answer the question. It was too big a question. There was too much to say, so he said none of it. She really became worried when he, a scholar and a man who liked science, began keeping a big stick behind their door. She asked another question.

'What do they want?' she asked.

'Everyone,' he said, 'wants diamonds.'

And, in respect of the Central African Republic and the roots of so much of the bloody turmoil, he was right.

There are many explanations for what has caused the chaos in the Central African Republic, just as there are still many theories about the causes of World War I, the French Revolution or the assassination of John F. Kennedy.

There are, however, a few reliable fixed points in the ground. The Central African Republic was formerly the French colony of Oubangui-Chari, part of French Equatorial Africa. It finally gained independence in 1960, and then suffered from a series of more or less corrupt and ineffectual presidents, including the infamous Jean-Bédel Bokassa, who crowned himself emperor in a ceremony with white horses, Napoleonic uniforms and a crown of diamonds that in total cost one-third of the country's entire GDP. It is easy, however, to mock post-colonial excess and extravagance in Africa and forget the deep scars of decades and centuries of colonial exploitation and enforced servitude.

Military misrule was replaced in 1993 by civilian control, but in 2003 the head of the armed forces, General Bozize, mounted a successful coup. There was deep dissatisfaction with Bozize's privileging of a narrow ethnic and political elite in the capital Bangui to the neglect and exclusion of the north-east of the country, which is predominantly Muslim. A number of rebel and bandit groups began fighting Bozize rule in that relatively remote region, which had weak Bangui control. This phase of the conflict came to be called the Central African Bush War. The rebel groups were involved in looting and plundering, particularly targeting the lucrative mining areas of the north-east. In 2012 several of these entities banded together to form an alliance – a 'seleka' in the local Sango language (sometimes the group's name is written Séléka). They began advancing towards the capital. They were principally Muslim in composition and contained adventurers and warlords from Chad and Sudan. In March 2013, the rebels having surrounded Bangui, Bozize fled to Yaoundé in Cameroon and Seleka's leader Michel Djotodia, a Muslim, suspended the constitution and dissolved the National Assembly.

Djotodia proclaimed himself head of state. There then followed a little under a year of violent and bloody Seleka rule.

But back in 2010 in Saira's town in the north-east, and despite her father's warnings, nothing seemed to happen. After several weeks, Saira asked her father whether the rebels would still come. 'He looks up to the sky, like this [she points her nose to the clouds], like he sees if there is something in the wind.'

And still for a while nothing happened. She went to school, though numbers were dwindling as many of her fellow pupils left. Then it all happened very quickly. Vehicles swept into town.

Jeeps and trucks. One was right outside their house. Two men kicked open the door. Her father grabbed the long stick behind the door. A man with a rifle hit her father a sickening blow to the side of the head. He collapsed. His glasses flew off.

'He says to my father, "Where are the diamonds?" This was my father's fear, that people speak about him and diamonds. The men pull my father up so he is kneeling. "*Go*, Saira, *go*," my father says, but quietly. "Where are the diamonds?" the other man says. "I do not keep diamonds," my father says. The man, he hits him with the rifle again. My father falls. The other man, he tries to grab me. I run through the door. So many people of our village are in the street. They lie there, face in the ground – right in the middle of the road. Men have feet in their back. They stand on them. I am running. I do not know where is my mother. I hear gunshots. I do not know what happens to my father.'

She ran up a small hill, and when she looked back from the higher ground, her home was burning like a torch. There were gunshots. Unseen people cried out. Smoke and flame rose – she could almost reach out and touch it all. She hid in the bush until dusk.

She wanted to go back, but there was a group of other villagers who told her in whispers that she would be killed. The rebel group had taken over the village. Smoke curled slowly over the huts. It writhed up into the darkening sky. Both of Saira's parents had been killed.

Just before I left the UK for Harvard, I acted as leading counsel in a murder trial at the Old Bailey in which a young man was brutally stabbed to death because one young man (not the victim) had not acknowledged another young man (not the accused) at a car wash in north-west London. It appeared such a senseless act. So when I encountered in Boston research about 'simulating murder', I wondered why there was a need to simulate it. Is there not enough to go round? A great proportion of my legal work involves homicide; all around Saira people were killing other people. As moral philosopher Judith Thomson – she of the philosophical thought experiment, the trolley dilemma – wrote in 1989, you don't need a microscope to observe human action – you just have to look around you to see what people do.

And yet the Gettysburg rifles, and a slew of other anecdotal military accounts, suggest that even in battle, people find it hard to hurt other people. As has been often stated, the human being itself is the greatest piece of war technology, but at the same time the human mind is the greatest impediment to war.

It was this fundamental paradox that impelled Fiery Cushman and his colleagues to bring human violence into the lab, get it under experimental control – somehow to test it. To simulate murder.

*

Blood does not just flow through our bodies, it must be pushed. And due to the resistance of the vessels (the veins and arteries), like water being pushed through a pipe, it requires work to flow. If these vessels get narrower, pumping the blood requires more work: it becomes harder to keep pushing it through. And this narrowing – vascular constriction – is what happens when we are under threat or feeling stressed. It is a physical phenomenon that is of particular value when examining how we feel about harming other people.

Scientific research has demonstrated that our negative moral judgements of harmful behaviour do not derive solely from deliberative reasoning, from highly 'rational', cognitive adjudication. Our condemnation of such actions contains a strong affective – emotional – element. Researchers have sought ways to measure the extent of our negative feelings towards inflicting harm, our aversion. Of course, they can simply ask the participant. In other words, gather self-report data. But they can go further.

One of the indicators of the level of negative stress response is the total peripheral resistance (TPR) – how difficult it is to push our blood through the vascular system. This can be calculated by attaching sensors to the research participant to gauge how their blood pressure and heart responds under stress. And this in turn can provide an indication of just how averse we are to hurting someone else – how much it troubles or stresses us. To test this, Cushman and colleagues conducted a number of studies to investigate the basis for our aversion.

But it's one thing to say we are reluctant to harm other humans, and another to understand why. When entering this critical scientific and moral conversation, Cushman recognised that the dominant view is that our aversion stems from empathy for the 'victim'. Put another way: if we don't inflict harm it is because of concern for the victim. That is certainly part of the answer in real-life situations – as we saw with the Perceiver of Pain. But there is something more.

Cushman's colleagues tested 108 participants by strapping them up with ECG and blood pressure sensors. First, they calibrated their individual characteristic response to stress, as there is some variation from person to person. To check this, they asked them to count backwards quickly in multiples of 7. It was a little like this:

Start at 1296.
Now count back 7.
The first one is easy: 1289.
But do it rapidly. Next?
1282. Next?
1275 . . . 1268.

In just typing this, I am conscious of what researchers call 'enhanced cardiac performance': my heart beating faster. I was also holding my breath. I'm going to guess you were pretty much the same. So the counting-back-in-sevens ordeal provides a pretty good baseline of the extent to which our individual bodies variously cope with stress.

Next, they invited the participants to perform 'simulated non-harmful actions'. Cushman's team devised some zingers. One research assistant wore what looked like an ordinary pair of trousers. The research volunteer then was given a real hammer. He or she was told to hit the leg of the lab assistant. Hard. It was made absolutely clear that there was a PVC pipe under the trouser leg. Hitting the research assistant as hard as possible would do no harm. But there was reluctance. It was hitting what looked like someone's leg.

In other simulations, the research assistant's hand had to be smashed with a downward blow from a rock. A real rock. A fake hand. But again reluctance. Real reluctance. Then a replica metal handgun, realistic in detail and weight, had to be fired into the assistant's face; a knife (rubber) had to be used to cut across the assistant's throat; a baby (fake) had to be smashed on the table edge.

Through all this, the experimenter emphasised that no harm was being done. Nevertheless, there was significant TPR reactivity: blood vessels were constricting. This vasoconstriction when no conceivable harm could be done tells us something of prime importance.

People are not just concerned with outcomes. It is not just about empathy. Their blood vessels narrowed, their blood pressure and stress levels went up, even when they performed acts they *knew* could not cause the slightest harm. The baffling battlefield phenomenon of the unfired rifles begins to make sense. There are certain actions that we just cannot bear to do. Actions that we deprecate even where there is no identifiable harmful consequence. For example, at Gettysburg the rifles could have been aimed high over the heads of the advancing enemy soldiers and fired without causing harm. But perhaps it was the mere act of pulling the trigger that added to the reluctance – whether or not anyone would be harmed.

Therefore firing (disabled) handguns; hitting a leg (in a PVC sleeve) with a hammer; cutting at people's throats with (rubber) knives; we find it stressful to do all this. It is what Cushman and colleagues call 'action aversion' – a reluctance to do the act itself, whatever the consequence. Thus it is certainly true that our moral condemnation of harmful actions in significant part comes from imagining the pain of others, but that is not the whole picture.

We also envisage what it would feel like *for us to perform the act.* It is our revulsion at imagining ourselves being the killer – and not just imagining the suffering of the victim.

The shadow side of this is what happens to us when the actions are not direct and visceral and recognisably associated with harm. What about surgically cold killings and executions by distant drones? Disassociating us – distancing ourselves – from our target makes it easier to kill. And that is a danger in itself – as is performing an act (like pushing a button) we don't commonly associate with tremendous harm. But highly mechanised remote killing is the exception. The pushing-a-button paradigm is a modern innovation, even if it is how we may think of modern warfare. But it is not typical. It is not, on average, how people kill other people in conflicts on the planet today.

Today's conflicts are predominantly not highly automated fantasies of virtual wars fought on computer screen at a remove of hundreds or thousands of miles. Most warfare today is the exact opposite. It is personal. It is one on one. It is often hand-to-hand killing, using knives and machetes. It is bloody and brutal. It is full of mania and mutilation. It is standing on someone lying face down in a village street and shooting them in the back of the head. It engages the kind of actions that research shows us we are highly averse to. And yet it happens. At this very moment in conflict after conflict around the world, just like in Saira's town. Why is this the case?

One way to gain insight into this is to ask a simple question: to what extent do we identify ourselves with insects?

FOUR

You'll Like Him

The kaleidoscope of chaos that swept up and destroyed Saira's family in the Central African Republic was a confusing jumble of letters. Acronym after acronym, different rebel factions with portentous names, distinguished by two things: their letters, and the brutality of their predation.

There was the UFDR, the Union of Democratic Forces for Unity (or the equivalent in French). They claimed to be protesting about the Bangui government's neglect of the great swathes of land in the north and east of the country up towards Sudan and Chad. As we know, one of their leaders Michel Djotodia would later take control of CAR. They were mainly comprised of the Gula ethnic group. In response to the sectarian violence directed against their particular ethnic group (the Runga), the CPJP, the Convention of Patriots for Justice and Peace, formed.

Mining communities in the rural areas began fleeing from this group. Were they freedom fighters? Whose freedom – and what would replace it? Were they merely criminal opportunists, bandits taking advantage of the absence of any kind of meaningful government and security to enrich themselves? For people on the ground, it made little difference. They stole diamonds. There was extortion, robbery, mutilation, bloodshed. Some local people fled into the bush. Some fled back to the main town. Some were not quick enough. Saira's family was right in the path of the armed group. They were engulfed. Saira had her family ripped away from her without truly understanding why. It was 2010 and she was 14 years old.

Central African Republic, showing Kotto River,
Bangui, Bossangoa and western border with Cameroon

And what of Patrice in all this? During the unrest in the north and east, he was in the capital Bangui. He had one goal: to make money.

The unrest and rebellion was not his fight. He did not even much understand what they were fighting about – certainly didn't believe the propaganda and claims of the various sides – and did not much care. Let them fight. So long as no one bothered him, let them fight and sort it all out. ('So there is fighting? *C'est la vie.* I wish I look like an American star. What am I to do – cry? No, *c'est la vie.*') He was still doing little deals, buying low – shoes, jeans, old phones, wind-up radios – selling a bit higher, keeping anything he liked. And he particularly liked Western designer clothes, as I found out when I finally met him.

'You'll like him,' François said. He laughed. François is huge; François is enormous. He sits in his old Mercedes like a genial Sumo wrestler.

'I like everyone,' I said.

A Sumo wrestler with a gold ring encrusted hand hanging out of the driver's window of an old white saloon that he calls his limousine. 'Maybe he even likes you.' He glanced over from the steering wheel like the proud master of a magnificent sailing vessel. I never understood what a car could mean to a man until I met François. Motown blasted, as Motown needs to be blasted.

'And everyone likes you back?' François asked.

'What's not to like?' I said.

His eyebrows knitted with confusion. He briefly touched the amulet – a battered dark leather pouch, no bigger than a credit card, stitched in yellow around the edges – that hangs from the rear-view mirror. We are both speaking our idiosyncratic versions of French. Perhaps what I said was lost in translation. François is a man who can source anything, find anything, help with anything in Cameroon. He is a fixer. What V. S. Naipaul said of his travels in Iran after the Islamic Revolution, someone to 'clear the path'. In places like Yaoundé, everyone needs a François – there are many paths that need clearing. We continued driving through the capital's crazy traffic, with battered yellow cabs buzzing around us like deranged insects, stoking up the street theatre. I tried another tack.

'*Ce n'est pas grave*, if he doesn't,' I said. I'd brushed up on my French a bit since Anthony and Michael, but still blagged a few irregular verbs. 'No one likes lawyers.'

François laughed, which was better. With the deftest flick of his wrist, he steered his limousine around a gaggle of goats traipsing up the road, floored the pedal and stroked the dashboard adoringly. Never since 1885, when Karl Benz hammered and welded together the world's first petrol-propelled 'Motorwagen', has Mercedes had a more devoted customer. 'No one likes lawyers? No one likes medicine,' he said. '*Then* they need *la medicament*, eh, English lawyerman?'

After over 20 years of legal practice, that was one of the best definitions of a lawyer I'd heard: we're medicine. François rapidly became not just fixer, but food adviser, philosopher of everyday life, friend. One time, we were driving around the business area when a kamikaze taxi, its oblivious driver pressing his mobile phone against his ear like a hearing aid, almost took off François's offside. François yelled out the window.

'What did you say?' I asked.

'I wish him a good day and his lady wife good health,' he replied.

'He didn't seem too pleased.'

'Maybe he don't like his lady wife.' That was François. I was glad to be with him – though later I'd see him in a different light, a sadder one.

I had been asking him about the scorchingly hot local sauce I'd tried in the hotel – *piment* (pee-*mahn*). In fact, we were arguing about it.

'Okay, okay, I admit it's pretty impressive,' I said.

'The hottest,' François said.

'Sorry, *mon ami*, but there's this hot pepper sauce in Barbados. It will blow your head off.'

François shook his head vigorously, '*Non, non, non*, I will eat this – baby Barbados food by the spoon.'

'That,' I said laughing, 'I want to see.'

His beloved limo cut out at some lights. He turned the ignition and cajoled the beast back to life, whispered softly like one might do to a reluctant lover, *stroked* it. Soon he pulled up near a shack-cum-café of some sort next to a lay-by or yard where trucks from time to time hauled in. We'd driven out from the centre of Yaoundé and there on some white plastic chairs we waited for Patrice. François ordered a coffee. I asked for tea – '*avec du lait froid*'. It was my best effort at asking for cold milk with it. I was brought a sachet of Nido Fortifié – Nestlé powdered milk – and a teaspoon. At least I got a teaspoon.

Patrice, when he languidly walked over, moving like mercury, didn't want anything to drink. He is tall: 6 foot 2, muscular with it, not an inch of surplus flesh, *sculpted* – like he and François have done a swap, with all the excess flesh lumped at various bulging places on François. I liked François. It was easy to like him. Patrice, he was different.

'You have cigarette?' he asked after we shook hands. It would be one of the few things he ever said to me purely in English.

We met at this venue as Patrice was trying to negotiate a ride out of the country – as ever with Patrice, as I would learn, on the cheap. Hence the truck stop.

'*Désolé, fume pas*,' I said. It was true: I don't smoke.

François obliged. Offered him one from an open pack of cigarettes. Patrice took two. He tapped one on the white plastic table and put the other in the chest pocket of his white shirt. He also had white jeans and black trainers. In his mid-thirties (my estimate: I never asked), with a fully shaven head and a face full of carefully cropped designer stubble. His nose was unusually sharp, suggesting just the hint of a beak, and his skin had a slight sheen like those space-grey iPhones. He had round black reflective sunglasses.

'*Les Sangaris*,' he said, exhaling a cloud of smoke, 'they have cigarettes.'

I'd heard about Sangaris before I'd travelled out to Central Africa: Judith Léveillée had told me about them. They are the French troops sent to the Central African Republic as peacekeepers. Their name derives from the famous butterfly found in CAR, glorious, but of short duration – like the French military intervention is meant to be. We'll see.

'*Les Sangaris*,' Patrice said, 'they always tell you they don't have nothing, but you never know. I am in a line at a checkpoint . . .'

'In Bangui?' I ask.

He doesn't directly reply. Not a good start. 'And there is this long queue, and I think, How can I get a cigarette?'

Sangaris butterflies have striking red wings and are also known as Blood Red Gliders. *Sangaris* are part of the *Cymothoe* genus, which contains 82 varieties of butterfly inhabiting the tropical African forests, especially the upper canopy.

'So I go to this older Sangari. He stands on the side with his gun across his chest – *comme ça*.' He gestures. 'Never choose the very young ones. They are too scared of us, they stick to the rules. So I go up to the older Sangari. I say, "Excuse me, *monsieur*, but do you have a lighter?" I take a packet of cigarettes out of my jeans and smile. He says yes and takes out a lighter.'

The wings of *sangaris* butterflies glow bright like fire. *Sangaris* and its related cousins started splitting genetically in the late Miocene, around 7 million years ago. It was a period of tremendous change: of cooling and deforestation, and changes in tropical ocean currents.

'So he offers me his lighter. Then I say, *"Mon dieu, qu'est-ce qui se passe?* The packet is empty. *Terminé."* I show him. I say, "Do you have a cigarette, *peut-être?"'*

The same period also witnessed our human predecessors finally genetically splitting off from the last common ancestor we shared with our nearest evolutionary cousins, the great apes.

'The Sangari, he is about to say he did not, when I say, "Well, you have a lighter – why does a man have a lighter without a cigarette? Maybe I don't understand. I understand little. But it would be a great honour for me to tell my village one of our honourable guests gave me a little cigarette."'

'Did he give you one?' I asked.

'He gave me two, and then said fuck off. And I thanked him for the cigarettes and especially for the fuck off. That empty packet, it does not work every time, but it got me many Sangari cigarettes.'

I laughed. François laughed. But Patrice was not laughing. In a quietly cold voice he said, *'Donc,* what are you doing in Africa?'

François shouted something at him I didn't understand.

'It's all right,' I said.

'He is here to help,' François said.

'Oui, oui, help. The international forces, they come "to help". In Bangui, there were Chadian troops with them. They would kill us. So in CAR we know about *les étrangers* [outsiders] coming in to help.'

There was an uneasy silence between the three of us for a while. In the distance music was faintly playing, a kind of Congolese dance beat, as if mocking us with its joviality.

Patrice paused before adding, '*Vous n'êtes pas d'ici.*' Not so much a question, not even a statement, but an accusation – 'You're not from round here.'

'I'm trying to understand,' I said.

'Understand what?' Patrice said. I could see myself dully reflected in his round black sunglasses.

'The Central African Republic,' I said.

For one of the very, very few times I can recollect, Patrice took off the glasses. He massaged his eyeballs. '*Bonne chance, monsieur,*' he said.

Although *sangaris* and its bewildering variety of cousins inhabit the great wet forests of Africa, they are found in syntopy: they live together in the same locality. However, male *sangaris* butter-flies devote an inordinate amount of their short lives to internecine combat. Living in syntopy has provided a similar challenge to the humans who inhabit the same geographical area a long way beneath the forest canopy.

Patrice looked me up and down, and without any great sign of approval. 'You have more jeans in your hotel?'

'Hey,' said François.

'Couple of pairs,' I said.

'He's not here for selling clothes,' François said.

'It's not a problem,' I said.

'You will like the price,' Patrice said. 'Not a high price. But a fair price.'

'But then what will I wear?'

'Then you will go home. You have more clothes at home, *peut-être.*'

He was right. Just as he was right when he said, *Vous n'êtes pas d'ici.* I felt a very long way from home on the fringes of one of the world's bloodiest conflicts that I found hard to understand. I wondered if anyone did.

Patrice and François started arguing loudly. François had warned me earlier, '*Don't* buy, *don't* sell anything with this guy, yes?' I told him I had no such intention.

Patrice pointed to François's Merc. 'Why you have that anti-Balaka thing?' he shouted.

I didn't understand at the time, but it was a reference to the amulet.

'Is nothing to do with your stupid militias,' François shouted back.

The argument continued and I didn't catch anything else they were saying. Patrice suddenly got up, was about to go. François pulled him back with his bejewelled hand. I allowed both of them time to settle. We all checked our mobiles. Or pretended to. Patrice stubbed out the cigarette.

There was silence for a while.

The woman from the café, perhaps seeing how aghast I was with the milk powder, brought me a roasted plantain. The long banana-like fruit was pleasingly warm to the touch.

'*Pardonnez-moi, monsieur*,' she said, giving me the peace offering.

'Please, there is no need to apologise. *Je suis anglais* – we like cold milk,' I said.

Of the many things that happened to me in Cameroon, I keep returning to her small act of kindness. Perhaps it is because it sharpened the contrast with how I was feeling about Patrice. The truth is that of the many people I have encountered during the course of this book – Dawn Faizey Webster, Anthony, Jane Nicklinson, Alan Pegna, Sheldon Solomon, even Miss L – I liked all of them from the start. Patrice was the exception. So in the end François was wrong: Patrice didn't like me. The feeling was mutual.

The smell of the plantain wafted around us faintly, like chestnuts roasting on a bonfire.

'Okay, okay, he agrees,' François finally said, 'he will tell you.'

'Tell me?' I said.

'About the diamonds,' François said.

Patrice reached into the pocket of his white designer shirt, slowly took out the second cigarette, lit it, and that's when I really noticed the faint space-grey sheen to his skin.

FIVE

How Similar Are You to Small Insects?

In psychology there is a concept called target similarity. It really does get in the way of killing. Or more precisely: it does so at first.

It suggests that killing comes at a cost. Obviously externally: the adverse outcome to the victim. But internally, when we kill there is a consequence for the inflictor of harm, an implication for the sense of self, the understanding of who we are, what we are capable of.

This is particularly true where there is a perceived similarity between the perpetrator and the victim – the 'target'. Was this, perhaps, one of the obstacles to the firing of muskets at Gettysburg, with communities rent apart and cousin fighting cousin? Clinical research suggests that for soldiers, post-traumatic stress disorder (PTSD) is critically linked to feelings of guilt and shame, and this distinguishes it from many other types of PTSD. As a psychologist treating the trauma of Vietnam veterans once put it: 'You recognized you did the unthinkable. You blasted away a piece of yourself.' And this is where bugs come in.

Or more precisely: pill bugs (which you may know as wood-lice). Or more precisely still: pill bugs and an extermination machine. The research was ingenious, gruesome and really rather disgusting. But from a scientific point of view, it provided invaluable insights.

Into what? Into our reluctance to harm others and the damage it causes to ourselves – our sense of self. The extermination machine was a macabrely adapted coffee grinder. A brass pipe was fitted to the side of it, providing a chute from a white funnel above, all the way down to the machine's grinder blades. At least that was what participants were told.

In fact a carefully concealed bung prevented bug extermination. Instead, scraps of paper were preloaded in the grinder to simulate the gruesome grinding of bugs. Thus the researchers could genu-inely say: no bugs were hurt in the conduct of this research. The bugs were presented to participants in little lidless clear plastic cups, so the half-inch bugs could be inspected before extermina-tion.

Researchers at Arizona State University carefully counted how many bugs people killed in 20 seconds – or believed they killed (the bugs had been secretly dropped unharmed into a sealed container). The research volunteers were asked to answer a ques-tion on a standard 9-point scale, from (1) not similar at all, to (9) extremely similar. The question was this:

Please rate how similar/different you think you are to small insects.

I am bound to raise a minor point: pill bugs, surprisingly, are not insects. Unlike butterflies, Blood Red *sangaris* or otherwise, which are flying insects, pill bugs are actually crustaceans. They have hard exoskeletons and are more closely related to shrimps and crayfish. They are also related to crabs – just like those Michael Goldsmith, the Western journalist imprisoned in the Central African Republic during Bokassa's time, imagined in his dream, crawling out of the sea, taking over the world. While this vision of crawling crabs deeply disturbed Goldsmith, so much so that he wrote to German director Werner Herzog about it, for the purposes of experimental validity there is no evidence that we associate ourselves any more or less with crustaceans as opposed to insects, that we fear one group of such creatures more than the other.

There were two test conditions. An 'initial kill' condition, in which the participant was led to 'grind up' one bug in the extermination machine as a practice run, to gain familiarity with the process. The other was a 'no kill' condition, in which there was no practice. Now here's the remarkable thing that happened.

In Condition 1, where there was no initiation into killing, no trial run, when the participants were asked to kill as many or as few bugs as they could in a 20-second controlled extermination period, the amount of bugs they killed dropped dramatically with the degree they identified with bugs. The more they identified with bugs, the fewer they killed. That was to be expected.

In Condition 2 – the initial kill condition, where the participant was induced to get a feel for killing bugs – something remarkable happened. Not only was there not a drop-off in killing with those people who strongly associated themselves with bugs, but there was something more: a small but discernible *increase* in bug kills. An *increase*.

The more they identified themselves with the bugs, the more they killed. This finding may provide an insight into what might be happening in the Central African Republic and elsewhere. To recapitulate: those people who identified themselves *more* with the little creatures fed down the chute for extermination now tended to kill *more* of the creatures they identified with. Why? What is going on?

Sangaris butterfly (*Cymothoe sangaris*)

A variety of converging streams of evidence suggests that most of us are simply not preprogrammed to harm and kill others. It is not our 'natural' or default state. Indeed there is a respectable case to be made that the opposite is the actual position. There is support for this proposition in how the number of bugs research volunteers killed dropped off with the degree the person associated themselves with the little critters. Except . . . what about the initial kill condition? It appears on first inspection to be baffling. Until we understand the mechanism at play.

Once killing has started, it causes a 'threat' to one's sense of self – that inner cost. One way to cope with that threat, para-doxically enough, is to carry on killing. And that is why those participants who saw something of the bug in themselves ended up killing more of them. The killing continues in order to cope with – to cover up – the initial sense of transgression, the violation, the appalling recognition that you've done the 'unthinkable'. You've blasted away a little piece of yourself.

With this small insight, we can return to internecine conflict, where people begin to kill the people directly around them, their neighbours . . .

Her parents having been killed, Saira made her way to the main town, many miles away, the place her mother's sister lived. There were some government soldiers there, but not many. No one knew what would happen next. There was nowhere else that Saira could go. She was otherwise alone in the world.

For two years, Saira lived with her maternal aunt and her aunt's boyfriend. At least she had a roof over her head. She worked hard, did all the housework, but at least she had food. Her aunt was there, and although Saira didn't like the boyfriend – he had a cruel temper and would sometimes hit her aunt – at least she had a place to stay.

The boyfriend – whose name was Ahmed – used a wooden stick to help him walk since he had suffered a road accident, coming off a motorbike, which landed on and mangled his right foot. So although he could be aggressive and menacing, Saira made every allowance for him: perhaps he was in pain from the accident. And he would drink a lot, which she also put down to the accident, so when he was violent, it was due to the pain and the alcohol, and not him. That's what Saira thought.

'One night,' she said, 'I am sleeping and you know how you wake up and you don't know what makes you wake up? This happens. I am going to sleep again and I realise I had waked up because he is in the room. Ahmed is in the room. At least I think it is Ahmed. It is dark. But I see him. He stands by the door. He looks at me. "What is it?" I say. He says nothing. He moves. Then I do not see him. Dogs are barking outside. Was it the dogs who wake me up? I try to go back to sleep. Maybe is the dogs. I wonder: did Ahmed wake me up or is it the dogs? Was he even in the room?'

The next day Ahmed said nothing, nor did Saira. Then about a month later, Saira awoke again in the night. This time it was a smell. 'His smell,' she said. 'Cigarette and drink. I wake up. He is sitting on my bed. I sit up. He says, "Saira, now you are beautiful. Now you are a young woman." I say nothing. "I like to buy you something," he says. I say I want nothing. I remember the golden box I left in my home. It is the only thing I ever wanted. But I say I want nothing. Still, I tell him thank you. I think if I am polite, I will be safe.'

She was not.

'Then after that, when he . . . visits, he leaves the stick next to my head. I think he will hit me with it. I think it can break my head. But he never hits me with it.'

He did not need to. Sometimes at night, she would hum to herself, as if it were a magical chant, and would keep him away. 'Sometimes it works,' she said.

But not always?

'Not always,' she said. 'But I had nowhere else to go.'

When the molestation began, Saira was 15 years old.

For a long time in our deep evolutionary past, human beings were the hunted as well as hunters, another animal in the long food chain, and not at its top. Indeed, when our ancestors moved into the open African savannahs due to the desiccation of the forests they lived in, they were particularly vulnerable to attack and predation. But there were also new opportunities.

Evidence exists of our human ancestors hunting smaller mammals all the way back to the Pliocene epoch (which ended

2.5 million years ago). This overlaps with the first evidence of tool production. And there was likely a simultaneous combination of gathering, scavenging of larger carcasses and the hunting of smaller prey. However, around 400,000 years ago several early human species engaged in a different kind of hunting: the killing of large animals – as evidenced by the group of early humans involved in the killing of the Ebbsfleet elephant.

The hunting of animals in the wild is an arduous endeavour, involving considerable hardship, pain and privation. But today people keep hunting in all parts of the world. In virtually every remaining forager society around the world today, people hunt. In the West, certain people make great efforts to find opportunities to hunt. In doing so, they have to pay not only the financial cost, but also the opportunity cost: so much else they could do. But they hunt. They speak of its 'thrill'. Are such people dysfunctional or deranged? Or is the process, the ritual, tapping into something more primal within us?

Studies, as we will see, indicate that hunting animals produces in human beings endorphins, serotonin and testosterone, chemicals that inoculate the hunter against hardship. They surge and flow through the blood as the hunter – or hunters (it is more pleasurable to hunt in a group, in a pack) – closes in on the prey. The chemicals ease the pain; they produce pleasure – even euphoria. And then the moment comes when the game is snared, or cut or killed. A moment of completion, elation, triumph. This does not, I emphasise, mean it is a good thing, or acceptable – I have for years represented people who have fought for animal rights and liberation – but this is the mechanism. We need to understand it.

It has been the same with our closest biological kin. Chimpanzees, sharing 95 to 98 per cent of our DNA, are ruthless hunters. Harvard anthropologist Richard Wrangham noted that when hunting for small monkeys, the aggression of chimpanzees is transformed into 'intense excitement':

> The forest comes alive with the barks and hoots and cries of the apes, and aroused newcomers race in from several directions. The monkey [prey] may be eaten alive, shrieking as it is torn apart. Dominant males try to seize the prey, leading to fights and charges and screams of rage. For one or two hours or more, the thrilled apes tear apart and devour the monkey. This is blood lust in its rawest form.

But maybe that is just chimpanzee aggression. Not us.

On the other hand, consider this account of fox hunting from the *Cheltenham Examiner* on 25 March 1909.

> Captain Elwe's two children being present at the death of a fox on their father's preserves, the old hunting custom of 'blooding' was duly performed by Charlie Beacham, who, after dipping the brush of the fox in [the fox's] blood, sprinkled the foreheads of both children.

In *Killing for Sport*, a humanitarian anti-hunting tract published in 1914 with a preface by George Bernard Shaw, there is a further account of 'blooding' of a child, here of a royal princess (the account is replicated from a London newspaper):

> A pretty little girl on a chestnut cob, with masses of fair curls falling over her navy-blue habit, was the chief centre of attraction at a meet of the West Norfolk Fox-Hounds at Necton. The pretty little girl was Princess Mary of Wales, and the day will be a memorable one in her life. She motored back to Sandringham

carrying her first brush . . . Princess Mary was 'blooded' by the huntsmen, and was presented with the brush, which was hung on her saddle.

That is what happens when humans – and our closest genetic relatives – give vent to some aggressive seam within them and hunt other animals. (Intriguingly, Wrangham and colleagues found the rates of lethal violence in chimpanzee and existing human forager or subsistence societies to be similar.) But what happens when humans hunt other humans? What happens to our aggression then?

SIX

Determination and Delight

When all that started with Ahmed, Saira stopped reading, even thinking of reading. It was as though her mind was too full up.

'This is happening for about a year,' Saira said. 'I didn't do — everything with him. But then he wanted to do everything, and I said no, and he says he will tell my aunt what I am doing. I was confused, so confused. The way he says it I am thinking: yes, it is my fault. Is it my fault? What have I done? I think my father will be ashamed of me and thinking of this makes me cry. People were talking of more war. People were leaving the town, but my aunt, she was going to stay.'

Saira made a decision. 'I drop so many tears, too many for one life. So I say, No — now you will stop. The tears will stop or you will be gone.'

She was scared of staying, scared because she thought she might actually kill Ahmed. She even planned it: have a knife under the mattress, and when he came in the night and lay with her — then.

It scared her because that thought was inside her. Where did it come from? Was she like the other young people joining the militias? Was she a killer? It's not who she ever believed she was. She didn't want to be that person.

Instead, Saira ran away.

For three days and three nights Saira travelled, as in a trance, along the rough roads alongside streams of refugees, walking through the shadows of trees, beside the shadows of people fleeing the violence and aggression. Only, the teenager was also fleeing a crisis of her own. 'Sleep would not come. I kept walking, walking to find it, find it, but sleep would not come.'

It was as though she was in a fever. But she was cold inside. It was like iced fingers spreading inside her. Once she stepped over a log in the road. Then she realised it was a body. A man. He'd been shot. In his outstretched hand, he clasped some torn white cloth. Who was he and what was the cloth? What did it mean? His eyes remained open.

The strange fever got worse and the world began to fade. Saira collapsed. The people in the nearest village took her to the men who were in charge of the area. They sheltered her, fed her when she came to, although at first she could not keep down the food. They gave her new clothes.

The group had swept down from the north-east of the Central African Republic in a sandstorm of violence. It was an armed militia called Seleka. They were a loose, complex, shifting alliance of dissident and disaffected groups, including Janjaweed militia all the way from Sudan's Darfur. Others were from Chad.

When Saira joined Seleka she was 16 years old.

The historic walled city of Konstanz perches on the edge of Lake Constance in the south-west of Germany at the Swiss border. The river Rhine, with its source in the Swiss Alps, passes through the lake, which is Europe's third largest after the nearby Geneva and Balaton in Hungary. And the lake is also the reason for another cause of Konstanz's celebrity: it is a UNESCO World Heritage Site.

For around the lake there is evidence of human habitation dating back to 5000 BCE in the form of remarkably well-preserved Neolithic pile-dwellings – wooden stilt-houses. These buildings – huts on platforms that rise above the marshy lands below on long wooden piles – were constructed as precautions against flooding, rodents and other dangers. And these ancient precautions against peril and predation find a thematic unity in the work being undertaken in the research labs of Konstanz's very modern university.

It is here in the Department of Psychology that Thomas Elbert is Professor of Clinical Neuropsychology. Now in his mid-sixties, Elbert is sturdy, bearish in a reassuring way – one might say substantial. He emits the aura of a substantial man and a man of intellectual substance. The closely cropped white beard and searching eyes seem appropriate to one of the world's foremost stress and trauma experts, a veteran of fieldwork in many of the world's most incendiary and dangerous conflicts. But despite the catalogue of atrocity Elbert has investigated, he possesses an infectiously positive disposition and a talent for encapsulating esoterically complex concepts in a non-stuffy turn of phrase.

'Okay, Dexter, you ask about child soldiers. You must understand how some of them function,' he says. 'They are specialised killers. They are like that because that is how they have developed – or have been developed. What do you or I do to relax? If we have had a frustrating day? We go home, we curse our colleagues or with you, perhaps, your opponent in court, and then we have a glass of wine or a beer. For these children in armed groups, it's the same. They feel the same about going out to kill.'

I don't understand what he is saying. I ask him to explain.

'Look, they know life in the bush with the militia, with the rebels, is terrible. At any time they could be injured, killed. They have little food, medicine, shelter. It is a terrible life. And the frustration builds inside them. And when it gets worse and worse, they turn to their drug. But it is not Chardonnay or Heineken. Their drug is "combat high". Their combat addiction takes over. They go out. They fight. They kill. The frustration subsides. Until next time.'

'Children?' I say.

Elbert pauses. 'Yes, you may see them between episodes and say, oh, these are children. And they are. But then it is time to do it again.'

Elbert studied psychology, mathematics and physics at Munich, gaining his PhD in 1978. With over 400 academic publications to his name, he is a member of the German Academy of Science. His inquiry into the human mind ranges from the neurophysiology of tinnitus – the ringing we hear when nothing is actually there – to the area that has absorbed a significant amount of his research time in recent years: mental health in war zones.

The list of Elbert's research sites reads like a map of world's most brutal conflicts: Afghanistan, Sri Lanka, Rwanda, Congo, Uganda, Somalia. He and his team have interviewed rebels in Colombia, perpetrators of genocide in Rwanda, child soldiers in Uganda and also, to provide a historic comparator population, German World War II veterans. They have spoken to over 2,000 combatants. And the number keeps rising.

We speak just after I have returned from west of the CAR border, just before he is to return to east Congo (DRC).

'The thing about the Kivu area over there in DRC,' he says, 'is that for all the bloodshed and suffering, it is an unbelievably beautiful place.'

I was going to ask whether that made it worse. Having visited a similar locale, a place on the fringes of great conflict, it is hard to imagine anything making the situation worse for the people caught up in it. And yet the CAR/Cameroon border region, like Kivu, *is* indescribably beautiful. Elbert's last answer reveals what is perhaps the unifying theme of his empirical and intellectual inquiry. Beyond the innovative examination of neural anatomy, Elbert has another, largely unspoken, ambition. It is to relieve human suffering. And ultimately it is for this reason he has intrepidly ventured into highly fraught areas where he has knowingly exposed himself to physical risk.

'Blood is interesting,' Elbert says. 'It is a strong biological cue. It can be appealing or disgusting.'

'Really? Appealing?'

'Yes, and that applies whether the individual is well balanced or dysfunctional. For example, when we were in Colombia there was a client [his disarming name for an interviewee], he was an ex-combatant, and he constantly kept going back to the local hospital.'

'The hospital?' I ask, mind beginning to race. 'To see the wounded, casualties?'

'Something more,' Elbert says. 'To drink blood.' Before I can properly absorb this fact, he continues, 'Commercially, we use the smell of blood to make sausages more appealing, even mushrooms. An artificial substance that produces a chemically equivalent smell is sprayed on certain products to make them smell and taste . . . fresher. This is because we human beings have a biological preparedness for that cue – the blood cue. It probably goes back to our ancestral hunting patterns. It's still there.'

Indeed the meat in European supermarkets is artificially kept vivid red – and thus 'bloody' – by treatment with a combination of gases, including carbon dioxide, nitrogen and oxygen. The supermarket industry 'treats' such meat on display shelves with a gas cocktail in a process known in the trade as MAP – modified atmosphere packaging. In the United States, the Food and Drug Administration authorises the use of carbon monoxide (banned in Europe), a potentially lethal component of car exhausts. Small quantities, but carbon monoxide nonetheless.

MAP is an elaborate and highly sophisticated technology, treating animal flesh with just the right amount of 'food grade gases'. It is big business. And it stems directly from something deep within us. The fact is, even if individually we are not partial to eating our steak rare, we want to buy our meat bloody. In other words, when we say we want fresh meat, we actually want meat that has been freshly killed.

Elbert returns to child soldiers. 'And so with some of these children who have been in combat groups, the violence, to them it's like heroin. They relieve frustration and the pressure within them by violence and killing. You will hear them sometimes speaking about their acts, what they have done. The injuries caused, the blood spilled. Unless we acknowledge and understand that addiction, we will not be able to counteract it. And they will still crave it.'

The blood lust, in other words, will still be there.

There is a lull in our conversation. We have covered a lot of ground. It is tough terrain, dealing with trauma. We discussed briefly the orthodoxy: how violence was related to trauma. Studies of Vietnam veterans, for example, show that those who killed suffered from higher levels of PTSD than those who did not. That finding can readily be understood; it melds with the

Cushman studies, our inhibition against harming others, in itself a stressful act.

'Are the pile-dwellings worth visiting?' I ask.

He laughs. 'We have just a couple at Konstanz. But there are many in the lakes region. These were built many thousand years ago, but tell us something of value. You see how resourceful the human animal is when it comes to survival. And that's the thing we found about the behaviour of these child soldiers: their behaviour is – strange to say – adaptive. Going out and killing: yes, it's destructive, yes, terrible, but in the field – out there – it helps them survive.'

'Survive?' I say. 'Survive how?'

'It inoculates them. It provides them with – it seems strange – resilience.'

To begin to unpack the mechanism at work, it is necessary to step backwards through time and space, far beyond the stilt-houses around Lake Konstanz from the Neolithic times, back further, perhaps to the formation of the glacial lake itself on the fringes of the Alps.

The most cursory survey of the animal world will reveal that aggression and predation is, and has been, an indispensable part of animal behaviour and survival for over half a billion years. Whether in terms of struggle for food, resources, territory, the protection of the young or the winning of mates (all of which are likely to be connected), animals of every conceivable genus compete and deploy aggression. This is not a new development.

The first available evidence of animal predation dates back 600 million years, to the Proterozoic era. In the fossil record we find *Cloudina* fossils, containing round holes of the organism that killed them. Shortly after (in deep-time terms), we find evidence of horseshoe crabs, one of the planet's first creatures and predators. They still exist today, virtually unchanged. For 450 million years these animals have crawled along our seashores. For this reason, they are referred to by the US National Park Service as 'living fossils'.

With the massive flourishing of life in the Cambrian period, there was also a multiplication of predators, including *Opabinia*, a waterborne animal with five eyes at the front of its head and a long proboscis, equipped with lethal grasping spines. So from the earliest times, in the animal kingdom predators have come in all shapes and sizes. And human predators still do. But human predation is complicated; human violence is.

Very often it is, from the outside at least, baffling – like that stabbing case I was counsel in that began with the smallest slight in a car wash in north-west London. While there is no universal consensus about the precise nature of human aggression, commonly psychological researchers divide human aggression into two broad categories.

As Elbert and his colleagues observe, the first type of aggression is in response to threat or perceived threat. This aggressive behaviour is reactive and retaliatory, defensive, protective. It is what we do when we protect our family, children, property, homeland.

Secondly, there is aggression that is instrumental. It is used in the service of gain or reward, to compete for or win resources, status, power, people – to secure victory in a battle of ideas. In Konstanz in 1415, in what now has every appearance of a genteel and civil city, the Czech cleric and philosopher Jan Hus was stripped, had a chain put around his neck, had that attached to a stake, had wood and straw piled to his chin, and then was burnt alive for some perceived breach of doctrinal orthodoxy. His ashes were cast into the Rhine.

This second kind of aggression is proactive. It is also common. For at the opposite end of the same spectrum as the execution of Jan Hus, lie the behaviours of the aggressive, offensive, pushy people around us. A mild manifestation of such aggression, but an example of it nevertheless. This kind of aggression has a planning element. As Shakespeare's Richard III, the epitome of his arch-schemers, says, 'Plots I have laid, inductions dangerous, by drunken prophecies, libels and dreams' to get the English crown, by tactics that are 'subtle, false and treacherous'.

But this second type of aggression may have a development – a mutation. A kind of altered aggression that is possibly a relic of our historic hunting behaviour itself. It is aggression that is *hedonic*. In other words, violent acts are committed which reward the perpetrator with pulses of pleasure. They provide enjoyment.

Such acts of hedonistic aggression respond to what Elbert and colleagues describe as 'hunting-related cues such as blood and the cries of the prey animal'. Indeed the sight of suffering comes to provide, as Elbert and colleagues observe, 'an essential reward for perpetrators'. Thus the experience of being aggressive transforms itself from being distasteful, repugnant and frightening, into an experience which is exciting. It is 'perceiving aggressive behavior toward others as fascinating, arousing, and thrilling'. It results in violence not being avoided, but approached, not reviled but revered.

Of course some people involved in armed conflicts must be, statistically speaking, psychopaths. Some indeed may be drawn to combat zones precisely because they are. But an accumulating body of research across the globe in conflict zone after conflict zone where atrocities have been perpetrated has suggested another

– perhaps more disturbing – explanation. Witnessing and perpetrating violence can become arousing. It can provide, for want of a more accurate word, pleasure.

This phenomenon has been documented by the Konstanz research team in conflict zones from Cambodia to Colombia, in South Sudan, Somalia, the Congo, Uganda and Sri Lanka. It transcends continental divides. It sails across seas. It seems blind to the cause of the conflict or which side one finds oneself on. It is not a rare or exceptional aberration. It is a mechanism that produces an adaptive outcome. It provides *resilience*.

Thus coming to feel that violence is exciting seems, at least to some extent, to inoculate the possessor of it against stress and trauma. But at the same time – and here is the problem – it is associated with acts of extreme cruelty.

Elbert's colleagues surveyed former guerrillas and paramilitary militiamen from Colombia's long internal armed conflict. In the north-east of the country, they interviewed former members of the infamous FARC guerrillas at demobilisation camps. They found that conceiving of violence as appealing or arousing may be 'adaptive' in increasing survival chances when one is locked in an environment of extreme threat and danger. But this inoculation comes at a cost: cruelty feeds off cruelty. Some of the participants even began to 'crave' it. It became 'addictive'.

These and many studies like them contradict the hypothesis that 'human predation is limited to a pathological subgroup, such as psychopaths'. For previous research proceeded on the basis that 'the purposeful hunting of humans was an activity carried out only by "psychopaths"'. In fact, finding enjoyment in violence 'seems to be a common facet of human behaviour, which surfaces in the context of war'.

With this kind of transformation in how violence is experienced, the inhibition against killing other human beings that Fiery Cushman's team found is overcome. And it is this development or mutation of the lust for hunting, particularly when unleashed on a collective scale, that may contribute to mass killings, mutilations, atrocities, genocide. It is the infliction of pain and suffering on other humans not only with determination but also, as Professor Victor Nell observes in his seminal research article 'Cruelty's rewards', with delight.

SEVEN

Diamonds

Sabrina Avakian has shoulder-length russet-coloured locks – the mass of curls some complex consequence of her mixed Italian and Armenian heritage. She was brought up in Ethiopia, the site of Italy's imperial ambitions in Africa, but studied and continues to practise law in Italy itself. Her paternal grandfather, an Armenian, fled by boat to Ethiopia to escape the 1915 genocide of his people, when 1 million Armenians were massacred. Presently she is head of UNICEF's mission in the east of Cameroon at Bertoua (pronounced 'ber-twa'). Bertoua is a frontier town: a long way from the capital; on the fringes of things; facing something immense and wild. That thing is the Central African Republic. From Bertoua, Sabrina Avakian provides support to a cluster of camps that house ten of thousands of refugees fleeing the bloodshed on the other side of the border in CAR.

However, the tremendous problems caused by this displaced persons crisis have met their match when confronted by Avakian. 'I have some African blood in me,' Avakian says. 'People can't see – they think: that crazy Sabrina woman, she is European. Perhaps I was dropped in a bucket of bleach, maybe. But my African blood, it goes right through my heart.' Avakian is irrepressible. She works endlessly, intrepidly.

Back in Rome she is a family mediation judge and an international expert on juvenile justice. 'But why stay in Italy?' she says. She points accusingly at an otherwise unoffending drainage ditch at the Gado Number 1 camp, 20 miles from the CAR border. 'No, no, Dex-terre, why stay in Rome when *here* is the problem.'

It was with Sabrina that I first made it to the UN refugee encampment. A mass of white tents on a slight incline, something like a Napoleonic army worn out and waiting for the next battle. A painfully bright (almost blindingly bright) day, even though it was July and the spinning earth was reaching its annual aphelion – the farthest distance from the sun. As we drove along the approach road in our white Land Cruisers, the sunlight completed its 95 million mile journey, bounced off the tent tops and into our squinting eyes. Like us, the baking occupants within knew that the conflict continues in large parts of CAR; the casualties keep coming; the tents are not sufficient; more canvas is needed. Sabrina Avakian is needed. Despite a terrible, traumatic incident (that we'll come to) she returned to Central Africa, which is how I met her.

Avakian is a veteran emergency and humanitarian aid professional. For example, she is fluent in Angolan Portuguese, knowing all the worst swear words, having worked with street children in the demilitarisation process following the Angolan war. When she speaks, it is a mixture of French, English, Italian, occasionally a few words of Portuguese and, frankly, I'm not sure what else. I came to call it Sabrina-speak.

'So, Sabrina,' I say, 'tell me about the Central African Republic.'

She laughs. Avakian, you will find, laughs a lot. But this particular laugh is not really a laugh. 'Many times, yes, I've thought I'd be killed,' the mission chief says. 'Oh, for sure. Boom. *Au revoir*, Sabrina. Gone. But here I am bugging you. So someone – something – up there likes me, or doesn't want to have to deal with me yet.' In the last decade Avakian has taken up Buddhism (she doesn't eat meat, believing it is ingesting suffering) – but also karate. 'You know me, Sabrinitta, she covers all the bases,' she says.

We are sitting in the Hotel Mansa in Bertoua on a balmy evening, having made the arduous 3½-hour journey back from the tented city of the Gado camps to Avakian's UNICEF head-quarters in Bertoua. Along the way we pass screens of dense green trees – the bush closing in on us – with delicate yellow flowers climbing into the branches. I keep meaning to ask Celine, our frighteningly confident driver, what the flowers are – she's from the south, near Equatorial Guinea. Occasionally young boys rush to the roadside holding sticks up high with mongooses haplessly dangling from them. They are said to be a delicacy. Every now and then a venomous green mamba – one of the deadliest snakes in Africa – slithers across the road ahead of us. And constantly clogging the road are huge trucks, their flatbeds full of massive butchered tree trunks – some of it the looted ancient forests of CAR. The great horn-bearing herbivore, the black rhinoceros, has been hunted to death there. It would all break Judith Léveillée's heart.

After the Kimberley Process, which regulates the world diamond trade, suspended the Central African Republic, militias intensified their illegal logging – going after 'blood timber'. The CAR forests are part of the ecologically critical Congo Basin rainforest, the world's second largest after the Amazon.

Back at Bertoua, the hotel is near the Red Box Bar with a sign proudly announcing its 'VIP Cabaret'. It is built along the shore of a small river. Avakian points accusingly once more, now at the unsuspecting water. 'See how beautiful? Like paradise. But no one knows what the river is called. I ask and they shrug.'

'Sabrina,' I say, trying to get back on track, 'about *Le Centrafrique?*'

'*Allora* – woooo – *mon père, mon père.*' Her French accent is heavily Italian. 'I arrive in October 2013 in the middle of the fighting and went to Bossangoa. In fact, you know what? I volunteered to go there. Hey, crazy, huh?'

In the bloody history of a bloody conflict, the area around Bossangoa witnessed some of the worst bloodshed. Avakian was housed in a building abandoned by a French NGO that left the town when one of its staff members was shot in the head for his mobile phone. She arrived during the short reign of the Seleka militia. Bossangoa is the capital of Ouham province, 200 miles to the north of Bangui. 'Practically no one else was there apart from UNICEF. I liaised with the Christian priest and the imam, we organised food for 40,000 starving people. Thousands of them children, badly, badly malnourished.'

Avakian's activities were not popular with the Seleka militia leadership.

'What would have happened if you hadn't provided the food?' I asked.

'People were already dying, you know. Many more would have died.'

'But Seleka didn't like what you were doing?'

'I don't care what Seleka or any militia think. I say to them, "Ha, okay, *désolé*, I'm sorry you don't like what I do, but people are hungry. I am going to feed them. Those are the people. This is the food. I don't care, Christian, Muslim, they are starving."'

Tensions kept rising between UNICEF and the militia, resulting in General Yaya, a notorious Seleka commander – one of the most ruthless – confronting Avakian.

'He comes up to me. He says, "Dottoressa Sabrina, *vous êtes courageuse.*" Then he puts a Kalashnikov in my face. Right to my head. I am kneeling. I feel the barrel pressed into my head.' She indicates the crown of her head, pushing two of her fingers into her curly hair.

'Why was the general so angry?'

'Because they want to say: *Regardez*, we are in charge. We run everything. Commander Yaya has to prove they have all the power.'

Over life; over death. Sabrina Avakian almost lost her life not because she harmed people, but because she saved them. And that's the Central African Republic. The irrationality and random-ness of life and death; arbitrary and awful. Hundreds of deaths averted by an Italian-Armenian, karate-practising, Buddhist judge.

While Saira was joining Seleka, Patrice was having a pretty good war in the capital.

People were desperate. They would pay more for things as the crisis deepened. If you kept calm, as Patrice did, if you did not take sides, as Patrice refused to do, there was money to be made, which was his goal in life. He didn't much care which crooks or bandits ran the capital – what difference did it make? He sold everything: radios, lighters, SIM cards, second-hand or third-hand mobile handsets, fuel canisters, plastic sheeting and other 'NFIs' (non-food items) provided by international agencies. Things got steadily worse.

The cycle of violence deepened when there was a backlash by the Christian majority against the new Seleka administration and the many abuses they perpetrated. Christian communities formed self-defence 'committees', militias called anti-Balaka. In the local Sango language it means anti-machete. Muslims were ruthlessly hunted in what was called Operation Clean-up. Things were spiralling out of control. The head of Seleka, Michel Djotodia, the new president, disbanded the Seleka alliance of armed groups.

When I asked Patrice about that period, he laughed. '*Bouff*,' he said, puffing out his cheeks. 'No one seems to have told Seleka that.'

Then after a mere eight months in office, Djotodia resigned. Seleka armed groups now officially became 'ex-Seleka'. Not that it made much difference. They continued to ravage and loot the countryside. Anti-Balaka squads, frenzied, fearsome, hunted Muslims pitilessly everywhere in retaliation. Murder and mutilation took over the country.

With all the madness in the capital, Patrice went north, to the region where his family ancestrally hailed from.

Patrice found that whole villages had been abandoned. He moved into a house, in fact a group of four buildings in an L shape beside a dirt road. They too had been abandoned. Muslims had once lived there. Not now. He had nothing to do with driving them out, but he was not going to let perfectly good houses go to waste. Then one day when he came back, he went to the outhouse, where he kept his stock. There in that fourth building he found a boy – hiding.

The boy sat on his haunches with his back against the wall in one corner.

'Get out,' Patrice said.

'Please,' the boy said.

'What have you stolen?'

'Nothing. I swear, nothing.'

'You are here to steal.'

'If I was stealing, I would be gone by now.'

The boy had fine features, with high cheekbones. He must have been around 17. Patrice could tell – it was just the process of living his life in CAR – that the boy was Muslim.

'Please,' the boy said. 'I do not steal from you.'

'Ha! Just good luck for me I get back in time.' The boy shook his head at Patrice, but Patrice ignored him. 'And bad luck for you I come and find you.'

'Please,' the boy said.

'Please, *please*,' Patrice said mockingly. 'You know nothing else to say?'

The boy paused. 'I wanted you to do it.'

'Do what?'

'Find me.'

Patrice stopped. He knew he was street-smart, he knew most of the angles, he'd prided himself on inventing a few for himself – he could deal with the militia, he could deal with UN soldiers, even Chadian warmongers – but he was confused. This boy confused him. ('*Fuck this boy*,' he later told me. 'I wish I never meet this boy.') He knew the boy must be working him, but – and this is something he did not understand even many months later – it did not *feel* like he was.

'Want, huh?' he said. 'Like you want the militia to find you?'

'No,' the stubborn boy said, looking at him unwaveringly. 'You. I meet two Muslims in the bush. They say . . . please . . .'

'Again – please, please – '

The boy stood up for the first time. He was not as tall as Patrice. He said, 'They say you are not like the others.'

'Others?'

'People here. Christians here.'

'Get out now or I find the militia,' Patrice said.

'They say, you don't care, this faith, that faith.'

This was true, but Patrice didn't want to answer, to get drawn into a further conversation, because what he really wanted was the boy out of his outhouse.

'Please. They will kill me. You know what they do to our people.'

'Our people,' Patrice said quietly. He was getting even more furious, but it wasn't just the boy – it was the whole mad situation that poisoned the country. '*Our* people? Which country you come from? Sudan? DRC? You are one of these Chadians who come cause trouble in this country?'

'*Le Centrafrique*,' the boy said, confused.

'So stop talking shit – your people, our people. All this stupidness. My people, their people – whose people. Every one of you, idiot people.'

'You know, please,' the boy said, 'what they do to Muslims.'

Patrice didn't need reminding. He didn't want reminding. About a month previously, there was a crowd in a town square and people were shouting, 'See here our Muslim brother.' A man was kneeling in the centre of the throng. People were looking on and then the anti-Balaka simply slit his throat. And the man said nothing. He did not plead with them. He did not beg for his life. But Patrice also noticed that other people did not try to save him. But worse: the look in their eyes. He thought: what are we? 'No,' he subsequently told me, 'that is wrong. I thought, now I understand: *this* is what we are.'

He said to the boy, 'You get me in trouble if you stay.' He grabbed him and started dragging him to the door. Then the boy uttered a sentence that changed everything.

'I know where there is something.'

'Something?'

'Something you want. The Muslims in the bush, they say, yes, that man, that man from Bangui, he is about business. He is the man. Him.'

Later, Patrice said to me, 'I was about to slap his face from his head. How did he know what I want?'

'So what did he say?' I asked.

'He says to me, "Please, I know you will want this."'

On the dirt track outside the buildings, pickup trucks were grinding to a halt. Their badly oiled brakes screeched through the air in protest. The anti-Balaka militia. The boy's eyes were desperate, glancing from Patrice to the door, back again, back to the door, where the men with machetes and blood in their nostrils were jumping off the vehicles and shouting.

'In the bush, I know where they've hidden them,' the boy said.

'What?'

'I will show you. I saw them do it. I was hiding.'

'Tell me now,' Patrice said. '*Now.*'

There was shouting, anti-Balaka screaming that there are Seleka rebels hiding in the area. The boy's eyes were wide.

Patrice said to me, 'I was about to open the outhouse door and show the militiamen this Seleka. And then he told me.'

'Told you?' I said.

'Told me. And then I thought, okay. Okay, this boy may live a little while longer.'

'What did he say?'

'He said he knew where the militia were hiding them. *Les diamants.*'

Diamonds.

*

324

There had been a pause in our conversation while Patrice went up the cab of a truck and asked the driver where he was going and how much a lift would be. The vehicle was heading out west to Douala, the port and biggest city, 150 miles away. It wasn't what Patrice wanted; it wasn't far enough. While this negotiation was unfolding, I saw that one of the other truck cabs had a rhino sticker on the window. I thought about that last rhino in CAR, just before they were wiped from the land. How long had it been alone? Did it see that there were none other of its kind left?

Patrice returned, smoking. 'There is always a ride,' he said. 'It's just how badly you need to take it.'

'That one is crazy,' François said. 'Charges too much.'

Patrice drew on the cigarette. '*Il faut vivre.*'

Which I took to mean, everyone's got to make a living. Something like that. 'That young person in the outhouse,' I said, 'how did you know you could trust him?'

'How can you trust anyone?' Patrice replied.

'Some of these children associated with combat groups,' I said – I'd read the literature – 'they can be . . . difficult.'

'*Difficile? Non,*' Patrice said.

I wondered if I'd used the correct French word.

'Not difficult,' he said. 'They are wild, dangerous. That doesn't mean you can never trust them.' He paused. 'Perhaps in your country, you can trust no one. Or everyone. People are people.'

He'd made his point. So, okay, I was willing to grant that there is something about human–human contact that means we process numerous minuscule cues to decide very quickly whom we can and cannot trust.

More jeeps were arriving; the sound of their engines was louder, invading the outhouse containing Patrice and the boy. The sound of boots, militiamen jumping down.

'Normally,' Patrice told me, 'I know what to do. But now I wasn't sure. I could say something to the anti-Balaka, and he would be dead. I remember looking at him and I thought, you could be dead. But then he would be dead and I would stay poor. Or . . .'

'Or you could look for the diamonds,' I said.

The men outside were screaming. 'Where are our Muslim brothers?'

'But now I have a problem,' Patrice said, 'because the anti-Balaka they are outside. I hear them banging on the doors of the other buildings with the end of their machetes. They are coming down the line, so I tell the boy to go out the back window. The militia are coming, coming. I open the door. There was a militiaman right there – right in my face.'

He had a belt of ammunition, studded with bullets, over his shoulder like a sash. Around his neck was a necklace of animal teeth. Some of the other men in the pickups wore wigs, one a horrid blond, ragged like wet straw. All of them wore amulets of varying size and shape. When I asked about the amulets in the refugee camp in Cameroon, no one much liked to speak about them as if they were jinxed. They were little purses, charms, tied together around their necks. They were said to protect the wearer from enemy bullets – part of the animist beliefs that made up the strange philosophy of the anti-Balaka. One of the men outside Patrice's house had a long-handled axe.

'The man at the door says to me, "My commander, he says I must search all these buildings." So I say, "Search? For what today?" He says, "We are hunting Seleka. There are Seleka in the area."'

The militiaman wore a green New York Jets T-shirt, the same colour as the forest canopy behind the buildings. He had watches on both wrists.

"'Ah, you are *hunting?*" I say. "You see, yesterday your colleagues come and you find nothing, the day before they come find the same, and every time it costs me money." I notice the watch on his right wrist is the wrong time. I say, "But today, maybe it is different, because today you are *hunting.*" He says, "This is what my order is." So I say, "*Mon capitaine*, you are too late." "Too late?"'

Patrice paused and said to him, 'You want a cigarette?'

'Give me,' the militiaman said.

'I gave him a cigarette,' Patrice said. 'I don't like giving my cigarettes. I lit it with my lucky lighter. It has a playing card on it.'

It was almost standard procedure: the militia asking, demanding, extorting tribute. Often it was cigarettes. On the roads there were *les barrages routiers* – roadblocks – and there would be a price for getting through: money, cigarettes, anything of value. When the militia came to your home, they rarely left empty-handed.

'Kneel out there, we search all the property,' the man said.

Patrice knew they would find the boy and it would be over. He thought of the Muslim man kneeling quietly in the square. He flung open the door.

'Come *in*, brothers,' he said with great politeness and courtesy. 'Come and search empty buildings which two of your patrols have searched, when Seleka criminals are driving through the country and killing our people. Yes, this is how to protect ourselves. Come in, come in. Oh, oh: let me see your hands. Let me see your machetes. Ha! You carry them like a child with a stick. No, you are not our saviours. Come back when you have blood on your blades. Then I will believe you are true patriots of our country.'

Patrice told me that it is always a tightrope. When you deal with militia you are always balancing, teetering, any moment about to fall. He worried that he had overplayed his hand.

The driver of the truck said, 'I know this one. He sold me a radio.'

They were wind-up radios, Patrice told me, the type that didn't need batteries. He'd got them cheap from a trader who'd got them – he didn't know where or much care. They were small green boxes with a rotating crank on the back.

'Yes, I remember,' Patrice said (although he didn't). 'I have many happy customers.'

'Did it work?' a man in the second pickup shouted.

'Piece of shit,' the purchaser said. 'I smashed it with a hammer.'

The men in the other vehicle were laughing.

'Let's go,' the driver said.

Suddenly the militiaman with the necklace of animal teeth said, 'What's that noise.' The men stopped laughing in an instant.

'I don't know,' Patrice told me, 'if the boy made a noise or if the man was dreaming. "Is a dog," I say. "A dog?" the militiaman says. "*Avec la rage* [with rabies]," I say. "But I'll eat him anyway. Give me your machete." I went to grab it.'

Again the men were laughing.

'Leave him,' the driver said. 'He's mad.'

The man at the door, the one with the machete, pressed his teeth hard together. He rubbed the flat part of the blade against Patrice's groin.

Patrice said, 'He whispers to me, "Next time? I kill you. Christian or no, I kill you." I say nothing. I know I say one more thing, one word more, I *breathe*, he kills me, there, *à ce moment-là*.

He kills me. I stand in the doorway. I do not move. I do not blink my eye. But I do notice: *yes*, the other watch, it does not work either. I *knew* it. These men, they don't care about time.'

Patrice stood and watched the receding dust storm as the trucks rattled and skidded towards the next village. The watches were probably looted from victims, just trophies. No need for them. The old kind of time, that had stopped.

'I take out my cigarettes, from my waistband, and light one. It is the best cigarette I taste in my life.'

Patrice slowly shut the outhouse door. He turned and went to find the boy.

EIGHT

With Open Eyes

After the AK-47 was pressed into her head in Bossangoa, Sabrina Avakian left the Central African Republic. She returned to judicial duties in Rome. The UN offered her counselling for the deep trauma of everything she had witnessed in Ouham province. And then one morning three months later she woke with a start. She knew she had to leave Italy; she knew she had to go back. 'I thought: what am I doing here? It's still going on.'

There was a three year-old girl she had particularly looked after in the camp at Bossangoa. This child was not only malnourished, but also suffered from mental health problems. She would follow Sabrina around the enclave where the Muslims were trapped, surrounded by anti-Balaka and certain death if they left.

'I felt,' Avakian told me, 'I'd abandoned this girl. I don't know why this was the one that got to me, no? Whether she was, how to say, the symbol for the bigger thing about CAR. One's head doesn't think like that. I just said, Sabrinitta, you my friend are going back. Pack *les valises*.'

And she did. When she returned to the UNICEF mission, the situation at Bossangoa had deteriorated alarmingly. 'About 1,500 families were trapped in the Ecole Liberté.' Neither of us commented on the glaring irony of the name of the school where 4,000 people were incarcerated. 'But we discover something else – people there were whispering things. They see me and trust me. They whisper, "Miss Sabrina, Miss Sabrina, they are now doing this."' Avakian shakes her head.

'What was the "this"?' I ask.

'Now it is the anti-Balaka doing all this – I'm sorry – *shit*. They were keeping Muslims prisoner.'

'You mean trapped in the enclave?' I said, slightly confused. 'Trapped at the school?'

Avakian shakes her head again – her russet locks fly everywhere and then settle back exactly where they previously were. '*More*,' she whispers. 'There were these metal containers, you know, *big* – like for freight or cargo. Muslims were being packed into them, just metal boxes, kept there in that terrible heat – how high? Ahhhhr, 45 degrees.'

She feared that people were literally being roasted to death.

'How do you explain this, what was happening in CAR?' I asked.

'It starts off with a struggle for power. Greed. People thinking, literally, this country of ours, it is a diamond mine. We want all of it.'

'Does it stay like that?'

'How can I explain?' Avakian says. We are in the nearly empty restaurant area of the Hotel Mansa. On the wall-mounted television behind her, a South American soap opera plays out loudly.

A woman in a black bikini is being dragged across a bathroom floor by a man with a moustache. Avakian sips a Sprite. 'I'm trying to explain, really I try.'

'Perhaps some things are inexplicable,' I said.

'With the war, it's like people become different people. Our UNICEF mission office was attacked, you know, completely looted, everything, *every*-thing taken, not by Seleka or anti-Balaka, but by the people we were trying to help. They turned on us. Violence, it feeds on violence. Abuse, yes, it grows more abuse. The old laws – *psshht* – gone.'

'And there are new ones?'

'Not laws that you the judge know, Dex-terre. New, old – let's say different,' Avakian told me.

As Navi Pillay, the then UN High Commissioner for Human Rights, said about CAR, 'The level of cruelty and disregard for life and dignity is horrifying, with public mutilation of bodies, amputation of body parts and genitals [and] beheadings . . . spreading further terror.'

Sabrina Avakian finishes her Sprite, then has a good-natured argument with the waiter about the puny amount of ice put in her glass for the next one. She likes ice. Everyone at Hotel Mansa knows that she likes ice. The waiter turns off the television: the man with the sinister moustache disappears. Outside, the river with no name continues to flow quietly into the bush.

'Yes, these different laws come,' Avakian says. 'Slowly, slowly, around you, you see these new people. Who are they? But here is the thing, yes? They are the *same* people. But now, believe this or no, also *not* the same people. And these calm, nice people, now violent – so, so violent.'

Now people are put in metal containers.

*

Thomas Elbert and his colleagues have called this kind of aggression 'appetitive'. In invoking that term they try to capture the fact that violence becomes addictive and arousing, enticing and enjoyable. To measure it, to provide empirical quantification, they have developed an Appetitive Aggression Scale. They have tested it with combatants in conflict zones across the world. They asked questions like:

> During fighting does the desire to hunt or kill take control of you?
> Once you got used to being cruel, did you want to be crueller and crueller?

We will come to the answers shortly. But these are questions that have been relevant throughout human history. Indeed one of the earliest accounts of human aggression can be found in Homer's *Iliad*, along with the story of arguably history's most renowned warrior.

In Book XXII, the champion fighters of each side – Hector, son of King Priam, the royal prince of Troy, and mighty Achilles, unsurpassed warrior of the Greeks – face each other in combat. After a titanic struggle, Achilles stabs Hector through the chest with his sword. But it is not enough for Achilles to beat Hector. Achilles wants not only to defeat his opponent, but to desecrate him.

> [Achilles] found a way to defile the fallen prince. He pierced the tendons of both feet behind from heel to ankle, and through them threaded ox-hide thongs, tying them to his chariot, leaving the corpse's head to trail along the ground. Then lifting the glorious armour aboard, he mounted and touched the horses with his whip, and they eagerly leapt forward. Dragged behind, Hector's corpse raised a cloud of dust, while his outspread hair flowed, black, on

333

either side. That head, once so fine, trailed in the dirt, now Zeus allowed his enemies to mutilate his corpse on his own native soil.

Homer depicts both the futility of human violence and yet, and at the same time, the terrible lust men sometimes have for it. One warrior after another falls, leaving thousands of human bodies, as the poet ominously warns in the very first line of the epic, 'as spoil for dogs and carrion birds'.

The massive research project that Elbert's team at Konstanz University in Germany has pursued has tried to examine scientifically our dark aggressive side. It has started to produce a stream of startling results. For researchers have found something remarkable about acts of extreme human violence.

For all the carnage they cause, they can also provide a demonstrable psychological benefit. Extreme acts of violence inoculate the perpetrator against certain mental harm. And this has been startlingly evident in children. In child soldiers.

So Patrice decided not to give the boy up to the militia. But who was this interloper, this young Muslim who was running for his life? It was Saira who had the answer.

So you joined the militia?

'They found me,' Saira said. 'After I was walking and collapse.'

Were you a soldier?

'I never have a gun. You can fight without a gun.'

What was it like, being in the militia?

'People, they think these militia, they are all animals. They help me. They take me in. But people think they are all animals.'

People like who?

She paused. 'Like you.'

But I don't know, Saira. I don't understand.

334

How did a girl, still in law a child, cope with being in a combat group? What was her life like? My reference points were severed. This was new terrain.

I'd really like you to help me. But only if you want. To understand. What was happening in this combat group. And why. What people were like. And how they changed.

And she did.

In the Seleka militia, Saira became 'wife' to a deputy commander, only the militia group didn't have ranks like that, or didn't stick closely to them. ('It wasn't an army kind of army.') And she wasn't married, but she was unmistakably his bride.

'I was "given" to him,' Saira said. 'That is what it is called. Given.'

His battle name was Tonnerre – Thunder.

It meant that none of the other men came near her like that, for which she was grateful. But he did. For which she was not. He had a hunting knife. It had many teeth. ('This is what he is very proud of, his knife.')

They fought their way from the north-east of the country towards the capital Bangui, sometimes on bush roads, sometimes on the *route nationale*. Somewhere before Bangui, she can't recall exactly where, she noticed that a boy of about 16 or 17 had joined their group. He was around her own age and Muslim also, as was virtually everyone in their group (except a couple). She really didn't have much to do with him. There was too much running around, housekeeping and cooking to do. What use was another boy? But then, after a raid on a village, he came to her attention.

There had been so many such raids over the months that this was nothing unusual. The village was a pitifully poor place and there wasn't much to be taken from it. Saira thought the raid was just so the men could cause some havoc. This is sometimes what they did.

'I was not there, so this is what they tell me,' Saira said. 'There was an old man in the village, and he has an old goat. He will not give it to our men. He says they can have anything, but they cannot have his goat. "It is not a problem," Tonnerre says, "we will have something else instead." The old man said that they can take everything, but they cannot take his goat. "Is not a problem," Tonnerre said, "we will have something else." The man tries to explain, the goat, it has been sick, but now he has made it better, and he begs them to let him keep his goat. "Is not a problem," Tonnerre says. "Take his hand. The one that holds the goat." The boy is given the job. The young ones often are. They are made to do bad things. He has to cut off the old man's hand. The boy, he picks up a machete. He moves to the old man. Then he stops. He says, "This is an old man and this is an old goat. We can find better goats. I will find you a better goat." Everyone is shocked. No one says anything. Tonnerre, they say, he smiles. He says that it is okay. And all is over. Then he turns around. He shoots the goat in the head. The old man screams. He shoots the old man in the chest. "It is an old goat," Tonnerre says. "We can find better goats."'

When they returned to the Seleka camp, the deputy, in front of everybody, beat the boy. He hit him repeatedly with a stick, on the back of the legs, over the arms. He hit him very hard. The stick broke.

'Tonnerre was saying, "Everything is now our property, everything now is ours. Even their hands are ours. But you, you do not give me their hands that belong to me. So I need another hand. Where is the hand you owe me?"'

There was a big rock.

The deputy said to the others, 'I will show you how our country will be.'

He took out his prized possession, his hunting knife. He told the boy to put his hand on the rock. 'I will show you,' he said, showing everyone the teeth of the knife. 'Put your hand there.'

He tapped the rock with the flat of the blade.

Saira said, 'I do not know this boy well, but I am crying inside. The boy, he puts his hand on the rock. He is nodding his head a little. I'm thinking, why is he nodding his head? What does this mean? Tonnerre lifts the knife above his head. High, high. I am crying, crying in my head. Tonnerre says, "See – here is my other hand." Then the commander comes. He says, "Leave him. He fires his gun well. Leave him." The boy has not moved. His hand is still on the rock. And I think: what sort of a boy is this?'

The boy was not given any food.

Late at night, after she had been lying with Tonnerre and he was asleep, Saira sneaked the boy some food she'd hidden as she was clearing up.

There was a little stream full of rocks. In the quiet of the night the running water made a kind of music over them. The boy was sitting against a tree with his hands tied behind his back: that was another part of his punishment.

When she offered him the scraps, he said, 'For why do you do this?'

'For why do you care about the old man?' she asked.

He greedily ate the food she fed him. But he seemed embarrassed to be fed, as if he was a child. For a while he was silent, staring intently at the stream. Then he said, 'Do you think they sleep?'

'The commanders are asleep,' Saira said.

'Not commanders.'

'So I ask who he means,' Saira said.

'Them – the fish,' the boy said.

He said what?

337

'He says, "Those fish, do they sleep?"' Saira said. 'And I say I do not know. But he already knows his answer, and it makes me angry because why is he asking me a question when he knows what is the answer?'

But what is the answer? I genuinely did not know, or wasn't sure.

'He says, "Fish sleep with eyes open." And I am confused,' Saira said. 'I think of the man lying dead in the road holding the white cloth with his eyes open. But he doesn't mean that. And I am angry. I say, "But why do you speak of these fish? I asked you why you care about the old man."'

And what did he say?

'Nothing,' she said. 'Just then he says nothing.'

They sat next to the cool water and barely spoke again. They did not need to: the stream continued its conversation with itself.

'That night I am lying, lying in the hut,' Saira said, 'and I am thinking so much about this. I keep thinking: why does he mention how fish sleep? I'm thinking about these things, and then suddenly it was there.'

It? What do you mean by it?

'Sleep. In so long, this was the first time I easily find sleep. And I think: who is this boy?'

That was the first time they talked.

NINE

4GW

As I write this, in the middle of the second decade of the new millennium, there are approximately 300,000 child soldiers around the world. In over 80 military conflicts across the globe, such children are frequently commanded to execute the most dangerous and gruesome tasks. Not only do they act as porters, guards, spies, housegirls (occasionally houseboys), but they are also exploited as sex slaves, or due to their expendability they are thrust into the front line, used to attract fire or use up enemy bullets, sacrificed as decoys, sent as advance parties through unknown territory to clear paths of mines with their feet and bodies.

The conflict zones across the continents create thousands upon thousands of detached, abandoned or orphaned children living in dire circumstances. Thus conflicts themselves are tremendously effective at recruiting sergeants. As Rachel Brett and Irma Specht, researchers who have examined the role of child soldiers in depth, state: the war comes to them. Moreover, as psychologists Thomas

Elbert and his colleague Maggie Schauer observe, 'Never before in history have child soldiers played such a prominent role'.

It is possible that this change is a component of what is called 4GW: fourth-generation warfare – a qualitatively different way in which wars are waged, with fighting dominated by irregular (non-state) forces. It is heavily symbolic warfare. It is directed not only against the body but the mind. One of its key weapons is to induce a form of terror.

It targets civilian populations with mass atrocities, systematic sexual violence, massacres and mutilations. Indeed the percentage of war casualties that were civilian increased throughout the 20th century. In this child soldiers have become essential to what ex-US Marine Corps colonel Thomas Hammes, a counter-insurgency specialist, labels as today's 'evolved form of insurgency'. Children across the world are deployed, exploited, used up. From Britain, they journey to Syria. In the Central African Republic, they are forced into armed groups or simply, like Saira, drift into them because of the chaos.

But not all children respond to their new life as child soldiers in the same way. With the atrocities they witness, there are the conditions for severe mental and psychological repercussions, for PTSD. However, with some children, as Elbert and Schauer found, it does not work like that.

For these young people there is a gradual transformation in how they see and experience the violence they have been made to perpetrate or witness. At first it is frightening. Consistent with the findings of Fiery Cushman's team, they find the infliction of violence deeply distressing. For example, Cori [name changed] was a young woman who was abducted by Joseph Kony's LRA militia in Uganda when she was 13. She was ordered by the commander to beat her friend to death with a stick.

I knew I did not want this. Doris was lying on the ground next to us on her stomach. We got up and lifted the sticks. They were about as thick as my hand wide and as long as my arm. We started beating her. On her buttock, on her shoulders, on her back. I heard her crying and shouting for help. Everybody was watching us … I felt so helpless. Then Doris cried out my name. She shouted: 'You are killing me, we are such good friends and now you are killing me.' I slowed down the beating as much as I could and I answered her: 'I did not want to do this, I am forced to do this. If it was me, I wish I would not have to do this.' After that she kept quiet. She was not crying anymore.

However, with repeated exposure to such experiences, the infliction of violence can become not just normal and acceptable, but fascinating. It can become arousing. It is this mechanism that Thomas Elbert and his colleagues have sought to understand in their appetitive violence research.

The vulnerability, inexperience and bewilderment of children incorporated into armed groups provides a fertile 'window of opportunity' for the transformation of violence into a form of arousal. Children have shorter horizons; they are less able to assess risk; they have less exposure to social norms and standards of moral behaviour. Their minds are malleable; they can be broken down, reshaped and built back up, recalibrated into alarming configurations. Consequently, they can be turned, as Elbert and his colleagues were told when they interviewed former child soldiers in northern Uganda, into 'terrible killers'.

As Richard MacLure and Myriam Denov from the University of Ottawa write of their research into former combatants in Sierra Leone, children were transformed into 'warriors' who committed acts of 'unspeakable brutality'. Elbert theorises that with child soldiers either the inhibition against killing other people breaks down in the brutalising environment they find themselves in, or in certain children it is simply not learned – especially where children have 'grown up' in armed groups.

Perhaps this is predictable. It appals. We prefer it were not so. But it can be predicted. Such vulnerable and isolated children are, after all, impressionable. It is in this sense that a senior officer in the Chadian army says, 'Child soldiers are ideal . . . when you tell them to kill, they kill.'

But what was a more surprising finding in the research investigations with child soldiers was that those who were more 'cruel', those who embraced brutality and bloodshed with surprising frequency, did not suffer the same rates of post-traumatic stress – even though they had been engaged in or witnessed exceptional violence, terror and death. This was a robust finding with child soldiers across combat zones from the West Nile and South Sudan, to Sri Lanka and back to the Congo and the Rwandan genocide. These children began behaving in very distinctive ways:

> . . . after they have killed someone, they sit together and talk about their killing stories like an adventure and re-enact the victim's suffering.

They scoff, Elbert found. They laugh.

Saira had to remain cautious about being seen to be friendly with the boy. It wasn't just that she was given to the deputy. It was because the adult leadership discouraged the young people and children from forming too close friendships. There was the constant concern that children would run away. Thus, a little like the experience of Michael and Anthony at Lake Volta, ominous threats of horrendous collective punishment were made should escape or defection be attempted.

This pattern has been found by researchers beyond the Central African Republic. In the Great Lakes region of Central Africa lies Burundi (the country of origin of Alan Pegna's extraordinary patient). After the assassination in 1993 of the first democratically elected president, a civil war between the majority Tutsi population and Hutu rebels claimed over a quarter of a million lives. Many thousands of children were conscripted into the warring factions. The vast majority of former child soldiers informed researchers that forming friendships was forbidden. In an almost Orwellian development, the personal was less important than the cause, the loyalty was to the group, not one another.

As Suzan Song and Joop de Jong found in their Burundian study:

> The rebel commanders constructed a culture in which friendships were forbidden and, as a consequence, were a potential source of stress, so the child soldiers learned to be quiet and to 'keep to ourselves.'

This depiction, while not identical to the world Saira found herself in, is one she would recognise. Getting close to the boy would be a risk, to both of them, and they knew it. So she'd have to be careful. But despite the risks, she became more and more determined. She would find a way to get to know the boy.

The two of them didn't speak alone again for weeks. They didn't even look at each other, as if they were both embarrassed for some reason. She kept thinking about what he did with the old man and the goat, what he said about the fish. What did he mean? Why did he do it? There was so much killing, what was the old man to him? He was an infuriating boy. She didn't understand him. She would sleep every night with the deputy and the boy would slide into her thoughts.

Then one day, after the boy had been on a long night patrol, he fell asleep with exhaustion at the next day's roadblock. They used to block the roads with vehicles and even rocks and logs, stop vehicles, then rob them. It was another way to get money, another part of the madness.

This time the deputy beat him with a belt. That was somehow worse. Tonnerre took the belt from his trousers to beat the boy and the other militiamen laughed. This time he was allowed to have food and the punishment was just being beaten with a belt like a child. His hands were not tied with wire.

Later there were welts on the boy's back like snakes. Saira brought a bowl of water in which she put a little salt. It was all she could think of.

'It will hurt,' she said.

'Yes,' he said.

There was dirt in the open wounds from where the deputy had kicked the boy around in the dust. The welts, angry red, reached right across his back. She used a cloth, the cleanest she could find. The boy winced with the sting of the salt, but was determined to make no sound. She finished cleansing the wounds.

'My father,' the boy said, 'he was not a brave man.'

'Why you speak of your father?' she said. She did not want to hear about fathers. She'd forced herself to banish the memories of her own for some time. Now it was like opening up a box. It was like putting your hand in broken glass – why would you do it?

344

'When the enemy attack our village, our men stand to fight them. But my father, he runs. He was shot,' the boy said. 'Many were. But at least they tried to fight.'

'Where are you from?' Saira asked.

'The same place as you,' he said.

Saira got angry. Did he think she was stupid? 'You are not from my town,' she snapped.

'You are not from your town,' he said.

She thought he was trying to say something important, but she was too worked up to think about it, struggling with the emotions he'd stirred by mentioning fathers. They just sat side by side on the ground, near the side of a pickup.

'Next time,' the boy said, 'I will kill him.'

'Tonnerre?' she said. 'You fight Tonnerre and they will kill you.'

The boy shrugged.

'Sometimes,' she said, 'Tonnerre cries at night. His family has been killed.' It was actually true. She said it because she didn't want the boy to get himself into more trouble and get killed.

'It doesn't matter,' he said, 'I will still kill him.'

'Better you do something else.'

'What?'

She'd been thinking hard about it since the first time they'd spoken, that night by the stream. And now she thought she had an answer.

'Leave,' she said.

By leave, did you mean leave the militia group?

'So he said to me,' Saira said, 'he says to me, "Leave? Leave here?" And I said to him, "Yes, leave here."'

The boy was silent for a long time, thinking. 'Will you come?' he said.

345

She did not respond; something inside her was not able to provide any answer. She wished she could answer, just say yes, but something she didn't understand inside was stopping her. To fill the big emptiness inside, she began humming, a tune from her childhood she had long known.

Everyone had been speaking about the big fight that was coming with the anti-Balaka enemies soon. Saira's group would join with local groups of Muslims who were intent on assisting Seleka. Many people would die. Everyone knew it; Saira knew it; she could be killed; the boy could be killed. They were heading towards the regional capital. Maybe that is how it would end, just suddenly die. And now, when she met someone she liked. She didn't know what to say, so instead she continued humming the song from her childhood.

And that was the second time they spoke.

TEN

The Burning Country

Nim Tottenham is Associate Professor of Psychology at Columbia University in New York. There she heads the Developmental Affective Neuroscience Laboratory. The work of the lab has pushed the boundaries of knowledge about how early life experiences, and particularly trauma, affect our behaviour. In particular, Tottenham's team examines the impact of stressors on underlying neurobiology – that is, how the structures of the brain actually change when exposed to trauma. Key to their research is the question of attachment.

'Human beings are not like sea turtles,' Tottenham explains. She speaks with poise and clarity. 'Sea turtles never meet their parents and are never expected to.'

'And the expectation with humans is that we form bonds with a parent?' I ask.

'The thing to understand is that the human child brain is not just a mini-sized adult brain. The neurobiology shows that it is a specific adaptation that maximises the survival chances of the infant human animal as it develops. And it depends crucially, critically on species-expected caregiving.'

And this is where the thousands of displaced, isolated and orphaned children in the Central African Republic create a potential powder keg for the future of the country. When we speak, Tottenham is immaculately turned out in a crisp white shirt. She has highly intelligent features and fine dark hair. Before Columbia she did her PhD at the University of Minnesota. Her seminal work has earned her a Distinguished Early Career Contribution Award from the American Psychological Association.

'The thing we're learning about trauma,' Tottenham says, 'is that it can be passed on in the genome. That's what the accumulating evidence tells us. Thus the damage caused to children enlisted in combat groups in CAR does not just remain with them. It will have consequences for their offspring – and the future of that country.'

Tottenham's team have explored in detail how trauma is caused by being deprived of appropriate parental contact and caregiving with children in institutional settings such as orphanages. Even in ostensibly 'good' institutions. Being deprived of a parent can create very distinct changes in the anatomy of the brain and that then affects behaviour.

'What about children that have been brought up in armed groups,' I ask, 'or who have spent long periods in them?'

'Think of the question of attachment,' Tottenham says. 'Human neurobiology is built to meet the needs of the developing human animal. Attachment is vital. If the attachment is to an armed group, then you might find that the child develops approach behaviour to what most would consider highly dangerous activities.'

'Like serious violence?'

'Yes, rather than aversive or avoiding behaviour, they walk straight into it. The sheer importance of attachment is such – however dysfunctional the "parental" figure – that you find that children being removed from deeply abusive parents are nevertheless highly traumatised by the act of removal.'

In this sense, the removal of an abusive parent comes to be not a relief, but a wrench.

'It seems,' Tottenham says, 'that we need something to attach to as we develop.'

'And if it is a combat group? If it is in an environment of violence?'

'Let me put it this way: the human brain is exquisitely – exquisitely – attuned for immediate survival. Physical survival. People who recruit children into armed groups – alarmingly enough to say – are doing exactly the right thing from a neurobiological point of view.'

'Why?' I ask.

At this point the air conditioning automatically comes on in Nim Tottenham's Columbia office. She gets up to silence it. When she returns, she says, 'The human brain up to the age of around ten is at the peak of its neuroplasticity. That means you can effectively sculpt how you want the brain to function. Then that functioning can become locked in. It's very hard to change. Not impossible, but hard.'

I explained to Tottenham my research with refugees from the bloodshed in the Central African Republic.

'From a neuroanatomical point of view, these people you're talking about, who run the combat groups, they're wise to go after children.'

'In what way?' I ask.

'If they want to build killing machines.'

The truth is, Saira didn't exactly know why she couldn't answer the boy's question and agree to run away. That not knowing made her want to weep.

Some months before there was a girl she knew — well, actually knew of, since it happened just after Saira joined and they didn't really get to know each other well — and this girl got pregnant. She didn't want to have the child in the group. She didn't want the child of the soldier she was being made to sleep with, but at the same time, it *was* her baby growing inside her and she wanted to have the baby — it was all so confusing. Then she miscarried. She cut her left wrist with a knife, straight, deep, quietly. She bled to death in the night. There were all kinds of escapes. The trouble was, Saira just didn't know where she could go if she left. Run away where? Escape where?

So many of the young people in CAR were orphans. The country was becoming one big open orphanage. Bodies were just left in the roads and villages. There were many orphans and many vultures. In Cameroon, an elderly woman I later met with Patrice, a woman who had lost her entire family in the Central African Republic, said to me, 'What is CAR? Our children are thin and our vultures are fat. That's our country, that's *le Centrafrique*.'

One night there were stars everywhere. The group was on the edge of fields and had joined with other Muslims. The big fight would happen the next day. That night, Saira noticed, people didn't know what to do with themselves, as was often the case before there would be much bloodshed.

Then something happened: lights appeared to fall through the sky — shooting stars. The commander, the big boss, said very knowledgeably that it was a sign that the sky could fall. Tonnerre immediately agreed and Saira nodded, but knew it was not true. She'd done too much reading. She wandered away from the camp alone, incensed by the sheer ignorance.

Saira stood on the edge of the fields: the crops had been burnt, she didn't know why or by whom. For the first time it was the boy who approached her.

'What is wrong?' he asked.

A terrible smell filled the air, the country burning. She started walking off and he followed her.

'Why do you want to walk with me?' she said.

He pointed back to the camp. 'Who is there to walk with there?' he said, smiling.

'Yes, that is the only reason?'

'That I think of. Maybe if we walk, I think of another,' he said. 'Maybe.'

It was her turn to smile. It just came on her face.

'So what is now wrong for you?' he said.

'I want to go back studying,' she said. She desperately missed her books. She wondered if she could even read any more.

'No one is studying in this country,' he said.

'Then I will find another country,' Saira said.

He was silent for a while, like he was swallowing the enormity of the thought. 'Does he hurt you?' he asked. 'Tonnerre.'

'No,' Saira told him, but she didn't pay enough attention to the question. She was thinking of her father. The box, his note. Anything is possible – maybe another country, that was really possible. Perhaps not Paris, not like her father had spoken about, not yet. Congo or Cameroon, yes – many people were fleeing to Cameroon, and after all the group had come hundreds of miles across the country and were now nearer Cameroon.

'Truly, he doesn't hurt you? Everyone knows he is cruel.'

'He *doesn't* hurt me,' Saira said.

'I was angry at his question,' she told me.

Why were you angry?

'I think: who is this boy, to ask me such things?'

I wondered whether she desperately wanted him to believe she was too valuable, too precious to be hurt. But she didn't say that.

'Let us leave after the fight,' the boy said.

'Yes,' she replied instantly, but suddenly a bad feeling crawled up her throat.

'Things will be all right,' the boy said.

And what did you say?

'I said nothing,' Saira said. 'But the feeling, it got worse.'

It was decided: in the very early morning there would be the raid, and then they would leave. That night, there was a moon, and then there was not. That was the third time they spoke.

ELEVEN

A Man of Business

The fighting the next day was like all the other battles, only their side lost. The men, most of them, got killed. Tonnerre and the commander, almost all the others she'd got to know over the previous months, all dead. She didn't know how to feel about it. The men who put down their arms and surrendered were killed too, even more brutally. Some of the women were taken by anti-Balaka. The boy, he disappeared. She did not know what happened to him.

Over the months of looting and plundering the senior officers in her Seleka group had accumulated a mass of money and diamonds, but the anti-Balaka had taken all of that. Now she did not know what her captors would do with her.

In the same region of the Central African Republic, about a week later, Patrice found a boy squatting against the wall in a corner of his outhouse. The militiamen had just driven off in their pickups, and Patrice, smoking the sweetest cigarette of his life, confronted the hiding youth behind the group of buildings in the shape of an L.

'So,' Patrice said, 'tell me about the diamonds.'

'There are many,' the boy said.

'Where are they?' The boy hesitated. '*Where?*' Patrice shouted.

Finally the boy said, 'The anti-Balaka have diamonds. Many Muslim diamonds they took from Seleka.'

'Where are they?'

'They are hidden in the bush. I know where. I saw them hide them. I escaped after the fight. But I keep watching what they do. In the bush, I watch. They don't see me.'

'Why?' Patrice asked.

'Because the anti-Balaka, they take someone I know.'

'What do you mean?'

'The anti-Balaka, they have some prisoners. I think they will kill them.'

And what did you say?

'I said I don't know what those idiot militia do – they all do crazy things,' Patrice said. 'But I said to him that it's not my problem who the anti-Balaka kill.'

Patrice told me that, although he hadn't heard of metal containers, he had heard that sometimes anti-Balaka kept prisoners, for little other reason than to amuse themselves.

'Then the boy says, "I want to go back because it is my friend. Will you help me go back and then I will show you the diamonds." I ask him why he needs me, and he says because he needs weapons and he has no weapons. But if I help him get weapons, he will show me the diamonds. Then I ask what is this friend. "A girl," he says. I shout at him, "I am not going back for a girl. Here there are many girls. There always are girls."'

354

Patrice made a gesture as if his head exploded. 'Then I say, "You are the stupidest youth I ever met. So stupid I want to kill you myself with these hands."

'I grabbed him. I shake him. He is thin, his shoulders, but I shake him hard. I say, "We cannot do anything for those prisoners. We cannot save your girl, do you understand?" He says, "She is not my girl." So I say, "Then why does it matter?" He looks down. "I don't know," he says.

'He doesn't look at me. I don't look at him,' Patrice told me. 'I thought, fuck this boy, fuck this youth. You know, many times I wish I never meet this youth.'

Even after all this time – all this happened well over a year previously – Patrice was breathing heavily just recounting it. His fists were clenched tight. I didn't say anything for a while. His breathing slowly became more regular; the agitation subsided.

So what happened?

'So,' Patrice told me, 'we went back.' *But why did you go?*

'The diamonds,' Patrice said. 'What *else*? I might just get some diamonds,' Patrice said. 'At least, you know, I want to know where they are.'

I didn't believe it – it was the way he said it. I'm not sure he ever did. But I let it pass. Instead I asked him where he got the weapons.

'In CAR,' he said, 'there is no problem finding weapons – paying for weapons, yes. But you can always find weapons.'

What weapons did you get? Did you actually get any?

'A hammer, a long knife, I already had these. Then a pistol, an old, old Chinese pistol. I pay for this. The boy, he says he knows about guns. More than me. I am a man of business. He checks it. He says, is okay. Not great. But okay.'

It has puzzled me for a long time why Patrice went to the anti-Balaka encampment. The boy wanting to return, I could understand from everything I had learned about him and Saira, but Patrice – why?

There were actually three camps in a small cluster. When Patrice and the boy arrived at the first one, two prisoners were tied up, hands and feet – hands behind their back, feet together. There was a campfire, and anti-Balaka militiamen were sitting around.

The way Patrice described it, one of the prisoners was kneeling, his hands and feet were still tied, but he was bleeding heavily from the face. Patrice and the boy listened to what was being said. It was difficult to understand what had happened. Every now and then, one of the militia would get up off a stump and kick the prisoner in the ribs, the prisoner would collapse, several of the militiamen would force him up again, so once more he was on his knees, and then everything would settle down. Alcohol, it wasn't clear what, was being passed around, there was more talking and laughing, more wood thrown on the fire, and in the glow, under the Central African night sky, full of stars, the blood seeping from the gashes in the prisoner's face could be seen.

Another militiaman, right in front of Patrice and the boy, advanced towards the fire. They could not see his face, just his broad back, then the swing of his assault rifle, couldn't see precisely where it landed, but then the crunch of the metal against the head of the prisoner.

'"They will kill him tonight," the boy tells me. We crawl away from the camp. I'm thinking hard. What to do? What to do? I ask him where is the girl. The boy says she must be at another camp because he cannot see her.'

There were two more encampments to try.

*

At the second camp there was only one anti-Balaka militiaman. He sat rather morosely in front of the fire, his chin was propped on his fists which were propped by his elbows on his knees. He stared at the fire, which was in the middle of a group of rudimentary huts. From time to time his eyes closed and his head, on which was perched a broad-brimmed hat (the way Patrice described it to me, it was something like a Panama), bobbed. This was a tedious job, the dullest detail – all the fun was to be had in the other place with the prisoners. He appeared alone save for a radio that blared music – but not the usual dance tunes, but something more mellow, and this added to the guard's drowsiness.

'She's not here,' Patrice said to the boy.

'That means there are many guns at her camp,' he replied.

That was a problem. Patrice tried very hard to think it through. Then he had an idea.

'All the guns are at the other camp.'

'So is she,' the boy said.

'So we need all the militia here.'

'How?' the boy said.

How. Further back towards the surrounding trees someone had parked a pickup. Jerrycans of fuel sat on its flatbed. Patrice thought that one would be enough. He began.

TWELVE

The Vortex

Patrice's feet pressed into the spongy red soil. There was a strong, unpleasant smell around this camp, but on the flatbed of the pickup he could see his target: jerrycans propped upright like soldiers. A lamp was propped on the bonnet of the vehicle, casting a halo of light.

Patrice had tried to let the war wash over and around him. Let the war get on with its business and he would get on with his. But there came a point, he said, when the two got 'stuck in a pipe' and one must go through the other. That's how he understood it. That was what was happening now. He was stuck in a pipe. *Malheureusement. Eh, bien, ça va, ça va.* Nothing for it. He didn't feel bitter. Get through to the other side. And blocking the way, sitting on a log by the fire with an AK-47 across his knees, was the anti-Balaka guard.

It seemed, now when he looked back at it, madness. But at the time, it was the most important thing he'd ever done. Over the years he'd wanted, *craved*, felt an almost painful need to have the best clothes, phones, *things* – but at that exact moment, he told me, there was nothing – *nothing* – he had ever wanted more in his life than to pull this off – rescue the girl.

And get the diamonds?

'Yes, yes, also the diamonds,' he told me. It sounded like an afterthought.

Don't forget the diamonds, Patrice.

'*Non, non, absolument pas.* Don't forget the diamonds,' Patrice said.

Only ... you see, you just did.

Patrice shrugged; for one of the very few times he faintly smiled. For one of the few times, I actually got him. Touché, *mon ami*, touché.

The militia guard's face shone in the flames of the fire. From time to time his eyes closed and his head bobbed. Patrice and the boy watched as the guard's amulets dangled from his neck. If Patrice could get one of the jerrycans he might be able to pull off his plan. He leaned back against a tree trunk in the undergrowth to think it through. He hated all these trees. Like all the vegetation, they just got in his way. And then this forest that was constantly in motion was suddenly silent and still. It held its breath. Patrice tried to steady his. The blood pounded in his head. He explained the plan to the boy.

'It is dangerous,' the boy said. 'But I believe we can do it.'

'You keep the gun. You shoot him if he sees me,' Patrice said. 'I am not a killer.' He was, after all, a man of business. Then he caught a bad smell again, a pungent, distasteful smell.

The warmth of the night, the comforting crackle of the fire, the deep vegetal smell of the forest – too much drink. The militiaman fell asleep. He was snoring, gently, but unmistakably snoring.

Patrice and the boy turned and crawled further around the fringe of branches. He saw them, lying there, cast aside like refuse. Behind the next bush, piled like timber were three decomposing bodies, the smell of them filling his nostrils. That made up his mind. Do it now or it would be too late.

Patrice turned onto his front and slithered flat out of the tree-line and towards the pickup. The boy covered him with the Chinese pistol. The radio kept playing its low lullaby. His stomach was scratched raw with the crawling, dirt filled his mouth, but he reached the back wheel of the pickup. Then he realised the flaw in his plan.

Opening the can would make a noise. Or rather, it might. He knew the canisters well – had sold some two years ago: they were 20-litre NATO cans, with a pouring spout and a flexible hose. But the old ones did make a noise when you cranked them open. These looked old. He was about to retrace his path, when he heard it: the guard snoring more loudly. Patrice got onto his haunches. His fingers moved nimbly, they flew over the lids of the line of canisters, his fingertips brushing over the grooved metal sides. He leaned into the flatbed of the pickup and opened the nearest one.

His breathing was quickening, his chest began to heave as the smell of petrol rose headily around him. He took the final can next to the back wheel, opened the lid. Very slowly, he began to pour. As he retreated back to the bush, stopping every couple of paces to ensure he could still hear the guard's snores, he kept pouring, a long trail of petrol that soaked into the soil but he knew was there. Before he knew it, he'd retraced the ten yards to the cover of undergrowth and was back with the boy. Now was the moment: now was the decisive moment of his plan.

'Yes?' he said.

'Yes,' the boy said.

Everything then happened at once. He recalls taking his lucky lighter out of his pocket, the one with the playing card on it. He remembers seeing the empty can next to vegetation – he did not want it too close to him – he saw, definitely, clearly in the firelight, the hunched figure of the guard, his head propped on his hands, his head now turned to the side, and he recalls that he was about to light a handful of dried grasses, indicating to the boy to get back into the undergrowth – that's what he remembers he was *about* to do, but what actually happened was that suddenly the whole place was in flames: a curtain of flame rushing along the clearing floor like a wave to shore, hissing, rolling, spreading outwards and upwards at the same time, launching itself into the air with the sudden bellowing of the petrol cans, spewing out fire, the guard suddenly awake, drowsy, disorientated, confused about what was happening, his hat blown off, the fire leaping onto the pickup, into the jerrycans Patrice had opened there, and the vehicle bucked in the air, in protest as if the earth had rippled – everything, *every* thing was dancing with flame.

'Have you seen how gasoline burns?' Patrice twirled his index finger horizontally in the air. 'Rolling, rolling.'

The fire leapt across the spaces between things, like bolts of electricity, connecting them in flame – he could actually see it. The huts were burning; the pickup was burning; the branches around Patrice were burning. It seemed that the night itself was on fire. Flames climbed up through the trees; they wound themselves around the branches. (He looped his fingers round and round like a vortex.) The fire growled like an animal. 'I thought, I have done all this.'

But then it got worse. A pile of ammunition – he doesn't know what – went up. The explosion convulsed the very trees around him. Razor shards of superheated metal tore through the vegetation – *tsssk, tsssk, tsssk* – shredding everything.

Patrice did not see how it had happened but the guard had been blown off his feet and lay on the ground barely moving, his eyes wide with horror. Fire covered him; he was in a pool of flame and unreachable. The fire began to consume everything, his clothing, his amulets — burning him up and he knew it.

'I look at him,' Patrice said, 'and he is not my enemy now. I look at him. His eyes are big. I never see such big eyes. Then he is gone. I have killed him.'

The noise and the chaos had the effect he wanted: he could hear the shouts and screams of the anti-Balaka rushing to the encampment. They began firing their weapons. 'All around me this noise: *schukk-schukk-schukk* .... *schukk-schukk* ... *schukk-schukk*. I look around — where is the boy?'

The two of them became separated in the bush. He is not sure how. There was gunfire everywhere, a torrent of it raining into the foliage around him. He ran as best he could, his skin getting ripped open by razor branches. He hid for a long time, pressing himself into the soil, wondering what to do.

Many hours later, when he was as sure as he could be that there were no anti-Balaka around, he crawled in a wide arc to the other side of the camp. Then Patrice saw him. Or rather, saw his body.

Patrice did not tell me what they had done to the boy. I did not want to know. I did not ask. It has meant that since that time I have regularly imagined the very worst about what happened. I have heard first-hand, from people who have directly witnessed the brutality, the stories of mutilation, desecration and decapitation in CAR. It is a mercy not to know what the anti-Balaka did to him. But my mind is filled with atrocity. This is something Patrice lives with every day.

He also has to contend with the fact that the return to the camps had ended in disaster in another way: he didn't find the girl.

THIRTEEN

17 Days

Patrice and I met again in the rubble-strewn truck stop outside Yaoundé. It was a muddy mess. It had rained in the night, angry tropical rain. Puddles formed in the cratered surface. They began emitting faint wisps of vapour in the heat. Birds squatted sullenly in roadside trees. They seemed dark blue in the early light, crosses between crows and jays, but in truth I didn't know what the birds in this continent actually were.

'Amazing morning,' I said.

He agreed by shrugging as if to say, What do you expect? I then tried to amaze him, by telling him about Jupiter – you know all that. He was underwhelmed; he was unimpressed. I was unimpressive.

'I will show you amazing,' he said.

He took out his mobile phone and I thought he was going to show me an app. And let me confess that I thought: Patrice, it better be a good app to beat my star chart one. So let's see, Mr Business Man, let's see. Men, it seems, can be competitive about almost anything. But instead he used his phone, can you believe, as a phone. He made a call. He didn't speak into it since he clicked off as soon as it was answered – some kind of arranged plan.

Two women emerged from behind the trailer of an enormous truck. One woman was elderly, her face deeply wrinkled, her features riven with sorrow. She stooped, edged forward, gingerly advancing in minute steps, her frame curved like a question mark. She approached me weeping, wailing, caterwauling in front of us.

'Her family were pulled off trucks trying to get out of Bangui, killed in front of her eyes,' Patrice said. 'I told her there is nothing you can do.'

What could the law do? What does it do in places where there is no law? I felt sharply the limits of lawyering.

'She wants to tell someone,' Patrice said.

Having being absorbed by the sheer grief of the old woman, I hadn't noticed that the second woman was suddenly, quietly, at the elderly person's side, clasping her hand, speaking softly in her ear, letting her know she was not alone.

'It's okay,' Patrice said quietly.

The young woman wore a yellow headscarf with green leaves; she'd knotted it loosely but with panache. Someone who cared about what people made of her.

'It's okay, Saira,' Patrice said. 'It's okay.'

On one hand, I have a new life and I have left the forest behind and also all the hardship of those days, on the other . . . sometimes at night I walk out of the building, especially when I get the dreams and stare at the sky.

K.K.G. (male, 16 years)
who spent three years with Mai-Mai rebels
in the Democratic Republic of Congo

*

Post-traumatic stress disorder is now a widely recognised phenomenon. It is characterised by the intrusion of flashbacks or nightmarish events so vivid and visceral that, as Thomas Elbert and Maggie Schauer write, 'the victims believe themselves to be back amid the atrocities'. It wasn't like that for Saira. Speaking to her, hearing her quietly recounting what happened, wasn't her going back. You got the sense she had never left. Saira was still there.

Sometimes when you are speaking to her, you see all those events in her face. You think you do. You sense her aunt's boyfriend standing silently in her bedroom, watching; the desert breeze from the north and east on which the rebels came; her father whispering *Go, Saira, go*, even as he realised he may never see his daughter again. And sometimes this exquisite young woman would listen to Patrice and myself talking and would be quietly humming to herself, barely audibly, slow notes coming out of her, like a kind of lullaby. And while she did this, over her head a vast arch of African sky connected the alien city to which the Fates had driven her, back to her abandoned home. Sometimes she drew fine circles with the tip of her sandalled foot in the mud, creating a strange hieroglyph. All the while, the sun kept rising. It would not stop.

In the end, as so often, after so much chaos, there was stillness and silence. Another armed confrontation took place two days after Patrice and the boy returned to the camp. In it the anti-Balaka group who had killed the boy were for the most part killed themselves. Patrice even went back to the house where he'd first encountered the boy. And nothing much happened. Not for 17 days. And then the pickups returned to his property.

But these vehicles belonged to the new militia, people that Patrice knew. They said they'd found something in the bush. On the flatbed of the third vehicle was an emaciated girl in clothes that were little more than rags. Her name was Saira.

Patrice looked after her, bought her new clothes, eventually after a few months came across the western border with her into Cameroon. It was a perilous journey. Many people did not survive it. They were killed or became trapped in enclaves, the leaving of which would mean certain death.

But Patrice and Saira got through. Several months after the crossing, he brought her to meet me. Later that night, I was in a car, driving through Yaoundé. I turned the handle and opened the window.

'What's wrong?' François said. 'I turn up the AC? Doesn't work good, but I try.'

'No, it's fine,' I replied. I put my face to the space where the glass had been and felt the breeze jetting across my forehead. It was warm and alive, in the way tropical air stunningly is. I asked him if he'd ever consider going to the Central African Republic. He puffed out his cheeks.

'*Pourquoi?*' he said.

'*Pourquoi pas?*' I said.

'*Parce que le CAR, c'est l'enfer.*' It's hell.

The warm air rushed across my cheeks, I felt it in my eyes, and although we careered through the concreted sprawl of the centre of Yaoundé, for a few moments I was sitting with Saira and the boy on the bank of the stream in the Central African Republic, by the cooling water with the sleeping fish.

'She can tell you more about him,' Patrice had said earlier that day at the truck stop.

And Saira could. And did.

'What was he like?' I asked her.

Patrice rubbed the side of his sharp nose and lit a cigarette with his playing-card lighter – it was a king (I forget whether of clubs or spades) – and it was almost like a celebration, a tribute in trails of smoke.

'He was very quiet,' Saira said, 'and also very brave. He did not speak much, but when he speaks, I listen. I like listening to what Omer says.'

I found my breath held tight in my chest. 'Omer?' I said.

'His name was Omer,' Saira said.

That boy in the Central African Republic, the child soldier killed in the bush, his name was Omer.

FOURTEEN

The Great Desert

I confess I found it difficult to hear all this. After I met the two of them, and for some days after I returned to Europe, I found it difficult, as Saira puts it, to find sleep. Although back in a relatively safe Western city, among those I know and love, I walked along the bush paths of my mind and sleep continued to elude me. It was difficult to divest my thoughts of the tales of madness and murder I was told by so many about the Central African Republic, the litanies of lynching and mutilation.

In the fervid way the imagination works, I kept associating the country's insanity with the large, orange crabs that plagued Michael Goldsmith, crustaceans crawling out of the sea and infesting the world. I began to associate the cries for help from the Central African Republic with that extraordinary cave in Argentina's Patagonia, now a World Heritage Site, a wall imprinted with outstretched human hands, reaching out towards us from our deep ancestral past. And yet there is so much beauty in the Central African Republic, for coexisting within the country's conflict-ravaged borders is that other CAR: a land beautified by great beasts, forest-dwelling elephants and almost extinct antelopes, a land traversed by thunderous rivers – the last place on earth. The country is, I began to realise, a world within the world.

Vast tracts of formerly populated areas now lie desolate. Human Rights Watch reported that it was possible to drive for hours in the area around Bossangoa without seeing a single person in their home. In December 2014 the United Nations Commission of Inquiry determined that 99 per cent of the Muslim population in the capital had either been killed or forcibly displaced. In CAR as a whole, 80 per cent of Muslims had been driven out of the country by the violence directed against them. Many have sought sanctuary in Cameroon, where I met one, Saira, and heard about another, Omer. Unlike the two of them, Patrice is Christian (not that he regards himself as devout); he is technically on the 'other side' (not that he acknowledges affiliation to either camp), but this sectarian conflict cannot be reduced to a simplistic Christian versus Muslim narrative. Seleka were not, for example, seeking to install a caliphate. And I must emphasise that it is not my intention to take sides. I believe Patrice is right: your people, my people, whose people – that thinking is part of the problem. A problem of fanning differences between people into justifications for slaughter. Unquestionably there have been atrocities of an unimaginable kind by both camps.

Indeed both anti-Balaka and Seleka have been named on the UN's infamous 'Annex 1', the list of parties of concern in armed conflicts. As such both the CAR factions keep inauspicious company with Mai-Mai affiliates in DRC, Al Shabaab in Somalia, combat groups in Myanmar/Burma and insurgents in Syria. Both Seleka and anti-Balaka are listed as using, recruiting, killing and inflicting sexual violence on children. Additionally, however, the UN has concluded that against the Central African Republic's Muslim population, anti-Balaka have pursued a determined 'policy of ethnic cleansing'. How many members of the general public in the developed world know about this calamitous human tragedy? I suppose it is impossible to care if we don't know. For a long time, I did not know.

The UN Secretary General reported to the Security Council in the summer of 2015 that 2014 was one of the worst years on record for the treatment of children in conflict zones. Child abductions were an increasing trend and extreme violence rose to unprecedented levels. In response, UNICEF has launched its 'Children, Not Soldiers' campaign. They have a tremendous challenge ahead of them.

Many enclaves of trapped and terrified people remained in CAR. As Sabrina Avakian told me at her mission headquarters in Bertoua, 'It's like what I saw in Kosovo all over again: they are prisoners in their own country.' I discovered that the man who put the Kalashnikov to her head, General Yaya, was killed in fighting around Bangui just before the fall of Seleka in 2014. But first he was complicit in seven farmers being tightly bound and then thrown into the rapidly flowing Ouham River to drown. Miraculously, three survived.

I left the refugee camps with a heavy heart. Gado Number 1 is now matched in size by Gado 2. People were still having to flee the CAR crisis; UNICEF and UNHCR keep having to do their humanitarian work. As Sabrina once said, 'It's still going on.'

The International Crisis Group has reported that with the withering of the failed state and the internecine turmoil, the Central

African Republic has become one of the world's principal sources for conflict diamonds – blood diamonds. Many are ghosted away through smuggling routes to the west, through Cameroon – along the very road I travelled from the CAR border to Bertoua, criss-crossed by green mamba snakes.

Patrice, Saira and I were sitting on the white plastic chairs at the makeshift café.

'So what will you now do?' I asked. As Patrice, cigarette in hand, systematically laid out his grand plan, I was slowly filled with another kind of concern. 'Do you have to do this?' I said. 'Everyone knows how dangerous it is.'

'And CAR was not?' Patrice replied.

'But you're here, Cameroon.'

He looked at me and I saw myself dully reflected in his round black sunglasses. 'Let me ask you: you want to stay here, Cameroon?'

'No,' I said.

'Why not?'

'Okay, I get it. But just because it's not your home – '

'If I can't be in my home, I find the best I can.'

I told him how our legal practice in London was involved in protecting those exploited by human traffickers, how we support and represent refugees and asylum seekers. Try to. It seemed so little, I admit. 'So I may see you in Europe?' I said.

'You will have those jeans for me, yes?' Patrice said.

I laughed. 'Sure, yes. And you'll give me a good price?'

'Fair price,' he said. 'I told you fair.'

We shook hands. So at the end of it all, was François right: did I like him, this man of business? It seemed to have gone beyond that. Saira slowly unfolded her hands and it was obvious she wanted to say something. Both of us became silent.

'*Pardonnez-moi*,' she said. 'But is it true what they say?'

'How do you mean?' I asked.

'That *les Européens*, they don't want us to come? That they hate us?'

What could I say? She looked at me with her intelligent, searching eyes, seeking to know. I felt she deserved the truth. 'Some people are like that,' I said. 'Many. Not everyone.'

'But many?'

'Yes,' I said.

'I love my country. But they try to kill me there.'

'I know,' I said.

And that is the tragedy of the refugee from chaos: both loving their home and needing to flee human aggression. I wandered with Patrice to François's Merc. We were alone as François spoke to Saira at the café.

'Do you have any idea,' I said, 'how you will cross the Mediterranean?'

'It must be boat,' Patrice said.

It was the last thing I wanted to hear, but Patrice, a pragmatist to the end, was resigned to it. 'It will be very tough,' I said. (*Très dur.*)

He ran a hand over his shaved head, wiping away the iridescent beads of sweat glinting under the Yaoundé sun. 'The desert,' he said, 'even worse.' I'd heard the stories: so many people died or were killed or kidnapped crossing the Sahara Desert. 'But I will know,' Patrice continued, 'who I can trust.'

I believed him; I trusted him. He trusted the boy. Of the people I know, there are few I'd back to pull off that journey. Patrice is one of them.

There are only one or two more things to add.

*

I got close.

The Gado camps lie a mere 20 miles from the Central African Republic border. I could feel its tremendously powerful pull. I desperately wanted to cross; was advised not to, not yet, not without proper security planning. Okay, I told myself, okay: be patient. In any event, it is still extremely dangerous to travel outside Bangui (and even in some sections of the capital), and I wanted to speak directly to ordinary people caught up in the madness and not just meet officials. In the UN's eastern Cameroon camps I was able to meet many who have survived the carnage.

The first thing you notice when you enter the camps is that they are awash with children (60 per cent of refugees are infants or youths). At Gado 1, in what was no doubt some kind of breach of protocol, I ended up playing football with more than 40 six- and seven-year-olds from the Central African Republic – I couldn't help myself. I won. I'm sorry, *mes amis*, but football is football. They understood. They surrounded me and all pretended to pound my head. It was blissful to have one's head pounded.

But even in that euphoric moment, I noticed a young boy in a ragged green shirt on the fringe of the empty dust patch we'd been playing football on. His slender frame tilted to the left as he leaned patiently on a makeshift crutch made of wood. He had lost most of his left leg beneath the knee. The medics told me that sometimes children in CAR have limbs amputated because there's been a complete absence of early medical treatment to prevent disease. But sometimes, as the UN has reported, children are mutilated as an act of war.

I spent time speaking – or more accurately listening – to displaced and dispossessed fellow human beings yearning to go home but too afraid to do so: over their shoulders, less than an hour away, the bloodshed continues. They spoke with pain and at the same time tremendous pride about their home. And all the time more blood is spilt and the forests are looted and lost.

Sabrina and I never made it to the Red Box Bar. Its VIP Cabaret remains a mystery. As do the delicate yellow flowers that climb high into the trees. At Bertoua and the camps, Sabrina continues to wage her unrelenting personal war on malnutrition, disease and homelessness. Permit me, just for one sentence, to slip into Sabrina-speak.

'*Allora*, Sabrina, *mon dieu*, I know you will hate this, okay, but, I am sorry, yes, but what you do for the Central African Republic, it is heroic. *Va bene*, Sabrina, *obrigado*.' Thank you.

And thus with these images slowly turning through my mind, I flew out of Yaoundé on Air France for Paris. There are no direct flights to the UK. The aircraft's flight map showed that we were heading right over the heart of the Sahara, passing Agadez in central Niger, a stopping point for those crossing the great desert; we sailed high to the east of Timbuktu, before finding water again at the Mediterranean and finally leaving the continent the shape of a human heart. I did all this in a safe, sanitised cabin in a couple of hours. It would likely take Patrice and Saira many weeks or months to do the same.

I have the palpably unnerving sense that the aircraft I travel back on is not the same as the one I came on – a different *kind* of machine; the magazines in the pouch in front of me are not the same kind of publications. We sail on over the ominous desert, over people inching towards the sea and Europe, clutching bulging bags and dreams. *There is always a ride*, Patrice once said. How much farther can it be across the great and ghastly sands? I snatch the magazine from the pouch in front of me. 'Your personal copy', the editors of the summer issue of Air France's *Madame* magazine generously announce. It is like a gift someone has left just for me. I flick through the glossy ads, not particularly absorbing anything until something strikes me: almost every other advertisement is for *joaillerie* – jewellery. I hadn't noticed the sheer extent of it before – not in that previous kind of aircraft and that previous kind of magazine, before Patrice and Saira. And something else.

From Cartier and Van Cleef & Arpels at the front, through Buccellati, Chaumet, Chopard, Boucheron, Piaget, Bulgari, Pasquale Bruni, to Chanel's full-page back cover, all of them, *les diamants* – diamonds.

FIFTEEN

The Cave of Hands

In the Central African Republic, it seems as though the Aggressor has been unleashed across the land. But that is not the whole story. It cannot be. The Seville Statement invites us to believe it isn't. We desperately want to believe that. And when in the last couple of years we hear report after report of atrocity and terror, we want to clutch to Seville like an article of faith. So what have we learned?

We must recognise that aggression is an adaptation. It is part of survival behaviour. It has been employed by animals for hundreds of millions of years. It pervades nature. It is within us, possibly part of us – but not the only part. Not even the most important part, but there. It does not define us; it does not determine us. It co-evolves with our culture: rules, restraints, compassions. But we must be clear-sighted in understanding what it is and what it is not. Intrepid people like Thomas Elbert constantly explore innovative and imaginative ways to combat the combat high, the addiction, how it spills into post-conflict life and society.

The implications of their work for post-conflict societies, for transitional justice, are enormous. That kind of aggression arises in very particular circumstances. The battle is on to neutralise it. But first let us honestly understand.

What else have we learned? I claim that during the course of this section we have encountered a number of extraordinary people, people who have in their exceptionally different ways – they could hardly be more different personalities – sought to overcome the world.

Sabrina Avakian, standing in the way of loaded weapons and saying people need to be fed.

Omer, who found it within him, in the midst of madness, to say no to the Aggressor, to be prepared to lose his own hand rather than take another's.

Saira, who risked being beaten or worse, by tending to his wounds.

Patrice – what can I say about Patrice? – who found a boy from a faith 'his people' were supposed to be at war with, and trusted him – went back with him into danger, who now carries that boy's memory around with him.

In differing ways these people have confronted the Aggressor; they have found fresh ways to be free.

Somewhere on the long, sad road from West Africa to Europe, just one speck in the long line of humanity snaking from the conflict zones of Africa to the safety of the North, perhaps in one of the dens of human exploitation on the fringes of the great and ghastly desert, or half-asleep and dust-encrusted on the back of a ramshackle truck, or on the crammed deck of an unseaworthy boat, bought by human traffickers and filled with desperate people, is a man who moves likes mercury, sporting round black sunglasses on his shaved head, who just as you view him lights a cigarette with a playing-card lighter, emblazoned on which is a black king. But on this journey, he will not be entirely alone.

Because he will be accompanied by another, a young woman whose father once bought her a golden box. Maybe she will reach Paris, even though her father never did. And the two of them, on this long and perilous trek, this new migration, for all the old reasons – betterment, respite, hope – will be followed by a shadow, that of a boy, whose name was Omer.

A youth who became a child soldier in one of our era's most brutal of conflicts, and while people around him were swallowed up in mutilation and madness, who found a way to stay true to something good in himself. Omer found his own way to stay free.

UNESCO is probably right: we are not genetically programmed to have a 'violent brain'. But still human violence against humans blights our lives and our communities, fills our news programmes and newspapers. The psychological mechanisms that incline us to kill, to overcome our aversion to inflicting harm on other human beings, mechanisms that facilitate our pouring of insects into the various extermination machines of the world, are at war with other instincts and impulses within us. The outcome of that conflict may be our actions, what in the end we do. If we have an Aggressor, it does not have a free rein, not in almost all of us, not almost all of the time. The ability to be aggressive *on occasion* has unquestionable survival benefit: to protect one's young, to defend against a potentially lethal attack. But the fact that we can be aggressive does not make us constitutionally aggressive. We have other qualities. There is sympathy; there is sacrifice.

Omer went back. He returned to save the young woman who tended his wounds, the bush bride of the man who beat him. She was his friend in the folly of their country's war. In the rage and rebellion all around them, something rebelled within Omer himself, something that rejected the worst excesses of the slaughter, at great cost to himself. In the end the ultimate cost.

In doing this, he set himself on one side of one of the central arguments we have perpetually been conducting with ourselves, an argument that evidentially stretches back 13,000 years, to Jebel Sahaba. Omer set himself against those who would massacre and maim. He had no appetite for it. It meant that the atrocities he witnessed would very likely have caused him deep distress and trauma. He would not have developed a resilience. He was not viewing it like a fish with eyes wide open but ultimately asleep. He saw it for what it was. His seeking to rescue someone else finally claimed his life.

It is irrational, I know, but I search the footage of African migrants pulled out of the azure Mediterranean by the Italian coastguards in their unnervingly white hooded overalls and face masks, wondering if I will see Patrice and Saira. I have related their history because I want it to be known, for just two of the many thousands who risk death in the crossing from Africa, where they have come from, and how their lives have been. Before we condemn, before we turn away, before we switch off.

I never met Omer, just as I never met Gareth, nor Anthony's friend Michael. But I see Omer as another link in the curious chain of life across time and space, connecting Gareth and Dawn's son Alexander and Anthony and Michael and now this lost boy in Central Africa, Omer.

379

I have also related this because of something else that psychologists Thomas Elbert and Maggie Schauer write. They observe that those of us not directly involved in conflict and chaos can do something of great use when we meet survivors:

> [D]ocumenting and acknowledging human-rights violations can dignify the hot traces left in the memory of those who have survived terror and organized violence.

There is another term for documenting: it is to bear witness. And that's what Thomas Elbert and his colleagues do. They are developing interventions against the enduring impact of conflict violence, against those manifestations of the Aggressor.

Judith Léveillée has tried to find creative ways to raise awareness of the plight of children in CAR, to forge new alliances. 'You know,' she says, 'we've been trying to fight this crisis with 19th-century methods – sheets and buckets. They are important, but we must be able to do better than that.' Prompted by her, I researched Stephen Hawking's project with 'science philanthropist' Yuri Milner. Nanocraft equipped with 'light sails' will be launched into what Hawking calls 'the great void between us and the stars'. At the project launch he continued, 'We are human, our nature is to fly. I believe what makes us unique is transcending our limits.'

'Oh, and mats,' Léveillée says. 'We use mats. Mats are important, but can't we do better than that for all these people? Is that the best we can do?'

The UN has called the Central African Republic the world's largest 'forgotten humanitarian crisis'. I remember what Saira said. 'Please tell them,' she said to me. 'Please tell them about my country.'

*

Once Patrice asked, 'Your phone has a map?' I said it did. We had been discussing his impending journey. 'Where are we?' he said. 'Show me where we are.' And I did.

The app produced a satellite map of Yaoundé. It showed our position as a blue circle with a white outer fringe.

'You can make it smaller?' I pinched the touch screen and we zoomed out. The *quartiers* of the city appeared, the *routes nationales* needled through patches of green forest, suddenly Douala appeared on the coast to the west, balanced by Bertoua on the other side near the CAR border. 'More,' he said. I zoomed further out, the Gulf of Guinea provided some cooling blue relief, clustered around it were Nigeria, Benin, Ghana. Further out and the Atlantic Ocean appeared, higher up North Africa kissed against the end of Europe at Spain – the Pillars of Hercules to the ancient Greeks – Egypt connected Africa to the Middle East, suddenly there was Iraq, then Iran, Kazakhstan, Mongolia. 'Again,' he said. I swept my finger across the glass and we glided past Japan, over the Pacific, into the heart of the American prairie lands, Kansas, Nebraska, past places I knew well – Boston, New York – then swiftly across the North Atlantic Ocean, where the United Kingdom, my little island home, sat like a strange afterthought off the European mainland; I scrolled down and suddenly, dizzyingly, we were back in Yaoundé.

'Where are we?' he said again.

He had made his point. This is where we are: together on an oblate spheroid-shaped rock silently spinning through space. Patrice and Saira are two people of the land, the first land, as her father called it, two people from the last place on earth, seeking another place to live. I wonder if they will make it. I wonder if they will survive. I hope that Saira's father was right. I hope *tout est possible* – that anything is possible.

Cueva de las Manos (Cave of Hands), Patagonia
Ancestral handprints, up to 13,000 years old

PART VI

THE TRIBALIST

Then said they unto him, Say now Shibboleth:
and he said Sibboleth: for he could not frame
to pronounce it right. Then they took him,
and slew him at the passages of Jordan.

Book of Judges, 12:6, King James Bible

ONE

The Isle is Full of Noises

This chapter was going to be a silence – a vacancy and a void. That's what Jeanne, my contact in Haiti, made me realise was the effect of what I had done – more exactly, of what I had failed to do. Created a silence. A vacancy and a void. I wanted to understand one of the most recognisable qualities of human beings: our rapid, sometimes irrational, tendency to form groups, subgroups, cliques, nations, networks – tribes. Is there something within us, a Type, that prompts us to form groups? Is there a Tribalist? I had a chance to find out on the ground in an exceptional human situation, practically a time zero. I had that chance, and lost it.

Life in court, conducting cases in public, is always performative – all advocates are aware of that. It's always a performance. But when I returned from Central Africa, something was changing. I was beginning to perceive the performative in life outside court too. It began with news that an undercover documentary was about to be broadcast. It was going to be big. Children in custodial institutions were still being hurt, physically abused, maltreated. We uncovered evidence of this at the inquest into Gareth Myatt's death. I knew it would happen again. Which is to say I feared it would. Pam told me it would. Why? That same haunting question. But now I was connecting it to something else: to what had happened to Anthony and Michael in Ghana; to Saira and Omer in CAR.

Let me be clear: I still *functioned*.

From the outside, no one would have perceived any difference. I appeared in court, advocated, sometimes acted as a judge. I was commissioned to write articles and met my deadlines, renewed my car insurance when it came up for renewal, opened the back of my printer and fixed an apocalyptic jam, made my famous Tuscan lasagne – a once-in-a-decade event – taught me by an 80-year-old lady in a farmhouse near San Gimignano with its medieval turrets, but I kept returning to those questions posed at the beginning of the book: *Who are we? What are we? Who is inside us?*

I thought about Michael swimming through a lake that is not a lake, looking at the fish as they look at him, about Omer putting his hand on that rock and not flinching. I was messaging Dawn. We were slowly becoming friends. She wanted to know about my travels. I wanted to know about hers. She had moved on from ancient history, and now the history of art of the entire planet was opening up for her. All this spooled around those frames of Gareth walking along that corridor in silence, turning left, shutting the door. What happened in that room?

I had planned to go to Haiti, was eager to: there were human rights projects that I hoped I could contribute to. Yet I couldn't bring myself to book a ticket. Why? It wasn't a direct flight: BA to Miami, connect next day via American to the Haitian capital Port-au-Prince. But that wasn't the reason for my reluctance. A night in Miami – what an imposition. That was not the reason.

I again contacted Jeanne, who lives in Port-au-Prince and works in human rights. We were going to develop my work in sub-Saharan Africa, trying to find better ways to protect the vulnerable – children, women. I was standing on the languid arch of the footbridge across the Thames that leads to the Tate Modern, a stone's throw from the back of the Old Bailey. Jeanne had put in a vast amount of work to make my trip work. She had arranged meetings, people for me to meet, to talk to, to understand. The phone rang. As she picked it up on the other side of the ocean, the bridge shook under my feet. Barges slipped by beneath; tourists took photographs.

'Jeanne, it's Dexter.'

'Hey, hey,' she said, 'so you're back from Africa?'

'I'm back.'

'With, I think, a tale to tell?'

'Tales,' I said. 'Several tales.'

'Ah, that is good, no?' She speaks French with an accent warmed by the Caribbean Sea.

'Yeah,' I said, flatly.

One of the gentlest voices you could hear. 'Are you okay?'

'I'm not coming to Haiti,' I said. 'I'm sorry.'

I braced myself. She had every right to be angry, to tear into me. I steeled myself.

'Ah, I'm sorry too,' she said. 'But are you okay, Dexter? What has happened?'

What had? I tried to step back, take stock. Central Africa had. I told her. About Patrice and Saira; about Omer. I told her about my visit to the refugee camps on the CAR border, the

387

tens of thousands of displaced people. How I met dozens of the children, played football with them, loved it – left. That act of leaving – I kept wrestling with it. But it was the conversation with Jeanne, that was the 'physician heal thyself' moment. I had been investigating the cognitive cost of compassion, writing on it. Surreptitiously, softly, it had crept up on me. I hadn't allowed myself to recognise the true effect of seeing these things, being exposed to them – a different kind of exposé. We try to control it, which is a form of both defence and denial.

'There is something beautiful in this,' Jeanne said. It was one of the very last things I expected to hear. 'For you to be there, to leave your life, to go, to observe.'

'But it's not enough,' I said, 'just to observe.'

There was a pause. 'Then what are you going to do?' she said quietly.

Her words reminded me of a question. After weeks of some of the most acrimonious and savage legal battles I have experienced in court, we obtained a 'good' verdict for Pam and her family. The jury gave us what we wanted, a narrative verdict that was a devastating condemnation of the way in which Gareth and other children in our custodial institutions were treated. So, yes, they gave us, the lawyers, what we wanted. But they did not give Pam her son back. And if she could not have that, then she wanted to stop other parents sitting where she had been sitting for week after week as the people authorised to care for these vulnerable children ran for cover and evaded responsibility.

With Jeanne's what-are-you-going-to-do comment, I knew I had to do more, find out more about the three key questions at the heart of the book. But at that point, it was too much. So I did not go to Haiti, not then. And so, for several months this chapter remained a silence, a vacancy and a void.

*

Imagine this. A little piece of hell in modern life: a noisy new neighbour has moved in next door. You moan, you complain. The noise is endless, unfathomable – what is going on in there?

Many animals are highly attuned to the noise their neighbours make. Noise is information. Evolutionarily, eavesdropping has a function. It can be adaptive, provide marginal but meaningful survival advantage. Female birds eavesdrop on noisy males as they compete with each other in song: a genetic *X Factor*. Female birds then seek extra-pair fertilisation from the 'winner'. Nightingales, Keats' 'light-winged dryad of the trees', eulogised for their song, use that noise as a form of territory defence, overlapping their song with intruding males as a form of aggression. On the other hand, male common nightingales (*Luscinia megarhynchos*) make less noise after they've mated.

So noise is more than just a din. But this noise from your new neighbour is too much. You complain to your family, to your friends. They want to know who this person is. What do they want to know? What do they actually *need* to know?

Whether your tormentor is male or female.

Approximately how old he or she is.

But there are other factors the conversation circles towards. There are other things we will want to know. Which part of the country they are from – perhaps; which part of social space they inhabit – possibly. We are liable to ask what they 'do'. Would, for example, the following picture be sufficient for you?

My annoying new neighbour is a she.

She's in her late twenties.

I'm not sure what she does.

Enough? Would more information help? Might another descriptor assist you?

1. My annoying new neighbour is a she; she's in her late twenties; I'm not sure what she does.
2. My annoying new neighbour is a she; she's in her late twenties; I'm not sure what she does; she is black.

That second answer – whether we like it or not – immediately creates a series of different mental images and associations (unless because of who we are and where we live we originally conceived of her as black – in which case substitute white, Latina, Chinese).

Research science has repeatedly found that certain repeating 'vectors' arise when we wish to have a rapid understanding of another person. So when encountering a new individual we typically classify them along those three vectors in social space: sex, age and race. The picture of how we conceive of our new neighbour in the hypothetical will differ dramatically depending on whether it is an elderly white man or a young black woman. They still generate the same un-neighbourly noise, but we conceive of them differently. Of course we do. Why?

As I write this, today is, ironically, the United Nations' International Day for the Elimination of Racial Discrimination, and issues around race have great saliency. In the United States there has been the 'hands up' campaign following the shooting of Michael Brown, an 18-year-old black man, by a white police officer in Ferguson, Missouri; there was Donald Trump's 'travel ban'; across the Atlantic, Europe is facing a different kind of crisis. In the UK referendum on whether to leave the European Union, survey after survey revealed that for voters the number one issue was immigration, a complex question that at its heart is inseparable from race – and difference.

But a group of evolutionary psychologists argue that of the three classification categories above, one should not necessarily be on the shortlist. One of those three vectors is not hard-wired into the mind. That vector is race.

Their argument is that in the deep evolutionary past, for countless thousands of years when our mental machinery was evolving, although humans have always formed groups – we *are* social animals – our ancestors would simply not have come across other humans who appeared on visual inspection to be of a different 'race'. Contrast that with life in any metropolitan area in the West today. Standing on the footbridge across the Thames to the Tate Modern, I am passed by Chinese tour groups, Scandinavian students, Arabic visitors, Americans, even a few Brits, all side by side, all in the space of a few seconds.

So if race appears so important to us today, how deeply rooted is it? A research team led by Robert Kurzban at the Center for Evolutionary Psychology at the University of California, Santa Barbara set about investigating how robust our awareness of race actually is. Are we really wired to be sensitive to race? How and why do human beings form groups?

My case collapsed. Murders sometimes do that. And so a chance to go was again suddenly there, unexpected: a month in a London court had disappeared. Almost, not quite, but almost, as swiftly as the events of 12 January 2010 – *le douze janvier* – when what was full instantly emptied, what was standing was crushed, when in a few cataclysmic seconds not only a world but the understanding of what the world is, for countless thousands utterly changed.

But first my murder collapsed. I was free, even if my client, who awaited a new trial date, was not. Not yet. I had to brush up my French. But even as I did so, I knew it would not be enough. I'd need Kreyol, and that would mean an interpreter. Which was interesting because my journey was also fundamentally, finally, about interpretation. How does one – how can one – interpret the astonishing wonder and woe that is Haiti?

I needed to get medicated up. So a return to the travel clinic in High Street Kensington. When I arrived, to my great dismay, it was boarded up. Curiously, a tall black man with a tight knot in his tie and an immaculate white shirt sat on a stool on the pavement outside.

'Do you want injections?' he asked.

'I'd be lying if I said I actually wanted them,' I replied. 'But I'm sure a doctor will tell me I'll need an armful.'

The man had a long golfing umbrella. He waved it towards the side street and the back of the building. 'Refurb. I'll show you how to get in the back.'

And so we headed for the tradesman's entrance, down some steps, past workmen with classical music on the radio. As it turned out, most of my jabs were up to date. What I was missing was cholera. There had been several outbreaks in Haiti since 2010, the disease having been brought, it was increasingly believed, by UN peacekeepers and emergency aid workers, possibly from Nepal.

'Haiti, Haiti . . . *Hay*-tee,' the nurse said, scrolling down the information on her screen. 'Just keep up the highest possible standards of water-food hygiene.' She pored over the fatality figures for the latest epidemiological week. 'Cholera is waterborne, so brush your teeth with bottled water. Oh, and don't drink your shower.'

'Drink my what?'

'Keep your mouth shut when you shower.' She tore open a sachet and added the mysterious white contents to water. It began to fizzle.

I gazed at it suspiciously. 'How hideous is this going to be?'

The doctor, trim beard, constant smile, said, 'It's not actually an unpleasant taste. Something like artificial fizzy drinks from the seventies.'

'As I said, how hideous is this going to be?'

'Remind me,' he said, still smiling, 'why are you going to Haiti?'

Of all the places I travelled to during the course of this book, I was given most advice about Haiti, much of it conflicting. About the security situation, the medical risk levels, where to go, where not to go, what to eat, what to avoid. But there was one piece of advice all agreed on: don't arrive after dark. Make sure you get a flight that lands in daylight. Simple as that. So suddenly there I was: Miami. The lull before the storm.

Only when I landed there was a fearful storm hitting Florida. Flattened clouds, more purple than I've ever seen, scudded in low across the wave-tops bringing horizontal sheets of rain that chased bathers from the beach as if they were being whipped. In the torrent, palm tree fronds were blown sideways like miserably sodden streamers. A flash of lightning set off an inconceivably deafening car alarm. This was supposed to be the lull.

But at least I was close. It was more last-minute than I'd have preferred. But trial lawyers can't be choosers. Our lives are governed by the glorious uncertainty of litigation, which is to say they are barely governed at all. I stood on the beach in the rain and gazed across the Atlantic waves. A few hundred miles to the south-east of this south-eastern rim of the United States lay Haiti.

Later, as I sat watching the furled umbrellas around the pool while the rain raged on, the waitress cleared away my Cuban club sandwich. She was in fact Dominican, from the other side of the island of Hispaniola that Haiti shares with the Dominican Republic.

'It's awesome you're going,' she said. 'How can one place have had to suffer so much? My brother, he is a medic, he went across in January 2010. He still won't talk to me about it. I kind of see it in his eyes, you know. All that.'

As I waited for the bill, she returned with a plate I had not asked for. On it were three beautifully cut slices of baklava. 'Our chef, he's Turkish,' she said. 'Everyone round here, they are having a good time and you're going over there. He wanted you to have these.'

I thanked her and bit into the first piece. It was the moistest baklava I've ever tasted. I asked her if she had any advice.

'Just get there, you know, before dark,' she said.

TWO

The Pier

The seventh book of the Bible, the Book of Judges, relates how two Semitic tribes, the Gileadites and the Ephraimites, went to war. After a monumental battle, the Gileadites installed a blockade across the river Jordan to trap fleeing stragglers from their enemy's troops. Since the two groups were visually indistinguishable, the guards at the crossing were instructed to ask each person seeking safe passage to pronounce a single word. The word was 'shibboleth'.

It had a number of meanings: an ear of corn or an olive branch, a stream of water or torrent. However, the significance of the word was that the Ephraimites had no 'sh' sound in their language. They could not pronounce it the same way. When they failed the test, they were slain.

But that was a biblical story. That kind of arbitrary test – what has come to be known as a 'shibboleth' – could only be a grand metaphor for human discriminative behaviour, for base tribal behaviour. Surely.

*

When on 6 December he landed on the island, he believed he had happened upon either Japan or even the legendary biblical kingdom of Sheba. Then a few weeks later, on Christmas Day 1492, his flagship ran aground further along the island shore. He named the place La Isla Española. The island itself, the tenth biggest in the world, is still known by the name Christopher Columbus gave it – Hispaniola.

The isle was not uninhabited. For several thousand years a population of farmers and fishermen had spread over the island and flourished. They were a Taino/Arawak people, part of the great migration that began thousands of years before, passing over the land bridge from Siberia to Alaska then progressing down through the Americas, possibly as far as South America, before making their way up into the Caribbean.

Still, the islanders warmly greeted Columbus and his troop of newly arrived Europeans. As Columbus himself wrote:

> They have no iron or steel or weapons, nor are they capable of using them, although they are well-built people of handsome stature, because they are wondrous timid. . . . Of anything they have, if you ask them for it, they never say no; rather they invite the person to share it, and show as much love as if they were giving their hearts.

There are a number of contemporary reports about what subsequently happened after Columbus's 'discovery'. One comes from Bartolomé de las Casas, the son of a small merchant from Seville, a city where centuries later world experts would gather trying to understand human violence. De las Casas left Spain for Hispaniola in 1502, reaching the island within a decade of Columbus's arrival. He wrote that the mysterious land across the great ocean was the 'most happy isle called Hispaniola, which indeed has a most fertile soil'. And to the European seafarers who had sailed west into the unknown, it must have seemed like a miracle, something of a paradise. Half the island even today remains covered in tropical moist forestation and teems with hawks and hummingbirds, kestrels, cuckoos, doves and parakeets.

And like Columbus, de las Casas was struck by the very particular character of the indigenous inhabitants. 'Now of the infinite multitude of humanity,' de las Casas wrote, 'these are the most innocently simple, guileless, the most devoid of malice . . . and live without the least thirst after revenge, laying aside all rancour, commotion and hatred.'

De las Casas was given a royal grant of land and documented carefully what he witnessed, later publishing his account back in Spain. In due course it would be banned. He wrote that his European countrymen began 'to carry out massacres and strange cruelties. They attacked the towns and spared neither the children, nor the aged, nor the pregnant women, nor women in child bed.' Indeed, he observed that among his fellow Spaniards

> . . . it was a general rule to be cruel; not just cruel, but extraor-
> dinarily cruel so that harsh and bitter treatment would prevent
> Indians from daring to think of themselves as human beings.

Consequently, the native population of Hispaniola was either killed or enslaved or died from the diseases the Europeans carried. Within a few generations of Columbus's *Santa Maria* running aground in what is now Haiti on Christmas Day 1492, and his establishment of the first European settlement in the 'New World', the indigenous residents of the happy isle had been all but eradicated.

*

Sitting in Miami International, waiting for the gate to open. But Haiti is already here. Kreyol being spoken all around me. At the security check, an elderly lady is asked to take off her hat. In fact, hats – she is wearing three, one on top of another. She wears also three coats.

'Madam, why are you wearing so much clothing?' the guard asks.

'Why are you wearing so little?' she responds instantly. 'I'm cold. Why is your airport so cold?'

She is correct, factually. Gloriously correct.

It is daylight when I arrive. But there has been some kind of incident in Port-au-Prince. The security staff won't let the driver picking me up into the airport. I call Jeanne. She tells me clearly, but unmistakably firmly, 'Go out of the double doors. Do not go beyond the double doors. Do not go into the car park. Do not speak to anyone. Do not look at anyone. Do not do anything except wait at the double doors. Don't let anyone touch your bags.' I waited. And then while the sense of menace built and built, suddenly he appeared through the mass of humanity pressing at the airport gates.

'Welcome to Haiti,' Jonel said, smiling broadly. It started pouring with rain, the same weather front I'd left in Miami and that stretched over the slivers of land we threaded through on the flight: the Bahamas, the northern shore of Cuba, to the east of Guantanamo. Jonel wore a T-shirt the colour of the sun that had just disappeared. He was about 40, thickset, short and endlessly smiling. 'Your first time in Haiti?'

'Yes,' I said.

'We hope you will come many, many times.'

We shook hands, and he was so openly welcoming, so disarmingly open, that I felt sick for feeling so threatened at the airport doors. There was something familiar about him, not just his features, but his aura. As I hauled myself up into his SUV, I glimpsed the woman with the hats in the car park, distributing them to her family as they greeted and hugged her. Such joy on their faces, a family reunited in the rain. They actually did need all those coats and hats.

As Jonel and I drove through the streets of the capital, he explained, as I suppose everyone has to when people visit for the first time, *le douze janvier* – the earthquake.

'Most of the tents are gone,' he said. 'But still some stay.' The rain smashed onto the car roof and gushed in turning torrents through side streets – everything seems on an incline in most of the city, what remains of it, hill after hill, water sluicing down them. I wondered what conditions would be like in those camps that still existed. I'd soon find out.

'You see, when it happened, no one here knew anything about earthquakes. What was this thing happening? People, they didn't know what to do. Some people in the street ran into buildings. Ohhh.'

That understandable instinct for shelter in a crisis turned out to be fatal.

'Do you know where the people brought to this island originally came from?' I asked. Slavery began with the Spanish. It intensified under the French. Haiti was a tremendously lucrative slave colony. Perhaps the most profitable.

'Africa, certainly,' Jonel said.

'I was just wondering where, if you know.'

He shook his head. 'The elders, they say from Central Africa. And Benin.' My eyes must have lit up. 'Benin?' I said.

'You know Benin?'

And suddenly I was back in Bukom, and a chicken was wandering past, and a boy with almond-shaped eyes was bobbing and weaving.

'I know someone from there,' I said. So: Central Africa and Benin. What would Patrice think? What would Anthony?

'And some came from Guinea,' Jonel said. 'And some from Ghana. You know Ghana?'

The rain kept falling. We passed the shells of buildings wrecked by the earthquake, stripped, crushed, crumbled. 'I know Ghana,' I said.

Today 20 million people live on the island that was once the home of the Taino. Numerically they are almost evenly divided into two, with the eastern two-thirds of the land mass forming the Dominican Republic, a Spanish-speaking nation of which about 10 per cent of the population are black. On the other side of the island is the first black republic, the site of the first black rebellion (victorious against Napoleon's army); it is a land of Kreyol- and French-speakers, 95 per cent of whom are black. They inhabit one of the poorest places on Earth – Haiti. And it is how the island is divided that is crucial. Historically it has marked and maimed Hispaniola. In many ways it still does.

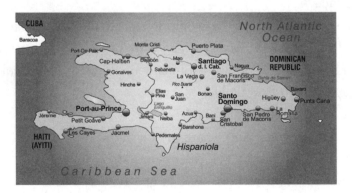

Hispaniola

Until January 2010, the event in Haiti that was most known to the outside world took place in 1937. It was a massacre.

In October 1937, Rafael Leónidas Trujillo, a Dominican militaristic dictator with fascist leanings, ordered the killing of Haitian workers who had settled across the border in the Dominican Republic, principally to work in sugar-cane production.

Trujillo himself, previously an official in the sugar-cane plantations, rose to power with the National Guard, trained by the US Marines. It was *la dominicaniȝación de la frontera*, the Dominicanisation of the border. To remove Them altogether; to leave the land for Us. For another way to view the project was one of de-Haitianisation – as Edward Paulino, professor of History at John Jay College, New York, puts it, an 'erasing the Kreyol'.

The conflict was deeply rooted, and complex. The border had been a contested region for over a century, with periodic military incursions by Haiti. The frontier was however porous, and people in the borderlands were often indistinguishable from one another. Some had been brought up speaking Spanish, others spoke French-Creole. It meant that language itself was seen as a kind of border, a distinguishing mark for two different tribes – a false distinction, as historically the people were intertwined and integrated. Nevertheless, as Haitian writer Edwidge Danticat put it in her novel *The Farming of Bones*, it led to a situation where people's words were taken to reveal 'who belongs on what side'.

To distinguish Afro-Dominicans from Afro-Haitians, the execution squads held up a sprig of parsley to the person at the end of the rifle barrel or with the machete at their neck. They demanded them to state what it is. The word in Spanish is *perejil*. But those who were not raised as Spanish speakers found it near enough impossible to roll or trill their 'r' – they couldn't pronounce *perrrr*-e-hil. It cost them their lives. So a shibboleth was used. Within the last 100 years.

People were shot, strangled or hacked to death with machetes. At the port of Montecristi, a thousand people were forced off the pier to drown in the waters that lapped the shores of Hispaniola, very close to where 445 years previously the *Santa Maria* had run aground.

How many died in the massacre of 1937, even after all this time, is still contested. The figures range from 500 to 35,000. But in the scholarly literature there appears to be a growing consensus of between 12,000 and 15,000 victims. In other words, the systematic slaughter of 12,000 to 15,000 people with rifles and machetes. Machetes were preferred as the weapon of butchery to convey the impression that this was a spontaneous response by the Dominican citizenry. In fact, it was a carefully coordinated military operation by the National Police and Army augmented by civilian volunteers. This action was, as the US ambassador stated in a cable to President Franklin D. Roosevelt, 'a systematic campaign of extermination . . . directed against all Haitian residents'.

Today the island still suffers from the scars of the divide. The Dominican Republic, according to Professor Edward Paulino of the City University of New York, remains in the grip of an 'exclusivist notion of Dominican identity', one that relegates the black peoples of Haitian descent to second-class status – to being seen as aliens and outsiders and even enemies on their native island. The Us and Them.

THREE

The Dogs

At the Center for Evolutionary Psychology at the University of California, Santa Barbara, Robert Kurzban and co-founders Leda Cosmides and John Tooby sought to investigate how intractable race is as a classification tool. Was it, they wondered, eradicable? To scrutinise this question, they used a memory confusion paradigm – an experimental device dating back to at least the 1970s.

Research volunteers were shown a number of photographs and also a series of textual sentences. The photographs were of players in a basketball game. The sentences were snatches of a heated argument around a foul during play. They were along the lines of:

You nail our guy in the face and expect to get away with it? That's bullshit. You have to play to the whistle. No whistle, no foul.

It was the usual trash talk that accompanies most highly competitive sport. And which, some would say, is part of the fun – the cathartic release of controlled violence (that is another story). For the research volunteers – all undergraduates at UCSB – the next task was to complete a memory test. First there was a one-minute filler/distraction activity – in later replication experiments, for example, volunteers were asked to identify the 50 states and state capitals of the US. Then they proceeded to the real point of the study: how successful were the volunteers in matching individual player to statement, to what he said in the argument?

The sentences were reshown in randomised order. Could the volunteer match sentence with player? If not, if there were mistakes in attribution, was there any pattern in the misattributions? One key feature of the set-up was that some of the players were white and others black (African American). Would that feature be represented in the results?

What Kurzban and his colleagues found was that when there was no obvious indication of which team each player belonged to, research participants comparatively rarely misattributed a statement to someone of a different racial group. In other words, race was salient: the white guys were saying this; the black guys were saying that.

The rationale of the memory confusion experimental model was that the kinds of memory mistake the volunteers made was revealing of how they were classifying people, the categories they were using to divide up the world. Race seemed a guide to recollecting who was saying what. The experiment was repeated.

But now the players were dressed in team kits – some yellow, some silver-grey – obvious indications of which group each person belonged to – coalitional cues were amplified and emphasised. Now on the repetition of the experiment there was a

significant change in how volunteers made mistakes. Few misattributions fell along group/team lines. The yellows said this;
the greys said that. Instead people made *more* mistakes matching
up the statements with the players along racial lines. The UCSB
hypothesis stated that when other coalitional (group affiliation)
information was given, volunteers would privilege categorisation
along those lines at the expense of race. Race became less salient.
It mattered less.

This finding has potentially far-reaching implications. It came
to be called the 'race-erased effect'. Was it really the case, as the
title of the Kurzban paper suggests, that race could become
'erased'? If so, what does that say about our innate sensitivity to
racial difference?

So fundamental was the UCSB result that more recently
researchers in the Netherlands sought to replicate the findings.
Using a similar methodology, they found that although sensitivity
to race was not entirely 'erased', it was indeed *reduced*. It seemed
that arbitrary cues or signals, such as the wearing of tops of
differing sporting teams to indicate affiliation, can perform a similar
function to race: they can be salient ways to divide and make sense
of the world – and in doing so, they can reduce the impact of
race.

As a result of these experiments, researchers have argued that
we do not automatically encode for race. On this analysis, race is
in fact a by-product of other coalitional cues. In other words, it
is a proxy or shorthand for defining our in-group and out-group.
This is because when presented with other and clashing coalitional
cues – when the subjects were primed about other categories – the
effect of race, while not eradicated, was significantly diminished.

This finding would be surprising if we are indeed 'hard-wired'
for race. Our race sensitivity network would be activated and we

would remain attuned to it. Yet this did not happen in the Kurzban experimentation, nor in the Dutch replication study. This was unquestionably a significant result. The paper Kurzban and colleagues produced has subsequently been cited several hundred times.

The Kurzban paper suggests that 'to the human mind, race is simply one historically contingent subtype of coalition'. The volunteers had been brought up in a modern world where race was a socially germane and prominent category, one of our prime classification methods. But it has not always been like that. Reaching back in evolutionary time, race would have been more or less irrelevant as our ancestors would not have encountered other 'races'. The world was just too sparsely populated and the human population too scattered.

The tribes our forebears met would have been very like their own tribe, genetically and visually. The differences would not have been racial. But the problem remained: how to decide whom to trust, whom to fear, whom to cooperate with, whom to flee. The eternal problem of dividing the world into Us and Them. On Hispaniola, on 12 January 2010, this problem arose with devastating effect.

It happened at seven minutes to five in the afternoon. Offices were about to close. Schools were emptying. It was one of the busiest times of day for humans on Hispaniola. There were people everywhere. First it came like something slithering through the grass. Like a snake. Its tail reached 8.1 miles below the surface of the earth. And then suddenly it was there. At Leogane, 15 miles southwest of Port-au-Prince, the subterranean thing centred and surfaced. It unleashed hell. It was savage, merciless. The earth quaked. It literally did.

But it didn't last long, somewhere between 30 seconds and one minute. It doesn't seem very long. Unless you were in it. And it is what happened in that unfeasibly short period of time that changed everything.

At 4.53pm on Tuesday 12 January 2010, an earthquake registering 7.0 on the Richter scale hit Haiti. More than 250,000 people were killed. Port-au-Prince was destroyed. Leogane, the epicentre, was levelled. Much of the southern part of the country was wiped out. The UN building in the capital, a six-storey administrative complex, was instantaneously squashed into a single storey as one after another, pile after pile of concrete smashed down with 100 people inside.

Kenneth Merten, the US Ambassador to Haiti, gave the best description of what had happened to the country. 'It looks,' he said, 'like an atomic bomb went off.'

Haiti is the poorest country in the western hemisphere. So says the CIA in its *World Factbook*. The CIA actually posts lots of facts online. I scroll down its Haiti page. Here's another: 'A massive magnitude 7.0 earthquake struck Haiti in January 2010, with an epicentre about 15 miles west of the capital, Port-au-Prince. Estimates are that over 300,000 people were killed and 1.5 million left homeless. The earthquake was assessed as the worst in the region over the last 200 years.'

The country collapsed.

People gathered outside churches and prayed. They congregated outside the rubble of government buildings and sang. There were bodies everywhere. Everywhere became an open morgue. The problems of life reasserted themselves in a new way: the old problems in a new way. Shelter, food, water, safety. Particularly safety. Danger everywhere: from the ground beneath your feet, from falling buildings and bricks above – from the people surrounding you.

Tented cities appeared. There were no communities. There were no streets. There were just fragments of families left, as if some giant inscrutable hand had randomly plucked people – you, you, *not* you – and in a heartbeat, a tremor of the earth, everyone else had gone.

As Naomy, head of one of the schools in Port-au-Prince, said, 'Suddenly – BOOOOM – there was no rich and no poor. Everyone was in tents in Place St Pierre, and it was a time for us to understand that we are nothing more than creatures. I saw a boy in the street bleeding. I tried to help him. I saw one of the teachers from my school lying in the street flat out. His back was broken. Broken – his back, completely broken. And I began crying. I didn't know what to do, and I was crying. And then there was a hand on my shoulder from behind. It was a woman I've never seen before or since. And she said quietly, "Don't cry. We must not cry. We have work to do. We all have work to do."'

This was true. So much work to do, just to stay alive. But other people put themselves to another type of work.

The world was new. How would people live? People in Haiti did what humans have probably always done: they formed groups. That part of us that is very old surfaced anew. Very quickly there were new associations between people with the old ways gone. A new Them, a new Us – new tribes. Some people gave food to strangers, to people who had in common with them the gift – the small miracle – of having survived. But there were others – looters. Looters would kill you for anything, for a bag of rice in your hand. They dragged people out of cars. Shot the driver. Took the vehicle. They didn't care. Some were former neighbours, but there was no longer anything resembling a neighbourhood. The world on this side of Hispaniola was new.

Dogs were running wild. Some died as other hapless animals in the city had died; others ran alongside the gangs of looters. The looters carried sticks, machetes, iron bars, sharpened pieces of wood, anything. Some shop owners armed themselves. They fired at the marauders, some were killed. People climbed into gutted buildings through windows, across collapsed rooftops, and dragged out mattresses, while bodies remained inside. People tied impromptu masks across their mouth and nose to allay the stench and airborne infection. Toothpaste became a highly coveted item: it was smeared under the noses to counter the smell of the bodies. With the dead everywhere, cars were turned into hearses. But even these were carjacked. The bodies tossed out, the vehicle taken. Gangs formed along roads and created roadblocks. They demanded money for passage. They instituted a new form of taxation. Sometimes bodies were piled up to form roadblocks.

How quickly it happens. But predictably? What was coming out? Gangs of thieves and looters were arriving from outside the capital. But many were already there. The main prison of Port-au-Prince collapsed. All 4,000 prisoners were able to escape. 'They took advantage of the disaster,' as the International Red Cross said. Criminal gangs fought what was left of the police. They fought one other. International aid agency doctors found that as well as those people needing their help for broken bones and head injuries there were others with gunshot wounds.

Some gangs 'charged' people for the right to loot certain warehouses. Another type of tax. They fought the residents of the capital for anything, candles, boxes of soap, everything. An international news agency reported a 'frenzy' of looting. Was that right? The word frenzy derives from *phren*, the Greek word for mind. Had people lost their mind?

At the Anglican church in the Carrefour district of Port-au-Prince, the Reverend Paul Frantz Cole said, 'If the people don't get food, they will have reason to give vent to the violence inside all of us.'

Who did he mean by 'us'? And was he right? What is inside?

FOUR

Like Peeling Fruit

In a side street hanging off a hill in Pétionville, historically one of the more upmarket neighbourhoods of Port-au-Prince, sits the office of Kanesof, a school collective run by women. They are building a wall. Bricks are neatly stacked alongside a pile of roughly broken rock. As I was to discover, many women's organisations in Port-au-Prince need to build strong walls. We park up alongside the rubble. The other side of the compound is encased in flimsy corrugated sheets leaning at a precarious angle. It's a meeting I've long wanted to have, to hear about their work, explore ways we can help support their human rights programmes.

Naomy is head of the collective. A small but strong woman in her forties, she has a confident air, and determination in her eyes. We sit in a classroom in the school Naomy and her team have built up. There are long wooden benches in a horseshoe config-uration, no glass in the windows, just a gap in the wall. The back of the room is painted vivid canary-yellow. The brickwork on the other sides is exposed. As the 20 or so women gather, a cooling breeze blows from nearby hills and mountains that surround the city.

'My mother inspired me,' Naomy says. 'My parents had nine children. None of us knew how to read and write. So my mother went to school herself, to learn. People made fun of her, an adult going to school. Even my father made fun of her. But she didn't care. She studied so hard, also bringing us up, and became a teacher. I was so proud to see my mother as a teacher. So when I grew up, I took it upon myself to teach women and children to read and write. I started teaching Restavek children. You were telling us about child slavery in Ghana, well, we have a form of child labour here in Haiti. These children are called Restaveks.'

The word Restavek comes from the Kreyol word meaning 'to stay with' (*rester avec*). They are children who are sent to stay in another family, away from their parents, if they have them. They effectively become chattels, someone else's property. It is a form of child slavery.

'It's so deep in our culture,' Naomy continues. 'I can't stop it. I want to, but I can't, so instead I was thinking, what can I do to help? Then I realised: I could teach these children to read and write. I started a class and had 35 children in it. But there were so many more. "Please help me read and write and then I will find a way to be free," they said. How was I going to help them?'

Naomy visited the mayor of Pétionville. In October 2002 she was giving classes for 182 children. A year later she had 255. Now she has 800.

'Most of these children don't have any food. We try to give them one hot meal a day. But some days I can't feed them and it is hell. I feel I've failed them. I can't sleep because I know these children will go to sleep hungry, and then how can I eat? How can I?

'On the afternoon of *douze janvier*, we had one of our Restavek groups. We have classes for them in the afternoon because in the morning they must work. That is their life. I don't like it, but that is it. My staff were taking the class, and I'd been feeling unwell all day. Like this pressure pressing down in my head. I had no cold or anything, but I was unwell all day. I was downtown buying some sewing machines for the children, and for some reason I phoned the principal and told him to let the children out at 4.30. I don't know why I did it. I said, "Let them out at 4.30." I came back to the school and the children had been let out so the school was nearly empty when BOOOOM. I didn't know what it was. The walls were shaking, like they were going to crash on us. Everyone was running.' She points at the wall we parked our car alongside when we drove into the Kancsof compound. It collapsed and killed five people. 'I ran to the main road of Delmar 75 and saw a bloodied kid, and he said "I want my sister. Where is my sister?" I didn't know who he was, who his sister was. And he was just there covered in blood saying, "I want my sister." Houses were falling, people were screaming, trapped, dying, and this child is saying, "I want my sister." Then I saw one of my teachers on the ground and his back was broken. He couldn't move. I started crying."

'After that, I started looking at life differently. We're not as important as we think. In 35 seconds the country lost 300,000 people. I understand people better after the earthquake. Soon I had 60 ["*soixante, soixante*"] people staying in my house. How was I going to feed them? But over the years I had found a way to feed hundreds, so I knew I would find a way again.'

Women had to queue up for emergency supplies. They were given access cards in a kind of voucher system. 'The security guards,' Naomy said, 'they sometimes demanded that women have sex for the use of the cards.'

Sex became a currency. People – men – with keys to the stores demanded payment. What was a desperate young mother to do? Or a teenage daughter with a father dead and a mother dying from her crushing injuries? The world divided anew. Two tribes: the haves and have-nots. In that Darwinian struggle for survival after the earthquake, humans did what humans invariably do: they formed groups. Our social brain, our intelligence and ingenuity, seeking out stratagems to survive, gravitated towards a very old solution: band together, form coalitions. Act in groups; see the world in groups. But in those dire few days full of fear and after-shock, the categories assumed new configurations. Some people had control over resources; others were without.

Another of the women gathered at the school, Madam Phisline, was without.

As we speak, Phisline adjusts the wide brim of the straw hat she wears. It gives her a jaunty, rustic air, in contrast to her sandals, which have a little faux silver brooch on the strap between her toes, a touch of glamour, a sign of something different. The brooch glistens in the sun, a minute detail that marks her out. She has the gaunt, wiry frame of someone constantly in motion. She is: she is a nurse and a midwife.

'When the quake hit us,' she says, 'the world, it ended. There was no safety, no fence, everyone was crammed together in a small area. You can't stop the bad guys getting in, running around everywhere. I never before understood how valuable this is,' she says, as she taps the wall behind her. 'How precious a thing is a door. A lot of girls who got attacked were attacked going to the bathroom at night. The men were watching. They were waiting.

'In the Champs de Mars, by the presidential palace, there were three camps. Everyone was living too close to everyone else. That is not good. People need space. We need at least some . . . distance. One minute I had a house, my own home, and I loved it, and then I was in a tent. How are people supposed to live in tents? Suddenly there was no rich and no poor, everyone was in tents. I lit a candle to have some light, because the darkness was when the men came. Light kept them away, but the tent caught fire, and started to burn.

'The men were outside. I could see them through the flames. They were waiting. Sometimes they wore masks across their faces, but you could still see their eyes, watching. They knew that with the fire we would go out to where they were. There was no light. Just the stars. The fire burning, and the men waiting for us to go out to where they were. This is how it was. Those in the tents, and those who were waiting.'

In the early 1990s, Madam Phisline was a young democracy activist. She was a fervent supporter of President Jean-Bertrand Aristide who had won Haiti's first free democratic election. Once he assumed office, he set about ending many of the human rights violations inflicted by Haiti's notoriously repressive previous regimes. But he was opposed. The rich and the powerful and their military supporters ousted him in a coup later that year. After that there were severe reprisals against those who continued to support him, seeking his reinstatement. Phisline did. She was seized and sexually assaulted. As a result, she had a son. At the time, she was 16 years old.

She sometimes worked at another women's support centre, Mercopek, situated in another part of Port-au-Prince. Phisline has shining, moist eyes, as if she is on the verge of weeping. Her long fingers claw the air as she talks, parting some invisible netting that appears to surround her. It is unbearably hot. Across the city, there is a power outage. Phisline carefully wipes beads of sweat from her face as she speaks. 'When the quake hit us, I was on my porch with two of my children. My husband didn't make it. Our house collapsed and he was crushed inside. It was Tuesday night. Everyone went out on the street. Tuesday was when he died.'

It became, as she described it, the most terrifying carnival in history. She spoke with intense fondness for what was lost: a land of flowers and trees, surrounded by a gentle sea, which was suddenly taken away from them. Suddenly they were living in a tent. The land was rubble and madness.

'*À vrai dire*, it was not even a tent. It was a sheet. We made our own shelter with sticks we stuck in holes in the ground. We used bedsheets from wherever we could find them. Sometimes, people had to take them from shops or the houses of people who had died. I am sorry for everything that happened, but we had to survive. When it rained, I crawled into our old house, what was left of it, and got a rug. I loved this rug, but it was now a roof. My children when they were small, just babies, used to play on this rug, roll around and laugh, and now it was our roof. It was all we had. This is how we lived. Me, my five children, including my daughter who was 17, living like this on the street on that night.'

'Which night?'

'The night the men came.'

She paused and took a deep breath. Then another. Her fingers knotted, curled together, were finally still.

'The earthquake happened on a Tuesday. The men came on a Thursday. So quickly all this badness comes out. You see, people were saying, "Beware, beware, the walls of the prison have fallen down."'

Hundreds of prisoners had escaped. Many of them were being held on remand, incarcerated before trial, some had not even been charged. Some had simply insulted or offended someone they should not have. Some were entirely innocent. But there were others.

Smelling an opportunity, looters in the capital formed gangs with those who came from outside Port-au-Prince. They armed themselves. There was no law, only these people who waited in the night and the people behind sheets with rugs as roofs.

'You must understand,' Phisline says, 'there was no electricity. They came out of the darkness, these men, if they were still men, and they were . . . operating right through the camp. No one knew what to do. If we left, my children could be in greater danger. They'd catch me. They'd catch my children. There was a police station nearby. But the police wouldn't come to help us. They wouldn't come into the camp. They didn't do anything to protect us. So I thought, okay: I can't run with my kids, so the only choice I have left is to do whatever I can to protect them. I could hear the men in the next tent. The people next to us were screaming, then silence. These men, we'd heard how they were attacking 6-year-old girls and 70-year-old women. They did not see us as human any more. Something happened. Something terrible happened in their heads.'

For these men, there were two groups: them and their victims. Everything had been reduced to that. Sometimes she spoke as if these men were starved, other times as if they were gorged and glutted. It was as if something that had been contained could no longer be; as if a sickness far worse than any virus or contagion were infecting everything; she spoke as if at night something dark and appalling spread its wings over the city. Old women prayed for the daylight to come again; people held their breath in the darkness. The intruders would appear with contorted faces, the hideous masks of nightmare and broken dream. People huddled behind sheets around failing candles and waited. There was nothing else to do.

'They came to our tent with machetes and shaving blades,' Phisline said. 'The blades cut the sheets they like were cutting a leaf or peeling fruit.'

They asked Phisline if she had any money. She said she did not. They said they had to take something. Since they had come, they had to take something: they could not go without taking something. That was the new law, their law, in this new Us and Them.

'I had hidden my daughter under all our clothes. I was thinking if they . . . take me, then they will go, they will move on. They . . . assaulted me in front of my children, including my son who came into the world because I was attacked when I was 16 fighting for democracy and Aristide. This is the world. But I protected my daughter. They did not find my daughter.' Madam Phisline looks down. There are no tears, or none that are visible, even though her eyes are moist. She gathers herself, looks up. She says, 'They did not find her and I would do it, do it, *do it* again.'

Later, in a side room of Mercopek, I have a meeting with the centre's leader, Pastor Aniya. Somehow they've got a generator to work. An ancient groaning fan blows a jet of cooled air at the back of my neck, fans the pile of victim statements on the desk in front of the pastor.

'Yes, this was the case, how it really was,' Aniya says. 'A lot of prisons broke, and suddenly these men were all outside and it was an open situation for them. Our office collapsed. But we had to persevere with our programme because even more women now needed our help. When we realised that all young girls were in danger, we decided, we the women, that we would organise ourselves. It was just us and the people who attacked us.

'People were desperate. They were looking everywhere to see if their loved ones were still alive, and yet these men were looking everywhere for girls. They would wait in the dark. They'd wait for girls to go to the latrine. And then they would move. They came out of the dark. That's where they hid. There was no electricity, you understand. Nothing. Us, the sky above, and these men in the dark, waiting.

'When you live in a camp, you don't know who your neighbour is. It could be anyone, everyone, a gang member, a rapist, a drug addict, a crazy person, anyone. But what could we do? We decided to do something about it. To fight back. One of things we did was to get whistles. Most of the latrines were outside the camp. We gave women training, told them that the whistle was not a toy but a tool, a weapon – our weapon. So we conducted some simulations of a woman in danger and using a whistle and other women running to protect her. I once took a CNN crew to one of the camps and blew my whistle. So many women came running, the film crew couldn't believe it.'

Earlier Naomy had told me something similar. 'Women's groups organised themselves. They got people who knew martial arts to train them. Women watched over the camps at night. They worked hard during the day to earn money to buy torches and whistles. At night, they fought off the men waiting to attack girls. They began to fight back. There was no one else to protect them, so they thought they will help themselves. What else can you do? The best part of that experience was that women spoke to each other, the mothers began to mother each other.'

'So we thought, why stop there?' Pastor Aniya continued. 'Women in the camps were also at risk from their husbands. There was so much stress that domestic violence went up. Men were raising their hands to the women. But these women now had whistles. And when their husbands attacked them, they began to whistle. Perhaps for the first time in their lives, they were making a noise about domestic violence. But we also knew we had to involve men in finding solutions to this problem. So we had 25 men who had daughters or wives sexually assaulted, and got them involved, asked them to speak to other men. We had all kinds of men: men with jobs, even gang members. It was good for them to tell other men that women are not a "thing", that it's a crime to hurt them, that we would ensure they would be arrested and put into jail. Having men talking to men, that really made a difference.

'We women in the camps couldn't rely on waiting for aid or help from the outside. We had to do it ourselves. We had to stand up for ourselves. Time moved on. But women were still being attacked. At first there were no courts, but slowly they started coming back. So we tried to develop programmes around prevention, accompanying and supporting women to get medical help and legal assistance in taking their case to court. But when we started helping in this way, our call centre started receiving threatening calls, then death threats. We've had people coming to our offices, threatening us. One of our workers was kidnapped. One of our co-founders has had to flee. I've seen emails announcing the death of Pastor Aniya. I'm Aniya. I'm also a pastor. But I'm not dead. If they want to do that, okay, I don't like. But I will not stop. I will never stop. Unknown men have come to our office asking for me. They wanted to find me, get me. The next day they returned and took photos of our receptionist, threatened her, asked where I was, and said they'd be back. My life is in danger. They want me to know that.'

'So why are you here?' I asked.

She pauses. Looks at her phone. 'We can't all run. We can't all go abroad. While we have been talking, I've missed calls from two survivors, two women who have been sexually attacked. Who is going to help them if I close down? If we don't help each other, if we close our doors, these men who do all this to vulnerable women, they will think, no one else is there, no one cares, and we'll put more women in danger, not just me. It isn't easy. But when was anything important ever easy?'

Back in 2010 Naomy argued and persuaded and badgered and borrowed until she was able to find a reliable supply of food to give to the women and children around her. Their collective grew. Within two months of the earthquake, Naomy started a microcredit scheme. With small grants, she was able to give each woman $64 to buy stock to start a business selling food and supplies on the streets. Even heavily pregnant women were working, carrying heavy baskets of food on their head, trying to sell something, anything, to feed their children or other children they'd decided to look after. The women shared the proceeds. They helped one another.

Now, six years later, some have built their own businesses worth $500. 'They will buy and sell anything,' Naomy says, 'but not themselves, do you understand? Not any more. No, not now, because now we are taking back control of our lives. We are going to change how we are treated.'

The fight takes many forms.

'We try to fight the fear inside our sisters,' Phisline told me. She stops when there is a sudden groan of machines as the power surges back. 'The fear eats them up. How can we stop the fear eating them up? That's what we were trying to work out. First, we make sure we let our sisters know they are women and they are wonderful and worthwhile and we will stand by them to help them stand up for their rights.'

Phisline and her colleagues go wherever transport will take them – wherever the ramshackle taxis, the tap-taps, go. Where the roads end, up in the hills, they walk. They offer cooking and sewing classes, and a safe house for victims who have had to go into hiding. They secure medical assistance and accompany and support women who take their cases to court. But this is risk-laden work. Phisline has herself had to go into hiding. The gangs are looking for her. They shot at her house. I asked why she continued her work.

'My parents died when I was 12. And other people helped me. And then when I was attacked and became pregnant as a teenager, people also helped me and my child. So anytime I am able to help someone else, I feel stronger. I have to give it back to others. I don't want other women and girls to experience what I have. I'll fight to the end and give all I can to stop this. So other women and girls will feel safer. *Plus fort ensemble.*'

But even if the Kurzban and Dutch experiments suggest that race is not intractable, as social psychologist Marilynn Brewer concluded, in-group favouritism, along with out-group indifference (even hostility), exists everywhere. See a football match. Go to a school. Go to a church. Martin Rees, former President of the Royal Society, possessed no theistic beliefs. Nevertheless, as he told Richard Dawkins, he goes to church (religiously?) as an 'unbelieving Anglican . . . out of loyalty to my tribe'. To test Brewer's claim, ask this simple question: has there been a society where this phenomenon has not existed? The quest goes on. Which groups do you belong to? As significantly, how aware are you of the groups that you do not belong to?

When we examine the behaviour of our biological cousins in other primate species groups, there are similar complexes of coalitional behaviour and conflict with out-groups. Kurzban's team suggested that this characteristic tendency of forging coalitions and designation of others to be wary of may predate our evolutionary separation from other primates and may be a feature of our particular branch of the evolutionary tree. The significance is that in-group assignment leads to our preferential treatment of our fellow group members. We tend to give more resources and 'goods' to those we view as 'one of us'; we tend to judge their behaviour more leniently. Which is another way of saying, comparatively, those on the outside are more harshly treated and judged.

This behaviour is extraordinarily – some might suggest frighteningly – easy to create. Experimenters have randomly divided strangers along entirely arbitrary lines with meaningless categories, or random ones – what are called 'minimal groups'. For example, people might be separated into groups depending on whether someone preferred a Klee or Kandinksy painting, or more arbitrarily still, when they were split into heads or tails groups after a coin toss. They have found that in-group preference almost immediately materialises, even though the groups have 'minimal social content' and effectively are baseless, meaningless or previously unheard of. Some of this behaviour is socially learned. But also, this rapid, often irrational, tendency to form groups appears to be generated by part of our neurocomputational kit, part of our mental make-up. It is likely to have been evolutionarily beneficial to form and be part of in-groups. The sheer prevalence of this behaviour is obvious: think office politics, playground politics, family politics – not to mention infighting within the same political parties. It rarely takes long for the lines to be drawn.

In distant evolutionary time, in the absence of racial difference within more or less homogeneous societies, other social signs and classifications would have been used to effect the subdivision. The world was seen to be divided into different same-race groups – let us call them 'tribes'. This part of our make-up, the equipment to make, recognise, process these divisions, the Tribalist, continues to affect us as we categorise and classify, form coalitions, contend, come into conflict with and fight against others. But in more recent centuries, with significant population movements in many parts of the world, race has been a way in which we divide up the world. Again and again, research findings show that along with age and sex, race is one of the most prominent vectors we use. In this context, the obvious significance of the findings of Kurzban and his colleagues is that race is not an immutable classification tool. It can be 'overwritten':

> Less than 4 minutes of exposure to an alternative social world in which race was irrelevant to the prevailing system of alliance caused a dramatic decrease in the extent to which they categorized others by race.

That is a remarkable result. And an encouraging one for how we may think about ways to work towards greater social harmony – or less damaging disharmony. There is an overwhelming weight of research evidence demonstrating our tendency to form groups. It is likely to be both culturally learned but also deeply wired. Group formation from the time of the savannah has undoubtedly provided survival benefits. In that unforgiving environment, it is likely that those who were able to pursue a coalitional strategy had greater survival prospects than the loners. And thus we are group-forming social beings. We are in this sense Tribalists. We tend to give preference to our in-group. We tend to be indifferent to out-groups, even wary of them, or hostile. We show remarkable loyalty to our tribes.

But the constitution of out-groups is not fixed. It is historically and geographically contingent – highly so. Racial sensitivity, then, is not innate. It is more probably a by-product of what are undoubtedly deeply wired mental mechanisms for assessing coalitions.

Such assessments are a critical part of our past and our present, and a key characteristic distinguishing mark of our functioning as highly social beings. Thus the Tribalist in us does not necessarily need to see the world in racial terms. And if it does, because of the specifics of our historical and geographical context, that can be worked on, dented and diminished, if not completely reversed. Race can be overwritten because it is one of a number of proxies for group membership. It is a recent historical thing. It tells us about who we are now, but not who we were or – perhaps more importantly – must always inevitably be.

It seems that in a bewilderingly complex world, we are looking for shortcuts. Ways for us to break down and understand the social space around us, to make reliable predictions about the likely behaviour of others. To do this rapidly in social interaction, we seek observable cues. We use markers, identifiers, codes, cultural passwords – shibboleths. These heuristics are means of social and cultural detection. In the modern multicultural world, one of the obvious ones, aside from age and sex, is race.

But we are not using a mental mechanism created to sensitise us to racial or genetic differences. Instead, our coalitional computation machinery, in order to make rapid assessments, uses race as a shortcut to infer social outcomes and behaviours. It doesn't have to be that way.

We all, despite our best endeavours, make race-based inferences. If we are honest, we all, in all likelihood, and to differing degrees, racially stereotype. Here is an interesting intersection between biology and culture. So when we think of all the problems this particular social categorisation has caused – and is causing – the notion that it is not immutable gives hope that we can overcome it. We can move on. We are not condemned to see the world through racial glasses. We are not as a species inherently, unalterably racist. That is good to know. We may see the world in 'tribes', but our tribes are not necessarily what we think. We have a need for something the tribe tantalisingly dangles in front of us – belonging.

The women at Kanesof experienced first-hand how quickly new groups can appear in human societies. In the post-quake chaos in Haiti in 2010, for a few frightening days people found themselves as close to year zero as almost anywhere on earth has been in recent times. In those first couple of days, everything was demol-ished, broken, destroyed. And new groups rose. But even as they did, there was a reaction. The women in front of me found a way. They formed groups of their own. They fought back.

As the session at Kanesof closes, I see that one member of the collective, a woman in her thirties called Marcie, is quietly weeping at the back of the room. Throughout the meeting, during all the discussions, she has remained at the rear of the classroom, quiet, attentive, always appearing on the verge of speaking, but never quite managing to bring herself to do so. Everyone else is milling quietly around, chatting, so I take the opportunity to speak to her.

'Thank you for coming,' I say. She looks at me but does not speak, twists the bangles on her wrist. An awkward silence falls between us; I try to find something innocuous to fill it with. 'It's been wonderful hearing about all your work.' Still silence. 'I was particularly interested in what Naomy was saying about . . .'

'No, listen. *Please* listen,' Marcie says. She grabs my hand, tightens her fingers around it with remarkable strength. 'When you told us about the children being sold in Ghana, I was crying inside. Because I have sent my child away to other relatives. It's like I've sold my child to the men with the boats in Africa. I am a bad mother. Naomy says you are a judge. Perhaps you should send me to jail. But I love my children and I was scared I couldn't feed them all and I didn't know what to do. But now what will my sent-away child think of me? How will I look in my child's eyes? I want my child to go to school. My relatives can send my child to school. My husband, he does nothing. Doesn't send us money. I never went to school. My father had cattle. He wanted to buy more cattle rather than spending money on educating a girl, so I could learn to read and write. But I know what I must do. I must get my child back. I will, do you understand?'

'Yes,' I said.

'I survived the earthquake. I survived the gangs. I made my business. Can I not now get my child back?'

She looked up at me, wanting me to tell her that she had done her penance. But who was I to tell her that?

'Can I not?' she repeated.

'I have met women in Africa,' I said, 'and they have sold their child to the labour agents. They have other children they believe will starve if they had not. They are not evil people. They say to me, "What can I do? My other children will starve."'

'They do?'

'Yes.'

'Can you forgive me, then?'

'It's not for me, Marcie. You must forgive yourself. Only you can forgive you. And your son. Get him back. Ask him.'

'What if he hates me?'

I thought of Michael, Anthony, all the young people I'd met in Ghana. 'What if he doesn't?' I said.

Marcie did not cry and did not smile; she did both. We held each other; I don't know why. There was nothing else to do. Here I was in Haiti and I was thinking, I confess, of Anthony and

Michael. I wanted to stay longer, but many of the women were vendors. They had to earn their living and did so brilliantly, defiantly on the streets of Port-au-Prince. Naomy asked everyone to retake their seats for the formal closing.

'What message,' I asked, 'do you want to send to the many women in Africa, fighting FGM and child slavery?'

I wanted something to take back across the sea they had come from all those centuries before, to the people they had come from, all those centuries before. They didn't give me an answer. They *made* me an answer. Without a single word between them, they were all suddenly on their feet, clapping, singing – I wish you could have seen it – and the song, a melodic chant, was this: 'Women are not sugar cane.'

At first I didn't understand. Their ancestors had been brought in holds of ships across the sea to islands like Jamaica, Cuba, and here, particularly, spectacularly, profitably, here in Haiti, to cut sugar cane. 'Women are not sugar cane,' they sang. Naomy whispered to me, 'Not to be chewed up, not to be spat out.'

'Women are not sugar cane,' they sang. Marcie also sang. She sang and clapped and wept for her lost child. Phisline sang in her straw hat, Naomy was at the very front, leading the song, so strong, firm, indomitable, like the mountains that rose dizzyingly in the distance, looming like pale ghosts around the city – like, someone told me, the ghosts of all their ancestors.

Where once this chapter was going to be a silence, a vacancy and a void, I can bring you this instead: 'Women are not sugar cane.' That is what they sang – a sound momentous enough to reach across an ocean. That is what they wanted me to take across that water. This is what I took.

PART VII

THE NURTURER

By 1699, however, it was necessary to place
a grille across the opening to prevent parents
shoving in older children as well.

Sarah Blaffer Hrdy, *Mother Nature* (1999)

ONE

Left, Right

S omething.
 Some deeply instinctual urging reaches down through the layers of sleep and drags you out of a dream. One you were kind of enjoying. Something about a forest in the summer. The White Mountains, New Hampshire, a place you once went. In your dream you were watching a bird skimming across the treetops and were trying to identify it from its wing flashes, bursts of burning gold, and then this thing – this *something* – it pulls you out of the forest and suddenly . . . you're awake. At home. In the darkness. Then you realise what's disturbed you.

A faint acrid unpleasantness in your nostrils. A scratching at the back of your throat. Smoke.

It can't be. You reach for your phone, tap it. A greenish halo radiates around the screen as it lights up: 4.34am. Was the forest burning in the dream – was that it? You reach for the glass of water beside your bed, take a cool sip. Maybe the forest was burning. Yes, that must have been it. Then just before the screen flicks off,

431

you glimpse it: seeping under the door, like a silent, sinister fog rolling into your life to smother everything – smoke. Real smoke.

Imagine you are at home.

And you have two children, two daughters.

Your partner is away for the night. Notionally you're in charge, but it doesn't mean that much because your family, like many others, just muddles through together. But now you're going to have to *take* charge. You've half-read the stats. Half-read them last week on that Twitter link from the Federal Fire Administration: 'Know the facts about fire – How fire can be our friend or foe.' All those little bullet points:

- Early human species started using fire 800,000 years ago.
- The control of fire was a turning point in human evolution.
- Every year fire departments respond to over 350,000 house fires.
- 2,500 people die each year.
- Children under four are particularly at risk.

Only this time, those children caught in a raging home fire, infernos burning at 1,100 degrees – hot enough to melt aluminium – they aren't just children in the news, they're yours. Your children could be the news. You go to turn the door handle, horribly scalding the flesh of your palm. More of those fire facts; more bullet points:

- *If the door handle is hot, don't open the door. Find another exit.*
- *Closed doors slow fires – closed doors save lives.*

Only your children are on the other side of that door. It's their lives that count to you. It's their lives you want to save. You grapple with the expert advice, ignore it, searing your hand as you clutch the handle. You open the door and the fire rages into your life.

The control of fire, a turning point in evolution? There's no control here. You stand in the corridor, choking on the smoke. The girls. Your two girls. Lisa to the left; Ruth to the right. You shout out their names, but there's no reply. Another fire fact:

- *Most fire deaths are caused by smoke inhalation.*

They're probably unconscious from the smoke. *You* feel light-headed, dazed, as the fumes swirl in your head. But you've got to think clearly. Because you have a choice. A life-and-death choice. Here it is:

> You can only save one of your children.
> Not both.
> One of your daughters only.
> Lisa to the left; Ruth to the right.

Their bedrooms lie at opposite ends of the corridor, but the fire is raging, alive, dancing sheets of flames all around you. And you just don't have time to get to both. But you can save one. You can *definitely* save one. So the situation amounts to this: whichever one you go to first, that one will be saved. Lisa to the left; Ruth to the right. You *can* save one. That much you can do. Do you turn left or right?

It's an impossible choice. Yet real parents are sometimes called upon to make it. It is the sort of decision dramatised in the film *Sophie's Choice*. And you're going to tell me – this is what I said: 'I can't choose between my children. I *won't* choose between my children.'

So let me help you. Because you have every right not to choose between them. That *is* your right. You love them equally and you

433

can't choose. The flames are rolling along the carpet towards you like a living liquid, feeding off the chemicals in the fabric. Your head is as light as your heart is heavy. Your deliberating is taking up time, eating away at life-saving seconds. You're thinking about *whether* you can choose instead of *whom* to choose. Lisa to the left; Ruth to the right. They're lying unconscious in their bedrooms surrounded by flames snaking toward their bodies. You're thinking that it's impossible for a parent to make the choice. So let me help you. Let me give you an equation:

If you make no choice, both die = 2 deaths
If you choose one (either one), one child lives = 1 death

That's your choice. I *can't* make that decision, you still maintain. How could I possibly select one child over the other? Let me give you some help. Because I haven't yet given you much information about the children. But then again, what possible information would allow you to make such a choice? Nothing could conceivably make a difference.

Could it?

Ruth is six. Lisa is seven. Not much difference there. Children under four are particularly at risk from fire fatalities, but Ruthie, well, she's six. Though those six years have been anything but plain sailing. In truth, they've been an ordeal. For you and your partner, but so much more so for Ruth. Leukaemia. But she's tough, courageous. You remember when she was born. How life comes into this world with pain. You recall her face. Crying a little but then a stoical, wise look: as if to say to you, her startled parent: 'It's going to be all right.' But you're feeling a different kind of pain now – now the house is burning down around your family. For the past six years, you've done all you can, in truth everyone has, your relations, the doctors, always professional, there to answer questions, never holding out false hope, but now Ruth is sinking fast.

The doctors, they didn't want to tell you exactly what they thought, but you pushed them and pushed them, because you wanted to know the truth, you deserved to know the truth. You said to the doctor, 'Look, you don't even need to say it, just write it down, that's all I want, so I can know, and prepare – just write it down.' And that is the number, the single figure written in green biro (why did she write in green?) on the back of a folded bill from a Chinese restaurant. You keep it in a book in the drawer next to your bed. *That's it.* The book is a bird-spotting book. Ruth bought it for your birthday. There's a bird with red-flashed wings on the front. And on the slip of paper inside just one number: 12. Twelve months with your beloved child. And now you've had three. And now the building's burning. Your home's ablaze, like 350,000 others in the United States every year, only this time it's yours.

But what about Lisa? She's a year older. In perfect health, always has been, which made the news about Ruth all the more shocking. She is fit and bright and beautiful. She is one of those golden children, a blessing and a boon. Lisa's room is to the left.

You've given in to the realisation that you *must* make a choice. Ruth or Lisa? Left or right. You cannot – absolutely cannot – save both. By trying to save both you will lose both. What other choice do you have? Turn in one direction – whichever direction – fight your way through the smoke and flame, stumble through the darkness, feel your way to that daughter's bed, pick her up, try to hold onto her limp body and fight your way out of the house before it's completely swallowed up in flames. You can do that. Rescue her, save her. You will have accomplished that – and you will leave your other daughter behind. The roof will collapse. The fire will consume the house and everything inside it. Here's the equation again:

If you make no choice, both daughters die = 2 deaths
If you choose one (either one), one child lives = 1 death

Which way do you turn? Time is running out. The smoke is now almost blinding. Its foul stench reaches down inside you with every pained breath you take. So which way do you turn? Left or right?

You Were Not Alone

I think I know what you'd do. In many ways, this is harder than the school. Why should that be? There are not 25 children's lives at stake now, but only two. But both are intimately connected to you. Both are your flesh and blood. More precisely, more scientifically – and this will tell us much – both have your genes.

Genes – what, you ask, have *genes* to do with it? We will shortly see.

So what did you do? And how do you feel about it? Is this the kind of person you thought you were? If it offers you any comfort, all I can say is that when I grappled with the burning building, I felt as soiled and conflicted as you probably feel right now if you've thrown yourself into the problem.

And yet I know that my instincts drove me to the only choice I believed it was genuinely – *humanly* – possible to make. I went left. I chose Lisa.

Did you? And if you did, then why? What was your reasoning? Perhaps like me you decided that the fact that Ruth had been given less than a year to live was decisive. You weighed that year against the unrestricted prospects of Lisa. Of course we all die. Nonetheless, this kind of choice seems one we are capable of making: one year or less against a likely 70-plus. So what do we now know? We can choose between human life. More: we can choose between our children.

But perhaps there is such an imbalance in the life prospects of the two girls that a clear decision can be made. So how could we rebalance the scales towards Ruth? What if she were given a prognosis of five years to live? Would that mean that you simply couldn't decide between left and right and would now choose between the girls more or less randomly? Five years might not be enough. What if the doctors said that at some point within the next ten years Ruth would die from her illness, but they were not able to say when. Would that change how you viewed the choice? It makes it much tougher, but does it mean that you would not save Lisa? By going through these questions we are getting a better sense of which kinds of human life we choose to prioritise – when . . . *if* . . . it comes to it, what we actually do.

But stop.

We? Who is this 'we'? Who is deciding these things? Who is it who turned your feet left rather than right? As you groped your way through the smoke of the burning building, you were not alone.

Your steps were accompanied, informed, influenced – driven? – by another of the Ten Types of Human.

What is this character in our head for? The Kinsman was there in the school with the gunman. The Kinsman impelled you to choose your flesh and blood over others – over many others. But now all the flesh and blood at risk is your own. The Kinsman cannot help you. The Kinsman is paralysed; you are paralysed. The Perceiver does anticipate the pain of a fire; it projects you into the pain of each of your stricken children. But it cannot decide between them. And the Tamer, it is whispering a bitterly regretful I-told-you-so: life contains this – the doors into death lie all around us. Be that as it may. Be that as it all may, none of this is going to help you. But something does. *Someone* does.

Another of your selves steps forward. It rises to your aid through the acrid smoke. It is a mental mechanism that evolution has shaped. It has developed through countless generations of human parenting and pain. It makes us smile in that slightly daft way at babies in the street. It has nurtured not only its own offspring, but also our species. It has on countless occasions driven dog-tired parents up through the night to their crying child. It has meant that we feel the blows they suffer as if they were our own. Why? Because in part, as we will see, they are. It causes us unquestioningly to pay for food and clothes, for holidays, haircuts and honeymoons for another – not always grateful – human being.

And now with a clarity that may surprise us, it's driving us to abandon one of our children. How could that be?

To understand, we must first see the darker underbelly of what it can do. Let's temper the romance of parenting with the ruthlessness of rearing. Let's call this self by its name. Let us spell it out – the Nurturer.

TWO

The Ruthlessness of Rearing

I am going to call her Anna.

    Obviously her name was not Anna. I have to protect her identity, and will, but for our purposes let's call her Anna. Something you need to know before we go any further is that I don't know what happened to Anna. The trail vanished. I was once out hiking with Harvard's Outing Club. We were walking up a New Hampshire mountain. On the way up we were joined by a group of female students from another college who were singing that Cyndi Lauper song, 'Time After Time'. There was a trail in the forest that suddenly went – nowhere. It just suddenly stopped. That was Anna.

    I first met her in Cambridge, Massachusetts, because Ubah, someone I was working with on FGM, kept telling me, 'You must meet Anna, you must meet Anna, she is so fantastic, everyone loves Anna.' They lived in the same part of downtown Boston, did a lot of temporary jobs, knew people in common – became friends. 'Everyone loves Anna,' Ubah said, having to sit down on the grand sweep of stone steps leading to Harvard's Widener Library. Sometimes Ubah has problems with her ankle. 'Everyone loves her. Only – she's always late.'

'Okay, I'll remember,' I said. 'What else?'

Ubah laughed. 'She *hates* cats.'

'Cats?'

'But she doesn't like the right chocolate.'

'There is a right kind of chocolate? Enlighten me,' I said.

Ubah paused. 'I told you before: you British, you have the best chocolate. Cadbury-dairy-milk-chocolate,' she said, as if each of the four constituent parts were equally critical.

'I'll try to remember,' I said.

And true enough, on the day that we eventually met, Anna was late. I waited in the lobby of my office block, William James Hall – WJH – with the quote from James himself imposingly engraved above the bank of lifts: *The community stagnates without the impulse of the individual.* Did I agree with it? Did I really understand it? I was forced to hang around for 15 minutes waiting for Anna. I'd checked my emails. So for something to do, I looked at the William James quote, a sign I passed a dozen times a day, unthinkingly. What did it actually mean – stagnates? Then suddenly Anna was there.

'Sorry, so sorry,' she said, smiling winningly. 'I will be late for my life.' She was always smiling, even – as I later discovered – when she was not. Her accent, although now largely Americanised ('Hollywood, my friends call it when I Skype home,' Anna once said), still carries the traces of her childhood and youth in East Europe. She clutched a couple of shopping bags, one from a German designer. Anna was now probably in her late twenties. I never asked her precise age; it was never relevant. She was one of those people who are not so much attractive as *disconcertingly* attractive. Her cheekbones can't be that high, you think; her skin can't be that perfect, you think; her hair cannot be that lustrous. It all was.

'It's a *tall* building,' she said, smiling, elongating the word.

William James Hall is one of the tallest buildings on campus – some say the tallest, and then there is an argument, so let's just call it one of the tallest. It houses a number of departments including Psychology and has 15 floors. It was designed in 1963 by Minoru Yamasaki, who also designed the World Trade Center. It's a white modernist block rising up on sculpted stilts into the Cambridge sky.

'Yes, pretty tall,' I said. 'We've got rather amazing views.' Which was true. Harvard had given me a fabulous office. It only had one problem: the constant air-conditioning draught. A vent seeped icy air continuously from behind the desk. I fought back: I covered it (against the rules, I'm sure) with piles of research papers.

'Where is your office?' Anna asked.

'On 14. Don't worry,' I said, pointing towards the lifts, 'I won't make you walk. Unless you want to.'

I got the sense – just a fleeting flash passing across her face – that something had unnerved her.

'I know,' she said, smiling again – had I misinterpreted it? – 'is such a nice day, why don't we go somewhere? The Spanish place. You know that Spanish place?'

'I know that Spanish place. But I can offer you a coffee in my office. It's not against Harvard regulations. Most things are, but not that. They make exceptions for the British.'

'I've been wanting to try the Spanish. A friend of mine works in a bar down by MIT. He knows all the Cambridge restaurants. He says try the Spanish place. You want to try the Spanish place?'

'I want to try the Spanish place,' I said.

It seemed a little odd, the sudden, subtle shift of plan, but I didn't think much more of it at the time. The significance of it all would only become apparent much, much later. But that's jumping ahead.

So we made our way slowly through the perfectly tended lawns of Harvard Yard, past John Harvard's statue, with the inevitable gaggle of tourists competing with one another to name the statue's three lies, past the Widener Library (I told her the tragic story of its origins and the connection to the sinking of the *Titanic*), across Massachusetts Avenue and onwards to the restaurant. And all the time I have to confess that a half-thought was bugging me: why didn't she want to have the meeting in my office? Still, I let it slide.

We got a table outside. It was still a glorious day but a bank of cloud was gathering beyond the Charles River. We sat on heavy wrought-iron chairs and ordered coffee. Or more precisely: she ordered coffee; I ordered tea. She had a stone in her shoe and took it off. A waiter, tall with sloped shoulders, watched her, transfixed, as if it were the glass slipper. I often still think of her like this and even though it was a scene filled with sunlight and warmth, when I think of it, it is as though someone turns down the lights and outdoors becomes indoors and Anna is alone, sitting at a table staring at a cup of coffee forever. It was only later I realised what I was seeing: that painting by Hopper from 1927, *Automat*.

But she had ordered coffee, that much did happen. She wore a breezy floral skirt and a vivid green cardigan which she tossed over the back of the chair, saying, 'You Brits, always drinking tea.'

'Not always. Just almost always,' I replied. 'So it's great meeting you finally. Ubah said you're busy on your course.' Everyone I met in Boston seemed to be doing a course.

'She's the busy one,' Anna said. 'She is amazing.' She is.

'The course is downtown somewhere?' I said.

'I go to a couple of places. Is very cool.'

'Photography, was it?'

'I want to be a photojournalist.'

'Okay, okay, interesting stuff.' There was a slight lull, as some-times happens when people meet for the first time. To fill it, I said, 'Ubah tells me you totally love cats.'

Anna burst out laughing. 'Please tell me, yes, you are not one of those men that likes cats? Or pretends they do.'

'I like both. I was brought up with dogs, but I'm pretty fond of felines.'

She shook her head violently. 'This old Croat woman in the apartment opposite, she has a cat. It is an evil cat.'

'How can a cat be evil?'

'It climbs in my window and poops in my plants.'

'Your plants?'

'The . . . pots?' she said, reaching for the word.

'Ah, the plant pots.'

'Is *not* funny,' she insisted, banging her palm on the table, but we both laughed. 'Only thing worse than cats – *men!*'

'What have we done now?'

'So this guy,' she said in a whisper, leaning towards me conspir-atorially, 'he's been bugging me like *all* the time on social media – he's working that cool bar near MIT.'

I knew the place. In the sense that I'd walked past it. It looked too uber-chic for a British barrister to venture into (not without a tattoo, new haircut and significant sartorial makeover, which quite frankly did not seem worth the effort). 'Yeah, I know it,' I said.

'So he says, "Anna, I love you, I'm falling in love with you, I love you, I love you."'

'Don't knock it. It's nice to be appreciated.'

'Yes, but it can all be *soooo* dull that you want to reach for the nearest bottle of — what you call — cleaning fluid and drink it. Anyway, I say to him, *really*, you really love me? And he goes, really. And I say how much? And he goes all this stuff as much as up to the stars and trash like that, which actually was quite funny, but I say, is not enough. So he says beyond the stars, and I tell him is not enough. And he says then what — how much? And I say, a Prada handbag, that's how much.'

I laughed. 'Nice move. Did you get it?'

'Haven't heard from him again,' she said. '*Men.*'

The waiter came with the drinks. He brought hot frothy milk for my tea: a travesty — in fact, a cultural crime. I asked for cold, which was as mystifying to him as if I'd demanded that he tap-dance in front of us.

Anna yawned.

'Sorry I'm keeping you up,' I said.

She laughed. 'Sorry, sorry. I'm just back from San Fran. Have you been?'

'Once,' I said. 'I went to Alcatraz. They wanted to keep me in. Had the best Chinese food of my life in Chinatown. Chinatown there is wild.'

'Is wild here too,' she said.

'In Boston — really? I didn't think it was that big.'

'I didn't say big. I say wild. You should listen, Mr Lawyer. They should keep you in Alcatraz.'

445

And we laughed. I liked her feistiness. I tell you all this about Anna because I want you to get a sense of the Anna I know, at least, one of the Annas I know. Because there is more than one. And it was that other Anna, the life-scarred one, the Anna of the *Automat*, that for the purposes of the Nurturer we must meet.

Of the Ten Types, perhaps the most relentlessly pursued by researchers is the Nurturer. The reason is simple. It is a part of us that exhibits behaviour that appears, at least on first inspection, disconcertingly contradictory. One minute caring; the next coldly callous. The parent we want to love us; the one who can walk away. This wounding schizophrenic behaviour by parents is an intrinsic part of the human story from its very origins.

Intrigued by conundrums such as these, experimental psychologist Janet Mann sought to corner this character. Mann studied how Canadian mothers interacted with preterm twins. These were 'high-risk' newborns, both seriously ill, but typically one of them had better prospects – a better chance of living. Essentially Mann was studying what's called 'parental investment'. It's the idea that we live in a world of finite resources, and parental time, properly understood, is another resource.

This is one of the great challenges of parenthood – and one of the most common paranoias and accusations of children: you prefer him/her to me. All parents understand the tremendous pressure to treat their children equally, to love them equally – perhaps hardest of all, to *like* them equally. Do we hold the line? Or do we succumb? In times of great strain do behavioural patterns begin to emerge about which child is prioritised?

There is a considerable anthropological record that in many traditional societies around the world, when children are born with defects or obviously poor prospects for survival, they suffer differing degrees of abandonment. Sometimes they're neglected. Other times allowed to die – or even killed. For example, reports about the Yanomami in the Amazon reveal how children born with defects can be suffocated with leaves in shallow graves, given poison or left in the rainforest. The Nurturer does not nurture. Why is that?

Is it a reflection of how, compared to us, such traditional societies continue to practise inferior 'primitive' ways? For example, the Yanomami believe children with defects do not have a soul. But is that what this is about – exotic and bizarre tribal beliefs? Because there's another way to view it. One that marks our pretensions of cultural superiority as not only insulting, but as an insupportable act of self-flattery. Children are abandoned in the West. Children are killed by their parents in the West. And indeed other reports speak of Yanomami parents who, rather than harming their sick and failing child when ordered by tribal leaders, attempt suicide by eating poison roots.

Of course, it can be argued, these deep Yanomami dilemmas occur in societies without the benefits of the modern medicine that has so transformed life chances. Indeed the miracle of Western medicine *has* changed the odds. Children with serious birth defects do not necessarily die. Children in very poor health can be cared for. And should be. But is that the end of the matter? That, in part, is what Janet Mann was studying. In a brave and sensitive research project, she studied how mothers of preterm twins allocated their time and efforts in caring for them. Of course Mann was studying a modern Western democracy on the cusp of the 21st century. But are there any traces of the more calculating attitudes mentioned above? Do we, despite our claims to 'civilisation', retain a ruthless residue?

It is essential to emphasise that there was no evidence of deliberate or conscious neglect by the mothers that Mann investigated. Indeed she was struck by how stunningly devoted they were in the most trying situations. But it is also important to recognise that distinct and discernible differences in the allocation of care emerged. By four months, a pattern was detectable. By eight months it was clear.

It wasn't so much neglecting the sicker child. It was preferentially 'investing' in the healthier twin. Mothers were more responsive to the cry of the healthier twin. It appears that in conditions of 'intense stress', where caring for two very sick children inflicts a draining and debilitating ordeal on parents, care is not allocated evenly. Mothers exhibited a clear behavioural preference in favour of the healthier twin. In a sense, they reserved the best of themselves for the child with the best life chances.

They turned left not right.

No one suggests that if the same mothers had a single sick child they would not have done everything they could for that child. As psychologists Margo Wilson and Martin Daly write, parental love is the 'most nearly selfless love we know'. But when they simply do not have the capacity to do that for both, when a choice has to be made, it falls in favour of the healthier child.

Does that surprise you? It surprised me. Remember: we are not arguing whether this is or is not a good thing. We are looking at the empirical question: what actually happens. So what are we saying? That parental love is conditional? Or perhaps that it is conditioned. If so, conditioned by what?

'So Ubah sees the mad woman in the apartment opposite,' Anna said.

'The Croat with the cat?' I asked.

Anna nodded her head vigorously. 'And Ubah says to her, "Excuse me, lady, your cat messes in our block again and I'm going to buy a gun. Thank you."'

'At least she said thank you.'

'Ubah is very polite.'

'But a gun,' I said, 'that's pretty extreme.'

'Half the people where we live have a gun. But you probably don't know these things.'

The waiter still hadn't corrected the great tea calamity: still no cold milk. With surprising rapidity the sky was beginning to cloud over. Banks of dark-bottomed cumulonimbus rolled in across the Charles. As the waiter passed, even before I could gently remind him, Anna smiled at him. It was like a laser beam. He came over immediately, smiling back.

'We ask for milk,' she said in a deadpan way, her forthrightness like a slap in his face. He retreated, confused. Anna pulled the vivid green cardigan she'd left on the back of her chair over her shoulders like a cape. There was something faintly elfin about her, a fragility that belied the bravado and bluster of her words.

'Fine him,' she said.

'Fine?'

'No tip. Look at his face. Imbecile. We ask for cold milk and he looks like we spit in his beer or something.'

'He probably hasn't forgiven us for Gibraltar.'

'What?'

'It's a long story,' I said.

We sipped our drinks and chatted about various aspects of FGM. Anna had asked to meet me because she wanted to do a photo-essay and Ubah had said that I was someone she should meet to understand the human rights aspects of the issue. I knew that she and Ubah lived in the same apartment block on the fringes of Chinatown.

'So how does FGM differ?' she asked.

449

'Differ?'

'You know, from other violence with children?'

I exhaled. Loudly.

'What?' she asked. 'Like an imbecile I ask the wrong question?'

'No, no. It's just such an enormous question. You know for FGM it's critical to understand how violence in the family works within a wider context of violence against children and violence against women.'

'Violence is violence,' she said.

This was an interesting question in itself. For a social theorist like the French sociologist Pierre Bourdieu, for example, there is not just racism, but racisms. I imagine Bourdieu would maintain something similar about violence.

I was beginning to articulate this when Anna said, 'Why do the mothers do it? To their children.'

'And fathers,' I added.

'But for mothers is different. They've carried the child nine months. They give birth to it. It's their flesh and blood.'

'It's the genes of the father too.' One of my ambitions has been to get more men to be part of the fight against FGM. Thus far they've got off too lightly.

Anna was quiet for a while. She brushed some stray hairs from her forehead. 'My father was a lawyer,' she eventually said.

'Okay.'

'Not like you.'

'Lucky him.'

'No, I mean he is a lawyer in the government. And we have a very bad government, but it was a good job and it meant we had a nice apartment. We lived in one of the tallest blocks in the capital. It was one of the better places to live. It had a balcony and from there you see the whole city. But it was high. Some of my early memories, they are that we live in the clouds. Some people see cars go past their windows, we used to see clouds. Is not totally true, but that's how I remember.'

Anna's country, which I do not name out of respect for her identity, had been through incredibly turbulent times, like much of the Balkans. I'm not sure how long she had been in the US, but it was several years. Ubah said she worked in a hotel downtown.

'Being a lawyer was too stressful for him,' she said. 'Because he knew all these . . . things that were going on and he was drinking. I think he was a good man, deep inside, a good man, but he knew all these things and he didn't like them. He used to love fishing. And then one day he stopped. He broke his . . .'

'Rods?'

'Yes, the sticks. He put them in the trash. He kept drinking, and in the end he gets ill, so ill.'

Behind us the cloud bank was filling out, darkening menacingly over the river. Anna didn't appear to notice. She told me about how her father died from not just the alcohol but the terrible stress he was trying to insulate himself against.

'So we lose the apartment,' she said. 'They wouldn't let us stay there and it was so unfair because that was our home, me and my two brothers, we never lived anywhere else. But my mother, she couldn't make rent any more. She took a job in the hospital. It didn't bring enough money and we have to move out. Our new apartment, it's this disgusting place full of rats and there are drunken men in the lobby. I was scared because you know how it is, they *look* at me as I pass. I was only 13 years old.'

'So your mother worked in the hospital?'

'She was a cleaner, she wasn't trained.'

Anna seemed to lose her train of thought, so I said, 'Ubah said you work in a hotel downtown?'

She didn't reply, lost, it seemed, in that time well over a decade before. 'I think she liked working there,' Anna said, 'meeting the patients – getting away from us. We were just running wild, crazy wild, my brothers and me. We had to cook our own meals and get ready for school if my mother works early shift. And she would come home and say, Poor Mr This, I want to find him something nice. What can I find him for something nice? And poor Mrs That, she asks me to stay after work and just talk to her, she is so lonely, and my mother stays. But her own children, we are at home and trying to grow up. Once my father died, it was like she wasn't our mother any more.'

'Perhaps,' I said, 'it was just too hard. She was worn out by the hospital.'

Anna shook her head. 'I think we reminded her.'

'Reminded her?'

'Of him. Of my father. She blamed us. She said he had to work so hard to feed us. She always said how happy they were when they married, before they had us. People say the happiest time is when you have babies. But that is what is supposed to be the happiest. Not what is. Bringing up children must be hard work.'

She broke off, looking towards the river. Her eyebrows knitted together and she rubbed her shoulders. She pulled her green cardigan around her throat. 'I'm never doing it,' she said.

'Doing what?'

'Having children,' she finally said.

THREE

Cases Like Mine

One of the oldest surviving sets of laws is the famous Code of Hammurabi, named after the sixth king of Babylon. On an imposing black index finger of stone over seven feet tall is the recognition of the sale by a parent of a child, engraved into the dark igneous rock in cuneiform. If the sale was in satisfaction of debt, the law decreed that the child would have to endure three years of forced labour.

Hammurabi reigned in Babylon somewhere around 1750 BCE. In Ghana, just a few years ago, Anthony's father sold his son into slavery. Whether it was in satisfaction of a debt, I don't know – Anthony does not. But it was an act that not only Hammurabi but a thousand years later a Roman father from the fifth century BCE would recognise. For the edict in the Twelve Tables, a foundation stone of Roman jurisprudence, states that if a father sells his son three times, he loses authority over him and the son is free of him. Selling one's son twice, it appears, would be acceptable.

And if we move forward just under another thousand years, the first Christian emperor of Rome – Constantine – in 313 recognised the legitimacy of the sale of a child. A little after this time, Basil of Caesarea, the Cappadocian saint, wrote with concern about the sale of children:

> How can I bring before your eyes the suffering of the poor man? . . . he has no gold and never will. What can he do? He turns his glance at length on his children: by selling them he might put off death. Imagine the struggle between the desperation of hunger and the bonds of parenthood . . .
>
> Then what are his thoughts? Which one shall I sell first? Which one will the grain auctioneer favour the most? Should I start with the oldest? But I am reluctant to do so because of his age. The youngest? I pity his youth and inexperience of life. . . . What horrible misery. . . . What sort of animal am I turning into? . . . If I hold on to them all, I will see all of them die of hunger.

Basil was writing in the second half of the fourth century, in Asia Minor, what is now Turkey. Move down through the Levant and we find Jewish legal tradition recognising the mortgaging of children. Move forward in time, pass over another thousand years – noting briefly below us the foundling hospitals of the Middle Ages that we will come back to – keep rolling through decades and generation after generation until we splash down in our troubled century. And here we find Anna, and what happened to her.

'He was a professor at the university,' Anna said. 'An assistant professor. I wanted to go to university eventually, but knew we couldn't make tuition, but he said I could do some cleaning and filing work for him. He was connected to our family and so wanted to help. It was a great opportunity for me. For all of us.'

'You mean an opportunity for the whole family?'

She nodded. 'My brothers were getting into trouble, especially the oldest. He was hanging around in the streets, sometimes he was even sniffing glue. That's what the street kids do. To get high. To keep out the cold. But not people like us. People like we used to be, before my father died. But we were just going down, down. Our lives were heading into the street, into the . . .' She pointed to the pavement, to the gutter.

'So you went to work with the professor?'

'It wasn't like a proper job. But, yes, he let me. And you must know that he was very kind to me also. He would say, Anna, you look thin, and he'd bring me a pizza – not like the pizza here. Or Anna, your clothes are so old, and he'd give me money to buy something new. And this is how it started. It made me feel – grown up. He was usually so gentle with me, and told me about Klimt and books, Balzac – I hadn't even heard of Balzac before.'

The faintest, most distant of smiles passed across her face, but disappeared, was used up. We spoke briefly about the Balzac novel I'd recently read. From his immense *Human Comedy*, his Lear-like book *Old Goriot*. In it Balzac wrote of his Paris, which was the world, how it was 'a valley of real suffering and often deceptive joys'.

'When he was drunk,' Anna said, 'he would shout and swear at me: what have you made me do? Like I was the devil. Like it was all me. I had done this to him.'

'Done what to him?' I asked.

'Made him have an affair. He was married.'

It was beginning to make sense. At least I thought it was: that familiar pattern. I was wrong.

'When he was kind, it was like there were all these doors behind him. Doors that opened to wonderful things: poetry, art exhibitions, music, things that we used to think about years before when my father was alive and then it was all gone. It was exciting because I thought he had the key. He could open them and then I go through and there is this better life on that side. But never,' she said. 'Never did I go through. Never did he let me.'

'Why not?' I asked.

'Because he was very, *very* jealous. He says to me, "Anna, understand what men want. Grow up, Anna. Understand what men want." Like he wasn't a man, not one of those men, and didn't want. But he did. He always did. He used to go out and play poker with his friends. "That's what men do, Anna," he says to me. He speaks like men are this different species, like they are dangerous and I must never go near them.

'And all the time it's him – *he* comes back from poker, *he* is drunk, he is the one that I must be careful of. Sometimes it gets really bad, and he is shouting at me and saying all this is my fault. You are a devil. So bad sometimes I hide in the cupboard. I go into the cupboard and hide, and he pulls open the doors. "Why are you hiding, Anna? What – you think I will hurt you, Anna?" He drags me out by my hair. Once he started hitting me with a metal hanger, around the arms. "What have you made me do?" he says. "Look what you're making me do."'

'Anna, you don't have to tell me this,' I said. 'You don't know me.'

'I know *me*,' she said. 'I want to.'

'I'm just a lawyer.'

'Lawyers see things. You've seen things?'

'I've seen things.'

I was later to judge a case where a man was charged with domestic violence and for reasons that were unclear, he couldn't get legal representation and so did his own advocacy in court before me – something I strongly advised him against as there was every chance I was about to send him to prison. The pre-sentence report had said that he bitterly regretted his actions (striking his common-law wife in the face with a blunt object while drunk, part of a pattern of abusive behaviour over the years). And yet as he addressed me on his own behalf, what he appeared really concerned with was what had happened to him, how he was also a victim, his bitter regrets centred around his lot. I did send him to prison.

'You've seen cases like mine?' Anna said.

'Too many.'

'So what do you know?' She said it like a challenge. I felt as if I were being auditioned, for what I didn't know. I thought about how I should deal with this. I thought I should tell the truth.

'I know that you blame yourself,' I said.

She didn't say yes or no. 'What else?' she asked.

'I know that after he hits you he gets very upset. He probably cries and you've gone to him and you comfort him and then it happens again.'

She was silent. 'You're wrong,' she said. 'He never cried.'

'But you comforted him?'

'He said I was the only one who understands him.'

'How old were you when this started?'

'Sixteen,' she said.

'You were a child, Anna. Why did he keep hitting you?'

'He was angry because of what I've done,' Anna said.

I waited for her to tell me, my mind racing, trying to think what this young woman could have done to the older man. She was plainly very upset.

'I'd got pregnant,' she finally said.

*

The phenomenon of parental attitudes towards their children was examined another way by other researchers in North America. In this study they examined which death provoked the greater grieving in parents: that of a healthy child or of one that was ill.

Hundreds of respondents were questioned under experimental conditions to assess their 'grief intensity'. The results were clear: the loss of a healthy child produced greater pain in the parent. Why would this be? Is it simply the fact that a healthy child is likely, on average, to live longer than an unhealthy one? What is the cause of this additional grief? We will shortly do an experiment of our own to find out.

But before we do, I should say that I cannot pretend that my grappling with dilemmas such as these completely overturned my view of who we are. But it has set it on edge. It left me wanting to understand more. Is not all human life equal? As a human rights lawyer and a researcher animated by social justice, this is what I passionately believe. But the evidence appears to suggest that we do not end up *acting* equally. And I want to face up to this and understand what is happening. Just because we don't like it, it doesn't mean it's not occurring. And if it does occur, it doesn't mean we can't try to change it. But first we have to understand what is going on. To recapitulate our decision in the burning building:

We have, the two of us, chosen to abandon one of our children.

We asked ourselves the question: how could any parent possibly do that?

But eventually we chose Lisa.

Implicit in this question is the suggestion that no decent parent could abandon their child. But the sobering reality of human life, as testified to by centuries of historical records, is that children have always been abandoned. And they continue to be abandoned. Shortly we will come to the empirical evidence revealing which kinds of children are more likely to be abandoned, or physically harmed, or killed. But for now we are beginning to see that in making our choice to turn left not right – that was the way you chose to turn, wasn't it? – that in choosing Lisa, we are not alone.

This is not to suggest that any life in itself is intrinsically less worthy than any other – that Ruth is in some way a lesser human being than Lisa. But is the burning building not telling us – we must face it – that in extreme circumstances we are capable of prioritising the saving of some lives over others? And recognising this, a further question demands an answer: by what principles can we possibly – *dare* we presume to – make such life-and-death decisions? What drives the turn to the left or the right in the burning house? What leads us inexorably and always to our child in the school's broom cupboard and away from the packed classroom?

By forcing us to pluck just one of our children from the flames, by making it a life-and-death decision, just as we did by inserting the prowling gunman in the school, we are stripping away the layers of decorum and etiquette. We are getting beyond polite or popular choices made to placate others, so they will think well of us – so we will think well of ourselves. Instead we are drilling down to our most fundamental motivations. We are having to make what researchers call 'biologically significant' decisions. That is never easy. Nor should it be. We are trying to grasp not what people might like to think they would do, but what they actually *would* do – and the ultimate reasons for it. Let me give you one further example.

Imagine that we have exactly the same situation. The building is burning. The flames are rising. The smoke makes it almost impossible for you to see.

- *When you're inside a fire, it isn't bright. It's pitch black.*
- *The black smoke creates darkness.*

You are reaching about in the smothering blackness. Like that line from Milton's *Paradise Lost*: what you see is darkness visible. It would be easier if in the blackness you did not know where you were and could not choose. But I can't let you off the hook. You *have* to choose. So you must think clearly. Somehow. Somehow you must think as clearly as you ever have in your life. That Twitter link, you wish you'd never read it. As though it's jinxed you, you and your family. Something else it said is happening: your T-shirt is smoking, it's catching fire.

- *If your clothes catch fire, stop-drop-roll.*
- *Stop where you are. Drop to the ground. Roll over and over.*

You drop, roll chaotically, put the fire out on you. What about your children? You have two daughters. They are in two bedrooms in cotton nightdresses amid the flames. Lisa to the left; Ruth to the right.

Now imagine both girls are 12. They are twins. But Ruth has one difference from Lisa. Ruth has a congenital problem that means she cannot have children. What I am going to ask you to consider is brutal. These two daughters of yours, they're identical — literally. Except one of them cannot have babies. Does that matter? *Should* it matter? Does that affect who lives and who dies? And if it does, why should it?

In fires, victims mainly die from smoke inhalation. The insatiable flames suck out all the oxygen in the air. The fire fills the air with poison. And it is this lack of oxygen that's so lethal. And this means you simply, immediately, have to make a decision. While you're agonising about whether fertility matters – in your mind turning left, turning right – the awful alchemy is at work, sucking the oxygen out of the air, sucking the life out of your children's bedrooms.

In every other respect, there is no – absolutely no – difference between your two daughters. They both are healthy. They both love you and are loved by you. They adore each other. But you must choose one of them. The flames are climbing the walls. The plaster melts and slides down in slow streams, leaving tear-tracks on the brickwork. There are two bedroom doors in the corridor. Behind each of them lies one of your daughters. They do not respond to your calls. They are unconscious. In every important respect for this life-and-death choice they are the same. Except one can have children. The other cannot. Which do you choose?

Left or right?

Lisa or Ruth?

FOUR

The Surface of Civilisation

It might have been a marginal thing, but I think I know your decision. If you chose Lisa once more, you are keeping company with hundreds of interviewees in scientific studies across the globe, from Toronto to Tokyo. The results show that we tend to grieve more for the loss of a teenager than for a baby. Why should that be? Of course, we would have got to know the young adult for longer, had greater opportunity to form stronger bonds. But is that all there is to it?

To answer that question, we need to consider two further things. Firstly, recall your answer: whom were you prepared to save? It was Lisa. Has Ruth been penalised because she cannot get pregnant? In what way does that diminish her claim to life?

Let's think about that again: after all, there is no guarantee that Lisa *would* have any children. There is no evidence that she was particularly inclined or wanted to. So what's behind our choice? Why is reproductive potential so important?

To understand, let's move forward in time. Ten years.

The two girls have grown up. They are both 22. Ruth is still infertile. But now it's Lisa who has been diagnosed with a terminal illness. She has ten years to live at a maximum. It could be less than that, but ten at the outside, the doctors say. Now – finally – are we going to turn right? Here's the choice:

Left = Lisa (22), ten years to live but can have children.
Right = Ruth (22), can't have children.

Now, at last, are we going to save Ruth?

I did. And it was almost a relief. We'd passed over the sick Ruth and the infertile one, but now that her sister is ill, the barren Ruth can be saved.

But we can change it back again by the addition of one simple fact. One additional fact will flip everything. You have already probably guessed what it is – haven't you?

Lisa is pregnant.

Whom do you save now? A terminally ill Lisa who is pregnant or Ruth who, through no fault of her own, is condemned to a life in which she cannot have her own biological children? Ruth could adopt, of course. She could be a mother like that, but she will never be able to give birth to her own biological children. Whom do you save?

If Lisa is eight months pregnant, are you going to save Lisa at Ruth's expense? What is the equation? Can we reduce it to its brutal basics?

Lisa (ten years to live) + baby > (infertile) Ruth . . .?

I want to tell you about another extraordinary study. In this set of experiments, adults were asked to estimate the grief of *other* parents when children of various ages died. So the genes of the

463

interviewees were not engaged directly. In this experiment something very interesting happened.

First, there was a more or less robust correlation between the estimated grief and the reproductive potential of the dead child. The closer the child was to puberty, the greater the grief at its loss. Given the other studies we've considered, that is now predictable. But then there was the real revelation: the grief curve mapped almost *exactly* the reproductive-potential curve of a particular population – in Africa. That population is the !Kung people who inhabit the Kalahari. Why should a research study interviewing subjects in Canada and Japan produce a series of choices that matched the reproductive life cycles of this traditional, desert-dwelling people?

The answer may lie in the fact that the !Kung are a hunter-gatherer people. They have a lifestyle more akin to the one that our ancestors lived for approximately 99 per cent of the human story. In this sense, they are more representative of historic human beings than we are. And what do we sophisticated moderns do? When we are asked to make decisions about something as raw and visceral as life and death, we make decisions in a pattern very similar to hunter-gatherers. That's pretty interesting. How could it come about?

For evolutionary psychologists these kinds of dilemmas provide us with insights into the deeper structures of our minds lodged away beyond the surface effects of 'civilisation' and modern living. By doing this we begin to get at the ultimate drive housed within us. Shorn of comforting euphemism, unadorned and unembellished, it can be starkly stated: *the need to survive and reproduce.*

So that was teenaged Anna's great crime: she had become pregnant. I thought of this fragile young person, dragged out of the cupboard she was seeking refuge in, terrified as he beat her with a hanger – and pregnant. And this is why I've told you about Anna.

'"Get rid of it, get rid of it. You're going to get rid of it," he says. I tell myself, Anna, you're going to get rid of it. But something inside, something inside me I didn't even know is there, it is saying in my head at the same time: you will not – what else you do, you will not. Me, I didn't understand. I didn't want a baby. I couldn't have a baby. The shame. But this voice in my head says you will not, you will not get rid of it. Maybe he saw something, maybe I was crying – I can't remember – but just as quickly he becomes the kind one again, like when he is not drinking, and so he's gentle and kind and says, "Don't worry, I will pay, I will look after you. No one will know. We will sort it out together. You mustn't worry. We'll do it together." He knew how. He knew doctors. And so is arranged. I will have an abortion.'

The droplets of rain were just becoming uncomfortable now. On the opposite side of the road, further up, was another restaurant and people who were sitting outside were asking for tables within. Along Massachusetts Avenue cars raced along the wide carriageway and then would suddenly screech to a halt when a group of Harvard students without even looking would step off the pavement in the sure and certain knowledge that the world would stop for them. Invariably it would.

'How old were you,' I asked, 'when the abortion happened?'

She shook her head. 'I didn't have the abortion.'

Once more the story came off the tracks.

'Didn't?' I said.

'I couldn't do it.'

We were both suddenly silent. I looked at her, and she looked away, and she appeared to be about to take it back, and then it

465

appeared to me that she realised there was no point in taking it back and I wouldn't believe it. In a way, she seemed relieved to have come out with it. Her hair sparkled with raindrops.

'I had his baby,' she said. 'Everything went crazy.'

'How old were you?'

'Seventeen,' she said. 'I got pregnant at 16.'

It was young – too young. But was it illegal in her country? I didn't have a chance to ask her.

'I tried to keep it quiet, but then finally I kind of broke down one day, even before I was showing real, real obvious, and told my mother. I'd been keeping it all . . .' She held herself tight.

'Bottled up.'

The wind got up; a stray sheet of newspaper rolled down the street like tumbleweed.

'Yes, hiding it all. This big terrible secret. And so I was kind of glad to tell her. But she just goes cold. She is frying fish. There was hot oil in the pan. I thought she'd throw it in my face. I thought she wanted to throw it in my face. But she hardly says anything. She tells me to get out. Is very quiet. She turns off the stove. "Get out," she says, really quiet. Then I start crying and say, "Please, Mama, forgive me." I am begging her, forgive me, but she screams, "Get *out*." She screams and screams, "Get out, get out, get out, get out, get out, *get out*." I say, "Mama, please look at me." She won't look. She looks at the pan. I pull her arm. She turns round. Then the face, the look, is not my mother there.'

The oil was so hot it kept sizzling, Anna told me. Her mother said that she disowned her.

'But surely you needed her help.'

'What I had done, it was too terrible.'

'But going through a pregnancy without your mother, a teen-ager, that's very, very hard.'

'She would never forgive me.'

'She was very religious?'

'He – the father . . .'

I was confused. '*He* was religious?'

'He was my uncle,' Anna said. 'Her brother.'

FIVE

The Surrendering

The evidence is unclear about where the first wheel was built. What is clear, however, is how much in demand the devices were once they were put in place. Such wheels came to have various names: *roda* in Portuguese, *tour* in French, *ruota* in Italian. They were not just any kind of wheels. The best way to explain it is to consider one of the most famous.

Filippo Brunelleschi was the second of three sons of a Florentine notary in the late 14th century. The young Filippo was a talented sculptor, and in the fervour of Florence's Renaissance competed with others for the high honour of designing the doors to the Baptistery. His entry was of one of the most celebrated child sacrifices of all time: Abraham's sacrifice of his son Isaac. But Brunelleschi lost. Fortunately for the Renaissance, he lost. It would have been little comfort even if he had known that he had lost to such a worthy opponent that a century later Michelangelo himself would view the doors designed by Brunelleschi's rival Lorenzo Ghiberti and say, 'Surely these must be the Gates of Paradise.'

So Brunelleschi turned his attention to something else: to architecture. This is why we know him today. For Brunelleschi solved the problem of how to build the dome of Florence's magisterial Duomo, the Cathedral of Santa Maria del Fiore. But it wasn't his first construction.

Brunelleschi's first commission was in fact for Florence's Ospedale degli Innocenti – the Hospital of the Innocents. The commission to design Florence's foundling hospital came from the influential and affluent Florentine guilds, like that of *seta* – silk. When constructed, it was the first institution in the world devoted exclusively to caring for children. It was much in demand. In Tuscany, as elsewhere in medieval Europe, children were being 'exposed' – abandoned.

Sometimes they were left in the street. Sometimes at the doors of churches. The deposited babies were prey to weather, scavenging dogs, chance. The problem became intolerable and an institutional solution had to be found. The Hospital of the Innocents was one concerted response to the problem of parents abandoning their offspring. It was built on the site of a farm. At first children were deposited in the marble basin at the front portico. But by the 17th century a *ruota* was installed – a wheel.

It consisted of a hole in the wall. Behind was a rotating wheel, laid flat. A baby could be placed in one side of it, then the wheel could be spun, and the child would disappear into the confines of the hospital, and the parent would remain anonymous. Such devices, permitting the depositing of children without the parents being identified, became very popular.

Where they started has been lost to us in the historical mists and missing records. Certainly when the first shelter for abandoned children was opened in France in 1180, it included a rudimentary wheel of some kind. In 1196 Pope Innocent III issued an edict that all foundling homes should contain one. By the start of the 19th century, 1,200 Italian cities, towns and villages had installed wheels for abandoning children.

As Sarah Hrdy, an evolutionary anthropologist from the University of California at Davis, writes, the marble basin in Florence's Hospital of the Innocents was replaced with a rotating wheel in 1660. By 1669, a grille had to be placed over the aperture to prevent parents forcing their older children through the narrow gap as well.

We are inside the Spanish restaurant, sheltering from the rain that is pouring down. Anna ties her hair back. It is slick with raindrops. She suddenly seems much older to me.

'Now you hate me,' she said.

'Because of your uncle?' I said.

'Because you judge me.'

'I don't, actually.'

'Yes, you do. People say they don't judge you and they do judge. I understand. I judge myself. I did a terrible thing.'

'You were a teenager, Anna. He was the adult.'

'I grew up with him. I knew he was married. I know his wife for years. No one liked her. She was very large, small and large. My parents, they called her the Beach Ball. Even her husband didn't like her. That's what he told me.'

The staff were going around the tables, lighting candles. It was like being in the glow of a cave lit by a series of small bonfires as the light faded rapidly outside.

'My mother said he deserves better than her. My mother always she protects him. He was the younger one, her baby brother, and he was always a kind uncle when we were growing up.' She shook her head slowly. 'Is madness. I still don't know how it happens. I should not let this happen.'

There was little point in my repeating that she was just 16. I've found in court that sometimes people simply don't want you to defend them; sometimes they act as their own prosecutors.

'I gave up my child,' she said. 'For adoption.' Anna stood up. She said very quietly, 'I don't want that you hate me.'

'I have no right to,' I said.

'I wish I believe you.' She moved towards the door.

'Don't go,' I said. 'Look at the rain.' When it rains in Boston, it can really rain. The sun was trying to break through but failing, clouds passing across its face like smoke.

'I wish I believe you,' Anna repeated, her eyes searching my face for a sign.

'Then do,' I said. The restaurant was full, but it was as if no one was there. With the thrum of the customers and the soft gypsy music it was as if we were cocooned and alone. My advocacy failed. She left.

It was only later that evening, when she called me to apologise for walking out – there was of course no need to apologise – that I understood why she thought I would hate her. I was trying to explain to her that while I didn't know the precise situation in her country, there nevertheless may be some kind of way to re-establish contact with her child, her son, in a carefully controlled fashion. I knew lawyers who knew lawyers in her country and I could find out if there was a legally sanctioned protocol. Over the last two decades there has been a gradual drift towards a greater degree of openness in adoption: there was growing recognition of the anguish and rights of birth parents. I knew that there was a pattern of grief caused by what the literature calls the 'surrendering' of a child that resembles that following a death. I was wondering if all this was why she had actually wanted to meet me in the first place rather than about FGM – to see if I could advise her legally on the adoption. But it was more complex than that.

The truth is that after she gave birth to her child, she did give him up for adoption. That much was true. But that wasn't the whole story. Anna sold her baby.

SIX

The Rose

The foundling wheels were a strange hybrid of cradle and turntable: the child was deposited in a cot-like space, turned, disappearing behind the walls of the hospital or orphanage, into a kind of institutional cradling. Professor David Kertzer of Brown University, states that the wheels functioned as a gateway between two worlds: 'On the outside lay nature and sin, on the inside civilization and salvation.'

We see here how these institutional arrangements, while on the one hand providing a solution for at-risk infants, were also a form of the policing of women, their bodies, their sexuality. It was all infused, as Anna found when she finally revealed her relationship with the older man, with severe moral condemnation.

Thus apologists of the wheel saw it as a means of safeguarding children from 'the impure atmosphere of corruption . . . [and] the contagion of vice'. For the woman giving up her child, it was a way of concealing 'the intruding witness of guilt and shame'. As Anna found, the focus remained relentlessly on her

— as it historically has, not on the men who made these young women pregnant. Thus the wheel embodied the notion that a child born in a world of uncontrolled sexuality, danger and lustful desire could be transported into a setting of institutional and moral safety. Of course, the reality was different. Many children died.

They died at varying rates, but they constantly died. What were parents actually doing when placing their babies in the wheels of foundling hospitals? Was it a de facto act of social infanticide – a way of effectively ending a life you couldn't bring to end yourself? Or was it the taking of a very, very risky bet – an impossibly long shot, but the only shot realistically remaining?

Sometimes tokens were left. In London in 1739, for example, at the Foundling Hospital, the mother of a child called Florella Burney left her a little piece of dotted cream cloth. It was embroidered with a red flower in full bloom. To this was pinned a note. On it, in remarkably even handwriting – who can really gauge the anguish Florella's mother was suffering? – she begs that 'particular care' be taken of her child, as she 'will be call'd for again'. The truth is, however, children like Florella Burney were rarely reclaimed.

In Italy the tokens were not just pieces of torn cloth but foreign coins, scraps of pictures, images of saints. They were called *segni di riconoscimento*: signs of recognition. What did they represent? A last hope or often, as David Kertzer argues, a denial of the brute reality of the act of abandonment.

How should we understand the actions of Kow's mother? They lived in one of the coastal communities that supplied the child slavers at Lake Volta. But Kow's mother had the perennial problem: how to feed all her children?

Kow's mother gave him up for a small sum of money. The money was vital. It helped her feed the others. But the price was Kow. The man with the money convinced her that Kow would be given useful employment, that her son would be well cared for. It was all lies. The man turned out to be a trafficker.

Kow was forced to fish on the lake. It was grinding labour; he was severely beaten during it. One day near the main settlement on the lake, the town of Yeji, Kow saw a boy dive into the water. He was trying to untangle a net. The child drowned. From that point, Kow was haunted by the thought that he would die like that boy, that he would be trapped under the water and the lake would never let him go.

Kow is now almost 14. He was on the lake for over four years. While he was there, he never got paid. He was regularly beaten. There was no school, no education, only work. That changed when a child who had been rescued from the lake told Kate Danvers's colleagues about Kow. Kate's team found him. From that time, they have provided him with shelter and support at the NGO's rescue centre.

Kow is still haunted by the lake. Perhaps he will always be. You get away from the lake. But it doesn't release you. Like the trees growing out of the water that don't release the nets. Or are the trees dead? That's the thing about the lake: it's hard to know what's alive and dead.

Still, he is starting school. He is learning. About the world beyond the lake, about himself, that although he was forced to work, he is not a slave, that his life can and will be different to that. It will be better.

Whether he can be resettled with the mother who gave him up – that is the question.

*

For selling her child Anna was paid $1,000. She sold it through an agency to a couple from 'the West', as she put it. I knew that in that period, in that region, there had indeed been a practice that came to be known as the 'baby trade'. There were thousands of children 'sold' to Westerners. Agencies sprang up. It was big business. Anna's child was one of them.

She told me that she didn't know what else to do. Some of her friends were, as she termed it, selling 'other things'.

'I knew it could be done. They go sit in lobbies of the international hotels – and wait. You pay security guards some money, and they let you wait. Some of them, they were the very clever girls. They wanted to go to the university, but didn't have money. This was how they make tuition. But sometimes they just spend the money on nonsense, designer goods.'

Prada handbags.

'My friends said, you did the best you can for your baby,' she said. 'But I think: what about what I did to my baby? That is it: what I do *to* my baby.'

The prosecutor in her head, indicting her again. I tried to come to her rescue as we spoke on the phone but she rejected any mitigation. Our conversation was more than ten years after it happened, but in her mind she was still guilty and guilty she would remain.

One day, about a month later, I was looking in my pigeonhole in the long corridor outside my office at Harvard, high up on the 14th floor of William James Hall. The pigeonholes in WJH are by the water coolers. From there you can see a panorama of the campus stretching towards the Charles River, studded with dorm houses with their white bell towers piercing the horizon. I found mailed to me a neatly written card. It was from Anna.

There was picture on the front of a white rose bush, almost too perfectly painted, like a pastiche. I didn't understand why she chose it. Maybe it was the only card in the shop. Maybe it meant nothing – but why a white rose bush? As I took the card out of the envelope, something fell out: a pressed white flower – just like the blooms on the front of the card.

Dexter, thank you for offering to ask your lawyer friends about my case. For a long time I pretend it is over and my son is not in my life but he is. I come to this country to pretend he is not but that is not true because he is. I know you will say again you won't judge me but really. I can't do the article of FGM. How can I when I am a terrible person, worst I know. I want the best things for my son. I think he is happy and a grown up big boy and I have no right to hurt him again. I thought I wanted you help me find him. But he would be ashamed. I would be ashamed. So I will not try & find him but thank you for saying you will help. Anna.

As I read and reread her card, I thought that perhaps the strange passions that bring us into the world do not necessarily accompany us on the journey through it. Therefore it is entirely possible that Anna's son will lead a perfectly contented and cosseted life in an affluent Western city; perhaps he will never have any idea of the turmoil and trauma his birth has caused. Like Anna, I hope that is the case. I placed the card and the pressed flower on the piles of research papers on the AC vent.

Mary Dozier, a psychologist at Delaware University, conducted detailed studies with colleagues to investigate which factors in nurturing affected children.

Researchers examined the relationship between 50 foster carers and children placed in their charge. The babies were aged between birth and 20 months. Having controlled for other variables such as socio-economic status and race, Dozier found that the best predictor of how securely the child was attached to the foster carer was one thing: how warmly and positively the caregivers felt about their own childhood experiences.

Secure attachment – that is, seeking out the comfort the child needs, in the confident expectation they will be soothed – is important. It is associated with successful future relationships, as the child grows, with other children and teachers. But how does a person's experience of childhood affect their future nurturing?

From the early 1990s, research has shown that parents with unresolved attitudes to how they were nurtured tend to behave in ways that frighten their children. This in turn leads their children to have their own problems with parenting. Trauma or abuse by attachment figures can overwhelm the behavioural system and lead to subsequent problems in parenting. It is sometimes known as 'attachment-related trauma'.

Trauma is traditionally understood in this context as intense fear, terror or helplessness. It could include what child psychologists Mary Main and Erik Hesse, who studied this phenomenon in the Bay Area in the 1980s, call 'a close brush with death'.

It was only later – and unexpectedly – that I understood how this related to Anna. For I thought I wouldn't see her again. Not after the card. Then out of the blue she called me. It was an emergency, she said. A real emergency.

There was once a boy called Frederick who was born in a tent in a public square. That he was born at all people found it hard to credit, because no one believed his mother could get pregnant.

But born he was, in a tent in a public square in 1194. But when he was three years old his father died. The next year, 1198, his mother Constance also perished. But just before she died, Constance made arrangements to deliver her only child into the care of one of the most famous men in medieval European history, Pope Innocent III – who had issued the foundling wheel edict. For Frederick's father, Henry VI, was one of the Germanic Hohenstaufen dynasty, King of Sicily and Emperor of the Holy Roman Empire, the sprawling ever-changing kingdom of the Franks and Germans that followed the coronation of Charlemagne on Christmas Day in the year 800.

Although for simplicity many authoritative sources, including the *Encyclopaedia Britannica*, refer to him as Holy Roman Emperor, the title only officially came to be used from 1254, shortly after Frederick's death. More accurately, then, he was Emperor of the Romans. This exemplifies the morass of intriguing ambiguity that besets the Holy Roman Empire, which was, as Voltaire famously said, not Holy, nor Roman, nor an Empire.

The decision of Frederick's mother Constance appeared baffling, if not perverse. For many years there had been a bitter struggle between her husband's Germanic family and the church in Rome, with the two power blocs vying for advantage. But now on her husband's death Constance was placing her son in the care of the very entity his father and grandfather had struggled against. What sort of nurturing was this? How is it possible to understand it?

Impossible – except for the fact that Constance appreciated that on her husband's death war for the spoils of Sicily would rage violently as the land descended into chaos, bloodshed and rebellion; because she appreciated that the very life of her son would be at stake, that on her death the boy king would be an orphan, surrounded by those who would slay him.

So from the moment of his birth, Constance did what she could to protect him. She gave birth to him at Jesi, a Roman town near Ancona in Italy's central Marches. What is a moment of agony and elation for a new mother, was turned by Constance into a public performance. She gave birth to Frederick in a tent, in the public square.

She did quell any doubts about her son's entitlement to the throne. For Constance was 40 years old and had been married to Henry for nine years. Rumours abounded about her inability to provide the king with an heir. So she endured her labour pains in plain view. And to make sure, she repeated the demonstration: to prove it was not a conjuring trick, she breastfed her child in public under the gaze of the town's great and good.

Constance was well acquainted with the violence that accompanied royal descent through her own bitter experience. She had recently been betrayed and imprisoned by her brother's (illegitimate) son Tancred in the bloody succession wars for the throne of Sicily. Thus bequeathing Frederick to the custody of the Pope was the act of a desperate mother protecting her child.

With the tremendous strain of it all, Constance succumbed 14 months after her husband. She died on 27 November 1198. But she had achieved what she set out to do: she had saved her son.

Once when he was on the shore of the lake, Samuel saw two spiders by the roots of a tree. The bigger spider ate the smaller one. That's how he thinks now of his childhood: eaten by something bigger.

When he was a young boy – he does not know the exact age – Samuel's mother sent him away from their coast town home of

Winneba to the lake. The plan was for relatives who lived at Volta to look after him. He would work, fish, but it was with relatives. Relatives would treat him better. That was the plan.

Things did not work out like that. Eventually his mother sold him to another person, unconnected to the family. He was trafficked and enslaved. When years later the rescue team reached him at the lake, he was reluctant to leave. His master had put fears in his mind that the people who claimed to rescue enslaved children in fact resold them or would treat them even worse.

After two hours' persuasion, Samuel relented. He went with the rescue team and left the lake behind. While he was at the lake, he did everything: casting nets, hauling them, diving to untangle the webbing from the black underwater branches. The lake was his life. After nine years, having started at so young an age, it was hard for him to imagine any other. But now he is retraining. He has swapped the nets for thread; a different kind of stitching. He is doing an apprenticeship as a tailor.

The lake is always in him. It's as if his memory is snagged like the fishing nets by the trees in the dull water. But the steady thrum of the sewing machine soothes him and hauls him back to dry land. He makes garments for other people and clothes himself with new things, like hope. He dreams of becoming a fashion designer. One day.

Once his tailor shop flourishes, he intends to use the income to fund the rescue of other children at the lake, trapped as he once was, when he was sold by his mother.

But sometimes he can't help thinking, as the sewing machine thrums, who was that big spider? Was it his mother or was it the lake? That is what he doesn't know. He thinks of the spiders as he weaves and sews.

*

I took the Red Line of the T all the way into Boston, riding it from Harvard Square to Downtown Crossing. But it wasn't Anna who needed help. It was Ubah.

Anna tried to explain it on the phone. 'She crashed,' Anna said. 'She had another flashback. You know her ankle's been hurting?'

'Yes,' I said. 'I've noticed.'

'Everything, everything, coming back.'

I'd seen it before. How it can happen with survivors. Ubah was a survivor of female genital mutilation. Sometimes people who have undergone FGM suffer the most gruelling flashbacks, to when – often as children – they were mutilated. It can be paralysing, debilitating, terrifying.

'I've got to go out,' Anna said. 'I just have to. I'm sorry. No one else is free for now. She trusts you. It's just a couple of hours – I've been with her all afternoon – then I will be back.'

'I'll be there,' I said.

I have related some of the detail of Frederick II's history because the machinations surrounding his mother and his bloodline might well have driven him to think much about why people are as they are and do the things that they do – and why children become the people they become, particularly when they are reared in straitened circumstances. As he had been, an orphan, his life constantly at risk.

Although notionally entrusted with the child's care, Pope Innocent III paid him little heed and only met him once. He wrote to the young Frederick, advising him thus: 'God has not spared the rod. He has taken away your father and mother. He has given you . . . a better mother, the Church.' Frederick was five years old.

But Frederick was a survivor. In 1212 he was crowned King of Germany. In 1220 he was crowned Holy Roman Emperor. In 1229, in the Church of the Holy Sepulchre, he crowned himself King of Jerusalem. But in truth Frederick was less preoccupied by the mysteries of the realm divine than the mystery of nature right in front of him – within himself. He set about investigating it. He experimented.

There is little doubt that he was an unusually talented individual. Nietzsche was later to call him 'the first European'. A contemporary chronicler called him *stupor mundi* – the wonder of the world. But within Frederick ran a streak of cold cruelty.

He authorised some of the first experiments on nurturing. He conducted experiments on children.

SEVEN

Life's Longing

Frederick wanted to know. What things are; why they are.
Soon dark tales of Frederick's 'curiosities' – or 'excesses' –
seeped out from his court.

Some are likely to be wild exaggerations, rumour feeding on
supposition, supposition feeding on fantasy. But it is unlikely to
have all been confabulation. The 13th-century Franciscan friar
Salimbene di Adam actually met Frederick. Salimbene's *Chronicle*
relates how Frederick was interested in the nature of nurture – in
children.

Why, Frederick wondered, are they as they are? How much of
it is inbuilt and to what extent is it a question of how we raise
them – how we nurture. Was this curiosity affected, perhaps, by
the early death of his parents, by the fact that he was brought up
by strangers? He ordered that there should be an experiment.

In the year 1211 children were placed with foster mothers and
nurses. They were permitted to suckle and bathe the infants but
no more. For that was the strict limit of the allowable contact;

their attendants were, as Salimbene tells us, 'in no wise to prattle or speak with them'. The children were brought up in isolation and silence.

Frederick wished to know if, deprived of stimulus or other human contact, children would instinctively speak Hebrew (which he believed to be the first language), Greek, Latin or Arabic – or even the tongues of the parents to whom they had been born. What was the 'language of God'?

Frederick's experiment ended in disaster.

Shorn of affection, deprived of something as simple as another person's 'gladness of countenance', the infants died. When news of the deaths of the children raised in silence reached him, did Frederick, I wonder, think of his mother? Given that Constance died when he was just four, could he even remember the woman whose devotion and determination saved his life – and may have shortened her own? On that, history itself is silent.

In his *Divine Comedy*, Dante places Frederick's mother in Paradise. After all Constance's travels and travails, her mortal remains lie in a tomb in Palermo Cathedral, Sicily, the island home of her father and grandfather. A few paces from Constance lies the body of the son she had given birth to in a tent.

Much later, when Anna returned, we sat in a Chinese restaurant south of Boston Common, on the fringes of Chinatown itself. It was a street or so from where Anna and Ubah lived. For a couple of hours, I'd sat quietly with Ubah. We just talked. Mostly it was about nothing, which was what she wanted. But now she was exhausted and had fallen asleep.

So Anna was back. The air roiled with the heady smell of roast duck and soy, with every now and then just the hint of the nearby harbour. Opposite us a red neon sign in the window of a

Vietnamese restaurant flashed that it was open for business. It was late and everything was in fact shutting down.

'So all was good?' Anna said. I detected that she had make-up on, subtly, unmistakably, as if she'd been on a date.

'All was fine,' I said.

The waiter brought us a squat white teapot of jasmine tea. He seemed to know Anna and smiled ingratiatingly at her. She quietly said something, just a couple of words, in what I presume was Cantonese. She waited until he moved off. 'When I called you,' she said, 'you thought it was about me?'

I didn't answer. We both knew the answer. The tea breathed a small cloud of fragrance around us. Ubah was sleeping. She had both our mobile numbers.

'Thank you for the card,' I said.

'Is just a card.'

'Well, I kept it. I liked the rose.'

'I shouldn't have sent you that.'

'Why not?'

'People think: Oh, pretty girl. Weak pretty girl.'

'Do they think that?' I asked.

'I'm not like I look.'

'What do you mean?'

'I can cope. With what happened to me.'

'Why do you just have to cope?'

She looked across the street towards the Vietnamese restaurant. Pedestrians passed on their way home. A street person begging for some leftovers tried to push his way into the Vietnamese. There was some shouting. Two waiters forcibly ejected him.

'In my country,' Anna said, staring at the scene, 'in the mountains, they tell stories, they say children are taken by wolves. Ubah and I, I know this sounds crazy, crazy, but we speak a couple of times about wolves, and then speaking to her I realise: the wolves, they're men. And women. But mostly men.'

Wolves are so alien to the modern British experience that later I looked it up. What happened to British wolves? Edward I's edict of 1281 led to the systematic slaughter of wolf packs in England. It is not known when the last English wolf was killed, but perhaps around 1500. They survived longer in Scotland. Some Scots took to burying their dead on offshore islets to prevent the graves being dug up and desecrated by wolves. The last Scottish wolf was reputed to have been killed by Sir Ewen Cameron at Killiecrankie in 1680. But while wolves have been wiped from the land in the British Isles, they still roam through Anna's region and can sometimes be heard in the darkness. As Angela Carter says in her *Company of Wolves*, 'One beast and only one howls in the woods by night.' Today's pan-European population amounts to 12,000. A significant number near Anna.

The street person in his tattered rags, once rebuffed, tried again and made a move towards the door of our restaurant. Our waiter, his face suddenly set hard and menacing, stood blocking the entrance. The man moved on.

'I always feel guilty,' she said. 'Like we should help that guy.'

'It's difficult,' I said.

'Is it?'

'No. But we don't.'

'Sometimes I think out there,' she said, indicating beyond the plate-glass window, 'is forest. But I don't know – are they the wolves? I think about this a lot when I think of what happened.' She paused. 'Are we? The truth is,' Anna told me, 'he scared me.'

'Your uncle?'

She shook her head. 'He hurt me. He hit me. People hit people.'

The stoical way in which she said it, with a mixture of resignation and world-weary acceptance, reminded me of that cryptic line from Marcus Aurelius' *Meditations*: 'Art thou angry with him whose armpits stink? What good will this do thee?' For Aurelius, for Anna, this was the way of the world.

'I'm not scared of him,' Anna said.

'I'm losing you. You said he scared you.'

'He is not *he*,' she said. 'Not that man. I am not scared of men like him. They do what they do.'

'Then who were you scared of?'

The waiter was piling chairs on the tables so the cleaners could vacuum the floor.

Tears welled in Anna's eyes. 'I was scared of my baby,' she said.

'But what could he do to you? He was a child.'

'Not what he could do.'

'Then what?'

'Then what . . . then what . . . then what,' I still vividly recall her repeating it like a mantra, staring down disconsolately into her white china cup, turning it round and round, sending the little white jasmine petals spinning. 'Then what I could do.'

'What could you do?'

'I could hurt him,' she said.

She paused for a very long time. 'I was scared,' she said, 'I would hurt him.'

She said it with such utter conviction that I did not challenge her. I was about to say: Anna, there's no reason to think you would hurt the child you've just given birth to, but I was actually worried. Sometimes people tell you things in a way that leaves no room for doubt. What I didn't understand was why she so completely believed it.

*

The research of Nim Tottenham from Columbia University extends to how nurturing and caregiving impacts the behaviour of children and the structure of their brain.

Seventeen researchers (and their colleagues) from a variety of academic institutions across the United States, from Cornell in Connecticut to California, collaborated in a significant body of experimental work involving children who were 'PI' – previously institutionalised.

There is a large literature on the behavioural difficulties that are associated with the prolonged raising of children from their early years in institutions rather than families. But what Tottenham and her colleagues wanted to explore was any neurophysiological changes that accompanied it. In other words, whether being brought up in an orphanage impacted the internal shape and structure of the brain.

Seventy-eight children were assessed. Of these, 38 had been previously institutionalised; the other 40, the control group, had never been institutionalised and instead had been brought up in their families. The real significance of the experiment was that those children who had previously been in orphanages had subsequently been reared in American homes with a profile that broadly matched that of the children in the control group. Both sets of children were now in families with similar household incomes (which was above the national average). So was being institutionalised in early years reflected in the shape and structure of their brains?

Nim Tottenham's team used MRI to scan the brains of 62 of the children. Would there be any structural differences? What would they be?

The PI children, despite having been brought up for years in adoptive families, had a greater incidence of psychological problems. Indeed 53 per cent suffered from at least one psychiatric disorder. Their amygdalae were also different.

The adopted children fell into two groups: early-adopted, those placed below the age of 15 months, and late-adopted, those leaving institutions above this age. The MRI scans revealed that late-adopted PI children had significantly larger amygdala volumes than either the early-adopted group or the children who had not been adopted. What did this mean?

As we have seen, the amygdala, that complex brain structure that extends its tentacles beyond its characteristic 'almond' shape, is associated with processing and reacting to threats, stress and other emotional cues. It is central to how we scrutinise how safe our environment is. What is more, in humans the amygdala develops rapidly in the early years, with its growth (certainly for girls) typically complete by the age of four. It is thus extremely sensitive to the developmental surroundings the child encounters. Researchers argue that it is at the period of swiftest development that a neurological structure like the amygdala is most vulnerable to environmental influence.

In an orphanage, the stress the child is exposed to is likely to take a very particular form. The person administering the care is constantly, necessarily, changing as staff members work in shifts. Thus the child is unable to form a consistent attachment to a particular caregiver – to a 'mother' figure. In place of the maternal attachment, a stress system fills the void: the amygdala is prematurely engaged and activated. If in early years it is constantly activated, or overactivated, or protractedly activated, there are consequences for the child – and for the brain structure monitoring the threatening situation itself.

Thus the stress of childhood institutionalisation is followed by overstimulation and abnormal growth of this neurological region.

Put more simply: prolonged placement in orphanages changes the anatomy of the child's brain. It physically grows the stress structures.

This institution-induced inflation remains years after the stress and trauma are ended. Nim Tottenham and her colleagues make the case that their research has profound policy implications. It underlines the need for what they call a 'rapid adoption process' for children in orphanages.

And what does this mean for Anna's decision? If she was going to give up her child, she was probably best to give him for adoption shortly after birth. She sold him. There is no escaping that. But the alternative, having him interned in an orphanage with notoriously poor care, waiting for adoptive parents who may never arrive, is likely to have been extremely damaging.

Faced with these dire choices, giving her son up at birth was likely to enable his better neurological development; he was more likely not to have his amygdala activated and overdeveloped by early stress; he was more likely not to develop associated behavioural problems in dealing with the day-to-day stresses of life. He was likely to have a more stable life.

And yet he was not with his mother. He had been exchanged for money. He may never fully know who he was and where he truly came from. That is also what Anna's decision meant. And it marked her.

'And so when I was born, I gave her a terrible time,' Anna said. 'My mother's labour, it lasts so many, many hours. It is a terrible birth. My mother loses so much blood. She nearly dies. After the birth, she is not the same. Is as though something in her . . .' Anna, I recall, made a kind of tearing motion with her two hands, as if she had a delicate paper napkin between them and she was very slowly ripping it in two. There was actually a napkin on the table. She didn't use it.

'So my mother is ill. Not just her body is ill, you understand? And the doctors, they are worried. She goes in and out of the . . . special hospital. Sometimes they are worried what she might do with me. So my father has to try to look after me. My grandmother comes, she lives with us. Is weeks while my mother is ill. Sometimes I am with my mother. Sometimes the doctors say, no, is not safe for the child to be with the mother.'

Finally the truth was emerging. But it wasn't anything like I thought. 'But she did come home?' I said. 'Eventually, you mother came home. The family was reunited?'

'My father, he could not cope. He would stay at the government offices. He would work on his cases until very late. He would drink. He began affairs with women there. I don't know how many. My mother never told me how many. But it was a lot, I think. And she was stuck with a small child in that apartment block, high up over our city. So my mother tricked him, I think. She gets pregnant again. He didn't want more children. But she tricked him with the dates and got pregnant. She thought maybe if she gives him a boy he will be happy with her. He always wanted a boy. But when he found out she was pregnant he is so angry. He says he wants to kill her. He said he was trapped. She trapped him. He left us. And so there is my mother. I am four years old. My mother is pregnant. My father has left us. And we are living up there in a tall apartment block on our own now. I can only remember small parts. But her brother told me too. And he was told by his wife, the Beach Ball, and she was told by one of our neighbours, and the neighbour was his wife's friend. So other people know what happened, so I am not mad.

'One night, my mother gets me out of my bed and she puts on my coat. Why she put my pink coat on me I never can understand. She puts on my coat and then she walks out of our front door into the hall. She goes to the elevator. But she doesn't get in the elevator. She goes to the staircase – the emergency stairs, the stairs that lead to the roof. And she and I walk up onto the roof, and she is holding my hand. And it is one of the highest apartment blocks in the city. And it is night. Below us is everything. The whole city, all the lights. We are up in the clouds. And she walks with me, holding my hand, and I'm wearing my pink coat, and we move slowly towards the edge.'

Anna stopped. I imagined the wind racing across the rooftops of the capital; the child's pink coat flapping in the breeze; the blinking stars; the concrete streets like thin ribbons of grey far, far below. I thought of my office at William James Hall, the one she didn't want to meet in, so far up also, all 14 floors up, with extraordinary but dizzying views of Boston. Like Anna's view, there it all was: the fullness of the city, the emptiness of the sky.

'Someone had seen her, seen us,' Anna said. 'They call the police. My mother, she had to go back to the special hospital. I was taken into care. I spend two years away. Nothing. Two years in care home, that terrible place.'

'I don't think she would've done it,' Anna said. 'I think she thinks about it, but I don't think she would've done it.'

Did Anna believe that she, Anna, would *actually* do anything like that to her own child? She was certainly scared. When I think how she was nurtured, perhaps she was right to be scared. It was a risk with her son's safety she did not want to take. I have come to see Anna's actions as a form of nurturing too. Not just nurturing her own child, but nurturing life. Like those lines from Gibran:

> Your children are not your children.
> They are the sons and daughters of Life's longing for itself.

The Polish for baby hatch, the modern equivalent of the foundling wheel, is *okno życia*: window of life. There are all sorts of hatches, all sorts of windows. Anna found her own window. She used it to make her child safe. The problem was she couldn't look through. But she figured that that blacked-out window was better than a rooftop, better than the sky. I wonder whether it's possible to see in what Anna did – in the very, very end – not just an act of nurturing but an act of love.

EIGHT

All the Annas

Something I've thought about again and again is what ways to be free there are to be found in Anna's story. For a long time I believed there were none. She had accused herself, convicted herself and passed a punishing sentence, a permanent exile from the hope of seeing her child again. How was that freedom in any way? And then I wondered if I was in fact looking at it through the wrong lens. What if I thought of her son? What he was spared. How by her act she had freed him from poverty and shame and stigma. Was there a kind of freedom in that? I imagine him growing up in a Western capital, going to a good school, reading books (even Balzac), playing tennis, going to art exhibitions – Klimt. I wonder if his new parents have told him the truth. Whether they ever will. Is there a way in which being kept free of the truth can ever be a kind of freedom?

Recently I represented a woman accused of murdering her life partner, someone who had for years physically and sexually exploited her. We got the case reduced to manslaughter and she pleaded guilty. I asked her why she had stayed with him. She shrugged. 'It just seemed impossible to do anything else,' she said. When she told me that, I thought of what Anna said about something suddenly rising inside her with irresistible, impossible force, something she didn't previously know was there, telling her with great resolution, even as she was beaten with a metal hanger, that she was going to continue with her pregnancy, she was not going to have an abortion. Whatever the name of that – whether we call it the Nurturer or something else – the sheer strength of that impulse permitted her to stand alone and give birth to the child, despite the pressure of the adults around her.

One day, some months after I spoke to Anna in the Chinese restaurant, Ubah and I met to discuss an international initiative to fight FGM. I was working on a briefing for the UN and wanted to run a couple of ideas past her, wanting to speak to someone who had personal knowledge of the problem. After skirting around the subject, inevitably we started talking about Anna.

We were in the John F. Kennedy Park that runs along the Charles River. Cars raced between traffic lights on Memorial Drive and across the water lay Soldier's Field and the enormous Harvard Stadium, standing out like a Roman amphitheatre. The park wasn't too far from where Anna and I had first met all those months before.

'Haaa, you don't look well,' Ubah said.

'Yes, I love you too, Ubah,' I replied.

'You are working too much. Work, work, work. When will all this work end? Maybe we change the world, maybe it changes us.'

Before I could respond, she continued, 'So are you listening to my friend Eunice, like I tell you?'

'I'm listening to Eunice,' I said. 'But how's Anna?'

Eunice – Eunice Kathleen Waymon – was Ubah's good 'friend', even though they had never met. I will come to all that. But not now.

'You *must* listen to Eunice,' Ubah said. 'What she says. That *voice*.'

'I agree, Ubah. But what about Anna?'

There was a sudden stillness around us, that strange stillness in a city when for a moment nothing moves and there is no sound. Ubah told me that for a while Anna had been seeing the guy from the bar near MIT. He did finally give her a Prada handbag – albeit a fake one. It made her laugh. But soon her money was running out and she couldn't keep paying for the photography course. She dropped out. I asked Ubah whether Anna had lost her job with the hotel. Ubah shrugged and then looked away towards the slow undulations of the water.

Now there was movement: two people, a man and a woman, were paddling ferociously in lurid yellow kayaks, sending halos of water splashing around them.

'What's Anna doing now?' I asked.

Ubah did not answer.

'What's wrong?' I said.

'Is not for me to say.'

'Oh, come on. You can't do that.'

'Anna, you know, she is my friend.'

'What's happened?'

For a short while Ubah was silent. To one side of us, traffic went racing past with the usual fanfare of engines, heading up to Massachusetts Avenue.

'All right,' Ubah said. 'Only because I know she like you.'

She was troubled. What she then told me was not what Anna had told her directly but what another friend, also from Anna's country, had told her from speaking to Anna. It was what we call in the law multiple hearsay. One of the most notoriously weak and worthless forms of evidence. As a judge, I would almost certainly have ruled it inadmissible. But it was the only information we had. So we had to go with it.

'You see,' Ubah said, 'Anna wasn't working in a hotel.'

'Where was she working?' I asked.

'Well, she *was*.'

'What?' Again Anna's story seemed to be slipping away from me.

Ubah took a deep breath. 'She was working in a lot of hotels.' She looked at me knowingly. 'A lot.'

Even before she repeated the words 'a lot', the penny had dropped. I felt stupid. I was supposed to be one of Her Majesty's counsel learned in the law, expert in forensic analysis and it had been staring me in the face all along. I had completely missed it. I thought of how Anna spoke of the 'clever girls' who went to the international hotels of her capital city, and waited. When I asked her about working in the hotel, she hadn't really answered. It was an innocuous question, and I had thought nothing of her evasion of it. I realised now where she had gone when she called me to relieve her when Ubah crashed – the make-up, the urgency, the work she had to do.

'So she wasn't doing a course?' I asked.

'No, she was,' Ubah insisted. 'She didn't . . . .. work all the time, but it took everything out of her.' Not at the time of my conversation with Ubah but later I turned over in my mind the lines from Wittgenstein (that Dawn Faizey Webster once brought to my attention) about how we never doubt what is there and observable because it is 'always before our eyes'.

'Once,' Ubah said miserably, 'they fly her to San Francisco for three days. Just three days. Some party on a big boat.'

'Yacht?'

'This big Chinese businessman owns it. She told me they had gold baths. I said can't be, but Anna said yes. She slept a week when she comes back.'

In my mind I could hear Anna speaking those few words of Cantonese to the waiter. I hoped she was safe. I hoped she wanted to keep herself safe, but was unsure. I didn't know how much she really cared about herself any more. Her inner prosecutor kept prosecuting. She was, she believed, the worst person ever.

Over the years, I've represented many women who are sex workers; I've been judge in cases with several more. There are many motivations – sometimes even a curious kind of lack of motivation, a hollowness or deadness inside, a running from something within. Sometimes there is a kind of complex distancing from themselves, from personal trauma – what psychologists call dissociative behaviour. There are unsettling research findings that victims can experience sexual trauma as a kind of 'out-of-body' experience: they 'stand' to one side and look on, observing, trying to break the link between the feeling, the pain, being inflicted on their bodies and themselves. These young women inhabit a world of loneliness, isolation and fear. There is a running from the wolf.

'She's taken all her things,' Ubah said mournfully. 'She's left Boston. No one knows where.'

I want to give you a better ending. I want to tell you something more concrete, but up to the point of writing this – now something like three years later – no one has heard from Anna again.

Edward Hopper, *Automat* (1927)

I am conscious that this is not a Hollywood ending. It's just a human one. But perhaps there is one more thing about Anna I can tell you. I was going to omit it; it didn't seem important – simply something she said. But now I think about it, it may be. I'll let you judge.

We were walking away from the restaurant in Chinatown. Street people were hunched in alcoves and shop doorways, seeking such shelter as they could from the icy wind blowing off the Atlantic. They looked stunned.

'There's no need to come with me,' Anna said.

I was walking her home. 'Force of habit,' I said.

She told me that a woman in the agency said that she should use the $1,000 to have a better life, the life she wanted. It was a gift from her child. Anna hardly spent any of it for a long time, except for emergencies. She eventually used it to buy a ticket to the US to get away from the money she wished she didn't have.

'Now,' she told me, 'I hardly remember his face. Not, you know, 100 per cent. His face was so small. I don't forget that. He looks at me. He keeps looking at me with his small face. Like he asks a question: who are you? Are you mine? But I can't remember if his face looks like this or looks like that. Is it some baby's face I remember, because I spend long, long times trying not to think about him. Because it hurts when I think like that. So I can't now say, yes, he looks like this. I see children with their parents on Boylston, and I think that can be him, that can be him, that. But . . .' she said. We stopped outside her block. I'd been there just two hours before. Now it looked different, impossibly tall. Music came out of a low window, a mariachi band. 'But I still feel how it feels when he touched my face,' Anna said. 'His fingers, they kept touching all over my face. Like they find out what is this thing lying next to him. I still feel that. How he touches my face.'

I go to the White Mountains of New Hampshire and climb a slope near the top of the treeline, thinking of Anna and the mountains of her home country which are stalked by wolves. As we steadily inch through the trails, a group of young women from another college sing (in an exaggeratedly ironic fashion) Cyndi Lauper's hit about getting lost, looking, finding each other – 'Time After Time'. I catch myself again and again going over that episode from Anna's childhood: standing on top of the frightening tower block, wearing a pink coat, clutching her mother's hand; the coat flaps and cuts the breeze; the concrete streets wait below; her toes creep closer to the edge.

But I am in the White Mountains. For the briefest of moments my eye is distracted by a bird, with flashes of burning gold on its wings. It disappears into the canopy of trees. The trail through the woods suddenly comes to an end. But Anna is not there. I want her to be safe; I want her child to be safe. But both are gone.

And what of freedom? Anna wanted to keep her son free from the wolves. She wanted to keep herself free from becoming one. The word nurture comes from the same root as to nourish, to feed. Anna tried to ensure her son was safe so someone could nourish him. She understood that it could not be her. The mental mechanism, that executive system, we have evolved that prioritises our offspring, privileging their wellbeing above almost everything else, spoke to her in a pitiless and plain way: make him safe. That single message. Burning through the pain, that message: save him.

A couple of days later I return to Harvard. It is night-time and I'm back in my office up on the 14th. I think about how Anna would have spared her son the damaging changes to his neuro-anatomy caused by the orphanage, not that she could possibly have known that. But something intuitively told her that it would hurt him. The Nurturer? The secret firing of neurons, the creation of affect – emotion, a feeling, visible, visceral. I am thinking about all this, take down from my shelf a book that some previous occupant of my room has left. It's called *Affective Neuroscience: The Foundations of Human Emotion*. Something like that. Then I notice. The cleaners have removed my piles of research papers from the air-conditioning vent. While I've been away, the slow, steady, sanitised gust has blown over Anna's card. It lies miserably on the floor. I search around frantically, under my desk, behind the waste-paper bin, for Anna's flower. It's nowhere. I put the heavy textbook down. I scrabble around. But the flower must have been swept up as rubbish, along with the paper clips and screwed-up Post-its. It is night and all the tens of thousands of lights of Boston lie beneath me. Anna was not a client, not a colleague, not a friend, but my contact with her was deeply unsettling. I want all the Annas to be safe: the Anna with the vivid green cardigan, the Anna on the yacht, the Anna in the cupboard, the Anna who gave up her child – the Anna in the pink coat. The Anna of the *Automat*. I think of that Cyndi Lauper song they were singing in the White Mountains: getting lost, looking, finding each other – 'Time After Time'. For a fraction of a second up high in my office, I see what Anna saw: the fullness of the city, the emptiness of the sky. It's like I am looking at it for the first time.

You are back in the burning building. Smoke seeps around every edge of the door frame in front of you. On the other side are your two children. Lisa to the left; Ruth to the right. You said to yourself that you cannot choose between them. That it's impossible for parents to choose between their children. But we've seen that people have always done that. Throughout history there have been times when parents have had to do that – all the way from Hammurabi, all the way through Basil of Cappadocia, and then the foundling homes and the spinning of their wheels.

You put your hand on the door handle. It horribly scalds the flesh of your palm. You stand in the corridor, choking on smoke, the fire is alive, flames leaping around you. You can only save one child. They're unconscious from the smoke. The fumes swirl in your head. But you can save one. Lisa to the left; Ruth to the right. You think of Anna. She only gave birth to one child, but she chose between two children. A child that would be brought up in the misery of the orphanage and one that would be sold.

If you had that choice, knowing everything we know now, everything that the research has told us about nurturing, how hard it is, or can be, how brutal, how ruthless, how complex and confounding – if the choice were this, if Ruth would be the orphanage, if Lisa would be sold, which way would you turn? Would you do as Anna did? Which way would you turn – to the left or to the right?

The grille on the foundling wheel,
Santo Spirito Hospital, Rome

PART VIII

THE ROMANCER

For lovers ever run before the clock.

William Shakespeare, *The Merchant of Venice*,
Act 2, Scene VI

ONE

The Gift

It started with an argument at a wedding. And a snub.

On Mount Olympus all of the gods were invited to the wedding of two of their immortal host: Thetis and Peleus, the parents of the greatest of all warriors, Achilles. But Eris was not invited. For she was the goddess of discord and was snubbed to avoid her fomenting strife. Nevertheless, she was determined to attend. She came to the celebrations. When she was summarily turned away, Eris – also known as Discordia – ingeniously created another way to create trouble. She used the simple expedient of a gift.

She rolled a golden apple from the Garden of the Hesperides, on the western edge of the world, among the goddesses present – a prize to be claimed by 'the fairest of them all'. Incited by Eris's provocation, three of the most beautiful heavenly beings, Aphrodite, Hera and Athena, vied for possession of the apple. But the argument could not be resolved. Zeus, intent on remaining neutral (Hera was his wife, after all), determined that a young Trojan prince, Paris, son of King Priam and brother of Hector, whom Achilles would kill and drag behind his chariot, should adjudicate. To lure him into coming down in their favour, each goddess offered Paris something different, which each calculated would have the most powerful effect on the mind of a man.

Hera offered him boundless worldly power, promising to make him king of Europe and Asia, effectively the known world.

Athena offered him might in war, skill in combat and wisdom to use these gifts unstoppably to vanquish his foe in battle.

But it was Aphrodite who won.

For she knew the secret source that unlocked the hearts of mortal men. She offered him what would prove to be, ironically, the Achilles heel of men: love. She offered him the most beautiful woman in the world.

Paris's decision precipitated the war against which all others have been measured. A war that, the archaeological evidence suggests, might even have taken place. Legend has peopled it with characters – heroes – that loom over all those that have followed in the Western canon in the next 2,500 years. For Paris's choice led to the launch of a thousand ships and the burning of the cloud-capped towers of Troy. He was to choose Helen; he chose love.

But to what extent does this story, gilded with metaphor and myth, represent some durable facet of human nature – particularly that of men? If the fundamental Darwinian drivers are survival and reproduction, then it should not surprise us if there is an executive system directed at the latter – a mating module. But what is of surprise is the sheer extent of bizarre behaviour that the Romancer will engage in. And I mean bizarre.

In 597, a Benedictine monk was sent to Britain by Pope Gregory. There in the south-east corner of the land this monk, Augustine, christened the king and founded the English Church in Ethelberht's capital, Canterbury. The area was chosen in one respect at least because of love: Ethelberht had married a Christian princess and was thus thought to be receptive to Augustine's overtures. Fourteen centuries later a curious little advertisement suddenly appeared on noticeboards in the drama department of the University of Kent in Canterbury. The ad sought 'observers' to participate in a series of experiments in the Department of Psychology that probed one aspect of the Romancer. These experiments needed the drama students for one principal thing: their face.

Volunteers were graded by ten students of the opposite sex for their attractiveness. The two drama students rated the most attractive overall – the fairest of them all – were chosen. One male, one female. They would be the observers.

The public behaviour of men – the boasting, posturing, performing, fighting – has caused many problems, not least for evolutionary theory. This has been particularly so because of one peculiar expression of such behaviour: male generosity. A growing body of evidence indicates that in public men tend to act more generously towards strangers than do women, whether in charitable donations or when intervening to help people in the street. There are a number of plausible explanations associated with men's relative greater economic and social capital, learned social norms (but where did they come from and why?), male physical formidability and confidence in public intervention scenarios (in part also a consequence of gendered inequality). It has also been suggested to be part of reciprocal altruism, giving in the expectation of a benefit in return. But the research team at Kent's psychology department sought to examine whether such male behaviour could also be connected to something rather different: to mating behaviour – to the Romancer.

After being involved in a random task and consequently earning money, the research participants were then given the opportunity to give a proportion of those earnings to charity. There was a desk and a computer screen and a chair and in the first (control) experimental condition they would be able to determine how much (or little) to donate in private. But in the other two set-ups they would be watched.

An observer would be seated next to them and able to watch the screen – and thus their donation decision. Some volunteers were watched by an observer of the same gender, others by one of the opposite sex. An *attractive* member of the opposite sex – the drama students rated by their peers the fairest of them all.

When female research volunteers came to make their donations, they displayed little difference between the three conditions in the proportion of their earnings they would give away – it was usually in the 40 per cent range. But men were different.

From donating around 35 per cent with no observer, that fell to around 30 per cent when watched by another male. However, when a female (an *attractive* female) was observing them, their donations leapt to around 60 per cent of what they had just earned.

The female observer did not say anything. She was not allowed to. She did not do anything. She did not have to. But the Kent experimentation revealed that male volunteers, when observed by an attractive female, gave more. Much more. Almost twice that amount, just by changing the gender of who sat in the chair doing 'nothing'. Aphrodite, surely, would have known this.

What accounts for this difference? What causes this male generosity and gift-giving? Is it a consequence of learned behaviour? Or is there a deeper or parallel contribution from fundamental neural systems? A further insight is to be had not in Kent, but north of the Great Barrier Reef, in the Coral Sea that washes the north-east coast of Australia. But before we get there, we need to revisit someone. An old friend.

The greatest gift he was ever asked to give, the greatest act of generosity he could ever have imagined – in fact it was beyond his imagination – something that to him was so shocking and sad that it took him several years just to tell one other person about it, was asked of him – demanded – by the only woman for whom he'd felt anything approaching love.

She would not leave her soil or her people, and she knew with a certainty more absolute and terrifying than any he'd ever encountered, that it was better to die than be captured or enslaved, which to her was the same thing.

He was one of the least likely people to have been possessor of this story and this strange gift request.

You already know him. I met him in Cameroon's capital Yaoundé, the Rome of Central Africa, with its tree-lush hills, when I was obsessing about another country, trying to get to know that unknowable place, the Central African Republic. His name is François.

On one of my last days in Cameroon, after he had introduced me to Patrice, François and I were driving in his gloriously ramshackle, arthritic old Mercedes through the teeming streets of Yaoundé. I had been telling him about the Gareth Myatt case, the terrible struggle we'd had to expose the truth at the inquest, all witnessed with mounting horror by Gareth's mother Pam. I remember when I first met her and she was delighted that the case was coming to court so people could explain what really happened. I had to warn her: it would be war. It was. A little like when I spoke of these things to Anthony in Ghana, such an account didn't sit well with François's rosy image of England.

'Will you tell her for me I'm sorry,' he said.

'Of course,' I said.

He suddenly veered towards the kerb right beside a stall. 'You hungry?' he said. We'd been listening to another of his Motown playlists.

'Please tell me you're not hungry again. François, we ate an hour ago.' Only a minor exaggeration. It was hard to explain the sudden change of tone, except that for François eating was a life-affirming thing, a kind of celebration.

'So, I starve myself when I'm gone,' he said. 'This, *the* best, best place for street food. I will get you Ndole.'

Ndole is an iconic dish in the area, an ingenious confection of peanuts, shrimp, beef and a spinach-like bitter leaf (the ndole itself). A clutch of obviously satisfied customers lingered around the stall. François didn't get out. He just talked through the window, speaking in English, no doubt for my benefit. He told the owner, 'Today, special, special offer. A ride in my limousine for two bowls of your ndole.'

The woman, adorned in a spectacular headscarf, said, 'Haa, I give you *three*. Three meals if you drive your dirty car far, far from my restaurant.'

They both burst out laughing. We drove off armed with said delicacy and parked up. When we were finished, I asked him about the recipe. He didn't appear to hear. He toyed with the small leather amulet dangling from the rear-view. He looked dead ahead – as if at something so far away it wasn't in Yaoundé or even Cameroon. François said there was something he wanted to tell me. 'Is only small, small thing,' he said. His thick arm was half hanging out of the Merc's open window, as it always did.

'Small is good,' I replied. He was silent, kept staring. To fill the uncomfortable void, I added, 'Small is beautiful.'

When I was at school I'd once read Schumacher's book by that name – in truth, I was forced to read it. The only thing I could remember as I sat with a door of an old Mercedes open in a central African city was the subtitle, something that struck me at the time, as a teenager: 'A Study of Economics as if People *Mattered*'. With all I'd learned about the Central African Republic and the atrocious conflict there, I had been forced to consider how much, in the grand, grotesque scheme of things, people actually mattered. But then again, through François I had met Patrice and Saira, and through them, indirectly, Omer. Whatever the carnage and chaos across the eastern border, they mattered.

'A small, small thing,' François said.

'Are we getting out or not?' I said.

'Very, *very*, very small thing,' he said. It was as if we were having two conversations. The face of my constantly cheerful friend had contorted, almost squashed into two-thirds of its normal size, in an uncharacteristic scowl. 'You know, sometimes men, they do the *fou* things.'

'Foolish – men?' I said. 'Humans?'

He jabbed his thick stub of a finger sharply towards me. I imagined the stab of it in the flesh of my chest. 'You, me. Men. Not women. Men.'

'Foolish?'

He very slowly shook his head. 'So, so *fou*, you will want to cry is so *fou*. But don't cry, *mon ami*, huh?' Finally the smile that remains my dominant memory of him reasserted itself. 'Life, she is too short for any more . . . I am not sure of your English word, Mr Lawyer, for any more *tristesse*.'

Then he told me what was troubling him. It made me see everything he'd said or done in my presence in a different light.

'You know,' he said, still staring ahead, 'I didn't tell you the truth.'

TWO

The Lie

If one journeys north along the gentle arc of the Barrier Reef as it shadows the Australian coastline, past Heron and Lizard Islands, and leave Marian Wong and her goby behind, eventually the land runs out. Australia ends. The northern tip of Queensland is divided from the southern reaches of New Guinea by a stretch of water just about 90 miles wide at its narrowest point, the Torres Strait, named after the Spanish explorer Luis Vaez de Torres, who navigated through the waterway in 1606.

Torres and his crew were required to keep their wits about them for the area is treacherously cluttered with dozens of islands and shoals. These clumps of rocks and sand may be all that remains of the land bridge that once connected Asia to Australia – the stepping stones over which the peoples that were the forebears of modern Aboriginals made their way to the vast, strange continent.

One of those islands in the Torres Strait, slightly off to the east, is called Mer. It's also known as Murray Island. Formed of an extinct volcano that was last active a million years ago, today it has an indigenous population of 450 islanders who speak a form of Creole. Europeans began to inhabit the island when in the 1870s the Reverend Samuel Macfarlane created his mission headquarters there. Born near Glasgow of poor parents, Macfarlane resolved to become a missionary and was accepted by the London Missionary Society. He journeyed around New Guinea, established several mission stations and founded a religious school on Murray Island itself. Macfarlane returned to England and in 1894 published his account of his adventures, which he called, in the idiom of the day, *Among the Cannibals of New Guinea*.

Today the islanders live by horticulture and tourism but also by an activity that they must have developed and honed while they were splashing their way south from Asia: marine foraging. And it is that last activity, the hunting by male islanders in the surrounding seas, which has been the cause of intense study by research scientists from across other more distant oceans.

'What didn't you tell me the truth about?' I asked François.

'You know, when I tell you that thing.'

'What thing?'

'My home. Cameroon.'

'Yes. So?'

'I *am* from Cameroon.'

'Yes, so?' I repeated.

'No, no, listen. *Now* I am from Cameroon. But at first, in the start, I am from CAR.'

'Hang on. You're going to have to tell me all that again,' I said. 'When we spoke before, you told me you'd never want to go there. You said it was hell.'

'That is because I *know* it. I know it because I am it. Some people, no, they hate things because they don't know them. But you also can really, really hate something you know. I *know* that place. What happens there – is happening.'

My thoughts were reeling from this, recalibrating the dynamics between him and Patrice, reviewing the conversations François and I had had during our time together. 'I thought you were from Cameroon,' I said. It was the best I could do for the moment.

His face contorted with anger. 'Do I look like I am from Cameroon?'

'Honestly,' I said, 'I don't know.'

He smiled a little. 'Is *pas grave*. How are you supposed to know, English lawyerman? But why you think *les centrafricains*, they trust me? I am one of them.'

'I thought you did it for the money.'

'I do it for the money *and* because I am one of them. Central Africans, we are allowed to make money. Why are we not allowed to make money? But is terrible thing. This country we love. What they are doing to it.'

The way he was to speak about CAR reminded me of a word the Poles have: *żal* (pronounced 'jhal' or 'zhal'). It is the word, famously, that Chopin used to describe his music, and embodied by many of his mazurkas, based on traditional Polish folk music. The word *żal* is capacious, containing more than just sadness and sorrow; it also has room for anger, compassion, regret, melancholy, nostalgia, rage, perhaps even, as in Chopin's music itself, the loss of one's native country – homesickness. François's feelings towards the Central African Republic, I would discover, contained all these things.

He began by telling me something he saw before he left. He was in his home town some distance from the capital Bangui. One day he saw all the birds flying out of the bush. 'So many birds, they fly right over the tops of houses, so many birds you cannot count. Like . . .'

He used a word I didn't know. Finally, I understood that he meant locusts. Like locusts. The people said it was an omen. But he knew it was men. Men killing other men as the latest civil bloodshed got closer. 'And I knew,' he said, 'the birds would be back because there would be bodies. The country was becoming like this. I could no longer stay.'

What is CAR? Our children are thin and our vultures are fat. That's our country, that's le Centrafrique.

Bodies lay still and untended in the street, around them the smouldering carcasses of schools and clinics, houses and hospitals, such terrible mutilations of people it was hard for him even to begin to explain it. He didn't want to and I didn't want him to. He had the unnerving thought: what if there were no more people? With the scale of the slaughter in CAR, what if all the people were killed?

In Europe in the 19th century, Chopin experienced something similar. In November 1830 the Polish people rose up against Russian rule. The insurrection was bloodily crushed, with tens of thousands of Poles killed or wounded. Chopin, who happened to be on a tour to Vienna, was destined to become an exile from his native land. He wrote to his schoolfriend from Warsaw, Tytus Wojciechowski:

> I think I am going away to forget my home forever. I think I am going away to die. How dreadful it must be to die elsewhere than where one has lived.

With the carnage in CAR, François thought: Very well, so this is the world. It didn't care, not about anything, not about life, people's liberties – him.

'But, okay,' he told me, '*I care* about me. If there is no one any more to care about me, I will care about me and I will care about no one.' And with that stark philosophy, he survived and flourished, even as war raged and the country consumed itself. He left CAR and crossed over into Cameroon. People said there was money to be made in Cameroon. And he would have stayed there, if it wasn't for his father, if it wasn't for the girl and the gift.

Males from most primate species do not contribute much of the food that is consumed by females and their young. Human beings, however, have evolved differently. Where in hunter-gatherer societies protein in the form of meat is vital, two features are commonly found. First, the hunting activity is principally conducted by men. Secondly, the sharing of the hunted animal becomes part of an elaborate public display by the successful male hunter.

In non-human animals, an approach to behaviour explanation known as signalling theory has provided robust and incisive understandings of what would otherwise be baffling behaviour. This analytical approach is centred on a simple but powerful organising idea: how creatures behave and look conveys significant information about them. Signalling has, for example, explained the curious behaviour of certain primates – male chimpanzees in the Bossou area of the south-eastern Republic of Guinea.

While these apes almost never share plant foods that grow wild, when it comes to crops that they have pilfered from human cultivation, the picture is markedly different. Then they share papaya fruit grown by their human neighbours, which they have stolen at considerable risk. This 'forbidden fruit', given the danger encountered to obtain it, becomes a highly desirable commodity. But rather than it being hoarded or consumed in Scrooge-like isolation, it is shared. Overwhelmingly this practice occurs among male chimpanzees when they permit fertile females to partake of the illicit goods. Such behaviour may well be part of a signalling strategy, a 'food-for-sex' gambit by the larcenous and lustful adult male chimp. Offering commonly available forest fruit would not provide the same level of allure. Anyone could get that.

In the last few decades signalling theory has been trained upon the human animal. It has produced a growing mass of ethnographic research suggesting that public displays by humans, including and notably acts of public generosity by males in hunter-gatherer societies, are linked to the acquisition of status and prestige which, crucially, may be translated into success of a very particular kind – reproductive success.

People were fleeing the killing in terror. It was bedlam.

With the crisis in the country caused by the marauding of the predominantly Muslim Seleka militia from their strongholds in the north-east, a mass of people was in flight. But François left the safety of Yaoundé and Cameroon and headed straight into the line of Seleka's advance. For that was where his father's home, their family home for as long as François could remember, was situated. There was no choice.

His father was gravely ill. He had not long to live and his cousin Aurore, who had been looking after him in François's absence, urgently contacted him and said that if he wanted to see his father alive again, he had to come back from Cameroon. Every month François sent money to Aurore (a cousin on his mother's side) for his father. It was not always easy, parts of the country were in meltdown. But there was a complex system of informal money transfer – there always is – and he managed to get money back to his cousin and she looked after his father.

While he was relating all this, and although François did not tell me directly as such, I sensed there had been a falling-out between him and his father. What it was about, I didn't know, and didn't have a right to ask.

Despite his best efforts, delayed for a day when he purchased an old jeep at the border that had then broken down, François couldn't reach his home town in time. By the time he arrived, his father had died.

In the days after the burial, François lingered in CAR, unsure what to do. He'd had very little contact with his father in the preceding years, but it still was a blow, hitting him much harder than he could have imagined. It derailed him, just being back in the area he grew up in, the place of so many memories he had tried to flee.

'Why didn't you come back to Yaoundé?' I asked.

He shook his head, his hands gripping the steering wheel of the Mercedes even though we were stationary. 'You have a parent that died?' he asked.

'My father too,' I said.

'So why do you ask me this?'

I didn't reply. I recalled returning to the town in which I had grown up after my father died. In my daze I left my bags on the train and just walked onto the platform. I had never done that before in my life.

He thanked Aurore, of course. She was constantly around his father's house, a bulky person, unfit, exhausting herself by just moving, puffing heavily as she fussed about tidying up, even though he could no longer see any point. Still, he thanked her for what she had done. However, what happened next crept over him slowly but unmistakably.

What she said about his father just didn't match what François remembered. People can change, naturally, and he'd been away from CAR a long time, but when he asked her if she was able to get his father the cigarettes and palm wine he liked with the money he'd sent from Cameroon, she said it had been difficult, but she had done it. He knew then that she was lying. It was a test. And she had failed.

His father had loathed alcohol and had once beaten François for getting his younger brother Georges to try palm wine. The more he probed, the more he was certain that Aurore had done very little to help his father. They had a vicious argument, and she was spiteful and cruel. She said he was an impossible old man who was never satisfied. She said François was a negligent son for abandoning his parent. He scolded her back. Then she said something I did not understand when first he told me, 'You're not even family. Don't you say one more thing because to me you are not my family.' She left.

In the aftermath of the row, a neighbour came by. She confirmed that Aurore had done very little, but had paid a young woman to tend to his father. The neighbour gave François a letter his father had written to him. The old man had not trusted Aurore with it. There in the town street, François stared down at his father's writing. It read:

François, the girl did not save my life, no one can save my life. I am too sick. But she did everything for me. Try to help her as I have nothing left. Her name is Marielle. See that she is safe.

He instantly recognised the writing, and just as recognisable, the absence of sentiment or ornamentation. It appeared that his father left no other final testament save this.

Eventually, in a meagre shack on the edge of the town, he found her. When François arrived, she was sitting on a stool in the shade of a tree, mending a white cotton shirt, the woman who had nursed his dying father.

THREE

Carriages and White Horses

'Are you Marielle?' François asked.

'Yes, monsieur,' she said.

'I am – '

'Forgive me, I know who you are,' she said, looking up calmly.

'How?'

'I have seen pictures. Your father showed me the pictures of you.'

François did not answer. She was perhaps in her early twenties. A smooth, trusting face. 'Is it true,' he said, 'you looked after my father?'

She put the needlework to one side, wiped her hands on the side of her dress, stood up. 'Yes, monsieur.'

'Why did Aurore not do it?'

'She was too busy.'

François exploded. 'Too lazy. She has nothing to do. She sits all day and gets fat.'

'I do not know,' the young woman said.

'Fat, lazy, stupid . . .' he caught himself cursing his cousin in the street. He stopped, was silent for a while. He moved from the sun into the cool pool of shade in which the girl was standing. 'You looked after my father?' he said.

'I tried,' she said.

He still found it baffling: his father, unreasonable and cantankerous, and this slip of a girl. 'How did you find him?' François asked.

'Your father, he taught me many things. I tried to help him as much as I can.'

'Really?' François said, still somewhat sceptical. 'What did you do?'

'Very little,' she said slowly but evenly. 'Most, I stayed by his side, got him water when he needed.'

'And cigarettes, I hope,' François said.

'He never smoked,' she said. 'Not with me. Perhaps in earlier times he smoked, but not with me.'

She was, he knew, telling the truth.

'Were you with him at the end?' François asked.

She looked down. 'I'm sorry,' she said.

'Don't be sorry,' he said harshly. 'Tell me what happened,' François insisted. 'Tell me how.'

'Please, monsieur, I don't want to say.'

'Tell me.'

'Please, monsieur.'

'He was *my* father,' François shouted.

Along the road, a stray dog sniffed its way along the gutter. Two children in far too small T-shirts were playing in a pile of broken-up furniture. François found himself breathing hard, painfully, like his chest was tightening. He bent over, put his hands on his knees and tried to regain his breath. The dog barked briefly at the children, then thought better of it and padded off.

'Please come in,' Marielle said. 'I can give you some water.'

He entered the shack – there was barely room enough for the two of them – and drank from a small orange plastic cup. It was all she had, but his breathing eased, regularised.

'So,' she said, 'this is how it happened.'

In the last day or two, his father's feet began to get very cold. It was so hot outside, suffocatingly so, but his father's feet were constantly cold.

'He asked me to rub them, just hold them in my hands, make them warm,' Marielle said quietly. 'I'm not sure he could feel it, but he makes like he can.'

At first the old man tried to raise his head in acknowledgement, but then when he was reaching that last staging post, he occasionally smiled briefly at the ceiling.

So that's how his father had died. And now there was this girl. This girl he'd never known existed. The armed militia were approaching the town, everyone said, and his father had asked François to help her, this quiet girl he'd never known existed.

'What do you want?' François said.

'Want?' she said confused.

'Want. Everyone wants.'

'No, monsieur.'

'Tell the truth, does Aurore owe you money?'

'A little.'

François took out his wallet.

'It doesn't matter,' she said.

'Maybe these things don't matter to you.'

'Do you need help?' she said.

'Help?'

'To pack away things in the house? Miss Aurore didn't want me to be there after you came. She didn't want you to see me.'

'It doesn't matter,' François said back to her. To him at that point, none of it mattered. 'What will you do now?'

'I will look for work.'

'Work? You know Seleka are coming?'

'Perhaps they don't come to our town.'

'They will come to *all* these towns, don't you understand?'

She shook her head. 'These are things that are not my business.'

'I can give you some more money,' François said. 'What you're owed, a little more. So you can leave. Do you have family in another place?'

'I have no other place. There is only me now.'

He paused, thought about it. What could he do with this girl he'd never known existed? 'Look, I can drive you to Bangui on my way to Cameroon,' he said. 'You can find somewhere there.'

'Why should I go to the capital?' she said. 'This is my home.'

'This is going to be a war zone,' François said.

'It is still my home.'

'Do you understand how many people are being killed? All over the country. Seleka will kill anyone.'

'But what have I ever done to them?'

'Yes, that is just how they work,' he said sarcastically, then when she kept looking at him evenly, with wide trusting eyes, he regretted it. Why was this girl getting under his skin? He turned his mind back to the job in hand, his father's letter, the wish contained in it. He thought how he could honour it. 'Listen, I will drive you to Bangui, or give you money. Your choice.' She did not respond, expressed no preference or interest. 'Or, okay, okay, I can do both,' he said, like a devastating final offer. Now it would be resolved, he believed. Give her both and be done with it.

'You are very kind. Like your father. But I don't need anything.'

'Ahhhhrrrr, you are *impossible*,' François shouted. 'I don't have much time.'

'Please, don't spend it on me. I wish you well. I liked your father. I'm so sorry for what happened.'

This enraged him further, but despite it all, she seemed genuine. She was clearly moved by his father's death. Her sorrow seemed simpler. But she didn't have to grow up with the old man and his discipline.

'There is no point in this,' François said. 'I'm going soon. If you want anything, come to the house and tell me. There is not much time. I'm not waiting for Seleka and I'm not waiting for you, do you understand? No waiting. I will just go.'

She nodded. 'I wish you a good trip,' she said.

And that infuriated him all the more.

That evening, however, she came. He was glad she had.

He was loading a few of his father's meagre possessions into his jeep when he suddenly noticed her standing very still a little distance from the house. He was glad not because he much wanted to see her – who was she to him? – but because it comforted him to know that the way of the world, its motive forces, which he had learned wheeling and dealing in the back-streets of Yaoundé, had not changed. People *always* wanted something. It was just a question of how long it took them to ask you for it, and how much it was. Always. And here she was.

'Yes?' he said.

'There is something,' she said.

'Yes, something,' he replied.

'Something I'd like.'

'Yes,' he said again.

He thought he had her worked out now. Yes, she was good: the soft sell. The apparent indifference to money. It was all a ruse. A negotiation. He had to give her credit: she was good. She finally came to it and asked.

On the volcanic outcrop of Mer Island (the local name for Murray Island) the islanders in the Torres Strait harvest fish and shellfish that inhabit the reefs and warm waters. It is a custom known as marine foraging. But of all the foraging, there is one activity that is valorised above all else: the hunting of sea turtles.

Historically, while Meriam women tended to engage in the laborious gathering of plant foods (the sheer bulk of their haul demonstrating their industriousness), men engaged in higher risk hunting for highly desirable foods that demonstrate skill and dexterity. On the reef they engage in the spearfishing of small fish, elusive, fleeting targets requiring tremendous patience and a steady nerve. But that pales in comparison to the grand quest for the green sea turtle.

This seagoing animal, *Chelonia mydas*, is celebrated on Mer as feast food. During the nesting season when the turtles come ashore, the community works together – men, women and children – to gather turtles from the beaches. But that is communal collecting. Quite distinct from this tradition is the practice of turtle hunting amid the waters surrounding the island. The animal, which can grow up to 4 foot in length, is tracked by small boats riding the tide. When one is spotted, one of the hunters at the front of the boat jumps onto the swimming turtle.

Compared to collecting, such hunting is harder. It is risky and time-consuming. It is expensive, with hunters having to pay out in fuel costs for the boat to track down these predominantly herbivorous sea animals as they drift around grazing on seagrass meadows on the seabed. In the non-nesting season, triumphant hunters broadcast their success by sharing their haul with the community at public feasts, attended on average by around 175 islanders – that is, approximately *one-third* of Mer's inhabitants.

Research over several years by anthropologists from the universities of Maine and Washington reveals that successful turtle hunters have greater mating and reproductive success than other men. The public pronouncement of their hunting via public sharing appears to be an efficient signalling of their formidability, and the prestige and status flowing from this is correlated with sexual success. What it comes to for the men in the boats chasing after turtles is this: successful turtle hunters have more sex and more reproductively successful sex with more female partners than other men on the island.

On these little lush outcrops on the remnants of the land bridge between Asia and Australia, men make costly investments in time and money to hunt turtles *and then give them away*. On one level it makes little sense. But when one introduces the concept of sexual competition and sexual selection, it makes sense. These lavish displays of generosity reap rewards. They make sense if one considers the Romancer.

What is it that drives this behaviour? The case of the Mer Islanders is not isolated. The broad finding that hunting success correlates with reproductive success has been seen in a range of other forager societies such as the Aché in Paraguay, the Hadza in Tanzania, and the Tsimane of the lowland forests of Bolivia. What about in the Global North? Is it reasonable to suppose that men who make public demonstrations of their generosity (indicating their resource-rich status) have greater mating success? Do rich men attract more beautiful women? And more of them?

Payments between families at the time of marriage have occurred for millennia – recorded evidence dates back to 3000 BCE.

It is likely that in one way or another they have taken place for many thousands more years previously. Marriage-related payments were known among the Incas, Mesopotamians, Egyptians, Hebrews and Aztecs. Today, perhaps the most well known such system is the dowry. Here the wife's family provides money or resources to effect the marriage of a daughter. However, it actually takes place in relatively few cultures. In 1967, the *World Ethnographic Atlas* brought together evidence from over 1,000 pre-industrial societies. Dowry arrangements occurred in only around 1 in 20 of the considered societies. More prevalent by far was the concept of bride price. Here the male or his family pay for the female. What are they paying for? Possibly in significant measure her reproductive potential. And to secure it, a tangible demonstration of resources is required.

Seen in this light, the public display of generosity by males is another form of demonstrating one's resource-richness. The evidence base provides a clear indication that such displays, certainly in subsistence societies, correlate with sexual success. But is it causative? He who gives also receives? (And *because* he can give?) If so, generosity displays are transactional; they're not one-off acts of beneficence; they're on a two-way street, fringe benefits coming back the other way – benefits that are possibly genetic.

François's father had been in the police. He was a young recruit in Bangui when Jean-Bédel Bokassa, the living embodiment of the pantomime African dictator, crowned himself Emperor Bokassa I and renamed – reimagined – his country as the Central African Empire, in a coronation which (notoriously) cost a vast proportion of CAR's annual budget, replete with a guard of honour in faux-Napoleonic uniform, carriages with white horses, and Bokassa posing as the great Bonaparte himself. François's father lived it. He was there. A wide-eyed young police recruit just keeping back the crowds, but there.

That was in 1977. In 1979 the police force rounded up schoolchildren who refused to wear the uniforms they were obliged to purchase from the Bokassa private family cartel. Amnesty International reported to an appalled world that around 100 children were murdered.

At that point, François was just born. His brother Georges would be born two years later. Therefore he can remember nothing of the Bokassa years, but he does remember his father and his police uniform, how proud he was of it, particularly when the family moved back to his father's home town beyond the capital Bangui and he was promoted in the police. François remembered how his father would toil diligently to keep the creases sharply pressed on his uniform and lecture his sons on the vital importance of responsibility and duty. But his father would never speak about those past times – what he saw or did in the Bokassa years. His scars slowly closed over them, and shut out the rest of the world, and his son.

Their relationship had deteriorated badly as François was growing up. But now he knew his father's final wish: to help the girl who had shown him kindness at the end. Now she stood in front of him, next to the old jeep he had bought at the Cameroon border.

'So what do you want?' François asked her.

'Is it true Seleka are coming?'

'They will come. I am certain of it,' he said.

She nodded, looked down, closed her eyes slowly and when she looked up said, 'Will you really try to help me?'

'My father wanted that.'

'Then I know what I want,' she said. But she didn't say anything else.

'Yes, tell me, what is it that you want?' he said.

'You are sure, Seleka are coming?'

'I told you,' he said.

'Then I want a gun.'

He laughed. He couldn't help himself. But she was earnest, utterly serious. 'I tried to do everything I could for your father. It was not a chore. I do it with sadness, but joy to help him too. I don't want money or to go to Cameroon, but before you leave, please do just one thing, please give me this gift.'

'A gun? A *gun*? What will you do with a gun? You think you can stop Seleka with one gun?'

'I fight them a different way.'

'How?'

'The way I fight, they cannot beat me.'

'Why?' François said, but a chill was slowly spreading through him, and he was unsettled. 'You are crazy.'

'It is crazy to be caught? I have spoken to others more now. It is crazy to be raped?'

'Come with me. I can take you to Cameroon.'

'I know you can,' she said.

'No, I mean I will. I want to.'

'You take me to Yaoundé, then I become one of those women. I can be one of those women here.'

'That's not what I'm trying to do.'

In one electrifying instant, she took his hand. 'I think you are a good man, like your father. But I will never leave my home, I will never leave my people, I will never leave our land. I'm sorry, Monsieur François, but –'

'Don't call me that.'

'I'm sorry, but I don't have the money to buy one. Please give me this gift.'

'A gun, a gun. You are crazy wanting a gun. I will take you to Cameroon.'

'I know. You have said that.' She looked fully up at him, her eyes gazing right into his. 'I know why you want to do this.'

'My father wanted me to.'

'No, I know,' she insisted. 'I know why you want to make me safe and it's all right.'

'Why? Why? What are you talking about, stupid girl? So you won't die, that's why.'

'But I *know*,' she said.

He paused. There was a silence between them, then he said, 'What are you talking about?'

She looked down. 'I know what happened.'

'You know? You know? You know *what*? What happened? When?' François shouted at her with increasing fury.

She let go of him. 'Your father, he told me,' she said.

François exploded. 'You don't know what you're talking about. This is none of your business.'

'I'm sorry.'

'Sorry about what?'

'About what happened,' she said.

'Stop your saying sorry. Stop speaking.' Now he was the one who took hold of her, grabbing her forcefully. 'Just *stop*,' he shouted, shaking her by the shoulders.

And so she did. She did not move, did not flinch in the teeth of his anger. It was like a huge wave, the fury that passed over him. He could do nothing until it crested and crashed. When his mind finally began to clear, he found he was still holding her. His breath was fast and heavy; drips of sweat ran down his nose and tumbled to the floor.

'What do you know?' he quietly said.

She looked up at him unafraid, unperturbed by his behaviour. 'I know,' she said, 'it wasn't your fault.'

FOUR

Something Beyond All That

Their father had returned after a long policing shift. It was the early 1990s, and the boys, now on the cusp of being teens, were bewitched by their father's prize possession: an old hunting rifle.

He'd got it in a terrible state of disrepair from a Congolese trader, who said in turn he'd obtained it from a French paratrooper who had fallen on bad times and was selling all his possessions. François's father devoted his spare time to the rifle. He oiled it, removed the rust, sanded and smoothed the butt, caressed it, *talked* to it, like he was resuscitating a body, bringing it back to life. In a way he was. He restored it and it restored him, helped take him away from the things he saw as a policeman.

But now their father was sleeping after a long shift. It was François's idea, to go into the bush with their father's prize possession and kill birds, animals, snakes, anything they could find – it was after all a hunting rifle.

All François can remember is that it was a very windy day. He told his younger brother, as if he were an expert, that they would have to make allowance for the wind direction when they were taking a shot. But that's about the limit of what he can recall. After all these years, he still does not know how the gun went off.

When he gave it to Georges he was sure that the chamber was empty. He was certain that he had checked. How it had gone off, how it *could* have gone off like that, he still agonises over today. One minute Georges was standing next to him, the next not.

After they buried Georges, things were never again the same between François and his father. Georges was the light of their life, a beacon at the centre of the family, and suddenly the light had gone out. Now François found himself back in his father's home, the strength vanished from his legs, leaning back against the jeep, as Marielle stood in front of him talking to him about these things he had buried for years.

'Your father said it was not your fault,' she said. 'He told me to tell you: I know, François, I know it was not your fault.'

'If that's true, why didn't he write this in the letter?'

'Sometimes people, they find it hard to say sorry, sorry to the person,' she said. 'He was sorry. He wanted me to tell you he was sorry. He told me to tell you he does not blame you. He should have properly fixed up the gun.'

'Everyone else,' François said, 'they blamed me.'

'Why, if is accident?'

'Because they knew the story. Where I come from.'

She looked at him quizzically.

'My father's parents, they had already chosen my father's bride. The bride price was agreed, everything. But then he meets my mother. She was the one he liked. But his parents say no, not that girl, she is from a poor family. They have agreed the bride price with another family, a richer family like them. But my father, he loved my mother. Really loved her. She became pregnant.'

'And he married her?'

'The other bride price was agreed,' François said.

When he told me this, I didn't at first understand all that he was saying. But in CAR, and even more so 30 years ago, parents often arrange the marriage. The future groom would work for some years for the nominated bride's family. His family would also pay a bride price at the end of it. But François's father had fallen in love. The child – François – was born out of wedlock. His father married the other woman. Years later, when François's mother died, he went to live with his father, who by now had a son. He was François's half-brother – Georges.

'The people,' François said to Marielle, 'they talk. They say I kill him because I am jealous. I was not the true son. That's why. That was the talk.'

'People always talk,' she said.

'I can't remember my mother,' François said. 'I was too young.'

For a long while after he said that, they were silent. That night, they slept together.

As François was telling me all this, the weather was changing. The sun had sometime before disappeared behind the bank of hovering cloud that filled the horizon. The sky turned a kind of coffee colour and the whole city skyline looked as if it were bruised. There was thunder.

'I can't see any lightning,' I said.

'No,' François replied.

'If there's thunder there must be lightning.'

'But you don't always see it. We get a drink?'

'Yes,' I said.

'You know,' he said, briefly touching the amulet, 'my mother, she kept the old ways. She believed everything was alive. Yes, all is alive, but she believed everything had a life, that's how my father explained it to me. The trees, the rivers. Our trees, our rivers. My father's parents, they wanted the new things, what the Europeans had. Cars, books, medicines. They wanted their children to live longer and so how can I say this is a bad thing? But my mother, they thought she was foolish, believing the simple ways, the old ones, that we are just part of the world and not even the most important thing in the land.'

He turned on the car engine. In its recalcitrant way the old Merc slowly grumbled into life. He didn't say it, but I wondered if the amulet, after all, was just as he told Patrice nothing to do with the militias. I was convinced François loathed them as much as Patrice. I wondered if the amulet was for his mother.

'*Voilà*,' he said.

'What?'

'You see? Over the hill – lightning.' And I did.

They spent the next day in bed. It was dangerous, irresponsible, joyous.

He stayed despite the risk. She'd wanted a gun. He gave her something else: himself – he stayed on.

She wasn't just a woman. She was *women*. His confused, troubled relationship with them, perhaps reaching all the way back to the mother he could not properly recall. He could never understand – not them, it was his own behaviour he didn't understand, the manic, messy polarities of how he behaved towards them. Stifling, possessive; detached, distracted, indifferent; he could do them all – had.

Nothing had worked. Relationships crumbled. His belief in a future life shared with a woman had also. And then there was

Marielle, who came out of nowhere and into his life. She had something. What? She had something but he could not say what it was, but he knew he wanted it – her. But Seleka were coming. The war was almost at their doorstep. Everything rational in his being said get out of there immediately.

He lingered. He stayed. With Marielle.

What *did* she really want? He offered her money and she didn't want money. He offered her safety and she turned her back. She plainly understood little about the bitter bloodbath that was engulfing their land. But she understood something more. Something beyond all that. He just didn't know exactly what it was.

She heard it first, the distant rumbling. The glass of water beside the bed began rattling on the stone floor.

They had been talking about his far-off city of Yaoundé, a place his father had spoken about with some contempt because it had taken his son from him. To Marielle, caught in a country that was sinking in war and death, it sounded heavenly.

'Are there really seven?' she'd asked François.

'They say this. Seven hills.'

Later he told me, 'I said to her "*Ça dépend*". It all depends, yes, on what you say is a hill.' And it was just about then that the glass started to rattle.

'And what do you want?' she asked.

'Want?'

'In your city of seven hills?'

He didn't have to think long because he knew. 'I want a Mercedes,' he said. 'A white Mercedes,' he said.

'I hope one day you will get this,' she said. 'No, I am wrong.'

'I won't?' he asked her as if she knew everything. At that moment he believed she did.

539

'I don't hope because I know. I know you will get this Mercedes that is white.' Then as soon as she said it, she put her hand over his mouth. If anyone in Yaoundé had done that just a few days ago, there would have been trouble. But he found he liked it. What was happening to him? 'Listen,' she whispered. At first he heard nothing. Then he understood: militia trucks, lots of them.

'You must go,' she said.

'Come with me,' he said.

'Why?'

'Because they will kill you.'

'Maybe they drive past.'

'But if they don't.' He grabbed her face, her cheeks between his flattened palms. 'Marielle, if you stay, I stay. It is simple.'

'I don't want you to stay.'

'Then we go,' he said.

She didn't protest.

'Really?' he said. '*Really?*'

Their eyes met each other. She smiled, blinked slowly. That was enough. François jumped out of bed, pulled on his jeans, a T-shirt. 'Grab what you can,' he said.

'There's nothing I want,' she replied.

It was extraordinarily hot, the heat pressing into your eyes, obscenely muggy. By the time he got to the jeep, his T-shirt was sodden with sweat. She got in next to him. No rush. Deliberate. They drove off away from the sound of the convoy behind them, and sped around the next bend in the road, straight into a Seleka roadblock.

The hail of bullets pierced the grille of the vehicle, bounced off the wing mirror, smashed the windscreen glass and Marielle. A bullet struck her shoulder, half turned her around, another thudded into her chest so she exhaled like she was coughing.

François tried to steer the jeep as bullets flew around his head, one hand on the wheel, the other reaching for Marielle as she slumped forward. He tried to turn the jeep around, skidded, the vehicle almost rolling over, but he salvaged it – to no avail: it nosedived into the drainage ditch that ran alongside the road.

His head smashed against the steering wheel producing a thousand bursting lights in his brain. Somewhere beyond these, he was vaguely aware, was Marielle, motionless. He was concussed, out of control like being impossibly drunk. Before he knew it, militiamen were all around him. So many. With wooden staves. They dragged him out of the jeep. There was no water in the ditch. It hadn't rained in so long. He called to Marielle, but there was no reply. As the blows began to rain down from what seemed like the clouds and sky, he was dimly conscious that they were dragging her out of the vehicle too.

They pulled him by the legs onto the road: it was easier to land the blows that way. He fought back as hard as he could, shouted Marielle's name, kicked out from his prostrate position before someone clubbed his knee, an awful crushing blow that was the most painful. He screamed out. They pulled Marielle onto the road next to him. They were trying to revive her for their own reasons. They gave up and pushed her body over. The lights of their vehicles were on full beam, even in the daylight, like eyes staring at him, like another insult. From behind the roadblock, a young Seleka member, no more than a boy, in shorts, flip-flops, brought out a rope, a thick hairy rope, swinging it back and forth. Perhaps they are going to hang me from a tree, François thought. Perhaps drag me along the road from the back of their trucks. He'd heard that Seleka did both things. They would do anything.

But in fact, with him at their entire mercy, what they actually did do was try to pull his jeep out of the ditch. When they could not do that, with François beaten and unable to move, lying there on the road next to Marielle, they left.

Marielle's feet were next to his shoulder, just the position of it all, how they had been dragged and discarded. Her ankles were touching neatly, as if she'd just clicked her heels. He reached up, despite the pain in his arms, and eased off her shoes, edging them over her heels. Her feet were still warm. He did not understand why, but his head was mixed up with the battering. Yes, her bare feet were still warm and he was confused because he could not compute how long the warmth of a body remains after death. Around him, very slowly, all sound seeped away. He lay there, knowing she was dead from the massive chest wound. His fingers, shaking with pain from the beating the militia had inflicted upon him, touched her skin as her body heat evaporated, as she already had.

FIVE

The Fever

That was all several years ago, at the height of the Seleka insurgency and *coup d'état*. I was torn by conflicting emotions as François told me all this: Saira and Omer would later be in some other Seleka combat group, in some other part of the country, but in Seleka nonetheless, and so on the other side to François and Marielle. Patrice, of course, was on a side of his own.

If I am truthful, I didn't know what to make of it all. I still don't entirely. The lightning flashed over the Yaoundé roofs, startlingly lighting up the tropical trees. Then the chaos in the sky over the many famed hills cleared; the thunder's gunshots moved on to trouble somewhere else, and we were in a hotel atrium bar in the Cameroonian capital by the time François got through telling me it all. Incongruously, there was tinny piano music piped through the speaker system. I tried to place it, gave up.

'Can I ask something?' I said. He nodded. 'Why did the militia just leave?'

'You mean, yes, why did they not kill me?'

I had been trying to put it delicately. But, yes. That. Precisely that.

'In that time there were so many people to kill. Me, maybe they think I'm dead. Or very soon. So maybe they don't want to waste a bullet,' he said. 'Maybe they think a bullet, that is too kind.'

On the low shiny black tables around us, a group of Russians casually dressed – chinos, sports jackets – were in a heated nego-tiation with a few Cameroonian men in immaculate suits. 'It is not *true*,' one of the Russians shouted, and banged the table. The Africans smiled respectfully, but did not seem to agree. Their truth was different from the Russians'.

François pursed his lips, rotated his glass tetchily on the coaster slipping smoothly on the ebony-black tabletop. 'Now Russians and Chinese everywhere,' he said. 'Everyone wants Africa.'

'Will you go back, to CAR?'

He took a deep breath. 'Yes,' he said. He said it with the settled resignation of a man who had never really left. He said it with *żal*.

I have thought often of the gift Marielle had asked of François. The gun – why? Did she really want a gun or was it a test of some kind? The gift he ultimately gave, of course, was himself. By staying right to the end, he very nearly gave his life. Why did he do it? For sex?

In evolutionary terms, his actions could be construed as an act of *generosity*; in signalling theory, a display, to demonstrate – to *evidence* – his clear commitment, to prove that he could be trusted. He had made a costly, risk-laden investment in her. The Romancer in him had, that part of our mental make-up that animated both Prince Paris and François. Only once she was reassured of that was she prepared to leave with him. Tragically, it was too late. For her; for them.

The research undertaken with the Mer Islanders did not, it seems, have a neuroscientific or fMRI component. But acts of conspicuous public generosity have been found in disparate – and unconnected – subsistence hunter-gatherer communities strewn right across the globe. That must at the very least create an inference. There might well be some mating module involved.

There is a significant and growing body of research science that documents the superficially bizarre behaviour of males once their mating mindset has been activated or even artificially primed. Drawing on dozens of groundbreaking studies into our 'subselves', psychologists Doug Kenrick and Vladas Griskevicius state that priming men to look at 'photos of attractive women or imagining going on a date or watching a romantic movie' produces a state of mind whereby men become 'more reckless, adventurous, creative, aggressive, heroic, independent, and inclined to spend money on flashy products'. If the brain is indeed modular, the existence of a mating module is one of the most obvious and likely candidates.

There is research with flies. Lots and lots of research with lots and lots of flies. In one type, *Drosophila melanogaster*, the male has a very precise mating routine. Perhaps many males do. This little animal, whom you'll know better as the common fruit fly, was studied in detail by Yufeng Pan, Carmen Robinett and Bruce Baker. The results were published in their 2011 article 'Turning Males On'.

In it, they brilliantly encapsulate the intellectual quest of neuroscience, 'to understand in molecular detail how neural circuits function to permit individuals to perceive the world and execute specific behaviors based on those perceptions.' What does this approach tell us about *D. melanogaster*?

Drosophila's mating routine is highly formalised and sequenced, consisting of 'orienting, following, tapping, singing (wing exten-

sion and vibration), licking, abdomen bending, attempted copulation, copulation, and culmination with ejaculation'. But what they
also found was that certain neuronal circuitry was implicated in
the behaviour. More than that: it could be induced. By the artificial activation of certain neurons, the hapless winged subject, in
isolation from any promising female, could be induced into an
amorous state. Indeed, Pan's team found that there may be parallel
or overlapping neuronal pathways in *D. melanogaster*. This would
make evolutionary sense. Given the critical importance of reproduction, building in redundancy would confer overall survival
advantages. If because of a genetic mutation one system did not
function, then that would not mean the end of the genetic line –
the parallel pathway to passion could kick in. The animal's genes
may yet be passed on.

We finished our drinks and I followed François out of the sterile
refrigeration of the hotel lobby and once more into the African
heat. It assaulted us instantly from all sides. The hotel concierge
staff had silently, with a sullen dismissive wave, forbidden
François from parking his Mercedes on the forecourt next to the
intimidating row of Lexuses, Porsches and polished 4×4s. The
Russians filed out. Their chauffeurs simultaneously opened
the back doors of the vehicles in imperial fashion. For our part,
François and I wandered down to the street where his beloved
limousine was parked. For the last time, I saw the amulet hanging
from the rear-view mirror. The noise of the city wrapped itself
around us. We were dwarfed by the crenulations of the high-rise
hotels and half-finished office blocks. Yaoundé was on the way
up; Africa was.

'I'm sorry about Marielle,' I said. One of the five most inadequate
things I've ever uttered. No mean feat: I'm a trial lawyer – I've

had my moments. Yet I wanted to say something. What do we say? What can we?

François straightened up his clothes. 'Was short, huh?' he said. He never really had the chance to get to know her, as with his mother. 'It was,' he said, 'like madness.'

'Sometimes, a little madness is okay,' I said.

'And with you?'

I laughed. 'I almost reached the CAR border, didn't I? I'm here with you, aren't I? Maybe I should have gone across.'

'Too *much* madness,' he said.

I was still obsessed with the place. I'd gone right to the edge, probed it. Would that be enough to purge the infection – did I know enough now of that unknowable place?

'But if you go,' François said, 'I can arrange. Good, good price.'

'Is there anything you can't arrange?' I asked.

He pretended to think hard about it and said, '*Rien du tout.*' I suspected he was right: in that place, at that time, there was probably almost nothing at all he could not have arranged. I also knew that the longing for CAR in the two of us, for differing reasons, was not totally satisfied.

He stood massively in front of me, nodding slowly. 'Is hard to understand what is in there,' he said.

'In CAR?'

'It is us. And people are scared of CAR, so they are scared of us. We should not be scared of us,' he said.

'No,' I said. I remembered what he'd once told me: in CAR, there was nothing and everything – both.

'But you promise, yes? If you go, I take you.'

'If the price is right,' I said.

'My price is always right,' he came back, smiling.

Around us, the city, the Rome of Central Africa, this city of seven sun-baked hills, did not stop, did not notice, did not care, but we laughed, shook hands, said goodbye nevertheless. And then without saying anything more, and for the only time, hugged.

I returned to the hotel lobby. The tinny piano music kept getting piped out into the ether, unremarked and unremarkable. On the table where the Cameroonian businessmen sat, there was a fresh round of drinks. Now that the Russians had left, they had taken off their jackets, loosened their ties; they were smiling, but not too much. At the bar, a Belgian man was slowly getting drunk.

I had to pack to head back to London. But I didn't want to return to my room, the single traveller's cell, not just yet. I kept thinking that I hadn't made it across the border. That secret siren song of the forbidden – the fever. Full of that appalling attraction E. O. Wilson writes of: the monster in the fever swamp. We as we are, as we can be. Everything; nothing. So: a failure? What is the definition of success?

I kept thinking of François and Marielle and that time when their world was on fire and they somehow found each other; then his father, and his love for François's real mother. I thought of François: born, I like to think, out of love, not duty and social obligation. I thought of the amulet. In the hotel lobby there was a commotion: a young waiter bringing over milk for my tea dropped the jug. A little slick of white spread like suddenly opening fingers across the highly polished Formica floor. The maître d' was furious with his young charge. I told him it didn't matter. Really, I didn't need milk. I'd drink it black.

Judith Léveillée of UNICEF – committed, intrepid, veteran of some of the world's most challenging places – reached a point when she had to leave CAR. Like many people I spoke to about the place, she was torn between finding ways to process the scale of the depredations she had observed and a deep, fierce affection for its resilient people.

'I miss the country and the people,' Léveillée says. 'The people touched my heart. You need to connect with humanity, but also know when to stop and recharge, manage your energy.'

She was depleted, knew she had to regroup to continue her work. 'It only really struck me when I got home, how things really are for us. I was back in Montreal and just went to the supermarket. That's all. I realised: the size of our warehouse in Bangui for essential humanitarian aid for the whole country was the same size as the supermarket. We were dispatching things to the four corners of the whole country. And I'm just wandering around with a cart in my local supermarket. So, yes, now I'm home and returning to "normal" life after CAR and I hear your Stephen Hawking talking about a big space project to seize the energy of light to explore the cosmos, to find out what's out there.'

Hawking is teaming up with billionaire investor Yuri Milner to launch a $100 million project called Breakthrough Starshot to develop a minute, light-propelled spacecraft capable of harnessing solar winds to reach our next neighbour star Alpha Centauri in 20 years.

'Yes, that's fantastic,' Léveillée says, 'I see that. I get it. But, you know, we only have one earth, only one place to live, so we need to be mindful of all this here.' She pauses. 'And mindful of each other.'

I ask what $100 million would have done in the Central African Republic.

'Don't,' Judith Léveillée says quietly. 'Don't.'

We pause for a while. 'Will you go back?' I ask.

This was a difficult question for Léveillée to answer. I don't press for a response. It's complicated. Back in Yaoundé, François's new home, I sat in the lobby bar and wondered something similar about him — would he ever return to his real home? Chopin, I knew, had not been so lucky after his exile from Poland.

He had actually visited Britain shortly before his death and his last public performance was at what is now Lancaster House in London, attended by Queen Victoria. His piano recital was sandwiched between crowd-pleasing bel canto staples sung by popular operatic stars of the day. In her personal diary, Victoria noted that the singers sang well. Then she added, 'Some pianists played.'

Within months Chopin was completely incapacitated by his deepening illness, possibly tuberculosis. It did not release him from its grip. He died in 1849 and was buried in Paris. His words to his friend Tytus proved tragically prophetic: how dreadful it must be to die elsewhere than where one has lived. As was his fervent wish, his sister Ludwika ensured that his heart was returned to Poland, where it was interred at the Church of the Holy Cross in Warsaw, near to where 39 years earlier her brother, arguably the person most associated with piano music of the Romantic period, had been born.

I returned to my hotel room. From the window you could glimpse the tropical trees clinging to the hills, part of a long line of them reaching all the way back to the CAR border, silent sentinels watching as the forests of CAR, which François's mother believed were alive — had *life* — were hauled before them on trucks.

We are here for a short time and then are gone. Our genes are passed on or they are not. Either through duty or love or romance or blood. The Romancer – that strategist and tactician – which aims to see that they are, succeeds or fails, can be generous or not, gives gifts or, like François and the gun, does not. The power of the drive that animates it is one the Greeks recognised and sang about in their songs and celebrated in their stories, as do we, as will those to whom our genes are ultimately passed. If they are.

PART IX

THE RESCUER

Well, I did warn you.

Fyodor Dostoevsky, *The Brothers Karamazov* (1880)

ONE

He to Hecuba

It is a while before you actually *see* Susan.

She was not in the lab's reception room, an office in the faculty building that had been given a hasty makeover to make it feel homely and cosily unthreatening: soft furnishings, potted plants, a scattering of lifestyle magazines. That made it worse, more sinister. Nor was she in the viewing room. You thought she might have been there since this is what you've come here for: to watch. To watch Susan.

On the other hand, this activity is, social anthropologists tell us, precisely what we spend an extraordinary amount of our waking lives doing: watching other people. But here you are paid to do it. Not much, but paid, for your participation in the experiment at the lab. So in you go.

Into the deliberately relaxed setting, meeting smiling research assistants, Steve and Jeff. It's all been meticulously scrutinised and approved by the ethics board. It's safe. Of course it's completely safe. But a part of you still wonders. At the end of the day, you are going to view someone getting shocked.

The electric shock that will be administered will be mild. And in the name of science. But you are going to watch very carefully as someone is being electrically shocked. This is how science sometimes proceeds. How we probe the edges of what is known, and what lies beyond. Little steps of carefully calibrated pain. There is nothing sinister about any of this.

'I want you not to worry about Susan,' Jeff, the lab assistant says. 'Some volunteers do. It's natural. But really it's all pretty straightforward and harmless.' He runs his fingers through his thick, wavy blond hair, 'And like you Susan is also a volunteer. She's pretty hyped to explore how the mind works.'

How our minds work. That's what captured your interest. When you answered the advert for lab volunteers. Do science; learn something; get paid. Yes. And it's Susan who's going to get shocked.

It would have been nice if Jeff had had a white lab coat. That's what you'd expected. Something sanitised and surgical. Instead it's so low key, so *opposite*: he is in jeans and a loose-fitting jumper. He is smiling reassuringly. Jeff has a great smile. On the wall behind him is a painting of a mountain. Where, you wonder, is that mountain? And why is there a picture of a mountain in the reception room? Or perhaps it was just there and no one thought to take it down. It doesn't matter, does it?

'Did you follow all that?' he says.

Your thoughts were up the mountain that doesn't matter. 'If you could just repeat that last bit,' you say.

'We're trying to establish how very slight static effects, the kind of faint pulses you might get from mobile phones or tablets, might over time cumulatively affect our ability to learn. It's about cognitive processing under challenging electrostatic conditions.'

'Oh,' you say.

You'd read something about all that, the study of task efficacy, in the introductory information. You didn't fully absorb it. You signed the consent form; you didn't fully absorb that. You never really read those things.

'So what I was saying,' Jeff continues, 'is that we have magnified the level of charge in this round of experiments and we want to see how Susan does. But it's all completely within authorised limits. Below the max. So if you don't have any questions, why don't we scoot over into the viewing room?'

From somewhere inside you – you're not conscious of thinking the thought before you hear yourself voice it – you ask, 'Where is the mountain?'

Why do you ask this? Distraction behaviour, avoidance, probably. To delay the viewing in the viewing room. Of Susan. The intellectually intrepid Susan, doing this in the name of science.

'Ah,' he says, momentary confusion giving way to his default smile, '*that* old mountain. It was just here. I can try to find out if you like.'

You don't answer. You ask, 'What will the shock be like? For Susan.' You wonder why you care about Susan.

'Right, lots of people ask. Volunteers say it's kind of like if you're walking along a nylon carpet and then press an elevator button. A little sting like that.'

'Have you done it?'

His smile is more nervous, reactive. Covering. 'Ah, we're not allowed to.'

'Like a sting?' you say. Why so many questions?

'Or if you're getting an injection – not even that.'

557

You think of that last injection you had. The needle point distending the skin, stretching the membrane of its surface like a balloon, then suddenly piercing through. 'She knows it's coming?' you ask.

'She's agreed to it,' he says. 'But it's random. She won't know precisely when. That's kind of part of the point. You can't anticipate and prepare.'

'And what do you want me to do?' you ask.

'Your instruction,' he says, smiling, 'is in the viewing room. Just carefully read the instruction in the viewing room.'

You enter. A room with nothing but walls, a chair, a desk, a screen. No window. No natural light. No pictures. No mountain. On the desk a laminated form:

Thank you for volunteering to participate in this important study. Your time is appreciated! As you watch the ongoing experiments via the webcam, please try to place yourself in the shoes of our volunteer undertaking the test. She has agreed to work under challenging conditions, but is perfectly safe. Imagine what she is thinking; imagine how she is feeling; imagine what she wants. Imagine what it's like for her. Write down on the paper provided anything you think important about how she feels. Please ensure you've switched off your phone.

Paper provided – what paper provided? You are about to call out, 'Excuse me, but there is no – ', when you notice that next to the screen is a buzzer. You press it, gazing at the instructions, finding again that exclamation mark unnecessary, inappropriate, patronising – get a grip: it's *only* an exclamation mark – when suddenly Jeff's loose-fitting jumper is behind you.

'Is there something wrong?' he immediately says. The smile has gone. Anxiety seeps through the genial mask.

'Paper?' you say.

'Ah,' he says. 'The old lack of paper problem.' You catch him glancing at the screen. 'I thought it was with the experiment.'

'It hasn't started,' you say.

And then it has.

Susan, a young woman with shoulder-length chestnut hair, and a pink plastic wristband — why does she have that wristband? — enters some other room. She sits at a desk. She watches a screen of her own. A short film plays and then she has to answer recollection and observation questions in rapid succession. You can't see what's on the screen. That's not your job. You're here to observe the observer.

Susan uses a mouse — how old-fashioned. How reassuringly quaint. Left click or right click — presumably yes or no. Her free hand, her non-dominant one, the one without the pink band, is actually only partially free. For a moment it's off-screen, then you see it again — flat on the desk. It's wired to something. There is a foil square on the back of her palm. It's taped in place. Wires protrude from it. They lead to some black box. The questions keep on coming. Every now and then Susan winces. So many details for her to observe. She obviously tries hard to concentrate but now and then she winces. She is being shocked. Random intervals. She can't predict them.

You have paper. You're writing. Your thoughts. About her thoughts. What you think she's thinking. She is wincing as she is shocked. She can't anticipate or prepare. But still she continues. Question after question. A buzzer sounds. End of Round One. She is allowed to take off the foil. She rubs her pale skin, the back of her hand. The shock site. With the shocked hand she coils the lurid pink wristband round and round the other wrist. What is the band — a bonus, a branding? Another buzzer. Round Two.

More rapid-fire questions. Left click, right click, feverishly responding. More shocks. The foil back in place. She's wincing. What is she thinking? What are you thinking she is? Susan concentrates hard on the screen. You concentrate hard on her.

Every time she's shocked and winces, something in you winces too. It's uncomfortable for her. But she perseveres. You admire her perseverance. She reminds you of someone.

A sibling, a cousin, a friend. That look of all-consuming concentration, determination. Who? For a fraction of a second, she glances up, towards the observing camera, towards you, from where she knows you're watching her. What are you going to write down about her beseeching look? It's as though your eyes have locked. Suddenly the buzzer. End of Round Two.

Susan asks for a glass of water. She is entitled at the very least to a glass of water. She takes off the foil. She rubs her hand harder. She is saying something to Jeff. Susan doesn't look happy.

Jeff is trying to reassure her. He does a lot of his sympathetic smiling. He has a great smile. Susan is not being reassured. What is she saying? You move your head closer to the screen. You try to make out the shape of her mouth, the words that are coming out. What is she saying? Has something gone wrong? With the calibration, with the pain level? You look closer. And then suddenly, the screen goes blank.

They keep you waiting. What is going on in that other room? No one comes for you, so you wander back to the reception area and the picture of the mountain on the wall. Suddenly Jeff breezes in, your notes in his hand. You recognise your writing.

'So sorry to keep you,' he says. 'I was just – '

'Is she all right?' you ask.

'Susan? She's just a bit tired.' He smiles. 'But she's fine and dandy.'

Dandy? 'How many rounds are there?'

'Uh, ten in all,' he says.

'Ten?'

'Well, eight more. We've done two.'

She's done two.

He is glancing at your notes, your observations. 'These are great,' he says.

You try to resist the glow. But we are social mammals. We respond to verbal grooming.

'Very interesting insights.'

'She has eight more rounds?' you say.

He's still reading, not looking at you as he says, 'I mean, you don't have to stay.'

'Stay?'

'Watch.'

'Watch?'

'Watch Susan. I mean,' he says, still perusing your notes, 'I think we have enough here. It's really useful,' says he, who hasn't been shocked. 'So you can get your payment. I'll tell Steve to cash you out if you like. The next observer's here anyway. They're a bit early, but they can take over if you want to go.'

'But Susan?' you say.

'Susan is fine. Bit tired.'

'She has eight more rounds?'

He pauses. 'Not necessarily.' He is now looking at you.

'How do you mean?'

'She doesn't have to carry on. Not if, well . . . so long as we have someone doing the quiz. So not if . . .'

'If what?' you ask, already knowing the answer. You are already wondering what the pink wristband will feel like.

'Not if you'd be willing to take her place,' he says.

You have, it seems, three choices:

1. Stay and watch as Susan is shocked for eight more rounds.
2. Leave, get paid for having watched her, and she continues to be shocked in your absence.
3. Take her place.

But who is Susan? Why should you possibly care about Susan? What, after all, is all this to you? That beseeching look she gave you, your eyes locking – so what? You don't *know* Susan. Like those words from *Hamlet*: 'What's Hecuba to him or he to Hecuba?' Why should we care about other people?

And yet. Think about what you're thinking. Is there something that turns you towards Susan? To replace her. To rescue. What does?

Who does? What is going on deep in your mind? What kind of human thing is it? You stare at the picture of the mountain. As if the answer lay there.

TWO

The Naming of Parts

S o: after Africa.

Back in the UK. Working. Restless. London becoming increasingly unfamiliar, a strange city, vast, full of new cars, clean cars, cars that *work*, none of them quite like François's limousine – that old white Merc as rare as a black swan. London seems less – *mine*.

I walk out of the judge's entrance at the Old Bailey where I've been presiding over a case. The high office blocks resolve themselves into steel carcasses with people standing above people above people obliviously. I thought I understood this city. I don't. Along the Thames I look at pleasure boats full of tourists; I *see* arrow boats on Lake Volta; in the crowds near Covent Garden, I glimpse their faces: Patrice, Saira, François, Anthony. Tony Nicklinson drops out of the blue sky, waving. Then my phone rings and I'm back.

'He'll speak to you,' the voice at the other end said, a male voice, faint and indistinct.

I'd been waiting for the call for days. Due to witness and juror difficulties, the case had finished early for the day, so I had the unexpected opportunity to do something I'd been meaning to do for a long time: visit the body.

'That is great news,' I replied. I moved to one side as a clutch of tourists headed towards the body. I was a little late. I'd hoped to get there at one minute past the hour because from the box in which the body is preserved, a photograph is taken hourly and then tweeted out to the world. What the body sees as we see the body. 'How would he prefer to talk – telephone or Skype?' I asked.

There was silence down the phone.

That was not promising. I tried to fill the void with enthusiasm. 'What he has to say is so important, I'm happy to wear the international call charges. Or he can make a reverse call from out there.'

'He *will* speak to you,' the disembodied voice said. I superimposed it onto the painstakingly preserved corpse within the glass box. Just for a flash of a moment, it was as if the great man who died in 1832 were doing the speaking.

'Yes,' I said again, 'that's great news.'

'But only face to face.'

Not great news.

The tourists had taken their shots. They wandered off. You can only look at a body for so long.

'Why?' I said.

'You know, Dexter, he is paranoid. It is what many people who have lived in these countries are like.' *These* countries?

Jeremy Bentham, what was left of him, the coiner of the phrase 'nature has placed mankind under the governance of two sovereign masters, pain and pleasure', was mummified and motionless before me. The father of utilitarianism had been that way for almost 200 years. In a glass box, in a college, in London.

'So I have to come out there?' I said.

'Yes, here,' my contact said.

And that is how it began again. Leaving London.

To understand her, and what she would later do, you have to go back to her beginning. If each of us has many beginnings, one of them is when we are given a name. Among her people, this is a big event.

So on the day of the naming ceremony, somewhere in the Central Asian grasslands that cover an area the size of Western Europe, before the child was placed in her cot, an elder of their clan, as was tradition among her people – a famously nomadic people – approached the newly born girl. The venerable patriarch, an elderly male from her horde, bent over the child (she would later inform her rescuer) and whispered three times in her ear, 'Lena, Lena . . . *Lena*.'

At the end of the street snow-capped mountains rise as if someone has painted a perfect mythical mountain range from Middle Earth and hoisted it as a backcloth. It is unnerving. It is too unfairly perfect to be true. When I first arrived in the city, overtired but excited after the overnight red-eye flight, I thought they were distant clouds – they are that high in your eye-line. Then you realise these white floating masses are in fact the snow-strewn tops of mountains. I didn't know their name.

'These are the Tien Shan,' the driver said.

It means, I later discover, the Celestial Mountains. The Tien Shan are one of the longest mountain ranges in the world. Yet I'd never heard the name. The sun beats down; it is late summer in Central Asia; there is snow on the peaks above and terrible traffic down below. The mood of the driver who just cut us up in his Subaru 4×4 is far from celestial. So I'd arrived. I was 'out there'.

I'm about to meet Vasily. It begins.

Earlier, when I had taken off out of Heathrow, I put on the in-flight entertainment's Moving Map to get an overview of where I was actually heading. It had been tight: at one point it looked like I might not make it. I'd been judging a case for weeks at the Bailey, and at the same time had been preparing a murder trial that was to take place outside London. One day I was taking the high-speed train down from St Pancras, when shortly out of London it suddenly stopped. I looked up and was delighted. Just the name of the station – a delight.

'It's *Ebbs*fleet,' I said to my travelling companion. Bafflement and silence. 'The site of the great elephant,' I added. She just saw Ebbsfleet International Station. I failed to generate any enthusiasm for the great creature whose bones we disturbed to get to the coast 30 minutes faster. Her double Americano was a dismal failure, it is true – but still. 'It was twice the size of the modern African elephant,' I tried, a detail that astounded Rana. My colleague said I needed to take a break.

So I found myself at 30,000 feet – it wasn't really a break – watching as the Moving Map screen filled with sinister waves of static. Drinks were served and then when the screen flickered into life, the writing was mainly Cyrillic. We were flying east across the vast Eurasian landmass that extends unbroken from Calais to Vladivostok for 5,000 miles – about the same distance from London to Los Angeles. It was our task to cross a good proportion of it. I saw that we had weaved our way north of Kiev and south of Moscow. At the far end of the flight path lay my destination, the old capital of the ninth biggest country on earth.

Scattered around it, like counters on a Risk board, are places of myth and imagination: Mongolia, Samarkand, Tashkent, Bishkek, Bukhara, and above them all, brooding sullenly, Siberia. Sullen Siberia. The Moving Map details three of Siberia's cities: Chelyabinsk — I recall that was where that meteorite crashed to earth a couple of years ago, the fireball captured on a hundred smartphones; Ekaterinburg — somehow I know that here was where the last tsar's family was imprisoned and then shot; and Novosibirsk. I knew nothing about Novosibirsk. Later, much later, I would find out that it meant New Siberia. But at that moment, as I was flying out to Central Asia, Novosibirsk meant nothing to me at all.

When I was back in the UK, as I was leaving Jeremy Bentham's body, my contact said, 'Enjoy yourself in Kazakhstan.'

I recall thinking: does one enjoy oneself in Kazakhstan? And then I thought, why shouldn't one? I had little idea either way. But all of a sudden, here I was. At the border control in Almaty airport, there was a customs official in pristine militaristic uniform and an enormously peaked cap. He gazed at my passport, gazed at me (it's not the best likeness, admittedly). A slip of paper fell out: the picture of Gareth Myatt. He looked at it impassively, looked at me, inserted it carefully into the back of my passport and said, 'Welcome to Kazakhstan.'

And now the Tien Shan are rising mute and magisterial in front of me. I look in astonishment at snowfields in the middle of summer. I wait for Vasily.

Pleasure and pain. The maximisation of one; the minimisation of the other. When Jeremy Bentham and his protégé John Stuart Mill sought to name the fundamental springs of all human action, those are the names they gave them. Pleasure and pain: our twin sovereign masters.

Philosophically, of course, utilitarianism; psychologically, the theory of psychological egoism. Incalculably influential. Underpinning vast fields of Western liberal economic and social theory. A view of human nature that is unsparing and uncompromising. When we appear to act in the interests of others, we are at the same time, within the inner recesses of ourselves, being motivated by our own ultimate self-interest: the maximisation of our pleasure, the minimisation of our pain. Do you doubt it?

Consider this simple prospect: are we surprised when people act selfishly? But when someone acts in a self-sacrificing and self-less way, do we not think them worthy of celebration and praise? And do we not, at the same time, surreptitiously, secretly, remain suspicious of their true motivations? Not always. But very often. 'He acted in a completely altruistic way,' we are told. What are we quietly thinking when we hear this?

Really – did he?

'No, really, he did.'

Did he?

Are we going to accept that, or will we want to know more before we dare believe? And if we recognise this line of reasoning, is it because our life experience tells us that people tend to be selfish? Or is it because we are constantly told that people tend to be selfish? Indeed, even when we ourselves act selflessly, charitably, we are more comfortable believing that we are in part acting in our own self-interest.

In a remarkable study by John Holmes, Dale Miller and Melvin Lerner, published in 2002, people were found to be prepared to give money to charity more readily and to give more if the act of giving was dressed up as an exchange. Thus if a small, largely worthless trinket (such as a candle) was offered in return for a charitable donation, people were more prepared to give up their money. The trinket – the 'disinhibition instrument' – created the fiction of an exchange. It gave donors 'the license to act on their sympathies'. That is why the published article was given one of the best titles of any social psychological publication: 'Committing altruism under the cloak of self-interest'.

Committing altruism – why are we like this? What is at stake? From one view it is an arid intellectual debate that has rumbled on for many decades – something as dry and shrivelled as Jeremy Bentham's corpse at University College, London. But from another, it is about something altogether more vital – the living truth of one of the most important facets of who we are. And that is why I needed to speak to Vasily.

What does it take for us to help other people – to be prepared to sacrifice our interests for the interests of someone else? Is there some part within us that will perform this task, and if so, why? To give a name to it: is there within us a Rescuer?

THREE

The Cairo

It does not start well. That's the first thing you should know.

We meet in one of Almaty's many parks, framed by the great mountains above. The Tien Shan watch. They wait. Judged by celestial Tien-time, the frenetic human comedy below them will soon pass. All of it. Certainly individual humans will. And the two of them that meet among the city's innumerable trees: Vasily and me.

The plan was for both of us to wear lots of red – his idea. I didn't have much red with me. If I'd known before I boarded the flight, I'd have got something in duty free. Thus it was that I ventured into a cheap Almaty супермаркет – supermarket, as you probably worked out – and bought a cheap red tracksuit. I refused to wear the trousers. They were hideous.

The Tien Shan were formed around 50 million years ago, when what is now the Indian subcontinent broke away from Africa and sailed north at an alarming rate, crashing into the great Eurasian plate, creating a catastrophic fold in the earth's crust. This was around the time of the K-T extinction event, the comet collision at Mexico's Yucatán peninsula that wiped out almost all the dinosaurs, and left what was left for mammals. For us.

The man who approached me wasn't wearing red. He called my name and said glumly, 'Vasily cannot come.'

This mournful messenger was tall, thin beyond athletic trim – that borderline undernourished look. Sunken cheeks, face riven with lines – even his nose was slightly squashed, as if it were sinking into his face. His hair was shaved very tight, and he sported – sprouted – an even stubble. There was a faint indentation on one side of his head. He was one of the Russian residents of Kazakhstan. Around 35 to 40 per cent are ethnically Russian – a legacy of Communism, and before that tsarist imperialism.

'He cannot come?' I say, trying to retain serenity, celestial-ness.

'He cannot come.'

'Did he say why he couldn't?'

'His little one. His little one, she is ill.'

'I'm sorry to hear that. And you are?'

'Vasily's friend.'

Evidently. I held out my hand. 'I'm Dexter.'

'I'm . . . Oleg.'

Just too long a hesitation. His name was decidedly not Oleg. 'Hello, Oleg,' I said. 'Oleg,' I said to not-Oleg, 'would you tell Vasily something for me. Would you tell him it's totally fine if he doesn't want to meet. But if he does, it's up to him. He can tell me what he wants. He can *not* tell me what he doesn't want. It's up to him. So to start, it's very simple, very quick, just a quick talk.'

Not-Oleg appraised me carefully, as if he had to make a thorough report to his friend. It was unclear whether I passed.

'Okay, I tell,' he said. He turned and began to leave.

I had without much thought reeled out a standard kind of speech I'd used from Boston to Accra to Cambridge. It's about reassurance, taking the pressure off a potential interviewee. But now it seemed inadequate. It seemed undercooked, given the setting. The mountains merited more.

'Oleg,' I said to not-Oleg, 'I'm just a lawyer from London. That is a long way away, I know, and probably means very little. But I *would* like to speak to Vasily. I think he may have something it's important to know. If I'm wrong, it's no problem. But I think Vasily has something and it's not good. But good could come of it. But if not . . . not. As I said, it's no problem. If he doesn't want to meet, I think I'll go up into those mountains.'

'Mountains?' he said, as if he'd never appreciated they were there.

'Oh, come *on*. Look at those mountains. They're so . . . *big*.' Yes, I won the Central Asian prize for stating the obvious. He thought about it, and thought my comment not worth replying to. Which was fine. I could see which way this was going. I really *did* want to go up into the mountains. They're still geologically active – still rising. There are regular earthquakes in the region: Almaty sits on an area of 'crustal stress'. A massive quake hit in 1911, devastating the city. The most recent was a couple of months before I arrived.

I squatted down on my haunches and broke a twig from a fallen branch. The soil nearer the tree trunk was slightly less baked. I started digging around with the twig.

'What do you do?' not-Oleg said.

'Oh, nothing. Just looking for ants,' I replied, adding no doubt another black mark in his report to Vasily. My rooting around had been provoked by a research article I'd read on Sente, the academic reference system on my MacBook, on the flight over. It was too much to explain to him.

I watched him wander off, framed by the Tien Shan, which across the border in Kyrgyzstan rise to 24,000 feet. I wondered what it would be like to stand knee-deep in the snowfield up there and gaze down at the baking summer city. So if the worst came to the worst, I'd go up there. But then again, I really did want to speak to Vasily because what happened to him may just provide a clue to a puzzle right at the heart of evolutionary theory. For right at its core lies a problem. The problem of the Rescuer.

You can find them in the looser soil under trees. You can track them from the trails – the 'doodles' – they leave in the sand. This happens all around the world, particularly in warm, arid areas. Although once fully fledged, they are winged insects visually resembling small dragonflies, it is when they are in the larval stage – an interlude that can last for up to three years – that they have attained a notoriety. Because the trails are the telltale signs of the antlions' search for a suitable site for one of their most character-istic activities: building traps to snare their prey.

During the larval stage the predatory larvae feed on a variety of insects and even spiders. But in large measure what they eat is ants. And this gives them the first part of their name. The second half may well be a legacy of their ferocity. For antlions possess hollow tusk-like protuberances at the jaw – the nightmarish stuff of the creature in *Alien* – which enable them to suck the life out of whatever victims they can trap. It was this I was looking for in the Almaty park.

The antlion builds a pit in the sand, the shape of an inverted cone. The gradient of the pit walls is designed to reach a critical angle – any steeper and the pit would collapse, any shallower and the prey could climb out. Therefore the sheer steepness is delib-erate: it is to ensure that once you fall in, it is impossible to escape.

At the bottom of the pit, submerged in the sand just below the apex of the cone, the antlion – and its jaws – wait.

A passing ant innocently wandering across a sandy terrain might stumble on the edge of a pit. The edge crumbles underfoot sending the hapless ant sliding down the precipitous side. The more it scrambles, the more the walls disintegrate around it, propelling it downwards, to what is waiting.

Sometimes the ant is consumed alive, its life juices sucked out by the hollow jaws. But other times the antlion misses. The ant can try to clamber back up, to safety, to life. But the antlion is not finished.

Its limbs gyrate furiously, unleashing a hail of flying sand that sends the fleeing insect sliding back down. It is slowly pulled under the sand and is gone. This desperate drama, repeated countless million times every day, evidences the pitiless struggle of evolution. However, the interest for us lies in another aspect of this tiny but titanic life struggle. For lethal as the sand traps are; terrifying as the antlion jaws may be; hopeless though the fate of an ant sliding down into the pit would appear, evolution has developed another mechanism. Rescue.

Waiting and waiting in the Cairo Café, Almaty.

Try not to look at the time on your iPhone. It slows time down. Really.

Try not to think you've been stood up again by Vasily. You will make it come true.

Try to keep cool. Literally.

It was stiflingly hot inside the cellar, probably deliberately, a device to conjure up an Egyptian bazaar, a little Nile fever. So I opted for the terrace. Patrons milled about, going from table to table, greeting one another with *salaam alaikums*. About 50 per cent of the Kazakhstan population is Muslim. In name, at least. We were in downtown Almaty, not far from Tchaikovsky Street. The café's terrace was little more than a tent slung across the pavement and sloping down to the busy road. Thus it was that trees grew out of the decked floor and up through the yellowing, smoke-cured awning. On the thoroughfare outside, blue and white electric buses plugged into energy-infusing overhead cables curiously echoed the clientele of the Cairo, hooked into their shisha pipes and hookahs.

This was not my pick, but if Vasily felt more comfortable here, I would put up with the smoke. I'm not a fan of smoke. And then someone quickly approached my table. My heart sank. It was Oleg again.

He sat down opposite me on the luxurious yellow and purple cushioning. Smoke wafted up towards the Tien Shan, as if billowing out from a dozen gun ports of a man-of-war.

'So, okay, you find the place,' he said, 'I'm sorry to be late. My little one, she has not been well.'

'Yours too?' I replied. 'I'm sorry to hear that, Oleg.'

'Yes, is sad.'

'It is, and don't take this the wrong way, but really I was waiting for Vasily. Please tell me he's hiding in all these clouds of smoke.' I was only marginally exaggerating. Some customers blew delicate smoke circles that tremulously hovered in the air before evaporating. Others drew heavily on the long, stringy pipe before bellowing out all-encompassing fragrant clouds. 'Impressive as these tricks are – and they are impressive – I really want to see Vasily.'

'You don't like smoke?' he said.

'Never have, never will.'

'You must be very brave man who can say never will.' He sat down opposite me.

'Oleg,' I said, 'I want you to tell me that Vasily is coming. Are you going to tell me that Vasily is coming?'

'*Who* you say?' He rubbed the creases of his forehead in a futile attempt to smooth them.

'Vasily – or are you going to tell me he can't come again, Oleg?'

'Who you mean "Oleg"?'

I was getting very confused. He knocked his knuckles on the dark wood table – little more than a trellis – and waited for me to speak next.

I decided to start again. 'Okay,' I said, 'very simply, what is the situation: Vasily can or can't come?'

'Vasily *can* come.'

Before I could say hallelujah, or its equivalent, my café companion suddenly shouted across the room extraordinarily loudly. 'Oya, Aliya.' (That's what it sounded like.)

The waitress, wearing a headscarf, glanced at him, scowled viciously and then pointedly turned her back.

'You see?' he said. 'She likes me.'

'Yes, definitely,' I replied.

'You see this Aliya,' he said. 'She is really good person, but she pretend to be – agggghhhrrr – nasty like policeman.' The said waitress reappeared and he called to her again and once more she ignored him. 'She like me,' he said.

'And Vasily?' I said. 'Where is Vasily?'

He extended his hand. 'I am Vasily.'

It was a sudden jolting moment when I did not know whether to feel angry or foolish.

'Okay, okay,' I said, going with it. What does one say at such a time? *You've got to be kidding.* (There was no kidding about it.) *I knew all along.* (I didn't.) Something smart. (And that would help how?) Instead, I said, 'Pleased to meet you, Vasily.'

Too English? Too bad.

'Yes, I know,' he said. 'I am *very* terrible person. Why would any person be careful when they meet strange lawyer from another country for first time?'

It was a fair point – and particularly in the context of the troubled country he came from. Not Kazakhstan, but originally Russia. I didn't say that. 'I guess London lawyers must seem strange,' I said.

He almost laughed: the deep lines around his eyes momentarily crinkled upwards; the deep horizontal lines on his forehead clustered together, before his face settled back into its resting position. 'You been to Kazakhstan before?' he asked.

'First time,' I said.

'Kazakhstan, this is best country round here. By long way best of the – in West they call them "Stans", yes?'

In scholarly literature they are sometimes referred to as CARs (Central Asian Republics), but a less formal shorthand for this group of five former Soviet satellite republics – Uzbekistan, Kyrgyzstan, Tajikistan, Turkmenistan, and the biggest of them all, Kazakhstan – is the Stans.

'Some people use the word,' I said.

'You been to any other?'

'No, this is my first Stan.'

'You not been to *any* Stan?' he said with greater incredulity.

'Well, not unless you count Stahn-well.'

'Stahn-well? Stahn-well? What is this Stahnwell? Such a place exists?'

'It's a question people in my country have often asked,' I said. 'But, no – I've been to no other Stans.'

'You know Afghanistan, of course. But you know also Dagestan?'

'Where?' I think I'd vaguely heard of it. I cannot pretend my knowledge was any more than that.

The waitress wandered near and he beckoned her over. We ordered – I held my breath as I ordered tea with cold milk.

'Did you say Dagestan?' I said.

Vasily gazed around the other tables suspiciously. People were occupied in drawing on the long serpentine pipes, chatting in huddled conversations, being slowly engulfed in clouds of smoke.

'I met this girl,' he said, 'called Lena.'

It was the first time he mentioned her name.

'Sometimes we do things that are . . .' he searched for the word, '. . . terrible.'

'Did you say Lay-na?' I asked. That was how it sounded to me. I repeated the question but he did not reply.

'Sometimes we do not mean to do these things that are terrible, but, you know, still this is what we do.'

He spoke as if I was not there, as if he were conducting a conversation with someone else, with someone invisible to me who was.

Two research biologists, Karen Hollis and Elise Nowbahari, have studied antlions in great detail. What they found is that sometimes when ants tumble into the trap, they are rescued by other ants. But not by *any* other passing ants. For the rescue behaviour is almost exclusively restricted to nestmates. So there is a genetic connection between rescuer and rescuee.

They found that almost no rescue was attempted where there was an ant from a different species altogether from the victim. But even where the passing ant was of the identical species, if it happened to come from another nest, even one only metres away, there was negligible rescue behaviour exhibited. It may be that ants rely on indicators of relatedness such as scent. If you've got the wrong scent, you're not going to be helped. The antlion would have its prey.

Equally the kind of home — the microhabitat — of the ant was critical. Rescue behaviour was observed where the ants inhabited terrain where there was a live risk of antlion traps. For example, loose sandy soil areas infested with predatory antlions and their pits as opposed to harder, more baked terrains where there were few traps. In other words, ants came to the rescue in circumstances where there would be an evolutionary advantage for selecting for rescue behaviour since the individual would be statistically at greater risk of being trapped and in need of rescue itself. Consequently, for these species, such as *Cataglyphis cursor* and *Cataglyphis floricola*, sand-dwelling ants found around the Mediterranean, evolution has selected for those ants which would be more inclined to rescue others.

The reason these various species of sand ants have been so intricately studied is because rescue behaviour, one animal risking itself for another, is the exception in the animal world. As Nowbahari and Hollis state, 'Rescue behavior is both fascinating and rare, precisely because there is not an immediate direct benefit to the rescuer.'

Indeed in the scientific literature there have been until recently only two analyses of animal rescue behaviour: in ants and rats. More broadly, observed acts of rescue by animals extended to dolphins helping an injured pod member in the fifties, and a capuchin monkey intervening to help a mother and child capuchin from attack by a rival group. That was a decade ago. Beyond these accounts, genuine reports of rescue behaviour in the animal kingdom are vanishingly thin.

The fact is, very few animals attempt to rescue members of their own species in distress. But sometimes, it is said, humans do. It is said.

FOUR

The Other Side of the Mountain

Vasily said, 'Everything here in Kazakhstan is horse, horse, horse. They love the horse. Always the horse.'

I had noticed. There is something of a Kazakh cult of the horse. At the same time, it was the only place I'd been where at the hotel buffet a plate of horsemeat sat alongside the breakfast bagels.

'Kazakhs *were* nomadic,' I said. 'It makes sense they're fond of horses.'

He waved his hand. 'Everyone was nomad, yes?'

He was probably right: our early ancestors, itinerant hunter-gatherer bands – probably.

'And here they don't like dogs,' Vasily said. 'Kazakhs *say* they like dogs,' he added, 'but they don't like dogs. They think dogs should stay outside. But we Russians, for us, is good to have dogs in house. Is no problem. Lena, you know, she is different. She likes dogs.'

When I later met my Kazakh interpreter and guide Marzhan, I asked her about this. 'Yes, your colleague is right,' she said. 'Dogs are dirty animals. They should be outside.'

'And Lena is Kazakh?' I asked Vasily.

He paused. The drinks had come. 'Dexter, you see, I don't want to talk about Lena today.'

Now he had me. Now I was gripped. But I was also worried about scaring him off – research like this is always a delicate dance. Back and forth, back and forth. I eased back. 'We British are like you. Dogs are a bit of a national obsession. A nation of dog-lovers, people call us.'

'You never do like what we did to Laika.'

'Laika?' I said. At first I thought he'd said Lena again, but no, it was Laika.

He pointed away to the west, in the general direction of the steppe. 'Over there, at Baikonur, in Soviet times, they launch our Russian dog Laika into space, from here,' he thumped the table, 'here in Kazakhstan.' His hand and eye rose slowly to the sky, a canopy of piercing blue that stretches from the Tien Shan to the vast sea of grass, the steppe, which extends west for thousands of miles.

As I found out that night, he was right. At Baikonur in the Kazakhstan steppe is the Cosmodrome, the world's first and largest space facility, the Soviet's statement of intent in the space race, one of the battlegrounds of the Cold War.

So it was that from Kazakhstan on 3 November 1957 – to commemorate the 40th anniversary of the 1917 Revolution – the Soviets launched an enormous tank of rocket fuel, Sputnik 2, up through the clouds with such a seismic shudder that, as Colonel Alexander Seryapin, doctor of medical science for the operation said, you could feel 'the very earth vibrating'. And sitting right on top of this enormously fantastical firework was a single passenger, a *Canis lupus familiaris* – a stray dog. She had been found on the streets of Moscow. Her name was Laika.

For those giddying hours and days after launch, Laika's celebrity outshone any actor or athlete on earth. The world held its breath. People gazed up at the skies. Prayers were said for little Laika. But then, as so often in Cold War politics, things became confusing and unclear.

'They lie for years about what happen to her,' Vasily said. He appeared to take it personally. It was a long time before I understood why.

And he was right about that also, I was to discover. For years – for 45 years in fact – the Soviets concealed the truth of what happened inside the nose cone of Sputnik 2. Laika – her name means 'barker' – was propelled around the Earth at dizzying speed. Her pulse rate went up to three times its normal rate. Round and round she went at approaching 18,000 mph, within her own goldfish-bowl glass helmet. She had short-cropped white fur, a dark face with a characteristically thin white flash running away from her nose towards her eyes – almost like a go-faster stripe.

'You know, they choose her, because she is . . . loose dog,' Vasily told me.

'Stray?'

'Yes, stray.'

'Because she was abandoned?' I said. 'Because she had no owner?' A surreal conversation, suffused in clouds of shisha smoke: here we were in the middle of Central Asia, in the second decade of the third millennium, discussing the fate of a stray dog who lived 60 years before – while what I really wanted to know about was Lena.

'No, no,' Vasily said, exasperated, 'they not choose her because she has no owner. Look, you know dogs?'

This was a serious challenge. 'I grew up with dogs,' I responded.

'Pure? Or street dogs?'

'Both,' I said. 'We had pure – pedigree – and a wonderful cross-breed. What we call in English a mongrel.'

'And what is she like? This . . . mongrel?'

'He. He was the most loving, gentle, calm dog.'

Vasily smiled. 'That,' he said, 'was Laika.'

And that's how I met Vasily – or properly met him, after the not-Oleg fiasco. Even on this second encounter, we had discussed absolutely nothing about why I'd hoped we'd meet: but at least I knew her name – Lena. That night in the hotel, I was in that infernal vampiric state where I was overtired, exhausted but unable to sleep. My time zones were messed up – it was still early in Western Europe. But I'd become obsessed, I'm happy to confess, with finding out more about the first living creature from our planet to voyage into space.

I discovered that something else Vasily had said was true: Laika *was* selected because she had a calm, even temperament, and because as a stray from the streets of Moscow she was tough. She'd learned to endure – and survive – hardship and hunger, the bitter Russian cold. Rumours circulated that the plan was to parachute the dog safely back to Earth after her heroic mission. As the world waited and wondered, the Soviets publicly stated that they would do everything to retrieve her. The truth was very different. The Soviets never intended to rescue Laika. It was a one-way ticket: they launched her knowing she was destined to die in space. But for almost 50 years they lied about what had actually happened. Due to a systems failure – something that could never be admitted during Cold War hostilities – Laika's capsule began to overheat.

Instead of the ambient temperature remaining around 20°C, it shot up to 41°. From that point, as Oleg Gazenko from the Russian Academy of Sciences said, Laika 'was doomed'.

It is not clear precisely when it happened. But sometime during the third or fourth orbit of the Earth, up there in the solitude of space, alone except for the slowly turning stars, nearby Mars, Jupiter, distant Pluto, Laika suffered what Colonel Seryapin concedes was 'a slow and painful death'.

Nevertheless Sputnik 2 kept spinning around the planet for another five months and 2,500 orbits. Then on 14 April 1958, with Laika's remains still inside, the space vehicle launched into space with such fanfare from the middle of Kazakhstan re-entered the Earth's atmosphere. It rapidly incinerated. Nothing was left.

Although Laika's story is undoubtedly tragic, I share it with you for two reasons. Firstly, because it was the first real thing that Vasily and I spoke about. But more than that, because it provides a sense of Vasily's strength of feeling about dogs. And that is essential for understanding what happened with Lena. For understanding the Rescuer.

Who she was and what actually happened, the remaining pages of this chapter will attempt to reveal. But let me begin by grounding what you are about to read in some solid points of reference.

Ethnically, Lena was Kazakh.

She lived in Almaty shortly before she met Vasily. (But where she actually came from, as you'll see: unclear.)

She was, as you will also see, tough.

As the capsule that contained the world's first space dog was hurtling around our water-washed rock, somewhere in the Great Steppe of Central Asia Lena's parents were living under Communist rule. It was one of Stalin's darkest legacies that the great wandering peoples of Central Asia that came under the sway of the Soviet Union should be yoked, tamed, tethered. Mass collective farms were forced upon Kazakhs – the fatal collectivisation that is one of Stalin's greatest crimes. Hundreds of thousands of Kazakhs died. It could have been up to two million. But Lena's grandparents and parents survived all this. In the 1980s, before the collapse of Communism, they gave birth to a child, a daughter – Lena.

The steppe is famously vast: one of the largest expanses of space on the planet – it is something to be proud of, to come from such a monumental place. Yet as Lena grew up, the boundless space at the same time, and in another way, seemed too small. There was too little going on. Real life, by which she meant exciting life, was happening elsewhere. Not out here in the gently rolling nothingness, but in the cities – Almaty, Moscow.

She came from the Middle Horde. There are three big divisions of Kazakh people: the Great Horde, the Middle Horde and the Little Horde. We use the term pejoratively, a legacy of Genghis Khan and the Mongol conquests. But horde simply meant one hundred. A communal group of one hundred. At least, that's how it started.

Lena's horde, the Middle, have historically inhabited – and roamed – the vast centre and north of the country. When she was a teenager, her grandfather spoke of the great city of Almaty where once he'd gone, a city of endless trees, as numerous as the blades of grass in the steppe. He said that behind the city, guarding it like giants, were mountains, and on the other side of the mountains Kyrgyzstan, with China behind this again. So that is where the young Lena was desperate to go – one day Moscow itself, but first Almaty.

Once, only once that she could remember, she dreamed she was sitting on the great white goose, the mother of all the people, as it glided over the endlessly stretching steppe, which was the world and their home. But she wanted to turn the great bird away, over the distant hills. Lena knew then for sure that she wanted to escape. Her father did not approve. He said the city was full of evil. He forbade her from going. But her grandfather – one generation closer to nomadic life – encouraged her roaming. Despite her father threatening to disown her, in the end she went. She would roam. She would explore the other side of the mountain. And that is when the trouble in her life started, when she fell into a slowly crumbling pit of a kind she could never have anticipated.

FIVE

The Road

It was one of the puzzles about animal behaviour that deeply troubled Charles Darwin, one he was not able to resolve before his death. Ants. Ants were just *puzzling*: why would they sacrifice themselves for one another? Why were some castes of ants, wingless female worker ants, sterile? Using the yardstick of survival and reproduction, it didn't make sense. Why did they spend their lives in slave-like drudgery to promote the prospects of ants that were not their own children? Writing as he did in the middle of the 19th century, Darwin, of course, could not have known about genetics. It would take a development of the laws of inheritance investigated by the great abbot Gregor Mendel and the cross-fertilisation of Mendel's ideas with Darwin's theory of evolution by natural selection for a more satisfying account of life to emerge. But that came too late for Darwin.

During the troubled years of intellectual doubt that plagued his life, Darwin knew ants were a serious problem. Indeed their self-sacrificing behaviour appeared to him to present 'insuperable' obstacles to his analysis. As he wrote in his *Origin of Species* itself, the problem of selflessly sacrificing ants may be 'fatal to my whole theory'.

It was not. Still, early suggestions for resolving the problem revolved around 'helping' behaviour being 'for the good of the species'. Elephants, for example, have long been observed to 'help' other elephants. There have been sightings of animals supporting an injured herd member, pulling tranquilliser darts from their flanks, sealing their wounds with mud and dust. To explain this behaviour, it was suggested that such actions were for the 'good' of elephants generally – for the group, for the species. It was called group selection.

Gradually, however, this theory was increasingly doubted. (Although there has been a revival in interest of group selection ideas that we will come to later.) Then in the sixties, Oxford academic Bill Hamilton produced an idea that some argue is the most significant development in evolutionary theory since Darwin. Group selection, Hamilton argued, was a 'misreading' of the theory of evolution. Darwin's theory certainly needed an overhaul, 'an extension'. (In fact, it needed two. We'll come on to the second shortly.) But group selection was not it.

The point of the extension was so that the kind of cooperative behaviour that so troubled Charles Darwin could be understood using a different lens, at a different level. The key was not the group. Not beyond the individual animal but within it. The key was the gene.

Thus, Hamilton argued, the degree of genetic *relatedness* was vital – literally. For the gene looks beyond, in Hamilton and his colleague Robert Axelrod's chilling phrase, 'the mortal bearer' of its code. It gazes on the alluring prospect of indefinite reproduction, on immeasurable replication, on – not to put too fine a point on it – immortality. In this vast vista, we, the frail human husks, will wither. But the reproduced and reproducing gene goes on.

Such is the seductive power of this alluring incentive that it drives behaviour that helps other related individuals who bear *some parts* of the same gene. The idea was called kin selection. In their seminal article 'The Evolution of Cooperation', Hamilton and Axelrod cite the 'suicidal barbed sting' of the honeybee worker, sacrificing itself for the hive, for its relatives. But let us return to ants.

The rescue behaviour of sand ants is a particularly costly form of helping. They risk their very lives for others. But viewed through the lens of kin selection, the rescue efforts of sand ants become intelligible: they risk themselves to try to save not just their fellow creatures, their nestmates, but their own genes – albeit a very small proportion of them. In the minuscule but titanic tussle with the antlion, the individual altruistic ant may fall. But a proportion of the rescuer's genes, literally within the body of the rescued individual, continues.

But that's ants. It doesn't entirely deal with the problem presented by us. For the conceptual difficulty presented by human beings is that rescuing behaviour is not restricted to genetic relatives – to our nestmates. It extends to those with whom we have no link in blood or gene. And to understand this further problem for Darwin's original thinking, a further upgrade to evolutionary theory is required.

'I searched up about Laika,' I told Vasily when we met once more the next day at the cacophonous Cairo. 'And you were right. Once they launched her into space, they never intended to rescue her.'

I'd arrived first. As ever. I looked up at the forlorn plants hanging down from the canopy stanchions. They were pretty much dead, fumigated into submission by shisha smoke. I'd got us both a glass of water and he swallowed a sort of beige freeze-dried pill which he shook out of a small plastic bottle. A pain reliever of some kind, I assumed, but I couldn't read the packaging. He took a precise sip of cool water in the overheated café.

'They find a dog in a cave up in the Altai,' he said quietly.

'The Altai?'

'The mountains, up in Siberia, they come down into Kazakhstan too.' (And Mongolia, I later discovered.) 'They say that dog could be the first dog,' Vasily said. 'Here in Kazakhstan is always, the horse, the *horse*, the horse is so special animal. The horse is our first friend. *No.* Is dog. The man and the dog.'

'Okay,' I said, 'the Altai? I'll check it out.' I was silently giving thanks for the existence of glorious Google, when Vasily veered off in yet another direction.

'I don't want to talk bullshit with you,' he said. 'I'm leaving Almaty. I have job driving. So I have not much time.'

'Same with me. I have little time in Kazakhstan, Vasily.'

'So I don't want to talk no bullshit with you. People tell me, Vasily, why you get so upset, Vasily? So the government lie about a dog, yes? They lie about the death of a dog. Don't get so upset, Vasily. And that is what I mean: they *even* lie about a dog. Human beings, they lie about anything. They will do anything.'

'You believe that?'

'Believe? What's to believe? I've seen.'

'Seen?'

'Human beings, they don't care — when I go to Dagestan, they do anything to other human beings. Anything. That's what you want to speak to me for, yes?'

It was complex. It wasn't as simple as that. Yet in a way it was. 'Yes,' I said.

'You want to know about the cargo, yes?'

'The cargo?'

'The human cargo.'

'The human trafficking, yes.'

'You want to fill here,' with his long pointer of an index finger, he tapped his deeply creased forehead hard, making a drumming sound, 'you want to fill it with all this things?'

'It's not that I want to,' I said. 'It's so important, I need – we need – to understand it more. But so few people know what it's really like.'

For a while the big Russian was silent. Then he said, 'Poor little fucking dog.' He pointed to the sky. To Laika. To him it was all connected.

So the dance between us took a new turn. Sometimes you sense that it is time. Sitting in the Cairo that day, as Almaty went about its business, I sensed it was time. His fingers came away from the little white plastic bottle. It said Feverfew.

'Let's do this Lena thing, Vasily,' I said.

'No bullshit?'

'No,' I said. I had no idea what feverfew was.

'Okay,' he said. 'Okay.' He ordered a shisha pipe. 'First, you see, there was this picture.'

'Picture?'

'This picture of a road.'

When he was a boy, and still living in his father's home, a modest apartment in Moscow, there was a cheap print on the wall in the front room. It was above the beloved chair that Vasily's father, who had served in the Soviet army, often sat in, particularly following his return from Afghanistan. The family had lived in Moscow for generations. One of Vasily's great ancestors was a labourer, rebuilding Moscow after the Russians burned their own sacred city to thwart Bonaparte. When Vasily first told me about the layout of their front room, the chair appeared more interesting than the print. But I was wrong.

The chair was low-slung with a slightly arched back, maybe a feline tribute to the material – fake – that it was covered in: some kind of leopard print. His father would sit in it for hours.

Above the chair was a cheap print – to many sensibilities as cheap and tasteless as the chair. But who is to judge? It had a dull glass front, or rather a glass over the print that reflected the world dully, so when Vasily as a boy stood in front of it – when he was younger he would have to stand on the chair – he could see a faint outline of himself. Sometimes if the light was right, it seemed he was inside the picture.

The print was of a road. A nondescript, unremarkable, unassuming road curling through fields and off into the distance. It has rained, and the clouds above have been captured, brought down to earth, and trapped in the slicks of water on the road's surface.

The young Vasily wondered about two things. Where was that road? What would it be like to travel endlessly on it? As things would transpire, he would find out.

SIX

The Problem of Us

How could evolutionary theory account for helping behaviour when there was no kin selection – no discernible genetic or family link? It was here that Hamilton's insights were later developed by a researcher at Harvard, Robert Trivers.

Trivers went to Africa. There he was struck by how male baboons interact – and cooperate. What he found was this: elder male baboons endeavour to have exclusive sexual access to certain fertile females. This naturally presents a problem for younger males wishing to fulfil their evolutionary destiny and propagate their genes. How could they defeat a dominant male? A head-on confrontation would inevitably end in disaster and maybe injury. But there was another way: form a coalition with another younger male. Together they can overcome the more formidable baboon.

However, this workaround in the wild only solves one part of the problem. Running off the dominant male is one thing, but it doesn't resolve which of the younger males can have sex with the female. It was here that the theory of altruistic behaviour was postulated. What if one of the two juniors cooperated in the attack in the anticipation of future assistance and a turn to copulate with another female? Rather than there being a direct benefit in the immediate promulgation of one's genes, there is a future benefit of another kind: the repayment of present helping acts by future acts of altruism and thus future reproduction. Thus the junior baboon's altruism would be repaid. It would be reciprocated. It is for this reason that Trivers's idea was called 'reciprocal altruism'.

Subsequently a number of animals were periodically cited as providing evidence of helping behaviour between animals that were not directly related – of reciprocal altruism. Grooming among primates. The sharing of blood among certain bats. Were these non-human animal examples of behaviour that represented helping of another for future benefit?

In recent years, however, these initially appealing examples of reciprocation have been doubted. For example, the 'altruist' in the pairs of Trivers's baboons did not simply stand by once the previously dominant male was defeated to await a future 'turn' (mating opportunity). Instead, further observation of baboon behaviour by ecologists has found that once the elder male was run off, there was a mad scramble for copulation between the two erstwhile cooperators. Neither took a back seat. The struggle for domination returned with the substitution of a different dyad of actors – those who had previously worked together. Thus the pact was not reciprocal altruism properly understood, but strategic alliance building – mutualism – to win the immediate opportunity to mate.

Therefore the growing consensus is that firm evidence of reciprocity in non-human animals is rare. It may even be to some extent illusory – behaviour that appears to be cooperative, but that in fact is a proxy for other things: mutualism (symbiotic

beneficial joint action) or manipulation (coercion by a more dominant individual).

But when you add the human animal into the equation, the
picture becomes murkier still. Our cooperative behaviour – and
there is no doubt that for all our war and crime and violence
and bloodshed, we cooperate enormously – presents life scientists
with a tremendous problem. The problem of us.

Vasily's parents were fighting. Again. Vasily did the shouting and
screaming that his mother did not. For the more his father hit her,
the quieter she became. Personally I'd seen it at the Bar, on the
Bench, how violence in a family can be like a black hole, sucking
everything into it. So Vasily's father was beating her and his
mother was silent. Both of them had been good-looking and, it
seemed, not long before in love. What had gone wrong in their
lives? What had happened?

Afghanistan had happened. After Vasily's father returned from
Afghanistan, everything changed. What had he seen there, what
had he done? He never said. Of course, one doesn't need a war
zone for there to be violence in a family. Some families, they are
a kind of war zone all of their own.

But once he returned from the war, Vasily's father condemned
himself to sit on his leopard-print chair. His sentry post. He
guarded the print of the road. Then, unannounced and unpro-
voked, something inside him would snap. Like a fan belt deep
inside a machine breaking, sending other parts flying in all directions. The direction would usually be his wife.

It's sometimes said we hurt the people we love the most. It is
said. Vasily's father simply hurt the thing nearest to him. It was
his wife. She made sure that at such times she stayed closest to

him. Always in the line of fire. Swallowing it up, absorbing it. Into the black hole. To protect her son.

On this occasion, Vasily had come in from playing outside. He was all muddy and was screaming at his father for hurting his mother. His father told the boy to go to the bathroom, to wash his hands. Vasily stood nervously at the sink, ran the taps, while his father loomed silently behind him.

'Fill the sink,' he said.

Vasily's hand trembled as he put in the plug. As the cracked old porcelain bowl filled with icy water, his father said, 'Wash your hands.'

Vasily put his shaking hands into the cold water.

'Use soap,' his father said.

Vasily couldn't keep the slim bar of dirty-white soap in his hands, such were his nerves.

'So many diseases we can avoid, if we wash our hands. That the army teaches us in Afghanistan,' his father said.

On one level, it made sense to the boy. He resolved to wash his hands more often. Yes, it made sense. In future, he would ensure he'd do precisely that. His father grabbed his thin neck, like the scruff of a dog, and suddenly Vasily's face was plunged into the water, his father punching him in his back, in the kidneys, forcing out the last precious pockets of breath. Water painfully shot through his nostrils, down the wrong side of his throat. He was choking him; drowning him.

'They say you can drown in ten centimetres of water, yes?' Vasily said to me. 'You can drown in a sink.'

You can also drown in a family. Just as the boy was about to black out, his father released him. Vasily collapsed in a heaving, rasping heap on the cold tiled floor, water spilling out of his nostrils, ears, mouth.

His father told him that this was what they did to Afghan insurgents. If it was good enough for Afghan insurgents . . .

For a long time Vasily did not tell his mother what had happened. And then he did. When he finally braced himself to do so, she said, 'Your father would never do that.' He told her again. 'Your father would never do that,' she said. His mother spoke as if he were insane, as if he hadn't heard her cries, seen her bruised eyes, as if he were mad. Was he mad? He was beginning to think he was.

After that, Vasily withdrew, like in a military operation. Like an insurgent in retreat. While there were periods of ebb and flow, his insurgency against his father's violence didn't end for years. His face was thrust into icy water until he could breathe no more. It started when he was ten years old.

Then his mother died. He was alone with his father.

A kind of truce entered the flat, uninvited. It was like it was not worth fighting any more, as if there was no longer anything to fight over.

'I told her,' Vasily said to me about Lena, 'she is so stupid. Her father, he love her. Do everything for her. She leave him, come to Almaty. My father he beat me. I stay. People are crazy, huh?'

He spoke as if they, he and Lena, they were somehow separated twins. That if you put the best of their lives together, you would get one happy one. Two tattered half-lives, if only they could have been stuck together. And that was the strange thing: circumstance, coincidence – fate – resulted in their coming together, not long after the dawning of the new millennium. Their lives were indeed stuck together. For a time. Not in Kazakhstan as I'd thought, but in southern Siberia.

The Altai Mountains of southern Siberia spread stony tentacles across the borders with Mongolia and Kazakhstan, and in many places they fold in upon themselves to create cavernous voids extending back through the rock. One of these, less than 50 miles from the Kazakhstan border, is known as Razboinichya Cave – Razboinichya means 'bandit'. The cave is an ideal shelter from the harsh Siberian climate and has been for countless centuries. Indeed bones found there, over 70,000 of them, attest to the fact that it was occupied by very early humans tens of thousands of years ago. But the human inhabitants may not have been alone.

An international team, including research scientists at the Institute of Archaeology and Ethnology at Novosibirsk University, determined that some of the bones, a mandible, a skull fragment, came from an early canid, a 'proto-dog'.

In other words, it was a dog, they claim, 'in the very early stages of domestication'. An incipient dog rather than an aberrant wolf. Using radiocarbon techniques at Oxford University, the team dated the animal in the Siberian cave to 33,000 years ago. And in doing so, the bones of this ancient animal, long sheltered from millennia of Siberian weather, were exposed to the harsh winds of academic controversy.

For it is widely accepted among scientists that the dog was the first animal domesticated by our forebears. But there the agreement ends. Controversy still rages about when it happened. Despite the use of the latest genetic, biogeographic and 3D-geometric morphometric techniques, the question remains unresolved.

When did we come to domesticate, and be domesticated by, dogs? Was it during the Neolithic period when we began to gather in permanent and semi-permanent settlements, around 15,000 years ago? Or was it significantly earlier, in the Pleistocene epoch, while we were still hunter-gatherers? If so, it could have happened between 30,000 and 40,000 years ago. That would be consistent with the finding of the Razboinichya canid.

The importance of all this is that the domestication of animals was a very significant stepping stone in human evolution. From that time dogs and humans co-evolved in parallel. They were used for hunting and guarding; they became co-predators and ultimately pets. Through dogs, and for the first time, we formed a close cooperative relationship with an unrelated other creature. We helped them; they helped us. The bonds were close, the affection clear from an early time. There is evidence dating from over 10,000 years ago of humans being buried with their dogs.

I relate all this – I'd looked it up because of what Vasily told me – not just because it seems that Vasily was right: one of the very first dogs to be domesticated by early humans could have been up there in the Altai Mountains, in Siberia. But also because this long history of man and dog played a pivotal part in the choice Vasily was destined to make.

After his mother's death, the Great Silence descended. And with the silence came a kind of truce. And a truce is often (albeit not always) better than war. His father would speak more in his sleep than he did during the daytime. War, young Vasily supposed, did that to you. Life sometimes did.

One day Vasily was playing truant. His father didn't seem to care. Only Vasily wasn't playing. He was deadly serious about it. Truancy was his life. While he was out on his rounds, he heard a strange sound coming from an alley strewn with litter and broken wooden crates. Vasily went to investigate. Investigating oddities in the street was his self-appointed job during his truant patrol. It was a dog. It was bleeding, with a trail of blood leading back to the road.

599

Vasily used one of the broken crates to carry the small tan dog home. He gave it water. He offered it scraps of food from the fridge in their apartment. It showed no interest. It lay there, its fragile breath pained. So absorbed was he with this failing creature before him, that he was unaware that his father was suddenly standing behind him. Vasily turned with a start, cricking his neck.

'It's a dog,' his father said.

'A car hit it,' Vasily said.

'Where was it?'

Vasily explained. When he did so, it was already the longest conversation they had shared in a year.

His father said, 'Get it . . .' Vasily braced himself for the worst. 'Get it help. Ask Yevgeny, he will know how to find a vet.'

Vasily did find Yevgeny; Yevgeny did know a vet; the vet did come. But the little dog quietly died. No one could save it.

'Why did you rescue the dog?' I asked.

'It was hurt,' Vasily told me.

'It wasn't your dog,' I said, trying to draw him out.

'It was hurt.'

To his great credit, his father never asked the question I had. The Great Silence lifted. A little. Vasily learned over the next few weeks something remarkable about his father: when his father was a boy, he had a dog. His father, Vasily's grandfather, sold it for money for vodka. It wasn't even enough to get drunk for one night. Maybe that explained some things about his father, young Vasily thought. He assessed all this carefully. It presented him with an opportunity. About a month after the dog's death, Vasily asked his father a question.

'Can we get a dog?'

His father took a step backwards and sat in his leopard-print chair. He thought a long time before he answered. 'No,' he said.

It was never discussed again.

The denial of a dog was a blow. There was no escaping it. But his father had thought about it — actually thought about something Vasily had requested. That was something.

After that, as far as Vasily can recall, his father never hit him again, nor thrust his face in the water. During the months after the street dog died, just occasionally, things started appearing in Vasily's room. First an apple. Then an old kopek, a Russian coin from decades before. It wasn't worth very much, but it looked ancient and mysterious. Then a whistle, the kind a football referee might use. In an unvoiced complicity, Vasily and his father never spoke about this. Each gift was gratefully received, silently accepted.

'Did you ever give him anything back?' I asked.

'Then he will know I know is him.'

'But it *was* him. There was no one else but him.'

'But then he knows I know is him,' Vasily said.

So the silent ceremony continued. A biro. Some marbles. Chocolate.

'Did you come across another dog?' I asked.

'In the street, I find many dogs. But my father say no, so is no. I respect that.'

Gradually Vasily began to go to school more often. He discovered that he was very adept at learning languages. One day, around the tenth anniversary of his father's stationing with the Soviet army in Afghanistan, Vasily came home and as usual his father was seated in his favourite leopard-print chair under the picture of the road. He'd had a massive cardiac arrest.

After the funeral, Vasily was sent north to live with relatives. To Archangel. That was where the road took him next. To Archangel.

SEVEN

All the Elaines

H er name was actually Elaine, not Susan.

In the experiments that were conducted over many years at Kansas University by C. Daniel Batson and his colleagues, the receiver of shocks in the experimental scenario with the viewing room and the experiment room was named Elaine, not Susan.

The actual experimental set-up used reflected the technology of the early eighties: the viewing of Elaine was not via webcam, but closed-circuit television; the footage of her performing the tasks was not digital but videotaped. But the purpose of the experiment was pretty much as per our hypothetical at the beginning of the section.

Would we swap places with the person being shocked?

Would we even contemplate it?

Why?

And if we do, is our action motivated by genuine altruism to ease Elaine's suffering or an act of disguised self-interest? In other words, to ease the distress *you* feel when (a) you know another sentient being you have seen is suffering; (b) you know you were considering doing nothing about it.

Of course, Batson and his colleagues did not actually electrically shock Elaine. But the research volunteers who observed her – and perhaps this is a testament to the acting skills of the various Elaines – believed that they had.

In examining the question of whether volunteers would trade places with Elaine, two aspects of the scenario were varied. One variable that was 'manipulated' was the level of empathy the observer felt towards Elaine. In our introductory hypothetical, for example, you received the high empathy prime. Why?

Because you were asked to imagine how she would feel, what it might be like for our equivalent of Elaine – Susan. The other factor that was varied was 'ease of escape'. Some volunteers were given the option of leaving after two rounds and not witnessing further shocks. You were. Others were told that they would remain for all ten. Would that affect their willingness to trade places with Elaine?

The reasoning of Batson's team was that if the motivation for helping Elaine was altruistic – to ease her suffering – then that should provoke a willingness to trade places whether or not it was easy to escape.

And that is what they found.

Further, if the true motivation was not about easing Elaine's suffering but about easing one's own distress at witnessing Elaine's suffering, then there should be a greater willingness to help when escape was hard. What is perhaps most remarkable is that the highest percentage of volunteers prepared to help occurred precisely when it was *easy* to escape.

That bears thinking about: when there was a choice to walk out, more people stayed and were willing to take the shocks. Over 80 per cent.

In conducting these experiments, Batson's team were going after big game. For the egoistic paradigm – the idea that we are disinclined to help others, or if we do so it is primarily to relieve our own distress – had largely 'prevailed for decades' as the dominant theory of human motivation. It was asserted with great confidence that ultimately, albeit sometimes surreptitiously, 'everything we do is ultimately directed toward the end-state goal of benefiting ourselves'.

The work of Batson's team laid a foundation for empirically challenging this orthodoxy. They argued that their experimental results suggested that our motivation for helping others was not necessarily a veiled way of helping ourselves. In fact, we can be concerned with the welfare of other people – not just or primarily our own. This is a very significant claim. If it is correct, our actions could in reality be directed at reducing another person's suffering, not our own.

Such was the challenge of the Kansas findings to established thinking, that other researchers were not going to let it pass. And they did not.

More Elaines were destined to be 'shocked'. And when this happened, when the experiment was replicated, the conclusions were markedly different. The picture that emerged of who we – deep down – actually are, was radically, dispiritingly different.

I was intrigued by the capsule Vasily took – had never heard of it. I put 'feverfew' into my iPhone browser and waited. The Kazakh connection was slow. I refreshed. Then a kind of daisy came up. *Daisies?* Why was Vasily swallowing the leaf of a kind of daisy? It reminded me of the pictures I'd seen drawn by stroke sufferers with hemispatial neglect. A fan of even white petals, the yellow yolk in the middle – white rays, yellow florets, the botanical texts more scientifically told me. The plant, *Tanacetum parthenium*: a herbal remedy for migraine.

Vasily spent several years in Archangel, then returned to Moscow. But the loss of his father, following on from his mother's death, had left a tiny, leaking hole at the very centre of his life. In Archangel, another city, another school, albeit with relatives, another family, the hole was stopped up – more or less. Once back in Moscow, it opened up again. His life began careering out of control.

Over 2,000 miles to the south-east of this, when Vasily had been back in Moscow for several years, Lena went to Almaty.

Suddenly she was in the old historic capital of the country. Only a few years before the capital had been officially moved to the north, to the newly flourishing city of Astana, but Almaty was where it was all happening: the greatest city not only in the country but arguably in all the former Soviet republics of Central Asia. There was a bewildering array of nationalities: every shade, complexion and inflection of humanity. So this is what the world was like.

Lena wanted to meet everyone, to find out everything about these distant lands. It seemed impossible to believe that all of this could be happening in the Kazakhstan that not much more than a decade before had been a tightly controlled Communist state. A secretive nuclear test site, a location of Soviet prison camps, a space centre. But now . . .

In Lena's apartment block was a young woman called Samal, also from the steppe. She befriended the bewildered new arrival and showed her around. Samal was doing very well, working in a telecoms company. Meeting people from all over the world. Going to parties. She took Lena to one of them.

It was here that Lena met a man from the Emirates – sometimes he spoke of Dubai, other times Bahrain, so she was not sure which one. It was complicated because he seemed to speak about them interchangeably. He had a small black wart on his nose, but she didn't mind as her grandfather had once told her such a thing was good luck.

The man from the Gulf was an engineer, and bewitched Lena with his talk. He had actually studied in Moscow, the very place she one day hoped to go, and was working on oil production in the West, at the Caspian Sea. He had flown from the burgeoning business-industrial city of Atyrau and was in Almaty for a big oil and gas conference. She asked him a hundred questions about Moscow, but what really fired her imagination was what he said about what was happening in the Gulf.

She could hardly believe it. Yet he was perfectly serious. He said they were building hotels that were like palaces, soaring high into the sky, and floating on the sea – on land that had been pulled out of the sea. How could this be true? She thought he was teasing her, but he said it in such a matter-of-fact way that she was convinced.

What a world. This was why she had left the steppe. She wanted to do just this: discover a world of palace hotels floating on the sea.

In Moscow, Vasily continued to lead a life of slow, steady self-destruction. Alcohol. Cannabis. Debt. More alcohol, greater debt. Debt to his cannabis supplier. Suddenly, before he knew it, he was out in the Moscow cold selling cannabis to pay back the money he owed.

He didn't have a dog. But his supplier, a man called Z, did. Part of the arrangement was for Vasily to take the dog out with him while he was selling for Z. In truth, it was no burden. Vasily would have *paid* to be with the dog. Its name was Kolya. His name was Kolya. A squat white dog as wide as he was long called Kolya.

It was not a good area of the city, and Vasily did not have his heart in selling drugs. From time to time Z would check up on him. He would drive by in his large white van, park up and berate Vasily for his poor performance. Whenever Z came by, Kolya cowered.

This day, Z had in fact been in a good mood. He had surreptitiously passed Vasily some more product, then was returning to the van. No rebuke today. As Z walked back to the van, Vasily watched, half-crouching down next to Kolya and patting his flat head, tamping down the couple of stray hairs that kept sprouting upwards no matter the weather. Suddenly Z turned. In an instant he was back at Vasily's side.

'Maybe no one buys from you because they are scared of this fucking dog,' Z said.

Kolya cringed on the ground before him. Z kicked at the dog's midriff, landing a sickening blow to its side. Kolya yelped.

'No, is not the dog,' Vasily said. He saw the snow under Kolya was leaching yellow with urine as the terrified animal braced itself for the next blow.

'I hate this dog,' Z said. 'I'm going to fucking shoot this dog.' He glanced up and down the street. No one else was there. He reached into his jacket.

'No, is not the dog's fault,' Vasily said. He moved between Kolya and Z.

'Why you care? Is my dog. I shoot it if I want.'

'Tomorrow I get more money. I promise. You will see. Tomorrow, more.'

Z pushed Vasily. He fell backwards, falling over the squatting Kolya hiding behind him. Vasily ended up prostate in the snow, just like Kolya. Z loomed over dog and man.

607

'Tomorrow. More,' he said. 'Or I shoot the dog. Or I shoot you. I don't give any shit which way.'

Z drove off, the white van merging into the falling snow and vanishing as if it had never been there. Vasily felt Kolya's side for injury. It didn't seem as if anything was broken. By some chance, the boot had struck flesh.

'Is not your fault,' Vasily whispered to Kolya. 'Tomorrow we sell more. Definitely more. And I will buy you meat, Kolya, okay? I will buy you so much meat, Little Czar.'

Kolya looked up at him and did not flinch as Vasily rubbed his side.

The next thing Lena recalled was waking up in a strange room.

It had a large double bed, piled with pillows – she'd never seen such a big bed in her life. The bed alone seemed almost as big as her Almaty apartment. Everything was neat and clean and modern. An international hotel. She was lying alone in the bed and was naked.

She saw an open suitcase, and to her horror noticed men's clothes – ties, folded shirts, a pair of impossibly shiny black leather shoes. Her mind filled with horror as the pieces began to slide together. She had a crushing headache, had never known one like it, and felt sick in her stomach. Her own clothes were strewn around the floor by the bed.

When he came back into the hotel room, she stood there with all her clothes on, every button and zip done up, even a soft white hotel towel tightly pulled around her shoulders. Nonetheless she had never felt more naked in her life.

'I went down for breakfast,' he said. 'I did not want to wake you. I order you room service?'

'Why am I here?' Lena said.

'Why do you think?' he said.

'*Why* am I here? What did happen?'

'What you wanted to happen.' He paused and then said quietly, 'What you *really* wanted to happen.'

'I'm not like that,' Lena said.

'You were last night,' he said.

Infuriating tears rolled down her cheeks. She did not want them, but they would not stop.

'Okay, okay,' he said, taking something from his pocket. 'You want money? Is this the problem?' It was his wallet he was fingering. It was full of dollar bills.

'I want nothing from you. You did something to me.'

'Get out,' he said.

'You did something to me. You put something in my drink,' Lena said.

'Get out or I get the hotel to call the police.'

Her head exploded. She tried to grab his face, his hair. She really didn't know why or what she would do. As her hands were in mid-air in the closing space between them, she felt it. The thudding blow of his fist striking her cheekbone and nose, kind of mashing the two together.

She had never been hit before, not seriously. Her parents, whose safe home she'd abandoned, had made it an unswerving principle not to use violence, something that made the child Lena feel special. She flew backwards under the blow and lay on the luxurious carpet with her legs sprawled helplessly. A trickle of blood leaked from her nose. Yet something deep in her nature impelled her to keep moving. She crawled, literally crawled, on hands and knees, with blood dripping from her nose and chin. She hauled herself up on the bed and looked him squarely in the eye.

'I never want this,' she said. 'You know I never wanted this.'

That was all she could think of. That was all she could do – let him know that despite everything she still knew the truth.

Suddenly she was out in the Almaty street: cars rushed by; one thousand trees swayed in the slight breeze whispering down from the Tien Shan mountains; her life had changed.

Her father was right: the city was full of evil. She now knew what evil was. Evil was whatever was in her drink. It was the money he offered her. It was that thudding blow that cracked the musculature of her nose. Evil was the way he looked at her and how pitifully little he thought she was worth. Without rushing and taking every precaution, she crossed the Almaty street and left her old life behind.

EIGHT

A Place of Myth and Legend

And so Elaine – all the Elaines – returned. Back in the experimental room; now at a different university, Arizona State. Back answering questions and getting shocked. Only you know, as the research volunteers at the Arizona State University who watched her did not, she was not really Elaine and she was not really being electrically shocked.

The research team of Robert Cialdini (he would later rise to fame with his international bestseller *Influence: The Psychology of Persuasion*) set about manipulating the empathy levels of the observing volunteers. Once more they used a high empathy prime. But their hypothesis was different from Batson's. The Arizona team hypothesised that empathising with Elaine and her suffering produced 'personal sadness' – distress – in the observer. And that tension was the motivating spring that induced someone to help. Not to reduce Elaine's suffering, but to relieve one's own. If this were correct, the motivation would be egoistic. They dubbed the idea 'negative-state relief'.

What they found was importantly at variance with Batson and Kansas. Their results indicated that helping was predicted by the level of sadness or distress the observer of Elaine felt and not the degree they empathised with her. But more than that, they used the ingenious device of a 'mood-fixing' drug to probe this. The drug was called Mnemoxine.

This drug possessed two qualities: it affected information processing and it also affected mood – in a very particular sense. Its impact was of relatively short duration, certainly in the small quantities carefully meted out during the experiment, lasting no more than 30 minutes. But during that brief window, the drug chemically acted to preserve and prolong whatever mood you happened to be in when it took hold.

Each volunteer was given a small medication cup of Mnemoxine. But it was in fact an entirely harmless placebo. It was made up of soda water and ginger ale. The volunteers, however, did not know (participants were probed for suspicions in the debriefing).

Subjects who had a high level of empathy for the suffering of the victim did not help her at commensurately greater rates – not if they believed their mood could not be relieved by helping because of the action of the drug. What this suggested is that helping carries a very particular kind of reward component and thus can be used by a 'helper' instrumentally to relieve a negative or distressed mood. But when subjects believed that their mood was chemically 'stuck' because of Mnemoxine, helping wouldn't help. And so in this manipulation volunteers would not be inclined to trade places with Elaine. It would make no difference to their mood. Put another way: there was nothing in it for them.

Thus, concluded Cialdini's team, the actions of their research participants were not selfless. Instead they were animated by a desire to relieve their own distress. They were egoistic.

They readily acknowledged the potentially profound significance of the Batson research endeavours. They accepted that the Kansas results would have offered the enticing prospect of the first empirical confirmation that we can act purely selflessly. As such this would have constituted a considerable development in the 'characterization of human nature'. Would have.

But Arizona and Mnemoxine seemed to have dispelled that. And once more the elusive grail of pure human altruism seemed to waver before our eyes and vanish. A thing of our imaginations; as illusory as all the Elaines.

One day, while Lena was trying to keep her life from falling apart in Almaty, Z's white van pulled up in the Moscow street. Kolya ran around the back of Vasily's legs. Z demanded the drug money. Vasily gave him what he could, what he had earned. Z looked down at it derisively.

He said, 'You're so fucking stupid, you don't know when you owe someone money, you don't decide when you pay it back. The man whose money you owe, he decide.'

'I'm not stupid,' Vasily said.

'No? Who is out in the street?' Z said. 'But is your choice. You can keep walking these fucking streets to pay me. Or do one thing.'

'One thing?' Vasily said. 'What thing?'

Z looked up and down the street. 'I need a driver.'

'I can drive,' Vasily said.

'Is a long journey,' Z told him.

'I can do long journeys.' Vasily had driven trucks and vans thousands of miles out of Archangel, down through the Ural Mountains, all over.

'And I even give you money as well. Kill the debt. And bit of money more.'

'I don't want money,' Vasily said. 'Just no more debt.'

'Ah, you're a man of honour?'

'No,' Vasily said. If he had any real self-respect or honour, he wouldn't be walking the streets for Z. 'But I want one thing.'

Z stared coldly at him. He didn't ask what.

'I want Kolya,' Vasily said.

Z burst out laughing. 'You want a fucking dog?'

'I want Kolya,' Vasily said. It's all he really did want.

Feverfew (*Tanacetum parthenium*)

She was alone in Almaty. Lena had defied her father and look what had happened. She'd tried to strike out for herself, to make something of her life by herself, and look what had happened. She could not bear to return home, to look her father, her grand-father, in the eyes, to see the steppe, the places she had grown up in. She had betrayed it all – in a hotel room in Almaty.

She realised that this is what children did not know: not maths, or spelling or science – what they didn't know was the tricks of the world. Every day she waited with a mixture of fear and dark wonder to see if she was pregnant. She told her friend Samal, and Samal said to tell the police – she felt terrible for introducing Lena to this man – but Lena didn't want anyone to know. She didn't want to admit it. All the time she wondered: is something growing inside me – something of *his*, this man who spoke of hotels like palaces floating on the sea. Samal told her how to sort it out, to end it, but Lena believed life was precious, too precious to waste, which was why she'd come to Almaty in the first place. What a mess.

She had very little money and felt ashamed to ask her grandfather for more – her father had effectively disowned her. One day the next week she was walking by the Green Bazaar and there was someone playing an accordion on the street corner and asking for money. He was playing a simple tune, almost like a lullaby, and her legs suddenly went weak and she stumbled and fell in the street. A woman quickly came up to help her. Lena was crying and crying. The tune reminded her of something her grandfather used to sing.

The woman helped Lena to a nearby café and bought her a cup of coffee – she insisted. She – Darya – was the kindest person Lena ever met.

'See?' Vasily told me. 'Just out of the sky her angel falls and finds her. This is how it goes, no? In a strange city – *zzzhuuumm* – there is her angel to save her.' Then he added, 'This Darya, she was Russian.'

Lena's angel was about 20 years older than her, a stout but attractive woman with her dyed-blonde hair always tied back. Over coffee, in her dazed, hallucinatory state, Lena told Darya what she simply could not tell her father. Darya became like a parent: her city parent. It turned out she had lost a daughter.

Although she was originally from Moscow, when she married she moved with her husband to live in Semey, a city in the north-east of Kazakhstan not far from the Russian border, where the Soviets had tested their nuclear weapons and who knows what else. In Soviet times, while it was called Semipalatinsk, the Soviets tested over 400 nuclear weapons near there: it was one of their principal experimental centres. The test site closed with the fall of the USSR in 1991.

Darya's daughter was born in this strange, secretive, contaminated place. She developed cancer. Many people did. The doctors said it was just one of those things, just a thing of statistics, like if you deal out playing cards someone has to get a black queen. That's what Darya was told, even though everyone knew it was because of all the chemicals and poisons that had seeped into the soil and air and everywhere. Everyone knew that. There were too many black queens. But for a long time the pretence continued because perhaps the truth was too awful. It is likely that tens of thousands of people had developed cancers. So Darya's daughter had died, and then suddenly Lena collapsed in the street right in front of her, and so Lena was like an angel to her as well.

Darya ran a cleaning agency and with the economic boom in Kazakhstan there were many apartments of rich people that needed cleaning. Rich people, she said, they act like pigs and expect to live like princes. That's the privilege of being rich – everything is done for you. It was always like that. Even in Soviet times, only then the rich were called Communists, but Lena was too young to remember how all of that really worked.

'So Darya says,' Vasily told me, 'the work is not very good pay, but it is okay, and there is lots – lots of rich people with dirty apartments — so if Lena want to work hard, she will never be hungry again.'

And that's what Lena wanted — to work so hard that the sheer fatigue would help her forget what had happened to her, help her sleep. The breeze kept rolling down from the Tien Shan mountains, and no one else seemed to know about her dark secret. How could they not tell just by looking at her? It mortified her and she punished herself for it.

For the next couple of months, all she did was work, seven days a week, no rest. She was going to make something of herself. Maybe it was not what she thought her life was going to be, but it didn't now matter — she'd make a new one. Things had been changing so fast in Kazakhstan after the fall of the Soviet Union and she would now change fast too. But she wouldn't have been able to begin this act of self-reconstruction if it wasn't for blind chance, for a woman in the street who had lost her own daughter, for her angel, her Rescuer.

One day, after Lena had worked the whole weekend, and had pushed herself through double shifts, Darya came up to her with tears in her eyes. She was not crying — or trying not to — but had tears in her eyes. She told Lena that she was so sorry but the company which was supposed to pay for the cleaning had not paid her. So she couldn't pay Lena straight away. She was totally devastated and seemed ashamed to be put in that position.

'Lena said to her that it doesn't matter,' Vasily told me. 'She told Darya she can, you know, wait because everything, everything she owes to Darya anyway. When she says that, Darya then cries and cries. She thought there would be a big problem and Lena would shout and scream at her and say she was trying to cheat her or something. But Lena says is okay. Says she owes Darya everything anyway. And then you know what? The very next day, Darya gives her the money. All the money. The company still does not pay, but Darya goes to bank, takes her own money out, gives it to Lena. She pushes the money in Lena's hand even though Lena says she can wait. Darya says, "Lena, you are so good. Not like the other girls. Pray for all of us, will you? Please pray for us, I never meet any girl like you."'

'And did Lena pray?' I asked.

Vasily shrugged. 'She never say. I never ask. Maybe I should of ask. You think this is important?'

'I was just interested,' I said.

The next month, when Darya was giving Lena her wages (she always gave the bundle of notes, *tenge*, neatly in a white envelope that she never did up, but always meticulously in an envelope because she liked doing things properly), the older woman was extremely excited.

'Lena, I think you *are* praying for us,' Darya said. 'There is some good, good news. You know you are my best worker,' she said.

Lena glowed with pride.

'Not one of the girls work like you,' Darya said. 'They work sloppy, leave the apartments with mess, I get complaints and then they lie to me and say they leave it good. But with you, never one complaint. Only praise. "Who is this new cleaner?" the clients ask. "Never before is the apartment so good. She make it a palace."'

Lena simply said, 'Thank you.'

So out of all the girls, Darya offered Lena the opportunity: to work in one of the biggest hotels, and not just as a cleaner, but as a receptionist – she'd have to train a little there first, learn how it goes – and then there may be the chance of something better, perhaps even some kind of hotel management diploma.

'I don't want to lose you,' Darya said, 'because no one but you are my best worker, but my family in Russia, they say, "Darya, we need someone very, very good for this special job," and they ask if there is anyone I trust who will not let them down.' Darya took Lena's hands. 'I know, Lena, I *know* you will never let me down.'

Lena started weeping. That someone would trust her with all this, she who was all despoiled within. And that was not even the best part. Darya had saved it for last.

'Lena,' she said, 'this big hotel, it is where you always wanted to go.'

Lena dared not even mouth the word in case it was all a dream, and the unspoken promise of the greatest city in all Russia would vanish. For the hotel was in Moscow.

It was dark by the time Vasily and I got together at the Cairo the next day. I said, 'So you met Lena in Moscow?'

'No,' he replied.

'But she was going to Moscow.'

'But that's not the place we meet.'

'Okay, where was?'

He paused. 'Is hard to explain.' So many things seemed hard to explain. To his credit, Vasily tried, 'Between Kazakhstan and Russia there is big border, no?'

'Sure.' I knew it was the northern rim of the country.

'How long you think that border goes?'

'I know it's big,' I said. 'Must be.'

'You know how big?'

I tried to estimate it using the UK as a yardstick. I happened to know that from London to Edinburgh was 400 miles since I'd once driven it to get to a wedding where I almost crashed the car – another story. So it had to be at least double that. I added a little more on top to be safe. 'A thousand miles,' I said. Even as I said it, it seemed an insanely long border.

Vasily snorted briefly as if he were disappointed in me. 'More,' he said.

I needed to recalibrate. I knew the distance from London to Boston is around 3,000 miles right across the Atlantic since I'd often gazed at the sign to that effect up in the departure lounge in Boston's Logan International Airport when going back and forth to Harvard. (In fact Boston–London is 3,250 miles, depending how you measure it.) Could the Russian-Kazakh border be halfway across the Atlantic? I went for it. 'Sixteen hundred miles,' I said.

'Three,' he said.

'Three thousand? Impossible.'

'Three times what you say.'

I wasn't having it. I took out my iPhone. Google would sort this out. I pressed the search button and then stared incredulously at the answer: 4,660 miles. It seemed inconceivable. I immediately entered a search for a list of distances from London. The closest I got to 4,600 miles was Denver. Could it really be that Kazakhstan's border with Russia was the distance from London to Denver, Colorado?

'Somewhere around the border,' Vasily said, 'that is where I meet Lena.'

I gazed out of the window of the café. A border more than the width of the Atlantic Ocean. I still couldn't compute it. Above us, unaccountably, searchlights scoured the dark metallic sky, until the Central Asian night finally swallowed them. There was a sliver of new moon.

'So in Russia?' I said.

'Not just Russia,' Vasily said. He shook out another capsule from the feverfew bottle. Then he thought twice about taking it. 'But this terrible place in Russia.'

For on the other side of Kazakhstan's impossibly long frontier with its northern neighbour, stretching, curling, straightening out, for thousands of miles, lies the Russian region that would determine everything for both of them, a place of myth and legend, fear and fevers – Siberia.

NINE

How it Happens

And then the Kansans fought back.

Batson's team performed further experiments casting doubt on the Arizona findings, providing alternative explanations for the results. They did not challenge the notion that *one* source of helping behaviour is the wish to end your own distress when witnessing someone else's suffering. But, they argued, it was more than that.

They artificially induced people to feel sad. This 'reminiscence procedure' involved asking subjects to dwell on an event or a situation in their own past that they knew made them feel sad. They were asked to focus on it for several minutes. This negative reminiscing did make people help more – helping 'relieved' that negative state. Helping helps the helper. When they are sad.

But Batson's team disputed that ostensibly altruistic behaviour was exclusively egoistic behaviour in disguise. Even where their experiments offered a 'mood-enhancement manipulation', high empathy subjects still helped. So their behaviour was not about seeking to reduce their own distress by the 'reward' of helping. There was, as Batson's team argued, 'more to it than that'.

And so the intellectual debate raged on. From the eighties, into the nineties. And then technology took over.

The availability of more penetrating and sophisticated scientific equipment provided a whole new dimension to the debate. Instead of looking at what people did from the outside and then inferring their motivations, it was possible to look within. For the equipment enabled researchers to reach inside the brain.

There was an explosion in the field of social neuroscience.

The next morning. The phone went. I had to get out of bed as my Kazakh phone was charging in a wall socket on the other side of the room. I glanced at my iPhone on my bedside table: 6.29am.

'Vasily, it's 6.29. The hotel breakfast buffet doesn't even open for another minute.'

'I was not going to tell you what really happen with Lena. But I said before, yes, no bullshit.'

I was standing facing the wall with the cheap Kazakhstan handset still charging in it. 'Yes, you said that,' I replied.

'I think all night, and want to tell how it happens.' He paused. I imagined him with another capsule of feverfew. 'I was not any hero, Dexter. I want you to know I could have done a lot different. A lot better.'

'Better?'

'For Lena,' he said.

He began to tell me about Siberia.

Vasily and Z had driven to Novosibirsk, the Siberian capital, in two vans and were waiting.

'You done quite good for me,' Z said. 'But job is only half done.' They were in a cheap hotel – soiled sheets and broken locks cheap – in the far Siberian south. 'Hey,' Z said when Vasily was silent, 'you drive good, maybe I don't shoot the dog, hey?'

'You said you give me Kolya,' Vasily said.

'I never actually say that.'

Vasily scrolled back through his memory. Had Z not? Maybe he'd overlooked that detail. Or maybe he'd mistaken silence for assent.

'But maybe I give you that piece of shit,' Z said. 'Or maybe I let you choose a watch.'

'I don't want a watch.'

'Want, want,' Z taunted him. 'Anyway, you haven't finished the job yet.'

What *was* the job? Why this waiting around in a horrid hotel in Siberia? It had taken them three days to drive east from Moscow: through the Ural Mountains, across hundreds of miles of southern Siberia, a tiny fraction of its land mass, towards the end of the journey shadowing but never crossing the border with Kazakhstan, until they arrived at Novosibirsk, the city on the magisterial Ob River, the seventh largest river in the world, rising in the Altai Mountains near Mongolia and finally emptying itself 2,000 miles later into the Arctic Ocean.

'The first girls arrive today from the east,' Z said. 'Then more tomorrow. We take some of them back to Moscow for work. Just cleaning and shop work. But there's lots of them.'

He knew Z was buying and selling all sorts of contraband. Cigarettes from Kaliningrad, Belarus, Ukraine, cheap, stolen, fake, he wasn't sure. Watches. No doubt Z was doing some drugs deals also. But also offering cheap transportation back to the capital – what was this?

Vasily had heard about young women from the distant provinces working in shops and cleaning companies for next to nothing. Some came from the far east of the Russian Federation: Kamchatka, Yakutia, Sakhalin, all the way across Siberia to the Pacific coast and Vladivostok, some of the most sparsely populated places on earth. Life was tough out there. No doubt Z would make money out of these recruits like he did with the drugs.

Vasily asked him when they would be returning to Moscow.

'Why hurry? You have nothing to do there,' Z said. 'Or maybe you not feed the dog.'

'Kolya is with a friend.'

'Bullshit. That dog's your only friend,' Z said.

Unbeknown to Z, Vasily believed this was one of the truest things he'd heard in his life.

'Tomorrow they bring the other girls up from the south,' Z said. He mentioned some more places, former Soviet Central Asian republics. Now all independent. In theory. But some of them had fallen on hard times with the collapse of the Soviet Union. Many people, Vasily knew, were desperate for work.

'So we leave tomorrow or next day,' Z said.

'Okay,' Vasily heard himself say. In truth he wasn't paying attention: he was thinking of Kolya.

'Go get drunk.'

'I'm tired. I think I sleep.'

As Z was leaving, some part of Vasily's consciousness registered that Z had said something about one of the Stans. Kyrgyzstan, was it? Vasily suddenly felt impossibly tired, as though great effort was required not just to put one foot in front of the other, but even to remain standing. So they would leave tomorrow or the day after and he would drive the van for thousands of miles back to Moscow. He reached his room with the soiled sheets and broken locks. No, it wasn't Kyrgzystan Z had mentioned.

'You know,' Vasily told me, 'then that place, it means nothing to me except a name. Kazakhstan. Kazakh-fucking-stan.'

So here was the hard truth Vasily had to tell: although his suspicions were raised about Z's intentions, Vasily wanted nothing to do with any of the girls. It was not his business. It was for that reason that he chose to drink coffee and smoke shisha in a café across the street from the hotel – that and the poor mobile reception in the hotel. It was because of a desire to mind his own business that he chose to eat alone. He wanted to keep himself to himself, wait for Z to do whatever Z had to do, and then drive Z and his passengers back to Moscow. That was his role. His job: drive a van and ask no questions. He was very good at both.

The road had taken him here, all the way to southern Siberia. The road would take him back to Moscow. And Kolya. And that was all he cared about. But then something came across his path.

From the late eighties, while the debate between Kansas and Arizona rumbled on, biologists and psychologists found common cause in trying to discover the neural bases for social behaviour, how we interact with one another, cooperate, help – or don't. Technological innovations presented enticing new possibilities.

Initially many of the studies focused on animal behaviour. But the coming of fMRI in the late 1990s fundamentally altered the landscape. And that landscape, of course, was our understanding of the human brain. Indeed, as Damian Stanley of the California Institute of Technology states, since the turn of the millennium the field of social neuroscience 'has exploded'.

Why 'social' neuroscience? It is because the primary initial aim of the infant mammal – and particularly the human primate – is to connect to a caregiver. Without this, it dies. But why should the caregiver, the Nurturer, care? Because evolution has selected for those that do and to promote this has made the provision of assistance 'rewarding' – pleasurable. Many parents will attest that the hardest job in the world is also the most rewarding, even during tempestuous teenage years. That process – the reward-reinforcing effect of helping others – may not be solely restricted to children or kin. It may extend to other unrelated humans. That, in essence, is what this debate is about. The nature of animating forces of behaviour towards other, particularly unrelated, human beings.

Why 'neuroscience'? Because the working idea was to study the neural basis of these helping human behaviours. It was proposed that social processing in primates recruits distinct systems of brain structures – literally, networks in the brain. With fMRI, it became possible to zero in on the neural circuitry. And this happened. With startling results.

The anticipation was that when we were able to look in our heads we'd be able to resolve this issue; when we looked in our heads, we would be able to see with a previously unattainable clarity what we actually are.

Towards the end of the next day, Vasily was in the café, sitting alone with his back to the rest of the restaurant, not bothering anyone, not bothering with Novosibirsk or Siberia, when someone slid into the chair opposite.

'Hello, you're Z's friend, aren't you?' she said.

Vasily looked up. A young woman. *Young* eyes. Intelligent-looking. Attractive in an unusual way: full of life. She smiled broadly. Then he realised she must be smiling at him. There was no one else. Why was this person smiling at him?

'I'm sorry,' she said. 'I ruin your steak? It looks like a good steak.' She paused, waiting, inviting a response. 'Is it a good steak?'

'Is a steak,' Vasily said.

The more she smiled, the more irritated he got. 'Z said you're driving one of the vans to Moscow?' Another pause, another invitation. When he declined, she said, 'Is that what you're doing?' When he was sullenly silent again, she said, 'You're a very quiet man, aren't you?'

'I'm eating steak,' Vasily replied, but as soon as he said it he was even more irritated, this time with himself. Why did this harmless young woman unbalance him?

'I'm sorry,' she said, suddenly embarrassed. 'It is bad that I come and talk to you like that.' She stood up. 'Enjoy your meal.'

As she turned to leave, Vasily said, 'What are you doing in Moscow?'

She sat down warily, as if he could snap at her again at any time, but slowly her smile returned. 'Hotel management,' she said.

Vasily nodded. 'Big job.'

'Well,' she said. 'That's what I hope in my future. But I will start cleaning rooms, I think. I don't mind. I'm good at cleaning. I did lots of cleaning in Almaty.'

'Almaty? Kazakhstan?'

'I'm not from Almaty. I worked there,' she said. 'You've been to Almaty?'

'Never.'

'You want to go?'

'Never,' he said, and they both laughed.

'Is beautiful city,' she said. 'Only the people, people in cities, you know . . .'

'I'm from the city,' Vasily said, and again they laughed.

'Please tell me, you are not from Moscow,' she said.

'Why?'

'Because Moscow is the place I want to go all my life. I grow up in the centre of nowhere. But one teacher I had, she studied in Moscow. She tells me how beautiful it is. What do you do, in Moscow?'

'And what am I to tell her?' Vasily said to me. 'What I can say then? That I sell drugs. That I sell them so bad, I got to come out here to Siberia, to drive a van thousands of miles, because I can't even sell no drugs to no one.'

'So what did you say?' I asked.

Vasily took the painkillers. With water. A blue and white bus slid past us, powered by the overhead cables.

'I have a dog,' Vasily told her.

'A dog?' she said. 'That is what you do in Moscow? You have a dog?'

'Yes, a dog.'

'My grandfather, he had many dogs,' she said. 'I love dogs.'

'Dogs love me,' Vasily replied. He held out his hand. 'So my name is Vasily.'

'I'm Lena,' she said.

They chatted about dogs as only people who love dogs can. In other words, to normal human beings – insufferably. He was intrigued that her grandfather used his dogs for hunting, amazed at the stories about how before him his father, Lena's great-grandfather, had hunted with eagles. Eagles. When she was about to leave, Vasily said, 'Good luck with your hotels. I hope you learn good how to manage them. Make sure the locks are not all broke.'

'I will,' she said. 'But I don't need luck.'

'Everyone need luck,' Vasily told her.

'Yes, that is true,' she said, nodding her head at the indisputable truth of his answer. 'Only, I also have Z. And Z, he promises to fix it for me. If I work hard, and I always work hard, Z, he promises to fix it for me.'

As she left, smiling, with the cold half-eaten steak still on his plate, Vasily kept telling himself: this is not my problem, this is not my business.

She turned one last time. 'What's his name, your dog?' she asked.

'Kolya,' he said.

'Kolya?'

'Or Little Czar. Sometime I call him my Little Czar.'

He'd never told anyone else in the world that. Why had he done so now? But he kept saying to himself that this, none of this, had anything to do with him.

TEN

The Choice

It was another heartbreakingly beautiful day in Kazakhstan when Vasily called. 'I must make our meeting later,' he said.

I could hear that he was saying something else, but I had to duck in sudden evasive action. I had been warned not to get too close to the fence. I'd got too close to the fence. I was distracted, steeling myself to try another Kazakh speciality: kumis – fermented mare's milk. It's said Tolstoy drank it for his respiratory problems. It cured his health *and* his relations with his wife. At least, that's the story 'I'm sorry, Vasily, what did you say?'

'My little one is ill. I can meet in Almaty, but late.'

A young Kazakh woman right next to me let out a yelping scream as an enormous beak darted towards her smartphone. She too had got too close to the fence.

'I can hear some big noise,' Vasily said.

What could I say? There was too much to explain. I just told him. 'It's a woman screaming,' I said.

'Screaming? Why she scream?'

Again, it was too much to explain. I just told him. 'Because of the ostrich.'

'Ostrich?' he said, tolerably accurately. 'What is ostrich?'

Have you ever tried to describe an ostrich? I turned and asked my guide Marzhan, a young Kazakh woman with glasses and a copy of Anne Rice's *Interview with the Vampire*, for the Russian translation. Phonetically it is something like 'strauss' (страус).

'You are seeing strauss?' Vasily said incredulously.

'I didn't want to see strauss,' I said.

I'd joined a group going along the great Silk Road that led from China. Along here for hundreds of years sinuous caravans of camels miles long carried not only the luxury that obsessed the Roman Empire – Chinese silk – not only gunpowder and precious stones, but that other precious commodity: ideas. And, it seemed, one of the latest ideas along the Silk Road was to start an ostrich farm.

After we left the farm and were driving back to Almaty, I asked Marzhan about some of the facts that Vasily had told me that I didn't entirely understand. She confirmed, for example, that the Kazakh naming ceremony does involve the new child's name being recited thrice. 'Just in case she forgets the first time,' Marzhan said cheerfully.

We were driving away from the mountains and the steppe far off to our right was slowly changing, losing its green lusciousness. Becoming something different again.

'What's happening?' I asked.

'You'll see,' Marzhan said, placing her bookmark into her paper-back.

'Can I ask you something?' I said. 'If a young woman from the rural areas wanted to go to Almaty, you know, leaving the steppe, would her father forbid it?'

'Is possible,' she said, but there was a slight hesitation in her voice.

'So much so that if she went, he'd disown her?'

'Disown?'

'Tell her that she was no longer his daughter.'

Marzhan put the Anne Rice novel neatly across her lap. 'It sounds strange.'

'Why?'

'Many young people come to Almaty from the villages to work. Mostly families support it. They benefit from it too. It brings money and how you say . . .' she raised her hand like an escalator going up.

'Social status?' I suggested.

'You know, in Soviet times, everyone was equal.' Then she burst out laughing. 'Now we embrace capitalism and everything is a fight to get to the top.'

'Outside my hotel,' I said, 'the expensive cars. It could be Beverly Hills.'

'People from other Stans, they say, Kazakhs, we like to show off wealth. They say we have become like Russians.'

'Hang on,' I said, looking out of the window. 'Are those sand dunes?'

'In the spring the steppe is full of red, red poppies and white desert candles.'

'But over there, Marzhan. In the distance, are those sand dunes?'

'Yes, here is semi-desert,' Marzhan said.

'Desert?'

'My grandmother up north, she used to have a camel.'

I let it pass, intriguing though the prospect was. I wanted to focus on Lena. 'So why would a father disown his daughter for going to Almaty, that's what I don't understand.'

Marzhan held up her copy of *Interview with the Vampire*. 'People,' she said, 'they are strange.'

She then got a call on her mobile. It rang with *The Simpsons* ringtone. I was left to look out of the window. In one direction the sand dunes rose like low dusky waves, receding quietly towards the horizon; in the other the steppe rolled endlessly on in a symphony of green. I tried to imagine it covered in blood-red poppies and white desert candles. I tried to assemble the pieces of what had happened in Lena's life, and the pieces didn't quite fit.

He couldn't get a signal. That's what caused Vasily's problem. Or more exactly: what set in motion the chain of small, tightly interlinked events that led to the disaster. It was an unremarkable beginning: a flickering bar on a phone screen that died. Tantalisingly appearing and then expiring, so that wherever he went in the squalid hotel, his phone was dead. The receptionist, an overweight youth with a fringe low over his eyes like a visor, was intently reading a glossy magazine of dubious content. He suggested Vasily go outside in the car park, even before Vasily had finished explaining the problem. For all the brusque discourtesy, it provided Vasily with some consolation: the signal problem wasn't with his phone. The temperature was plummeting, but he had no intention of being more than a few seconds on the call – he wanted to find out how Kolya was. He could have sent a text, but what he really wanted was to have the phone held to Kolya's ear so he could say something. If that meant he was crazy, so be it.

So he trudged out into the car park as a couple of people, who'd plainly been on the same mission, returned. He found a heating vent, a box grille sticking out of the side of the building like an exhaust pipe. He wasn't sure precisely what it was expelling, but it was warm. He'd take warm. Now the tricky part: making the call in the sub-zero temperature. The number he needed was the last number dialled (after a host of calls back and forth with Z), so it was easy to find.

He ripped off his glove, pressed redial, pulled it back on before the searching Siberian air, could even begin to eat through the flesh with frostbite. Friends of his had lost tips of fingers, a thumb. Frostbite was a fact of life. He held the phone as close to his ear as he could without the surface touching the skin: in the cold sometimes they'd stick together. Decidedly unpleasant. But at least he got a signal. At least he was connecting to his friend, Kolya's minder. At least . . . he put the phone down.

From the next window along, on the other side of the grille, he could hear talking. Z was talking. In a low voice, but unmistakably Z. The cool confidence, the understated menace. Vasily listened.

'You choose one,' Z was saying. 'It is my gift. You choose one.'

'Is not a good selection,' the unknown man said.

For the last couple of days, Z had been pushing his watches, Chinese fakes but good quality ones, to anyone he could. It was a nice little sideline.

'You are a good friend,' Z continued. 'So I give you first choice.'

Vasily knew this was not true: Z had been badgering people relentlessly.

'First choice?' the man said, perhaps privy to the same information as Vasily.

'Of course, first choice. Sometimes I have good selection, sometimes no,' Z said. 'This time is good selection.'

'You always say that,' the man said.

'I like my product,' Z said and they both laughed.

635

Vasily was about to go — what did he care if Z ripped off someone else? — and find somewhere else to make his call, but then there was another of those little links, another minute piece of the chain curled itself around the previous one and locked. It was not just what the man said, but how he said it. He seemed hurt, aggrieved, as though he were being cheated out of something.

'I don't like any of them,' the man said. '*Any*. I prefer to choose a Rolex.'

'No,' Z said. 'The Rolex, they are for Moscow. My boss he will choose from them. So instead I offer again. You choose any girl.'

'Is poor product.'

'The product is the product,' Z said. 'Sometimes good, sometimes not so good. Like weather.'

'Like watches.'

Again laughter. Vasily found himself rooted, transfixed. He tried to move one foot and it was as if the ice and snow were sucking the soles of his boot. It seemed to make a fearful din, like breaking glass, as the ice cracked around him.

'It is just a gift,' Z said. 'Because we do good business. I like you. But I don't like you that much. I am not going to have your fucking children.'

'Fuck you,' the man said.

'So what you like?'

There was silence. The man was reconsidering his options, recalibrating his desires. 'That quiet girl.'

'Which one?' Z said.

'The one like a schoolteacher.'

'She will be dead, like corpse. She knows nothing.'

'I like her.'

'Another. Not her. We have plans for her in Moscow.'

To this day, Vasily does not know about whom they were talking. He cannot say for sure it was Lena. He doesn't know. But he believed that it was.

That night Vasily and Z were in the café next to the cheap hotel on the edge of Novosibirsk. Z had just had a steaming coffee delivered. Vasily had been nursing a soft drink and smoking. He hadn't planned or wanted to meet Z, but Z had come looking for him.

'You *know* something,' Z said to him. It was not a question. It was a short indisputable statement of fact.

'What I know?' Vasily said.

Z released Vasily's face from his icy stare and looked at the steaming black coffee in front of him. 'Yes, you *know* something.'

Next to Vasily's table was a hookah bubbling away with the shisha solution, the pipe for smoking the tobacco lay on the table between them. Every now and then the contraption let out an impatient puff of smoke.

'Is very bad for you,' Z said. 'Smoking.' He took a teaspoon and piled sugar on it, tipped it into the coffee, did it again. He did it a third time, the overfilled teaspoon hovering inches over the disturbed black surface.

'And he looks at me, yes,' Vasily told me, 'like I must choose if he puts in next spoon of sugar. Me. The spoon is over the cup and he is looking at me.'

Suddenly it was all down to Vasily what would happen next. It was only a spoon of sugar, and yet Vasily did not know what to do. Z smiled. He meticulously tipped the granules into the chrome sugar pot and slowly stirred what he had.

'Someone saw you in car park,' Z said. 'No,' he continued before Vasily could say anything else. 'Don't lie.' Z carried on stirring.

637

'You know,' he said, 'There was one time a driver. Not good driver like you, but this driver. And I brought him out here. You know what he does?'

Vasily remained silent.

'I bet you know what this driver does,' Z said. 'He fall in love with one of these girls.' Steam curled slowly up from the coffee; streaks of condensation leaked down the street window; simultaneous movement in opposite directions. Vasily said nothing. 'Ask me what happened to him,' Z said. Vasily said nothing. Z's voice grew quieter, barely more than a whisper. '*Ask* me what happened to him.'

'What happened to the driver?' Vasily asked.

The other man's eyes once more crawled over Vasily's face. He lifted the squat white china cup and in one draught poured the still steaming liquid down his throat. He carefully put the cup down and with great care wrapped the pipe from the hookah back onto the stand.

'What driver?' Z said.

So the driver disappeared; and if Vasily did anything he would disappear. Z had been clear enough about that. Vasily kept telling himself that none of this had anything to do with him. Like the research volunteers in Kansas and Arizona, Vasily had a pass: he could walk away, escape, and simply get on with his life. That's what he thought he would do. That's what he told himself he wanted to do. Definitely that.

ELEVEN

The Line to Almaty

How do you tell someone everything in their life is about to change, to be destroyed, desecrated?

But as he saw her in the hotel lobby, as he gestured to her to come across the street, as he took her to another café well away from the hotel, he was thinking that it was not only her life that was about to change. Because he knew that the minute he told her, so would his. And if his life changed, so would Kolya's.

The café they went to was dark and doubled as a bar. They ordered coffee.

'You are quiet,' she said.

'What is wrong with quiet?' he replied. The enormity of the situation had closed up his throat. He was used to sitting in silence, he'd done so for years with his father, but this was different.

'I like quiet. Most people speak rubbish,' she said. 'Not businesslike, not professional. I will have to learn proper speaking in Moscow.'

639

Vasily looked at her and thought: she knows nothing – *nothing*. He gazed carefully at her youthful, fresh face and suddenly superimposed on it was another Lena: purple-bruised cheeks, addict-thin, black circles around her eyes. It was like there were two Lenas right in front of him. One was smiling, still dreaming. And the other was Z's Lena. Vasily was about to tell her when she had to take a call – was it Z? He didn't want to know. He went to the lavatory. In the mirror he saw a weak man. One who regretted not saying a thousand things to his father before he died. Suddenly, he can't recall how, he was sitting in front of Lena again and she was saying something he did not hear, could not hear. He heard himself saying, 'Tell me, how you know Z?'

'Z?'

'Z.'

'Why does it matter?' she said.

'Maybe it does not.'

The smile disappeared from her face. 'How do *you* know Z?' she asked.

'And,' Vasily told me, 'I'm thinking of Kolya. I'm saying in my head, please, Kolya, please Little Czar, forgive me.'

'How do you know him?' Lena repeated.

'I sell drugs for him,' Vasily said. 'I owe him money. So I agree to drive the van to Siberia and back to Moscow.'

Silence descended between them. It was like there was now a glass right there between them. Like the glass in front of that road in his father's apartment.

From the other side, Lena said, 'I don't believe you.'

'Why I tell you this then?' Vasily said.

'I don't know,' Lena said.

'Z is a criminal. Not right at top. But is dangerous. He sells drugs. I don't know for sure, but I think he sells . . . girls.'

Lena got quickly to her feet. She looked at him with fear and hatred. 'I will ask Z.'

'Yes, ask. And he will lie. But before, think how you know Z. Think what big story people tell you so you are not with your family, not in your home, but here, in Siberia, with some man like Z.' Vasily got up too. 'I don't tell you these things so you will like me.'

'I don't like you,' Lena said.

'I'm going,' Vasily told her. 'You will never see me again now. But at least I try to tell you.'

He moved to go. 'Sit *down*,' she said quietly. 'Please.'

The snow was falling more heavily. Their coffees went cold.

'I met this woman called Darya,' Lena began. And told him everything. The more she spoke, the more the sheer hollowness of the job offer became obvious: there was no contract, no agreed salary, no location, not even a name of the hotel. How had she been so gullible? The story of human trafficking around the world tells that people dreaming of a better life are like this – desperate to believe. It is the lifeblood of the trade in human beings.

'You have this Darya's number?' Vasily asked.

Lena got out her phone, scrolled quickly through the contacts. 'What shall I say?'

'Tell her you're worrying. You want to speak about the job. You have questions. Some of the other girls, they are talking all sort of nonsense. Don't mention you worry about Z. Understand?'

Lena nodded. She pressed dial. She listened. She put down the phone.

'Goes to voicemail?' he said. 'I bet it goes to voicemail.'

'It is dead,' Lena said, and in that moment the decision was made.

They would escape.

TWELVE

Outliers

Research in social neuroscience has mapped out the characteristic patterns of neural activation when people act because they are merely feeling the coercion and compulsion of a social rule (norm). Further, functional neuroimaging techniques have identified the neural patterns and pathways when the choice expresses a *genuine* preference. Neurologically speaking, these are two different processes. Different systems are triggered. In fMRI terms: different parts of the screen are lit up.

Therefore when you make a choice, not because you are eager to act that way, but because you are following a social norm, the brain engages circuitry that inhibits desire. This involves lateral parts of the prefrontal cortex: the side areas of the front of your brain. But when we act following a genuine preference another neural network is activated. It includes structures linked to the brain's reward system, including the ventral striatum. (The striatum is made up of three substructures: the caudate, the putamen and the nucleus accumbens. These are entirely different structures located much 'farther back' in the brain.)

This important distinction permitted James Rilling and his team at Emory University to examine what happens when we cooperate. Their subject group was exclusively women: 19 in one experiment and 17 in the next. They were then asked to play the well-known Prisoner's Dilemma game. In it, players can choose to cooperate with each other or 'defect' (not cooperate or effectively betray the other and cheat – gain at the other's expense). In a nutshell, usually it is more advantageous not to cooperate, to defect.

It would be expected that if the volunteer's real preference was to act selfishly, the striatum should have been activated when they obtained more money by defecting. Equally, if they were only cooperating because they were being subservient to a social norm, then when they did reluctantly cooperate, there should have been activation of prefrontal areas that inhibit desire. However, the Emory team found the reverse of this.

Even where the volunteer playing the game was earning less by cooperating (she could have earned more by defecting/not cooperating), she was neurologically experiencing enhanced activation of her brain's reward system – the striatum complex of substructures. As importantly, the prefrontal region was not activated when she cooperated. This suggests that the decision to cooperate was a genuine – and internally rewarding – one, not due to social coercion.

But perhaps the most intriguing confirmatory evidence in the Emory research was discovered when the game was played by one of their human subjects against a preprogrammed computer. The set-up of the game remained the same, the various advantages and pitfalls of cooperation remained the same, only the volunteer was informed that she was playing against a computer. Now even when the volunteer chose to cooperate with the machine, the human reward system did not trigger.

This has enormous potential significance. The various interlocking threads of evidence suggested that cooperating with other humans is rewarding, even when it comes at a personal individual *cost* to the actor. This indicates that as the Batson team had concluded 20 years previously, but without access to such sophisticated neurotechnology, we *are* capable of genuinely altruistic acts, acts which are not a front for buried self-interest. At Emory, they claimed they may have actually found the 'pattern of neural activation', the pathways of the brain, that sustain our cooperative selves.

These systems operate by rewarding us when we cooperate with others.

They may inhibit our impulse to act in our own narrow selfish self-interest.

They offer the tantalising prospect that we have evolved neural systems that make such altruistic behaviour 'rewarding'.

They make us feel good.

And if this is correct, an even more fundamental question remains: why has evolution selected for such neural structures? What is the advantage of our evolving in this way? Why are humans like this?

The strength of the plan was its simplicity. They took the van. They drove the van.

'I take you back to Almaty,' Vasily offered, as they were heading out of Novosibirsk.

'I'll never go back to Almaty,' Lena said.

'I take you back to Kazakhstan.'

'I don't want go to Kazakhstan.'

'Then where?'

'Anywhere. Where are you going?'

'Archangel,' he said.

'So am I.'

'But first I must go somewhere else.'

'Where?'

'Moscow.'

'Moscow?'

'I must get Kolya.'

'Let's get Kolya,' Lena said.

Snow was falling, monotonously brushed away by the wipers. The headlights shone steadily at the Siberian road ahead. She asked him to tell her about Archangel. He spoke of how in summer there were the White Nights, and it was light even until midnight, how people would take picnics and go to parks or out into the forest and the world was awake and asleep at the same time and it was like dreaming with your eyes open. He told her about these things. And that is what they planned to do — after they'd got Kolya.

Later that evening, after I'd been speaking to Vasily for several hours, I was in the hotel lobby, with its massive burgeoning of potted plants, restrained in straitjackets of ornate brass. I thought about what he'd done. It represents, as economists Ernst Fehr and Bettina Rockenbach vividly state, 'a spectacular outlier in the animal world'. Why are we this way? It is easy to scoff, to decry ourselves. I think that's what Vasily did to himself, that inner critic and persecutor. But what he did contains a clue. Some hint about human outlier behaviour. For outliers are interesting: they tell us something invaluable about what they lie without.

I look around the hotel lobby in Almaty. People on plush over-filled sofas, gazing at screens, but they contain the capacity for the remarkable. What draws it out? What enables us to choose as Vasily chose, risking everything he had in his life, literally everything, for someone he barely knew?

THIRTEEN

The Turning

He drove as fast as he could. He wanted to put as much distance between them and Z as he could. Vasily's calculation was that Z would think they had headed back down to Kazakhstan. It would make sense. Take Lena back to Almaty. Would he guess that they would head right to the very place Z wanted to take Lena all along? There was always a risk: Z knew how much Vasily thought of Kolya. But would anyone believe they would actually do it?

In any event, there are two principal routes from Novosibirsk to Moscow. A more direct one, faster — that was the one they'd used to come to Siberia in the first place and intended to return on. But there was a more northerly route, further up through the Ural Mountains. It was a bit longer, but safer. That's the route they took. It was as Vasily and Lena were driving through this chain of mountains that divide Asia from Europe that the storm struck.

*

There were fewer and fewer other vehicles. People were taking heed and getting off the road. But then they were in a different situation: they did not have to get to Moscow so urgently.

'It will pass?' Lena said.

'It will pass,' Vasily replied, carrying on driving.

It didn't.

As they came to the Urals – where the Urals should have been – there was only white. It wasn't as though the world had disappeared. Instead they had entered another world. It was only snow, nothing but that. It felt like they were like falling endlessly through a cloud. The van was getting stuck in the drift.

'There were some buildings a couple of kilometres back,' Vasily said. 'Did you see those buildings by that turn, a couple of kilometres back?'

'I saw something,' Lena said.

'Back or forward?' he asked her. 'Which way we go?'

'Back,' Lena said.

Vasily nodded. 'Back.'

He turned the van around. It was slightly easier. It was downhill. They drove and drove. They came to a side road.

'Was it here?' Vasily said. 'The buildings?'

'I think it was here,' Lena replied.

But they could see no lights.

'Where are the buildings?' Lena said.

'It must be the snow,' Vasily said. 'I think it was here.'

'I think so also.'

'We turn?'

'Let's turn,' Lena said.

'I'm sure it was here.'

'It has to be here.'

'What other place?' Vasily said.

'No other place,' Lena agreed.

They turned off the main road. They didn't get more than several hundred metres when the van gave out. They stared at each other. They were silent, equally fearful. The snow was silent also. Slowly burying them.

Siberia stretched as only Siberia can, unrestrained and uncaring, across one-twelfth of the land mass of the earth, the greatest space, the vastest void, unrelentingly severe, almost as if some frozen desolation from the recesses of space had by mistake been dropped onto the surface of an unsuspecting world. It is difficult to conceive how big it is. If you were to randomly travel the world, every twelfth step you took, that would be a Siberian one. Imagine. And in this void, in this overwhelming white emptiness, two specks painfully moved, a man and a woman, together. They sought shelter, and thus life. They were almost at the end.

Of course they'd both tried their phones. But there was no signal. Maybe it was the snow, obliterating everything. They lost their sense of direction. The wind now got up, severe, swirling, Siberian, and if it wasn't for their feet being below them, they would not have known up from down.

It was a white-out. Visibility was nearly zero. The engine had given up in the van. They would freeze to death in there. They had to keep moving, find habitation, help, life. But the wind was blowing them over. When they got up, it blew them left and right. It became impossible to know whether they were retracing their steps, going around in circles, going anywhere at all. Vasily no longer had any idea where the van was. They were dying.

The blizzard blew Lena over, then blew over her, almost imme-diately burying her. A hand reached out from the instant shroud of snow, Vasily reached down, clasped it. She used Vasily's upright frame to haul herself up. She clung to him. 'I'm sorry. I'm sorry, Vasily,' she shouted above the gale. 'I do this to you.'

'You do nothing,' he said.

'No, listen. If we don't find the road,' she said, 'I'm sorry I do this to you.'

Then suddenly they saw some trees. A screen of trees.

'The lights,' Vasily said, 'they were by trees. Lena,' he said, trying to wipe the driving snow from his eyes, hoping it wasn't some cruel kind of sub-zero mirage. He screwed up his eyes, against the wind, against the snow. There were some rocks, a small outcrop where they were. He climbed on one for a better view. Yes. There were trees. He was sure this was where the little cluster of buildings was. 'Lena,' he said, 'the *trees*.'

He turned, elated. Joy pumping through his heart. Suddenly he didn't feel the cold. 'Trees, Lena, *trees*,' he shouted.

When he turned, Lena was gone. He didn't see her at first. What he saw was the snow: how it flushed crimson. Blood spread out in crystal tentacles, a red tracery through the whiteness in every direction, from a single point – the back of Lena's skull.

Her body was horribly contorted, a gentle but unnatural curve the wrong way, like the brow of a distant hill, like the shape of the Urals themselves from a long way off. He rushed to her, lifted her head, causing a greater gush of blood. He put his hand over it. Her warm blood seeping out of her, onto him.

'My legs,' she said. 'Where are my legs?'

She had lost all feeling in them. He feared then that she had broken her back. She'd fallen backwards on a rock.

When I returned to London I found out from a friend who is a medical consultant that the higher up the back that injury occurs the more severe the consequences of the fracture. Damaging the vertebrae at the top of our spine – C1 to C4 – and the associated nerve roots can cause paralysis of the limbs. In Lena's case, it was her legs. On the Siberian rock she had dashed her head and caused crushing trauma to her upper back. Medically, it might have been diagnosed as paraplegia caused by traumatic injury to the spinal cord and cervical nerves. But such textbook definitions mean little. The reality was Lena was paralysed, immobile – trapped in the snow.

FOURTEEN

A Year in the Life

The ground was frozen too hard for Vasily to bury Lena. So the young woman from the vast inner grasslands of Central Asia would not have a proper grave. But Vasily did what he could.

At first he was going to put a cross made from two sticks tied with a bootlace, but then he thought, no, she is Muslim. Using his remaining reserves of energy, he dragged a foliage-covered branch from the treeline and covered her with it. At her head, he put a stick, the straightest stick he could find. He jammed it in hard, pointing straight up into the sky. He wanted to put something to mark the place, to say here was a person, here was someone. He didn't know what else to do. He stood there in silence.

It was only months later that he realised what he really wished he'd done.

'I wish before I cover her face with snow,' he told me, 'I wish I say those words she said to me.'

'What words?' I asked.

'You know what they say to her that time.'

'What time?'

'How that man, when she was born, he says in her ear, "Lena, Lena, Leh-na." I wish I said that.'

Vasily set off again for the lights. But they had disappeared. Had he just imagined them? He staggered on. Past the trees. Through the snow. To where he imagined the lights to be. As his strength failed, he wished he was back with Lena. If this was how it would end, he wished it was not alone. He did not know where he was or what he was doing, only that he was near his death. The snow smoked in front of him, rose as well as fell. He waded more and more slowly through the mounting Siberian drift. His body was closing down, just as his mind was opening up. He thought about his father, sitting in his fake leopard-print chair, gazing at the spot where the street dog had died. He tried not to think of Kolya. It was too painful to think of Kolya. He thought of his father and the chair, and the print of the road, behind the glass, always behind the glass. If only he could find the road. He sprawled on his four limbs in the snow.

He was no longer falling through the clouds. The clouds had all fallen.

When he woke up, all he saw were glasses. Thick, old-fashioned glasses. Peering at him, the eyes behind them moving slowly, over his face. He tried to get up. Something – the glasses barely shifted position – held him down.

'You must not move,' the glasses said. 'You almost died.'

He sank back into a kind of oblivion.

When he woke the next time, there was no one else in the room.

Vasily dragged his weakened body out of bed and hauled himself up to the window, his fingertips clutching the sill like a man clinging to a raft. He looked out of the window for Lena. He would later learn that he had drifted in and out of consciousness for nearly two days. The blizzard had reduced everything to a white void: the world wiped out, a pitiless sameness. After the terrible storm, he would have as little idea where Lena lay as trying to find a single pebble on a beach that stretched in every direction to the distant horizon.

He collapsed again.

The next thing he was aware of was voices from another room – there must be another room beyond the door on which hung a tatty pink dressing gown with little white flowers. There were voices, not women's voices, several of them, speaking to the same person. They began to resolve themselves into a talk radio station or maybe a TV channel. He couldn't be sure, the voices were too low. But they were arguing. What were they arguing about? Life is so short, he realised, so precarious, at any moment liable to be covered up and forgotten, so what on earth were they arguing about? Didn't they know? Didn't they realise – did no one under-stand apart from him?

He became aware of the glasses again. Not for long. Who was she? Was she even real, his rescuer? If he'd been asked to describe her – *identify* her – all he could relate would be the glasses. Or maybe, he thought, this is what it is like once you have died. People constantly arguing and someone watching you.

He sank back into the emptiness of his mind. Another kind of white-out.

When he awoke next, it was because he was being gently shaken out of sleep. This was different. The sky, such as was visible through the little postcard of the high window, had changed colour and was now brilliant blue. The weather was improving. Was he?

The white inferno had passed, leaving him behind, taking Lena. He was being shaken, gently, but shaken. There were no glasses. He almost missed the glasses. He tightened his neck muscles, turned his head, tilted up his eyes and looked into the face of Z.

Vasily tried to leap out of the bed. He felt a sharp tearing as his muscles and joints met resistance. His feet were tied to the bed. His hands also. Thick coils of rope snaked around his wrists and ankles, biting the skin when he moved.

'Tell us where the girl is,' Z said.

Behind him were two other men. One of them had a gun.

Vasily stared back at them, silently.

'Tell us where she is,' Z said, 'and we let you go.'

Vasily said to them, 'I will never tell you.'

One of the traffickers got out his gun, a heavy Glock. He pointed it at Vasily's face. Then Z nodded imperceptibly, a minute flickering of the eyes. The man raised the weapon high and smashed it down on Vasily's head.

Today, there is still a slight indentation in his skull where the butt of the Glock struck him. He wears it like some kind of badge, and a memory.

The next time Vasily was conscious, he found himself in the back of a van. He was tied with his hands behind his back, his feet wrapped tightly together with some kind of tape. He felt like a fish.

Z was on the seat that ran along the length of the rear of the vehicle. He looked down at Vasily. The van was moving, fast. Vasily could hear other vehicles. A motorway, perhaps.

'We found the girl,' Z said. 'Your stupid stick. It shows us where. You *care*. It makes my heart bleed.'

Vasily was silent.

'But how do we find you? That's what you don't know. You can drive anywhere in Russia, Siberia, Kazakhstan, and we find you.' He moved his eyes close to Vasily's face. 'That's what you want to know, isn't it? How.'

Vasily remained silent. But he did want to know. Maybe there was a flicker in his eyes.

'Ah, yes,' Z said, nodding. 'How? How did I make this miracle?'

Vasily thought he knew. But he wanted it spelled out. He wanted to know it was not his fault.

'When they find you,' Z said, 'you have your phone. Of course, you have blocked me. I ring you and ring you. No luck. But you don't clean your history. All those calls between us. So the people . . .' Vasily's rescuers . . . 'They call me, they're worried. They think you're dying. And I'm so worried too. So happy. They found my brother. Please take care of my brother. I will come. I will pay you well to save my brother.' Z paused, relishing his good fortune, Vasily's opposite. 'You know how people are when you pay them well. So now you wonder where you are going.' Z paused and looked towards the front of the vehicle, the wind-screen. 'A terrible place. And you wonder what is the future. A terrible life. I could kill you. But this will be worse. I want what is worse.'

There was another pause.

'And still you say nothing,' Z said. 'That is good. I don't want your questions. Either you do this for a year, to pay me back, and then we have no debt, nothing any more between us. Or you run. You can run. But if we hear you run, then we will spend time finding you. And you will live all your life wondering if I find you. You can choose either one of these. Which, I don't care. Really. I do not.'

For a long time Vasily was silent, until finally he could contain himself no more. He said, 'You know, I'm thinking just how big a man you are. So important, so very big. Because it take a big, big man to get these girls, to sell their bodies, to take the money. What a big, big man.'

Z laughed. 'That is how you think? You think we have come *all* this way, drive from Moscow to that shithole in Siberia – why? Just so we can make money selling them? That's what you think?'

'No, you're going to give them nice jobs in Moscow,' Vasily said.

Z laughed again. 'You understand nothing. Really – that's what you think – we come all this way to sell them?'

'Then what?'

'You understand so fucking little, huh?'

'*What?*' Vasily said more angrily. 'Then what?'

'We do all this, we come all this way, to see whether, these girls, any single one of them, are even *worth* selling.'

Vasily told me that he was silent. Outside vehicles rumbled along, racing he knew not where. He was sick to his stomach in a way he could not remember ever being before.

Z continued, 'Most of them, these girls you think *so* much about, most of them, they are worthless. They are most of them nothing. Don't you understand, there are thousands, millions, just like that and they are nothing. Sometimes, men, yes, they will pay some dollars for them, but they are still nothing – and you who care so much for them, you are less than nothing.'

Vasily wanted to scream. He wanted to kill Z. He stayed utterly silent.

'No? I am wrong, you think?' Z said. 'Think who really killed her – me or you? Now you tell me, huh, you tell me, who is the big man?' Z kicked him a sickening blow to the face – no, it was more of a stamp that gashed his cheek, but not deeply.

'I've sold you,' Z said.

Sold.

'One year. You work for one year. Real terrible work. One year. Then is over. You can make a big thing, go to the police, your choice. You see what happens when you do. No one cares about people like us.'

Us.

He worked 14 or 16 hours a day, usually seven days a week. Back-breaking labour. First he had to work to pay off his 'travel costs' to the place. Then ongoing payment for board and the pitiful food. It seemed impossible to clear the debt. He understood the game. But in a sense he was working to pay off another debt, one of his own. For what had happened to Lena. For his own kind of penance.

He had been taken to the Caucasus, the southern reaches of Russia between the Black Sea and the Caspian. There he worked in all but name as a slave labourer, first in construction, then as the weather improved in farming down towards Azerbaijan and Dagestan, a mainly Muslim republic of Russia, where there were Dargins, Avars, Kumyks, Lezgins and Chechens.

A few years previously, in 1999, Russia invaded neighbouring Chechnya after the Islamic International Brigade made a military incursion into Dagestan from its Chechen bases. 'You know in this part of Dagestan, they think Russians like me,' Vasily said, 'we are the enemy. They treat me like I am captured enemy.' Other workers were from various ex-Soviet Central Asian republics, with many from Uzbekistan, duped by so-called 'employment agencies'.

They were enslaved in another way. He told me how once one of his co-workers in Dagestan tried to escape. 'This Uzbek,' he said. 'They catch him and bring him in front of all the workers. They almost beat him to death. That,' Vasily said to me, 'is how it goes.'

So Vasily was a labourer, like his great ancestor who rebuilt Moscow. Vasily ended up at Volgograd, formerly Stalingrad. Buildings were soaring skyward everywhere. No one much asked who was building them, the conditions they worked in, how they were used, abused. And then, suddenly, it was over. One year had passed. He was free. No one owned him. It was little consolation. He barely wanted to own what little was left of himself. It was like being in Archangel constantly: awake and asleep at the same time.

What he did want was to get out of Russia. Once more, he stared at the road, just like he'd done as a boy standing on the leopard-print chair, gazing into his father's picture. Where would it go now? The nearest border was 100 miles away. It was Kazakhstan.

My time was running out with Vasily.

'So,' I asked him, 'did you go to Kazakhstan because of Lena?'

He pursed his lips. 'I would never even think of this place, not if I don't meet Lena,' he said.

My exchange with Marzhan near the sand dunes had kept eating away at me. 'A Kazakh friend of mine,' I said, 'she said it was a bit strange, that Lena's father cut her off —'

'Cut off?'

'Said she was no longer his daughter, because she left for Almaty. She said many young women leave the villages, the rural areas, for Almaty and Astana.' I kept telling myself I was not cross-examining a witness. But I did want to get to the truth.

Vasily was silent.

'Did Lena say anything about that?'

He instinctively ran his hand over his tightly cropped hair, where the dent is. He looked down as he spoke. What was he looking at? What did he see? 'In the van, when we are driving, we are talking, talking. Talking about everything. And she says that they were in Uzbekistan.'

'Uzbekistan?' I said.

Vasily looked up, his eyes wide and pained. 'She did not tell me everything. There was not enough time. The snow it comes, we leave the van.'

'She was an Uzbek?' I said.

'Kazakh,' he said emphatically, '*Ka-ʒakh*. But maybe they had family in Uzbekistan. I'm not sure. She had been to both. I'm not 100 per cent.'

Later I found out that there is a significant Kazakh population in Uzbekistan, the next country to the south. Marzhan had family in Tajikistan. Kazakhs were everywhere.

'It might explain why her father was so angry,' I said. 'If she is going to Almaty, to another country.'

'This I don't know,' Vasily says. 'She was telling me all this when the snow, it becomes so bad . . .'

That they abandoned the van. He didn't finish the sentence.

'What was her full name?' I asked.

'She never say.'

'What about her passport?'

'Her papers, they were in van. Z takes the van.'

I was desperately trying to put it together. Trying to do what — find the real Lena? 'So when she said she didn't want to go back to Kazakhstan, maybe it wasn't her home. Maybe . . .'

'I not sure I have everything right,' Vasily said. 'This is what I remember. I did not tell you about Uzbekistan because I do not know for sure. I'm sorry, I don't know for sure.'

'It's all right,' I told him. 'Vasily, really, it is all right.'

It had been a long session. Vasily was exhausted. I had pages and pages of scribbled notes. A documenting, of two people's lives, how they came together and parted. One from the country to the north of Kazakhstan and the other from the country to its south – perhaps. Or maybe from Kazakhstan itself – it was impossible to say. We stepped out into the Almaty street with all this racing through my mind. A police siren screeched unseen nearby.

'And Kolya?' I said. 'What happened to Kolya?'

'Next time,' he said. 'Now too tired. Next time.'

I nodded, but despite it still being summer and gloriously warm in Kazakhstan, I was thinking of the Siberian snow, seeing it slowly falling, covering a young woman's face, and I was thinking: Lena, who *were* you?

FIFTEEN

Take the Weather with You

At our last meeting Vasily was beside himself with excitement. It was the only time he arrived at any of our meeting places before me. It was where we'd first met – where I'd met not-Oleg – in the park. It was late afternoon. He had brought his 'little one' with him.

The object of his affections was tan and had a long curly tail and a pointed snout and was thin and elegant. It could not have been more different from Kolya. Still, he was very proud of her. She had been ill but now seemed to be recovering. I bent down to stroke her as the odd leaf tumbled across the grass in the breeze coming off the mountain. The dog's sleek coat was warm in the late afternoon summer sun. Rescue is not only about outcome; it is also about our reasons for intervening, also about reprieve.

'They say,' Vasily said, 'sometimes, these girls, they fly to USA and Rome. They have a lot of money and clothes.'

'They are flown. They are made to fly,' I said. 'Vasily, they are not free.'

He bent down next to me to pat the dog's haunches. She liked him boisterously ruffling her coat – the rougher the better – and I joined in, the young dog in bliss with all the attention. And under the celestial gaze of the slowly rising Tien Shan, the snowfields of which were turning pink with the setting sun, the young dog's long tail slowly thumped the Almaty grass. Finally, Vasily told me about Kolya.

He never saw him again. Not after he left for Siberia.

When he did not return from the trip to Novosibirsk, the people who were looking after him were approached by mutual acquaintances – someone who knew both Vasily and Z. They took Kolya. No one knows what happened to Kolya after that. When he spoke to me about his beloved Little Czar, sometimes it was as if, and despite the differences in gender and generation, Kolya and Laika had merged the one into the other. In different ways both had suddenly disappeared without trace somewhere in the ether and no one much knew where.

There are several explanations for where the term Kazakh comes from. Kazakhs are Turkic people, and one theory is that Kazakh originates in the Turkish word *qaʒ* – it means to wander.

Lena's wanderings took her from the steppe (whether in Kazakhstan or Uzbekistan or possibly both) to the city to Siberia to her death. Why did she do it? Because, I think, she wanted to know about the world. I have written all this, chosen this story out of several other candidates for the chapter on the Rescuer, because I want the world to know something about how young women like her are treated.

All this happened more than a decade ago, and when you research the grim machinations of human trafficking, you see that there are tens of thousands of vulnerable young women like Lena teetering on the cusp of disaster at this very moment. Therefore there are many Lenas. And of course there is only one.

Where are they? Which places do they inhabit?

This chapter has journeyed from Kazakhstan to Siberia to Dagestan and back. But there is another country it has travelled. It is a country that has no borders and no anthem. It has no language, and almost every one of them. It has no government, but operates by its own laws. Armies cannot defeat it. Police forces fail to stop it, and are sometimes part of it. This place has one common currency: the systematic exploitation of fellow human beings.

Through its secret trails and tributaries flow people, like water through a pipe. It now has a higher turnover than the arms trade and only stands behind drugs as the most lucrative transnational crime in the world. It is easy to visit this place. You simply need to go to one of our towns and turn left instead of right; enter a side street you wouldn't normally enter; climb a staircase you wouldn't normally climb. Make a call to a number you wouldn't normally call. You'll find an encyclopedia of its telephone numbers on the Internet, just waiting. And into this other country, this part of the province of human trafficking, Lena was slowly drawn. Until Vasily spoke to her in a Siberian café. Why did he risk his life by doing that?

The picture that emerges from the research science is that the brain processes that are involved in cooperative behaviour and helping others overlap with fundamental neural building blocks.

They engage networks that are used for learning, reward and punishment.

This scientific picture illuminated by neural imaging demonstrates how in important respects some of the pivotal assumptions of economic theory, predicated on the rational self-interested individual, do not reflect what is actually found, how our brains actually work.

Cosmides and Tooby, pioneers in the development of evolutionary psychology, argue that so pervasive and reliably recurring is the evidence of conditional helping, that the simplest explanation, the most parsimonious, is the true one: that there is a computational adaptation that has evolved within human beings over evolutionary time. It is directed at one of our fundamental life puzzles: how to deal with, cooperate and socially exchange with other members of our species. As the Emory University team reminds us, 'Cooperative social interactions with non-kin are pervasive in all human societies.'

From the time that hunter-gatherer groups expanded beyond narrow kinship clusters, having to cooperate with non-kin conspecifics is likely to have been one of the major puzzles our ancestors have had to solve. The solution, Cosmides and Tooby maintain, is a specific evolutionary adaptation, a mechanism in our mind, that facilitates our social interaction.

It crosses cultures and time, seas and centuries.

These neural networks are about more than behaviour that is solely for our own benefit. They reward us for cooperative behaviour. For helping others. Giving up something valuable to oneself to help someone else actually makes us feel good. It is not an illusion. It is not the pernicious posturing of our deeply buried egoism, only fulfilled if we are also secret beneficiaries. This part of our brain – this one of our many selves – is, Cosmides and Tooby claim, 'one component of a complex and universal human nature'.

It is part of who we are. Or rather, a demonstrable part of who we have evolved to be.

Let's return to where we started. To Susan.

What did you want to do? Were you genuinely considering swapping places with her and taking some of the shocks? I suspect that you might have been.

If so, you would be among the majority of human beings who would. Recall that over 80 per cent of the Kansas volunteers were prepared to swap places, even where 'escape' (walking away and washing one's hands) was easy. We must recognise that part of the impulse to help is to relieve the distress we feel at the prospect of witnessing the suffering of another human being. That much is clear. But there is, as the Batson team forcefully argues, more to it than that.

Neuroscience has confirmed that when we act in a way beyond our narrow self-interest the neural reward systems of our brain are activated. Even though we might receive some low-level but distinctly unpleasant electrical shocks, our brain would reward us for sacrificing ourselves for Susan.

If these systems have evolved, they are likely to provide some survival benefit. It may be that they promote our social interaction with others beyond the narrow circle of our kith and kin. That social impulse is one we do not always acknowledge or valorise. Indeed, we know from the charity-giving study, that we are more inclined to be charitable if we believe our act is more akin to an exchange and dressed up as not purely altruistic. That is interesting. We want to tell ourselves that we are acting out of our own self-interest even when we are not. We are more comfortable with that. Even when we are acting altruistically we prefer to cover it up with the fig leaf of a fictional exchange.

But then again, it *is* a kind of exchange. To return to Robert Trivers, whom I was fortunate enough to meet and speak with after a lecture in London, it is 'reciprocal'. Trivers wrote a groundbreaking paper in the early seventies entitled 'The Evolution of Reciprocal Altruism'. It proved to be one of the most influential papers in the development of evolutionary biology and the understanding of human behaviour.

Trivers wrote, 'One human being saving another, who is not closely related and is about to drown, is an instance of altruism.' How and when might that behaviour – and it unquestionably is part of human behaviour – prove to be adaptive? How and why might it spread and survive in human society?

Trivers concluded that there may be circumstances in which our helping of non-related others may prove an adaptive choice. If there was a prospect of the gesture, the favour, the rescuing, being returned. If the trait spread and it became part of the social ecology. Of course, the risk is of a beneficiary not reciprocating – of cheating. Therefore, Trivers concluded, there was the evolution of sophisticated mechanisms to be alert and police and punish cheating:

> . . . natural selection will rapidly favour a complex psychological system in each individual regulating both his own altruistic and cheating tendencies and his response to these tendencies in others . . .

Cheating will be selected against if the costs of cheating have adverse consequences for the defector that outweigh the cost of taking the benefit and not repaying. If, for example, a cheater is frozen out, or is punished, scorned, shunned, isolated. If so, Trivers writes,

> The system that results should simultaneously allow the individual to reap the benefits of altruistic exchanges [and] to protect himself from gross and subtle forms of cheating,

All this is a long run-up to the wicket, as they say in cricket, to return to Vasily and Lena.

Vasily could see it before his eyes: Lena was drowning.

What should he do? It is likely that Vasily would have been more able to deal with his helping behaviour towards Lena if he disguised it as some kind of exchange – as in some sense in his own self-interest. But how, objectively viewed, was it? What was he going to get in exchange for risking his life and his future for Lena?

Holmes and his colleagues, who devised the charity 'exchange fiction' experiment, concluded that 'appearing too sociocentric can make one suspect'. We are suspicious of people who appear too good. We inevitably believe they are too good to be true. The deep irony of Vasily's life is that the person who viewed his actions with the deepest suspicion was himself. He did not believe he was a good person, or had any real good within him.

The choice Vasily had to make was not an easy one. People might scoff that choosing between a human being and a dog was a simple matter. He didn't really know Lena. He'd only just met her. In evolutionary theoretical terms she was non-kin, unrelated, the kind of person we are slower to help. On the other hand, I have no doubt whatsoever that Vasily *loved* Kolya.

The bonds between man and dog reach back far into our ancestral past. If we think about the incipient canid, the early dog from the Siberian cave 33,000 years ago, we begin to grasp the sheer extent of our shared lives with dogs, and our deep attachment to them. Put another way, because it is difficult to envisage how long a period this is, think of all the centuries we would have to travel across to reach the birth of Jesus Christ and the stabbing of Julius Caesar. Think of that vast track of time. And then multiply it by 15 or 16. That's how long ago the Razboinichya dog was with us.

Or to put it another way still: at the time of the Razboinichya dog, we still shared the planet with other kinds of humans – Neanderthals. So Vasily's dilemma about whether to risk himself and Kolya for this young woman he had only just met contained a degree of complexity that might not at first be apparent.

For his choice he suffered terribly. And he continues to feel the pain today. What happened in the Siberian snow when Lena died has not left him. He carries it around with him. Wherever he goes it is unmistakably there, like the Tien Shan with their never-melting snowfields high above Almaty.

And so what is the lesson of the Rescuer? It seems that we are very likely to have evolved very complex executive systems that sensitise us to intervening to help others. The latter arrangement would be adaptive in the sense that natural selection would select it over situations where individuals are invariably inveterate cheats. Such a system would be unstable and would crash and burn. But the 'rescuing' behaviour is likely to have developed not out of pure, unmitigated altruism in the sense of Zen-like selflessness, but from a subtler reality that helping with the genuine prospect of being helped at a later point, when we need it, is simply a better system. It is likely to be more evolutionarily successful. On average, more of our genes are likely to get through. Reciprocal altruism can work.

Therefore if we as a species are capable of producing Zs, we also have the Vasily within us – troubled and tormented, admittedly; imperfect and inconsistent, without doubt; but capable it seems, on the evidence, both scientific and personal, of risking ourselves for someone else. Such human behaviour is not a mask or disguise for pure self-interest. In fact it is the claim that we are *only* capable of acting in service of our best interests that is misleading. It is more complex than that.

An impulse within us wants to relieve the suffering of others, whether of fictional creations devoid of real flesh and blood like Susan; whether of someone we've never met before and who is only playing a role like Elaine, or someone we are unrelated to and may never see again like Lena; or whether it is another animal being maltreated which actually belongs to someone else, like Z's dog Kolya. I think this is good to know.

I do not think that the fact such a system or sentiment has evolved because of an overall evolutionary benefit devalues it. On the contrary, we can with confidence refute those who say life is a merciless war of all against all with everyone just in it for themselves. The science is increasingly not supporting that. We are social beings; we can show compassion; we can sacrifice ourselves for others.

I once asked Vasily if what he did – I approached it obliquely, given the sensitivity of the topic – could have been motivated by an attraction to Lena. His response was, 'She was not the kind of girl I like.' He paused, added, 'She *is* the kind of person I like.' But human motivation is complex, and as the law and psychology tell us, motives can be mixed. But I believed Vasily. Their story seemed to me to be greater – *grander* – than sexual attraction.

As to Lena's story, I recognise that it would be nice to have neat narratives. It would be nice for us to have neat lives. I am conscious of the gaps in the information I have provided you with. There are several important informational holes. And yet we try and make do. One of the biggest holes, it seems to me, lies somewhere within Vasily. In the part in which he thinks, and thinks badly, of himself. The riddle of the Rescuer lies somewhere near the heart of the human mystery. The unfolding solution to it affords us the opportunity to see ourselves differently, as *better* than we usually believe that we are. I wish Vasily could understand that. But nonetheless I think that through him, at the very end, Lena – whoever she was – did.

The total number of people who are at this moment victims of human trafficking or modern-day slavery is not precisely known. For obvious reasons, it can't be. The official estimates from international agencies such as the United Nations and the International Labour Organisation range from 20 to 30 million people – 20 to 30 million modern-day slaves. It is generally agreed that there are more slaves in the world than at any time in history. It happens, as the UN's Office on Drugs and Crime states, everywhere. Statistically, it is happening near you.

Part of this is our burgeoning population. But also trafficking in persons is a highly lucrative, relatively low-cost, low-risk alternative to other illegal activities for crime organisations. It feeds on social instability, economic turbulence, chaos. We've had plenty of all of this in the last two decades.

The US State Department estimated in 2009 that each year something like 600,000 to 1 million *more* people are trafficked across borders to join the ranks of those who are already living in forced servitude and slavery. Today it is likely to be closer to a million more slaves annually. Lena was to be one of them.

In some ways she was typical: the majority of human trafficking is across at least one national border; between 70 to 80 per cent is for sexual exploitation; almost every one of those victims of sex trafficking is a woman or child. In international law trafficking means being subjected to coercion, force or fraud for the purposes

671

of commercial sexual exploitation or forced labour or similar kinds of servitude. It is about exploiting the vulnerable, about power and profit.

For reasons you now know, Lena was particularly vulnerable when Darya entered her life in Almaty. Traffickers prey on this kind of isolation, insecurity and fragility. With Lena the trafficking started off with fraud: she was deceived by Darya and then Z. No doubt, if Vasily had not intervened, her exploitation would have continued in Moscow with coercion and force. That is highly characteristic of sexual exploitation, which invariably entails the controlling and breaking of young women.

The UN has identified over 500 trafficking flow routes around the world. One of these exploitation superhighways runs from the former Soviet Central Asian Republics – the Stans – up into Russia, where victims are exploited or moved on – sometimes through a trafficking 'hub' like the Baltic states (Lithuania, Latvia, Estonia) – possibly to Western Europe. Lena may not have remained in Moscow. She may have ended up in a city like Frankfurt, Paris or London, this young woman from the Central Asian steppe who dreamed of seeing what was on the other side of the mountain. Such is the global nature of this form of exploitation – why it is an issue for all of us.

Every year thousands of young women or girls who have been trafficked for sexual exploitation die from neglect, or are used up by disease or are killed. Many just disappear. Like Lena.

In his book on modern-day slavery *A Crime So Monstrous*, Benjamin Skinner estimates the annual deaths at 30,000. But we don't actually know. This has been the story of one of the disappeared.

'I'm not a hero,' Vasily once told me. He is right. To rescue is not necessarily to be heroic. It is to be, in an overlooked and underappreciated way, human. Vasily chose to help Lena; when it came down to it, he did not falter; he chose, I like to think, for us.

William Faulkner tells us that thing about the past is that it's not even past, and so Vasily continues to travel with it, a white plastic bottle of feverfew capsules in his pocket. The Rescuer on that road his father guarded, where even at the height of the Central Asian summer, he takes that same weather with him: the Siberian snow, in which he lost not just a year of his life, and a squat dog from Moscow called Kolya, but a young Kazakh woman whose name was Lena.

Man and Dog
Cave art, Altamira, Spain

PART X

AGAIN CAME THE KINSMAN

There is a great deal of unmapped country
within us which would have to be taken
into account in an explanation of our
gusts and storms.

George Eliot, *Daniel Deronda* (1876)

ONE

The Wolves

How quickly our lives turn.

It doesn't take long. All it takes is a text.

Like the character in the hypothetical in the Preface to the book – the parent who ventured into the school corridor with the gunman – I was waiting, filling in time, wasting it as we all do casually glancing at my mobile screen, emails, tweets, texts.

It was a recess in a murder trial. I was doing my other job, as barrister, and the case had been going well (in the circumstances), our case theory winning the day, opposition witnesses crumbling, being exposed as liars. It was looking good. One of those (all too rare) times when the legal momentum has tangibly turned and the tide is running in your direction. I was sitting with my junior Sadiq, an enthusiastic young Asian barrister from the north. We'd brainstormed and laboured for months in pre-trial prep for just this. All was good. I was a long way from home, but still all was good – when the flurry of messages appeared on my mobile.

Coming out of court, I'd switched it on and there they were: message after message after message.

Ring me.
RING asap.
Pls ring immed.

Something had happened. I rang. I was told, as people always are in such situations, to do the impossible: 'Try not to worry, but your daughter has been involved in an accident.' I disobeyed; I · failed to follow the instructions. I did worry. And in that moment, everything changed. It didn't take long.

Sadiq was in the middle of a blow-by-blow retelling of a crunch concession we'd extracted from a key opposition witness when I got the first message. Later Sad told me how suddenly, unnervingly, when he looked up, it was a different person standing in front of him.

Even as the chaos was unfurling around me, one part of my mind was somehow analysing what was actually taking place. I ask for no credit and deserve none: it was almost certainly displacement behaviour, trying to intellectualise the situation, anaesthetise myself from it in those first few raw moments when nothing seems real.

During the preceding weeks of the murder trial, my headspace – what Harvard economics professor Sendhil Mullainathan calls 'bandwidth' – had been completely taken over, used up, by the most minuscule details of the case evidence. During a trial you live it, breathe it. It is your reality for those days and weeks. Everything else recedes. And then instantaneously it is overrun. By what on this occasion? By, I think, the Kinsman.

Suddenly it was impossible for more than a few seconds for me not to think of my daughter lying in a hospital trauma unit being fed morphine. Biology beat the Bar.

This wasn't supposed to happen. This wasn't what parenthood promised. I went to see the judge in private immediately. As it happens, he was in private session with an undercover police officer and the prosecution Queen's Counsel. Our forensic triumphs in court had opened up a whole series of important questions. There was sensitive information – police intelligence – the prosecution had to share with the judge. I had to intrude upon this.

I explained the situation. 'Go, go,' he said. 'Why are you still here?' I set off immediately for the other end of the country. Several hundred miles away my daughter lay in an emergency ward. She was born in our home, came in a glorious rush. So we didn't have to go to the hospital. And now we did. This wasn't what parenthood promised. I realised I was still wearing my court wig. It is convention when you enter the judge's private chambers to take it off when the judge is not wearing his. For the only time in my career, I forgot.

I'd spent a significant part of the previous weeks of the trial accusing the investigating police officers of lying. As I sped towards the south-west on the overnight train, they sent their best wishes via Sadiq. Everyone was brilliant. Everyone got it. Everyone understood.

What did they understand? What can we?

What happened in an accident on a country lane in the south of England, while I was cross-examining in a murder trial in an industrial city in the north, triggered the Kinsman. Again it came.

When I began writing this book, all that time ago, sitting on my 14th-floor perch high above Harvard, I never imagined that the Kinsman would have entered my life with such ferocity. It is,

I know you'll understand, a dismaying sight to see one's child in an A&E bed with a morphine drip to control her pain and metal rods to force straight her shattered leg. Around her, aside from the unnerving purr of machines and monitors, silence. For those few fraught days, that became my world, and all of the world I could imagine being part of.

Which leads me back to the school corridor. And the gunman. When I wrote the book's Prologue, the first hypothetical, it was the one-year anniversary of Sandy Hook. More or less. Since then there has been atrocity after atrocity, shooting after shooting. The gunman isn't just in our head, he is stalking America with his weapons. I sit on an irritatingly squashy blue sofa in a hospital an ocean away to write this on my MacBook, trying to fill my head with something other than the thought of my daughter in the operating theatre five floors below.

We are surrounded by other children, sick, injured, in pain, but I can more or less – shockingly enough – zone them out. It is like when I spoke to Roz, one of the inconceivably kind nurses on the first evening, when I was more alive to the deluge of images and impressions around me and hadn't learned how to screen them. I asked her how she coped with so much distress, so many children in pain.

'Yes, people often ask us that. And it's not easy,' Roz said, 'but then again it is, isn't it?'

'It *is*?' I said. 'Easy – really?'

'They're not my children, are they? I do a 12-hour overnighter, I have to try to soothe children in so much pain, and sometimes I just can't, and it's terrible, and I want to cry. Sometimes, even after all these years, I want to, and then . . . then I go home. The shift is over. Your shift,' she said, looking at me, 'it doesn't really end, does it?'

Part of that shift was for me to watch endless movies with my daughter as she tried to distract herself from the pain, the thought of the imminent operation. We watched the film *Juno*, about a feisty teenager, only five years older than my daughter, who gets pregnant. Terrifying. It had a brilliant soundtrack. We sang one of the catchy nursery rhyme-like songs together. The other part of my shift was to join the porter and nurses to wheel the state-of-the-art electric bed through linoleum-smooth corridors, all the way from the children's ward to the operating theatre. In the OT's antechamber the anaesthetic is fed into her body. I have to put on a blue surgical gown and a plastic cap. I'm told I look silly. I'm glad I look silly. It's the best thing I can do. I want to excel in silliness. I look into her eyes and she into mine. I'd prepared a dozen things to talk to her about to distract her, but I can't remember any of them when she asks, 'Dad, what's happening?'

I'm just about to tell her I'm still here, let her know she's not alone, when somewhere in her bloodstream the chemicals drag her away from me and her eyes flicker, shut.

'It's all right,' the anaesthetist tells me, 'she's gone.'

Suddenly I'm out in the corridor. I'm the one alone. What is happening to my daughter behind those closed doors? The sheer terror of it is something that perhaps only a parent who has seen their child go in for major surgery can imagine. I walk along the smooth corridors barely making a sound. Everything mixes up in my head, as if I've inadvertently absorbed some of the anaesthetic: this corridor, the school corridor with the gunman, Gareth – constantly walking in silence down that corridor of his own.

My thoughts drift to the last time I was so abjectly terrified: when she came. How one minute she was where she'd been safely ensconced for nine months, and then suddenly she was arriving, so quickly that all plans went out the window, no time to even

681

get out of the front door to leave for the hospital – no time to even get down the stairs. She was born in the bath at home. I continue my dazed walking down the corridor and think that's how life can sometimes come, can't it, in a rush. I console myself with how we coped, which is to say she had, and how if we got through that, we could get through this, which is to say she could. I think again and again of that song from *Juno*: Velvet Underground's 'I'm Sticking With You'. Think of it as I walk away from her.

The operation goes on and cruelly on. The two hours they told us it would take becomes four – then more. I'm still sitting on the horrid squashy sofa. I think of her first faltering steps (she wasn't an early walker), but then how she seamlessly took to gliding elegantly on her scooter – I'm showing off, you understand – and now the bone in her leg is crushed. Still no news from the operating theatre. On and on. I return again to that school corridor, and now know more than ever what I would do if that gunman was stalking. I reassess what my personal number would be, how many others I would let go to save just this one. I take my daughter to the operating theatre, see her eyes flicker and close, and know that my number goes up.

I try to feel the neural pathways in my head performing these tasks, the biology of the brain, the firing of electrical signals, little scintillating sparks of thought. Why has evolution selected for this? What has it shaped us for?

For survival, for our genes. Those things we cannot see that are simultaneously us and something other than us, that will go on, that will progress, proceed, when we are gone, as they always have, and as they always will, in the long chain of being, reaching out in two directions at once, with us, here temporarily, so fleetingly, at the fulcrum, before our genes are passed on and we are passed over.

In the quiet corners of the children's ward you see them. In pairs, usually. Parents, often not even talking, just holding each other, trying to get through the pain that is not theirs, but at the same time is. Often they are joined by family, by kin. Sometimes by friends, but mainly it is family, mainly it is kin – that gene thing.

We gather around the coffee station – the hospital thoughtfully lays on unlimited tea and coffee – and smile at one another. We know what we share in common, how it feels. What we have in common is the Kinsman.

You remember Ubah. Anna's friend in Boston. I know you do. I said I'd return to her, and here we are.

'Yes, your Cadbury-dairy-milk-chocolate, that's the best,' she said. We were seated across from each other at a metal table on the concourse of Boston's South Station, among the scattering of chairs in front of Dunkin' Donuts.

'I never realised,' I replied.

'See. What I always say.'

'What?'

'Lawyers don't know anything.'

The station is downtown in the Leather District, near the water-front, across from the Children's Museum. Before I could respond, defend the honour of the profession, or decline to do so, she changed the subject. 'What colour shirt are you wearing?' It was just about the last question I was expecting at our first meeting.

'What – *this* shirt?' I said.

'One you're wearing.'

I'd bought it in a sale off Boston Common. Ridiculous reductions. 'Duck egg blue, I think.'

683

'Duck? You wear duck?' she said, 'Which duck?' and laughed, a hearty, exceptionally loud laugh. 'Once,' she said, 'I see so many ducks.'

'Really? Where?'

'When I went to Alaska.'

'*What!*' I cannot recall a recent time when I have been more surprised by something someone said. 'Alaska?' Then I add quickly, 'Why shouldn't you go to Alaska?'

Ubah, a striking woman from Africa, wears a bright blue and red headscarf. She has meticulously painted long crimson nails. There is a painting I saw by Picasso in one of the Harvard Art Museums. It is from his Blue Period, painted in 1901. It is simply called *Mother and Child*. I mention it because in Picasso's painting a woman is sitting with her back against a wall while she holds her child. Like Ubah she wears a headscarf; Ubah, like her, is wearing a luxurious gown of intensely iridescent blue. It struck me immediately when I saw Ubah: what she's wearing, it's something out of Picasso. It was so incongruous sitting there at Dunkin' Donuts. But still: what she was wearing, that deep, deep blue, *was* something out of Picasso.

We both had coffee. She'd got there first and bought me a latte – I don't drink coffee but nursed it. She also had a chocolate doughnut of some kind. She never ate it.

'An African in Alaska,' she said, laughing. 'I know, is funny, yes?'

'No,' I said.

'*Yes*,' she replied. 'But you didn't ask me why I went to Alaska.'

'Ubah,' I said, 'why did you go to Alaska?'

She looked around the concourse of Boston's throbbing terminus, at the people, the unrelenting bustle. 'You know,' she said, 'they hunt things in Alaska. Back home, my country, we hunt things too, so I was kind of understanding that. But up there, they hunt wolves. And I was speaking to this guy who hunts them and he says, you know, wolves, they are like children. You see their tracks in the snow and before you know it, they are gone. Children, wolves; there, gone. You know there is an African saying, it takes the village to bring up a child.'

'Yes.'

'Okay. But. It is because of the village that they do things to a child. Because of the village, these things they do, on and on.' She looked around the teeming station. 'Some villages, they're just bigger. But that's the thing with people. We're scared of what people in the village think. We do things we must know are wrong because of what people in the village think. And that makes humans dangerous. So the wolves, you see, that guy says, they avoid us. They know we are so dangerous animals, the most dangerous animals.'

She nervously adjusted her headscarf; her eyes darted around us. I should emphasise that the scarf Ubah was wearing was not for religious reasons. She no longer had any truck with that. She wore it because she did not want to be seen. For speaking about what you're about to read, she had received death threats. 'We're like wolves that go bad. And one day,' she said, 'the wolves, they can come for you. Or you go to them, and you don't know before that they are wolves. Both. Wolves, they do both.'

I was trying to keep up. 'Both things?'

But she introduced another. 'You like music?'

'Love it.'

'Then I have something for you.' Only she didn't say what it was. Then.

TWO

The Storm

Above us the Arrivals and Departures board clicks away quietly. A long queue for the train to Washington, DC snakes in front of us, people mostly in silence, waiting. Ubah's Amtrak to New York has not been called yet, but she is anxious, glancing up at the board.

'Is no *big* thing,' she says. 'We're all going to die. But they're not going to find me. Never find me. They won't stop me speaking up. Shouting up. For my sisters.'

'You have sisters?' I say.

'All women, my sisters.'

'Okay.'

For starting to speak out about what had happened to her, she had received death threats. She was ostracised and cast out and threatened.

'I do have a sister,' she says. 'She's a year older. And she was there, on the day it happened. This crazy, quiet day. All these people gathered in our house back home.' She mentions the place.

The capital of her country. I cannot name it. 'So they come and come, all these people, and I knew most of them. Family. But there were others I didn't. And it was crazy, weird because they took my sister and I into different rooms. She was the older girl. She goes first. And so I wait. I'm waiting there. And I'm thinking: good she goes first, good I'm younger. Usual – I hate, really *hate*, being the youngest. This is the first time I ever think I like it better I'm the younger. And then it's all silent. Silent, so silent. Then I hear her. I hear her screaming. And it makes me cry. I cry out her name. I run to the door. I try to open it. But I can't get out. And I don't understand because the door is not locked, but I can't open it. Then I understand – there's someone outside. They are *holding* the handle. So I can't get out. It's not locked. It's open, but I can't open it, you understand? And my sister is screaming. And then the screaming suddenly stops. Then is silent again. Then the door opens. And they come for me. And when I was in Alaska, the other end of the world to this place – that's why I went to Alaska, the other end of the world to this place – that's what I think, when I think about what happened that day, when they come to get me, in Alaska I finally understand: the wolves, they come for me.

'And they grab me, but that's not it, that's not fair, because it's not hard how they do it, like they're trying not to hurt me. And no one will look at me. Like they cannot, not one of them, look in my eyes. They take me. They drag me because my feet won't work. My legs won't work. They take me to the bedroom. It's my parents' bedroom. But they're not in the house. I don't see them. There's aunties. There's my grandmother. And I'm crying out for my mother. But she isn't there. And they put me on the bed. And I'm looking at the ceiling. And they hold my legs. And they hold my arms. And this big woman. She kneels on my chest.

Sitting on my chest. Big, heavy, sweaty woman, I never seen before. And she's got something. She has something in her hand. But I don't know what it is. What *is* this in her hand? And then I hear this screaming, and I'm thinking: they're cutting another girl. Which other girl – I've not seen another girl in the house. And then I realise: the screaming is me. Screaming, screaming, so loud. And the woman tells me, Be quiet now, eh? Be a good girl, eh? Do not disgrace your lovely family. Do you want to disgrace your lovely family, eh? Don't you want your presents? Don't you want to be a good girl? But I don't want to be a good girl. I don't want to be any girl. I just want the pain to stop.'

But it didn't stop. The pain did not stop in Ubah for years and never may. When she was genitally mutilated on behalf of her family, Ubah was six years old.

Robert Quinlan of Washington State University claims that two of the major decisions in life are (1) whether to reproduce and (2) how much a parent will invest in any offspring. These two fundamental decisions, he argues, are sensitive to what he calls 'environmental risk'.

To assess this phenomenon, he analysed the 'standard cross-cultural sample' (SCCS), a vast database of 186 cultures, selected in the 1960s by Yale anthropologist George P. Murdock, which Murdock developed with associate Douglas R. White. It is comprised mainly of pre-industrial peoples who subsist by hunter-gathering, pastoralism and horticulture. They are drawn from different continents and include the Tiwi indigenous Australian people, inhabiting islands off the Northern Territory (around the coast from Murray Island and the Torres Strait); the Azande people in the heart of Central Africa (including the south-east corner of the Central African Republic – on the same side of the country

688

as Saira and Omer); the Kuna people of Colombia and Panama, and the Aleut of the Aleutian Islands, scattered across the northern Pacific from Alaska to the Kamchatka peninsula of Russia.

The point of the SCCS project, an initiative in comparative anthropology, was to glean data from different cultures that had little contact and therefore were subject to a lower chance that their customs and cultural norms would be cross-transferred (or contaminated). It is a resource for examining commonalities in societies with relative 'cultural independence'. Of course, given the nature of our species, this is impossible: ancestors of the Aleut may have journeyed through the Americas and ended up, eventually, on Hispaniola. But there is a sliding scale and some cultures have less contact with others. For example, in respect of the Azande of Central Africa and the Aleutians, it's hard to envisage how much cultural transmission there has been from one to the other.

Assessing data from these varied sources, Quinlan examined the evidence around what he maintained were those two central life decisions. He found that parental 'effort' was inversely associated with extrinsic risk. In situations of severe war or famine, where prospects for survival are limited, parents invested *less* of their time and resources in their offspring, and when they did, they focused on those with the best prospects of survival.

A similar pattern was found in times of severe disease (high 'pathogen levels'). In such situations, infants were weaned earlier and there was less maternal care. Further, the level of involvement by the fathers decreased as the level of surrounding disease escalated. In environments that are intrinsically harsh, excruciating life choices habitually have to be made by parents.

One controversial example of this surrounds the question of whether and to what extent Inuit populations have practised female infanticide.

Although the high incidences of the practice that early Western ethnographers claimed to have found – up to 66 per cent – appear exaggerated, there remains evidence that these populations surviving on the very fringes of the habitable world have previously engaged to some degree in female infanticide, albeit at significantly lower rates. Thus it is likely that parents in these Arctic populations in the past have deliberately killed certain of their female offspring.

In a seminal study in the mid-1990s, human demographers Eric and Abigail Smith examined the available empirical evidence that covers the five decades from approximately 1880 to 1930. They concluded that while the practice has disappeared, the evidence revealed that female infanticide did occur among a number of Canadian and North Alaskan Inuit populations. It was a practice undertaken, Smith and Smith suggest, by parents to align the gender ratios given variable risk and mortality rates. In the risk-laden environment inhabited by the Inuit in the far north, males who went out hunting were more likely to die.

In such a practice of gender manipulation, of course, the Inuit would not be alone. One thinks of the current imbalance between males and females in the Chinese population – estimated by the Chinese Academy of Social Sciences to be more than 24 million men of marriageable age, and 50 million overall. This accounts for nearly all of the 60 million more men than women living in the world at present. In significant part the situation in China is due to sex-specific abortions. The introduction of ultrasound scans in rural China in the late 1980s exacerbated the practice by allowing parents to screen out and terminate baby girls.

Humans, Quinlan concluded, are highly sensitive to external 'environmental' risks. They have to be. For example, in a study reported in the journal *Human Nature*, James Chisholm and colleagues in Australia investigated the reproduction strategies of 100 women and girls (aged 14 to 36) in a hospital in a metropolitan area. They found that there was a strong correlation between early life stress and menarche, the onset of menstruation. Further, young women who had experienced such early life stress characteristically gave birth to their first child at a significantly younger age.

The reason for the findings, the authors argue, is that from an evolutionary perspective it would make sense in environments of higher risk and uncertainty for women to adapt their 'life strategies' to have children earlier – which they on average do. To facilitate that, there is the need for earlier menarche, which in fact demonstrably happened in the Chisholm sample.

The majority of studies that have examined this phenomenon have sampled women of European descent who inhabit Western industrialised countries with low fertility rates. In a study published at the end of 2015, Kermyt G. Anderson of the University of Oklahoma examined the effects of childhood stress on early sexual maturity from a mixed racial sample of young adults in Cape Town. While no effect on early menarche was found (thus not replicating the findings of Chisholm and colleagues), the Cape Town Panel Study sample did show a link between childhood stress, as measured by father absence or intermittency by the age of six, and the age the child first engaged in sexual activity and/or became pregnant. Anderson's study also showed a link between childhood exposure to violence (another form of psychosocial stress) and early reproductive behaviour.

These phenomena are not restricted to humans. A study of rhesus macaque social groups at the National Primate Research Center in Lawrenceville, Georgia found that there was considerable within-sex variation in the interest showed by macaques in infants. Those monkeys that had been exposed to negative and haphazard maternal care in infancy demonstrated a higher level of interest in infants than controls. In Wistar rat populations, those animals experiencing less maternal care were observed to be more likely to become pregnant at a younger age.

Hence there is a tangled connection between biology, behaviour and environment. In the environment in which Ubah was raised, it was the norm for parents to have their children undergo FGM. The incidence rates are astronomically high: the vast majority of girls are mutilated, part of the 200 million women and girls who are living with the legacy of this practice, according to the latest UNICEF and UN estimate.

In my work around this subject, it is clear that many of the parents who arrange for their daughters to undergo the procedure are not 'monsters'. They are otherwise loving and caring – and yet they do this. Why?

Ubah grew up in an African country little known or understood in the West. You are likely to have heard of it in passing. If you are able to place it on the map, you will be the exception. You will be in a very small minority. I do not name it in order to protect Ubah's privacy and safety. I do not name it because Ubah does not want me to.

She grew up in a remote part of her land. As she became a teen and on through puberty, the pain from the FGM remained. It just wouldn't go. In the end, that may have been the point. Ubah wanted to do something about the pain, but not for herself.

'It is too late for me, but my daughter is not going to suffer like this,' she told me.

'But I thought you don't have children,' I said.

'The daughter I want to have, she won't suffer like this,' she said.

It was the rainy season and the roads were bad, disintegrating into muddy messes. Ubah went quietly from village to village on foot, watching with amusement as motorbikes and the odd truck slid and spun their wheels in the mud. She spoke to other young women in small gatherings, in private. She said that they had to do something. This couldn't go on. 'I say to them, "Are we really going to cut our children like we have been cut? And they will do that to their children also? And it is to go on? And when will it stop?" And the others say to me, "But, Ubah, when will it stop?" And I say to them, "When *we* stop it. We can stop it here."'

There was a village by a stream. As she entered, children playing carefree, wild games suddenly stopped. They stared fiercely at her, like they secretly knew her work, *demanded* she do it. It wasn't gratitude and she didn't want it anyway. In that moment, everything seemed to hinge on her. It made her more determined.

Many of the young women she spoke to were sympathetic, but they were scared. Ubah left them to think about it and promised to return. She had to leave early because another storm was coming. But someone must have spoken to the senior village elders. As Ubah left the village, the men were waiting.

'There were six of them,' she said. 'I remember, I count: one, two, three, four, five, at first it seems five, then a sixth one, smaller, he is hidden behind. One, two, three, four, five, six.' She counted them out on the middle three fingers of each hand. 'And I know what they want. I don't need to ask these men what they want.'

'Why?'

'Because they have sticks and axes. I say to them, "So it takes six men for one woman, huh? This is what men in this village have become?" And they say to me, "You must now pray because soon you will die." And I say to them, "No, you must pray because you are going to kill an innocent woman." They say, "Why you make this trouble? Why you want to stop girls doing our tradition?" I said, "Because cutting is wrong." They said, "It is the law." I said, "Whose law? It is not in our Holy Book." They say, "The elders say it is our duty." And I say, "To cut children? To take off what God has given children on their bodies? Why is this our duty? Do you think these parts would be put on our bodies for you to cut it off?" I look at each of them. I look them in the eye. "Will you do it? Will you take a knife or a nail? Will you hold down your daughter and cut her with it? No. You can't even look at me. You will not do it. I know you will not do it. So you get women to do it for you. And you don't do it because you know it is wrong. But you keep allowing it to happen because it has always happened and people say it must keep happening. But if we stop, then soon we will have a new 'it has always happened', then you will beat people who try to cut your child. That is all it is. You see that is all it is. It is what we have always done. We must change this 'what we have always done'. But I make a promise: I will not any more try to stop it, no, not me, not any more." I look at them, all of them, and I say, "Will you stop it? I will never say anything more if *you* will try to stop it. Are you going to try to stop it?" They said nothing. "Then I will not stop," I said.'

Ubah didn't see the first blow. One of the men behind her hit her on the back of the head.

'He hit me on the neck and ear, but it was like someone hit me on the legs, because suddenly my legs were not there.'

694

She fell. Then they set about her. They smashed one of her ankles. They broke her forearm. They gashed open her head. Blow after blow raining down on her bones. And then suddenly it stopped. At first she did not know why. They loomed above her, a canopy of hate-filled faces, and then somehow she was face down in the mud. She could barely see anything, her vision blinded by pain, when as suddenly as they started the blows stopped. The men disappeared and she was alone. What had happened? There was no one else around. No one had come to save her. But the onslaught had suddenly stopped. She sensed she was about to pass out. One part of her wanted to pass out, because then she would not feel the pain.

'But why did the beating stop?' I asked. 'Why did the men disappear?'

Above us on the vast mechanical screen, place names clicked round. Destinations of the trains hauling themselves out of South Station. A long, ragged line of passengers was sucked towards the gleaming metal tube of the Amtrak to New York City. I knew she had to go.

'I don't understand,' I said. 'Why did the beating stop?'

'Because it came,' she said, 'suddenly the storm came. At first I didn't even know, don't even feel it, the rain. But soon I saw that it was so heavy – heavy, heavy rain, like the sky broke. And this is why I am here with you, Dexter. Because these men, these brave men who protect our community, our traditions, they did not want to get wet in the rain.'

She lay there in the rain, alone, but still felt the fierce eyes of those playing children on her. There was no sound except the rain falling through the trees of the surrounding forest, swelling their roots. And now every time it rains in Boston, Ubah gives silent thanks for the rain. 'Maybe I am the only person who does, but I greet the rain, my friend.'

It is around ten years later and Ubah keeps speaking out against FGM, despite the threats. Because somewhere around the world, another girl is mutilated every 11 seconds. As you have read this chapter, 200 more girls have been mutilated. And the clock keeps ticking.

What happened to Ubah and her sister is replicated 3 million times a year, according to WHO statistics – that is five populations of Boston. Every year. Or imagine the entire heaving population of that great and noble city is young and female and is, every single person, genitally mutilated every ten weeks. Sometimes Ubah's ankle still hurts her. It plays up. 'It talks to me in the cold weather,' she says. 'So I talk back. I say you be quiet now, I have work to do.'

'And does that do the trick?' I ask.

'Sometimes it is stubborn. It kicks like a horse. But, okay, I try to understand. I like horses.'

Ubah has been recently told it is unlikely she will have children. Not impossible, but unlikely. That is one of the potential consequences of certain types of FGM. But despite the risks to her personal safety, she continues to speak out to protect her children, the ones she is unlikely to have. Something inside her keeps driving her on, something deep and mysterious she doesn't entirely understand and doesn't necessarily want to, that impels her to keep fighting for her daughter, the one she has in her mind, her dream girl, her ghost child.

THREE

Silent Flight

If there was one word (apart possibly from love) that would fill you with a sudden deluge of mixed emotions – joy, pain, hurt, elation, sadness – I'm going to guess what it is. Let me put it this way: all I need do is pose a simple question.

How do you feel about your family?

When I ask this in lectures the most common response I get is laughter and groans and heads going into hands and the shaking of heads and as one woman in the north of England said to me (and an audience of about 200 people), 'Don't get me started – we haven't got long enough today.' Someone shouted from across the hall, 'We haven't got long enough this week, luv,' and the audience fell about. All because I mentioned a single word: family.

Of course humans are not the only animals to have families. In New England I came across a particularly voluble member of a family. In fact, this animal is one of most vociferous of its kind.

697

So much so that its name, both in English and Latin, reflects that particularly characteristic trait: noise.

Its taxonomical name of *Charadrius vociferus* was included in Carl Linnaeus's *Systema Naturae* of 1758. The English name 'killdeer' derives from its characteristic *kill-deee* call. You will find it sharing terrain with humans; you may find it in railway sidings or concreted playgrounds or airports. It is a member of the plover family and is found throughout North America. Killdeer, like other plovers, have short bills. Overall they are tawny birds with white markings around the beak and throat, while two very noticeable black bands are striped across their white chest. The truth is, however, I noticed none of this when I almost walked right over one.

It was up in the deep woods of New Hampshire on a hiking trip. It was in the concreted car park. At first we did not know the killdeer was there. We were not looking for it; we were looking for the campsite. We parked in an empty overflow car park. Basically, we didn't know where we were going. As we left the vehicle we heard a sudden shrill sound. It was repeated again and again: *kill-dee, kill-dee, kill-deeeee*, over and over. For a moment there is paralysis: you want to move away from the distressed bird and yet the agitation and tumult are fascinating. The killdeer decided the issue for us. It began to run fast along the concrete with its tail fanned, all the time calling out. The bird is a ground forager and moves swiftly across the terrain. But then it suddenly stopped. It began to repeatedly flap its left wing. The wing appeared broken – damaged at the very least. I was concerned that somehow our 4×4 had inadvertently collided with it. The bird began gyrating on the ground in a state of sheer helplessness, flapping its wing but unable to take off. It was just feet from us, completely vulnerable, at our mercy – there for the taking. It glanced towards us, managed to scramble a few further paces away, then repeated the agonised wing flapping.

'Let's go back to the rig quietly,' one of my fellow travellers whispered. For some reason, she always referred to the 4×4 as the rig.

'Can't we help it?' I said.

'She doesn't need help,' my companion, who was from Utah, said. 'She needs us to leave.'

When we got back into the 4×4, she said, 'That killdeer hen, she just risked her life.'

'Risked?' I said.

'See over there?' She pointed to the rough stony ground on the fringe of the car park. 'Over there is her nest. She just risked her life to lead us away from her eggs or her chicks. Her wing is just fine. She was pretending, so we'd go for her and not her young ones.'

'That was not real?'

'That was very real. A very real act. To dupe you. As real as life and death. Back the rig out exactly the way we came in.'

And I did. That night around the large communal campfire, I repeated the story again and again to whoever would listen. It was a cloudless night full of stars, which somehow seemed fitting.

Killdeer nest on open ground. Their nest is barely even that. It is a slight depression in the stony ground. It is rarely adorned or lined. It is barely distinguishable from the rough ground. And that is the point: they hide their eggs and offspring from predators in plain sight. But it does not always work. And then when the nest is threatened, the parent killdeer engages in the elaborate behaviour we witnessed in the New Hampshire car park, what in ethological terms is called a 'distraction display'. It is the risking of the parent's life for its young.

Of course, the adult bird could simply fly away and leave the nest, the eggs or the chicks, to their fate. It may be that the inter-loper or predator would not see them anyway. The eggs are grey, speckled, extremely hard to distinguish from stony ground. So the parent killdeer could leave. It could think about future broods in other seasons, other years. But it stays. It fights for its offspring's lives by risking its own.

Analytically, a distraction display is behaviour that acts to divert or deflect predators from the animal's nest or young. It is a form of 'nest defence'. Such behaviour has intrigued naturalists since Aristotle. Its significance is that nest predation is one of the most significant – if not the most important – factor affecting fitness. Indeed, of North American passerine (perching) birds, 66 per cent of nestlings were killed by predators. In the never-ending arms race – Darwin's 'constant struggle going on throughout nature' – between predator and prey, distraction displays have evolved as a key weapon for the defence. Thus it was that ornithologist and churchman Edward Allworthy Armstrong, in a seminal paper on the ecology of distraction display from 1954, called behaviours such as the killdeer's 'broken wing' display acts of 'remarkable realism'. The killdeer in the New Hampshire woods convinced me. It was a mesmerising performance. It was meant to be. It had to be.

'After that,' Ubah said, 'I tried my best to speak out. I was given a chance by an international [Western] radio broadcaster. I would make little pieces about human rights, especially women's rights. It was freelance. I did it without pay. But the risks grew worse. People were threatening me when they heard what I was saying.

Sometimes, I had to move every month. I used different names. I went through seven different countries. I had to hide. Once I hid in the bushes.' She paused a long time. 'You know, sometimes, they do a second or third mutilation as punishment for those who do not do as they say, or protest about it all.'

'So why did you do it?' I asked.

'I've held women and children who have died from FGM. I've held them as they bleed to death, and we've tried to stop it and can't. And for what? What? Why are their parents doing this? What is the purpose?'

In a research paper from 1932 published in *Ibis*, the international journal of avian science, evolutionary biologist David Lack, for many years director of Oxford's Institute of Field Ornithology, reported his observations of another ground-nesting bird, the nightjar (*Caprimulgus europaeus*). He was interested in the relationship between a parent and its young.

The nightjar is a nocturnal and crepuscular bird renowned for its almost silent flight (the result of its extraordinarily soft feathers). Down the centuries it has been vilified because of apocryphal suggestions that its silent flight enables it to approach goats unnoticed and feed on their milk (the Latin name *Caprimulgus* means goat-milker).

In the summer of 1930, Lack made several night trips to the sandy heaths around Holt, a market town in north Norfolk near the North Sea, to find these aviators of the dusk and darkness. He went to Kelling Heath near Holt and waited and watched. It was midsummer so there were several nightjar pairs which had returned to this spot in the east of England after wintering in Africa. On Lack's approach to one nesting site, a female nightjar engaged with Lack.

She led him around the nest several times but did not seek to lead him away. One moment she drew closer to the nest, the next further from it. So somewhere on the north Norfolk heath, the nightjar and the evolutionary biologist circled each other, just a few feet from the nest.

The episode attained a certain celebrity in avian science circles. Nightjars, like killdeer, were known to perform distraction displays as a form of nest defence, but what was the hen nightjar that Lack encountered doing? Several years later, Edward Armstrong hypothesised that the behaviour of the bird evidenced the profound conflict between two of the most fundamental life drives: self-preservation and offspring protection. The bird was caught between its desire to escape and its need to protect its progeny. As Armstrong puts it, injury-feigning displays may be 'a ritualised compromise activity': a difficult balance between saving one's young and saving oneself.

Viewing the human family through an evolutionary lens places family conflict not only as inevitable but central to the dynamic. Such a positioning is, according to psychologists Marco Del Giudice and Jay Belsky, 'possibly the single most important contribution of evolutionary biology to the study of families'.

Such a stance understands the parent–child relationship as an endless cycle of both cooperation and conflict. It is a confrontation, Catherine Salmon and James Malcolm from the University of Redlands, California argue, that begins in the womb. For mother and fetus do not share an identity of interest. Generally, as Robert Trivers noted in his seminal paper on parent–offspring conflict, written when he was at Harvard in 1974, the offspring will want more than the parent is prepared to offer. For the offspring is thinking only of itself. The parent has to think about (a) the offspring, (b) itself, (c) any other present offspring, (d) other possible future offspring. That is a lot to think about. No one said parenting was easy.

Yet for all the conflicting impulses between protection and self-preservation, the nest defence stratagems of nightjars are so deeply engrained that, as David Lack put it, 'I have never found a Nightjar which did not feign injury at some period'.

Lack's female nightjar may not have got it entirely right in the protection of its offspring, but then again we are bound to ask: do human parents?

It still lives with her.

'You see me, the strong Ubah. And when I'm speaking in public, I'm strong in a crowd. Then I go back and I'm alone. I relive it all again. Again I'm that girl and I'm thinking: how can parents allow this to happen?'

And that time in Boston, when Ubah crashed, that is, I think, what happened. She became the other Ubah, the child, terrified in that room, turning the door handle, hearing her sister scream.

FOUR

For 16 Years

Peggy St Jacques is a researcher in psychology at Sussex University, having completed her PhD at Duke, and postdoc at Harvard. Her subject is memory. Her particular interest is autobiographical memory. 'Our brain has a number of regions that support memory,' she says. 'But there is one area of great interest, the hippocampus.'

'Hippocampus?' I say. 'As in sea horse?'

'Yes, it's Greek for sea horse.' I later discover that the name comes from *hippos* meaning 'horse' and *kampos* meaning 'sea monster'. However, these delicate, upright prancing fish, about three dozen species found around the world, are far from monstrous.

'This brain structure actually does look like a sea horse. It is uncanny,' St Jacques says. 'The early anatomists were right.'

The hippocampus is found in the medial area of the brain's temporal lobe and is a constituent part of the limbic system that regulates emotion. I tell St Jacques about Ubah's experience of public speaking – and when the memories come.

'When someone is narrating a memory in public,' St Jacques says, 'it is an effortful act, she is having to do quite considerable work to put the memory out there. When she is telling her audience about what happened, she is working hard and that may well suppress her amygdala, an emotion centre of the brain. Then when she is at rest – when she is offstage – she can enter a stage of "mind-wandering".'

That is an interesting phrase, and I ask St Jacques about it, since the origin of the word 'hallucination' is precisely that: from the Latin *hallucinari* – to mind-wander. So is that what it is like? When she is off guard, these things appear in her mind?

'There is an intriguing overlap between memory and hallucination. What are we doing when we remember? We suddenly see things that are no longer there. So if the memory comes, if it is not something she has summoned, she has less control. She becomes in an important respect vulnerable to it.'

'A victim of it?'

'Well, memories tend to come to us when we are unaware, and that can be more troubling, even debilitating.'

In certain cases, it can be devastating. 'Where do these memories come from?' I ask. 'Why do they come?'

St Jacques sighs deeply. 'These are *big* questions. I'm not sure science can yet completely answer them. Research shows that cues in the environment may trigger the recollection. They do not have to be identical, but something that partially overlaps with stored memory traces – a car backfiring may overlap with the sound of fighting in a civil war on another continent. What we know is that the hippocampus is thought to store our deep, historic memories. It has been said that it houses memories that are resistant to forgetting.'

But what if we want to forget? What if, like Ubah, we need to?

'We don't generally choose to have memories,' St Jacques says. 'And we can't choose to forget them.'

At the moment, there is no definitive explanation for FGM. Although it is often believed to be – and dismissed as – a Muslim practice, that assumption is wrong on a number of levels. First, FGM is not restricted to Muslims: adherents of Christianity (including Egyptian and Sudanese Copts), Judaism and animism also practise it in different parts of the world. Next, it is not specifically ordained or prescribed by the Koran. Some Islamic 'scholars' (often self-appointed) claim that in various of the Hadith (reported sayings) of their prophet there is authority for the practice, but such claims are intensely contested by reputed scholars within Islam itself. Finally, FGM predates Islam. Its origins may reach back to ancient Egypt, and conceivably beyond. It is at the very least a Pharaonic practice in antiquity.

But whatever its historical provenance, why were Ubah and her sister – along with the 3 million more young women and girls every year – mutilated?

Fifty years ago, evolutionary biologist Ernst Mayr published an article on cause and effect in biology. It has proved to be tremendously influential – as well as controversial.

What Mayr was trying to get at was a better understanding of the various ways in which we can understand why things happen in the lives of living things. To do this, he drew a conceptual distinction between those causes that can be attributed to immediate – what he termed 'proximate' – factors and those which are deeper: ultimate causes. This latter level has sometimes been called 'distal', connoting a more fundamental or distant originating cause.

Mayr asked why was it that the warbler on his summer place in New Hampshire flew south and migrated on the night of 25 August. He said that there were four levels of causation, all 'equally legitimate'.

First, ecologically, the bird feeds on insects and has to fly south or die of starvation.

Second, genetically, the imprinting in its genetic history induces it to react to environmental cues.

Third, physiologically, the bird exhibits photoperiodicity, triggering migration when the number of available daylight hours falls to a critical level.

Finally, externally, on the night of 25 August a mass of cold air passed over his New Hampshire property significantly reducing the temperature.

Mayr concluded that for all but the simplest biological phenomena, there are likely to be what he called 'sets of causes'. Life is complicated. Experientially. Anecdotally. Analytically. But that should not drive us, Mayr warned, to embrace non-scientific explanations for what living organisms around us do and are seen to do. For what we do. We should still strive to understand using the best science and analytical tools we have. To acknowledge the sheer complexity of what Mayr called 'the science of the living world' is not an admission of defeat because, as he wrote, 'often this is about all one can say.' He cited biophysicist Max Delbrück, one of the founders of molecular biology. Delbrück wrote, 'Any living cell carries with it the experience of a billion years of experimentation by its ancestors.'

Mayr died in Massachusetts in 2005, aged 100. In the spirit of his determination to get closer to the factors that produce and reproduce biological phenomena, we can say that proximate observable causes of FGM include the need to 'protect' the social standing and marriageability of the girl or young woman by ensuring she is 'cut' and therefore regarded as 'clean'. Indeed Leyla Hussein, one of the UK's leading survivor-activists, speaks about how when she was at school in Somalia, girls would insist on seeing the genitalia of other girls to see if they were cut and thus 'clean' and thus not 'sluts'. Respectable girls would only play with girls who were cut. Some girls would pretend that they were cut to avoid the social ostracism.

The fact is that in some communities in developing countries a young woman who has not undergone FGM is nigh on unmarriageable. Thus this behaviour, physically dangerous and degrading though it is, may be construed as an act of seeking to safeguard the interests of the girl. This is, of course, deeply paradoxical. But biology is, as Mayr would remind us, complex.

Parents in FGM-practising communities are often under intense pressure from the extended kinship group to preserve the status of family by ensuring that a new daughter conforms to the social convention and does not bring opprobrium upon the family. In other words, there are girls – in the world today – who are having their genitals mutilated to uphold the 'honour' of their family. Thus we have another proximate cause: the avoidance of stigma for the kinship group.

Layered around and upon this are a range of myths and traditional beliefs about the supposed dangers of the clitoris. How it may supposedly affect the health of the baby or the well-being of the man. Many parents are understandably – and terribly – torn by all this. Like Ubah's mother and father, they are unable to be present at the cutting. They cannot bear to hear for themselves the cries of pain of their daughters. And yet they give their child up for mutilation: protecting the social standing of their daughter, knowing FGM will cause her great pain, feeling the pressure of the family circle to avoid being shunned, wishing to preserve their own place within society and their families.

Sometimes daughters are given up for FGM only after tremendous agonising and vacillation. Like the nightjar David Lack witnessed, the parents circle around and around the problem, caught, confused, conflicted by competing impulses: protection of the child's physical safety; preservation of her social standing; upholding of the family's 'honour'.

And yet in ever-growing numbers there are women from FGM-affected communities who are refusing to carry on this tradition. Ubah is one. Leyla Hussein is another.

But the question remains. While the above proximate explanations provide causes for FGM on an immediate level, what about a deeper explanation – the distal level? Who are these people who do it and to whom it is done? Where does it happen and why? What kind of a human thing is it?

No critical consensus has yet emerged. One approach is to think about what FGM really involves, which part of the female anatomy is targeted, and what the effect of that targeting is. Then we begin to understand. It is frequently said that FGM is the social control of women. But controlling which aspects of female behaviour and how?

Very commonly, when FGM survivors are asked to describe what they associate sex with, they use one word – pain. In their mind, sex is often associated with excruciating pain. In some communities withstanding FGM denotes that the woman has been able to survive and cope with great pain, a foreshadowing of childbirth. The more severe forms of the practice accomplish two things. First, by removing or damaging the clitoris, sex is disassociated – severed, literally – from pleasure. It tends to discourage premarital sex or sexual exploration and thus increases the prospects that the girl or young woman will be a virgin when married. Second, the fact that sex becomes not only an empty, dully mechanical act, but one that is positively painful, significantly reduces the likelihood that women who have undergone the procedure would seek sex elsewhere beyond the marital bed. They are unlikely to 'stray'. Thus from an evolutionary point of view, the act reduces paternity uncertainty. It reduces the risk that a husband is 'investing' – devoting financial or other resources and time – in a child that is not genetically his own. We can see in all this the glaring link between FGM and patriarchy.

For animals that are fertilised internally, this is always a risk. It is a risk to humans throughout the world. A study in the UK of what is called 'paternal discrepancy' found that around 1 in 25 fathers in Britain may not actually be the biological parent of the child they believe to be theirs. In genealogy this is called a 'non-paternity event'. As the old saying (some say originating in the Deep South of the United States) has it: 'It is mother's baby and father's maybe.'

The converse of this phenomenon is that the level of paternity confidence is positively correlated with the amount of investment a male makes in the child. Knowing it is your child – or at the very least having confidence that it is – affects the behaviour of men.

FGM is only recently beginning to receive sustained critical scholarly attention. Having worked on this harmful social practice for a number of years in various ways, I am convinced, as are the academics and survivors I most respect, that FGM is at its very core one of the world's most physically harmful and pervasive forms of patriarchy.

It is surrounded by a complex of immensely powerful social forces and interests. Challenging it is a risk. Ubah received death threats for speaking out about FGM in her community. Several other of my colleagues have experienced the same. But for all the threats, and the deeply rooted social forces they are seeking to challenge, the dangers have not stopped more and more mothers from trying to protect their children from it.

We would do well to acknowledge that the groundswell of resistance to FGM originates in women in sub-Saharan Africa and elsewhere who refuse to let their daughters suffer as they have suffered. Notwithstanding the risks. Notwithstanding the cost. They have dared to stand up against society and tradition for their child.

In the UK, it took Leyla Hussein seven years of struggle with producers and channel controllers before she finally persuaded them to make a film about FGM. But in many ways, it was on the night that her groundbreaking programme *The Cruel Cut* finally aired Channel 4 in 2013 that her struggle really began – or was taken to another level altogether. She was inundated with death threats.

'They began even before the programme ended,' Hussein says. 'They were beyond anything I could have imagined. What they said they would do to me, to my daughter. And all of this because I said hurting children is wrong, hurting our daughters is wrong.'

Hussein had to be given a personal alarm by the police; a panic alarm was installed in her home.

'My daughter is now a teenager and googles me. She reads some terrible stuff about me online. Made up things. Lies. Things people say they will do to me. To us. I can't shield her from all the things on the Internet. Teenagers will find it. So we are just honest about it and talk it through. I try to tell her again and again why I am doing this, how I am doing this for her – so she won't go through what I went through.'

When speaking to Hussein, it is not long before she is back in Somalia on the day it happened to her.

'It is the wedding you never talk about,' she says. 'A day when no one takes any pictures. I woke up one morning and there were caterers in the house. *Caterers*. All the women in the family were gathering, and mothers in the community with sons were coming round.'

'What did you think was happening?'

'You kind of know and you don't. It's too much for your brain to absorb.'

When it happened to her, she was a year older than Ubah. Leyla Hussein was seven.

'It's the day you are put on the shelf, on the market. Usually the child's mother is not present because they cannot bear to hear their child scream. And I did cry out. I was not given sweets because I made too much fuss. After that my body shut down. I didn't cry for 16 years.'

Psychologically she managed the trauma by blanking out the experience. A few years later, when she was a teenager, her family relocated to the UK. But the trauma could not be contained. It surfaced again with an uncontrolled ferocity when she was pregnant with her first child.

'I started having flashbacks,' Hussein says. It's what Peggy St Jacques calls 'mental time travelling'. For Leyla Hussein, that journeying began at an unexpected moment. 'It was just out of nowhere. I went through the medical check-ups that all the other young mums were going through, but as soon as I was examined, I fainted. Like my body was remembering what had happened.'

'It's a massive disregulation,' Nim Tottenham says. Speaking from her office in upper Manhattan at Columbia University, the Associate Professor of Psychology continues, 'First, there's the physical trauma, the near-death experience. And there's the additional trauma of the breach of trust, the betrayal by the parent. This can increase the likelihood of psychological problems, mental illness and anxiety – you can become hypervigilant. The threat detection systems are in high-gear survival mode. They can lead to the reorganisation of the architecture to make them more vigilant in the future. The brain is not stupid. I don't want to get too much into the weeds, but the stress hormones that are produced can change the biology, reconfigure the neural pathways. It changes you. Your brain.'

When I toured the country for the NHS lecturing on FGM, one of the initiatives to raise awareness, a clinician told me that flashbacks like Leyla's are real. In that moment, the person is back in the trauma situation. They are not remembering it; they are not even reliving it; they are *living* it.

'I would faint and fall and it was all there again,' Leyla says. 'I didn't want my daughter going through this. I was *not* going to allow my daughter to go through this.'

Speaking to Hussein, you become aware of two Leylas in front of you: woman and child. I wondered what they would say to each other. I ask.

'I would tell the seven-year-old Leyla that I still share her pain, that the part missing from her is still missing from me. I would tell her – I *do* tell her – I wasn't able to save you. I say I wasn't able to save you, but I will save your daughter. Even if it costs me my life, I will save your daughter.'

And she has.

FIVE

Always in

The storm that hit Angie was of an entirely different kind to Ubah's. But it swallowed up everything and changed her family forever. The storm, for storm it was, was in her son's head.

Angela – Angie to all and sundry – has almost waist-length hair. Her slender, wiry frame is constantly in motion. There is always something to do in her life. When her son Ricky was born 17 years ago, there were so many complications. Years and years of them followed. By the time I met her, it was yet another one – a new one. I hadn't even heard of the condition Rick was being treated for. My daughter had just undergone major surgery. I was numb with shock. Angie and I happened to be at the beverage station of the children's ward at the same time. For the beleaguered parents of the patients on the ward, these precious water-cooler moments act as an invaluable respite, precious minutes 'off duty'. You pass the milk, you smile, you hang around and very quickly get out of the way the inevitable, necessary exchange of information: why you both are there – or more exactly, why your children are. You don't say what you've both been thinking: this isn't what parenthood promised. It wasn't in the instruction manual. Angie mentioned some name.

'Don't think I've even heard of that,' I said.

'Neither had we,' she replied. 'Now Rick's got it. Can you believe it?'

Frankly, I couldn't.

'Even the doctors here didn't really know what to do or what it was. They looked at his hand and thought, "Cor, blimey", you could see it and then they rushed off to look it up on Google. I don't think they've dealt with PGS before in this hospital.'

'That's what they call it, is it? PGS?'

'Do you want to see?'

It's always a sensitive issue in children's ward politics: you want to appear concerned; you don't want to pry.

'Okay,' I said. And we went into Rick's room.

It was opposite the central nursing station. Ricky, because of the numerous problems he has to endure, had one of the hallowed single rooms. My daughter, a fracture (albeit a serious one), was in a general open ward.

'All right, Ricky?' Angie said. 'Got a visitor for you, friend I met making a cuppa. He's a judge.'

'Part-time,' I said.

Rick made a sound unlike any I had heard in my life. And then again, there was a faint resonance – I couldn't place it. Rick lay out on a bed, more or less helpless, dependent on his parents, a 17-year-old boy. His thumb, which was what I'd been invited by Angie to see, was completely purple. Not a pinkish-bruising purple – almost black. And Rick's discoloured thumb, the result of PGS – purple glove syndrome – is but the end of a long line of trials for this young person and for his mum.

It all began his lifetime ago, with that storm – the one in Ricky's head.

'I was fine at carrying babies,' Angie says. 'Carrying them, schlepping them around inside me, no problem. But it appears I couldn't give birth to a baby. I couldn't dilate.'

One morning, in her 37th week of pregnancy, Angie was woken up by a contraction. 'I thought, "Oi, oi, hello – what's going on here, Ange? So I jabbed Pete in the back. I felt a bit mean because he was just a student then and he'd been off climbing a mountain with some mates and had got back at three in the morning and now it was 6am and he'd had just three hours' sleep. But I had to, just in case, because I felt that contraction. Boom. We rushed to the hospital, but I just knew there was something wrong. By the time we got there, they couldn't hear a heartbeat, they thought I'd lost my baby already.'

Angie was rushed to the operating theatre for an emergency Caesarean. 'All I remember was there was a lovely man there who said, "I'm sorry, I'm really sorry, but you may not have a baby to come out." I asked them to try, to please try. Please, please try.'

Those vital minutes meant that her baby – it turned out to be a son – had been critically deprived of oxygen.

'I'm not a medic or anything, but the way they explained it, it meant that various parts of his brain were hurt, killed off.'

Her son had his first seizure within minutes of being born. He now has cerebral palsy. His epilepsy means that he has had 20 or 30 seizures a day, every day, throughout his 17 years. Each day, one or two of the seizures are bigger, more serious ones. And every couple of years he has a more major seizure. Angie and her husband never know when one of them starts whether this is going to be the one. Any of them could be.

The serious damage to Ricky's brain has meant that he has spent 20 per cent of his life in hospital. And so has Angie. In and out of hospital, operation after operation.

'Hips, back, stomach, thumb, oh – hang on. Let me start again: they had to put a tube in his stomach to feed him. Then there were tonsils and adenoids. Then thumb number one when he dislocated it during a seizure, then another thumb operation, and now this thumb problem – and we only hope it won't be amputated. Then a couple of years ago he had his spine straightened. And also they had to break his hips as both were completely dislocated and were causing him a lot of pain. Then they had to tie the top of his stomach to stop acid reflux. And then he had a pump fitted to feed muscle relaxant into his spine 24 hours a day because he's been in so much pain. There's an op about every 18 months, give or take.'

Due to Rick's seizures he had to have large doses of phenytoin, an anticonvulsant drug, administered intravenously through a catheter in his left hand. While it successfully relieved the symptoms – controlled the seizure and calmed him down – there was a complication. The drug interacted adversely.

First it discolours the injection site. Then it spreads to the distal limb – in Rick's case, to his thumb. The doctors did what they could to relieve the symptoms. They elevated his arm, applied gentle heat to the thumb.

Day by day Angie and I watched for signs of a turning of the tide, of the threateningly dark colour leaching out, going back to 'normal'. Purple glove is a rare complication. It is not certain what the aetiology is, the mechanism that causes it. The pathophysiology remains elusive. Basically, it is poorly understood. It may be a vasoconstriction and soft tissue irritation caused by the chemical solvents (ethanol and propylene glycol) used to make the drug soluble. Other researchers regard it as the result of mechanical

vessel damage. It could be due to the crystallisation of the phenytoin itself on contact with the blood. But whatever the cause, it
only occurs in as few as 2 per cent of cases.

That it should happen to Rick, with everything else he has to
contend with – with everything Angie has to contend with on his
behalf.

'I try to stay positive,' she says. 'It's another thing in our basket
to carry, isn't it, Ricky? He's such a good lad. He doesn't really
complain or get grumpy.'

And nor does Angie.

I ask her how she manages it, the unrelenting hospitalisations
and operations, the seizures and anguish. The other parts of her
life have been more or less replaced by this cycle. She found my
question mystifying. She was silent for a while, her mind off
wandering – she has to contend with so much.

'Angie?' I say. 'I was asking –'

'Why wouldn't I?' she said, cutting me off. 'After Ricky was
born and was about six weeks old and we realised that he would
survive, we went to see the consultant. They asked us whether
we wanted to take Ricky home. Pete and I looked at each other
and said why wouldn't we, we're his parents. There was no doubt
in our minds whatsoever. As soon as he was born we had to
resuscitate him three times. He was a crash section. I was unconscious. They had to resus him twice even before they got him to
the critical care unit. Then once more when they got him there.
So it was obvious he was starved of oxygen. So we knew there
was going to be a problem.'

And there have been problems piled on problems for Rick, Pete
and Angie ever since. 'My life stopped 17 years ago. I don't live,
Dexter, I exist. It's quite hard. There's no time for you, not really,
but I try to do the crossword or walk the dog.'

719

'So what actually is Angie-time?' I ask. 'Apart from walking the dog?'

'It isn't even my dog,' she says. 'It's just life. I just get on with it.'

'I've seen you,' I say. 'When you're exhausted. When Rick has had another episode. I can't imagine how frightening it is to see your own child going through that, somewhere on the inside, looking out at you as everything in his body is out of control, and you're there, you go back in.'

She smiled. A pursed lips kind of smile. 'You know, hate to say it to a QC and judge and all that, Dex, but you're wrong.'

'Wrong? About what?'

'When you say I go back in.'

I was confused. 'I've seen you.'

'No, you're wrong.'

'I've seen you. You're out here in the corridor, and it's all kicking off, and you go back in.'

'That's where you're wrong. I don't go back in because I'm already in. It doesn't matter where I am, I'm already in. I'm always in.'

And that, too, is the Kinsman.

The intense laser-like staring that Angie and I exposed Rick's thumb to – willing, commanding, beseeching the discoloration to go away and find some other place to make a nuisance of itself – seemed to work. Slowly the base of his thumb started to turn pink. It was a definite improvement.

Finally, I placed where else I'd heard the noise that Ricky made. It was when I visited Dawn, when her glorious sound caught me unawares – what she calls her 'Wookie' voice. But it was all disorientating because Rick was close in age to Dawn's son Alexander, and in my mind Rick joined that chain that connected Anthony and Michael and Alexander and Omer and now Ricky to Gareth.

A week after my daughter was discharged from the children's ward, Angie texted me. Rick had to go back in. He was hospitalised again: the healing had stalled. There was necrosis – the death of the body tissue due to lack of blood flow.

'There was just nothing else they could do,' Angie told me, 'nothing else for it.' Ricky's thumb had to be amputated.

Overall, Rick's prognosis remains uncertain. He may continue like this for years, or it may suddenly end. 'He has intractable epilepsy,' Angie says. 'One day it will kill him because he will have a fit they cannot stop.'

That Big One could hit anytime, anywhere. 'Really, you just never know,' Angie says. This is how they live, Ange and her son. But whichever way it goes, she will be there. She's in and will remain in for as long as it takes.

One of the distinguishing features of our species – what in part makes us human – is the sheer intensity and duration of our parent–child relationships. Of all the relationships in this book – the dynamics and dyads, between the Rescuer and rescuee, the Perceiver and person in pain – it is perhaps the parent–child relationship that is most emotionally charged. When it is put like that, our initial response is: how could it be any other way? But it could be. For much of the animal kingdom it is that other way. Human beings have evolved along with a few other species to have an extended, deeply involved connection between parent and child.

It is fulfilling. No doubt. Unlike anything else. But it is also full of trauma and pain. It is ultimately about cooperation and conflict; sacrifice and the self. The prime resources of life – time and energy – are limited. How we choose to dispense them cannot be properly understood without understanding that parenting entails a benefit to the child at a cost to the parent. A cost of a particular kind in evolutionary terms. For the investment is a zero-sum distribution of resources: the more a mother or father (or both) invests in one of their offspring, the less there is to allocate to another existing or future child.

When we saved our child in the school corridor at the expense of other equally deserving but not genetically related children, we were acting on the imperative of this urge. We were driven by it. We fought to provide a benefit to our child in the teeth of a number of associated costs: the risk to our own life (we could have run in the opposite direction, just as the killdeer or the nightjar could have flown off); the loss of the life of other children (we could have saved them instead); the social and reputational cost to us that not saving those other children will cause.

However, and despite all this, I am yet to meet a single parent who after talking it through who would not preferentially save their child. It is only the number of others who would be lost that gives us pause. This is our make-up, our brain, our biology. A significant part of what George Eliot called the 'unmapped country' within us is the Kinsman.

The Kinsman is unsparing. It is a taskmaster. It is terrifying, this mental machinery, a kind of madness, when we think about it. When we think about what we are capable of doing to promote the survival of our genes. The Kinsman makes no excuses; it offers no consolation. It drives us down the corridors – in the school with the gunman, in the hospital paediatric ward – always to our child.

Ubah and I stood up and joined the slowly shuffling queue heading towards the Amtrak at Boston's South Station. We inched along. Ubah's ankle was playing up.

'You didn't drink that coffee I buy you,' she said.

I'd hoped she wouldn't notice. Ubah notices everything. 'Thing is, I don't really drink coffee,' I said. 'I drink tea.'

'Some places round here, I think they put mud, stir it, and charge five of my beautiful dollars. I will make you coffee. *Our* coffee,' she said. 'Then you will drink coffee.'

Weeks later, she did. It was a revelation. We met on her return from her anti-FGM activism around the country. We met not too far from the MCZ at Harvard, the Museum of Comparative Zoology. Within it is a library named after Ernst Mayr. Ubah would suggest I meet a friend of hers. It was someone called Anna.

'Did you ever see a wolf?' I asked; she was about to get on to the train. 'In Alaska.'

She looked hard at me. 'Do you *know* how cold it is up there?' she said. 'I never wanted to come out the hotel. That cold, it is an evil thing. Hah, how people live in it? Yes, *that* I respect. But no, no wolves.'

We said goodbye as the train's cylindrical metal exoskeleton throbbed before us, straining for travel. Invisibly, the air rippled with it.

'I know you fight FGM with us,' Ubah said. 'But, you know, we must fight harder.'

'Yes,' I said. 'We must.'

As Ernst Mayr wrote that time, often this is about all one can say.

'So . . .' she said. 'You like music?'

'I love music.'

'You know, many times, I'm here, and I'm alone. And I listen. To this song, over and over. One day, I'm going to go down to those Carolinas, because that was where she was born.'

'Who?'

'Eunice.'

'Eunice?'

'My good friend Eunice. I never meet her once, but I hear her sing and she is now my good, good friend, this Eunice.'

'Eunice?'

'Eunice Kathleen. Eunice Kathleen Waymon.'

'Eunice Kathleen Waymon,' I said, just to repeat the name. It is a great name.

'You know her,' Ubah continued.

'No.'

'You *know* her, Dexter.' I realised it hadn't been a question. She squeezed my hand. 'You like music? Then you do.'

Once – later – when she returned and was in my office at Harvard, I asked her what she would be doing if she'd had the chances that I'd been given. Ubah has received virtually no formal education. But she knows things. *Knows.*

'Me? You see, me, I'd be sitting next to a beautiful African woman and working out how I can stop FGM. We will end it. Never let any person tell you we won't. Is just time. How much time. How many people want our fight.'

At South Station on that first meeting, she looked at me very sternly. 'You're going to get me Cadbury-dairy-milk-chocolate?' she said.

'How much do you want?'

'How much is legal?'

'I'll look into it,' I said.

I watched Ubah's iridescent blue gown disappear into the Amtrak carriage before turning to make my way back through the concourse and out into Boston, thinking of Alaska, thinking of wolves, the deep woods, the killdeer. There is a particular line from *Company of Wolves*, where Angela Carter says that the great howling of wolves, the wolfsong, is 'the sound of the rending you will suffer'. Boston was cold and beautiful. But no snow, no gusts, no storm. Snow would come soon, and terribly, but not today. I love this great city, but just then I saw it as a village; the eyes of children seemed to stare fiercely at me as they once stared at Ubah. Yes, I thought, we must try harder. For Ubah. For her ghost child. For all of them. I entered my own phase of mind-wandering. I thought about my own girls, 3,000 miles away, and about who Eunice Kathleen Waymon may be.

Killdeer and young

Epilogue

Here is how the story begins . . .

Popol Vuh, The Mayan Book of Counsel

Wonder; Terror

The great white goose shook out its feathers and took flight over the endless steppe. She surveyed the silent world below. While she was serenely gliding over the vast green space, the light of the sun impregnated her and turned her into a princess; her offspring, the product of her labour and pain – for human life is printed with pain – was the first man, the first Kazakh.

The two great deities, Tepeu and Gucumatz, thought of the world and it obligingly formed out of the void. They thought of skies to cover it and mountains and rivers and forests to mark it and all these things appeared from their minds. But they realised they needed living beings to tend to their vast and strange dominion. They made animals of all stripes, but animals could not talk; they could not praise their creators. And so the gods made man. The first were made from clay, but they crumbled back into the dust whence they came as weak men are wont to do; the next were made from wood and were more robust, but they had no soul. Eventually the two great gods, Tepeu and Gucumatz, made men out of maize and they became the great Mayans.

About 4 million years ago an insignificant creature left – or was forced to leave – the shelter of the dense forests due to the vagaries of planetary spin and the vicissitudes of wind and rain. These creatures ventured into the savannahs. Around this time they developed (or may have recently partially developed) the ability to walk upright most of the time. They freed up their front limbs. These primates, a type of ape, began losing their hair and were able to cooperate with one another in small groups. They were, or became, social animals, usually linked by a variety of family and close kin connections (the Kinsman). Eventually – a million or more years thereafter – they regularly began to use tools. They not only lived in the world, they were able to *shape* it. This process intensified when, another million or more years after that, they began to master fire.

The savannah-based ape, foraging, hunting, surviving, experienced an extraordinary surge in the size of its brain. How and why it happened is still not resolved. The connection between this unprecedented surge and the control of fire, leading to the ability to cook meat and thus more effectively digest high-quality protein (the hunting of which involved more sophisticated cooperation) is something the descendants of these apes – remarkably fewer generations down the line than you would imagine – are still working out.

The size of their craniums and their upright gait meant that babies had to be born earlier to safely navigate the birth canal. These human offspring were not precocial (ready for independent life, like killdeer young), but altricial: they needed intense, prolonged nurturing (the Nurturer). It was difficult for a mother to do this alone. There were greater prospects for survival in bonded pairs. Human males made ostentatious displays, including those of generosity, to gain favours with a female or females (The Romancer). Certain physical configurations, certain character attributes, were found to be more attractive: possible cues to health or fertility or caregiving (The Beholder). But they also recognised that there are many types of beauty. When the males became fathers, they contributed to providing nutrition and protection for these otherwise helpless young; human fathers were more involved in the provisioning and caring for the offspring than in most other species. The creatures found that small family groups could share the workload. Slightly bigger social groups even more so, and these larger aggregations could provide the numbers for coordinated hunting. In these groups, they would use forms of social control: they would shun, cast out or banish disruptive transgressors (the Ostraciser). They spent an inordinate amount of time thinking about what other people were thinking; they could sometimes sense their hurt and pain (the Perceiver of Pain). They became fiercely loyal to their groups (the Tribalist). Sometimes they would sacrifice themselves for their groups. Sometimes they would strategically use or threaten violence to protect it (the Aggressor). And sometimes they would rescue others in the hope that others might one day rescue them (the Rescuer).

Up to a few tens of thousands of years ago, there were other early human species living at the same time. One by one they died and disappeared. We were alone.

The blankets of ice two miles high advanced and withdrew in a slowly destructive dance. The remaining humans – us – began to domesticate animals around them: horses, cattle, camels. Some descendants of wolves began following human camps. They became dogs. Humans started using fire to burn the land and clear it for their animals to graze. Some of these animals were little more than walking larders; others became friends; one would be launched into space. Their human owners hunted; they harvested; then they began to *plant* crops. Their nomadic lifestyle was given up to care for the land that would care for their nutritional and energetic needs. Children were lost to disease and predators and other humans; some of their offspring were beyond hope and had to be left behind. They buried their dead, leaving trinkets in the graves. They looked up at the stars and wondered. They sought ways to cope with the realisation that they, and everyone around them, would die (the Tamer of Terror).

Some of their dwellings perched on pilings above lakes for protection, like those near Lake Konstanz. Others clustered together for security; the clusters became villages; villages became towns; towns turned into cities; vast associations of humans were forged; they became countries; people fought amongst themselves within them; they fought with other countries beyond them. Sometimes the world was on fire. They also used fire to alleviate the bleakness of winter nights; to burn tobacco and ingest its smoke; to burn other human beings.

They returned to the forests, but now to cut them down; the trees that once were their home ended up on the backs of wagons, then trucks, long lines of them, like the forest funerals coming out of the Central African Republic. Civilisations and cities crumbled; their men and women fell; nature watched; the weeds waited. There were revolutions – political, mental, technological – and these creatures, now almost completely hairless, exclusively walking on two feet, now only very, very rarely surviving by hunting and gathering, began systematically searching deep space – they had not stopped looking at the stars – for where their world and its encompassing universe began. They also looked into themselves, for where their thoughts and actions began.

Because at the very heart of this evolutionary epic, this grand and gruesome cosmic sorting process, it was the brain of this world-shaping ape that marked it out in the unsparing battle for existence in a world of scarcity and limit. Not only the brain's size (Neanderthals had a slightly bigger cubic capacity), but its proportions, *where* the development came – in the frontal and temporal areas (the neocortical ratio); and *how* it developed, the sheer complexity and sophistication of it – how a multitude of different networks of neurons, functional executive systems, provided survival benefits when confronting certain, serious, real and recurring life problems.

Genetic evolution shapes our body and our mind. The modules that developed in this process were adaptations. They spread through natural selection. They are in us. They are a critical part of us. In many ways, they are us. And we will pass them on. Among them are the Types met in this book – perhaps all ten.

As I write this, the International Space Station, a microgravitational laboratory with a crew of six of the descendants of those savannah-dwelling apes, is about to pass overhead. This Earth-hewn craft is larger than a six-bedroomed house and orbits the planet every 90 minutes. Think: a large house hurtling around its entire world every hour and a half. I know it will pass overhead because my iPhone app, the one I showed Patrice in Cameroon, charts the ISS's streaking trajectory through the night sky. A palm-sized rectangle of plastic, glass and silicon that I keep in my pocket shows me where humans are floating above us in space. The spacecraft is below the horizon but will appear, like clock-work. As a species, we've come a long way. But many of our survival problems in their intrinsic nature, if not their environmental contexts, are little altered. We have in our heads the mental modules, the executive processing systems, to face up to them.

Pictures tweeted by Tim Peake, the British astronaut, show a planet below electrified by a tracery of light. It looks like some living thing, breathing, seething, which of course it is. It looks like the MRIs of neuronal activity in our brain, the torrent of tiny electric sparks which have made it possible for us to point our mirrors and radio telescopes into the recesses of space-time and look for clues about the creation of the universe.

Have we risen so far from that carpeting of savannah because of mental modules like the Ten Types that inhabit our brain or in spite of them? You and I continue the grand experiment. If this book has engaged with some of the more troubling things that humans do to other humans, it is because they are true, and real, and happening, but also because I believe we can find ways to stop them. But before that we have to understand. And before that we have to know – just know.

The picture of who we are, where we came from and what our place in the world is, has constantly changed. From the Kazakh white goose creation myth, to the Mayan's *Popol Vuh*, their grand account of their existence on earth, to those accounts in the holy books of the Abrahamic religions, humans have striven to explain where they have come from and who they are. In the second decade of the third millennium, revolutionary technology and techniques in neuroscience combined with various cutting-edge branches of experimental psychology in a second Darwinian revolution are granting us privileged access to our brain – and thus to ourselves. To our *selves*. What are the implications of all this? I must return to where the book started, to that originating case, bring it back to the boy in the corridor.

On Monday 19 April 2004 at around 2100 hours, a 15-year-old boy was in a place whose name conjures shaded streams, gently running with rainwater: Rainsbrook. He was making a toastie and refused to clean the toaster afterwards. He should have cleaned it, frankly, but he was upset because others had used it as well as him and he was being asked to do it because he was the last user. Beyond that, he *was* a teenager. He was told to go to his room. Unfortunately, for what happened next, his room was in a prison.

In my mind I can see it: a small boy – he is 4 foot 10, weighs 6½ stone – pads along a corridor in silence. My view is from a high CCTV camera in the corridor, black-and-white footage, no sound, and the boy walks slowly with his back to me towards a room, which is his cell. He turns left, enters. I never see his face. Can you be haunted by a face you never see? He disappears, shuts the door. Minutes later, two prison officers walk, much faster, along the same corridor. They walk in silence, but the sheer rapidity of their walk seems to fill the frame with noise, with chaos. They also turn left, enter the cell, shut the door. A third officer enters the room, shuts the door. Within minutes, the boy is dead. His name was Gareth Myatt.

What happened in that room? What happened in the minds of those officers who inflicted dangerous physical restraint upon a child who was unusually small for his age, when he was crying out that he could not breathe? He was asphyxiating in their arms during the application of that restraining hold, that Seated Double Embrace – that embrace. 'I shouldn't have PCC'd [restrained] him, he was half my size,' one of the officers said. 'It was rather like having run over a cat . . .' What went on in Gareth's mind in those last moments, desperate not to lose the piece of paper with his mother's number on it? These questions have haunted me.

I never met Gareth, but I represented his mother Pam at the inquest into his death. Pam is one of the most dignified and coura-geous people I have ever met. She sat for weeks listening to people ducking the truth and attempting to evade responsibility for the numerous catastrophic errors that contributed to Gareth's death. The jury were often in tears. Pam largely remained in court. She was determined to hear everything she could, find out everything that happened to her son.

The jury returned a devastatingly critical verdict – a historic one – identifying a catalogue of serious failures in the care and treatment of detained young people in prisons – in the treatment of children. Failure after failure, from the behaviour of front-line officers – giving themselves those names: Clubber, Crusher, Mauler and

Breaker – to the Star of Week award for the most forcibly restrained child, to failures to safeguard the young detainees, to failing to listen to their complaints and concerns, to the creation by the government of an inherently dangerous and potentially lethal system of restraint and control. Failure after failure after failure at all levels, that's what the jury found. Why was this happening? What was going on in the minds of those officers? In the minds of the injured children?

Yes, we do the case. Finish it. Move on. But the case isn't always finished with us. All this led to the first faint intimations of the three questions set out at the beginning of the book:

Who are we?
What are we?
Who is inside us?

Shortly after Gareth's case, I was asked to represent the mother of Adam Rickwood. Adam was also restrained and deliberately hurt by officers (he was hit in the face causing a nosebleed) in another child prison. Adam hanged himself. At the time, Adam and Gareth were the two youngest people to die in our custodial institutions. Throughout the process that has led to this book, I've been accompanied by not only the picture of Gareth, but Pam's simple question – why?

On the night I write this, I am standing in a sodden field in Cambridge with a clutch of stargazers near the university's Institute of Astronomy. It is a night filled with stars. The International Space Station streaks over, from one horizon to the next. What do the humans inside it see? It was here in Cambridge that my research began to answer Pam's question. Then after that Harvard; thinking, probing, trying to understand. This book is a continuation of that endeavour.

735

What can we say? How can we begin to answer her question? Having journeyed with the people whose life stories we have shared during the course of the book, we are in a better position to respond on both a scientific and a lived human level. One of the objectives of the book has been to provide an account not only of the science, but of actual human lives affected by it. It has looked at scientific theories and the statistics that systematic experimentation has produced. It has also looked at the people who live and breathe these facts and figures in their everyday lives.

What then do the numbers tell us; what do the people; how shall we answer that first question: who are we?

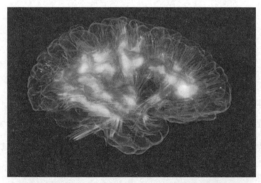

Earth from International Space Station and
3D modelling of human brain activity

Through the individual narratives within these pages, we see the truth Sophocles saw when he wrote, 'Many things are both wonderful and terrible, but none more so than humankind.' That monster in the fever swamp. Or as Pascal in his inimitable way less charitably put it, we are the 'glory and scum of the universe'. So here in the 21st century, 2,500 years after Sophocles, let us record some of what we know, a progress report.

Humans propelled the New Horizons space probe through 3 billion miles of silence and darkness for nine lonely years, so that on 14 July 14 2015 it swooped by the dwarf planet Pluto and beamed photos back to Earth. Pluto, it seems, has mountains.

The ice mountains of Pluto, equatorial Pluto
New Horizons space probe, July 2015

We have found ways to see mountains on the last world in our solar system some 3 billion miles away – 3,000,000,000 miles. We will launch nanocraft into the void, with 'light sails' harnessing solar winds, heading for Alpha Centauri, our next-nearest star. Here are some other images that for precisely the same instant in the history of life on Earth we could beam the other way to Pluto and beyond:

Humans condemn several million children every year to lives of slavery and degradation; we also risk our lives to rescue them from their servitude.

We genitally mutilate three million young women and girls every year in what the World Health Organisation calls a 'global epidemic'; we also refuse to be cowed by death threats issued for publicly opposing it.

We traffic hundreds of thousands of girls and young women for sexual exploitation annually, and maybe 30,000 of them die; we risk our careers and our lives to protect them.

We attack woman with acid for daring to stand up to suffocating social norms; we fight to change the law to reduce the chances that others will similarly suffer.

We enlist several million children to fight as front-line combat troops or as concubines for commanders in our bloodiest wars; we risk our lives to free them.

We do not permit our citizens who have been struck down by strokes and who are trapped within their own body to choose to end their life with dignity; we watch with astonishment as others like Dawn Faizey Webster fight and flourish and refuse to be daunted or defeated.

Therefore we have seen the extent that human society, as it is actually lived, carries the potential for both the flourishing that Aristotle thought was the purpose of life, and suffering – the haemorrhaging of human life. Like Balzac's beloved Paris, it's both 'a valley of real suffering and often deceptive joys'. Philosophers, bloggers and chat-show hosts will at no point soon stop opining about whether human suffering is inevitable. Maybe it is. Or is not. They will argue about whether we are intrinsically good or evil. Gustave Flaubert excoriated purveyors of such simplistic approaches, calling such either/or reductionism *'deux impertinences égales'*: two equal impertinences. In the meantime, in the real world, we know some things we can be getting on with: we know that (1) human suffering blights the lives of many millions of our conspecifics, our fellow human beings; (2) we can do things to reduce certain manifestations of it.

We can, for example, dramatically reduce the number of young women and girls every year who are genitally mutilated. I am convinced we will. We're already on it. The direction of travel is the right one. It is a stubborn problem, because it engages fundamental parts of who we are – Types. The Nurturer and the Kinsman are conflicted: torn between protecting the child on the one hand, and preserving her social status and that of the kinship group on the other – the Tribalist. Families who resist the practice face shunning, social sanction and threat – the Ostraciser. We need to understand these mental mechanisms better. Fish, Frisbees and FGM. Marian Wong's goby, Kip Williams's Cyberball research, the experiences of Leyla Hussein, Ubah, other survivors. We're trying to put it all together better.

When we do, when we honestly engage with the subject, we can talk about other less harmful ways to uphold family honour, and find better methods to circumvent the mechanisms of social rejection and ostracism that oil the continuation of the practice; we can begin to change these social norms and better protect girls who otherwise, like Leyla Hussein and Ubah, would be unnecessarily and irreversibly mutilated. But, as Ubah said, we must do more. We will end FGM. As Ubah said, it's just a matter of time. How many people want the fight.

In this momentous task we are helped by the intrinsic nature of our neuronal heritage. Our brain is extraordinarily adaptable. It has exceptional 'plasticity'; it can reconfigure and rewire itself. It can change. We can. So these dedicated Types that help us to process life problems, drive but do not dictate solutions. The outputs can alter. Our behaviour can. We can.

To turn to the second question: what, then, are we?

We are, it seems, not entirely alone. We carry within us a number of evolved mental modules, which are associated with certain highly characteristic behaviours. I have called them Types. They inhabit our mind. They inform our decisions. This book has been about ten. To pose the question asked at the start of the book: what kind of human thing are they?

They are not 'real'. 'Let me introduce you to my Rescuer, my Tamer of Terror.' Yet the effects of the mental modules, the evolved executive systems of our mind, very much are. Real and relevant and rippling through our lives. We are, in important respects, an aggregation of the decisions of these modules and mechanisms, with their secret firings of neurons through deeply grooved pathways of mind. Our lives are shaped by the choices that we, with them, have made. One way to view them is as being the latest iteration – the long and ongoing unbroken production line – of mental equipment that reaches back to the brains of that savannah ape. We are a consequence of both our anatomy and our neuroanatomy – and how they interact with the anatomies and neuroanatomies of others. To quote again molecular biologist Max Delbrück, 'Any living cell carries with it the experience of a billion years of experimentation by its ancestors.' I like that about us. Not everyone will. Some will want us to be possessed of unbridled free will and rationality;

others will serenely turn to some deeper destiny, an invisible and great Guiding Hand. I like evolution. I like the fact that it has shaped our body and our mind. So long as we combine that with the social forces around us.

The Ten Types as we now possess them are not immutable; they have not been there or the same forever; they are what we have – and have been given – as a result of a vast project of human experimentation. In what? Principally in living, that is, surviving and reproducing. And thus these parts of our psychological make-up are deep-rooted and powerful. We are not always aware of them. But sometimes, if for example we are placed in the school corridor with the gunman, they press forward and suggest actions that have been repeated for generations. But we do not *have* to follow them. They may begin to steer us, provide us with an instinct to go towards our child, even at the expense of others. But directing is not determining. Human beings are reflective. They are not just instinct-driven. We can reason. And it is that interface – conflict – between fundamental instincts and urges and our ability to think things through that many of the people you have met in the course of this book have had to deal with. In ways that are usually less extreme, we all do. Whom to prioritise, whom to protect, whom to love; what to do in the face of wrongdoing, how much to risk, when to fight, when to flee. This is the stuff of life. It is really just a matter of degree.

But within us is the imprint of a billion previous decision path-ways our ancestors have taken over several million years. The silent shadows of these forebears loom over our lives. And with not too much difficulty we can imagine them, deciding whether to stand and fight or turn and flee, agonising over whether to save one child and risk losing them all, not in a school, but on the immense and once immaculate savannah.

So on to our third and final question: who is inside us?

It is likely that we possess not just a few mental modules but many. Our mind is likely to be *massively* modular. These modules, computational programmes or executive systems, built not of wires and solder but neuronal networks, carrying, processing, transmitting information, coalesce around specific survival problems. They perform different evolutionary work. They have different jobs. They are highly specialised. Sometimes, for even long stretches of our lives, they lie dormant. They wait. Sometimes more than one of them is activated and we are torn by competing (survival) urges. We are often, usually, mostly, unaware of what they are or that they even exist.

When they are primed, it feels as if there is something, *someone*, driving us in a particular direction. Remember this is an idea, a way of thinking about an immensely complex process. A way of trying to understand it better.

The activation of these Types may be due to something as severe as having to contend with a gunman or a terrorist in a public building or street (whatever the objective situation, the world *feels* a lot less safe at the moment). But their activation may be as innocuous as at the University of Kent when male students doubled their donations by having an attractive female student sitting silently in the room with them. Analytically, there is an equivalence: a life decision being confronted and the triggering of an evolved mental module – a Type. Not every male student doubled their charitable donations when a female drama student was in the room, but on average they did. As Ernst Mayr wrote in 1961, due to the 'high number of multiple pathways possible for most biological processes . . . causality in biological systems is not predictive, or at best is only statistically predictive.'

Therefore human behaviour is not determined; it is not dictated. There is variation and individuality and quirk and character and personality. Therefore none of this is infallibly predictive; it is at best irksomely probabilistic. But: young men *do* tend to give more when a beautiful woman is in the room. They really do.

An awareness of our rich evolutionarily assembled mental machinery can help us understand otherwise mystifying behaviour. It can help us understand others; it can help us make sense of ourselves. We can be more tolerant of others; we can be more lenient with ourselves. I wish I could have more adequately communicated that to Anna in Boston; to Marcie in Haiti; to Vasily in Kazakhstan.

Genetics is not a complete picture – far from it: culture is also critical. It has to be: we are unashamedly, inescapably, social beings. Our behaviour is influenced by genetics and our hereditable traits (liking or loathing of cauliflower), but also by our environment, social learning – our own exploration and experience of surroundings, what we are taught, what we model. It's no longer heretical or even greatly controversial to state this. Indeed, our learning mechanisms are also likely to be the result of evolution (that *is* an ongoing controversy). However, we've come a long way. Remember that we would have been burnt alive for professing what I have just written about evolution. As was Jan Hus in Konstanz in 1415 for another heresy, with straw piled to his chin and the pyre lit.

But it is socially good to understand that we are built to perceive the pain of others, so long as we are not exposed to it to a psychologically crippling extent. This recognition can be the basis for promoting prosocial behaviour. We don't have to suffer the collapses of compassion Paul Slovic warns about. But we need to protect the Perceiver. It is precious. As is an appreciation of the fact that we are fundamentally social creatures. We must combine empathy and compassion with reason. Much as we wish to retain

743

and express our individuality, our inescapably social side not only explains the irresistible rise of social media, of Twitter, Snapchat, Instagram (or whatever the hot app will be when you read this), it can help us counter arguments that 'everyone is always and only in it for themselves', that it is 'nature'. It is not. It is more complicated than that. Human beings find cooperating with other human beings rewarding in itself – even if there's no material advantage, even if there is a cost. We get the glow. When we give, we really do receive. It's in there. We're possibly wired like that. I like that also. We need to broadcast it from the rooftops and high viral platforms of social media.

What we have seen from the record of experimental investigation of these phenomena is that we can trigger or bring forth these parts of us, as when research scientists 'prime' volunteers by activating a particular kind of self. That knowledge has the potential to be of great use in the countering of harmful social norms and practices. Thinking of FGM again, a sustained collective campaign directed at recalibrating the human behaviours and states of mind that produce and reproduce FGM, combined with an emphasis on other core instincts we value, such as the protection of a child, can act to change the landscape. That certainly is the UN's model of 'collective abandonment' of FGM amongst practising communities. From what we know about how humans are designed and function, it makes good analytical sense. Here is the first lesson we can learn:

Lesson 1

These types are not just an evolutionary relic, they are a *resource*.

744

They can be tools to tackle social problems, to reduce the sum of social suffering, to effect social change. They can help us be free; they can help us free others. This has been one of the biggest revelations to me while researching and writing this book. The sophisticated equipment we have inherited by the process of natural selection not only attunes us to the social suffering around us, but equips us with the means to find solutions for it. If we want to.

Along with colleagues working in human rights here and in the developing world, I have sought to provide a different account of what have been regarded as intractable social problems, such as female genital mutilation. I have sought to emphasise some of the other constituent parts in the 'set of causes' Ernst Mayr wrote about. I've tried to speak about not only the proximate causes but the deeper, distal ones, the underlying mechanisms. The evolutionary logic. Our emphasis has been on moving away from dangerous and deprecating denunciations that these are acts of 'barbarism'. It has been a recognition that we need to trigger other selves, other Types. Thus our stance has been uncompromisingly grounded in human rights and in social psychology, in particular the absolute prioritising of the protection and welfare of the child. That approach may jar with the demands for group loyalty with the Tribalist, but will resonate with the Kinsman and Nurturer. It is, we believe, beginning to work. It is an outrageously presumptuous ambition to try to change the world. But there it is. Some things in the world need changing.

We helped persuade the UK government following our submissions to a parliamentary inquiry to change the law on FGM and create a raft of preventative powers to protect at-risk young women and girls, to focus resources on their safeguarding *before* mutilation. We have lectured and presented here and abroad to thousands of front-line professionals, nurses, doctors, midwives, teachers, class assistants – those who regularly come into contact with the at-risk young women and girls – to bring them these insights. Sometimes there is pushback. It's good that there is. Sometimes the debates get heated. That is a consequence of democracy – a celebration of it. We want the heat. We are finally talking about these difficult things. We are bringing them out of the shadows.

The work has also taken us to sub-Saharan Africa. We have endeavoured to support and publicise the work of hundreds of thousands of women there whose courage is the fuel that is driving this massive social change. We sense communities and a world in flux around us. Whole populations – people like Patrice and Saira – are on the move. Their bodies are; thoughts and belief systems also. This should not surprise us. The sheer plasticity of our brains provides an opportunity for relearning and recalibrating. And this is the second lesson:

Lesson 2

Our brains are not obstacles but
opportunities.

But what kind of opportunities? Here are some ideas:

The Perceiver of Pain

Am I my brother's keeper? It is one of the first recorded questions we have asked ourselves. It is documented in the very first book of the Bible. In important ways, much of the book you have just read has been about this question from Genesis. So what's the answer? We need to draw a distinction between how we do treat other people and how we *should*. The first is an empirical question. Look around. During the course of the book we have examined various ways in which humans harm other humans – FGM, child soldiering, human trafficking, Violence Against Women. We began in West Africa. We began with child slavery. And that has helped us look at the second question, the normative one – the 'should' question. How should we treat others, what are our responsibilities? This question is at the core of *Donoghue v Stevenson*, the most famous case in English law, and was simply put by Lord Atkin thus: who is my neighbour?

As Anthony and Michael found at Lake Volta, when we perceive the pain of others, we perceive something about ourselves: we are not alone, not trapped in the skin we're in. But it's not just a question of mirroring the other person's pain. The key, it seems, is to reach out with compassion and think through the ramifications. The minor miracles of science have meticulously granted us the opportunity to understand compassion in a new way. It is not a one-way street. If compassion costs, that cost can be worth paying, since as we give, we receive; we are rewarded, neurologically, demonstrably. But, as I wrote in my notebook, we must protect the Perceiver. The new research insights in Part I are providing new understandings of our response to the brother's keeper question. There are different levels of response: there is the fMRI response, and then there is Michael's. On the shores of the biggest man-made lake in the world, from the precarious platform of an arrow boat, Michael provided an answer of his own, diving again and again into the opaque waters to protect his friend. Am I my brother's keeper? his short life at the lake asked him. Michael, a child sold into slavery in sub-Saharan Africa, said yes.

The Ostraciser

We are the Ostraciser; we are its victim. Social groups often have a 'pay-to-stay' condition that ostensibly safeguards the overall social health of the group. We are lured into paying it by our deep need to belong. Whether it's Marian Wong's goby, fasting once they get to the 9-3 limit, or Sree Dasari desperate to find a niche in the Big Brother House. But as Kathy Bolkovac decided in Bosnia, it doesn't mean we have to pay that price, not if the group is dysfunctional. Ostracism can be used to preserve power; it is ultimately a form of social control. So standing out, speaking up is difficult: the Ostraciser targets our deep insecurity, our fear of not belonging, of being alone. Exclusion is indeed a pain 'that keeps on giving'. Here we can rely on the Perceiver to help us. When we reach out to help those being exploited or harmed by the group – like the young trafficked women in Bosnia – for all the group opprobrium, we are rewarded neurologically. And is there an opportunity too? If it is inevitable that we will ostracise, can we form groups, alliances, to seek to ostracise harmful behaviours? As Kathy Bolkovac said, 'Right is right and wrong is wrong. I think it pretty much comes down to that.'

The Tamer of Terror

The terror in our life takes many forms. It comes to us in many ways. It stole up on Dawn Faizey Webster as she was sitting on a sofa; it entered Tony Nicklinson's head in a hotel room in Athens, not far from the Agora where the ostracisms used to take place. That kind of terror can lock you in. But there is another kind of terror to tame: for we can be locked out, by the press of life and its daily demands and dictates. The secret everyday battle to make meaning in our lives, the sheer exhausting weight of it, can blind us to what life actually has to offer, what it can also mean. As I sit here writing this to you, it is an early March day; the sky is a very pale blue wash; high above an aeroplane, just a silhouette, silently glides more like a galleon sailing on a very still sea, maybe like Columbus and his small fleet on the way to Hispaniola. The aeroplane flashes in the sun, its undercarriage suddenly illuminated by light that has travelled 93 million miles and then bounced right into my eye; light from a star, our star, that gives us life and will, as Miss L reminded me, eventually take all of it. My daughter comes down. She makes toast. It warms the air. 'What are you doing, Dad?' A crow flies above us in the opposite direction to the aeroplane. The toast pops up. I get a text message from Dawn. She has an interview for her PhD. All this will pass, the Roman Stoic philosophers tell us, all this is vanity. I think of Miss L; I counter Marcus Aurelius and the Book of Ecclesiastes with a desire to enjoy it while we're here. I want Spinoza to be right: everything generally does endeavour to persist in its own being. The butter melts on the toast. My other daughter comes down. She is recovering from a follow-up operation, still on crutches, but her leg will heal. She will. She mashes avocado on her slice of toast (her idiosyncrasy). Taming the terror can also consist of loving life, being lenient towards it, as I hope Miss L eventually was – being lenient towards ourselves. We can stare down the blank face of oblivion; we can face directly into the sun. So this was my taming of terror on that March morning: the indescribable joy of watching my daughters eat toast.

The Beholder

Wordsworth wrote in his *Intimations of Immortality* that we come into the world 'trailing clouds of glory'. We also come with preferences for certain configurations of features. As Alan Slater says, beauty is 'not simply in the eye of the beholder, it is in the brain of the newborn infant from the moment of birth and possibly prior to birth.' It is a powerful impulse. So powerful that when it is taken away, there can be a backlash. Rana and Hanifa suffered that lash.

The Beholder in us looks at others and judges; it looks at itself and judges with equal – greater? – severity. How do we learn self-leniency? Hanifa found a way. She found the strength to look at herself again. She came to understand that she was more than the face she lost. She learned to love herself, the new kind of freedom she found, the new voice that came out of her new face. As Proust wrote, the real voyage of discovery lies 'not in seeking new landscapes but in having new eyes' – that act of creation, constructing a new kind of beholding.

The Aggressor

Let us grant that UNESCO is right: we are not genetically programmed to have a 'violent brain'. But human-on-human violence blights our world like almost nothing else (except famine – but that is also frequently exacerbated or even significantly caused by violence). And yet almost all of us have an aversion to inflicting harm on other human beings. Therefore there remains a deep tension between this revulsion of violence and one element in our mental make-up, the Aggressor, that can respond to social and survival situations with subtle modes of threat and violence. Almost all of us do it. Viewed thus, the Aggressor is not *who* we are; we are not determined or defined by it. Aggression, properly viewed, is just one of the things we can do. We have other qualities. We have sympathy; we sacrifice. Omer was prepared to sacrifice his hand for an elderly man he had never met before and who loved a sick goat. Saira risked herself to give Omer food. Patrice joined with Omer in trying to save her, a girl he had never met. My friend Sabrina Avakian stood in the way of a loaded gun and said that people needed to be fed. This is an argument we have been having with ourselves for at least 13,000 years, since the slayings at Jebel Sahaba. And if it cannot be ultimately resolved, we can say that we are not the Aggressor; the Aggressor is not us; and if anything, that reductionist misrepresentation is one of the most vital things we must fight against.

The Tribalist

Our survival and success as a species has been connected to the remarkably social nature of our brain. It has been a recursive thing: intelligence leading to cooperation and coalition and flourishing and fighting and complexity and nourishment and resources and greater opportunities for development, individually and collectively. One of our most characteristic behaviours is group formation. The groups in our lives may be 'minimal', having little rational basis, making little sense. Yet we press to join them. It has always been thus. We know because the wise have warned us about this vice and this virus for centuries. In the very first few lines of his *Meditations*, the great Roman philosopher Marcus Aurelius passes on to us the advice he in turn was given by his governor: 'Be neither of the green nor of the blue party at the games in the Circus, nor a partisan either of the Parmularius or the Scutarius at the gladiators' fights.' No one today much cares about the Parmularius, let alone the Scutarius. But we have our own gladiators; we enthusiastically observe or are trapped in Circuses of a hundred different kinds. As was evident in post-quake Haiti, tribes can rapidly form for good and for ill.

We are acutely aware of sameness and difference. We are classifying creatures. Very often it begins as a heuristic: a way to rapidly make sense of a complex world. But once imbued with power and significance and an ordering these groups can act to produce and reproduce inequality, discrimination and disadvantage. It has been against such things that much of my work has been directed. But at this precise moment, there is a growing feeling of despair. I cannot pretend otherwise. There has been a reaction to the project of tolerance and multiculturalism. We have Brexit. We have Trump. But here, deeply paradoxically, the true nature of the Tribalist offers some comfort. We must not forget that the sharpest divide, the one that appears to be slicing communities apart – race – may not be inevitable as a classifying tool; it may just be a more modern heuristic, a shortcut for dividing up the world as it appears now. It may be a surface effect. The research suggests that we are not predisposed to view the world in racial (let alone racist) terms. So here is an opportunity to counter and contest reductionist suggestions that we inevitably must be racially divided.

The Nurturer

Gibran tells us that our children are not our children: they are life's longing for itself. Anna never forgot how her son's fingers kept touching her face, how he was trying to find out what was this thing lying next to him. The tragedy was that she would not lie beside him for very long. Anna gave him up. Was that an act of abandonment or an act of love? The Nurturer urges us to offer those gentle ministrations we associate with mothering and fathering. It can also be fierce. Children have always been abandoned. One child is sacrificed so others can be saved, the agony of so many mothers in Ghana's fishing communities when the fish don't come and the hunger does. In medieval Europe there was a hole in the wall. And in that hole was a wooden wheel. It had a cot-like space, a confusing combination of cradle and disposal chute. In this a desperate parent would place a child. I often think of how it would feel, I mean actually *feel*, on the tips of your fingers as they touch that worn wood and spin the contraption as your child slowly disappears from your sight, probably for the last time. Anna was paid $1000 to place her child in a more modern type of foundling wheel – adoption. I want you to know that I do not criticise her for that. What I saw in her was the daily devastation of what she did, and the unswerving belief, which compounded her misery, that her child was better off without her. The Nurturer has not only raised our children but also our species. It has done so with a mixture of succour and steel. Understanding that complexity may offer us the opportunity to be more tolerant of failure and frailty. It's something I constantly witness when I'm sitting as a judge.

The Romancer

The Greeks sang about it in their songs. They recognised its power, to shape our lives, to launch a thousand ships, to burn the topless towers of Ilium. François felt it too. He stayed in the Central African Republic as mayhem advanced. He stayed for Marielle. We are here for a short time and then are gone (as Marlowe's Dr Faustus beseeches Helen of Troy, 'Sweet Helen, make me immortal with a kiss'). Our genes are passed on or they are not. Either through duty or desperation or ritual or romance. The Romancer can be generous or not. What is this urge to reproduce? As François told me their story on that storm-swept day in Yaoundé, I thought of Pablo Neruda's love poem, *The*

Morning Is Full. Neruda narrates how the wind in the trees is like a language *llena de guerras y de cantos* – full of war and storms. And that, I think, captures something of the power and potency of the Romancer, the effect it's had on us through the generations. Should we try to rein in the Romancer? How do we harness it – how do we harness ourselves? Of all the surprising things that I learned during the writing of the book, the fact that François would have risked his life for love is among the most extraordinary. In the vast vista of chaos and carnage that is CAR, a small story about two people and that most tremulous of things, love, is one I will not forget.

The Rescuer

Somewhere in Southern Siberia, two other people met. I would like to think they fell in love, but Vasily never gave me any indication that they did. He liked Lena; he admired her. He wanted, there can be little doubt, to save her. Why? What is it in us that produces that desire – what is the Rescuer? We don't much like thinking of ourselves as altruistic. But the work of Robert Trivers suggests that our helping non-related others may be adaptive. We live in a world of risk. The more risk-laden our environment, the more need there is for mutual help. That is certainly what has been found with Mediterranean sand-dwelling ants inhabiting regions full of predatory antlions. But what about humans? Why did Vasily do it? His childhood had been full of risk and hurt and pain. Most of it was in his family. I've come to think that it was this specific understanding of the world that inclined Vasily to risk his life to help Lena. He was like those sand-dwelling ants inhabiting regions of risk, and offering help to another in the hope, belief, longing that someone would one day help him. Who helped Vasily in his life? I like that think it was Kolya, with his squat frame and unruly hair. When Vasily was on the streets hating his life, hating himself, he was given focus, he was rescued, by an otherwise unloved dog. But this, I emphasise, is just conjecture. An attempt to understand a man who loves dogs and exposed himself to the horrors of modern day slavery to prevent someone else, a young Kazakh woman he barely knew, from falling into a trap and disappearing.

The Kinsman

When I penned the hypothetical about the parent receiving a stream of messages out of the blue at the beginning of the book, it never crossed my mind that it would happen to me. Life changes so quickly. But without my daughter's accident, I would never have met Angie and Rick. I saw in them the sheer intensity of the parent-child relationship that is one of the distinguishing features of our species. You may have felt something of it when grappling with the gunman in the school. What was your number? After reading this book, has it changed? The bonds with our closest genetic relatives are among our most fulfilling relationships, yet are filled, simultaneously, with contention, heartache, trauma and pain. Let's test it. Let me ask that single, simple question again: how do you feel about your family? Is your heart filled with joy, did you groan, was there exasperation in your response, and, yes, real pain? As Angie says, with our families, with our kin, with are 'always in'. Genes can do this. Few others things come close. So let me turn to the third and final lesson, and see how we can begin to put the Types to work.

Lesson 3

We can counter damaging behaviour of one type by triggering another.

When we have spoken to theatre groups who have wanted to produce works around FGM, we have asked them not to think of the parents who subject their daughters to this practise as monsters. We have asked them to think of the human and evolutionary dilemmas that FGM has presented through the centuries. Think about the human; the dilemma; the deep, deep causes – the Type. Challenging the harmful behaviour associated with one of the Types is facilitated by triggering another; not just a renunciation of what is bad but an activation of what is good.

This runs contrary to some of our entrenched intuitions about how to 'confront a problem', with the desire to show resolve by meeting it head on. If, however, the aim is to reduce the levels of social suffering caused by it, we can enlist not only those who oppose the practice, but other parts within those who believe in or have been brought up to subscribe to it – we can enlist other Types *already* inside them.

When we say, colloquially, we must 'appeal to their better nature', analytically, psychologically, what we are doing is priming another part of their mental make-up, another module in their mind, another Type. In some senses, our lives, our worlds, are battlegrounds where these Types, and their clashing priorities and imperatives, contend. Clash and contend, yes, but we also cooperate, show compassion, perceive the pain of others – we also have wiring for that. When Michael dived from the boat for his friend, when Vasily spoke to a young woman in a Siberian café. Then.

These Types can be triggered in ways we do not envisage. Ubah was on the point of being killed by men from the village she had visited. They relented not because of her appeal to other Types within them, but because high above, nature had conjured a storm that unleashed the torrents of rain that triggered their homeostatic systems of wanting to preserve their ambient condition. They did not want to get wet. Life, human beings – extraordinary.

So what of the people we have met?

Alan Pegna has taken a research sabbatical from Geneva and has ended up in Queensland, not far from where Marian Wong researched her goby. He continues to explore the unknown reaches of the human brain – and in particular the concept of 'reach' itself: brain cells respond to objects differently depending on whether they are within the reach of our fingertips or just beyond, a feature that may be a primate peculiarity dating back to our time in the trees.

Alan Pegna's patient is still working as an MD. Patient A is back in Burundi, where the security situation deteriorates as violence spreads. They urgently need doctors. Still using a nurse as his 'eyes', Patient A continues to do what he can to alleviate the suffering around him that he cannot (visually at least) see.

Kate Danvers is back in the UK after two years in Ghana working with children rescued from Lake Volta like Kow and

Samuel. She has a post as a community psychologist in London providing support and counselling for adolescents with mental health problems. But she still finds herself thinking about the children and the fishing. As she says, 'You never leave the lake.'

My legal practice's social justice fund contributed to one of the projects that Kate Danvers worked on at the lake, a micro-financing initiative on the coast at Winneba that enables women to smoke and freeze fish in times of plenty and thus have a more reliable income stream in harder times. The idea is to help alleviate the problem 'upstream', to reduce the pressure to sell or trade children into forced labour when, as always happens, there are fluctuations in the fish, times of feast and famine. Over a hundred women are already using it. The hope is to scale it up. The thought is that perhaps Kow and Samuel's mothers would not have given them up if facilities like this had been available.

Kip Williams presses on with his research on ostracism and social rejection. I have consulted him as we try to think about effective mechanisms to bypass and beat the ostracism of those in affected communities who refuse to inflict FGM on their children. He offers a free download of Cyberball 4.0 where you can play it for yourself: https://cyberball.wikispaces.com.

Kathy Bolkovac has returned to her native Nebraska after some time in Amsterdam. She has finished a degree in political science at the University of Nebraska-Lincoln as part of the process of finding another way to apply her talents and drive. She is working in emergency response training ('Everything from terrorism to tornados – we have tornados in Nebraska'), but continues to speak whenever she can about the plight of the hundreds of thousands of young women still being trafficked today. Her work and sacrifice resulted in her being placed on the long-list of nominees for the Nobel Peace Prize.

The situation in the Central African Republic has been referred to the International Criminal Court and a domestic Special Criminal Court investigating the atrocities has been created. Elections were scheduled for Valentine's Day. The world held its breath. Sabrina Avakian is still working in the refugee camps with refugees. She is still surrounded by adoring children. She has returned to Italy, and plays a prominent role with UNICEF rescuing imperilled children crossing the Mediterranean. When I spoke to her again after a year or so, and after we basically screamed at each other with joy down the phone, she said, 'Hey, now don't forget, yes? Make sure they spell my name right, Dex-terre. It's Armenian. It's with an "N".' I assured her they will. I assured her that people will find it hard to forget her. Sabrina still thinks about her – that girl she left behind when she returned to Rome.

Judith Léveillée has also left CAR and is working in Montreal on a project reorganising mental health services across Canada to better meet the needs of young people, particularly those in the Far North from Inuit and First Nation backgrounds. I can think of few better people to do such a crucial job.

Thomas Elbert continues his groundbreaking work around the understanding and rehabilitation of child soldiers. He and his team are in the throes of implementing a demobilisation and rehabilitation project for former child soldiers in the Kivu region of DRC. His commitment to deeply traumatised children, his 'clients', remains undimmed and unrelenting. He is an exceptional scholar and human being.

The marvellous Marian Wong has another fish. She is researching the beautifully striped humbug damselfish (*Dascyllus aruanus*), also found around Lizard Island, where the unprepossessing goby still get on with their remarkable little lives.

Hanifa Nakiryowa is still in the US. Her campaign has contributed to changing the law back in Uganda to make it more difficult to obtain toxic substances, and in particular acid. She continues to campaign for better criminal laws to protect the vulnerable from acid attacks. She still gets up at 3am every morning to do as much academic research as she can before her children wake. 'On snow days,' she says, 'my children have to come with me, so they become the youngest research assistants in the university.' Once she finishes her research degree, she aims to work in international development and human rights to empower women to speak out about abuse and domestic violence.

Rana hopes to begin her studies next year on the long road to becoming a teacher. She has still not bought her dress, but that day is coming ever closer.

Nim Tottenham is still at Columbia University We have discussed ways to gain a better understanding of the neuroanatomical changes caused by developmental shock and trauma such as FGM, with a view to more effective psychosocial intervention and support.

Peggy St Jacques has generously offered to assist with her expertise in the effects of biographical memory.

Jane Nicklinson is trying to keep the campaign going for the recognition in law of the right to assisted dying, in memory of her husband Tony. She continues to believe that dying with dignity is a basic right. Life after Tony remains hard. 'I lost my husband,' she says. 'But I miss my friend.'

Leyla Hussein keeps campaigning against FGM. Together we continue to lecture around the country and do our 'double act' on stage, in colleges, community centres, to whoever will listen. On occasion young women from the audience have quietly come forward afterwards and disclosed that they are FGM survivors. After years of isolation, fear and pain, they have sought help. Leyla has done that.

Ricky continues to have seizures, but is learning to communicate more effectively with the help of a computerised eye-recognition system. The DynaVox EyeMax system tracks his eye movements and has helped his carers and family begin to understand what he really wants. As Angie puts it, 'Before the "contraption", our communication with Ricky was 90 per cent guesswork. You get to know your child, of course, but we were still basically guessing. Now he can show us on-screen exactly what he wants and in what order: bath – telly – teeth – bed. It is more than magic, it's basically a miracle.'

It occurred to me that this is a similar method of communication to the one Dawn Faizey Webster uses. I suggested they get in touch.

So then there is Dawn. Who won our bet from the beginning of the book? I won't brag because it was not a fair wager. I already knew. I had her on my bench. As part of her master's degree, Dawn explored how to curate an online exhibition of Scythian (ancient Kazakh and nomadic) art. The Open University have been using her to front some of their advertising campaigns ('I've become a poster girl. I need an agent.'). The short video clip about Dawn has at the time of writing received several million hits ('Gangnam Style watch out. Make way for Faizey Style.').

Dawn and I are in contact every week. Invariably, she won't mind my saying, it is about nonsense. But sometimes it is about the really important stuff. For example, as I write this, we are debating whether it was Albanian or Libyan gangsters who shot

Doc Brown in *Back to the Future* – I've just conducted an Albanian Mafia murder trial at the Old Bailey. We riff on art and architecture and critical theory, and always have what we call the Bin of Spurious Ideas close at hand. She's teaching me her A-H-N-T language – I'm pretty awful – and is planning a trip along the Silk Road through China and Kazakhstan ('Hellishly difficult for me, that's why'). I sometimes forget that she ekes out her side of the conversation one blink at a time. Extraordinarily, provocatively, irrepressibly, her life opens out in a myriad directions.

As I was writing this concluding section of the book, I received a text from Dawn. It simply said, 'I'm in.' She had been accepted on a PhD programme at the University of York – well done, York. It was such a historic moment that, unusually, I called the Faizey home. Her father, Alec, answered. 'I'll put you on to Dr Dawn, then, shall I?' he said. I just spoke down the phone and she just listened. I told her how proud I was and other woefully inadequate things. What lies ahead is an academic collaboration the likes of which, I suspect, the world has rarely seen. 'Ah, well, I suppose there's that,' Alec said. 'She brightens up our lives, don't you, eh, Dawn?'

Just as Dawn and I have grown closer, I have lost touch with others. Some, for their own reasons, which I respect, do not want me to say any more and thus I do not. I hope you will understand. They have given their stories, given of themselves; they are moving on. They have sent their dispatch.

Ubah has gone back to Africa; Vasily is still driving. I hope to meet them again one day. I wish them rest.

Gareth's mother Pam has spent the years since that night at Rainsbrook trying to come to terms with her son's death. Occasionally she finds herself speaking to him and that helps. She says that she gets through thinking, 'No one can hurt him now, he is safe.'

When he was approaching the early peak of his fame and public adulation, one of the most remarkable of all *Homo sapiens* began to realise with growing horror that one of his critical faculties – to him perhaps the most critical – was fading. He came from a modest family, not unfamiliar with hardship and tragedy. His father was a violent alcoholic, his mother the daughter of a cook, and regularly the child was locked in a cellar for hours, slapped or punched (as Vasily's father once did to him). Later the boy, his name often shortened within the family to Louis, developed a habit of thrusting his head in cold water – again, something that happened to Vasily. Certainly in the last seven years of this remarkable person's life, while he had to communicate through written notes, he was severely deaf. He did not let it defeat him.

After his death, reports circulated of the stricken and desperate Ludwig van Beethoven being reduced to sawing off the legs of his piano so he could continue to compose by feeling the vibrations coming through the floor. Whether or not that was true, the clamour of the world had cruelly receded, and Beethoven was condemned to live in a cocoon of silence and vibration. He refused to capitulate to his fate. He refused to surrender.

In those final years before his death, although virtually unable to hear the music he had created, Beethoven composed the late piano sonatas, one of which I tried to play after my father's death, and the string quartets; he finished the staggering *Missa Solemnis* and he retrieved from somewhere deep inside himself the revolutionary Ninth Symphony. In short, while the world outside his head became silent, he composed some of the greatest music humankind possesses. As he famously wrote, despite his miserable condition and torment, he refused to 'leave the world until I had brought forth all that I felt was within me'. Along with Shakespeare, that chapel ceiling in Rome, perhaps *Anna*

Karenina and *War and Peace* and the art of Picasso (you will have your own picks), Beethoven's music from this period sits near the summit of human creative endeavour. Created when he was devastatingly deaf.

What was he doing? What was he saying? In one way, it was very simple. Beethoven was saying to us: Can you hear me?

In a sense, this book has been a series of vibrations, of human resonances across both time and space. The thing about humans, the carriers of the Ten Types, is that for all their maddening behaviour, they are extraordinarily tenacious and resourceful. Those attributes are, no doubt, along with their frontal brain capacity and social or sociable instincts, the keys to their evolutionary success, to ours. We compete; we also cooperate. We strive for individual distinctiveness; we also want to belong. This book has been about the children who work in slavery on the lake, and those who fight for survival having been enlisted in combat groups in bloody internecine wars, about the young women who are sold into sexual exploitation, about those who live their lives having suffered FGM or who are at constant threat of it. It has travelled to frontiers of the human condition, places that often seem impossibly remote. But we can be forcibly transported there, as Dawn Faizey Webster found, in a heartbeat or two. While we're sitting on a sofa. As Anthony found, when he went to the store to buy a Coke; when Rana was out buying her mother a present. So, yes, life has that capacity: to assault and ambush. What are you going to do? That is the question life asks. How are you going to do it? The book has shown the answers given by a number of unconquerable human beings. People who, in the words painted on that sign by the sea wall in Old Accra, have 'overcome the world'. Because experience, Sophocles also tells us, unbaffles us. Through their struggle these people have shown some of the ways; they have revealed what lies often unknown within us, the glory and gore, the wonder and terror, of being human – the Ten Types.

At a pivotal moment in the final movement of Beethoven's final completed symphony, a lone voice suddenly sings, '*O Freunde, nicht diese Töne*'. Friends, enough of these sounds. Instead of despondency and despair, the exhortation is to join in a carnival of life. Slowly, steadily, this solitary voice is joined by another, then more, a small group, then a chorus, as the music rises and rushes into what is arguably the swirling climactic storm of noise and sound about the human condition.

This book has sought to connect with those sounds. And I want to introduce a final one. The sound of the voice of Ubah's 'friend', the one she never met, Eunice.

Eunice Kathleen Waymon was born on 21 February 1933 in Tryon, North Carolina. She died, aged 70, in France. She came from a modest black family. In fact, somewhere within her lay so much of the history of not only that region but also of that country. Her great-great-grandmother was a Native American, a survivor of a people who were, as Eunice later wrote, 'destroyed to make way for the plantations and railroad.' This young indigenous woman married an African slave and then had a daughter with him, also born into slavery. A couple of generations later, the family had a girl of remarkable talent. They named her Eunice. She started playing the piano at the age of three. She aspired to attend one of the nation's most eminent music schools, which was in Philadelphia, but was rejected because of her race – that's what she always believed. She studied hard, learning Brahms, Bach and Beethoven. At her first recital, her parents, sitting proudly in the front row, were forced to move to the back. She refused to play until they were allowed to return to the front.

Eunice went on to fill the world with blues and soul, jazz and R & B, singing, writing, playing the piano. She was a civil rights activist, whose song, the one Ubah played over and over again, became one of the anthems of the civil rights movement in the US, one of its defining sounds. We know her better as Nina Simone. It was the simplicity of that song Simone sang that got under my skin and became a kind of soundtrack for this book. I suspect you will recognise it too: the smooth, haunting piano introduction, the quiet clicking of fingers, before Simone's voice soars with her song, 'I Wish I Knew How It Would Feel to Be Free'.

If you haven't listened to it for a while (or ever), please do so.

And if you do, think of Patrice and Saira, and Dawn Faizey Webster and Tony Nicklinson, and Miss L and Anna – all these parallel lives – Vasily and Lena, Ubah and Omer, my fantastic, fanatical friend Sabrina, François and Marielle, Hanifa Nakiryowa and Rana, Anthony and Michael, all of them beside the lakes and rivers, the steppe and cities and strange seas of our human-infested world. All their stories, rising up in a chorus, their massed voices reaffirming and reconnecting us with our capacity to find fresh ways to endure, to resist, to rise up, to be free – to believe, as Saira's father did, that *tout est possible*. So while the book has explored hidden parts of our mental make-up that can dispirit and dismay, it has also been about those other parallel parts that dignify our lives.

We know some of the facts about the human mind. We don't know them all. That adventure lies before us. It is arguably the next great frontier of science. We will uncover and spy with extraordinary clarity more and more executive systems that make up our mind. We will be looking more clearly at ourselves. In doing so, as Manuel Castells exhorts us, we will unveil the presence of harmful powers in the workings of our mind. When we do so, we will better be able to challenge – even, eventually, change – them.

It is the nature of human nature that these twin processes – the dispiriting and the dignifying – seem to go hand in hand. How to make sense of it? The subtitle of the book captures its most urgent purpose: to understand. To understand who we are, with a view opening the door to the myriad, marvellous possibilities for who we can be. At the very heart of it is a desire to utilise this under-standing as a gateway. To what? To tolerance. Why is this neces-sary? Why is this *urgent*? I write this to you as a kind of postscript to the book. As I was finalising the typeset manuscript I went to see the fiftieth anniversary production of Tom Stoppard's extraor-dinary take on *Hamlet* and the meaning of life, *Rosencrantz and Guildenstern Are Dead*. Afterwards, we treated ourselves to a taxi home, driving through moonlit London, enthusing about the play, when suddenly we crossed the Thames, as we'd done one hundred times before. The Houses of Parliament rose stunningly into view. Only now it was different. There were flowers all along Westminster Bridge. We were following the route of the vehicle used by a terrorist two days before, a terrorist who had killed and injured so many innocent people. On the other side of the river was a policeman. At first it looked like he was guarding the Palace of Westminster. But he wasn't. He stood alone in tears near to the place where his fellow officer was killed. There are many ways to grieve such things. One is to be a beacon of tolerance in an increas-ingly intolerant world. We can each start to do that by under-standing ourselves and others better.

This book has been about those three questions posed at the beginning: who we are, what we are, who is inside us. It has been about hearing the voices of those Types within us, and harnessing their world-overcoming power, in different ways, in different places, on different scales, to find fresh ways to help ourselves and others to be free. We are exceptionally evolved organisms with exceptionally evolved minds, shaped as the rest of the natural world is by natural selection. We are genetically linked to that abundant, astounding natural world. We are part of it. As Max Delbrück also says, we are, 'one thread in the infinite web of all living forms, all interrelated and all interdependent.' We have a duty to that web. It's a kind of family loyalty. This is our true place in the world. But time is short, the water is rising; yet if we listen, then I believe we can hear, and can say: here is how the story begins once more.

It begins again as Patrice and Saira seek a new land across a great desert, and Dawn Faizey Webster embarks on a new research degree; as Leyla Hussein speaks about FGM and Ubah saves another girl from cutting; as Hanifa endures another operation, and Rana dreams of the Roman Forum; as Vasily finds another road to travel, and François invites another person into his 'limousine'; as Ricky's machine makes his secret thoughts come alive, and Anthony, the boy who thought he was nobody, quietly makes his way home. The story begins again as two human brains, yours and mine, perform that extraordinary feat their ancestral family sitting by a savannah fire would never have dreamed of and yet, through an untorn ribbon of human life, helped make happen: communicating across time and space through a series of shapes on a page or a screen. It begins again as I write and you read these words, and we hear Eunice Kathleen Waymon's song, 'I Wish I Knew How It Would Feel to Be Free'.

The Sound of the Book

The following pieces of music somehow became attached to the book. Some have provided support or inspiration to the people within it.

PART I – THE PERCEIVER OF PAIN
'A Real Hero' (feat. Electric Youth) – College & Electric Youth
'Poor Wayfaring Stranger' – Natalie Merchant

PART II – THE OSTRACISER
'Beyond the Sea' – (a) Bobby Darin; (b) Kathryn Williams &
    Adam Lipinski
'Paid My Dues' – Anastacia [*chosen by Kathy Bolkovac*]

PART III – THE TAMER OF TERROR
'Forever Autumn' – Jeff Wayne (feat. Richard Burton) [*selected
    by Dawn Faizey Webster*]

'Mad World' – (a) Tears For Fears; (b) (feat. Gary Jules) – Michael Andrews

PART IV – THE BEHOLDER
Piano Sonata No. 30 in E Major, Op. 109: III Andante – Ludwig van Beethoven
'I Am Not Alone' – Kari Jobe [*chosen by Hanifa Nakiryowa*]

PART V – THE AGGRESSOR
'I'm Gonna Be (500 Miles)' – The Proclaimers
'Shine Bright Like a Diamond' – Julie Anna

PART VI – THE TRIBALIST
'America' – Cast, *West Side Story* (Original Motion Picture Soundtrack)
'Wicked Game' – Chris Isaak

PART VII – THE NURTURER
'Time After Time' – Cyndi Lauper
'Reach Out, I'll Be There' – Four Tops

PART VIII – THE ROMANCER
'Bang Bang (My Baby Shot Me Down)' – Déborrah 'Moogy' Morgane
Mazurka in A Minor, Op. 68, No. 2: Lento – Frédéric Chopin
'Do You Love Me' – The Contours [*suggested by François, for Marielle*]

PART IX – THE RESCUER
'I Wanna Be Your Dog' – The Stooges
'Weather With You' – Crowded House

PART X – AGAIN CAME THE KINSMAN

'Fix You' – Coldplay [*chosen by Angie, for Ricky*]

'I'm Sticking With You' – (a) Velvet Underground; (b) The
Decemberists

EPILOGUE

'Here Comes the Sun' – The Beatles

Symphony No. 9 in D Minor 'Choral': Ode to Joy – Ludwig
van Beethoven

'I Wish I Knew How It Would Feel To Be Free' – Nina
Simone [*suggested by Ubah*]

Bibliography

This is a small selection of key texts I've leaned on in the composition of this book. To make it more accessible, I've divided the list according to the book's ten parts, and then further subdivided it into topics within each part so you can drill down into what really interests you for further exploration. The references are then ordered alphabetically within each topic. Some of the most provocative and thought-provoking research and analysis in the last 150 years lies below. I wish to express my particular gratitude to the seminal work of John Tooby and Leda Cosmides on evolutionary psychology; Rob Kurzban on modularity; Doug Kenrick and Vlad Griskevicius for their ingenious work on 'subselves'; and Steven Pinker for explaining to the world how the mind actually works. As previously mentioned, the full list is on the book's webpage at the penguin.co.uk website. Enjoy.

From the Author

Methodology

Bourdieu, P. (1987), 'The Force of Law: Toward a Sociology of the Juridical Field', *Hastings Law Review*, 38, pp. 814–53.

Bourdieu, P. et al. (1999), *The Weight of the World: social suffering in contemporary society*, Cambridge: Polity Press.

Bourdieu, P. and Wacquant, L. (1992), *An Invitation to Reflexive Sociology*, Cambridge: Polity Press.

Chomsky, N. (1998), *Profit Over People: Neoliberalism and the World Order*, New York: Seven Stories Press.

Chomsky, N. (2012), *How the World Works*, London: Hamish Hamilton.

Foucault, M. (1984), 'Nietzsche, Genealogy, History', in P. Rabinow (ed.), *The Foucault Reader: An Introduction to Foucault's Thought*, London: Penguin.

Lukes, S. (2005), *Power: A Radical View* (2nd edn), Basingstoke: Palgrave Macmillan.

Singer, P. (2000), *A Darwinian Left: Politics, Evolution and Cooperation*, New Haven, CT: Yale University Press.

Wacquant, L. (2004), *Body and Soul: notebooks of an apprentice boxer*, Oxford: Oxford University Press.

Wacquant, L. (2005), 'Carnal Connections: On Embodiment, Apprenticeship and Membership', *Qualitative Sociology*, 28(4), pp. 445–74.

Protective Measures

Berendt, J. (1994), *Midnight in the Garden of Good and Evil*, London: Chatto & Windus.

le Carré, J. (2016), *The Pigeon Tunnel: Stories from My Life*, London: Viking.

Obama, B. (2007), *Dreams From My Father: A Story of Race and Inheritance*, Edinburgh: Canongate Books.

Sacks, O. (1991), *Awakenings*, London: Picador.

Sacks, O. (1985/2015), *The Man Who Mistook His Wife For a Hat*, London: Picador Classic.

Yalom, I. (1991), *Love's Executioner and Other Tales of Psychotherapy*, London: Penguin.

Prologue

General

Castells, M. (2009), *Communication Power*, Oxford: Oxford University Press.

Delbrück, M. (1949), 'A Physicist Looks at Biology', *Transactions of the Connecticut Academy of Arts and Sciences*, 38, pp. 173–90.

Dick, P. (1987/2000), *We Can Remember It For You Wholesale*, London: Millennium.

Wilson, E. (2013), *The Social Conquest of Earth*, New York: Liverlight.

Child Restraint (and Gareth Myatt)

Carlile, Lord (2006), *An independent inquiry into the use of physical restraint, solitary confinement and forcible strip searching of children in prisons, secure training centres and local authority secure children's homes*, London: Howard League for Penal Reform.

Carlile, Lord (2011), *House of Lords public hearings on the restraint of children*, London: Howard League for Penal Reform.

Carlile, Lord (2016), *The Carlile Inquiry 10 Years On: the use of restraint, solitary confinement and strip-searching on children*, London: Howard League for Penal Reform.

Foucault, M. (1977), *Discipline and Punish: The Birth of the Prison*, London: Penguin.

Goldson, B. (2006), 'Damage, harm and death in child prisons in England and Wales: questions of abuse and accountability', *The Howard Journal of Criminal Justice*, 45(5), pp. 449–67.

Goldson, B. and Coles, D. (2005), *In the Care of the State? – Child deaths in penal custody in England & Wales*, London: INQUEST.

Howard League (2011), *Twisted: the use of force on children in custody*, London: Howard League for Penal Reform.

Medway Improvement Board (2016), *Final Report of the Board's Advice to the Secretary of State for Justice*, [online]. Available at https://www.gov.uk/government/uploads/system/uploads/attachment_data/file/523167/medway-report.pdf [most recently accessed 6 October 2016].

Office of the Children's Commissioner (2011), *Young people's views on restraint in the secure estate*, London: OCC.

Pounder, R. (on the application of) v HM Coroner for the North and South Districts of Durham and Darlington, the Youth Justice Board and others [2009], EWHC 76 (Admin), High Court.

United Nations Committee on the Rights of the Child (2002), *Concluding Observations of the Committee on the Rights of the Child: United Kingdom of Great Britain and Northern Ireland*, Geneva: United Nations.

Part I – The Perceiver of Pain

A – The Argument

Evolution

Coyne, J. (2009), *Why Evolution Is True*, Oxford: Oxford University Press.

Darwin, C. (1859/2004), *On the Origin of Species by Means of Natural Selection*, London: Macmillan Collector's Library.

Darwin, C. (1871), *The Descent of Man, and Selection in Relation to Sex*, London: Murray.

Darwin, C. (1872/2002), *The Expression of Emotions in Man and Animals*, New York: Oxford University Press.

Dawkins, R. (1976), *The Selfish Gene*, Oxford: Oxford University Press.

Dawkins, R. (1986), *The Blind Watchmaker*, New York: W. W. Norton.

Dennett, D. (1995), *Darwin's Dangerous Idea: Evolution and the Meanings of Life*, New York: Simon and Schuster.

Dunbar, R. (1992), 'Neocortex size as a constraint on group size in primates', *Journal of Human Evolution*, 20, pp. 469–93.

Dunbar, R. (1993), 'Coevolution of neocortical size, group size and language in humans', *Behavioral and Brain Sciences*, 11, pp. 681–735.

Dunbar, R. and Shultz, S. (2007), 'Evolution in the social brain', *Science*, 317, pp. 1344–7.

Hamilton, W. (1964), 'The genetic evolution of social behaviour, I and II', *Journal of Theoretical Biology*, 7, pp. 1–52.

Pinker, S. (2002), *The Blank Slate: The Modern Denial of Human Nature*, New York: Viking.

Shermer, M. (2006), *Why Darwin Matters: The Case Against Intelligent Design*, New York: Times Books.

Tattersall, I. (1998), *Becoming Human: Evolution and Human Uniqueness*, New York: Harcourt Brace.

Evolutionary Psychology

Barkow, J., Cosmides, L. and Tooby, J. (eds) (1992), *The Adapted Mind: Evolutionary Psychology and the Generation of Culture*, New York: Oxford University Press.

Barrett, L. et al. (2001), *Human Evolutionary Psychology*, Basingstoke: Palgrave Macmillan.

Buss, D. (2005), *The Handbook of Evolutionary Psychology*, Hoboken, NJ: Wiley.

Buss, D. (2016), *Evolutionary Psychology: The New Science of the Mind*, New York: Routledge.

Workman, L. and Reader, W. (2014), *Evolutionary Psychology: An Introduction*, Cambridge: Cambridge University Press.

Modularity

Barrett, H. (2012), 'Evolutionary Psychology', in Frankish, W. and Ramsey, W. (eds), *Cambridge Handbook of Cognitive Science*, Cambridge: Cambridge University Press (pp. 257–74).

Barrett, H. and Kurzban, R. (2006), 'Modularity in Cognition: framing the debate', *Psychological Review*, 113, pp. 628–47.

Carruthers, P. (2006), 'The Case for Massive Modular Models of the Mind', in Stainton, R. (ed.), *Contemporary Debates in Cognitive Science*, Oxford: Blackwell.

Chiappe, D. and Gardner, R. (2011), 'The modularity debate in evolutionary psychology', *Theory & Psychology*, 22(5), pp. 669–82.

Cosmides, L. and Tooby, J. (2002), 'Unraveling the enigma of human intelligence: evolutionary psychology and the multi-modular mind', in Sternberg, R. and Kaufman, J. (eds), *The evolution of intelligence*, Mahwah, NJ: Erlbaum (pp. 145–98).

Fodor, J. A. (1983), *The Modularity of Mind: An Essay on Faculty Psychology*, Cambridge, MA: MIT Press.

Kenrick, D. and Griskevicius, V. (2013), *The Rational Animal: How Evolution Made Us Smarter Than We Think*, New York: Basic Books.

Kurzban, R. (2012), *Why Everyone (Else) Is a Hypocrite: Evolution and the Modular Mind*, Princeton, NJ: Princeton University Press.

Kurzban, R. and Aktipis, C. (2006), 'Modular minds, multiple motives', in Schaller, M., Simpson, J. and Kenrick, D. (eds), *Evolution and Social Psychology*, New York: Psychology Press (pp. 39–53).

Pinker, S. (1997), *How the Mind Works*, New York: W. W. Norton.

Ramachandran, V. S. and Blakeslee, S. (1999), *Phantoms in the Brain: Human Nature and the Architecture of the Mind*, London: Fourth Estate.

Sperber, D. (1994), 'The modularity of thought and the epidemiology of representations', in Hirschfeld, L. and Gelman, S. (eds), *Mapping the Mind: Domain-specificity in Cognition and Culture*, Cambridge: Cambridge University Press (pp. 39–67).

Tooby, J. and Cosmides, L. (1992), 'The Psychological Foundations of Culture', in Barkow, J. et al. (eds), *The Adapted Mind: Evolutionary Psychology and the Generation of Culture*, New York: Oxford University Press (pp. 19–136).

Counter-Arguments/Criticisms and 'Adaptationism'

Dupre, J. (2012), 'Against Maladaptationism: or, what's wrong with evolutionary psychology?', in Dupre, J., *Processes of Life: Essays in Philosophy of Biology*, Oxford: Oxford University Press (pp. 245–60).

Fehr, C. (2012), 'Feminist Engagement with Evolutionary Psychology', *Hypatia*, 27, pp. 50–72.

Gould, S. and Lewontin, R. (1979), 'The Spandrels of San Marco and the Panglossian Paradigm: A Critique of the Adaptationist Programme', *Proceedings of the Royal Society of London*, B 205.

Nature/Nurture

Gander, E. (2003), *On Our Minds: How Evolutionary Psychology Is Reshaping the Nature-Versus-Nurture Debate*, Baltimore, MD: Johns Hopkins University Press.

Pinker, S. (2004), 'Why nature & nurture won't go away', *Daedalus*, 133(4), pp. 5–17.

Ridley, M. (2003), *Nature Via Nurture: Genes, Experience, and What Makes Us Human*, London: Fourth Estate.

Smith, A. et al. (2016), 'Food fussiness and food neophobia share a common etiology in early childhood', *Journal of Child Psychology and Psychiatry* (October 2016).

Tooby, J. and Cosmides, L. (1990), 'On the Universality of Human Nature and the Uniqueness of the Individual: The Role of Genetics and Adaptation', *Journal of Personality*, 58, pp. 17–67.

Wertz, A. and Wynn, K. (2014), 'Selective social learning of plant edibility in 6- and 18-month-old infants', *Psychological Science*, 25(4), pp. 874–82.

B – Anthony and Michael

Child Labour and Child Slavery

Acred, C. (2014), *Child Labour & Exploitation*, Cambridge: Independence Educational Publishers.

International Labour Office (2012), *ILO Global Estimate of Child Labour*, Geneva: ILO Publications.

Empathy and Compassion

de Waal, F. (2012), *The Age of Empathy: Nature's Lessons For a Kinder Society*, New York: Three Rivers Press.

Faulkner, W. (1936/1995), *Absalom, Absalom!*, London: Vintage Classics.

Pegna, A. et al. (2005), 'Discriminating emotional faces without primary visual cortices involves the right amygdala', *Nature Neuroscience*', 8, pp. 24–25.

Pegna, A. et al. (2008), 'Visual search for facial expressions of emotion is less affected in simultanagnosia', *Cortex*, 44(1), pp. 46–53.

Pegna, A. et al. (2008), 'Electrophysiological evidence for early non-conscious processing of fearful facial expressions', *International Journal of Psychophysiology*, 70(2), pp. 127–136.

Russell, C. et al. (2016), 'Motivation and attention following hemispheric stroke', *Progress in Brain Research*, 229, pp. 343–66.

Slovic, P. (2007), '"If I Look at the Mass I Will Never Act": Psychic Numbing and Genocide', *Judgment and Decision Making*, 2, pp. 79–95.

Singer, P. (1972), 'Famine, Affluence and Morality', *Philosophy and Public Affairs*, 1, pp. 229–43.

Singer, T. et al. (2004), 'Empathy for pain involves the affective but not sensory components of pain', *Science*, 303, pp. 1157–62.

Smith, A. (1759/2010), *Theory of Moral Sentiments*, London: Penguin Classics.

Part II – The Ostraciser

Fish (and Other Animals)

Clutton-Brock, T. (2009), 'Cooperation between non-kin in animal societies', *Nature*, 462, pp. 51–7.

Clutton-Brock, T. et al. (2002), 'Evolution and development of sex differences in cooperative behaviour in meerkats', *Science*, 297, pp. 253–6.

Clutton-Brock, T. et al. (2005), '"False feeding" and aggression in meerkat societies', *Animal Behaviour*, 69, pp. 1273–84.

Solomon, N. and French, J. (1997), *Cooperative Breeding in Mammals*, Cambridge: Cambridge University Press.

Wong, M. et al. (2007), 'The threat of punishment enforces peaceful cooperation and stabilizes queues in a coral-reef fish', *Proceedings of the Royal Society B: Biological Sciences*, 274 (1613), (pp. 1093–9).

Wong, M. and Balshine, S. (2011), 'The evolution of cooperative breeding in the African cichlid fish, *Neolamprologus pulcher*', *Biological Reviews*, 86, pp. 511–30.

Ostracism

Baumeister, R. et al. (2002), 'Effects of social exclusion on cognitive processes: anticipated aloneness reduces intelligent thought', *J. Personal. Soc. Psychol*, 83, pp. 817–27.

Baumeister, R. et al. (2006), 'Social exclusion impairs self-regulation', *J. Personal. Soc. Psychol.*, 88, pp. 589–604.

Bolkovac, K. and Lynn, C. (2011), *The Whistleblower: Sex Trafficking, Military Contractors and One Woman's Fight for Justice*, Basingstoke: Palgrave Macmillan.

Gruter, M. and Masters, R. (1986), 'Ostracism: a social and biological phenomenon', *Ethol. Sociobiol.*, 7, pp.149–395.

Kurzban, R. and Leary, M. (2001), 'Evolutionary origins of stigmatization: the functions of social exclusion', *Psychological Bulletin*, 127(2), pp. 187–208.

Eisenberger, N. et al. (2003), 'Does rejection hurt: an fMRI study of social exclusion', *Science*, 302, pp. 290–2.

Eisenberger, N. and Lieberman, D. (2004), 'Why rejection hurts: the neurocognitive overlap between physical and social pain', *Trends in Cognitive Sciences*, 8, pp. 294–300.

Hobbes, T. (1651/2008), *Leviathan*, Oxford: Oxford World Classics.

Leary, M. et al. (2003), 'Teasing, rejection, and violence: case studies of the school shootings', *Aggressive Behavior*, 29, pp. 202–14.

MacDonald, G. and Leary, M. (2005), 'Why does social exclusion hurt? The relationship between social and physical pain', *Psychol. Bull.*, 131, pp. 202–23

Williams, K. (2001), *Ostracism: The Power of Silence*, New York: Guilford.

Williams, K. (2007), 'Ostracism', *Annual Review of Psychology*, 58, pp. 425–52.

Williams, K. (2007), 'Ostracism: the kiss of social death', *Social and Personality Compass*, 1, pp. 236–24.

Williams, K. et al. (2000), 'CyberOstracism: effects of being ignored over the Internet', *J. Personal. Soc. Psychol.*, 79, pp. 748–62.

Part III – The Tamer of Terror

Terror/ Terror Management Theory

Becker, E. (1973), *The Denial of Death*, New York: The Free Press.

Gilderdale, K. (2011), *One Last Goodbye: sometimes only a mother's love can help end the pain*, London: Ebury Press.

Hirschberger, G. et al. (2010), 'Looking away from death: defensive attention as a form of terror management', *Journal of Experimental Social Psychology*, 46, pp. 172–8.

Landau, M. et al. (2006), 'The Siren's Call: Terror Management and the Threat of Men's Sexual Attraction to Women', *Journal of Personality and Social Psychology*, 90(1), pp. 129–46.

Landau, M. et al. (2007), 'On the compatibility of terror management theory and perspectives on human evolution', *Evolutionary Psychology*, 5(3), pp. 476–519.

Owen, A. et al. (2006), 'Detecting Awareness in the Vegetative State', *Science*, 313, p. 1402.

Rosenblatt, A. et al. (1989), 'Evidence for Terror Management Theory: I. The Effects of Mortality Salience on Reactions to Those Who Violate or Uphold Cultural Values', *Journal of Personality and Social Psychology*, 57(4), pp. 681–90.

Roth, P. (2002), *The Dying Animal*, London: Vintage.

Solomon, S. et al. (1991), 'Terror management theory of self-esteem', in Snyder, C. and Forsyth, D. (eds), *Handbook of Social and Clinical Psychology: The Health Perspective*, New York: Pergamon Press (pp. 21–40).

Solomon, S. et al. (1991), 'A terror management theory of social behavior: the psychological functions of self-esteem and cultural worldviews', in M. P. Zanna (ed.), *Advances in Experimental Social Psychology*, New York: Academic Press (vol. 24, pp. 93–159).

Solomon, S. et al. (2016), *The Worm at the Core: On the Role of Death in Life*, London: Penguin.

Locked-in Syndrome

Laureys, S. et al. (2005), 'The locked-in syndrome: what is it like to be conscious but paralyzed and voiceless?', *Progress in Brain Research*, 150, pp. 495–511.

Nizzi, M. C. et al. (2012), 'From armchair to wheelchair: how patients with a locked-in syndrome integrate bodily changes in experienced identity', *Consciousness and Cognition*, 21(1), pp. 431–7.

Part IV – The Beholder

Acid Violence

Acid Survivors Trust International (2016), *Justice? What Justice? Tackling Acid Violence and Ensuring Justice for Survivors*, London: ASTI.

Kalantry, S. and Getgen, E. (2011), 'Combatting Acid Violence in Bangladesh, India and Cambodia', *Cornell Legal Studies Research Paper*, pp. 11–24.

Faces

Aharon, I. et al. (2001), 'Beautiful Faces Have Variable Reward Value: fMRI and Behavioral Evidence', *Neuron*, 32, pp. 537–51.

Daly, M. and Wilson, M. (2005), 'Carpe Diem: adaptation and devaluing the future', *The Quarterly Review of Biology*, 80(1), pp. 55–60.

Eberhardt, J. et al. (2006), 'Looking Deathworthy: Perceived Stereotypicality of Black Defendants Predicts Capital-Sentencing Outcomes', *Cornell Law School research paper*, no. 06–012, Ithaca, NY: Cornell Law School.

Foucault, M. (1988), 'Technologies of the Self', in Martin, L. et al. (eds), *Technologies of the Self: a seminar with Michel Foucault*, London: Tavistock.

Halberstadt, J. and Rhodes, G. (2000), 'The attractiveness of nonface averages: implications for an evolutionary explanation of the attractiveness of average faces', *Psychological Science*, 11, pp. 285–9.

Langlois, J. et al. (1987), 'Infant preferences for attractive faces: rudiments of a stereotype', *Developmental Psychology*, 23, pp. 363–9.

Langlois, J. and Roggman, L. (1990), 'Attractive faces are only average', *Psychological Science*, 1, pp. 115–21.

Langlois, J. et al. (1991), 'Facial diversity and infant preference for attractive faces', *Developmental Psychology*, 27, pp. 79–84.

Quinn, P. et al. (2008), 'Preference for attractive faces in human infants extends beyond conspecifics', *Developmental Science*, 11(1), pp. 76–83.

Slater, A. et al. (2000), 'Newborn infants' preference for attractive faces: the role of internal and external facial features', *Infancy*, 1, pp. 265–74.

Slater, A. and Quinn, P. (2001), 'Face recognition in the newborn infant', *Infant and Child Development*, 10, pp. 21–24.

Slater, A. et al. (2003), 'The role of facial orientation in newborn infants' preference for attractive faces', *Developmental Science*, 3, pp. 181–5.

Wilson, M. and Daly, M. (2004), 'Do Pretty Women Cause Men to Discount the Future?', *Proceedings of the Biological Society*, 271(4), pp. 177–9.

Part V – The Aggressor

Aggression

Adams, D. et al. (1990), 'The Seville Statement on Violence', *American Psychologist*, 45, p. 1167.

Anderson, C. A. and Bushman, B. (2002), 'Human aggression', *Annual Reviews of Psychology*, 53, pp. 27–51.

Batson, D. et al. (2003), '"As you would have them do onto you": does imagining yourself in the other's place stimulate moral action?', *Personality and Social Psychology Bulletin*, 29, pp. 1190– 201.

Buss, D. (2006), *The Murderer Next Door: Why the Mind is Designed to Kill*, New York: Penguin.

Cushman, F. et al. (2012), 'Simulating Murder: the aversion to harmful action', *Emotion*, 12(1), p. 2.

Grossman, D. (1995), *On Killing*, Boston: Little, Brown.

Hammes, T. (2006), *The Sling and the Stone: On War in the 21st Century*, St Paul, MN: Zenith Press.

LeDoux, J. (1996), *The Emotional Brain*, New York: Simon & Schuster.

Martens, A. et al. (2007), 'Killing begets killing: evidence from a bug-killing paradigm that initial killing fuels subsequent killing', *Personality and Social Psychology Bulletin*, 33, pp. 1251–64.

Pinker, S. (2011), *The Better Angels of Our Nature: Why Violence Has Declined*, New York: Viking.

Singer, T. et al. (2004), Empathy for pain involves the affective but not sensory components of pain', *Science*, 303, pp. 1157–62.

Webber, D. et al. (2013), 'Using a Bug-Killing Paradigm to Understand How Social Validation and Invalidation Affect the Distress of Killing', *Personality and Social Psychology Bulletin*, 39(4), pp. 470–81.

Wrangham, R. et al. (2006), 'Comparative rates of violence in chimpanzees and humans', *Primates*, 47, pp. 14–26.

Central African Republic

Gide, A. (1995), *Voyage au Congo*, Paris: Gallimard Éducation.

Lombard, L. (2016), *State of Rebellion: Violence and Intervention in the Central African Republic (African Arguments)*, London: Zed Books.

Titley, B. (2002), *Dark Age: The Political Odyssey of Emperor Bokassa*, Montreal: McGill-Queen's University Press.

Child Soldiering/Appetitive Aggression

Amone-P'Olak, K. et al. (2007), *South African Psychiatry Review*, 10, pp. 76–82.

Brett, R. and Sprecht, I. (2004), *Young Soldiers: why they choose to fight*, Boulder, CO: Lynne Rienner.

Child Soldiers International (2017), 'What are child soldiers?', [online]. From https://www.child-soldiers.org/about-the-issue [most recently accessed 8 March 2017].

Coalition to Stop the Use of Child Soldiers (2010), *Mai Mai child soldier recruitment and use: entrenched and unending*, London: Coalition to Stop the Use of Child Soldiers, pp. 1–17.

Elbert, T. and Schauer, M. (2002), 'Psychological trauma: burnt into memory', *Nature*, 419, p. 883.

Elbert, T. et al. (2006), 'The influence of organized violence and terror on brain and mind – a co-constructive perspective', in Baltes, P. et al. (eds), *Lifespan Development and the Brain: The Perspective of Biocultural Co-constructivism*, Cambridge: Cambridge University Press (pp. 1–36).

Elbert, T. et al. (2010), 'Fascination violence: on mind and brain of man hunters', *European Archives of Psychiatry and Clinical Neuroscience*, 260(1), pp. 100–5.

Friedman, M. (2001), *Post Traumatic Stress Disorder*, Kansas City: Compact Clinicals.

Heckler, T. et al. (2012), 'Appetitive aggression in former combatants – derived from the ongoing conflict in DR Congo', *International Journal of Law and Psychiatry*, 35(3), pp. 244–9.

Maclure, R. and Denov, M. (2006), '"I Didn't Want to Die So I Joined Them": Structuration and the Process of Becoming Boy

Soldiers in Sierra Leone', *Terrorism and Political Violence*, 18, pp. 119–35.

Pham, P. N. et al. (2009), 'Returning home: forced conscription, reintegration, and mental health status of former abductees of the Lord's Resistance Army in northern Uganda', *BioMed Central Psychiatry*, 9, p. 23.

Song, S. and de Jong, J. (2013), 'The Role of Silence in Burundian Former Child Soldiers', *International Journal of Adv. Counselling*, 36, pp. 84–95.

Tottenham, N. et al. (2009), 'A developmental perspective on human amygdala function', in Phelps, E. and Whalen, P. (eds), *The Human Amygdala*, New York: Guilford Press (pp. 107–17).

Tottenham, N. et al. (2010), 'Prolonged institutional rearing is associated with atypically large amygdala volume and emotion regulation difficulties', *Developmental Science*, 13(1), pp. 46–61.

Tottenham, N. (2012), 'Human Amygdala Development in the Absence of Species-Expected Caregiving', *Developmental Psychobiology*, 54, pp. 598–611.

Weierstall, R. et al. (2013), 'Relations among appetitive aggression, post-traumatic stress and motives for demobilization: a study in former Colombian combatants', *Conflict and Health*, 7, p. 9.

Part VI – The Tribalist

Noise

Dunbar, R. (2004), 'Gossip in Evolutionary Perspective', *Review of General Psychology*, 8(2), p. 100.

Étienne, D. et al. (2004), 'Public Information: From Nosy Neighbors to Cultural Evolution', *Science*, 305 (5683), pp. 487–91.

Hansjoerg, P. et al. (2007), 'Vocal Interactions in Common Nightingales (*Luscinia megarhynchos*): Males Take It Easy after Pairing', *Behavioral Ecology and Sociobiology*, 61(4), pp. 557–63.

Otter, K. et al. (1999), 'Female birds then seek extra-pair fertilisation from the "winner"', *Proc. R. Soc. London*, Ser. B266, p. 1305.

Groups

Allport, G. (1954), *The Nature of Prejudice*, Cambridge, MA: Addison-Wesley.

Brewer, M. (1979), 'Ingroup bias in the minimal intergroup situation: a cognitive motivational analysis', *Psychological Bulletin*, 86(2), pp. 307–24.

Sherif, M. (1967), *Group Conflict and Co-operation*, London: Routledge.

Sidanius, J. et al. (2004), 'Social dominance theory: its agenda and method', *Political Psychology*, 25, pp. 845–80.

Tajfel, H. (1970), 'Experiments in intergroup discrimination', *Scientific American*, 223(5), pp. 96–102.

Tajfel, H. (1974), 'Social identity and intergroup behaviour', *Social Science Information*, 13, pp. 65–93.

Tajfel, H. (1981), *Human Groups and Social Categories*, Cambridge: Cambridge University Press.

Tajfel, H. and Turner, J. (1986), 'The social identity theory of intergroup behaviour', in Austin, W. and Worchel, S. (eds), *Psychology of Intergroup Relations* (2nd edn), Chicago: Nelson-Hall (pp. 7–24).

Haiti

Dandicat, E. (1999), *The Farming of Bones*, London: Abacus.

Farmer, P. (2011), *Haiti After the Earthquake*, New York: Public Affairs.

Kidder, T. (2011), *Mountains Beyond Mountains: From Harvard to Haiti*, London: Profile.

Paulino, E. (2005), 'Erasing the Kreyol from the Margins of the Dominican Republic: The Pre- and Post- Nationalization Project of the Border, 1930–1945', *Wadabagei: Journal of the Caribbean and Its Diaspora*, 8(2), pp. 35–71.

Paulino, E. (2006), 'Anti-Haitianism, Historical Memory, and the Potential for Genocidal Violence in the Dominican Republic', *Genocide Studies and Prevention*, 1(3), pp. 265–88.

Race

Kurzban, R. et al. (2001), 'Can race be erased? Coalitional computation and social categorization', *Proceedings of the National Academy of Sciences*, 18 December 2001, 98(26), pp. 15387–92.

Voorspoels, W. et al. (2014), 'Can race really be erased? A pre-registered replication study', *Frontiers in Psychology*, 5, p. 1035.

Part VII – The Nurturer

Motherhood, Nurturing, Parental Investment

Basil of Caesarea (1998), in Boswell, J., *The Kindness of Strangers: The Abandonment of Children in Western Europe from Late Antiquity to the Renaissance*, Chicago, IL: University of Chicago Press (pp. 165–66).

Crittenden, P. (1988), 'Family and dyadic patterns of functioning in maltreating families', in Browne, K. et al. (eds), *Early*

Prediction and Prevention of Child Abuse, Chichester, England: Wiley (pp. 161–89).

Bugental, D. et al. (2013), 'Outcomes of parental investment in high-risk children', *J. Exp. Child Psychol.*, 116(1), pp. 59–67.

Daly, M. and Wilson, M. (1981), 'Abuse and neglect of children in evolutionary perspective', in Alexander, R. and Tinkle, D. (eds), *Natural Selection and Social Behavior*, New York: Chiron.

Daly, M., and Wilson, M. (1984), 'A sociobiological analysis of human infanticide', in Hausfater, G. and Hrdy, S. (eds), *Infanticide: Comparative and Evolutionary Perspectives*, New York: Aldine de Gruyter (pp. 487–502).

Daly, M. and Wilson, M. (1988), 'The Darwinian psychology of discriminative parental solicitude', *Nebraska Symposium on Motivation*, 35, pp. 91–144.

Daly, M. and Wilson, M. (1995), 'Discriminative parental solicitude and the relevance of evolutionary models to the analysis of motivational systems', in Gazzaniga, M. (ed.), *The Cognitive Neurosciences*, Cambridge, MA: MIT Press (pp. 1269–86).

Dozier, M. et al. (2001), 'Attachment for infants in foster care: the role of caregiver state of mind', *Child Development*, 72(5), pp. 1467–77.

Gibran, K. (1926/2013), *The Prophet*, London: Vintage Classics.

Hrdy, S. (1999), *Mother Nature: Natural Selection and the Female of the Species*, London: Chatto & Windus.

Hrdy, S. (2011), *Mothers and Others: The Evolutionary Origins of Mutual Understanding*, Cambridge, MA: Harvard University Press.

Lupien, S. (2009), 'Effects of stress throughout the lifespan on the brain, behaviour and cognition', *Nature Reviews Neuroscience*, 10(6), pp. 434–45.

Mann, J. (1995), 'Attachment and maternal compensation with high-risk infants: an ethological study', *Human Behavior and Evolution Society*, Santa Barbara, CA (June–July).

Mann, J. and Plunkett, J. (1992), 'Home observations of extremely low birthweight infants: maternal compensation or overstimulation', paper presented at the International Conference on Infant Studies, Miami, FL (May).

Main, M. and Hesse, E. (1990), 'Parents' unresolved traumatic experiences are related to infant disorganized attachment status: is frightened and/or frightening parental behaviour the linking mechanism?', in Greenberg, M. et al. (eds), *Attachment in the Preschool Years*, Chicago, IL: University of Chicago (pp. 161–82).

Quinlan, R. (2007), 'Human parental effort and environmental risk', *Proceedings of the Royal Society of London*, B274, pp. 121–5.

Quinlan, R. (2008), 'Human pair-bonds: evolutionary functions, ecological variation, and adaptive development', *Evolutionary Anthropology*, 17, pp. 227–38.

Sear, R. and Mace, R. (2008), 'Who keeps children alive? A review of the effects of kin on child survival', *Evolution and Human Behavior*, 29, pp. 1–18.

Tottenham, N. et al. (2010), Prolonged institutional rearing is associated with atypically large amygdala volume and difficulties in emotion regulation', *Developmental Science*, 13(1), pp. 46–61.

Trivers, R. (1972), 'Parental investment and sexual selection', in Campbell, B. (ed.), *Sexual Selection and the Descent of Man 1871–1971*, Chicago, IL: Aldine (pp. 136–79).

Wells, P. (2000), 'Medea or Madonna?', *Times Literary Supplement*, London, England (17 March).

Winking, J. et al. (2007), Why do men marry and why do they stray?', *Proceedings of the Royal Society*, B274, pp. 1643–9.

Foundling Wheels

Boswell, J. (1988), *The Kindness of Strangers: The Abandonment of Children in Western Europe from Late Antiquity to the Renaissance*, New York: Pantheon.

Fuchs, R. (1984), *Abandoned Children: Foundlings and Child Welfare in Nineteenth Century France*, Albany: SUNY Press.

Kertzer, D. (1993), *Sacrificed for Honor: Italian Infant Abandonment and the Politics of Reproductive Control*, Boston: Bantam Press.

Tilly, L. et al. (1992), 'Child abandonment in European history: a symposium', *Journal of Family History*, 17(1), pp. 1–23.

Frederick II

Abulafia, D. (1988), *Frederick II: A Medieval Emperor*, London: Allen Lane.

Einstein, D. (1949), *Emperor Frederick II*, New York: Philosophical Library.

Kantorowicz, E. (1967), *Frederick the Second, 1194–1250. Authorized English version by E. O. Lorimer*, New York: Frederick Unger.

Masson, G. (1957), *Frederick II of Hohenstaufen. A Life*, London: Secker & Warburg.

Sex Work

Kaysen, D. et al. (2003), 'Living in danger: the impact of chronic traumatization and the traumatic context on post-traumatic stress disorder trauma', *Violence and Abuse*, 4, pp. 247–64.

Ling, D. et al. (2001), 'Silent killers of the night: an exploration of psychological health and suicidality among female street sex workers', *Journal of Sex and Marital Therapy*, 33, pp. 281–99.

Wolves

Carter, A. (1979/2006), *The Bloody Chamber and Other Stories* ('The Company of Wolves'), London: Vintage Classics.

Part VIII – The Romancer

Anderson, S. (2007), 'The economics of dowry and brideprice', *The Journal of Economic Perspectives*, 21(4), pp. 151–74.

Buss, D. (1992), 'Mate preference mechanisms: consequences for partner choice and intrasexual competition', in Barkow, J. et al. (eds), *The Adapted Mind: Evolutionary Psychology and the Generation of Culture*, Oxford: Oxford University Press (pp. 249–66).

Buss, D. (1995), *The Evolution of Desire: Strategies of Human Mating*, New York: Basic Books.

Darwin, C. (1871), *The Descent of Man and Selection in Relation to Sex*, London: John Murray.

Fehr, E. and Fischbacher, U. (2003), 'The nature of human altruism', *Nature*, 425, pp. 785–91.

Griskevicius, V. et al. (2007), 'Blatant benevolence and conspicuous consumption: when romantic motives elicit strategic costly signals', *Journal of Personality and Social Psychology*, 93, pp. 85–102.

Kenrick, D. and Griskevicius, V. (2013), *The Rational Animal: How Evolution Made Us Smarter Than We Think*, New York: Basic Books.

Kimberley, J. et al. (2007), 'Chimpanzees share forbidden fruit', *PLOS ONE*, 2, p. 9.

Pan, Y. et al. (2011), 'Turning males on: activation of male courtship behavior in *Drosophila melanogaster*', *PLOS ONE*, 6(6), e21144.

Murdock, G. (1967), *Ethnographic Atlas*, Pittsburgh: University of Pittsburgh Press.

Smith, E. et al. (2003), 'The benefits of costly signaling: Meriam turtle hunters', *Behavioral Ecology* 14(1), pp. 116–26.

Van Vugt, M. and Dunbar, R. (2008), 'Showing off in humans: male generosity as a mating signal', *Evolutionary Psychology*, 6(3), pp. 386–92.

Part IX – The Rescuer

Elaines (Altruism/Empathy/Egoism)

Axelrod, R. and Hamilton, W. (1981), 'The evolution of cooperation', *Science*, 211, pp. 1390–6.

Batson, C. et al. (1981), 'Is empathic emotion a source of altruistic motivation?', *Journal of Personality and Social Psychology*, 40(2), pp. 290–302.

Batson, C. et al. (1988), 'Five studies testing two new egoistic alternatives to the empathy–altruism hypothesis', *Journal of Personality and Social Psychology*, 55(1), pp. 52–77.

Batson, C. and Shaw, L. (1991), 'Evidence for altruism: toward a pluralism of prosocial motives', *Psychological Inquiry*, 2(2), pp. 107–22.

Cialdini, R. (1991), 'Altruism or egoism? That is (still) the question', *Psychological Inquiry*, 2, pp. 124–6.

Cialdini, R. et al. (1973), 'Transgression and altruism: a case for hedonism', *Journal of Experimental Social Psychology*, 9, pp. 502–16.

Cialdini, R. et al. (1987), 'Empathy-based helping: is it selflessly or selfishly motivated?', *Journal of Personality and Social Psychology*, 52, pp. 749–58.

Cialdini, R. et al. (1997), 'Reinterpreting the empathy-altruism relationship: when one into one equals oneness', *Journal of Personality and Social Psychology*, 73(3), pp. 481–94.

Fehr, E. and Gächter, S. (2002), 'Altruistic punishment in humans', *Nature*, 415, pp. 137–40.

Fehr, E. and Fischbacher, U. (2003) The nature of human altruism. *Nature*, 425(6960), pp. 785–91.

Hill, K. (2002), 'Altruistic cooperation during foraging by the Ache, and the evolved human predisposition to cooperate', *Human Nature*, 13, pp. 105–28.

Holmes, J. et al. (2002), 'Committing altruism under the cloak of self-interest: the exchange fiction', *Journal of Experimental Social Psychology*, 38(2), pp. 144–51.

Rilling, J. et al. (2002), 'A neural basis for social cooperation', *Neuron*, 35(2), pp. 395–405.

Trivers, R. (1971), 'The evolution of reciprocal altruism', *Quarterly Review of Biology*, 46, (March), pp. 35–57.

Van Lange, P. (2008), 'Does empathy trigger only altruistic motivation? How about selflessness or justice?', *Emotion*, 8(6), pp. 766–74.

Canines, Ants

Hollis, K. and Nowbahari, E. (2013), 'A comparative analysis of precision rescue behaviour in sand-dwelling ants', *Animal Behaviour*, 85(3), pp. 537–44.

Ovodov, N. et al. (2011), 'A 33,000-year-old incipient dog from the Altai Mountains of Siberia: evidence of the earliest domestication disrupted by the last glacial maximum', *PLOS ONE*, 6(7), e22821.

Part X – Again Came the Kinsman

Humans

Anderson, K. (2010), 'Life Expectancy and the Timing of Life History Events in Developing Countries', *Human Nature*, 21(2), pp. 103–23.

Anderson, K. (2015), 'Father absence, childhood stress, and reproductive maturation in South Africa', *Human Nature*, 26(4), pp. 401–25.

Chisholm, J. et al. (2005), 'Early stress predicts age at menarche and first birth, adult attachment, and expected lifespan', *Human Nature*, 16, pp. 233–65.

Del Guidice, M. (2014), 'Life history plasticity in humans: the predictive value of early cues depends on the temporal structure of the environment', *Proceedings of the Royal Society*, B281, 20132222.

Del Guidice, M. and Belsky, J. (2011), 'Parent-child relationships', in Salmon, C. and Shackleford, T. (eds), *The Oxford Handbook of Evolutionary Family Psychology*, New York, NY: Oxford University Press (pp. 65 et seq.).

Mayr, E. (1961), 'Cause and effect in biology kinds of causes, predictability, and teleology are viewed by a practicing biologist', *Science*, 134(3489), pp. 1501–6.

Mullainathan, S. (2014), *Scarcity: The True Cost of Not Having Enough*, London: Penguin.

Nettle, D. et al. (2013), 'The evolution of predictive adaptive responses in human life history', *Proceedings of the Royal Society*, B280, 20131343.

Quinlan, R. (2007), 'Human parental effort and environmental risk', *Proceedings of the Royal Society of London*, B274, pp. 121–5.

Quinlan, R. (2008), 'Human pair-bonds: evolutionary functions, ecological variation, and adaptive development', *Evolutionary Anthropology*, 17, pp. 227–38.

Non-human Animals

Armstrong, A. (1954), 'The ecology of distraction display', *The British Journal of Animal Behaviour*, 2(4), pp. 121–35.

Cameron, N. et al. (2008), 'Maternal influences on the sexual behavior and reproductive success of the female rat', *Hormones and Behavior*, 54(1), pp. 178–84.

Fernandez-Duque, E. et al. (2009), 'The biology of paternal care in human and nonhuman primates', *Annual Review of Anthropology*, 38, pp. 115–30.

Montgomerie, R. and Weatherhead, P. (1988), 'Risks and rewards of nest defence by parent birds', *Quarterly Review of Biology*, pp. 167–87.

Ricklefs, R. (1969), 'An analysis of nesting mortality in birds', *Smithson. Contrib. Zool.*, 9, pp. 1–48.

Epilogue

General

Balzac, H. (1835/1951), *Old Goriot*, London: Penguin.

Delbrück, M. (1949), 'A Physicist Looks at Biology', *Transactions of the Connecticut Academy of Arts and Sciences*, 38, pp. 173–90.

Miller, M. and Taube, K. (1997), *The Gods and Symbols of Ancient Mexico and the Maya,* London: Thames & Hudson.

Neruda, P. (1924/2007), *Twenty Love Poems and a Song of Despair,* London: Penguin.

Olcott, M. (1995), *The Kazakhs,* Stanford, CA: Hoover Institution Press.

Gene-culture Coevolution

Arjamaa, O. and Vuorisalo, T. (2010), 'Gene-culture coevolution and human diet: rather than acting in isolation, biology and culture have interacted to develop the diet we have today', *American Scientist,* 98(2), pp. 140–7.

Laland, K. et al. (2010), How culture shaped the human genome: bringing genetics and the human sciences together, *Nature Reviews Genetics,* 11, pp. 137–48.

Richerson, P. et al. (2010), 'Gene-culture coevolution in the age of genomics', *Proceedings of the National Academy of Sciences of the United States of America,* vol. 107, supplement 2: 'In the Light of Evolution IV: The Human Condition' (May 11, 2010), pp. 8985–92.

Eunice Kathleen Waymon

Simone, N. and Cleary, S. (1991/2003), *I Put a Spell on You,* Cambridge, MA: Da Capo Press.

Acknowledgements

I think there is another Type I should mention: the Ower of Debts. The plain fact is that during the course of the research for this book, I have become one of the most indebted men alive. If you have journeyed with me through these ten parts, you will already have sensed the sheer mountainous scale of my indebtedness to so many astonishing people. I cannot name everyone. Nor can I adequately express my thanks to any single one of them. This is the attempt of a lawyer, researcher and writer to tackle that daunting task, but it is one I welcome. I emphasise that irrespective of all the generous assistance outlined below, I alone remain responsible for this book.

On the Gareth Myatt case, I want to thank Gareth's mother Pam, my brilliant junior Brenda Campbell, our solicitors Mark Scott and Raju Bhatt, and the co-directors of INQUEST Deborah Coles and Helen Shaw. During the case, our good friend and colleague Gilly Mundy tragically passed away. He is deeply missed by all who knew him and was a fearless champion of human rights. Dr Alan Pegna is an exceptional researcher and an exceptionally warm man. I am grateful for his generosity and advice. Profound thanks to Kate Danvers, David Schley and Jonny Whitehead in Ghana, along with

JA, W, Austin F, LP and of course the incomparable Anthony. Kip Williams and Marian Wong were indispensable, intellectually stirring, tremendous correspondents, and are just so talented, undertaking research that is crucial. Ruth Thomas Suh directed and produced the stunning film on ostracism, *Reject* – watch it on kanopystreaming. com. Kathy Bolkovac's courageous indomitability is an inspiration to so many. Sheldon Solomon was always generous with his time and ideas and is engaged in vital research. I want to thank Saimo Chahal QC of Bindmans LLP and Jane Nicklinson. All the Faizey Websters stunned me with their mutual affection and resilience: Alec, Shirley, Alexander, Mark and, of course, my good friend Dawn – I will return to Dawn. I want to thank Rana, the extraordinary Hanifa Nakiryowa, and Jaf Shah (of ASTI). What happened in the Central African Republic (and its overspill in Cameroon) changed how I viewed the world. I wholeheartedly thank the amazing Judith Léveillée, also Daniela L., GH, Celine, UL, François, Patrice, Saira, Stevie S, 'Monsieur M', and of course my friend and companion, the incredible Sabrina Avakian – you are an inspiration. Thanks also to Sally Davies at Unicef UK. The innovative work of Thomas Elbert and his team alleviates the suffering of some of our most traumatised children: I am indebted to Thomas for time and advice. In Haiti, I am delighted to acknowledge Jeanne V., Jonel, Gunn Benjaminsen at the UN, Pastor Aniya, Naomy, Marcie, RR, CB and MT. In Kazakhstan, I am indebted to my contacts who opened my eyes to the realities of trafficking in people: T, AD, SK, KU, Marzhan L. and of course Vasily. Angie and Ricky were a source of support and companionship at one of our most challenging times, and a model of quiet valour. Nim Tottenham from Columbia University not only fielded my many neuroscience and neuroplasticity questions but made invaluable suggestions for further investigation and reading. Nim was always available, despite her busy schedule. I'm grateful to Peggy St Jacques from Sussex University for her advice on memory and trauma. For an extended part of the research arc of the book, I was assisted in my parallel legal work by a stream of some of the finest junior barristers at the Bar: Clare Davies, Peter Dahlsen, Imran Shafi, Paul Clarke, Paramjit Ahluwalia, Alex Rose (for so many extraordinary cases), my Cambridge colleague Cameron Miles, and the veteran of three cases we've successfully fought together, Richard Reynolds. One of those was the Jake Hardy inquest, where I not only made our legal team work inhuman hours, but inflicted some of the dilemmas from this book on them night after night over dinner at a Holiday Inn in Bolton. Therefore thanks also to the wonderful Helen Stone, Anita Sharma and Shona Crallan. At the Bar Human Rights Committee and the Working Group on FGM I chaired, I want to thank in particular my legal colleagues Kirsty Brimelow QC, Zimran Samuel, Charlotte Proudman, Dr Theodora Christou, Sam Fowles, Felicity Gerry QC and Courtney Perlmutter. Also, in terms of our UN report, Gráinne Mellon from Garden Court was of immense assistance, and continues to be so as we develop our VAWG work, as does Emma Nash our clerk and our senior clerk Colin Cook, who has clerked me ever since I've been at the Bar. When we took the fight on FGM to Parliament, I was delighted to work with Baroness Molly Meacher and Seema Malhotra MP and her team. More generally around the issue of FGM, it has been a pleasure taking the fight forward with the irrepressible Hilary Burrage and Tobe Levin (of Harvard and Oxford) as well as the wonderful Nancy Durrell McKenna of Safe Hands for Mothers. Also, thanks to the incomparable Sarah Jane Morris for writing a stunning song about FGM and my good friend HHJ Maureen Bacon QC for introducing us. I want to thank the Recorder of the Central Criminal Court, His Honour Judge Nicholas Hilliard QC, for his constant support and encouragement. At Cambridge University, I am grateful to an exceptional group of people:

Professor Loraine Gelsthorpe, Dr Caroline Lanskey, Dr Nicola Padfield (Master of Fitzwilliam College, who along with Loraine co-hosted an FGM awareness event at Fitz) and Dr Ben Crewe and Professor Alison Liebling for the intellectual stimulation over the years and the various invitations to talk, lecture and provoke. All are or have been engaged in cutting-edge and crucial research. I would also like to thank the staff at Cambridge's 'UL' (University Library) and Radzinowicz Library, and especially Stuart Stone and (previously) Mary Gower. At Harvard, Professor James Sidanius provided me with the invaluable opportunity to step back and think, and was so generous with his time and sage advice. Jim is an exceptional scholar and person. Dr Mariska Kappmeier was a friend, supporter and source of novel ways to think about conflict and war zones – thanks, Mariska. At Sevenoaks School, it has been a pleasure to create innovative events for young people to explore human rights issues with two tireless teachers, Wendy Heydorn and Chris Harbinson, supported by the school's inspirational head, Dr Katy Ricks. My close colleague and friend Leyla Hussein has been a tower of strength to so many for her courageous resistance to FGM. One of the joys of the last few years has been going around the country and sharing a platform with Leyla – what she calls our 'double act' – while making the case for the bodily integrity and protection of all girls and young women. We will change this social harm. As I've learned from Leyla and the dozens of extraordinary women in sub-Saharan Africa I've worked with: *continue to believe*. That should be one of the mottos of this book. I'm grateful also to Antonia Mulvey, the Executive Director of Legal Action Worldwide and her contacts at United Nations Women. On that, I am also grateful to Tuula Niemenen for initiating our collaboration with UN Women, National Committee UK. Good friends Victoria and Ross MacDonald provided a stream of advice on all things Africa. Dawn Grantham (another dear friend) kindly invited me to address the UK Council for Psychotherapy. The wonderful Jocelyne Quennell invited me to address the Open Forum on Children and the Law. I've pressed this manuscript – and imposed myself – on a small group of fabulously fanatical readers. None of them realised going in how enormous a commitment of time this colossal text would demand, but they never baulked or complained, and kept coming back for more. Helen Fospero, an inspiring television journalist and social justice campaigner, and Nicola Bensley, an exceptionally talented photographer, both constantly floor me with their enthusiasm for the project. I'm also grateful to Nicola for the profile picture. Tony Stark, a talented film-maker, possesses an eye for detail and nuance that helped me focus the superordinate point and purpose of the project. Kate Vick provided decisive advice right at the very outset, assisted in the articulation of the most fruitful lines of development and was a willing sounding-board throughout. Nicole Brannan and Bridget Bullick very kindly read an early draft. Emma Brookes somehow fitted the book into her numerous family and professional commitments. (Lord) Mark Malloch-Brown read the proposal and suggested where to send it; Trish Malloch-Brown shared a formative brunch with me in Manhattan's magnificent Grand Central. My literary agents at the Wylie Agency, Andrew Wylie in New York and James Pullen in London, have been tireless advocates for the book and the importance of the issues it seeks to tackle. I want to thank the whole team at Penguin Random House. But in particular the brilliant publicity director Kate McQuaid and the person who first read the proposal for the book and acquired it – got it – instantly, Jason Arthur. As Publisher, Jason has steered this project through a course of three intense but always enjoyable years. Special thanks go to my frontline, coal-face, down-and-dirty editor Tom Avery, Editorial Director at Heinemann. I cannot even begin to tell you the number of times Tom and I have talked and corresponded, via Skype or

WhatsApp or phone or email, from the edge of combat zones in sub-Saharan Africa, refugee camps, the steppe of Central Asia, the devastation of post-quake Haiti, the edge of the Kalahari desert, and sometimes just in good old Vauxhall Bridge Road. His calm, incisive vision and acute intelligence have immeasurably improved the text, and helped me draw out from the mass of words and stories generated by my research the human in the human rights issues that are so close to my heart. Thank you, Tom – your contribution has been pivotal. Throughout this process, I have been supported by my mother Valerie, my brother Michael and his wife Tamara, including attending stimulating neuroscience and psychological research events with Mike and Tamara. So back to Dawn Faizey Webster: not only is Dawn creating history with her unrelenting determination to add to the sum of human knowledge notwithstanding her stroke, she is writing (architectural) history in her PhD. Somehow she finds the time to message me in ways that are gloriously irreverent but never entirely irrelevant – there's always a link to what we're discussing – and fills her communications with hilarity, edification and joy. I *know* I must have omitted many exceptional people, so please speak out if so and I'll rectify any oversights in later editions.

Finally, I cannot take my leave without expressing my thanks to the three remarkable, and remarkably different people this book is dedicated to. I wouldn't – and couldn't – have written it without you, Katie, Fabi, Hermione. I began my research when Hermione was two years old. She is now almost a teenager. I mention this to explain how long 'the book' (not always a term of endearment) has been part of their lives and how patient they have had to be with me. At every stage, as I met Anthony, Angie and Dawn; Vasily, François and Saira; Patrice, Ubah and Anna, they patiently awaited dispatches from my latest venture. Therefore, gladly, unreservedly, I end by professing that this is not only a book for you three, it is in truth your book.

List of Illustrations

Grateful acknowledgement is made for permission to use the following pictures. Every effort has been made to contact all copyright holders, and any errors or omissions brought to the publishers' attention will be corrected in future editions.

p. 382 Cueva de las Manos (Cave of Hands), Patagonia Ancestral handprints, up to 13,000 years old: © Shutterstock.

p. 400 Map of Hispaniola: © Shutterstock.

p. 436 Image of a burning house: © WIN-Initiative/ Getty Images.

p. 500 Edward Hopper, *Automat* (1927): © Des Moines Art Center, Iowa, permanent collection. Photographic copyright © De Agostini Picture Library/ Bridgeman Images.

p. 504 The grille on the foundling wheel, Santo Spirito Hospital, Rome: credit to Warburg.

p. 614 Feverfew (*Tanacetum parthenium*): © Shutterstock.

p. 673 Man and Dog, Cave art, Altamira, Spain.

p. 725 Killdeer and young: © Danita Delimont/ Getty Images.

p. 736 Earth from International Space Station: © ESA/ NASA.

p. 736 3D modelling of human brain activity.

p. 737 The ice mountains of Pluto, equatorial Pluto, New Horizons space probe, July 2015: © NASA/ Johns Hopkins University Applied Physics Laboratory/ Southwest Research Institute.

If You Want to Get Involved

This book has explored several harmful human behaviours. As we've seen from the narratives of the remarkable people we've met, people are fighting back – they are making a difference. You can help. If you want to get involved, here are some suggestions. These are three organisations that are operating nationally and internationally to reduce the sum of human suffering. I strongly commend them all. On the book's dedicated page at the penguin. co.uk website, there is a longer list of NGOs fighting poverty, injustice and discrimination, along with latest details of how you can get involved with the three organisations below.

Organisation 1 – INQUEST

The impetus for my research and thus the book was what happened to Gareth Myatt at Rainsbrook Secure Training Centre. I represented his mother Pam at the inquest into his death. Throughout the arduous proceedings, Pam and her family were supported (as was I, brilliantly) by the multiple award-winning human rights organisation INQUEST. I've been working with them for around twenty years on cases where citizens have died in contentious circumstances in the care and custody of the state. It's hard to overemphasise the importance of what they do. The organisation is, without question, one of the jewels in the human rights crown in the UK. Director Deborah Coles and her team work tirelessly to get the truth. As did former co-director Helen Shaw. Bereaved families, grieving over the sudden death of their loved ones, would be lost without them. For over three decades INQUEST has had to find out the hard way what works and what does not to get the facts when the state is implicated in the death of a detained person. We have few more important areas of collective scrutiny. That's what INQUEST does. They are now seeking to develop their work internationally, so people in other countries can benefit from their expertise. Please support them – or get involved yourself.

Organisation 2 – ActionAid

As you've seen, one of the human rights issues I've been deeply involved in for several years is FGM. To combat it, to protect the 3 million more girls who will be cut in the next twelve months (one every eleven seconds), we need to join forces. One of the key organisations working to fight the harmful practice of FGM is ActionAid. As a leading international charity operating in over forty-five countries since 1972, ActionAid has been fighting poverty and working with the poorest women and girls in the world to change their lives for good. It offers practical, hands-on help to develop a long-term, sustainable impact. It advocates an ethos of supporting women to lead their communities out of poverty and participate in civil and political life as the strongest way to build a peaceful and just society. ActionAid works directly with women's rights organisations in ten different countries, providing funding and support to their efforts to stamp out FGM in their communities and, ultimately, to enable girls to build a future of their own choice. These countries are Kenya, Ethiopia, Ghana, Liberia, Nigeria (in some states), Senegal, Somaliland, Sierra Leone, the Gambia and Uganda. You may wish to contribute to ActionAid's direct support of women and girls who have escaped FGM. They train women to form Women's Watch Groups to report cases of FGM, and work with women's rights organisations to lobby governments to pass laws to end FGM and all other forms of Violence Against Women and Girls. I strongly commend ActionAid to you.

Organisation 3 – Unicef

I couldn't leave this section without mentioning Unicef. So many parts of the book have looked at what we do to children. So does Unicef. It works to ensure that we protect children better. It is Unicef's hope – and its unalterable demand. It makes it on behalf of some of the most vulnerable children on the planet. Unicef works unrelentingly to stop children being used as combat troops. I've seen what Unicef does. I've played football with children on the borders of the Central African Republic who, without Unicef, might not be alive. I've seen the classrooms Unicef has built, and in them the paintings of the children on the walls, depicting their lives and their dreams. One of the paintings I saw in the Gado camp was simply a hut with a smiling child standing next to it, next to a river, next to a tree, and what was stunning about it was what was not there: no guns, no jeeps, no blood, no bodies. It was a child being allowed to be that most precious yet fragile thing: a child. That's what Unicef strives to do. There are a number of ways to get involved with Unicef, whether by joining its campaigning or making a simple donation. Unicef has a project called the Girls' Investment Fund Taskforce (GIFT), a collective movement uniting philanthropic investors with Unicef in advancing the survival, protection and development of girls. In any of these ways, you can help Unicef with its crucial work today.

About the Author

Dexter Dias QC is a barrister who as Queen's Counsel has been instructed in some of the biggest cases of recent years involving human rights, murder, terrorism, crimes against humanity and genocide. He has been instrumental in changing the law to better protect young women and girls at risk of FGM and works pro bono internationally with survivors of modern-day slavery, human trafficking and violence against women and girls.

He is also a prize-winning scholar of Cambridge University, having been elected to a Foundation Scholarship at Jesus College and winning the Lopez-Rey Prize for the highest Distinction in his research degree at the Faculty of Law's Institute of Criminology, where he critically analysed the use of state coercive force on vulnerable young people in custody. He has researched and given lectures at Cambridge and held a visiting research residency at Harvard. He has addressed major international conferences and spoken on many national platforms around human rights and social justice issues and violence against women and girls. He chaired and co-wrote the influential Bar Human Rights Committee Report to the Parliamentary Inquiry into FGM and significantly contributed to changing the law to strengthen the national protective mechanism. His research was cited in Parliament and paid tribute to for its critical analysis of the defects in the UK's rights protections. He has written reports to the United Nations, briefed the UN's Special Rapporteur on Violence Against Women and Girls and advised parliamentarians in both the Commons and Lords.

He acts as governor, ambassador and advisor in respect of several human rights NGOs, sits as a part-time judge in the Crown Court (including at the Old Bailey), and is authorised to try Serious Sexual Offence cases. He was finalist in Liberty and JUSTICE's prestigious Human Rights Lawyer of the Year Award and won the TMG Award for Outstanding Contribution to Advocacy and Justice.

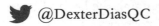 @DexterDiasQC